D1765073

A HISTORY OF THE
COMMON LAW OF CONTRACT

A HISTORY
OF THE
COMMON LAW
OF CONTRACT

The Rise of the
Action of Assumpsit

BY

A. W. B. SIMPSON

CLARENDON PRESS · OXFORD

*This book has been printed digitally and produced in a standard specification
in order to ensure its continuing availability*

OXFORD
UNIVERSITY PRESS

Great Clarendon Street, Oxford OX2 6DP

Oxford University Press is a department of the University of Oxford.
It furthers the University's objective of excellence in research, scholarship,
and education by publishing worldwide in

Oxford New York

Auckland Cape Town Dar es Salaam Hong Kong Karachi
Kuala Lumpur Madrid Melbourne Mexico City Nairobi
New Delhi Shanghai Taipei Toronto
With offices in
Argentina Austria Brazil Chile Czech Republic France Greece
Guatemala Hungary Italy Japan South Korea Poland Portugal
Singapore Switzerland Thailand Turkey Ukraine Vietnam

Oxford is a registered trade mark of Oxford University Press
in the UK and in certain other countries

Published in the United States
by Oxford University Press Inc., New York

ISBN 0-19-825573-X

PREFACE TO PAPERBACK EDITION

THIS paperback edition reprints the text as originally published in 1975, with only minor typographical corrections. Since then there has been a modest amount of writing on the history of contract; in particular the following pieces need to be noted. At a general level S. J. Stoljar's *History of Contract at Common Law* appeared in the same year; it covers a longer period, necessarily in less detail. On the medieval law R. H. Helmholz' important 'Assumpsit and Fidei Laesio' (1975) 91 L.Q.R.406 also appeared too late to be taken into account; it would have led me to modify the account of the enforcement of contracts in the ecclesiastical courts. D. J. Ibbetson has published an important article on the early history of the action of covenant in 'Words and Deeds: The Action of Covenant in the Reign of Edward I' (1986) 4 Law and History Review 71. The original edition also unaccountably failed to include references to W. M. McGovern's valuable writings on medieval contract law, 'Contract in Medieval England' (1968) 54 Iowa Law Review 19, 'The Enforcement of Oral Contracts Prior to Assumpsit' (1970) 65 Northwestern University Law Review 576, and 'The Enforcement of Informal Contracts in the Later Middle Ages' (1971) 59 Californian Law Review 1145. For this I take this opportunity to apologize. M. S. Arnold's 'Fourteenth Century Promises' (1976) 35 Cambridge Law Journal 321 and his 1986 Selden Society edition of fourteenth century trespass actions (*Select Cases of Trespass from the King's Courts 1307–1399*, Selden Society Vol. 100) are both important, the latter including a number of assumpsit cases. For the sixteenth century J. H. Baker's Selden Society edition of *Spelman's Reports* (Volumes 93 and 94 for 1977 and 1978), and in particular his introduction to Volume 94 at pp. *255–298*, fills in many details in the establishment of assumpsit for nonfeasance, without I think radically affecting the account I gave. The evolution of the doctrine of consideration remains controversial and has been discussed by J. H. Baker in a contribution to *On the Laws and*

Customs of England: Essays in Honor of Samuel E. Thorne (edited by M. S. Arnold and others, 1981). He disagrees with my interpretation, but I remain unconvinced. The late J. P. Dawson's *Gifts and Promises* (1980), though primarily an essay in comparative law, is also relevant here. D. Ibbetson has published two articles on *indebitatus assumpsit* and *Slade's Case*, and these also have something to say on the history of consideration. They are 'Assumpsit and Debt in the Early Sixteenth Century: The Origins of the Indebitatus Count' (1982) 41 Cambridge Law Journal 142 and 'Sixteenth Century Contract Law: Slade's Case in Context' (1984) 4 Oxford Journal of Legal Studies 295. Both derive from a Cambridge doctoral thesis, *The Development of the Action of Assumpsit, 1540–1620*, based on extensive study of unpublished materials; this both refines the history in detail and advances criticisms of the general interpretation presented here in some important respects, though not to my mind wholly convincingly. The Statute of Frauds has been the subject of an article by P. Hamburger (27 American Journal of Legal History 354) which is concerned with its conveyancing provisions rather than its contractual ones, though these are of course interrelated.

University of Chicago   A.W.B.S.
August 1986

PREFACE

THIS book comprises the first part of a history of English contract law; in due course I intend to complete the study with a second volume covering the period between the passing of the Statute of Frauds in 1677—the terminus of this volume—and the end of the nineteenth century. The central concern is with the body of doctrine evolved around the action of assumpsit, and this volume deals with the period which saw the origin of that action and its development into the principal vehicle of contract law. Doctrinal legal history, with which I am concerned, is a special branch of the history of ideas, of their reception, evolution and interaction, and the study of these processes in the context of contract law has, as it seems to me, an importance wider than that of merely illustrating the detailed elaboration of the complex moral principles which underly one particular legal institution. Additionally it contributes to an understanding of how a sophisticated legal system works and, at a more profound level, in what it consists. Much of what is offered as legal theory seems unsatisfactory because it has been constructed around the model of an instantaneous legal system, a model more appropriate to the working of a legal system than to its understanding. In general however I have avoided explicit discussion of general theories of legal history, especially of the type favoured by legal sociologists; the omission is deliberate. Such theories are of scant value unless based upon regular historical investigation and attention to evidence; at this stage my aim has merely been to provide the basis which much theorizing has conspicuously lacked.

Many colleagues and pupils have in one way or another contributed help; I must especially mention Mr. G. D. G. Hall, President of Corpus Christi College, with whom I have had many discussions over the years. I am grateful also to Mr. S. W. Bickford-Smith who acted for some time as my research assistant. My wife is largely responsible for ensuring that this volume, which has been on the stocks for many years, has actually been brought to completion. So far as institutions are concerned, I am particularly grateful to the Law School of Dalhousie University, Halifax, and to Lincoln College, Oxford, for much assistance by way of facilities for research.

Two chapters of this volume have previously been published in more or less the same form—that dealing with conditional bonds in the Law Quarterly Review (Vol. 82 at p. 392) and that dealing with the equitable doctrine of consideration in the University of Toronto Law Journal (Vol. XVI at p. 1).

A.W.B.S.

University of Kent at Canterbury
27 January 1975

CONTENTS

TABLE OF STATUTES

TABLE OF YEAR BOOK CASES

TABLE OF CASES

ABBREVIATIONS

THE following books are frequently cited, using these abbreviations. Other works mentioned are listed in the bibliography, and the standard forms of legal reference are not included in this list.

AMES—J. B. AMES, *Lectures on Legal History and Miscellaneous Legal Essays*. Cambridge, Mass., 1913.

BAKER—J. H. BAKER, *An Introduction to English Legal History*. London, 1971.

BARBOUR—W. T. BARBOUR, 'The History of Contract in Early English Equity', Vol. IV, *Oxford Studies in Social and Legal History* (ed. Vinogradoff). Oxford, 1914.

BROOKE—R. BROOKE, *La Graunde Abridgement*. London 1573.

FIFOOT—C. H. S. FIFOOT, *History and Sources of the Common Law. Tort and Contract*. London, 1949.

FITZ.—A. FITZHERBERT, *La Graunde Abridgement*. London, 1516.

H.E.L.—W. S. HOLDSWORTH, *A History of English Law*, 16 volumes. London, 1922–66.

KIRALFY—A. K. KIRALFY, *The Action on the Case*. London, 1951.

MILSOM—S. F. C. MILSOM, *Historical Foundations of the Common Law*. London, 1969.

PLUCKNETT—T. F. T. PLUCKNETT, *A Concise History of the Common Law*, 5th ed. London, 1956.

P. and M.—F. POLLOCK and F. W. MAITLAND, *The History of English Law Before the Time of Edward I*, 2nd ed. Cambridge, 1968.

SHEPPARD—W. SHEPPARD, *Actions on the Case for Deeds*. London, 1662.

S.S.—*Publications of the Selden Society 1887*–. (References to volume-number and name of editor.)

BIBLIOGRAPHY OF PRINCIPAL
WORKS CITED

THE edition is the one I have normally used; for further biblio-
graphical information see *A Legal Bibliography of the British Commonwealth of Nations*, by W. H. MAXWELL and L. F. MAXWELL, 2nd ed.
London, 1955.

ASHLEY, W. J., *An Introduction to English Economic History and Theory*.
London, 1894–1906.
ATIYAH, P. S., *An Introduction to the Law of Contract*, 2nd ed. Oxford,
1971.
BACON, F., *Collection of some of the Principall Rules and Maxims of the
Common Lawes of England*. Printed in Spedding's edition of Bacon's
Complete Works. London, 1868–92.
BACON, M., *New Abridgement of the Law*, 5 volumes. London, 1736–66.
BIRKS, M., *Gentlemen of the Law*, London, 1960.
BOICEAU, J., *Traité de la preuve par témoins en matière civile*. Paris, 1759.
BRISSAUD, J., *A History of French Private Law*, London, 1912.
BROWNLOW, R., *Declarations and Pleadings in English: the Forms of
Proceeding in Courts of Law*. London, 1652 and 1654 (in Latin 1693).
BUCKLAND, W. W., *A Text-Book of Roman Law from Augustus to
Justinian*, 2nd ed. Cambridge, 1950.
BULLEN, E., and LEAKE, S. M., *Precedents of Pleadings in Actions in the
Superior Courts of Common Law*, 3rd ed. London, 1868.
BULLER, F., *Introduction to the Law relative to Trials at Nisi Prius*.
London, 1772.
CHITTY, J., *Forms of Practical Proceedings in the Courts of King's Bench,
Common Pleas and Exchequer of Pleas*, 7th ed. London, 1856.
COHEN, H., *A History of the English Bar and Attornatus to 1450*. London,
1929.
COKE, E., *Booke of Entries; containing perfect and approved Presidents of
Courts, Declarations, etc.* London, 1614.
—— *The First Part of the Institutes of the Laws of England, or, A Com-
mentary upon Littleton*, 18th ed. London, 1823.
COMYNS, J., *A Digest of the Laws of England*. London, 1762–7.
DAUBE, D., *Studies in the Roman Law of Sale*, Oxford, 1959.
EMDEN, A. B., *A Biographical Register of the University of Oxford to
A.D. 1500*, 3 vols. Oxford, 1957–9.

—— *A Biographical Dictionary of the University of Cambridge to* A.D. *1500.* Oxford, 1963.

FITZHERBERT, A., *The New Natura Brevium.* Dublin, 1793.
[This work was not in fact written by Anthony Fitzherbert, though traditionally associated with his name.]

Fleta: seu Commentarius Juris Anglicani. London, 1647.
[A new edition by Richardson and Sayles is being published by the Selden Society, of which two volumes containing Books I–IV (S.S. 72 and 89) have appeared.]

FLETCHER, E. G. M., *The Carrier's Liability,* London, 1932.

GAIUS, *The Institutes of Gaius,* ed. de Zulueta, Oxford, 1946.

HAAS, E. de, *Antiquities of Bail.* New York, 1940.

HALL, G. D. G., *The Treatise on the Laws and Customs of the Realm of England called Glanvill.* London, 1965.

HARE, J. I., *The Law of Contracts,* Boston, 1887.

HASTINGS, M., *The Court of Common Pleas in Fifteenth Century England.* New York, 1947.

HAWKINS, W., *Pleas of the Crown,* London, 1716–21.

HAYES, J., *Le Statute of Frauds en droit anglais.* Paris, 1924.

HEYDON, J. D., *The Restraint of Trade Doctrine.* London, 1971.

HOLDEN, J. M., *The History of Negotiable Instruments in English Law.* London, 1955 (Vol. III in the University of London Legal Series).

JACKSON, R. M., *The History of Quasi-Contract in English Law.* Cambridge, 1936.

JONES, GARETH, *History of the Law of Charity, 1532–1827.* Cambridge, 1969.

KIRALFY, A. K. R., *A Source Book of English Law.* London, 1957.

LAWSON, F. H., *Remedies of English Law.* London, 1972.

LITTLETON, T., *Tenures,* ed. E. Wambaugh. Washington, 1903.

MAITLAND, F. W., *Bractons Note-Book.* Cambridge, 1887.

—— *Collected Papers,* 3 vols., ed. Fisher. Cambridge, 1911.

NICHOLAS, B., *An Introduction to Roman Law.* Oxford, 1962.

NOONAN, J. T., *The Scholastic Analysis of Usury.* Cambridge, Mass., 1957.

NOY, W., *Treatise of the Principall Grounds and Maximes of the Lawes of this Kingdom.* London, 1641.

PERKINS, J., *A Profitable Booke treating of the lawes of England.* London, 1621.

PLUCKNETT, T. F. T., *The Legislation of Edward I.* Oxford, 1949.

POLLOCK, F., *The Law of Torts,* 15th ed. London, 1951.

—— *The Principles of Contract,* 10th ed. London, 1936.

PUFENDORF, S., *The Law of Nature and Nations.* Oxford, 1710.

PUGH, R. B., *Imprisonment in Medieval England.* Cambridge, 1968.

PUTNAM, B. W., *The Enforcement of the Statute of Labourers during the First Decade after the Black Death.* New York, 1908.

RASTELL, W., *Colleccion of entrees, of declarations, barres,* [etc.]. London, 1566.

REEVES, J., *History of English Law from the Saxons to the end of the reign of Hen. VII,* ed. Finlason, 3 vols. London, 1869 (with continuation to reign of Elizabeth I).

Registrum Omnium Brevium, London, 1531.

ROLLE, H., *Abridgement des plusieurs Cases et Resolutions del Common Ley,* 2 vols. London, 1668.

ST. GERMAIN, C., *The Doctor and Student,* ed. Muchall, Cincinnati, 1886. [A Selden Society edition is soon to appear.]

SALMOND, J., *Essays in Jurisprudence and Legal History,* London, 1891.

SHEPPARD, W., *Touchstone of Common Assurances.* London, 1641.

SIMPSON, A. W. B., *An Introduction to the History of the Land Law.* Oxford, 1961.

SOMERS, Lord, *Collection of Scarce and Valuable Tracts.* 16 vols. London, 1748–51.

SPENCE, G., *The Equitable Jurisdiction of the Court of Chancery,* 2 vols. Philadelphia, 1846–50.

STATHAM, N., *Abridgement.* Rouen and London, c. 1490, published without author or title. A bad translation by Klingelsmith was published in Boston in 1915.

STEPHEN, H. J., *A Treatise on the Principles of Pleadings in Civil Actions,* 3rd ed. London, 1835.

STREET, T. A., *Foundations of Legal Liability,* 3 vols. New York, 1906.

SUGDEN, E. B., *A Practical Treatise on the Law of Vendors and Purchasers,* 8th ed. London, 1830.

TAWNEY, R. H., *Religion and the Rise of Capitalism.* London, 1949.

THAYER, J. B., *A Preliminary Treatise of Evidence at the Common Law.* London, 1898.

VEALL, D., *The Popular Movement for Law Reform, 1640–1660.* Oxford, 1970.

VINOGRADOFF, P., *Essays in Legal History read before the International Congress of Historical Studies.* London, 1913.

VIOLLET, P., *Histoire du droit civil franacis.* Paris, 1903.

WATSON, A., *The Law of Obligations in the Later Roman Republic.* Oxford, 1965.

WINFIELD, P. H., *Chief Sources of English Legal History.* Cambridge, Mass., 1925.

—— *History of Conspiracy and Abuse of Legal Procedure.* Cambridge, 1921.

PART I
THE MEDIEVAL LAW OF CONTRACT

INTRODUCTION

THE modern English law of contract has grown up around an action known as the action of assumpsit, and this book is primarily concerned with the conceptual history of this action. Although the origin of assumpsit can be traced back into the fourteenth century, it was not until the sixteenth that it achieved any great prominence as a remedy for broken agreements, and not until the seventeenth that it became the regular common law contractual action. Long before the rise of assumpsit the common law courts were exercising an extensive jurisdiction over private contracts, and had built up a considerable and sophisticated body of contractual doctrine. Some knowledge of this body of doctrine, which I shall call the medieval law of contract, is essential to an understanding of the evolution of assumpsit; hence the first part of this book is concerned with this more ancient law of contract which was in part superseded, in part assimilated, and in part left untouched by the more modern form of action.

This older law of contract was, in its main essentials, very fully developed by the end of the fifteenth century (hence 'medieval'), whereas the law of assumpsit was largely evolved after the end of the medieval period. The title I have given it could, however, be misleading if it were to suggest the notion that the old law passed into oblivion shortly after the battle of Bosworth Field. Nothing could be further from the truth, for the rise of assumpsit was a very gradual process; more ancient contractual institutions retained a very considerable importance even into the eighteenth century. This is the reason why the first part of this book contains references to cases (and some to statutes) of the sixteenth and seventeenth centuries. Indeed, the sheer *corpus* of live materials on the medieval law of contract vastly exceeded in bulk that dealing with assumpsit until the mid-eighteenth century, as is apparent from the old abridgements and reports.

I shall not attempt to trace the early history of the old law, and therefore only occasionally refer back before the year-book

period.[1] One other limitation in the scope of this part of the
book needs emphasis—my main concern is with the *common* law
of contract and its doctrines. Now even today the law of the
royal courts is not the only law in England even under a very
narrow concept of law. Thus undergraduates in Oxford are
subject to a special system of laws and regulations administered
by the University Proctors, and these laws and regulations
differ considerably, and some have thought lamentably, from
the general law of the land. In medieval England there were
many courts of law in addition to the courts of common law.
Some, like the courts christian, were run by professionals, and
administered a doctrinalized system of law; others, such as the
courts of piepowder held in markets and fairs, applied relatively
unsophisticated systems of customary law. By the time of
Glanvill,[2] that is in the twelfth century, the royal court had
already acquired a considerable jurisdiction over criminal law
and property law, but had hardly begun to handle private
contracts. The author of the *Tractatus de Legibus et Consuetudinibus
Regni Anglie* (traditionally attributed to Rannulf Glanvill[3]) thus
excuses his handling of the subject:

> 'We deal briefly with the foregoing contracts which are based
> on the consent of private persons because, as was said above,
> it is not the custom of the court of the lord king to protect
> private agreements, nor does it even concern itself with such
> contracts as can be considered to be like private agreements.'[4]

In the course of time the jurisdiction over private contracts was
progressively extended, but the process was by no means
complete by the end of the Middle Ages—actions for breach of
promise of marriage, for example, only began to be heard at
common law under the Commonwealth, having previously been
the exclusive concern of the courts christian. In view of this it is
well to remember that the mere fact that the common law
provided no remedy in a particular case does not mean that
no remedy could be had, nor does it mean that the common
law judges were opposed to there being a remedy; often all

---

[1] i.e. before *c.* 1290.
[2] Rannulf Glanvill (ob. 1190) became Justiciar to Henry II in 1180. The date
of his birth is unknown.
[3] See G. D. G. Hall, *Glanvill*, xxx et seq.
[4] Hall, *Glanvill*, 132. cf. 124 and see a note at 189.

that was involved was a jurisdictional rule. We may here compare the way in which today jurisdiction is parcelled out between the High Court and the County Courts, noting, however, that today both apply (or at least are supposed to apply) the same system of legal rules, whereas in medieval England the law applied in non-common law courts could be different. Furthermore the Chancery in late medieval England exercised an extensive jurisdiction over contracts which went a considerable way in supplementing and correcting the deficiencies of the common law.[1] From time to time I shall refer to the existence of remedies outside the common law; I must emphasize, however, that this book is largely confined to the law of the common law courts, and this limitation must not be allowed to suggest the idea that the common law of contract was the only law upon the subject.

The medieval common law was a formulary system, whose content and basic structure were determined, to a very considerable extent, by the catalogue of original writs in the Register. In so far as it was possible to bring contractual actions in the common law courts, the possibility depended upon the existence of a suitable form of action. Inevitably the way in which medieval lawyers thought about contract law was very powerfully influenced by the formulary system with which they worked, and which provided them with their categories. We must not expect to find them thinking of their law of contract in the same way as we think of our law of contract; in the course of the centuries very considerable changes have taken place in the ways in which consensual transactions are classified, analysed, and named. Thus to a modern English lawyer a 'contract' means an agreement supported by consideration, the notion of agreement being analysed in terms of the doctrine of offer and acceptance. Medieval lawyers had never heard of either the doctrine of consideration (which evolved in the sixteenth century) or the doctrine of offer and acceptance (which evolved in the nineteenth), and to make matters more complicated, their general term for 'agreement' was 'covenant' and not 'contract'. Consequently any attempt to investigate

---

[1] Fifoot, Ch. XIII, contains an excellent general account of contract outside the common law. See also Barbour *passim*, and S.S. Vols. 2, 6, 10, 11, 18, 21, 46, and 49.

the medieval law of contract in terms of modern legal theory would be perfectly futile, for it could only lead to the ridiculous conclusion that no law of contract then existed. Thus the American Restatement of Contracts defines a contract as:

> 'a promise or a set of promises for the breach of which the law gives a remedy, or the performance of which the law in some way recognises as a duty'

and this would exclude from consideration entirely the standard form written contract—the conditioned bond—of medieval Europe. Such a definition is not doctrinally neutral, and perhaps a neutral definition, which does not reflect current ways of looking at the law, is not attainable. The only practicable method is to adopt for the purposes of the inquiry a loose working definition of contract law as the law governing the legal effect of those consensual transactions which have been regarded as giving rise to a relationship of obligation, normally confined to the parties to the transaction, and see how such transactions were handled by the old lawyers in their terms. Even this method involves an author in some inconsistency of treatment.

Though certain other forms of action also contributed to provide litigants with a common law remedy where agreements were not performed, the three most important forms of action which concern us are covenant, debt, and detinue. These three actions, which I shall discuss in order, formed the backbone of the medieval law of contract, and determined its basic divisions. Covenant, which was normally an action for unliquidated damages, lay to provide a remedy for the tort or wrong of breaking an agreement to do something other than pay a debt; it could only, however, be used in the case of formal agreements under seal. Informal agreements (also called 'covenants') were only remedied to a very limited extent in medieval law, though, as we shall see, some classes of informal agreement (typically sale of goods) fell into the category of 'contract', not 'covenant', and as such were provided with common law actions. Debt was an action which lay for the specific recovery of sums of money or things due to creditors; it lay on both formal and informal transactions, such transactions being called 'contracts'. The easiest way to understand the old conception of a contract is to think of it as involving reciprocal gifts—thus a sale was a contract, one party giving the other property in return for money; this way of looking at sale or barter survives in modern English usage—'I'll give you £200 for your car'. Just to make life difficult the action of debt was sometimes called detinue when a chattel, rather than money, was due—for example, a horse sold. What may be called detinue proper lay on the type of transaction which we and the old lawyers agree in calling bailment.

I

COVENANTS

1. FORMAL COVENANTS

THE writ of covenant became available *de cursu* (as a matter of course) in the thirteenth century, later than the writ of debt; before 1200[1] the intervention of the Crown in cases of covenant had been unusual and was probably bought at great cost. By Bracton's time it was well established.[2] It could be had in the form of a *justicies* to the sheriff, or it could initiate litigation directly in the royal court, following the ancient *praecipe* formula. In the Statute of Wales (1284) the model writ runs thus:

'Rex vicecomiti salutem. Praecipe A quod juste et sine dilatione teneat B convencionem inter eos factam de uno messuagio X acris terrae et V acris cum pertinencis in N etc., et nisi fecerit etc. tunc summone praedictam A quod sit . . . ostenturus quare'

The King to the sheriff, greetings. Order A that justly and without delay he perform for B the covenant made between them concerning one messuage, ten acres of land, and five acres of land with its appurtenances in N . . . and if he does not do so . . . summon the aforesaid A that he be before . . . to show why he has not done so.

This form was not changed in any significant way throughout the Middle Ages.[3] The writ was varied as the subject-matter of the covenant required, and forms were developed to cover

---

[1] See S.S. Vol. 77 (Van Caenegem), pp. 256 n. 1, 264 n. 2, 493 n. 154, for early examples of royal intervention in matters of covenant.

[2] See Maitland, 'The History of the Register of Original Writs', *Collected Papers*, II, p. 110. A very early example appears in 1200; see S.S. Vol. 67 at 293 (pl. 3096). There are sixteen cases only in Bracton's *Note Book*. For examples see *Early Registers of Writs*, S.S. Vol. 87 at pp. 15, 27, 79, 231-4.

[3] F.N.B. 145A et seq., and S.S. Vol. 87 (De Haas and Hall), pp. 231-4 giving orms taken from a Register compiled 1318-20, p. 26 (a *justicies*), and p. 78.

such special situations as actions by or against executors or administrators.

The original scope of the action, and its restriction to formal covenants

Maitland, with some caution, suggested that at first covenant could only be used in the royal courts when the covenant concerned land; indeed he went so far as to say that the action was almost always an action on a lease.[1] The lessee for years could not use the assize of novel disseisin, and it could well be that covenant originally lay to remedy this situation. The exclusive association of the writ with land has been doubted by Sir Cyril Flower and Mr. Fifoot[2], and the latter has certain shown that the action was not originally confined to actions taken on leases. But whatever the position may have been in the early thirteenth century, no trace of any restriction survived into the year-book period. A register of writs of 1318–20 gives forms appropriate to actions for covenants dealing with corodies, building contracts, and suit of court[3]. The subject-matter of the covenant was by then apparently immaterial.[4]

In the developed common law the writ could only be used by a plaintiff who could produce a sealed instrument (a 'specialty') to witness the covenant; failure to produce ('make profert') the specialty had the consequence that the action failed *in limine*. In the thirteenth and early fourteenth centuries this rule was not clearly settled; indeed as late as 1346[5] there must have been some doubt on the point. This suggests that originally the action lay on mere parole covenants, and that a new and restrictive rule was introduced into the law in Edward I's reign, or thereabouts. But I doubt if this would be a justifiable interpretation, for there never seems to have been a time

---

[1] P. and M. II. 217.

[2] Flower, *Introduction to the Curia Regis Rolls*, S.S. Vol. 62, p. 285 et seq. Flower's argument is not convincing, since the cases he refers to are not actions of covenant, but merely actions concerning covenants. Fifoot 255–6.

[3] S.S. Vol. 87 (Haas and Hall) at pp. 231–4.

[4] S.S. Vol. 87 (Haas and Hall), pp. 231–4. I sampled Vols. IX, X, XII, and XIV of the published Curia Regis Rolls, and it does appear that all actions concern land; the indices are, however, very defective.

[5] In that year the King's Bench on a writ of error reversed a decision allowing covenant without specialty. Thereafter the rule was settled. See Y.B. 20 Edw. III (R.S.), Vol. II, p. 263, and cf. 44 Edw. III, M. f. 42, pl. 46.

when the royal courts regularly allowed actions to be taken on parole covenants; indeed there is a case in the Curia Regis Rolls as early as 1234[1] where it seems that an action of covenant failed because the plaintiff had no charter or chyrograph. What appears to have happened was that an old restrictive doctrine was for some considerable period under attack; if this explains the cases where the point is raised,[2] and occasionally the rule not observed,[3] it is still not easy to see why the common law judges resisted the pressure to extend the scope of the common law action.

Professor Milsom[4] has suggested that an explanation may lie in a conflict of views as to the proper jurisdiction of the royal courts. About this time—that is in the late thirteenth and early fourteenth centuries—there is evidence of a certain degree of resistance to the flow of cases from the local to the royal courts; a shift in jurisdiction was taking place, and not everybody liked it. The insistence upon a specialty, according to this interpretation, represents a compromise, for it reserves actions on parole contracts for the local courts, and thus limits the extent of royal jurisdiction over cases of covenant. Although there is no direct evidence in favour of this, nor even direct evidence of any pressure upon the common law judges to limit their jurisdiction over covenants, the suggestion is very plausible. It removes the specialty rule from the field of substantive law— the common law judges were not giving expression to the notion that only formal agreements should be actionable and legally valid, but merely saying that only formal agreements should be actionable in the royal courts.

There are other possible explanations. One is suggested by a case decided in 1311.[5] One Alice held lands in dower, and

[1] Found by Maitland in C.R.R. No. 115, m. 7, and noted in P. and M., Vol. II, p. 220 n. 1.

[2] Curia Regis Roll No. 140, m. 15d (noted in P. and M., Vol. II, p. 220 n. 1). Y.B. 20 Edw. I (R.S.), 222, 487 (probably a plaint in the nature of a writ of debt); 32 and 33 Edw. I (R.S.), 199; *Anon.* (1321) printed from Lincolns Inn MS. Hale 141 by Kiralfy, *Source Book*, 180; S.S. Vol. 86, p. 287; 15 Edw. III (R.S.), 454; 18 Edw. III (R.S.), 22.

[3] In 32 Edw. I (R.S.), 296 a lessor was allowed to sue a lessee without producing a deed in covenant on the ground that the lessee had the specialty in his possession. This came to be a settled exception to the requirement that a deed, if relied upon, must be produced. See *Read v. Brookman* 3 T.R. 151.

[4] Milsom, 214.

[5] S.S. Vol. 42 (Turner) at 71.

leased them *pur autre vie* to John de la Rokele, who wasted the lands. Alice was sued by the tenant in fee, Elaine, who recovered triple damages from her for the waste. Alice thereupon sued John in covenant to recover the damages; since she was a dower-ess and did not hold in fee she was unable to use the writ of waste. She was unable, however, to produce a specialty, and her action was objected to upon this ground. Bereford C.J. nevertheless allowed the action to proceed, and justified this by pointing out that Alice was not seeking to impose upon John by covenant any liability over and above his common law liability for waste; it was John who needed to produce a specialty to justify *his* conduct which was prima facie wrongful at common law. Behind Bereford's argument lies a general theory of legal liability which was common enough at the time; it was that a specialty, and only a specialty, could impose obligations, confer rights, and create legal relations which were *special* in that they departed from the *general* rules of the common law.[1] The same theory was applied to the entailed interest in real property. It could well have some connection with the doctrine applied to the writ of covenant, if only because it provided a substantive justification for the rule.

Another possible explanation seems more plausible. The possible alternative to the production of a specialty in actions of covenant was the production of suit, that is witnesses to the transaction. Now strictly speaking neither specialty nor suit was offered as *proof* on the trial of a contested issue. As Thayer points out,

'It was the office of the *secta* [i.e. suit] to support the plain-tiff's case, *in advance of any answer from the defendant*.'[2]

He goes on to show that profert of sealed instruments served the same function, showing that there was a claim which merited an answer; a plaintiff who offered neither suit nor specialty could be met by the submission that no answer was called for at all. Only if the action passed beyond this prelimin-ary stage did any question of pleading to an issue requiring trial arise, and trial in actions of covenant was trial by jury. In

---

[1] This idea was enshrined in such tags as *convencio legi deroget, convencio vincit legem*, and even gets into a statute (West. II, c. 46).

[2] Thayer, *Evidence*, 13.

deciding whether the specialty rule should be relaxed, and suit allowed as an alternative, the courts were only therefore dealing with a preliminary matter, and at this stage in the history of the common law it would never have been suggested that the bare assertion by the plaintiff of a covenant, unsupported by any-thing else, would be sufficient to put the defendant to answer. For it was then accepted that no man need answer the plaintiff's *nude parole*.[1] Now in the early years of the fourteenth century, when the possibility of offering suit as an alternative to a specialty was being canvassed, the production of suit was becoming an empty formality, and the practice of examining and questioning the suitors was falling into disrepute.[2] Why this was so is obscure, but there is no doubt that the common law courts were allowing the institution to degenerate. In conse-quence it is not very surprising that they refused to allow the production of suit as an alternative to the production of a specialty. There may indeed have been a risk of the specialty rule being applied to actions of debt as well.[3] These explanations are not necessarily mutually inconsistent.

Once the specialty rule was settled, it became a permanent feature of the law governing the action of covenant, immune from frontal attack. Had the decisions gone the other way the consequences would have been very far reaching, and we should surely never have heard of the action of assumpsit.

Covenant and damages

In the period covered by the year-books the action of covenant is regularly regarded as an action to recover unliqui-dated damages for wrongful or tortious breach of covenant; the only exception to this is that a lessee for years can recover his term, if unexpired,[4] from his lessor—though from nobody

---

[1] Thayer, *Evidence*, 10–16, P. and M., II. 605–10. See Y.B. 20 Edw. I (R.S.), 69.

[2] In 1314 (Y.B. 7 Edw. II, 242) it is said that the suit could not be examined. This was firmly settled by a case in 1343 (17 Edw. III, f. 48, pl. 14).

[3] Suit was acceptable in a writ of debt in the fourteenth century and thereafter. In 20 Edw. I (R.S.) 222 (1292) in debt for money lent it was argued that the creditor must proffer a tally or writing obligatory; held that suit was enough. Earlier Fleta, written in about 1290, supposes a record or writing to be essential; see Fleta, II, c. 60, s. 25.

[4] F.N.B. 145L, and see 24 Edw. III, f. 24, Dyer 257. In 38 Edw. III, M. f. 24 Serjeant Belknap argued that the lessee of a tenant in tail could recover his term by covenant from the issue in tail, so long as they took assets by descent, but this view was not accepted by Skipwith J., only damages being recoverable.

else. But this had not always been the position. In common with other early writs the writ of covenant, by its very terms, seems to be designed not so much to initiate proceedings directed towards compensating the plaintiff for wrong done, as to ensure that what was wrong should be put right; what seems to have been envisaged was specific performance rather than damages. Indeed in the thirteenth century, specific relief was in fact granted where some definite thing was in demand.[1] The common law courts used various techniques for ensuring that specific performance in fact took place; the defendant could be encouraged to perform by distraint, or security for performance could be taken from him. In some cases the sheriff could be ordered to take appropriate action. But in cases where the covenant was purely personal, no specific thing being in demand, it was more or less settled in Bracton's time that damages should be awarded.[2] The practice of granting specific relief soon afterwards passed out of use; thus in *Brevia Placitata* (*c.* 1260)[3] it is noted that only a term, and never right or fee, can be recovered. In a case in 1324 this principle is applied, though Serjeant Toudeby told the court that he had seen fee tail recovered.[4] A case in 1334 seems to suggest that a restrictive covenant not to build a mill might still be enforced by something in the nature of a mandatory order to demolish.[5] In 1345[6] the court rejected a belated attempt to persuade the justices to order distraint of an Abbot.

There is a neat illustration of the consequence of this development in a case in 1364.[7] A Prior brought covenant against an Abbot on a composition under seal concerning the payment of tithes, and the action was objected to upon the ground that since the cause of the composition was tithes, which were spiritual in

---

[1] See Fifoot 259 et seq. and the authorities there cited. S.S. Vol. 60 (Richardson and Sayles), pp. 127f. (1260–1). cf. S.S. Vol. 2 (Maitland), p. 36 (1290) for an example of an order for specific performance of a covenant to grant a lease in the Manorial Court of Ogbourne, Wilts.

[2] For discussion see Plucknett, 678–9, Hazeltine, 'Early History of English Equity', *Essays in Legal History* (ed. Vinogradoff), 261.

[3] S.S. Vol. 66 (Turner and Plucknett), p. 204. cf. *Casus Placitorum*, S.S. Vol. 69 (Dunham), p. 42.

[4] 18 Edw. II, P. f. 602.

[5] 7 Edw. III, M. f. 65, pl. 67, and see M. 4 Edw. III, f. 57, pl. 5, S.C.

[6] 19 Edw. III (R.S.), 422, and see 16 Edw. III (R.S.), 288.

[7] 38 Edw. III, P. f. 8, pl. 2.

their nature, the litigation should be conducted in an ecclesiastical court. Thirning C.J. overruled the objection:

'He has taken this action on a covenant fashioned by your own deed (*taille par votre fait desmesne*) and he can recover no tithes by this writ.'

Thirning's argument has two limbs. The first is that the royal court has jurisdiction over actions brought on deeds—which is the obverse of the rule that it *only* has jurisdiction where there is a deed; the second is that the action can only lead to the recovery of damages, and not specific performance, so that the action is, as it were, primarily concerned not with tithes but damages.[1]

Was the deed dispositive or evidentiary?

Originally the deed was regarded as what we could call evidence of the covenant, and the function of producing it (making profert) was regarded as a 'proof'. This is illustrated by the way the matter is put: the deed is said to 'witness' the covenant, just as the production of suitors served as witness or proof of a transaction.[2] Although, so far as the common law was concerned, the profert of a deed as witness of a covenant became essential, so that the action would fail *in limine* if no deed was produced, medieval lawyers do not appear to have come to think of the deed as a dispositive document in the fullest sense.[3] The best evidence that they did not think in this way is linguistic, and can be understood more easily if we consider a modern example, namely a will. Today a properly executed and witnessed will is a clear example of a dispositive instrument, and the way in which we view the matter is clearly illustrated by the fact that when we use the word 'will' we mean the actual and tangible document, not the wishes it expresses. Thus to destroy a 'will' means to destroy a piece of paper. Once upon a time (before writing was essential) a 'will' just meant the

---

[1] For illustrations of the rule in operation see 47 Edw. III, T. f. 3, pl. 4; 7 Edw. IV, H. f. 25, pl. 2.

[2] See *Anon.* (1313) S.S. Vol. 27 (Bolland), p. 13; S.S. Vol. 60 (Richardson and Sayles), p. 27; 2 Edw. II, M. ff. 49–50; 10 Edw. II, H. f. 307.

[3] For an exception see 40 Edw. III, H. f. 5, pl. 11, where Finchden speaks of a covenantor being 'bound by his deed [*fait*] to do a thing . . .', 'deed' here probably referring to the document itself.

wishes or desire of a person; hence a document was not itself
a will, but merely proof of what the testator's will was. In those
days to talk of destroying a will would have made no sense,
except as a reference to brain-washing. Medieval lawyers used
the word 'covenant' not to mean 'agreement under seal' but
simply to mean 'agreement'.[1] Very approximately we can
say that 'covenant' once meant what 'contract' means today.
In the course of time the usage changed; 'covenant' came
to mean 'agreement under seal'. This change did not occur
until after the medieval period, and of course in non-legal
contexts the older usage survives, with a hint of archaism. We
may still make a covenant with the devil without executing a
deed.

The fact that the deed, which had to be produced in a common law action of covenant, was not viewed as dispositive in
the fullest sense is not of purely linguistic interest; it has a wider
theoretical importance in the history of contract law. 'Covenant' was, as I have said, the medieval common lawyers' word
for agreement, and if by 'covenant' the lawyers had also meant
'something necessarily under seal' it would follow that they
were committed to the view that only formal agreements ought
to be legally sanctioned, or perhaps even that only formal
agreements really counted as agreements at all.[2] It is indeed
the contention of some writers that in early forms of society
formal agreements are indeed the first to achieve recognition, or
at least legal recognition (which is not quite the same thing).
Whatever truth there may be in this thesis in general, it is
quite clear that in the year-book period the common lawyers
had no doubt whatever that there could be agreements which
were not under seal, and that they had no objection to such
agreements being legally actionable, though not necessarily at
common law. Thus in 1448 and again in 1482 it is pointed out
in the year-books that in the city court in London an action of
covenant lies without specialty.[3] The common law rule that he
who sued by writ of covenant must produce a deed is not the

---

[1] For examples see 2 Hen. IV, M. f. 3, pl. 9; 3 Hen. VI, H. f. 36, pl. 33; 14 Hen.
VI, f. 18, pl. 58.
[2] See generally on this point Milsom, 'Not Doing is No Trespass', 1954 C.L.J.
105, 'Reason in the Development of the Common Law', 81 L.Q.R. 496, *Historical
Foundations of the Common Law*, III, Ch. 10.
[3] Fitz. *Covenant* 11; 22 Edw. IV, f. 1, pl. 6.

expression of a general formalistic theory of the nature of contract, and an appreciation of this fact is very relevant to the evolution of assumpsit.

Covenant and the writ of debt

If a plaintiff claimed a specific sum of money and based his claim upon an instrument under seal, the correct writ was the writ of debt,[1] not covenant; the species of debt used was called debt *sur obligation*, 'obligation' being the name given to the sealed instrument which bound the debtor to pay the sum due. Although the position eventually changed, the medieval lawyers did not permit the writs of covenant and debt to overlap; hence a transaction, in so far as it gave rise to a debt, was not a covenant. Occasionally cases may be found which at first sight appear to violate this rule, but if properly considered they merely illustrate its operation. Thus there is a case in 1477[2] where a lessee for years of a manor sued his lessor on a covenant whereby the lessor agreed that:

'he would acquit him [i.e. the lessee] during the term of all charges issuing out of the said manor during the term.'

This might appear to be a case where debt was the proper action, but the explanation was presumably that where there was a lease for years the lessee was the debtor, and the received doctrine was that one transaction could only produce one debtor. Again where a rent was granted by the compromised personal action known as a fine, an action of covenant based upon the court record lay to recover the rent; one might expect the action to be debt.[3] The explanation is that the personal action used for the fine was covenant, and a covenant could only give rise to an action of covenant, not to a debt; hence the action of debt was not available. Another illustration is the case of a guarantee under seal of a debt; the guarantor must be sued in covenant, for since there was only one debt, there could be only one debtor.[4] The one possible exception is the

---

[1] See below, p. 70.
[2] 17 Edw. IV, M. f. 5, pl. 4; T. f. 14, pl. 38.
[3] 22 Edw. IV, P. f. 1, pl. 6.
[4] On sureties see F.N.B. 146B; 39 Edw. III, 9. cf. 10 Edw. II, H. 307, where on an agreement under seal to pay money to a third party the third party's action is covenant, not debt, since the covenantor was not debtor to the third party.

case of a lease; Fineux C.J. in 1505[1] was of opinion that the
lessor could use debt or covenant for the rent at his election,
but earlier authority[2] is against his view. In the end debt and
covenant did become elective remedies; this development is
discussed later in connection with the action of debt.

Where debt was brought on a sealed instrument—called a
'bond' or 'obligation'—the instrument was regarded as dispositive in the fullest sense. It *was* the 'obligation' or 'bond', and,
since it conferred a right to the specific recovery of the debt,
it was treated as analogous to a deed of grant.[3] Partly because
debt and covenant did not overlap, and partly because specific
performance in covenant was largely abandoned, the action of
covenant came to be regarded primarily as an action for
compensation (assessed by a jury) for the tort or wrong of breach
of covenant, in sharp contrast to the recuperatory nature of the
action of debt. The character of the later action of assumpsit
resembled the character of covenant: it too was conceived as a
personal action for compensation for the wrong or tort of
breach of promise.

The theory of covenant

The old lawyers were perfectly well aware of the fact that
covenants involved agreement; as Bromley said in *Reade* v.
Bullocke (1543), 'each covenant implies agreement'.[4] Indeed
'covenant', as we have seen, was their word for 'agreement'.
Now a modern lawyer does not call every transaction involving
agreement a 'contract';[5] for example, a licence to enter property
for a picnic, or an undertaking which makes a person liable for
negligent mistatement would not usually be so described; we
are brought up to confine the use of the term 'contract' to those
transactions which can give rise to actions categorized as
actions for breach of contract, and the actions available in the
illustrations I have given are traditionally thought to be tort
actions, which we like to distinguish from contract actions.
Similarly the term 'covenant' tended to be used to describe the
sort of agreement which could give rise to an action of cove-

[1] 21 Hen. VII, M. f. 16, pl. 45.
[2] 22 Hen. VI, T. f. 58, pl. 7.
[3] See below, p. 95.
[4] Dyer 56b.
[5] For discussion of the conception in modern law see Atiyah, *Contract*, 23.

nant (provided a specialty was available). This action was a
compensatory action for a tort or wrong, the tort of breach of
covenant. Hence the theoretical function of the covenant was
to make future conduct, which would otherwise be lawful,
tortious and actionable, in much the same way as an undertaking of responsibility in modern tort law may have the effect
of making tortious otherwise lawful future inactivity or carelessness. But the effect of the sort of agreement which was
actionable by writ of covenant was not to confer upon the
covenantee any enforceable right to the possession, either
immediately or in the future, of any definite thing, be it a debt,
a chattel, land, or a person; a covenant did not operate as any
form of transfer. This scheme of thought may seem peculiar to
moderns, for it seems to be making the law of covenants into a
subdivision of the law of torts; nevertheless it was the way in
which covenants were analysed, and it found expression in the
doctrine that covenants were 'executory', as opposed to 'executed'. The gist of this doctrine, which is somewhat difficult to
express in modern legal terminology, was that 'covenant' was
by definition an agreement to do something in the future, and
as such could be contrasted with other consensual transactions
which actually conferred or released rights in things. Transactions which did this included those called by contemporaries
contracts. For example, a sale of goods, which had the effect of
transferring rights to the thing sold and the price, was a typical
'contract'.

   Thus a covenant could be contrasted with a grant, which
operated to transfer some form of immediate right or interest
in a thing to the grantee; in consequence it was arguable that
a document whereby one man *promised* to pay another money
was in terms future looking, and could not be construed as
conferring upon the promisee a right to the debt, the debt being
recoverable by writ of debt, but only a right to sue in covenant
for damages[1] if the promisor wrongfully failed to perform his
promise. Again an agreement under seal which permitted a man
to enjoy the property of another for a fixed period did not
create a lease; a lease required a grant, and a grant required
words of grant and not merely words of agreement.[2] Similar

---

[1] See Vavasour in 22 Edw. IV, M. f. 22, pl. 1.
[2] See Brooke, *Covenant* 26 and 21 Hen. VII, M. f. 37, pl. 45 and below, p. 45.

reasoning lies behind the judgment of Danby J. in *Alice's Case* (1458).[1] Here debt was brought, and the plaintiff declared that it had been agreed by parole (*concordatum est*) that one J, the plaintiff, should take the defendant's daughter Alice in marriage, and that the defendant should owe the plaintiff a hundred marks. Danby J. said,

> 'It seems to me that he cannot have an action, for it is neither contract nor accord, but is merely a covenant, upon which no action can be brought without a specialty. For the writ[2] is *"concordatum est"*, and this is neither contract nor accord, being merely covenant. . . . For I put it to you that if this matter had been written in an indenture like this: *Haec indentura* etc. *quod concordatum est, quod praedictus J accipiet in uxore A filiam Praedicti S et praedictus S debet ei C marcarum* would he now have an action of debt on the deed?' [As it were he said he would not, since there is no word of grant.]

Another case which illustrates the doctrine is reported in 1505.[3] An action of debt was brought on a bond; the debtor pleaded in bar to the action a document under seal whereby the creditor bound himself not to sue or vex the debtor by force of the bond before the Feast of St. Michael, which had not yet arrived. The point at issue was whether the document counted as an acquittance or release of the debt, that is to say as a kind of grant, so as to discharge the duty; if not it could not be pleaded in bar to the action. Fineux C.J. and Tremaile J. thought it did not:

> 'the words cannot be said to amount to a release or acquittance so as to determine the duty, for although he has granted that "he will not sue him before such a feast", yet these words cannot be otherwise construed than as words of covenant, and [not] of grant, in which case although the party has covenanted [not] to do such a thing, yet by this the thing for which the covenant is made cannot be determined, but the party in whose favour such a grant is made will have his remedy by writ of covenant.'

[1] 37 Hen. VI, M. f. 8, pl. 18 (F. 249).
[2] Presumably a mistake for count.
[3] 21 Hen. VII, T. f. 23, pl. 16, and cf. 21 Hen. VII, M. f. 30, pl. 10.

The theory of covenant is also neatly illustrated in cases involving the distinction between a condition and a covenant, which is well stated in the argument of Norwich in a case in 1523:[1]

'And sir, there is a great difference between a covenant and a condition, for by a condition a thing may be executed, but not by a covenant ... thus if I enfeoff you on condition of payment or non payment, now by this condition is your estate determinable on the condition; but if I lease lands to you for term of years and then by another deed make a covenant that if you pay me a certain sum of money by such a day you will have fee, although you perform this you will not have fee.' [i.e. you can only sue for damages for breach of covenant.]

This distinction may also be illustrated by a case in 1448.[2] Debt was brought in the Guildhall for rent due on the lease of a house for years. The lessee pleaded in bar to the action a custom requiring the landlord to repair the house, and he averred that the house was ruinous for lack of repair. The court held that the custom was to be regarded as in the nature of a covenant rather than a condition; hence it did not operate so as to discharge the lessee's obligation to pay rent in the event of breach. Therefore the action was not barred; the lessee must pay the rent due and have recourse to an action for breach of covenant. However, had the lessor been the King, the custom would have been construed as imposing a condition, for only thus could injustice be avoided; it would be idle to put the lessee to his action of covenant if no such action could be. brought,[3] and you could not sue the King.

In the early sixteenth century the traditional theory of covenant began to break down, for, after a considerable period of doubt, it came to be settled that a covenant could in certain circumstances pass a use in lands (i.e. a trust interest) to the covenantee, and thus operate to transfer an immediate interest in property; this development is discussed elsewhere in this

[1] 14 Hen. VIII, H. f. 18, pl. 7 at f. 19.
[2] 27 Hen. VI, T. f. 10, pl. 6.
[3] 31 Hen. VI, H. f. 21, pl. 3.

book.[1] Some lawyers[2] indeed were prepared to contend that any covenant concerning a chattel could operate to confer on the covenantee a right to the possession of the chattel, but this view did not prevail; in general it remained law that a covenant was merely 'executory'. But any rational analysis of the nature of covenants was hindered by the fact that such transactions as sales and leases, which did operate as grants in that they conferred rights to things, were also consensual transactions, and therefore could be called agreements or covenants.

The late medieval theory of covenants as 'executory' seems to reflect a conceptual distinction between (as we would say) *contract* and *conveyance*.[3] The analysis of this distinction in modern legal theory is beset with very considerable difficulties, for it involves the disputed question of the nature of rights *in rem* and rights *in persorlam*. It would be a mistake to suppose that medieval lawyers were familiar with such mysteries as intrigued Hohfeld or Kocourek. To their way of thinking such things as grants, conditions, and releases could operate so as to transfer or release rights in things; in contrast, the only effect of a covenant was to make future conduct, which would otherwise be lawful, tortious and actionable in damages. This contrast is not necessarily connected with the idea that some transactions can give rise to rights against the whole world, and others only to rights against limited classes of person, and for this reason it would be a mistake to think that the analogy between their distinction between covenant and grant, and the modern distinction between contract and conveyance, is particularly close.

Formality and Covenant

Though in theory merely evidentiary, a specialty was essential evidence if an action of covenant was to be maintained at common law; as Finchden C.J. explained in *The Prior of Bradstock's Case* (1371),[4]

[1] See below, p. 348 and see A. W. B. Simpson, 'The Equitable Doctrine of Consideration and the Law of Uses', 1965 Toronto L.J. 1.
[2] In particular see the argument of Deinshil in 27 Hen. VIII, T. f. 14, pl. 6 at f. 16; f. 28, pl. 16.
[3] See below, p. 187, for attempts to distinguish 'covenant' and 'contract'.
[4] 44 Edw. III, M. f. 42, pl. 46, Fifoot 247.

'. . . the action is taken on the deed, and without a deed it cannot be maintained.'

As a general rule the plaintiff must rely upon the precise terms of the deed, setting them out in certain and declaring precisely in what respects each covenant had been broken.[1] In certain exceptional situations it was possible to rely upon implied covenants. Thus if a master retained a servant by indenture, the servant could sue the master by writ of covenant if he failed to provide food and necessaries, for the master was bound by 'very right' to provide these.[2] Or again, a customary implied covenant in a lease was actionable by writ of covenant.[3] But in both situations it was essential that the main transaction be witnessed by deed; implied covenants could only be parasitic.

The deed rule in covenant, though evidentiary, attracted the general formalistic principle that a deed must be met with a deed. This was natural; it would hardly be fair to require the plaintiff to produce a deed if the defendant could advance defences substantiated merely by parole averment. Hence the action of covenant has been called 'strict'. But the strictness of the action can easily be exaggerated and misunderstood,[4] particularly if false analogies are drawn between covenant and the action of debt, for in covenant the insistence upon *contrarius actus* was not carried to great lengths.

The simplest illustration is the defence of performance. It would clearly have been wholly impracticable to insist that this defence should be supported by the covenantor producing a deed saying that he had performed; hence all he need do is to aver performance. The plea 'lay in parole averment'.[5] This was quite unlike the position in actions of debt, where a plea of payment of the debt was never acceptable.[6] The covenantor must, however, plead performance specially, or, as we would

---

[1] 6 Hen. IV, H. f. 8, pl. 34.
[2] 34 Hen. VI, H. f. 25, pl. 3.
[3] 27 Hen. VI, T. f. 10, pl. 6.
[4] See, for example, Fifoot 258 n. 21 and 247.
[5] 6 Hen. IV, H. f. 8, pl. 34; Brooke, *Covenant* 35 (31–3 Hen. VIII), 33 (26 Edw. III). This would on principle be subject to an exception if the performance of the covenant involved a matter of record or the execution of a deed.
[6] 40 Edw. III, P. f. 24, pl. 27, and 1 Hen. V, T. f. 6, pl. 1 illustrate the fact that even in the case of a parole contract a plea of payment as such was no answer to the action, though in such a case a plea of *nihil debet* lay in parole averment.

say, in detail.[1] Thus if he was sued for the breach of a number of distinct covenants in an indenture he was not permitted to plead generally that he had performed all and singular the covenants in the indenture. Instead he must set out in certain how he had performed each one of them. Issue could then be taken on each covenant severally, and damages awarded separately for any covenant broken.[2] The issue was determinable by a jury, who would also determine the quantum of damages for breach. The law on the plea of performance reflected the peculiar nature of a covenant action, which involved both matters of specialty and matters of fact. A specialty was essential to prove that there had been an agreement, and to prove its terms; whether or not there had been a wrongful breach of covenant could only be treated as a matter of fact, triable by jury on the basis of the averments of the contending parties.

A case in 1535[3] illustrates the way in which a fairly straightforward action of covenant worked.

'William Holgyl, Master of the Hospital of the Savoy, brought a writ of covenant against J.S. because the said J.S. covenanted with the plaintiff that he was the very owner and possessor of certain lands in E. in the County of Middlesex called Huddon's Close, and that he would make a sure and sufficient estate of the same lands to the plaintiff before the festival of Easter. Note that in the declaration he recited all the indenture, which contained many other covenants besides these. And after, he showed how the defendant was not the very owner and possessor of the same close, and that he had not made estate to the plaintiff. The defendant said that he was the very owner and possessor of the same close, and had made estate to the plaintiff. And on this they were at issue. And now at the distress the jury appeared at the bar, and on evidence given on the day it appeared that the defendant had made estate to the plaintiff of certain lands call Huddon's Close, and that the defendant was very owner and possessor of this close, and this was well

---

[1] Brooke, *Covenant* 35 (31–3 Hen. VIII).

[2] Brooke, *Covenant* 34, citing Fitz. *Issue* 86 (13 Hen. VI), and see 10 Hen. VI, M. f. 23, pl. 80, Brooke, *Issue* 52, (14 Hen. IV).

[3] 27 Hen. VIII, M. f. 29, pl. 19.

proved by substantial witnesses (or "evidence"). Thereupon Fitzherbert J. said to the plaintiff's counsel, "What do
you say to all this, for if it be true you have no cause of
action?" Brown, who was counsel for the plaintiff: The truth
is that we have had an estate made to us by the defendant of
certain lands called Huddon's Close, but this land is not so
valuable as the land to which he is bound by his covenant,
for his covenant is that he ought to make us an estate before
such a festival according to a schedule annexed to the same
indenture, which schedule among other things contains this—
"Item, certain lands called Huddon's Close to the annual
value of £10." The land that we have is only worth five
pounds a year, and so the close that we have cannot be
understood as the close in the schedule; consequently he has
broken his covenant with us. And the indenture was examined, and it had the schedule annexed, and it was as Brown
said. Fitzherbert J. to Brown: Now that what you are saying
becomes clear, it is obvious that this action is not maintainable when brought in the form in which you have brought
it.'

Parole discharge and variation

In principle there could be no doubt that a mere parole
discharge or variation of a covenant under seal could furnish
no defence by itself, and this was never doubted. Difficulty was
raised, however, in situations when the covenantee both discharged the covenantor and made it impossible to perform the
covenant. The point arose on demurrer in a case in 1478.[1] The
plaintiff sued on a covenant to build a house for a payment of
£10. The defendant pleaded that he had come to build the
house, and was ready to do so, but that the plaintiff ordered
him not to build it; he therefore departed. The plaintiff
demurred to this plea. The court held the plea bad:

'And the opinion of the court was that the defendant would
only have the plea if he said that the plaintiff would not
permit him, for if the defendant had pleaded the plaintiff's
agreement without specialty [it would not suffice]. For he
cannot plead in bar without specialty where the plaintiff

[1] 18 Edw. IV, T. f. 8, pl. 12; 19 Edw. IV, M. f. 2, pl. 6.

counts on a specialty. But if the defendant said that the plaintiff would not suffer him to raise the house on his land, then this would be good, for the defendant cannot come upon the land without the consent of the plaintiff.'

A similar problem could arise if a servant by indenture was discharged by parole; clearly he could not serve his master if his master was unwilling to let him do so, nor could he compel his master to give him a deed of discharge. The cases[1] seem to say that parole discharge was nevertheless no plea. Thus Vavasour in 1485[2] said:

'For in an action of covenant against an apprentice it is not a plea on the apprentice's part to say that his master has discharged him from his apprenticeship, since his action is founded upon a specialty, which requires a reply of an equally high nature as it is.'

However, since a licence to enter property to perform the contract was essential to performance, its revocation, if valid, could be pleaded in answer to the action;[3] by parity of reasoning a plea of prevention of performance (as opposed to discharge by parole) was presumably good.

Where the covenantee did not discharge the covenantor and prevent performance, but requested and even voluntarily accepted some substituted performance from the covenantor, he was nevertheless entitled to sue for breach of the original agreement. Prisot C.J. and Danby J. in a case in 1455[4] laid down this rigorous rule in these terms:

'Suppose that I make a covenant with a carpenter to make me a house, and set out the location on my property where the house is to be built, and also specify all the manner of building in detail, and then it seems to me that another location on my property more needs to be built upon, and so I ask the carpenter to build me a house in a different place to the same specifications as are comprised in the indenture,

[1] 21 Hen. VI, H. f. 31, pl. 18; 1 Hen. VII, P. f. 14, pl. 2; 4 Hen. VII, P. f. 2, pl. 6. Note, however, that this rule was not wholly unfair, for the apprentice himself had a counter action. A servant discharged by parole could similarly sue for his salary; 21 Hen. VI, M. f. 7, pl. 16.
[2] 1 Hen. VII, P. f. 14, pl. 2.
[3] 18 Edw. IV, T. f. 8, pl. 12; 19 Edw. IV, M. f. 2, pl. 6.
[4] 32 Hen. VI, H. f. 31, pl. 25; M. f. 7, pl. 15,

and in consequence he does so at my request. This matter will not discharge him against me in a writ of covenant. . . .'

This seems extraordinarily harsh, and represents the high-water mark of the refusal to allow the defendant to meet a deed with a mere parole agreement. The carpenter could, of course, have insisted upon a new deed, and it was to this extent his folly not to have done so.

Arbitration and accord and satisfaction

Both the plea of an informally agreed submission to arbitration, and the plea of accord and satisfaction, if tendered in answer to an action of covenant, involve the general question of whether to allow an action based upon a specialty to be met by a parole agreement discharging the covenant. The former plea was offered in a case in 1405.[1] Covenant was brought against a man for failure to find a chaplain to sing divine service; the covenantor pleaded in bar an informal agreement between the parties (reached at the instigation of the Archbishop of Canterbury after the proceedings had begun back in 1400) to submit all their disputes to arbitration. Reade, the counsel for the plaintiff, replied,

'You see well how this is an action of covenant, which is not maintainable without a deed, and so you will not be received to avoid this action by an arbitration, which lies in averment. . . .'

The court agreed with this argument; dicta in 1605[2] suggests, however, that in post-medieval law the rule was otherwise, though there is authority the other way.[3] Since an action of debt lay on a parole submission to arbitration, there was good sense in allowing the plea; the point was not, however, likely to arise often, since it was more usual to make a formal submission, and to bind the parties to perform the arbitrator's award by penal bond.

Whether or not accord and satisfaction could bar an action of covenant seems never to have been raised for decision in medieval law. The question eventually came up in *Blake's Case*

---

[1] 6 Hen. IV, H. f. 8, pl. 34, continuing 2 Hen. IV, M. f. 6, pl. 25.
[2] *Blake's Case*, 6 Co.Rep. 43b.
[3] 1 Rolle 265, citing *Middleton* v. *Chapman* (1605).

(1605),[1] where an accord[2] and satisfaction after breach was pleaded in bar to action for breach of a covenant to repair.

> 'And it was objected, that this action of covenant was founded on the deed, which could not be discharged but by matter of as high a nature, and not by any accord or matter *in pais*; for *nihil tam conveniens est naturali aequitati, ut unumquodque dissolvi eo ligamine quo ligatum est.*'

It was held, however, that the plea was good. The basis for the decision was that the cause of action in covenant only arose when the covenantor committed the wrong or default of breach of covenant. Breach of covenant was a matter of fact; hence the plea of accord and satisfaction for breach of covenant only met a matter *in pais* with a matter *in pais*. Furthermore, in accordance with earlier dicta, the court took the view that in actions where damages only were recoverable for a wrong,[3] accord and satisfaction was a good plea, and, for the reason stated, claimed this did not involve any contradiction of the doctrine that a deed must be met by a deed. *Rabbet* v. *Stocker* (1620)[4] carried things one stage further by holding that an accord and satisfaction before breach was a good plea. In reality, however, the acceptance of submission to arbitration, and accord and satisfaction, as defences to actions of covenant, represent an inroad upon the principle that formality must be met with formality; both defences can be viewed as permitting parole variation of covenants under seal. Indeed the decision in *Rabbet* v. *Stocker* amounts to allowing any executed parole variation of a covenant to operate as a bar.

Since a specialty was essential to an action of covenant it naturally followed that the defendant could undermine the plaintiff's case by showing that the instrument produced was not a deed at all (in which case he would demur), or was not *his* deed, or that the deed was voidable for duress (defences of this character are discussed later in this book in connection

---

[1] 6 Co.Rep. 43b.

[2] The 'accord' was the agreement to take something in satisfaction, and the 'satisfaction' was the receipt of that thing. An 'accord' alone was never thought enough, since no action lay upon a mere accord in medieval law.

[3] e.g. *Andrew* v. *Boughey* (1552) Dyer 75a, Fifoot 355. The theory is that covenant is a 'tort' action, the function of the specialty only being to substantiate the characterization of the defendant's conduct as tortious.

[4] 1 Rolle Ab. 265. 2 Roll. Rep. 181.

with bonds). Similarly he could answer a deed with a deed, as by producing a release or acquittance under seal. General defences based upon mistake, undue influence, or fraud were never admitted.

Excuses for failure to perform, illegality, impossibility, and absence of fault

An illegal covenant was void, so that the covenantor had a complete defence to any action taken upon it; the rule is obvious, though authority is scanty on the point, for the law will clearly not allow its process to be used to encourage illegal performance.[1] The subject is more fully discussed in connection with bonds, where the principles applied were identical.

More difficult problems are involved when a covenantor wishes to excuse his failure to perform by a plea which involves the contention that the breach of covenant is not the result of any default on his part; it has to be established one way or the other whether a plea of this general character counts as an answer to the action. The simplest case, though rare in practice, is where the covenant is from the outset impossible of performance. Here authority is scanty. In the case of conditioned bonds where the condition was impossible the bond was good and the condition void;[2] thus if Robert was bound to pay Peter £100 unless he flew to the moon, Robert had to pay. The view taken seems to have been that just as an impossible *condition* was void, so too was an impossible *covenant*, though the consequence was that the covenantor was *not* liable in an action for breach of covenant, though he would be liable if a bond had been executed for performance of the covenant. This doctrine is stated by Pollard J. in 1523[3] thus:

'And also if I covenant to make you a house before a certain day, and also that I shall go to Rome in a day, or that I will overturn Westminster Hall with my finger, or make Thames run through Westminster Hall, or other impossiblities, there

[1] See 14 Hen. VIII, P. f. 25, pl. 7, where it is suggested that if an indenture contained a number of covenants, some illegal and some not, the legal covenants could be severed from the illegal. See *Henry Pigot's Case* (1615) 11 Co.Rep. 26b, a case which contains the interesting information that John Shuter of the County of Wilts died at the age of 115 years.
[2] Discussed below, p. 110.
[3] 14 Hen. VIII, P. f. 25, pl. 7.

the deed is void so far as these covenants are concerned, and good as far as the others which are possible are concerned. . . .'

Cases involving wholly impossible covenants are not, however, likely to arise in practice, and so it is hardly necessary for the law to possess a settled doctrine on the matter.[1]

A problem more likely to arise in practice is that of a covenant whose performance involves the co-operation of a third party, over whom the covenantor has no control. If the third party refuses to co-operate is the covenantor discharged upon the ground that his default has not brought about the breach of covenant? This point arose in a case in 1455.[2] The defendant had covenanted by indenture with the plaintiff to marry the plaintiff's daughter, and enfeoff four persons of lands to her use; he had done neither. When sued by writ of covenant he pleaded that the daughter had refused to marry him and the feoffees had not turned up to have the land conveyed to them; to this plea the plaintiff demurred. The court held the plea bad; so long as the thing to be done was lawful and in principle possible, and performance had not been prevented by the covenantee, the covenantor was liable, although it was not his fault that performance had not ensued. Analogous cases concerning conditioned bonds,[3] where the same rules applied, justified this doctrine by saying that the contracting party had only himself to blame for making an agreement whose performance was out of his control.

Some event occurring after a covenant had been made without fault on the covenantor's part might render performance either wholly impossible, or at least very onerous, although at the time when the covenant was made it might have seemed that performance would present no special difficulty. In the case of supervening *impossibility* (excluding cases involving co-operation by a third party) presumably the covenantor had a defence; granted that initial impossibility makes the covenant void, supervening *impossibility* as a defence follows *a fortiori*.

---

[1] See on the subject Pollock, *Contracts*, 233 et seq.
[2] 33 Hen. VI, P. f. 16, pl. 7.
[3] See below, p. 108. If the covenantee prevented performance, as by validly revoking a licence essential to performance, the covenanter had a defence: see 18 Edw. IV, T. f. 8, pl. 12.

This was the medieval rule for conditioned bonds. There is no direct authority except on the effect of the death of the covenantor, a clear case of act of God. Here the rule was that death discharged a covenant for personal service, as one which by its terms could only be performed by the covenantor in person.[1] Again the problem is unlikely to arise in practice, which is the reason for the absence of clear authority.

There are, however, cases where some supervening event has made performance very onerous. Such a case was discussed inconclusively in 1355.[2] Land was leased for years subject to a covenant that the lessee would leave the buildings in as good plight as he found them; covenant was brought, and the defendant pleaded that a wall on the property had been blown down by the great wind (probably a reference to a particular storm) and by tempests. It was argued on one side that such a 'sudden adventure' or 'adventure of God', and 'adventure of aliens' (i.e. act of enemy aliens) ought to excuse the covenantor, since it could not in such circumstances be said to be the covenantor's default which caused the breach of covenant averred; on the other side Finchden put the argument thus:

'But a man is liable to do a thing which is within the power of a man; hence when he bound himself to the lessee to repair them, notwithstanding that [the wall] be destroyed by the wind, or by other sudden adventures, yet you have power to repair [it] and can do so, and thus you have broken the covenant, and you could have made provision in advance for such sudden adventures, and excluded such liability by express covenant.'

Though the point is not mentioned in the case, the two categories of supervening event emphasized—acts of God and acts of enemies—are peculiar in that no remedy over can possibly exist. Though the case is inconclusive, Brooke,[3] writing in the mid-sixteenth century, treated it as authority for the view that there would be liability unless performance became wholly impossible—for example, if trees were blown down it would be

[1] Though Brooke, *Covenant* 4, took 40 Edw. III, H. f. 5, pl. 11 to support the view taken in the text. See also 47 Edw. III, M. pl. 50, f. 22; 10 Hen. VII, P. f. 18, pl. 4; 15 Hen. VII, H. f. 2, pl. 5.
[2] 40 Edw. III, H. f. 5, pl. 11.
[3] Brooke, *Covenant* 4.

wholly impossible for the covenantor to make them grow again, and he would not then be liable. In accordance with some earlier authority[1] he distinguished the effect of a private contract where liability was self-imposed from the effect of the general law; a man by private contract could make himself strictly liable, whereas if his liability was imposed upon him by general law he would not be liable in the absence of default; for example, act of God was a defence to an action of waste.[2] As Finchden had pointed out, a party to a private contract could by express covenant exempt himself from strict liability if he wished to do so.

A case in 1537[3] before Shelley and Fitzherbert JJ. adopted this point of view. Meadow land had been leased, subject to a covenant requiring the lessee to maintain banks against flooding; 'un graund, outrageous et sudden floode' broke down the banks. They held that the lessee was not liable to pay an immediate penalty for a breach of covenant occasioned by such an act of God, which could not possibly be resisted; nevertheless the lessee was still liable to repair the banks, something he *was* able to do, and if he did not do this he would be liable to an action for breach of the covenant. In effect this meant that supervening total impossibility was a defence, but the mere fact that performance had been made more onerous by an act of God did not excuse the covenantor.

Brooke's theory, based upon the distinction between self-imposed liability and liability imposed by general law, enjoyed considerable popularity in the sixteenth and seventeenth centuries; it is exemplified, for example, in the earliest decision on the liability of common carriers[4] and in the well-known decision in *Southcote* v. *Bennet* (1601).[5] To some lawyers it seemed

---

[1] See below, p. 109.

[2] 12 Edw. IV, H. f. 5, pl. 11.

[3] *Anon.* Dyer 33a.

[4] *Anon.* (1553) Dalison 9, holding *inter alia* that a carrier who was compellable to carry should be under a less stringent liability than a carrier who voluntarily carried goods.

[5] Cro. Eliz. 815, 4 Co.Rep. 83b, 13 Harv. L.R. 43. The case involved the liability of a bailee under the general law, and held that robbery (i.e. *vis major*) was no defence; the bailee could, if he wished, accept goods on a special bailment to keep as his own goods, in which case robbery was a defence. Robbery or theft, unlike act of God or the King's enemies, did involve a remedy over, and *Southcote* v. *Bennet* did not deny that where there could be no such remedy a bailee who accepted goods generally would not be liable.

harsh to impose liability where there was no default,[1] but in the leading case of *Paradine* v. *Jane* (1648)[2] Brooke's theory eventually triumphed. That case involved an action not of covenant but of debt brought on a lease for years, but the doctrine enunciated there was intended to apply in actions of covenant as well. Three years' rent was in arrears; the defendant pleaded that

> 'a certain German Prince, by name Prince Rupert, an alien born, enemy of the King and Kingdom, had invaded the realm with a hostile Army of men, and with the same force did enter upon the Defendant's possession, and him expelled and held out of possession. . . .'

during the most part of the three years. The plea was held bad on demurrer; the chief ground for the decision was this:

> 'And this difference was taken, that where the law creates a duty or charge, and the party is disabled to perform it without any default in him, and hath no remedy over, there the law will excuse him . . . but when the party by his own contract creates a duty or charge upon himself, he is bound to make it good, if he may, notwithstanding any accident by inevitable necessity, because he might have provided against it by his contract.'

This preserves the excuse of *absolute* impossibility (hence the words 'if he may') but makes the contracting party liable, in the absence of an express provision to the contrary, if the contract becomes more onerous through an act of God or the King's enemies, these being the two cases where no remedy over can exist; *a fortiori* a contracting party would be liable in the absence of fault where a remedy over is in principle possible.[3]

Causes and conditions

By the light of nature one would naturally suppose that a covenant could be conditional and expect to find cases dealing

---

[1] See, for example, *Richard Le Taverner's Case* (1544) Dyer 56a, where there was a considerable division of opinion on a similar question.

[2] Aleyn 26.

[3] See on *Southcote* v. *Bennet* and the history of the bailee's liability S. Stoljar, 'The Early History of Bailment', A.J.L.H., Vol. I, 1, an article which contains an interesting discussion of the cases, with much of which I fear I cannot agree.

with defences based on conditions; curiously, there is practically
no authority on conditional covenants. The explanation for
this may be that the highly technical concept of a condition
was not usually thought to be applicable to covenants.[1] As we
have seen, conditions and covenants were differentiated in
medieval legal doctrine, on the ground that the former, unlike
the latter, could operate to transfer rights; consequently it
may have been felt to be inappropriate to couple the two notions
together. It is noticeable that in the one case which deals with
the question of reciprocal covenants, which one might expect to
find discussed in terms of conditions, the court employs the
notion of 'cause' instead. It is reported in 1500:[2]

> 'Note, by Fineux C.J. If one covenants with me to serve me
> for a year, and I covenant with him to give him £20, if I
> do not say "for the same cause", he will have an action for
> the £20 although he has never served me; it will be other-
> wise if I say that he is to have the £20 for the same cause.
> Thus if I covenant with a man that I shall marry his daughter,
> and he covenants with me that he will make an estate to me
> and his daughter and the heirs of our bodies begotten, if I
> then marry another woman, or his daughter marries another
> man, yet will I have an action of covenant against him to
> compel him to make this estate. But if the covenant had been
> that he should make estate to us for the same cause, then is
> he not to make the estate until we are married. And so was
> the opinion of the Court.[3] Rede J. said this was beyond
> doubt.'

Hence it appears that a defence could only be based upon an
express cause—expressed that is in the specialty upon which the
action of covenant was brought. This is hardly surprising: to
allow a cause not so expressed to be relied upon would allow an
action upon a specialty to be met by a mere parole averment,
and this would never be permitted; it would involve varying the
terms of a covenant under seal in a wholly improper manner.

---

[1] In 1535 (27 Hen. VIII, M. f. 14, pl. 6) Pollard J. does talk of a conditional
covenant, but this is the only example I know if one leaves aside cases involving
leases which are peculiar since a lease was a 'contract' in the old sense.

[2] 15 Hen. VII, T. f. 10, pl. 17. The 'cause' of a covenant could also be relevant
in the law of uses; see below, p. 348.

[3] This indicates that there was a decision.

Where a covenant under seal was expressly made subject to some proviso ('to build a house *if the moon turns blue*'), then, if the covenantee did not rehearse the proviso in his count, presumably the covenantor could demur to the count upon the ground that it was at variance with the terms of the specialty. If he did rehearse it, and the covenantor wished to base a defence on the fact that it had not been satisfied, he could perhaps plead that he had not broken the covenant. In neither case would he be basing his defence upon a condition distinct from the covenant; on the latter situation the covenantor would merely be relying upon the proviso to qualify his undertaking to build the house.[1]

Parties and privity

Normally covenants would be made by indenture, the parties retaining one part each of the deed, which was cut apart with a wavy line.

'The indenting, or cutting *in modum dentium*, which is usually at the top, ever supposes two parts, being made in order that the parts when joined may be authenticated by the sameness of the cutting.'[2]

Only a deed thus indented counted as an indenture; the mere fact that a deed called itself an indenture was not enough. An indenture was the appropriate form for a deed *inter partes*, and would usually be bipartite, but there was no objection to indentures to which there were more than two parties. Where covenants were made by indenture the parties would be identified as parties by the terms of the instruments, and the person entitled to sue for breach of covenant was the covenantee (or covenantees) so identified and named as a party in the instrument. The covenantee need not himself seal the instrument; being named as a party was what was needed,[3] the general principle being that only a party so identified was entitled to sue. Even if some other person was mentioned in the instrument as a person in whose favour the covenant was made, and that person sealed the instrument, he could still not

---

[1] 1 Rolle. Ab. 518 suggests this way of looking at the matter.
[2] Co. Litt. 143 n. 3, 229a.
[3] 1 Rolle Ab. 517.

sue upon the instrument unless named as a party; this rule was settled in *Scudamore* v. *Vandestene* (1586)[1] and accepted by Holt C.J. in *Salter* v. *Kidgly* (1689),[2]

> 'Holt C.J. held, that one Party to a Deed could not covenant with another who was no party, but a meer stranger to it. . . .'

A covenant could be made by deed poll. 'A deed poll', said Coke, 'is that which is plain without any indenting, so called because it is cut even, or polled.'[3] Such a form of deed was appropriate for a unilateral act, and was not made *inter partes*; it would not normally therefore be used in cases of covenant, for covenants involved two parties. If, however, a deed poll was used, then an action of covenant could be brought upon such a deed, but it was essential that the person bringing the action be named in the deed.[4] If an agreement was made by deed indented, but the instrument was not expressed to be made *inter partes* but used the form of a deed poll, the rule governing deed polls applied, so that a person named as a beneficiary of the covenant could sue upon it.[5]

The person primarily liable as covenantor was the person who sealed the instrument, whether the instrument was a deed *inter partes* or a deed poll. In the case of a deed *inter partes* it might happen that some person sealed the deed who was not named as a party to the instrument, but who purported to covenant with a party; in such a case the person sealing was liable to be sued by covenant.[6] The rule here originated in cases where a surety sealed an instrument in which he was not named as a party.[7]

Thus in the context of the covenant under seal the contractual instrument identified the persons who could sue and be sued upon the covenant.

These rules identify what may be called the primary parties who can sue and be sued for breach of covenant. In certain circumstances, however, both the benefit and the burden of

---

[1] 2 Inst. 673.
[2] Carthew 76. Holt 210
[3] Co. Litt. 229a.
[4] 1 Rolle Abr. 517, *Green* v. *Horne* 1 Salk. 197.
[5] *Scudamore* v. *Vandestene* (1586) 2 Inst. 673.
[6] *Salter* v. *Kidgly* (1689) Carth. 76; *Nurse* v. *Frampton* (1670) 1 Salk. 214.
[7] 40 Edw. III, H. f. 5, pl. 11.

covenants could be transmitted to other persons. I shall consider first of all the transmission of the benefit.

The transmission of the benefit and burden of covenants

(a) THE BENEFIT OF COVENANTS

(i) *Executors or administrators*

In the course of the fourteenth century the executor came to replace the heir for many purposes as the representative of the deceased. In the case of a covenant to perform a 'personal thing', such as to build a house, or train an apprentice, the executors could sue for breach of a covenant made in favour of the testator,[1] and presumably their right of action supplanted that of the heir. This was certainly true in the case of a lease; since a lease was a chattel interest the lessee's action of covenant passed to the executor, not to the heir.[2]

(ii) *The heir*

A covenant real, such as a covenant to convey an estate in fee simple, could be sued upon not by the executor, but by the heir,[3] provided that the covenant was made expressly in favour of the covenantee and his heirs. This at least was the general rule, though it may have been subject to some qualification, as we shall see, when the benefit of the covenant was annexed to land of the covenantee which the heir did not possess.

(iii) *Assigns*

Similarly a covenant real expressed in favour of the covenantee's assigns could be enforced by an assign in his own name;[4] an example would be a covenant to convey Blackacre to Robert, his heirs, and assigns. Whether such a covenant expressed in favour simply of Robert and his heirs could be validly assigned is uncertain. The closest analogy is an annuity so granted, which was held, after considerable doubt, to be assignable.[5] An

[1] F.N.B. 145D; Fitzherbert cites the Register of Writs.
[2] *Anon.* (1311) S.S. Vol. 20 (Maitland), p. 148.
[3] F.N.B. 145C, citing *Sir Anthony Cook's Case* (1576).
[4] F.N.B. 145C, *Middlemore* v. *Goodale* (1639) 1 Rolle Abr. 521.
[5] Co. Litt. 144b, n. 1, and cases there cited.

annuity was, however, treated very much like a legal estate of inheritance, and whether a covenant real would also have been so treated seems very uncertain. A personal covenant was probably not actionable at the suit of an assignee even if made expressly in favour of assigns.

(iv) *Freehold covenants running with land*

A covenant real might take the form not of a covenant to convey land but of a covenant capable of benefiting freehold land of the covenantee. If, as would normally be the case, such a covenant was expressly made in favour of the heirs of the covenantee, the heir would seem to be the obvious person with the right of action. A possible rival to the heir would be an assignee of the land benefited, for it could sensibly be argued in such a case that title to sue should depend upon the plaintiff having the land rather than upon his being heir. The problem was discussed in two important medieval cases, those of *Pakenham* (1367)[1] and *Horne* (1400),[2] which cases are the root of the doctrine that the benefit of a covenant affecting freehold land can run with the land so as to be actionable at the suit of an assignee of the land benefited.

In *Pakenham's Case* one Laurence Pakenham brought covenant against a Prior for the breach of a covenant made between the Prior's predecessor and his own ancestor (whose heir he claimed to be); the covenant was that the Prior should sing divine service weekly in a chapel in his manor for him and his servants. The defendant's counsel, Belknap, pointed out that Laurence was not heir, since he had an elder brother; Laurence's counsel replied by saying that even if he was not heir he was both tenant of the manor where the chapel was and at least privy to the blood of his ancestor. Precisely what was decided in the case is not at all clear, but the court seems to have been of opinion that the plaintiff could maintain the action as tenant of the land so long as he was privy in blood to the original covenantee, and therefore *capable* of being heir to the original covenantee.[3] The case does not say whether the elder brother could also have sued; it does, however, suggest the idea that

---

[1] Also called *The Prior's Case*; 42 Edw. III, H. f. 3, pl. 14.

[2] 2 Hen. IV, M. f. 6, pl. 25. See also 1 Hen. V, H. f. 1, pl. 2.

[3] An alternative suggestion, which is not relevant here, is that Pakenham might have a good claim by prescription.

title to sue might depend not on being heir, but on being terre-tenant and, if not heir, privy in blood.

In *Horne's Case* (1400) one Henry Horne brought covenant against the Master and Brothers of a religious house for breach of a covenant made between his ancestor and the Master's predecessor to find two chaplains in perpetuity, one of whom was to sing divine service daily in a certain chapel at the altar of Our Lady, or some other nominated altar in the chapel. Horne counted that he was lineal heir, and claimed that for eighteen years the covenant had not been performed. Serjeant Skrene for the defendant offered to plead that the plaintiff, though heir, currently possessed no interest in the manor where the chapel was, except in right of his wife, who was tenant in fee simple at the time of the action. Thirning C.J. thought this a good answer to the action, for he took the view that the right to sue on such a covenant depended not upon the plaintiff's being heir, but on his being in possession either of the chapel or of the manor with which the chapel was associated. Markham J., however, disagreed: unless the covenant was expressly made in favour of the covenantee as tenant of the manor (in which case the right of action might depend upon the plaintiff being terre-tenant) the plaintiff could only sue as heir:

> 'In a writ of covenant it is necessary that he be privy to the covenant if he is to have a writ of covenant or be aided by the covenant. But perhaps if the covenant had been in favour of the Lord of the Manor, who had an inheritance in the manor, or could be so construed, it would be otherwise. Which was conceded.'

Hankford J. then argued that the fact that the plaintiff was not tenant of the manor was irrelevant, since in the indenture of covenant the chapel had not been described as parcel of the manor. Nor did he think it relevant that the plaintiff had no possession of the chapel; whoever possessed it, divine service celebrated there would still confer spiritual benefit on the plaintiff. He supposed that the only person who could sue on a covenant was one who, like the plaintiff, was privy to the covenant as heir. Having listened to this somewhat confusing discussion Skrene dare not rest upon the plea[1] that the plaintiff had

[1] More correctly a demurrer.

no interest in the manor or chapel, and passed on to an alternative defence.

To extract any clear doctrine from these two cases is impossible; the following propositions seem, however, to indicate their general trend:

(*a*) If a covenant is not purely personal, and is expressed in favour of the covenantee and his heirs, prima facie the heir can sue if performance of the covenant is beneficial to him.

(*b*) If a covenant of such a character is also expressed to be in favour of the covenantee and his heirs as terre-tenants, then a subsequent tenant of the lands can enforce the covenant so long as he is of the blood of the original covenantee.

(*c*) In the situation described in (*b*) perhaps the heir cannot sue unless he is tenant of the lands.

Brooke[1] found the last two propositions peculiar, for he saw that there could be cases where the covenant became unenforceable by anyone—the situation envisaged is one where the heir cannot sue because he is not tenant of the lands, and the tenant cannot sue because he is not of the blood of the original covenantee. After Brooke's time the courts came round to accepting the view that the benefit of a covenant affecting land could be annexed to the land and thereafter enforced by an alienee of the land even if he was not privy to the blood of the covenantee. This doctrine is laid down in Coke's Report of *Spencer's Case* (1583),[2] and justified by Coke by some manipulation of the medieval cases, introduced in typical Coke fashion thus:

'Observe Reader your old Books, for they are the Foundations out of which these Resolutions issue, but perhaps by these differences the Fountains themselves will be made more clear and profitable to those who will make Use of them.'

(v) *Covenants in leases*

After a lease has been granted, either the landlord or the tenant may assign his interest to a third party, the interest assigned being the reversion in fee or the lease respectively. In

---

[1] Brooke, *Covenant* 17.
[2] 5 Co.Rep. 16a at 17b.

sixteenth-century law the general rule was that the benefit of
covenants in a lease ran both with the reversion and with the
lease; the leading authority on the question is *Spencer's Case*
(1583),[1] which became the basis of the modern law on the
matter. The extent to which the benefit of covenants in a lease
ran with the lease or the reversion in medieval law is quite
uncertain; there is a curious absence of authority on the question.[2] So long as the covenant was expressly made in favour of
assigns it is difficult to see any reason in principle which would
prevent an assign suing. A case in 1534[3] held that the *burden* of a
covenant in a lease ran with the lease, and it seems inconceivable that such a decision could have been given unless it
was then true as a general rule that the benefit of covenants
ran.[4]

(*b*) THE BURDEN OF COVENANTS

(i) *Executors*

Executors were in general liable for a breach of a covenant
made by their testator; this was settled by the late fourteenth
century. Thus in a case in 1373[5] executors were sued on a covenant made by their testator, who had agreed to place his son
apprentice with the plaintiff, a draper, for a term of seven
years. The plaintiff alleged that after the testator's death the
son departed without leave and came to the executors, who
harboured him in breach of covenant. The deed of covenant
did not purport to bind the executors, and it was objected that
the action did not lie. But the court held that the executors were
liable, and Finchden said that this had been the law for the
last twenty years, though this was denied by Wich. The executors could not, however, be sued for a breach occurring after
the testator's death in the case of every covenant, for the death
of the original covenantor might determine the covenant. This

---

[1] 5 Co.Rep. 16a.
[2] See on the subject, *H.E.L.* III 157 et seq., VII. 287. A case in 1500 (15 Hen.
VII, P. f. 18, pl. 12) reveals that even as late as that doubt existed as to the extent
to which the assignee of the reversion could sue for rent by writ of debt.
[3] Brooke, *Deputie* 16.
[4] Covenants of warranty are not discussed here, as the law governing them
belongs more properly to the land law:
[5] 47 Edw. III, M. pl. 50, f. 22, which appears to be the same case as 48 Edw. III,
H. f. 1, pl. 4. See also 32 Hen. VI, H. pl. 27 f. 32.

would be so in the case of a covenant involving personal service, or a covenant which could, for some other reason, only
be performed by the original covenantor.[1] The liability of
executors represents a peculiar exception to the general principle that *actio personalis moritur cum persona*; indeed in a case in
1537[2] Baldwin C.J. expressed some doubt as to the propriety
of the rule. A lessee for years covenanted for himself to build a
house in three years and died, the covenant unperformed;
Shelly and Fitzherbert JJ. held that his executors could be
sued although not named in the indenture.

> 'But Baldwin said secretly that there is a diversity between
> an obligation, in which no mention is made of the executor,
> for that is a duty: but covenant is executory, and sounds
> only in damages, and a tort which (as it seems) dies with the
> person.'

When informal covenants became actionable by assumpsit it
was, as we shall see, at first the rule that liability was not
passively transmissible; Baldwin C.J. would have approved.

(ii) *Heirs*

Brooke remarked in his *Abridgement*[3] that in the Register of
Writs no writ against an executor is to be found; for this the
explanation presumably is that before the rise of the executor
liability on a covenant would pass to the heir. In the late
fourteenth century the relationship between the liability of
heirs and that of executors was not clearly worked out; thus in
1364[4] it was said the lessee of a deceased tenant in tail who was
ousted by the issue in tail should sue the heir and not the
executors, which was denied a few years later.[5] It came to be
settled in fifteenth-century law that the heir could be sued
only if the covenantor expressly covenanted for himself and his
heirs, and the heir had assets in fee simple by descent.[6] In the

---

[1] See the case cited above and 10 Hen. VII, P. f. 18, pl. 4; 15 Hen. VII, H. f. 2,
pl. 5.

[2] Dyer 14a.

[3] Brooke, *Covenant* 37.

[4] 38 Edw. III, f. 24.

[5] See the case cited, p. 83, n. 1.

[6] 32 Hen. VI, 32 and see Brooke, *Covenant* 38. See also 11 Ric. II (Ames Series),
p. 40.

case of a restrictive covenant affecting land the heir may only
have been liable if he retained the land burdened.[1]

(iii) *Covenants running with land*

There exists no medieval authority on whether the burden
of a covenant could be annexed to freehold land so as to bind
an assignee; authority on the analogous topic of warranties
suggests that this would have been regarded as impossible.

(iv) *Covenants in leases*

The earliest authority holding that the burden of a covenant
in a lease runs with the lease is in 1534,[2] and has already been
noted; the modern law on the running of burdens with the
lease and with the reversion depends partly upon the Statute of
1540[3] and partly on the doctrines laid down in *Spencer's Case*
(1583).[4]

**The rarity of actions of covenant
on formal covenants**

It was common enough in medieval England to make agreements by executing indentures under seal; the 'formality'
involved was no more irksome than those involved today in
making a hire-purchase agreement, and much less than taking
out a life insurance policy. Nevertheless the writ of covenant
was not at all commonly used to enforce agreements; indeed it
was something of a rarity. After 1352 the process in covenant
was relatively unsatisfactory, since a statute in that year which
extended process by *capias* to the personal actions generally
(including debt) did not apply to covenant; this, however, was
not the cause of the disuse of covenant, for it was already little
used.[5] Instead of relying upon actions of covenant for damages,
contracting parties adopted instead the practice of entering
into bonds which obliged them to pay penal sums of money,

---

[1] 4 Edw. III, M. f. 57, pl. 71; 7 Edw. III, M. f. 65, pl. 67, *sed quaere*. A restrictive
covenant might be void as in restraint of trade.

[2] See above, p. 42.

[3] 32 Hen. VIII, c. 32.

[4] 5 Co.Rep. 16a. The whole subject of the history of covenants which can run
with land is complex, and the reader should consult *H.E.L.* Vols. III and VII for
fuller discussion. A modern textbook such as Megarry and Wade, *Real Property*,
forms a good introduction.

[5] See Milsom, 217 and 25 Edw. III, st. 5, c. 17.

recoverable by writ of debt, unless they performed the covenants in the indenture. The use of bonds is explained and discussed more fully later in this book.

There were, however, certain purposes for which the action of covenant was used. One was associated rather with the law of real property than the law of contract. A much used form of conveyance in the Middle Ages was the fine, a method of registered land conveyance which involved the use of a compromised personal action. Besides being used for straightforward conveyancing, the fine was also used as a method of barring entailed estates, and for this function survived until the nineteenth century. The form of action used in levying fines was normally covenant. It has indeed been suggested by Mr. Meekings[1] that one possible reason for the unpopularity of the action of covenant as a contractual remedy was its association with conveyancing.

The action of covenant was also of some practical importance as a remedy for tenants for years who had been ousted of their terms. A lessee for years, or termor, could not use the assize of novel disseisin, or any other real action, if he was ejected; he therefore must use some form of personal action for his protection.[2] In the thirteenth century he came to be able to use the action of covenant against his lessor, and the action known as *quare ejecit infra terminum* (in some circumstances) against third parties; so long as the term had not ended, both remedies could lead to specific recovery of the land. We are not here concerned with the early protection of the lessee for years, and I shall therefore confine myself to stating the position as it existed in late medieval law.

In general (though there existed important exceptions)[3] a lease for years was good by parole; in such a case there was no question of the lessee using covenant, which was of course only available if the plaintiff could produce a specialty. For there to be a lease by deed it was not sufficient for a person merely to show a covenant under seal that he should enjoy the property for a fixed period of time; the instrument must contain words

[1] See S. F. C. Milsom 'Reason in the Development of the Common Law', 81 L.Q.R. 496 at 510 n. 26.
[2] For a short account of the history of the protection of lessees for years, see Simpson, *Land Law*, 68 et seq., 87 et seq.
[3] For a discussion see 20 Hen. VII, M. f. 12, pl. 22; 21 Hen. VII, M. f. 36, pl. 45.

of grant, for a lease was not a mere executory agreement but a conveyance of a present interest in property. A person who could not show suitable words of grant, but a mere covenant under seal permitting him to enjoy property for a term, could sue on the covenant for damages just like any other covenantee, but he was not a tenant for years. The courts were, however, fairly generous in deciding what words would count as words of grant:

> 'Words to make a lease be, demise, grant, to ferme let, betake; and whatsoever word amounteth to a grant may serve to make a lease.'[1]

Hence in 1546 and again in 1552 it was agreed that where

> 'J.N. *convenit et concessit* to W.S. that he should have twenty acres in D for twenty years that this was a good lease for this word *concessit* is as effective as *dimisit* or *locavit*. . . .'[2]

Notice, however, the implication that *convenit* alone would not suffice; agreeing to do something, and granting something, were distinct conceptions.

Supposing that suitable words of grant were used and the grantee entered,[3] there would exist a lease. As lessee the tenant could sue his lessor by *quare ejecit* if ejected; so also could a tenant by a parole lease, and recover the land.[4] In fifteenth-century law he could also sue his lessor by action of *ejectione firmae* (also known as the action of ejectment), and recover damages; in sixteenth-century law he could recover the land in this action.[5] If ousted by a third party who derived title through the lessor, typically a purchaser of the lessor's reversion, he could sue the third party by *quare ejecit*. He could also perhaps use *quare ejecit* against certain other third parties who were regarded as bound by the lease, such as a lord taking by escheat.[6] If ousted by a mere stranger he could sue by *ejectione*

[1] Co. Litt. 45b.

[2] Brooke, *Leases* 60, and see 21 Hen. VII, M. f. 36, pl. 45.

[3] Entry was necessary to perfect a lease; until entry the lessee had a mere *interesse termini*.

[4] F.N.B. 198I. The terms of the writ confine its use to cases where a third party ousts the tenant, claiming the land by a sale by the landlord. But it seems that the allegations of a sale were not traversable, and immaterial.

[5] F.N.B. 220H, and see cases cited below at p. 46, n. 1.

[6] F.N.B. 198F, G, K.

firmae, at first only for damages, but in sixteenth-century law for the recovery of the land.[1] Naturally if ousted by a stranger whose title was paramount to the lessor he had no action against the stranger, who would then not be a wrongdoer. None of the remedies so far mentioned depends upon the lessee being a covenantee; his right to use these remedies depends upon his being a lessee, to whom an interest in property has been granted, and who has been dispossessed of the property.

Where the lease was by deed, and included an express covenant warranting the land to the lessee (i.e. guaranteeing quiet enjoyment), the lessee, if ousted by the lessor, could also sue upon the covenant and recover the term if it was not yet passed, and damages for the period during which he had been dispossessed of the land.[2] He could also sue the lessor even if there was no express covenant.[3] We would say here that he was suing on an implied covenant; I think a fifteenth-century lawyer would have justified the right of action in covenant by saying that a lease was both a grant and a covenant.[4] If the lessee was ousted by a stranger then he could only sue in covenant against his lessor if the deed included an express covenant of warranty,[5] and then only if the stranger took possession by title paramount to the lessor.[6] If the stranger was a wrongdoer, the lessor was not liable; the reason for this rule was that the lessee in such a case could sue the stranger by *ejectione firmae* directly, and, if he were given an action of covenant against the lessor as well, he would recover twice over for the one wrong, a result thought to be contrary to reason.

In the post-medieval period the action of covenant came to

[1] 33 Hen. VI, M. f. 42, pl. 19; 7 Edw. IV, P. pl. 16, f. 5; 21 Edw. IV, M. f. 10, pl. 2. F.N.B. 220H. See Simpson, *Land Law*, 87.

[2] 46 Edw. III, H. f. 4, pl. 1; here it is pointed out that covenant and *quare ejecit* are alternative. The introduction of *quare ejecit* is there attributed to *special ley* (i.e. statute).

[3] This is implicit in 46 Edw. III, H. f. 4, pl. 1, and is expressly stated by Littleton in 32 Hen. VI, H. f. 32, pl. 27.

[4] Support for this view is to be found in Fineux C.J.'s remarks in 21 Hen. VII, M. f. 36, pl. 45, and negatively in the absence of any mention of the notion of an implied covenant before the mid-sixteenth century.

[5] 26 Hen. VIII, T. f. 3, pl. 11; the rule is laid down clearly by Littleton in 32 Hen. VI, H. f. 32, pl. 27.

[6] 26 Hen. VIII, T. f. 3, pl. 11; Fitz. *Covenant* 26 (34 Edw. I); 22 Hen. VI, P. f. 52, pl. 26.

be used much more frequently, and the reports of the seventeenth century contain many actions on agreements under seal started by writ of covenant—on covenants of title,[1] covenants to repair,[2] apprenticeship articles,[3] charterparties,[4] and a variety of other matters. Covenant also came to be used as an alternative to debt in actions for rent,[5] It is difficult to explain the revival of the action, but it may be connected with the inroads made upon the use of penal bonds by the Chancery at this time and by the extension of *capias* to the action of covenant, originally by the device of starting the proceedings by a feigned action of trespass.

II. INFORMAL COVENANTS

THE medieval common law provided some form of remedy upon many informal agreements by the use of the writs of debt and detinue; the scope of these remedies is discussed in its place.[6] The evolution of the action on the case on an assumpsit, and the action on the case on a deceit also permitted certain agreements of an informal character to be sued upon at common law; these actions also are discussed later in this book.[7]

If, for the moment, we exclude all such agreements as fell within the scope of these remedies it is generally true that informal covenants were not actionable at common law. Thus an informal agreement for the sale of land was not actionable at the suit of the buyer if the seller failed to convey the land. There was, however, one particular branch of the law, namely the law of master and servant, where a remedy for the breach of a parole covenant was developed; the action in question was known as the action for departure, and lay at the suit of a master whose servant broke an informal covenant of service by departing from his service without leave or lawful excuse.

This action for departure was based upon the second article of the Ordinance of Labourers (1349) interpreted in the light

---

[1] e.g. *Hayward* v. *Duncombe and Foster* (1641) March 176.
[2] *Conysbie's Case* (1639) March 17.
[3] *Anon.* (1660) 1 Lev. 12.
[4] *Bellamy* v. *Russel* (1681) Jones 186.
[5] See below, p. 72.
[6] See below, p. 146.
[7] See below, p. 244.

of the Statute of Labourers (1350–1).[1] The Ordinance provided that:

> 'If any reaper, mower or other workman or servant, of whatever state or condition he be, retained in any man's service, do depart from the same service without reasonable cause or licence before the term agreed, he shall have pain of imprisonment. . . .'

Nothing whatever is said about any action for damages. Although the Ordinance was not made into a statute until 1378,[2] it was always treated by the courts as having statutory force. The Statute of Labourers (1350–1) provided that servants should be *allowed* to serve by a whole year, or by other usual terms, but not by the day, and this provision was read into the second article of the Ordinance of 1349. The earliest reported action for departure seems to be in 1355,[3] where a joint action against a servant for departing and a third party for retaining the servant was described as being 'founded on the statute'. A similar action is reported in the following year:[4]

> 'One William Brewer[5] of Holborne brought a writ founded upon the Statute of Labourers against a man and his wife, and against their daughter, one M. And he supposed that whereas this same M had made a covenant on a certain day and year to have remained in his service for the next seven years, she had departed therefrom within the term without reasonable cause, and the husband and wife had retained her against the statute. . . .'

It could be that the action for departure came into the law as accessory to the action for retaining or harbouring a servant which lay against third parties, the servant himself being viewed as a joint wrongdoer.[6]

Precisely what types of employee could be sued in an action for departure provoked considerable argument. There was no doubt that the action lay against a common labourer, who could

---

[1] 25 Edw. III, st. 2, c. 1.
[2] By 2 Ric. II, st. 1, c. 8.
[3] 28 Edw. III, M. f. 21, pl. 18.
[4] 29 Edw. III, M. f. 27.
[5] i.e. William, a brewer.
[6] For another early example see 45 Edw. III, M. f. 13, pl. 11.

indeed be compelled to serve in husbandry (for example, as a ploughman or shepherd) without his consent under the statutory regulations.[1] More difficult was the case of an artificer, a man skilled in an art, craft, or mystery, who would normally be a member of one of the craft guilds. In a case in 1364[2] an action for departure was brought against such an artificer, who was an embroiderer, and it was argued that since the Ordinance only spoke of labourers and servants it did not cover artificers; the action was nevertheless allowed, and in fifteenth-century law the same view was taken.[3] Apprentices formed a distinct category, and were not properly to be regarded as servants; hence an action did not lie against an apprentice, as such, for departure.[4] The difficulty could, however, be got over if the master described the apprentice as a servant in his count;[5] the rule here was somewhat artificial, for by entering into apprenticeship the apprentice also became bound to *serve* his master faithfully. A chaplain, though he might be retained by a man, was not regarded as becoming his servant; he remained a servant of God. Hence the Common Pleas, with the advice of the Justices of the King's Bench, held in 1366[6] that no action lay against him for departure, and this view was adopted in 1431.[7]

For the action to lie it was not necessary that there be an actual entry into the master's service. This was decided in a case in 1364,[8] where in an action for departure the defendant pleaded that he was never in the master's service. Finchden C.J. in this case indeed explained the rule in these terms:

'At common law before this statute [i.e. the Ordinance of Labourers] if a man took my servant out of my service, I would have an action of trespass, *provided that he was physically*

---

[1] An action for damages lay against one compellable to serve who refused to do so: see 39 Edw. III, P. f. 6, pl. 2; 40 Edw. III, 39; who quite was compellable provoked much litigation; there was some doubt about carpenters: see 8 Edw. IV, f. 23, pl. 1.

[2] 47 Edw. III, M. f. 22, pl. 50.

[3] 38 Hen. VI, M. f. 30, pl. 13.

[4] 39 Edw. III, M. f. 22, and cf. 45 Edw. III, M. f. 13, pl. 11; 21 Hen. VI, H. f. 31, pl. 18.

[5] 9 Hen. VI, P. f. 7, pl. 8.

[6] 50 Edw. III, T. f. 13, pl. 3.

[7] 9 Hen. VI, P. f. 10, pl. 28.

[8] 47 Edw. III, M. f. 15, pl. 15.

in my service. Now the Statute was made to deal with this
mischief, so that if he never came into my service after he
had made a covenant to serve me, and he absented himself
from me, I should have such a writ [as the one in this case],
to suppose that he was retained in my service, and departed
as this writ is here. Therefore it must be necessary to answer
to the retainer.[1] The whole court agreed with this.'

For there to be a retainer there must therefore be a valid
covenant to serve,[2] and not merely *de facto* service;[3] unless the
covenant was good, there was no tort committed in departing.
But there was no need for the covenant to be under seal. Thus
in 1372[4] the servant pleaded that the covenant was conditional,
and the condition had not been performed. Fencot for the
master objected that no specialty had been produced proving
the condition, but Winchingham replied,

'Since the action of covenant is maintainable without
specialty, it seems that for the same reason he may aver the
manner of the covenant on his part without specialty.'

The covenant might, however, be invalid on some other ground,
such as duress,[5] or infancy; thus in 1400[6] an action against a
'petit damosel' of under ten years of age failed, for although the
child might perform *de facto* service she was at this time thought
to be unable to make a valid covenant until she was 12.[7] The
covenant must also involve an agreed retainer for a term,[8]
normally for a year,[9] though there was some authority in favour
of the view that a minimum of six months counted as a 'usual
term' within the Statute of 1350–1.[10]

The need to show a retainer for a term imposed an important
restriction upon the scope of the action. Though regarded as a
tort action in the nature of the action of covenant, the action

---

[1] i.e. a plea that he was never in service was no answer to the action.
[2] 41 Edw. III, M. f. 20, pl. 4; cf. 21 Hen. VI, M. f. 9, pl. 19.
[3] *de facto* service could, however, be the basis of an action against a third party.
[4] 45 Edw. III, M. f. 15, pl. 15.
[5] 9 Hen. VI, P. f. 10, pl. 28.
[6] 2 Hen. IV, P. f. 18, pl. 7.
[7] See below, on capacity, p. 539.
[8] In 11 Hen. IV, f. 33, pl. 60, there is a hint by Hill J. of a fiction, whereby one who entered another's service was 'deemed' to have entered service for a year.
[9] 29 Edw. III, P. f. 27, settled that a term longer than a year was good enough.
[10] 47 Edw. III, M. f. 27, pl. 53.

under the Statute was an action for *departing from service*, and not in terms an action for a breach of covenant. In form the master's complaint is much the same as the Queen's complaint that a soldier has gone absent by leaving her service without lawful excuse or leave. The form of the action was dictated by the terms of article 2 of the Ordinance, but the courts treated the action as in substance an action for breach of covenant. Thus a refusal to obey the master's order was treated as a departure,[1] and, as we have seen, breach of an executory covenant to serve, though there had been no entry into service, sufficed. There is some slight evidence that the retainer for a term may have been treated fictionally in the early fifteenth century.[2] But in 1443[3] it was said that a retainer in service for a term was an essential element in the cause of action, and could be specially traversed. In the same case it was said by many that a retainer to serve for a year when required (as opposed to a retainer in service) was merely a covenant,[4] and no action under the statute for departure lay in such a case. Hence, according to these dicta, the action could not be used against what we would call an independent contractor, but only against a person taken on to the master's staff. Thus, to use a common year-book illustration, no action under the statute lay against a carpenter who covenanted informally to build a house and failed to do so; an action would only lie if a carpenter was retained in the master's service in the office of a carpenter for a term.[5] This, if it was the law applied, severely restricted the scope of the action, and the gap in the scheme of remedies which resulted was in the end filled by the action of assumpsit for nonfeasance, which could be brought against an independent contractor in such a case.[6]

The servant could defend the action by showing a licence to depart, which could be quite informal.[7] He could also plead that

[1] 3 Hen. VI, H. f. 37, pl. 33.

[2] See Fitz., *Labourers*, pl. 12, Trin.; 2 Hen. V, unreported; 2 Hen. IV, M. f. 3, pl. 9 (Fifoot 340); 11 Hen. IV, M. f. 33, pl. 60 (Fifoot 340).

[3] 22 Hen. VI, M. f. 30, pl. 49.

[4] The retainer was said to be *nudement en covenant*.

[5] For an example of such an action see 11 Hen. IV, M. f. 33, pl. 62. Curiously this case is reported next but one to the well-known case of nonfeasance, *Anon.* (1409) (Fifoot 340), which is plea 60 of the same term.

[6] See below, p. 260.

[7] 6 Edw. IV, M. f. 2, pl. 4; 10 Hen. VI, M. f. 23, pl. 78.

he had a lawful excuse for his departure—for example, that his salary was in arrear,[1] or that his master beat him, or refused him meat and drink, [2, 3]

[1] 13 Ric. II (Ames Series) 31.

[2] F.N.B. 168L.

[3] Generally on the Ordinance and Statutes of Labourers see Putnam, *The Enforcement of the Statute of Labourers*, *H.E.L.* II. 460–4; G. H. Jones. 'Per Quod Servitium Amisit', (1958) 74 L.Q.R. 39.

II

THE WRIT OF DEBT

THE most commonly used of the medieval contractual actions was the writ of debt. Strictly speaking, the action of debt was not confined to sanctioning claims to debts due on account of consensual transactions, and was therefore not solely a contractual action; nevertheless, since it was chiefly used to recover contract debts, it is not seriously misleading to regard the action as contractual in nature. Unlike the writ of covenant it was available on both formal and informal transactions, so long as they bound a man to pay a debt, that is, a definite sum of money owed. A formal transaction which gave rise to a debt actionable by the writ would involve the execution of an instrument under seal, usually called a 'bond' or 'obligation'. Such instruments, which were dispositive, were regarded in legal theory as contracts in themselves, and for this reason were sometimes called 'contracts'. They were, however, more usually called simply 'bonds' or 'obligations' to distinguish them from those informal transactions which gave rise to debts, and commonly the term 'contract' in medieval legal literature is used to refer only to such informal transactions; an example would be an informal sale of goods.

I shall first of all discuss certain general characteristics of the action of debt, and then go on to discuss its use as a remedy sanctioning formal transactions under seal. By this time the chapter will have become rather dauntingly long, so I shall devote a separate chapter to the use of debt as a remedy on informal transactions.

I. GENERAL CHARACTERISTICS OF THE ACTION OF DEBT

The writ of debt appears in the twelfth century, and is the earliest writ of a contractual nature to be regularly issued. This is perhaps not surprising, for in a money economy the duty to pay money will most commonly be the outstanding contractual

obligation, money credit being more usual than any other form
of credit. Indeed the institution of the loan (unlike, for example,
that of sale) entails an outstanding obligation. The early
evolution of a royal action of debt was also connected with the
conflict between Church and State in Henry II's reign; this
appears from the fifteenth article of the Constitutions of
Clarendon (1164) which provided that:

> 'Placita de debitis, quae fide interposita debentur vel
> absque interpositione fidei, sint in iustitia regis.'[1]

Glanvill, writing his account of the newly evolved writ procedure at some time in the late 1180s[2] gives this as the form of
the writ:

> 'Rex vicecomiti salutem. Praecipe N quod juste et sine
> dilatione reddat R. centum marcas quas ei debet ut dicit,
> et unde queritur quod ipse iniuste ei deforciat. Et nisi
> fecerit, summone eum per bonos summonitores quod sit
> coram me vel justitiis meis apud Westmonasterium a clause
> Paschae in quindecim dies, ostenturus quare non fecerit.[3] Et
> habeas ibi summonitores et hoc breve.'

> 'The King to the Sheriff, greeting. Command N to render
> to R, justly and without delay, one hundred marks, which
> he owes him, and which, he complains, he is unjustly with-
> holding from him. And if he does not do so, summon him
> by good summoners to be before me or my justices at West-
> minster on the third Sunday after Easter to show why he
> has not done so. And have there the summoners and this
> writ.'

The form of the writ is at first sight rather curious; it begins
with an order, to be transmitted through the sheriff, to pay the
debt, and ends, as a sort of afterthought, with a passage which
recognizes that the recipient of this order may question its
justice and seek adjudication upon his liability to pay. This
furnishes a clue as to the early evolution of procedure by writ,

---

[1] 'Pleas concerning debts, whether they be owed with or without pledge of
faith, are to be in the King's justice.' For discussion see P. and M. II. 198, and Hall,
Glanvill, p. 191. See also Glanvill, X. 12 (Hall, p. 126).

[2] See Hall, *Glanvill*, suggesting *c.* 1187–9 is the date of compilation. On Glanvill's
claim to authorship see Hall, op. cit., xxx et seq. I use Glanvill as the name of the
author to avoid clumsy periphrasis.

[3] Glanvill, X. 2 (Hall, p. 116).

and Van Caenegem[1] has shown how the very earliest writs were simply executive orders issued by the King ordering somebody to do something; only by degrees does it become the function of a Royal writ to summon a person to an adjudication. The form of the writ of debt reflects this development; it is a hybrid, transitional in form.

Another striking feature of the writ is its close similarity to the writ *praecipe in capite*,[2] which was used to assert claims to freehold land:[3]

'Rex vicecomiti salutem. Praecipe N. quod juste et sine dilatione reddat R. unam hidam terre in illa villa unde idem R queritur quod predictus N. sibi deforciat. Et nisi fecerit, etc. . . .'

'The King to the sheriff, greeting. Command N to render to R. justly and without delay, one hide of land in such-and-such a villa, which the said R. complains that the aforesaid N. is withholding from him. And unless he does so, etc. . . .'

Furthermore Glanvill does not differentiate between writs of debt where money is claimed and writs of detinue claiming chattels; his writ of debt is available for either type of claim. Glanvill's failure to mention a distinct detinue writ form cannot be explained away as a non-significant omission, for certain passages in his text make it quite clear that his concept of a debt could include a chattel debt. Thus in discussing the contract of sale he says: 'Debetur enim precium ipsi venditori et res empta emptori'.[4] Again in listing the possible *causae debendi* he includes, along with transactions giving rise to money debts, both deposit and loan for use, which can only give rise to a chattel debt.[5]

The use of a single writ form for claims to land and to debts is probably without conceptual significance; the *praecipe quod reddat formula*, as Plucknett[6] has put it, was 'the current blank form' for writs in the twelfth and early thirteenth centuries.

---

[1] S.S. Vol. 77, *passim*, but see especially pp. 105–94, and on debt pp. 254–9.
[2] For an elementary discussion see Simpson, *Land Law*, Ch. II.
[3] Glanvill, I. 6 (Hall, p. 5).
[4] Glanvill, X. 14 (Hall, p. 129) 'For then the price is owed to the seller *and the thing sold to the buyer*'.
[5] Glanvill, X. 3 (Hall, p. 117).
[6] Plucknett, 363, where the point is discussed.

The use of the word *deforciat* may look slightly curious in a debt writ, but again its use in all probability is not significant. Mr. Hall, in his edition of Glanvill, translates it as *withhold*, and if this correctly catches the sense there is nothing in the least peculiar in the idea of withholding a debt. Glanvill's failure to differentiate between an obligation to pay money and an obligation to hand over chattels is somewhat more problematical, and is discussed later in this chapter.[1]

The evolution of the form of the writ of debt

In the thirteenth century the expression *unde ei deforciat* was dropped from the writ, presumably because it was felt to be inappropriate, and there was a progressive elaboration of the rules governing the writ form, which reflected in part the slow separation of debt and detinue. The Statute of Wales in 1284[2] prescribed different forms for claims for money and claims for chattels, and gave examples. In a writ for money the correct form was this:

'Praecipe A. quod juste et sine dilatione reddat B. centum solidos quos ei debet et iniuste detinet. . . .'

A writ for chattels, however, was not to say *debet*, but simply allege detention, and the price of the chattels in money was to be included; it had already been established (indeed it may always have been the law)[3] that the defendant had the option of returning the chattels or paying for them.[4] The writ form therefore was this:

'Praecipe A quod juste et sine dilatione reddat B unum saccum lanae precii decem marcarum[5] quem ei iniuste detinet. . . .'

---

[1] See below, p. 75, and for discussion see Milsom, pp. 219 et seq and the same author's 'Law & Fact in Legal Development' (1967) Toronto L.J., p. 1.

[2] 12 Edw. I, c. 6. See also S.S. Vol. 87 (de Haas and Hall), esp. at pp. 221 et seq.

[3] Glanvill, X. 13. (Hall, p. 128) notes that a reasonable price for a thing bailed for use is payable if the thing is lost or perishes, where the thing still existed there may have been thought to be a right to specific restitution at first; indeed Glanvill says as much. But by Bracton's time (see Bracton at f. 102b) the option to pay the value was established. See Fifoot, p. 25 n. 8, citing *Wulghes* v. *Pepard* (1310) Y.B. 4 Edw. II (S.S. Vol. 26), p. 14 (Fifoot 37).

[4] In detinue of Charters, however, the value of the Charters (i.e. title deeds to land) was fixed at the value of the land to which they pertained, a rule which in effect would compel specific restitution if this was possible.

[5] 'One sack of wool, price ten marks.'

Detinue is still, however, regarded as a subdivision of debt; thus the relevant section of the statute is headed *Breve de Debito*. This notion persisted throughout the medieval period. Thus in the Register of Writs[1] writs of detinue are to be found classified under the general heading *De debito*, and the same practice persisted on the plea rolls[2] long after counsel had for many purposes come to conceive of debt and detinue as quite distinct forms of action.[3] The persistence of the older idea is strikingly illustrated by a decision in 1343,[4] where a reference to the writ of debt in a statute of 1335[5] was construed as including detinue as well. For most purposes, however, debt and detinue were regarded by medieval lawyers as distinct actions.

In the Statute of Wales the writ form was made to depend upon the subject-matter of the claim, one form being appropriate for money, and another for chattels. The underlying idea is that there is a distinction in principle between claims to money, which has no specific identity, and claims to chattels, which can be identified specifically.[6] In the course of time this idea was developed. The detinue form was proper where specific coins were claimed, as in a case where money was deposited for safe keeping in a sealed box or bag which the depositee was not entitled to open,[7] or where uncoined silver or gold was in demand.[8] Conversely the writ of debt was

[1] *Registrum Brevium*, f. 139b. In the form there given the notion of 'value' has supplanted 'price'; the writ claims *catalla ad valenciam centum solidos*.

[2] See Milsom, 'Sale of Goods in the Fifteenth Century', 77 L.Q.R. 257 at 273, citing Y.B. 17 Edw. III (R.S.), 141, 14 Hen. IV, H. f. 27, pl. 37.

[3] 30 Edw. III, H. f. 2. There is an instance of the way in which the differentiation of debt and detinue was still by no means worked out fully. An action was brought by an heir claiming on the basis of a local custom the principalities (i.e. the best bed, the best pot, etc.). The action is described as detinue; in the writ the plaintiff used the form *quod reddat catalla ad valenciam quae ei debet*.

[4] 17 Edw. III (R.S.), 144; the case concerned an action *de rationale parte*, which was treated as being an action in the nature of detinue. cf. 18 Edw. III, H. pl. 19.

[5] 9 Edw. III, st. 1, c. 3.

[6] It must be admitted that explicit reference to the importance of specific identity is curiously rare in the year-books; for examples see 34 Hen. VI, M. f. 12, pl. 23 and 20 Hen. VII, M. f. 8, pl. 18 (Fifoot 351). It was most important in actions of detinue of charters, which only gave the defendant the choice of returning the specific charters claimed, i.e. the title deeds to land or the value of the land.

[7] 13 Edw. III (R.S.), p. 244, where Schardelowe J. makes the point 'He gave the defendant no permission to take the money out of the bag'. See also 6 Edw. II (1313), S.S. Vol. 43, p. 65; 18 Hen. VI, M. f. 20, pl. 5.

[8] 2 and 3 Edw. II, S.S. Vol. 19, App. I, p. 194, where Bereford C.J. makes the point that the action was for the box, as one entire thing.

proper where fungible goods—goods not specifically identified
—were claimed by number, weight, or measure, as for example
in a case in 1306[1] where debt was brought for ten quarters of
wheat which had been sold to the plaintiff.[2] Where debt was
brought for chattels there was a complication, as a year-book
reporter notes in a case in 1455,[3]

> 'But note, that those in the Chancery are not willing to
> make any such writ in the *debet* for any kind of thing except
> money only, by which it seems that such a writ must be in
> *detinet*.'[4]

Because of this chancery practice, which seems to have been
established in the fourteenth century,[5] a writ of debt for
fungibles resembled in form a writ of detinue in that it alleged
only that the defendant unjustly detained (*detinet*) the goods; it
was *classified*, however, as a writ of debt (though 'in the *detinet*')
and it was probably unnecessary, though not objectionable,[6]
to include a statement of the price or value of the goods, though
it was only a money equivalent which the plaintiff appears to
have been entitled to recover.[7]

In the opinion of some fifteenth- and early-sixteenth-century
lawyers it was correct to classify as actions of debt (and not
detinue) actions for the recovery of specific chattels which
had never been in the plaintiff's possession, and which were
claimed as due to the plaintiff by force of a contractual grant.
The typical example of such an action is the claim of a buyer
for a specific chattel sold to him; other examples would be

---

[1] 33–4 Edw. I (R.S.), p. 150. cf. 20–1 Edw. I (R.S.), p. 139—debt for twenty
quarters of corn as rent due from a leaseholder. See also 6 Edw. IV, H. f. 11, pl. 6,
20 Hen. VII, M. f. 8, pl. 18.

[2] Barbour, p. 27, suggests that 'in the early Year-Books this distinction has not
obtained a firm footing', but the cases he cites for this do not seem to support him.

[3] 34 Hen. VI, M. f. 12, pl. 23. cf. 11 Hen. VII, M. f. 5, pl. 20; *Reg. Brev.* 139b;
F.N.B. 119M; Brooke, *Dette* 211 citing a case in 9 Edw. IV which I cannot trace,
unless it is intended of 6 Edw. IV, H. f. 11, pl. 6.

[4] The reference is to the chancery clerks.

[5] 50 Edw. III, T. f. 16, pl. 8: '*Hanim*: This is an action of debt for rent reserved
on a lease, the term being still in existence, and although the writ is *detinet* only
without *debet*, it is good enough, for a dead chattel or a living chattel it is otherwise
than for coins. For a man can have no other writ in the Chancery, which was
agreed by all.'

[6] 34 Hen. VI, M. f. 12, pl. 23.

[7] Brooke, *Dette* 211.

claims to chattels or foreign money granted by deed.[1] This classification means that the mere form of the writ is not regarded as critical in determining the correct identification of the form of action which the writ initiated. The form of a buyer's writ for a horse sold to him will be indistinguishable from a writ claiming the return of a horse bailed; the basis of the claim, revealed in the count or declaration, will, however, identify the buyer's action as an action of debt, and the bailor's action as an action of detinue. Whereas the buyer is claiming the horse upon the ground that he first became entitled to it by virtue of the contract of sale which gave him a right to it (and was thus a form of grant), the bailor is claiming the return of a horse which was his before he bailed it to the defendant, and is not relying upon any form of grant.

This way of classifying the actions is adopted in Fitzherbert's *Natura Brevium*[2] and seems more rational than any other; I have therefore adopted it in this book. It should not, however, be assumed that all contemporary lawyers would have accepted it;[3] indeed since it frequently made no difference whether one regarded an action as debt or detinue there was commonly no need to take sides on the matter.

Debt in the *detinet* for money claims

In some circumstances the word *debet* had to be omitted from the writ even when a straightforward money debt was in issue. The rule applied to actions brought by or against executors or administrators in their representative capacity;[4] it did not, however, originally apply to actions brought by or against heirs.[5] The reason for this, where representatives are bringing the action, is explained by Shardelowe J. in a case in 1343:[6]

---

[1] See Milsom, 'Sale of Goods in the Fifteenth Century', 77 L.Q.R. 257 at pp. 273–5, and in particular 34 Hen. VI, M. f. 12, pl. 23.

[2] F.N.B., 119G.

[3] For examples of the view that the buyer's action was detinue see 20 Hen. VI, T. f. 34, pl. 4 (*Doige's Case*, Fifoot 347); 17 Edw. IV, P. f. 1, pl. 2 (Fifoot 252).

[4] *Reg. Brev.* 138b; F.N.B. 119G; 30–1 Edw. I (R.S.), 391, *Casus Placitorum* (S.S. Vol. 69) lxxxvi, No. 27 (applying the same rule to an action against a surety); 16 Edw. III (R.S.), 382, 21 and 22 Edw. I (R.S.), 215, 615.

[5] There was some doubt over this, see 16 Edw. III, Vol. II (R.S.), 383. In later medieval law the writ was framed in the *detinet*; see F.N.B. 119G.

[6] 17 and 18 Edw. III (R.S.), 355.

'The reason why a writ of debt brought by executors on their testator's contract shall have the word *detinet* only is that the property is supposed to be in the testator,[1] and even though the executors after the testator's death sell the goods of the deceased, and take an obligation, yet the goods and the property in the debt which is to be deraigned by that obligation belongs to the deceased, and the executors have to account for them in the Court Christian.'

The rule thus reflects the Christian belief in life after death; the executors are to administer the assets of the deceased for his benefit in the afterlife, and money debts remain due to him, to be recovered for his benefit. It would thus be inappropriate for representatives to use the word *debet*, which would suggest that the debts were due to them. Similar notions are behind the rule where representatives are being sued—it is not *they* who owe the money, but the deceased whom they represent, and whose debts they must pay to the extent of his assets. The position of heirs was quite different, for the heir was not a representative but a successor. This was explained in *William Clare's Case* in 1339,[2] where one heir sued another in debt on a specialty, the writ being in the *debet et detinet*,

'*Gayneford*: Judgment of the writ; the writ has the word *debet* whereas when one demands what was due to another the words of the writ should be *iniuste detinet*, without *debet*.

'*Trewith*: Your maxim is false, for in a case where a man demands as heir, this is a profit due to himself, in which case he should say *debet*, but in the case of executors, there, where they should recover to the use of the testator the writ should only say *iniuste detinet*.'

Though there is no decision in this case, Trewith's view of the matter was probably correct.[3]

Though the principle seems clear, it gave rise to many difficulties of application; thus where the duty to pay arose after the testator's death,[4] or through the act of the representatives,

---

[1] i.e. it is the testator who is beneficially entitled.

[2] 12 and 13 Edw. III (R.S.), 168.

[3] See 16 Edw. III (R.S.), 382.

[4] 14 Hen. IV, H. f. 27, pl. 37 (an action for rent); 20 Hen. VI, M. f. 5, pl. 16, f. 4, pl. 14 (debt for the arrears of an account found before auditors after the testator's death).

as where the representatives through misconduct became liable to have execution levied on their own property,[1] it was arguable that the writ should say *debet et iniuste detinet*. Thus, to take one example, suppose executors were sued for rent due on a lease for years to the testator, the rent having fallen into arrears after the testator's death; it could be argued that the executors were liable because of their own occupation of the land, and should therefore be sued in the *debet et detinet* and be made personally liable. After a long dispute it was finally settled in 1504[2] that in such a case the writ should be in the *detinet* only, since they were in occupation in their representative capacity as executors.[3]

The need to claim a 'sum certain'[4]

The medieval conception of a debt was a 'sum certain'—a definite, liquidated sum of money or quantity of chattels due in law from debtor to creditor. In consequence a plaintiff in an action of debt must claim in the writ one entire sum, which he must specify, and because of the provisions of the Statute of Gloucester the sum *claimed* must be at least forty shillings;[5] in order to get the case into the royal court it seems to have been a common practice to claim precisely this sum.[6] In his count or declaration—which corresponds to the modern statement of claim—he must show the ground for his claim, and he was allowed to claim in one action a total sum made up of a number of smaller sums due on different grounds. Thus in his writ he could claim a debt of £20, and show in his declaration that this

---

[1] This provoked a long and inconclusive discussion in 11 Hen. VI, M. f. 7, pl. 12; f. 16, pl. 9; f. 35, pl. 30. Debt was brought on an obligation against an administrator who, it was said, had converted the deceased's property to his own use, thus making himself liable to suffer judgment in his own goods (*de bonis propriis*) and not merely in the deceased's goods. cf. 30 and 31 Edw. I (R.S.), 391, where debt in the *detinet* was upheld in an action against an executor who had bound himself as executor for the price of the goods of the testator which he had sold.

[2] See 14 Hen. IV, H. f. 27, pl. 37; 11 Hen. VI, P. f. 26, pl. 35; 10 Hen. VII, M. f. 5, pl. 10; 19 Hen. VIII, T. f. 8, pl. 10.

[3] For the form of the writ in an action against a Prior on a transaction concluded by his predecessor see 47 Edw. III, M. f. 23, pl. 57; 13 Hen. VII, M. f. 2, pl. 2 The writ must be in the *debet et detinet* if the goods came to the use of the house; if not the action did not lie at all. Liability rested on receipt, not on any notion of agreement through an agent.

[4] The accounts given by Ames, Holdsworth, and Fifoot all overemphasize the 'strictness' of debt, as Milsom has pointed out in 77 L.Q.R. at p. 258.

[5] 6 Edw. I, c. 8.

[6] See Milsom, 77 L.Q.R. at 258 et seq.

sum was made up of £10 due on a bond, and £10 due on a parole contract.[1] Thus in *Sandford* v. *Askham* (1410) the plaintiff claimed *un grand sum* made up of rent due on a lease, the price of goods sold, and remuneration for the carriage of goods.[2] In a sense therefore the 'debt' claimed in the writ might be made up of any number of different 'debts', the action being used to claim what was, in effect, the credit balance of an account. Naturally writ and count must be consistent, as Hankford J. explained in a case in 1412:[3]

> 'If in an action of debt for £40 the plaintiff shows an obliga-tion for £10 and counts on a contract for only £9, now his whole writ abates, because such a writ in such a case is false in part.'[4]

The principle of internal consistency was carried to somewhat surprising lengths. Having claimed one entire sum in the writ the plaintiff must never at any stage in the pleadings enter a plea which was inconsistent with this claim—he must fight for the whole sum, and if he failed to do so the whole action failed. Thus in a case in 1424 the plaintiff sued for £10 due on an obligation; the defendant admitted the claim in part, but pleaded an acquittance by deed of £2. The plaintiff prayed judgment for the amount admitted, but said nothing about the acquittance, and, when asked why, his counsel, Fulthorpe, explained,

> 'We can say nothing, for if we were to admit this, we should then abate our writ, for by this we should have to count that our action was bad in part, which would abate our writ in its entirety.'[5]

This was conceded. The severity of the rule must not be exaggerated; if the writ abated, the plaintiff could always try again, claiming the sum which was in fact due. But a creditor was frequently forced to claim more than was due—if, for example, as in this case, the debt was due on a bond, his claim

---

[1] e.g. 3 Hen. IV, M. f. 2, pl. 8.
[2] 11 Hen. IV, H. f. 55, pl. 38.
[3] 13 Hen. IV, f. 11.
[4] On the same point see 11 Hen. VI, M. f. 5, pl. 9, *Smith* v. *Vowe* (1588) Moo. K.B. 298.
[5] 3 Hen. VI, T. f. 48, pl. 6. On the same point see 4 Edw. IV, M. f. 32, pl. 15.

must be for the sum named in the bond, and he had to leave it to the defendant to plead the acquittance in part. Had he claimed only £8 there would have been an inconsistency between the claim and the bond, which would have been fatal.

So long as the plaintiff fought for the entire sum there was no general principle which prevented him recovering only part of the sum claimed.[1] Thus in a case in 1400[2] for £20, of which £10 was claimed on a bond and £10 on an informal contract, the defendant successfully waged his law (i.e. defended the action by oath swearing) on the informal contract, but lost on the bond; the plaintiff had judgment for £10. However, if the case went to a jury, and the jury found that *more* was due than the sum claimed there was a difficulty, and, as Martin J. explained, the plaintiff got nothing,[3]

'If I demand only £20, and the inquest says that the defendant owes me £40, the Justices cannot give judgement here. They cannot give me judgement for the £40, because I did not demand £40 ... and for the twenty pounds they cannot give me judgement, because they cannot sever the judgement from the verdict, which does not speak at all of the £20, but of £40 ... nor can they portion it out from the verdict.'

A more serious limitation is illustrated by the case of *Bladwell* v. *Sleggein* (1562).[4] Here debt was brought for £20, alleged to be due on a contract for the sale of woods; the jury found that the price was in marks, so that only £13 4s. 0d. was due. In conformity with medieval precedents the defendant obtained judgment, the reason being 'because it cannot be intended the same contract'. The plaintiff must try again, and although the rule seems harsh, it is not irrational; the price was an essential element in a sale, and the simple point is that the plaintiff is only entitled to recover on the contract upon which he sues.[5]

---

[1] *H.E.L.* III. 423, thought that if the plaintiff failed to prove that the exact sum claimed was due the action would be lost, but this view is incorrect.

[2] 3 Hen. IV, f. 2, pl. 8. See also 3 Hen. VI, H. f. 37, pl. 38, T. f. 48, pl. 6; 11 Hen. IV, H. f. 55, pl. 38; 19 Hen. VI, M. f. 8, pl. 19.

[3] 3 Hen. VI, M. f. 3, pl. 4. Similarly if the plaintiff claimed say £10, and the jury found £5 due and said nothing about the balance.

[4] Dyer 219b. *Anon.* (1562) Moo. K.B. 49. Dalison 49 is taken by the editors of Dyer to be the same case, but this seems dubious.

[5] See 21 Edw. IV, P. f. 21, pl. 2, and for the rule in assumpsit see below, p. 68, n. 1.

Similarly, if in detinue[1] the plaintiff declared on the bailment and detention of a horse, and the jury found that the beast involved was a cow, the action failed *in toto* and a new action must be brought.[2] The same doctrine was later adopted in assumpsit.[3]

The nature of the action of debt ruled out any possibility of the plaintiff claiming an uncertain sum by way of *quantum meruit* or *quantum valebant*; in the writ a precise sum must be demanded, and the count must conform to the writ. So much was never doubted, but the pleading rule leaves open the question how the certain sum in demand may be rendered certain, and here the law was not so clear. Thus in *Johnson* v. *Morgan* (1599)[4] debt was brought on a bond in these terms:

'Be it known that I, William Morgan, do acknowledge myself to be indebted to J. Johnson, for all such sums of money as A.D., my brother-in-law, did owe the said J. Johnson.'

The plaintiff claimed £45, averring in his count that this was the extent of the indebtedness. The propriety of this divided the court of Common Pleas. Walmesley and Kingsmill JJ. thought the action maintainable,

'although it be uncertain in the words of the bill, yet when it may be reduced to a certainty, it is well enough.'

But Anderson C.J. and Glanvil J. disagreed. Where work was done, or goods supplied, in circumstances where remuneration was expected, but no precise sum agreed upon, somewhat similar problems arose, and the medieval rule seems to have been in conformity with the view expressed by Walmesley and Kingsmill JJ., for in a case in 1482[5] Brian C.J. said this,

'. . . if I bring cloth to a tailor to have a robe made, if the price is not made certain beforehand how much I shall pay for the making, he shall not have an action of debt against

[1] 21 Edw. IV, P. f. 21, pl. 2.
[2] *Ab hypothesi* the judgment in the first action could be no bar to another action on another contract.
[3] See *Bagnal* v. *Sacheverell* (1592) Cro. Eliz. 292; *Simms* v. *Westcott* (1589) Cro. Eliz. 147; *Billingesley* v. *Anon.* (1567) cited by the editors of Dyer 219b *in margine*.
[4] Cro. Eliz. 758. Ames, p. 89, cites this case for the proposition that 'a promise to pay as much as certain goods or services are worth would never support a count in debt'; this goes well beyond the authority.
[5] 12 Edw. IV, P. f. 8, pl. 22. Fifoot 230, cites 4 Hen. VI, P. f. 19, pl. 5, on the same point, but the case seems not to deal with it.

me, but for food and drink in a tavern it is otherwise, for the price is made certain by the clerk of the market.'

Thus so long as the price could be fixed somehow, it did not have to be fixed by agreement, and in medieval times many prices were fixed by law independently of agreement; in such cases the plaintiff could demand the sum due at law. Thus the wages due to a common labourer were fixed by the justices of labourers.

The inability to use a *quantum meruit* (or *quantum valebant*) count would bear most hardly on the skilled artificer, who must make his own bargain in situations where freedom of contract prevailed; it was not, however, so serious a defect in the law as would appear to modern eyes, and the question discussed by Brian C.J. was in all probability of only theoretical interest. The rule only governed the pleading of an action of debt, and would be satisfied if the plaintiff *claimed* a certain sum. Thus suppose he did this, and averred in his count an agreement for the sum claimed, and the case then went to a jury on a plea of *non debet*; the jury would presumably find for the plaintiff if the sum claimed seemed to them to be fair. If the defendant opted for defence by wager of law there was nothing the plaintiff could do about that, but his problem here was not in any way aggravated by the 'sum certain' requirement. There was no question of the defendant pleading *specially* that there had been no agreed sum fixed in advance; in actions where wager was possible the general pleading rule was that a special traverse of the contract was a bad plea.

In the late sixteenth century it came to be settled that the action of assumpsit would lie where the plaintiff averred a promise to pay an uncertain sum,[1] and this development reacted on the law governing debt, so that in the early seventeenth century there are dicta in favour of applying the same rule in the action of debt. Thus in *Rogers* v. *Head* (1610)[2] it is said that a 'contract'

---

[1] The earliest case appears to be *Floyd* v. *Irish* (1587) Sheppard, 71. In *Royle* v. *Bagshaw* (1589) Cro. Eliz. 149, an action was brought on an express promise to pay *tantum quantum meruit*, with an averment *quod meruit tantum*. See also *Shepherd* v. *Edwards* (1613) Cro. Jac. 370; *Hall* v. *Lallard* (1621) Cro. Jac. 618; *Ive* v. *Chester* (1619) Cro. Jac. 560. The case of *Warbrook* v. *Griffin* (1609) 2 Brown 254, Moo. K.B. 876, though always cited in this context, is only marginally relevant. See below, ch. viii.

[2] Cro. Jac. 262.

to pay a reasonable sum was 'good enough', and this means that debt would lie. The availability of debt is also insisted upon in *The Six Carpenters' Case* (1610).[1] Eventually, in *Waring* v. *Perkins* (1621),[2] there was a decision. This did not mean that the creditor *claimed* an uncertain sum; he claimed a sum certain, but in his count he would justify this claim by an averment of an agreement to pay *quantum meruit* coupled with an averment that he deserved the sum claimed in the writ. But the propriety of such a count in an action of debt was never really established.[3]

It is commonly said, and said in general correctly, that where money was due by instalments debt could only be brought to recover the whole sum, and that the action could only be brought after the last instalment became due.[4] But this requires some qualification. One clear exception applied where debt was brought upon a recognizance,[5] such as a statute merchant;[6] here instalments could be demanded as they fell due. Another rule, which looks as if it might be an exception, is perhaps better viewed as defining the scope of the principle. Where debt was brought to recover an annual rent due on a lease for years, each year's rent could be demanded once it fell due, and there was no need for the landlord to await the end of the term and sue for all the arrears of rent in one action. The reason for this was explained by Strange in a case in 1428.[7] His client had brought an action for seven-years' rent in arrear on a ten-year lease; counsel for the tenant objected that he ought to sue for the whole rent due on the term, just as if he were suing on a

[1] 8 Co.Rep. 146a at 147a; this case is not concerned with the law governing assumpsit. See also Sheppard, p. 23.

[2] Cro. Jac. 628. Fifoot, p. 360, n. 12, calls this a 'strange decision' and a 'belated aberration', but there is really nothing very surprising about the case.

[3] Thus Ames, 89 n. 9, notes that although a precedent for a count in debt on a *quantum meruit* is given in Chitty, *Pleading*, I, 7th ed., 351, 721, it has been doubted whether it lies. The doubt as to whether debt lay is the reason why in later law the action upon a *quantum meruit* or *quantum valebant* count was by way of special and not *indebitatus assumpsit*.

[4] Co. Litt. 47b, 292b, *Taylor* v. *Foster* (1599) Cro. Eliz. 776, 807. *Slade's Case* (1602) 4 Co. Rep. at 94a.

[5] F.N.B. 131B.

[6] Debt did not lie on a statute staple; see 15 Hen. VII, M. f. 14, at f. 16, pl. 6, but the action did lie on a statute merchant, 3 Edw. IV, M. f. 27, pl. 24, the creditor having an election between the statutory and common law remedies.

[7] 7 Hen. VI, P. f. 26, pl. 14.

bond, where it was conceded that he must sue for the entire debt. To this Strange replied,

'Debt on an obligation is one entire duty: therefore it must be demanded entirely, where parcel is paid. But here the duty is as it were several, because for each term or each year he can have a writ of debt.'

The rule then was that for one debt only one action could be brought, and this one action could only be brought when that one debt was due. Thus if a debtor bound himself to pay £100 by deed, and the deed provided that this debt was payable in four quarterly instalments, the creditor could only sue for the whole sum, and this only became due at the end of the year; in consequence the provision for payment by instalments was unenforceable. But this doctrine gave room for some delicate reasoning upon whether the court was confronted with one single debt, or a number of different debts, for in the latter case each debt could be recovered as it fell due. Thus in *Anon.* (1591)[1] the defendant was bound by a bill under seal to pay a sum of £20 by four instalments of £5. The instrument went on to provide that if he fell behind in the payments he 'covenanted and granted'[2] to pay the whole of the residue at once. The debtor defaulted in the instalments and the creditor sued for the whole sum, and the court upheld the action; the default provision ranked as a distinct and separate grant of a distinct debt. Had the instrument, however, not included such a provision, the creditor would have had to wait until the last instalment fell due before suing, for only then was the entire sum demandable.

The rationale of the instalment rule depends upon the notion that the action of debt was recuperatory; its function was to enable a creditor to recover the debt which the debtor had granted to the creditor. It followed that if the debt granted was, say, a debt of £20, its recovery could only be permitted when £20 was due, and not before. The debtor who defaulted upon the instalments had, it is true, failed to do what he had agreed or promised to do, but the action of debt was not regarded as an

---

[1] 1 Leon. 208. See also *Hunt's Case*, Owen 42, Cro. Eliz. 118, 2 Leon. 107.

[2] The case is largely concerned to rule that these words amount to a grant sufficient to warrant the use of debt.

action which provided a remedy for loss suffered through breach of a promise or agreement; to this extent the creditor's complaint in an action of debt was that he was being kept out of his own rather than that he was the victim of a broken agreement to do something for his benefit. When, in the sixteenth century, the action of assumpsit for breach of promise was evolved, it soon[1] came to be used as a remedy upon instalment contracts where debt would not have been available, and since it was not viewed as a recuperatory action, but as an action for compensation for breach of promise, it was soon settled that it was not subject to the limitations of debt; once the defendant broke his promise in any particular the action accrued. The distinction between the character of the two forms of action was emphasized in a long line of cases. Thus in *Foster* v. *Taylor* (1599)[2] a sum of £100 was payable in two equal instalments; the plaintiff sued in assumpsit when the defendant defaulted in the first payment, and it was argued that, as in debt, he could not sue until the whole sum was due:

> '*Sed non allocatur*, for true it is it is so in debt upon an obligation, where the entire sum is to be recovered, but not in this action, or in covenant, where damages only are to be recovered.'

Again in *Milles* v. *Milles* (1631),[3] on similar facts, it was held that,

> 'the action well lies before the last day, being an action upon promise or covenant, for the breach is immediately for the first £10 not being paid at the day, and for this breach the action well lies. But we held it to be otherwise in debt, the contract or bill being entire.'

The rule governing instalment cases in debt also reflects a peculiar principle according to which one act in law, be it the

---

[1] The earliest case is *Peck* v. *Redman* (1555) Dyer 113a. See also *Joscelyn* v. *Shelton* (1557) Brooke, *Action sur le case*, 108; 3 Leon. 4, Benloe 57, Moo. K.B. 13, *Hunt's Case* (1587) Owen 42, Cro. Eliz. 118; 2 Leon. 107, *Taylor* v. *Poston* (1601) 1 Rolle Abr. 29; *Slade's Case* (1602) 4 Co. Rep. at 94a; *Beckwith* v. *Nott* (1618) Cro. Jac. 504; *Peck* v. *Ambler* (1633) Cro. Car. 349.
[2] Cro. Eliz. 776.
[3] Cro. Car. 241.

execution of a document under seal (a 'deed') or the making of a contract, could only give rise to one single duty. This was expressed in the case of contracts by saying that a contract was an 'entire thing' (*entire chose*).[1] The underlying idea is well illustrated in a case in 1478.[2] A husband was seized of land in right of his wife, and sold the defendant 400 oaks growing on the land for £20. The defendant cut 200, and then the wife died; the husband then became tenant by the curtesy and as such had no right to allow the defendant to cut any more. He sued for the whole purchase price, and once it became apparent that he had had sufficient time to cut all the oaks in the lifetime of the wife, it was agreed that he was liable to pay the full price. It was, as Littleton J. explained, a question of all or nothing—'The contract is an entire thing, and cannot be severed'.

In short the rule was one contract, one debt, one action, and the 'all or nothing' approach was thought to exclude, at least as a general rule, any question of the court apportioning or severing a single contractual obligation. Thus if a servant was employed for a year at a salary of 20s., and was discharged within the year with his consent, he was entitled to no wages;[3] the contract was entire and the court would not award him a rateable proportion of the agreed salary.[4] In certain circumstances a duty to pay rent might be apportioned, as where the reversion was severed, or the tenant evicted from part of the land by a third party claiming by title paramount,[5] and there was some authority[6] in favour of the view that a tenant might have his rent rateably reduced if he lost all benefit from part of the land through an act of God. The rules governing leases were, however, exceptional, and the 'entire contract' doctrine

---

[1] 9 Edw. IV, P. f. 1, pl. 1; 7 Hen. VII, M. f. 4, pl. 5.

[2] 18 Edw. IV, P. f. 5, pl. 30; H. f. 21, pl. 1.

[3] 20 Hen. VI, P. f. 23, pl. 2, Brooke, *Apportionment*, p. 17 (1538).

[4] Where assumpsit was brought on instalment contracts this doctrine caused considerable difficulty. According to one view, once an instalment was not paid on time, the agreement was broken and the promisee could sue once, and once only, both for the arrears and for future instalments. According to another view, the plaintiff could only recover damages for the time passed, and must bring successive actions for subsequent breaches. The dispute may be followed in the cases cited above, p. 68, nn. 1–3.

[5] See 1 Rolle Abr. 235–6, title *Apportionment*, where the authorities are collected.

[6] *Richard le Taverner's Case* (1543) Dyer 56a. The doctrine there apparently adopted was rejected in *Paradine* v. *Jane* (1647) Aleyn 26, Style 47.

passed into the law of assumpsit;[1] indeed in a much qualified form it still forms part of modern contractual doctrine.

Debt and covenant

Granted that a quantified sum of money was in demand, the general principle was that the proper writ was debt.[2] There was an important exception in the case of actions to recover rents; debt could not be used to claim rent service due from a freeholder, where the proper remedy was a writ of customs and services,[3] nor to recover any other form of rent enjoyed for a freehold estate, where the proper action was by writ of annuity.[4] This was thought to be inconvenient; in 1405 Thirning C.J. sadly remarked,

'It would be good law if a man could maintain a writ of debt for rent service, but I well know that the law is otherwise.'[5]

In consequence the exception was narrowly constrained and gave rise to some delicate distinctions; there is authority, for example, for the view that, although debt could not be used to recover the annuity itself, it could be brought to recover a penalty payable upon default in paying an annuity,[6] and that after the freehold determined debt lay.[7]

A consequence of this general principle was that debt and covenant did not overlap in medieval law; on an agreement under seal to pay a definite sum the action available was debt, not covenant. This was well settled, and a case in 1443 provides a curious illustration.[8] An action was brought by writ of debt to recover a penalty from a lessee who had agreed under seal to pay this penalty if he fell into breach of the covenants in the lease; the breach of covenant relied upon was his failure to pay

[1] Notably in the well-known decision in *Cutter* v. *Powell* (1795) 6 Term Rep. 320. Notice also the refusal to apportion under the common law doctrine of frustration.

[2] 20 Edw. I (R.S.), 222 and 487 might indicate that this rule was not then settled, but the fuller report of the case conforms to the view expressed in the text.

[3] F.N.B., 355B.

[4] F.N.B., 280H, 356H, and see 8 Hen. VI, M. f. 6, pl. 15; 37 Hen. VI, f. 35.

[5] 6 Hen. VI, H. f. 7, pl. 33; 10 Hen. VI, H. f. 5, pl. 17.

[6] 17 Edw. III, M. f. 48, pl. 12; 4 Hen. VI, T. f. 31, pl. 10; 8 Hen. VI, M. f. 6, pl. 15, *contra*. See also *Newdigate* v. *Capell* (1563) Dyer 227a.

[7] 10 Hen. VI, M. f. 11, pl. 38; 19 Hen. VI, M. f. 27, pl. 49, f. 41, pl. 85; 11 Hen. VI, H. f. 14, pl. 4; 15 Hen. VII, f. 1. Debt also did not lie in general for scutage, or to recover an aid or a relief: Co. Litt. 47b.

[8] 22 Hen. VI, T. f. 57, pl. 7.

rent. The action was held to be misconceived, for payment of money was not a covenant—*cel paiment est nul covenant*. The correct form of action was not determined by the expressions used by the contracting parties. Thus Yelverton in an undated case in Statham's *Abridgement*[1] says,

'. . . if an indenture be made between us by these words, *viz*, 'so it is covenanted between us that J.C. shall pay to me twenty pounds at the end of Easter' upon that I shall have an action of debt.'

Covenant could, however, be used where the person to whom the debt was due was not suing; thus if B bound himself to A to pay money to C, A could not sue in debt, for the money was not due to him. His remedy therefore was covenant, and not debt.[2] Certain other apparent examples of election between debt and covenant have already been mentioned.[3]

Eventually debt and covenant became elective remedies. Quite when this happened is not entirely clear.[4] The first sign of the development is an ill-reported decision in the King's Bench in 1585.[5] Debt was brought on a bond expressed in these terms:

'I am content to give W. £10 at Michaelmas and £10 at our lady's day . . .'

What was actually decided was that debt lay on this bond, the words employed being sufficient to impose the duty, for, '. . . it did amount to as much as, "I promise to pay"'. The court also said that covenant lay in addition at the election of the plaintiff, no reason for this being given. The ruling probably depends upon the special facts of the case, and was not meant to warrant election in general. The explanation may lie both in the peculiar terms of the bond and in the fact that the debt was payable by instalments; there is some later authority[6] for the view that

---

[1] Covenant 9.
[2] 10 Edw. II, H. f. 307.
[3] See above, p. 17.
[4] The point is discussed by Ames, 152–3; he detected a conflict between the King's Bench and Common Pleas on the point. The cases do not, however sustain this view.
[5] *Anon.* 3 Leon. 119.
[6] The idea is suggested, but not accepted or rejected, in *Anon.* (1591) 1 Leon. 208 in the Common Pleas. See also *Hare* v. *Savill* (1609) Brownl. 19, perhaps the same case as *Strong* v. *Watts*, (1609) 1 Rolle Abr. 518 pl. 2.

covenant, like assumpsit, could be brought for each instalment
as it fell due so long as the bond contained words of covenant;
debt, as we have seen, was only available when the last instalment became payable.[1] Thus Coke said in *Mordant* v. *Wats*
(1609 or 1619),[2]

> '... when an express covenant is made to pay rent at divers
> days, an action of covenant will lie before all the days of
> payment be past, but an action of debt will not lie until all
> the days be past.'

In the early seventeenth century there is some authority
which could be interpreted as allowing completely free election
between the two actions; thus a note of a case in 1609[3] baldly
states that if a man covenants with another to pay him £20 at a
day, debt or covenant will lie. But the general current of
authority is against this interpretation, and shows that there
was a period of hesitation; even as late as 1660[4] it was held in
Norrice's Case that covenant would lie on a bond in these terms,
'I oblige myself to pay so much money', but doubt was expressed
by the Chief Baron as to whether the action would have been
available on a bond in the old traditional form, *teneri et firmiter
obligari*, 'for that those words sound in debt and not in covenant'.
Decisions such as *Sickelmore* v. *Simonds* (1600),[5] *Strong* v. *Watts*
(1609),[6] *Fisher* v. *Ameers* (1610),[7] and *Brown* v. *Hancock* (1628)[8]
indicate that the courts in the earlier seventeenth century
adopted a compromise position. It had long been the law that
debt lay on instruments couched in the language of covenant
(i.e. 'I promise to pay', 'I covenant to pay)'. In such cases, and
such cases only, the early-seventeenth-century courts allowed
an election between debt and covenant. This compromise can
be illustrated most simply from the law of leases. If land was

---

[1] By this time there was no doubt that assumpsit would lie, and since the action
of assumpsit on parole covenants was regarded as the twin of covenant on formal
covenants it may have been thought only consistent to allow the latter action on
an express covenant to pay a debt by instalments.

[2] Brownl. 19.

[3] *Anon.* 1 Rolle Abr. 518 pl. 3.

[4] *Norrice's Case* (1660) Hard. 178.

[5] Cro. Eliz. 797, C.P.

[6] 1 Rolle Abr. 518 pl. 2.

[7] Brownl. 20.

[8] Hetley 111.

leased for years by indenture reserving rent, the only action for the rent was debt, the words in the *reddendum* amounting to a grant of the debt. If, however, the indenture included in addition an express covenant to pay rent, then covenant would lie in addition to debt, for the indenture would then contain both words of grant and words of covenant. When it came to be settled in the later seventeenth century that any words in a lease under seal could be construed as a covenant,[1] the need for an express covenant to pay rent became unnecessary; then at last debt and covenant became in practice purely alternative. It is interesting to note that even today it remains the custom to impose the obligation to pay rent twice—once in the *reddendum* and again in the tenant's covenants—a remarkable instance of the persistence of a conveyancing practice of inserting 'words of covenant' centuries after its original rationale has been forgotten.[2]

The wide scope of the action of debt

Though subject to the limitations which have been mentioned, the scope of the action of debt was remarkably wide; if a sum certain was due in law then debt lay to recover that sum, for the writ was not trammelled by any inbuilt substantive restrictions. Typically the action lay to enforce bonds—sealed instruments which bound or obliged the debtor to pay a sum certain. It was also brought to recover debts due by informal contractual transactions—to recover money lent, the price of goods sold, rent due from a tenant for years, remuneration for services. It could also be used in circumstances which would seem to us to have little or nothing to do with contract. Thus the action could be used to recover damages awarded in a real action, such as the assize of novel disseisin,[3] the basis of liability here being the judgment of the court enrolled on the record; a sum certain was due, and debt lay to recover that sum. One could even bring debt to recover a sum adjudged due [in an action of debt; debt on debt seemed 'marvellous' even to contemporaries, though the rule was quite settled.[4]

[1] Sheppard, *Touchstone*, 80; Comyn, *Abridgement*, Covenant A2.
[2] See also *Anon.* (1647) Style 31, where it was held that covenant lay in circumstances in which the availability of debt was doubtful.
[3] Y.B. 43 Edw. III, f. 2.
[4] Y.B. 11 Hen. IV, P. f. 56, pl. 2.

Debts due by custom could also be recovered; thus in 1494 it was agreed that the action could be used to claim a penalty of £3 0s. 9d. due by local and particular custom for pound breach.[1]

One of the more surprising uses of the action had its origin in statute. The Statute of Westminster II (1285)[2] made a gaoler or sheriff liable to an action of debt for suffering one found in arrears of account before auditors and imprisoned to quit the prison; the Statute of Merchants[3] in the same year imposed a similar liability upon gaolers for the escape of a debtor imprisoned on a statute merchant; the draftsman remarking menacingly,

> 'And let the keeper of the prison take heed that he must answer for the body or the debt . . .'

A statute in 1377[4] extended this form of suretyship, making the Warden of the Fleet liable for the escape of any person committed to his charge at the suit of the party. The courts generalized this liability of gaolers and sheriffs, and indeed went so far as to impose liability for escape upon anyone who became the guardian of a prisoner.[5] Actions for escape which were not directly warranted by the three statutes were sometimes justified as coming within the 'equity' of the statute,[6] and sometimes said to lie at common law,[7] and the development was assisted by the general air of vagueness as to which statute was being referred to and what the statute actually said.[8] In some situations debt was supplemented by the action on the case.[9] A corollary of the custodian's liability was the idea that the prisoner's escape discharged the debt, as Fineux C.J., with the approval of the whole court, ruled in 1498:

[1] Y.B. 11 Hen. VII, H. f. 14, pl. 8. Debt also lay to recover an amercement in a Court Baron: *Speake* v. *Richards* (1617) Hob. 209.

[2] 13 Edw. I, c. xi.

[3] 13 Edw. I: Statute of Merchants.

[4] 1 Ric. II, c. 12.

[5] 9 Hen. VI, T. f. 19, pl. 13; 15 Edw. IV, H. f. 18, pl. 8.

[6] *Platt* v. *Sheriffs of London.* (1552) (a bill of debt) Plowden 35; Y.B. 15 Edw. IV, H. f. 18, pl. 8; 7 Hen. VI, M. f. 5, pl. 9, Brooke, *Escape*, pl. 28.

[7] *Whiteacres* v. *Onsley* (1572) Dyer 322a.

[8] e.g. Y.B. 7 Hen. IV, M. f. 4, pl. 26; 33 Hen. VI, H. f. 1, pl. 3 (*The Case of the Marshalsea*) on which see a note by Fifoot, 168 n. 58. See also Fletcher, *The Carrier's Liability*, App. IV.

[9] Y.B. 16 Edw. IV, P. f. 2, pl. 7, where the sum due was uncertain. See also Brooke, *Escape*, pl. 9, abridging Y.B. 7 Hen. VI, f. 5, f. 23.

'If one be condemned in debt or another action, and his body put in execution for the same debt or damages, and he breaks prison and goes at large, the party shall never have execution of him, or of his body, or of his goods, but it put to his action against the gaoler.'[1]

One debt, one debtor. This somewhat extreme application of theory fell into disfavour in later law.

The 'proprietary' character of the writ of debt

A number of writers, notably Pollock and Maitland[2] and Barbour,[3] have argued that the action of debt enshrines an archaic conception of the nature of a debtor's liability. The creditor's claim, it is said, was conceived to be proprietary in character, for early common law lacked the concept of a personal obligation. Thus Barbour said,

'Debt represents an archaic conception. The active party appears at first as a demandant rather than a plaintiff, and the action is itself "petitory". One claims what is *his own*'.

Barbour goes on to argue that the separation between the actions of debt and detinue reflects the emergence of the distinction between 'obligation' and 'property'. Thus he says,

'Roughly speaking, the distinction (between debt and detinue) was between obligation and property. Where the plaintiff's right was *in personam*, that is, where he was enforcing an obligation to pay money or chattels, the proper remedy was Debt. But if he sought to recover *specific* property of which he claimed ownership, Detinue was the proper form.'

Pollock and Maitland put forward a somewhat similar interpretation, and laid particular stress upon the similarity between the early action of debt and the action *praecipe in capite* to recover land:

'The bold crudity of archaic thought equates the repayment of an equivalent sum of money to the restitution of specific land or goods. To all appearance our ancestors could not

---

[1] Y.B. 14 Hen. VII, M. f. 1, pl. 1.
[2] P. and M. II, 204–7.
[3] Barbour, 26–8.

conceive credit under any other form. The claimant of a debt asks for what is his own.'

Now unfortunately it is not at all easy to understand precisely what all this amounts to, for neither Barbour nor Pollock and Maitland explain what they understand by the distinction between 'obligation' and 'property'. A related difficulty, which is for ever causing trouble in legal history, is that both interpretations are presented in terms of concepts which would not have been used by medieval lawyers. Barbour, for example, describes the action of detinue as an action in which the plaintiff claims 'ownership'. Not only is it not clear what Barbour meant by this, which is confusing enough; in addition one may search the year-books in vain for any passage in which a contemporary lawyer says that 'ownership' is asserted in detinue. 'Ownership' was just not one of the counters used at that time in legal theory. Hence it is a question whether it is even possible to evaluate such an interpretation in a satisfactory way.

The starting-point for the theory adopted both by Barbour and by Pollock and Maitland (though with varied emphasis) is the account of the form and scope of the action of debt which is given in Glanvill's *Tractatus*. As we have seen, the specimen writ which he gives is similar to the writ *praecipe in capite* by which claims to the specific recovery of freehold land could be sanctioned; furthermore, in Glanvill's time trial in debt could be by battle. The writ of debt was certainly *petitory*. What this means is that the creditor *demands* (*petit*) what is his due, and does not *complain* (*queritur*) that he has been the victim of a wrong; he does, however, assert that the debtor has done wrong in that he withholds (*deforciat*) the sum of money of the chattel due. But whether these formal and procedural similarities are of any theoretical significance seems very dubious; all that can be said with confidence is that the procedure for claiming debts closely resembled the procedure for claiming chattels, and this is not very surprising. There is indeed an intelligible sense in which debt was a real action.[1] It had as its end product the restitution of the debt itself, and not some substitute for the

---

[1] Though both Bracton (f. 102b) and Fleta (S.S. Vol. 72, p. 200) regard debt and detinue as personal actions.

debt, so that the plaintiff would recover the very thing which was his due. But, granted a society which has the institution of money, an action of debt is inevitably a recuperatory action leading to specific recovery. That indeed is how credit can exist.

Glanvill's account of the circumstances in which the writ of debt can be used does not, it is true, attach any significance to a distinction between claims to money debts and claims to chattels. He says,[1]

> 'is qui petit pluribus causis[2] debitum petere potest. Aut enim debitum quid ex causa mutui aut ex causa venditionis aut ex commodato aut ex locato aut ex alia iusta debendi causa'

But this passage only appears curious because we insist on translating *debitum* as 'debt' and consequently make it seem as if Glanvill is employing *our* concept of a debt in a peculiar way. To catch the sense of the passage we must translate,

> 'the demandant can demand that which is due for several causes. For something can be due on account of a loan for consumption, or on account of a sale, or on account of a loan for use, or a hiring, or a deposit, or any other just cause whereby something may be due.'

Translated in this way the passage ceases to be problematical. For Glanvill does not appear to have assimilated claims to money to claims to chattels; rather he saw both as depending upon the existence of what we would call a duty or obligation. Since the *causae debendi* which he enumerates are all contractual in the sense that they depend upon the entry into some sort of consensual transaction, this was a straightforward and understandable analysis.

After Glanvill's time, as we have seen, a distinction grew up between the form of the writs of debt and that of detinue, which

---

[1] X.3 (Hall, p. 117).

[2] For a discussion of Glanvill's account of a *causa debendi* and a *causa petendi* see Hall, *Glanvill*, p. xxxviii. criticising views expressed by H. Kaufmann in *Traditio*, XVII (1961), 108–13. Note that Glanvill does not, as Hall contends say that the performance of the plaintiff of his part of the transaction is the *causa debendi*; the causes listed are contracts. When Glanvill says that in a sale the cause is either sale or purchase (*ex causa quoque emptionis vel venditionis debetum aliquid*), I imagine that he only means that the terms are alternative. *Sed quaere.*

was based primarily upon the subject-matter of the claim. This
was reflected in the writ form in two ways. In an action for a
chattel the inclusion of the word *debet* was thought to be
inappropriate; in addition, the value of a chattel had to be
stated since the courts would not (and sometimes could not)
insist upon specific restitution, but would only give a conditional
judgment for the chattel or its value. But the rules governing
the writ form were quite unrelated to the basis of liability; your
writ was 'in the *detinet*' because you were claiming a specific
cow, not because you were claiming that you owned a
cow. In origin at least, the distinction between debt and detinue seems to have been quite unrelated to any consciously held
theory that detinue was proprietary in contradistinction to
debt. No such theory appears in the sources, nor is it in the least
clear that such a theory would have been even understood by
contemporaries. In the later medieval period it is true that there
is evidence of what might be called a substantive distinction
between the actions of debt and detinue, which was not determined solely by the subject-matter of the claim (and therefore
the writ form). This distinction was never very clearly worked
out, nor did it possess much practical significance, but, so far
as it went, it seems to have involved distinguishing claims to
things which had previously been in the plaintiff's possession
from claims to things which had not. Thus whether detinue[1]
was brought on a bailment, a trover,[2] or some other form of
devenerunt count the plaintiff in most cases relied in part upon
his own prior possession to sustain his claim; in ordinary actions
of debt, and in an action for a specific chattel sold (which some
called debt),[3] the plaintiff did not and could not rely upon his
own prior possession of the thing in demand. This distinction
does not correspond to any distinction between proprietary
right and contractual right.

After debt and detinue separated, it was also sometimes said
that the action of debt was based upon the existence of a 'duty',[4]
and also that in detinue the claim was based upon the plaintiff

---

[1] Of chattels, Detinue of charters has to some degree a separate history.

[2] i.e. on an allegation, which might be fictional, that the plaintiff lost the chattel
and the defendant found it.

[3] See above, p. 58.

[4] For example, see 14 Hen. IV, H. f. 27, pl. 37 at f. 28; 20 Hen. VI, M. f. 5, pl.
16, f. 4, pl. 14.

having 'property' in the thing claimed.[1] But it is dangerous to invest these terms with a significance and precision that they do not possess. All that 'duty' seems to mean is 'duty to pay a debt'; showing 'duty' just means showing indebtedness and nothing more. Thus if Jones owed Smith £20, the 'debt' was £20, and the 'duty' the state of owing £20. Though the contrary has been suggested, there is no warrant for the idea that by 'duty' was meant 'duty imposed by law'; a 'duty' could arise either through operation of law or as a consequence of a consensual transaction. 'Property' is in medieval common law a term of varied significance. When it is said that a plaintiff in detinue asserts 'property' all that is certainly meant is that he is entitled to, or has a right to, the possession of a specific, identifiable thing; clearly you had to be entitled to so much if you were to claim that thing by writ of detinue. It could indeed be said that a creditor had 'property' in a debt;[2] the force of saying this was that the creditor was personally beneficially entitled. Thus in the Register of Writs it is said that an executor suing for a debt due to his testator must not use the word *debet*, which supposes property in him; this usage misled Vaughan C.J. into calling the action of debt 'an action of Property',[3] meaning by 'property' something like the modern 'ownership', but this was in the late seventeenth century.

Medieval lawyers did, however, conceive of the nature of a debtor's liability and a creditor's right in a distinctive way. Ames[4] expressed this by saying,

'A simple contract debt, as well as a debt by specialty, was originally conceived of, not as a contract, in the modern sense, that is, as a promise, but as a grant.'

This requires perhaps some further explanation. In modern legal thought a contract is regarded primarily at least as an agreement (or a set of promises) binding the contracting party to do something in the future—the future action may be paying money or performing some service or whatever. The party in whose favour the action is to be performed is thought of as

---

[1] 50 Edw. III, T. f. 16, pl. 8; 18 Hen. VI, M. f. 20, pl. 5; 20 Hen. VI, T. f. 34, pl. 4; 18 Edw. IV, H. f. 23, pl. 5.
[2] e.g. *Registrum Brevium* 140a; 17 and 18 Edw. III (R.S.), 355.
[3] *Edgecombe* v. *Dee* (1670) Vaughan 89 at 109.
[4] Ames, 150.

acquiring a right to future performance. This was not at all the way in which a consensual debt transaction was looked upon in the old law; such transactions were thought of as giving, granting, or transferring a thing to the creditor. This 'thing', the debt, he could claim by writ of debt because the transaction had entitled him to it; the vice of the debtor who failed to pay up was not that he had failed to do something which he had said he was going to do, but rather that he was detaining or withholding something to which the creditor was entitled. He was guilty of misfeasance, not nonfeasance. This way of thinking derived its plausibility from the fact that a debt was a sum certain which could be specifically recovered. Of course it was realized that a debt was only a thing in a somewhat abstract sense; the creditor could not lay claim to any particular coins and say that they, and they alone, were the coins to which he was entitled. But this obvious fact cannot have seemed to be particularly important, and understandably so, for the whole point of having coined money is to make the specific identity of coins immaterial to their value as a medium of exchange.

Viewed in this way, a debt transaction was, as we have seen,[1] differentiated from a covenant remediable by writ of covenant for damages. What a covenantee (and later a promisee in an action of assumpsit) complained of was a tort or wrong, and for such a tort or wrong he was entitled to compensatory damages; the effect of a valid covenant was that it bound the covenantor to future performance in the sense that a future failure to perform ranked as a tort. This more closely resembles our way of looking at contract, but with the difference that one would not then have spoken of the covenantee's becoming entitled to performance, or having a right to performance; the explanation for this is the general absence of any specific enforcement of covenants at common law. What the law does not allow a plaintiff to get cannot be viewed as something to which he is legally entitled.

The assignment of debts

The general principle of the medieval common law was that a *chose in action* could not be assigned, such a 'thing' being regarded as being incapable of being granted effectively. There

---

[1] See above, p. 70.

was an exception in favour of the King. The explanation for this rule is controversial. According to one view,[1] expressed by Coke in *Lampet's Case* (1612), the point of the rule was to avoid 'the occasion of multiplying of contentions and suits, of great oppression of the people, and chiefly of terre-tenants, and the subversion of the due and equal execution of justice'. This bombast connects the rule with the general discouragement of maintenance, and there is some earlier evidence of favour of this view,[2] which makes it clear that Coke did not invent this explanation. Other writers, however, have preferred the explanation put forward by Spence,[3]

> 'that the credit being a personal right of the creditor, the debtor being obliged toward that person could not by a transfer of the credit, which was not an act of his, become obliged toward another'.

Another possibility is that the severity of the mechanisms for enforcing the debtor's liability made it unfair to allow assignment, which could substitute a more cruel creditor. Whatever the explanation may be, there could be no question of assigning a debt. An instrument under seal granting a debt (i.e. a bond) could perfectly well be granted by the creditor to another, and this grant would vest the property in the instrument in the grantee, but the debt remained due to the original creditor, for the duty was incapable of being granted.[4]

To a limited extent, however, the practical effect of assignment could be achieved by the creditor giving the intended assignee a letter of attorney to enable the assignee to sue for the debt in the name of the original creditor. This practice seems to have been in use at common law in the fifteenth century, if not earlier,[5] but it came into conflict with the law against maintenance, for the third party could be regarded as intermeddling with a cause which did not concern him, particularly

---

[1] 10 Co.Rep. 46b at 48a.

[2] Brooke, *Chose in Action*, pl. 3; 34 Hen. VI, M. f. 30, pl. 15; 15 Hen. VII, H. f. 2, pl. 3; *Penson* v. *Hickbed* (1590) Cro. Eliz. 170.

[3] Spence, *Equitable Jurisdiction*, II. 850. See also Ames, Lect. XVIII and *H.E.L.* VII. 534 et seq.

[4] *Anon.* (1533) Dyer at 5a, citing *in margine Kelset* v. *Nicholson* (1595) and Co. Litt. 232b. See also 2 Rolle Abr. 46, Cro. Eliz. 476, 496.

[5] See Ames, 213 n. 2.

if it could be shown that he had prosecuted the suit at his own expense. In order to escape the charge of maintenance the third party had to show a just cause for the 'assignment'; the standard instance of such a just cause would be the fact that the creditor owed him a debt, and that the assignment was made in satisfaction of that debt.[1] Thus an assignment by way of gift, or a speculative purchase of a debt, would fall under the ban of maintenance. This remained the law until the eighteenth century,[2] though Hale C.J. in 1674[3] seems to have been prepared to hold that an agreement to transfer the benefit of a debt, as opposed to the debt itself, giving the assignee a right of action in covenant (and not debt) could not be regarded as involving maintenance unless this was specially found.

Transmission of rights and liabilities on death

Originally upon the death of a debtor liability to pay the debt, if transmitted at all, passed to the heir; this was the law in Bracton's time;[4] similarly the right to sue passed to the creditor's heir and not to his executors. In Edward I's reign the executor acquired the right to sue and the liability to be sued.[5]

'A change as momentous as any that a statute could make was made without statute and very quietly. Early in Edward I's reign the chancery had framed and the king's court upheld a writ of debt for executors and a writ of debt against executors.'[6]

This development left the rights and liabilities of heirs somewhat uncertain. So far as liability is concerned, it was established in

[1] 34 Hen. VI, H. f. 30, pl. 15; 15 Hen. VII, H. f. 2, pl. 3 (on which see Brooke, *Chose in Action*, pl. 3).

[2] *Penson* v. *Hickbed* (1590) Cro. Eliz. 170, 4 Leon. 99 suggests that some judges may have been prepared to allow the purchase of debts, and only regard as objectionable assignments where the assignee was to keep only part of the debt. But, as Holdsworth points out, the suggestion was not followed. See *South and Marel's Case* (1590) 3 Leon. 234; *Barrow* v. *Gray* (1597) Cro. Eliz. 551; *Harvey* v. *Bateman* (1660) Noy 52; *Loder* v. *Chesleyn* (1665) 1 Sid. 212, Note (1667–72) Freeman Ch. Cas. 145.

[3] *Deering* v. *Farington* 3 Keb. 304.

[4] Bracton f. 407b. See generally P. and M. II. 345 et seq.

[5] P. and M. II. 347, citing 20–1 Edw. I (R.S.), 375; 21–2 Edw. I (R.S.), 258, 598, 33–4 Edw. I (R.S.), 62, 294; 30–1 Edw. I (R.S.), 235.

[6] P. and M. II. 345.

the fourteenth century that the heir was only liable if he had assets in fee simple by descent from his ancestor on the day that the writ was purchased.[1] In the fifteenth century there is some authority for the view that even an heir with assets was not liable if he could show that the executors possessed chattels sufficient to satisfy the creditor.[2] If this was accepted law it amounts to a recognition that the heir's liability was secondary to the liability of the executor. That this was the way the matter was conceived is illustrated by a case in 1410.[3] Debt was brought on an obligation against an heir, and the defendant pleaded that the plaintiff was in fact his ancestor's executor and had the deceased's chattels in his possession. This plea appears to have been regarded as an answer to the action.

Similarly the heir's right to sue was whittled down. Thus a case in 1430,[4] which in fact concerns detinue rather than debt, was regarded by the author of *Natura Brevium* as authority for the view that the heir could not sue upon a bond in favour of a man and his heirs if the executors were living, and the rule laid down in the case is certainly consistent with this view. In 1440 Markham, then a sergeant, opined that,

'If a man is obliged to me and my heirs, my heir will never have an action of debt.'[5]

But this is perhaps an exaggeration, for the principle seems to have been that the heir could sue if there were no executors.[6] Another situation where the heir could sue was in a case where the right to the debt was thought to be in the nature of a heritable interest,[7] or appurtenant to such an interest, as where land was leased for years and the reversion descended to the heir at law.[8]

The transmission of liability to pay a debt to the debtor's executors was, however, severely restricted, for the executors could only be sued in cases where the testator in his lifetime

[1] 42 Edw. III, P. f. 10, pl. 12; 43 Edw. III, H. f. 9, pl. 27; Fitz., *Debt* 140 (13 Edw. III), F.N.B. 120B.
[2] 7 Hen. IV, M. f. 31, pl. 10.
[3] 12 Hen. IV, P. f 21, pl. 11.
[4] 9 Hen. VI, H. f. 58, pl. 4.
[5] 19 Hen. VI, M. f. 41, pl. 84.
[6] 49 Edw. III, P. f. 11, pl. 5 at f. 12. See Brooke, Dette pl. 47.
[7] 11 Hen. IV, T. f. 84, pl. 34.
[8] See 5 Hen. VII, P. f. 18, pl. 12.

could not have defended the action by a procedure known as compurgation (or wager of law). This procedure, which is more fully discussed later in this book, involved the debtor in taking an oath that no debt was due, and was available in most actions of debt based upon informal contracts. Hence in general the position was that it was only in cases where the debtor was bound by an instrument under seal that his executors or heirs could be sued; debts due by informal contracts died with the debtor, though the executors might be bound in conscience to pay them. The rationale of this peculiar state of the law is discussed below.

Leases and privity

In general there was no question of the assignment of the liability to pay a debt; the debtor could neither make a third party liable in addition to himself nor transfer his own liability to a third party with that party's consent.[1] The position where there was a lease and the debt due consisted in rent issuing out of the land introduced some complication, as might be expected. Primarily the persons who were privy to the lease were the original lessor and lessee, and since an action of debt was thought to require privity between the parties there was felt to be some difficulty in permitting either the assignee of the rever-sion to sue, or the assignee of the lease to be sued for the rent. It must first be noted that although the problem is closely analogous to the problem raised by covenants in a lease (where there has been assignment) it is not the same problem, for the obligation to pay rent was not enforceable by action of covenant. Second, the notion of 'privity of estate', which today means the existence of a tenure between two persons, and which is currently treated as the basis of actions between assigns of the reversion and assigns of the lease, had not yet been evolved as a justifica-tion for liability in this context; in any event it was hardly settled that a lease for years created a tenure at all. When 'privity' is mentioned in connection with debt it appears to express the idea of being party to, or being involved in, the transaction giving rise to the debt.

It was settled in the fifteenth century that an assignee of a

---

[1] 44 Edw. III, T. f. 21, pl. 23; 9 Hen. V, M. f. 14 pl. 23.

lease for years could be sued for rent. This was stated as if it was established law by Strange in a case in 1430:[1]

> 'As in the case where I lease lands to you for term of years, rendering to me certain rent, and you grant your term to another, if the rent be in arrear, afterwards I [may] bring my action against the second lessee, because he has the same term, and this is sufficient privity between me and him.'

The rule that there must be an assignment of the whole term, and not a sub-lease, is implied by Strange's statement of the law, and recognized expressly in Henry VII's time.[2] The same rule probably applied if debt was brought against the assignee of a lease for life or *pur autre vie* (which could only be done when the freehold had determined).[3] Rede in 1490[4] rationalized the rule by saying that it would be contrary to reason if any act of the lessee should adversely affect his lessor without his consent. This idea, and the emphasis upon the fact that the assignee is liable because he has the term, perhaps depend upon the conception of rent as *reserved* when a lease is granted, and as something issuing out of the land, which the lessee *renders* (i.e. returns) to the lessor. A lessor was conceived of as having granted the land but as having kept back some part of the issues of the land; upon an assignment his position would be prejudiced if he could not continue to get hold of what he had reserved from the only person able to transfer to him some part of the issue of the land; clearly that person was the assignee.

If the matter was looked upon in this way it becomes less surprising to find that as late as 1565[5] it was thought very doubtful whether the original lessee remained liable for rent falling due after he had assigned the whole term.

> 'And it seemed to divers justices and to Catlyn[6] that the action did not lie, because the privity between the lessor and lessee is gone and determined by the assignment of the whole term, and a new privity created which goes with the land

---

[1] 10 Hen. VI, M. f. 11, pl. 38.
[2] 5 Hen. VII, P. f. 18, pl. 12.
[3] See the case cited above, p. 70, n. 7.
[4] 5 Hen. VII, P. f. 18, pl. 12.
[5] Dyer 247b.
[6] Who was Chief Justice.

between lessor and assignee, yet *quaere* whether the privity
of contract does not remain between the parties to the first
contract, because it is personal.'

In *Marrow* v. *Turpin* (1601)[1] indeed it was held that if the lessor
had notice of the assignment, and accepted rent from the
assignee, he lost any right of action against the original lessee.
This decision perhaps turned upon the acceptance of rent, for
in *Walker* v. *Harris* (1586)[2] it had been decided that the lessee
remained liable. In Coke's[3] report of the case the basic objection to the action was that

> 'the land was debtor, and not the person, but in respect of
> the land'.

Walker's Case, as reported by Coke, was the basis of the modern
law, and rests the liability of the original lessee on privity of
contract, and the liability of the assignee on privity of estate.

The right of an assign of the reversion to sue in debt also
provoked doubt and difficulty. In 1430[4] Paston and Strange
disagreed on the question, Paston taking the view that, although
he could distrain for rent, he could not sue in debt, since he was
a stranger to the lease. The point arose for decision in a case in
1490,[5] where a devisee of the reversion under the custom of
London brought debt for rent against the lessee. Rede, counsel
for the tenant, took exception:

> 'whether this action lies at the suit of the devisee or not,
> because he lacks privity, and is not a party, and because an
> action of debt cannot be maintained without privity the
> action is not good at the suit of the devisee. But executors
> can have an action of debt, because the law makes them
> privy, but not so in this case. And the heir can have an action
> of debt, if the reversion descends to him.'

But the court was not persuaded, and held that any person who
lawfully acquired the reversion could sue, since the law made
him privy. This decision settled the point.

---

[1] Moo. K.B. 600.
[2] Moo. K.B. 351.
[3] 3 Co.Rep. 22a.
[4] 9 Hen. VI, T. f. 16, pl. 7.
[5] 5 Hen. VII, P. f. 18, pl. 12. 19 Hen. VI, M. f. 41, pl. 86 suggests that the
assignee could sue, in Paston J.'s opinion.

According to Brooke[1] the lessor, even after assignment of the reversion, could still sue the lessee for rent in the opinion of Newton C.J. in a case in 1432. This view seems never to have been acted upon. Brooke cites a decision in 1489 against it; the reference is incomplete, and I suspect that he was in fact referring to the decision in 1490 which has just been discussed.

The enforcement of the debtor's liability

At common law a debtor's liability to pay could be enforced against the debtor's chattels (which could be sold by the sheriff under a *fieri facias*), or against the issues of his lands which could be taken under a *levari facias*, or alternatively the debtor's lands could be distrained upon. The Statute of *Acton Burnell* (1283) introduced for the first time recourse against the body of the debtor, who could be imprisoned until he paid or reached a compromise with the creditor. But this was only permitted if he did not possess sufficient chattels to cover his liability. The Statute of Merchants (1285) carried matters considerably further; imprisonment became automatic, and lasted until the debtor paid, whatever other pressure was brought upon the debtor. Ordinary judgment debtors were not generally liable to imprisonment until 1352.[2] Thereafter, however, statutes merchant and staple were no longer peculiar in allowing the creditor to have his debtor imprisoned. They continued to give the creditor a more extensive right of recourse against the land of the debtor. By the Statute of Westminster (1285)[3] a judgment debtor (including a debtor by common law recognizance) was liable, if the creditor chose, to have half of his lands seized by the creditor; the creditor's remedy here was called *elegit*,[4] since the writ recited the fact that the creditor had *chosen* to proceed in this way rather than by *fieri facias*. A debtor by statute merchant or staple, however, could have all his lands taken as security for payment.[5] Such statutes were used fairly extensively

---

[1] *Abridgment*, Dette, pl. 178, citing 11 Hen. VI, M. f. 7, pl. 12, H. f. 16, pl. 9, which as reported in the printed year-books does not support him.

[2] 25 Edw. III, st. 5, c. 17, which allowed *capias* to issue in debt, detinue of chattels, and actions for the taking of beasts. See generally Plucknett, *Legislation of Edward I*, 149 et seq.

[3] By c. 18.

[4] The creditor who took possession was called 'tenant by *elegit*'.

[5] The creditor who took possession was called 'tenant by statute merchant' or 'tenant by statute staple'. The right of redemption was enforced by *scire facias*.

(as was *elegit*) to create what were in fact mortgages of real property.

II. FORMAL DEBT TRANSACTIONS

A. OBLIGATIONS

F AR and away the majority of actions on contracts brought in the common law courts in medieval times were actions of debt *sur obligation*; in such actions the plaintiff had to produce a sealed instrument whereby the defendant had acknowledged himself to be the debtor of the plaintiff. Such instruments were called 'obligations', 'bonds', or 'writings obligatory'.[1] They were commonly written in Latin, the debtor called the 'obligor' confessing himself to be bound and obliged (*se teneri et obligari*) to the creditor ('obligee') as in the following example, which is taken from a precedent book printed somewhere around 1510:[2]

> 'Noverint universi per praesentes me R.B. teneri et firmiter obligari J.N. in centum libros sterlingorum solvenda eidem J.N. aut suo certo attornato seu executoris suis in festo nativitatis sancti Johannis Baptisti proximo futuro post datum presentium ad quam quidem solutionem bene et fideliter faciendam obligo me heredes executores meas et omnia bona mea per praesentes sigillo meo signatas datas anno regni . . .' etc.

Bonds could also be executed in any language, and bonds in English are sometimes distinguished by being called bills. Latin bonds persisted until they became invalid in 1731.[3] The standard form of bonds did not change significantly over

---

[1] Quite a considerable amount has been written on the history of bonds in England; it is, however, scattered. See in particular the following: Postan, 'Private Financial Instruments in England' (1930) 23 *Vierteljahrschrift für Sozial- und Wirtschaftgesichte* 26; J. B. Ames, 'Specialty Contracts and Equitable Defences', 9 H.L.R. 49, reprinted in *Lectures in Legal History* (Camb., Mass., 1913), Lect. X; R. W. Turner, *The Equity of Redemption* (Camb., 1931), Ch. II; D. E. C. Yale, *Lord Nottingham's Chancery Cases*, Vol. II, S.S. Vol. 79, intro., pp. 7–30; L. F. Salzman, *Building in England* (Oxford, 1952); J. J. Rabinowitz, *Jewish Law: Its Influence on the Development of Legal Institutions* (New York, 1956).

[2] *Carta Feodi*, printed *c*. 1510 by Wykyn de Worde.

[3] 4 Geo. II, c. 26, and 6 Geo. II, c. 14, which statutes more or less completed the job (begun in 1357) of making English the language of the law. Lord Gardiner has, I believe, expressed the view that something remains to be done, which is a pleasing thought after six centuries of effort.

the centuries; having found a reliable formula, lawyers stick to it. The formality of bonds can easily be exaggerated, and the common law courts kept the formalities to the minimum. Thus the prevailing view was that no particular form of words need be used. In *Core's Case* (1536)[1] the 'resistance of formalism is exemplified:

> '... if a man makes such a bill as this: "This bill witnesseth that I, A.B., have borrowed ten pound of C.D." without more, this will charge the executors just as much as an obligation ... The law is the same in this case: "*Memorandum quod talis debet* to A £10", without more, if this bill be sealed and delivered as a deed, it is a perfectly good obligation. And Portman J. said ... that although these words, *teneri et firmiter obligari*, are commonly inserted in every common obligation, yet when other words, which carry the same effect and meaning, are expressed in writings, the law construes them as having the same efficacy.'

Since, however, a bond was regarded as a grant of a debt, it is not surprising to find that some lawyers felt that 'words of grant', as opposed to mere 'words of covenant' were essential. Thus in a case in 1482[2] Serjeant Vavasour argued,

> '... as it seems to me there is another cause why he should not obtain judgment. For he has counted against him as a sealed bill,[3] which is in this form "Memorandum that I Master Jo. Hatchy (who was testator) have received of W.K. etc., the which £20 I the said Master J.H. promise to pay to R. of A. (who is now plaintiff) In witness whereof etc. I set my seal'. And Sir, it seems to me that here there are no words of obligation, for a promise is not a matter of obligation.'

But this argument was emphatically rejected by the court, Catesby J. saying that he knew no better word of obligation than 'I promise'. There was also a school of thought which insisted that a *testimonium* was essential, a doctrine eventually rejected in *Goddard's Case* (1583).[4] Latin bonds would frequently be drawn by scriveners or other ignorant of the niceties of

---

[1] Dyer 20a at 22b.
[2] 22 Edw. IV, M. f. 22, pl. 1.
[3] The 'bill' was an early form of promissory note.
[4] 2 Co.Rep. 4b: 3 Leon. 100. cf. *Anon.* (1535) Moo. K.B. 3.

grammar, but false Latin, or English, did not impair the validity of the instrument.[1] The essentials were the use of parchment or paper,[2] sealing by the obligor, and delivery as a deed, normally witnessed and attested.[3] Sealing was no great chore; it corresponded to signing today, and, although the seal could be a grand affair, a blob of wax with some sort of impress on it sufficed. Loss of the seal, or any material erasure or alteration of the bond rendered the bond invalid,[4] as did any suspicious circumstance, such as the fact that the bond had been smoked[5] or the seal glued back on to the label;[6] the courts were prudently suspicious of any signs of monkey business.

Conditional bonds

A bond could be *single* or *simple*, both terms meaning unconditional; alternatively it could be made subject to a condition, and this was more usual, for it was by the use of conditioned bonds that important agreements were made actionable in the days when the bond was the basic contractual institution. Let us take first what was called the common money bond. Suppose Hugo proposes to lend Robert £100. Robert will execute a bond in favour of Hugo for a larger sum, normally twice the sum lent, thus binding himself to pay Hugo £200 on a fixed day; the bond will be made subject to a condition of defeasance, which provides that if he pays £100 before the day the bond is to be void. This condition will normally be endorsed on (i.e. written on the back of) the bond. What is essentially the same technique could be employed in the case of a contract for the sale of land, or indeed any agreement where what was desired was the performance of some act, or the granting of some forbearance. Thus if Hugo is to convey Blackacre to Robert, Hugo will bind himself to pay a sum of money, the bond being subject to a condition of defeasance if he conveys the property

---

[1] 8 Hen. VI, P. f. 35, pl. 1; 9 Hen. VII, H. f. 16, pl. 9; 24 Edw. III, f. 24. On false English *see James Osborne's Case*, cited in Rolle's *Abridgement*, Vol. II, 147, pl. 17.

[2] Perkins, *A Profitable Book*, Faits, pl. 129; *Goddard's Case* (1583), cited above.

[3] 3 Hen. VII, T. f. 5, pl. 20. Thus debt lay on a statute merchant, since it bore the debtor's seal, but not on a statute staple; see 15 Hen. VII, M. f. 14, pl. 6 (continuing 2 Ric. III, M. f. 7, pl. 14).

[4] Lib.Ass. f. 6; 14 Hen. IV, H. f. 18, pl. 16; 3 Hen. VII, T. f. 5, pl. 20.

[5] Perkins, op. cit., Faits, pl. 128.

[6] 7 Hen. VI, H. f. 18, pl. 27.

before the day fixed; reciprocally Roberts can execute a money bond for twice the price, subject to a condition of defeasance if he pay the price on the agreed day or before. Once the two bonds are executed and delivered, both parties are bound to pay what are in effect penal sums, but each will have a defence if he performs his part of the underlying agreement of sale.

A more sophisticated method, which was very commonly employed in the case of bilateral agreements, was to set out the terms of the agreement in the form of covenants in an indenture under seal; both parties could then retain one part of the indenture which they had executed. They could then both execute bonds of even date with the indenture, binding themselves to pay a sum of money unless the covenants in the indenture were performed. An example of such a condition, taken from the dorse (i.e. back) of a bond I possess of 1634, runs as follows:

'The condition of the within written obligation is that if the within bounden Richard Norman his heirs executors administrators and assigns and anye of them truelie and faithfullie hold observe fulfill performe and keepe all and singuler the covenants promises agreements articles clauses and sentences which on the part of the said Richard Norman his heirs ... etc. ought to be held observed fullfilled performed and kept mentioned specified and ordeined in one part of indentures bearing equall date with these presents made between the said Richard Norman of the one part and within named James Younge on the other part according to the true intent purport and meaning of the said indentures that then this present within written obligacon to be voyd and of none effect or else to stand remaine and be in full force power strength and virtue.'

There was, of course, no need to be as long-winded as this about it.

In the standard conditioned bond the condition was distinct from the deed which imposed the obligations. Though written on the same piece of parchment (or paper) it formed a separate part of the instrument, either written on the face of the instrument after the *testimonium*, or endorsed upon it (i.e. on the back). It was not itself either sealed or witnessed or signed. The rule that the condition need not be sealed was laid down in 1367.[1] It appears to have been based upon an idea akin to the principle of estoppel; the plaintiff creditor, by suing upon the instrument, was estopped from denying that the whole document was one entire deed. Presumably a condition not written on the same piece of parchment or paper would be ineffective, but I know of no case on the point. It must, however, be written; at law (though not in equity) a parole condition to an obligation under seal was wholly ineffective,[2] except perhaps in the case of a lease.[3]

The pleading of conditions

Although in form the condition was expressed to be both resolutive and suspensive, it was in general treated as resolutive; the bond was good and imposed the duty upon the obligor, but it could be made void by performance of the condition. In consequence, if an action was brought upon a standard conditioned bond, the obligee need do no more than base his declaration upon the bond (which he must produce) and say nothing about the condition.[4] He could, if he wished, go further than this and aver that the condition had not been performed; such a form of declaration, though not favoured, was unobjectionable. Where a bond was conditioned upon the performance of a number of covenants in an indenture, the obligee could sue on the bond, rehearsing the condition, and aver generally that the covenants had not been performed without specifying which covenants had been broken, or in what respect they had been broken; authority favoured such a declaration, though some thought such a count bad for duplicity (or worse). The obligor could then plead in reply that all the covenants had been performed; the next move was for the obligee to specify by way of replication a particular covenant which he claimed had been broken, and issue joined upon this single breach could be submitted to the jury.[5]

---

[1] 41 Edw. III, H. f. 10, pl. 7.

[2] *Esthalle and Herliston* v. *Esthalle*, 6 and 7 Edw. II, S.S. Vol. 19, p. 22; Fitz. *Debt* 169 (Trin. 4 Edw. II); 7 Hen. IV, M. f. 1, pl. 1; 8 Hen. VI, H. f. 26, pl. 15; 6 Hen. VII, M. f. 12, pl. 11.

[3] See 1 Hen. V, T. f. 6–7, pl. 1.

[4] 36 Hen. VI, f. 2, pl. 2; 6 Hen. IV, H. f. 8, pl. 34.

[5] 3 Hen. VI, M. f. 8, pl. 7; *Anon.* (1570) Dyer 297a; and see Brooke, Count, 3.

If the more usual form of declaration was employed it was up to the obligee to plead the condition and its performance. This conformed to orthodox doctrine. Normally the performance of the condition would be to the advantage of the obligor (since it saved the penalty) and its performance would require action on his part; it was standard pleading doctrine that one who sought to take advantage of a condition should plead it, and also that one who was to perform a condition should plead it, and its performance.[1] In substantive terms the position thus was that the plaintiff obligee did not have to undertake the burden of pleading the breach of the agreement which entitled him to his penalty; instead the defendant obligor had the burden of pleading by way of defence that he had not broken the agreement. This state of affairs was good for contractual plaintiffs, but not very agreeable for contractual defendants, whose lawyers naturally enough cast about for some pleading device which would in substance place the burden of pleading the breach of agreement upon the plaintiff. The need for such a device was particularly felt when a bond was conditioned upon the performance of all the covenants in an indenture; clearly no defendant would want to have to plead in detail that he had performed each and every one, when he knew that if in the event a single one was found to have been broken he would forfeit the whole penalty. Furthermore there was always the risk of losing the action on some technical flaw; the less one had to plead the less the risk of a mistake. There was no question of pleading substantial performance to save the penalty; the condition must be performed *in toto*, and a plea which did not aver this was demurrable.[2]

To deal with this problem (only in the case of bond to perform a number of covenants in an indenture) fifteenth-century defendants adopted the practice of pleading the condition, and averring generally that they had performed all the covenants. This device was accepted by the courts in a long line of cases,[3] and it had the effect of forcing the plaintiff obligee into

[1] See *Colthirst* v. *Bejushin* (1550) Plowden 32b.
[2] 21 Edw. IV, H. f. 78, pl. 1.
[3] 11 Edw. IV, H. f. 10, pl. 5; 22 Edw. IV, T. f. 15, pl. 40; 2 Ric. III, M. f. 17, pl. 44; 5 Hen. VII, P. f. 22, pl 4; 10 Hen. VII, H. f. 12, pl. 3; 13 Hen. VII, P. f. 18, pl. 1; 16 Hen. VII, P. f. 18, pl. 1; and see Brooke, *Condition* 16. There were qualifications: the covenants must be in the affirmative, their performance must

pleading a replication which identified which particular covenant had been broken;[1] hence the contracting party who sued
for the penalty was driven to accept the burden of pleading the
breach of the substantial agreement upon which he relied.
Though accepted in fifteenth-century law, this device fell out of
favour in Henry VIII's reign, when the law moved back in
favour of plaintiffs; such a general plea was held to be demurrable, and the defendant was required to plead his performance
of each and every covenant in detail.[2] This change must have
seriously increased the severity of the law. There was a long
dispute as to whether the defendant must produce the indenture
containing the covenants; the final rule seems to have been that
he must, which seems in principle correct and in practice
just.[3]

Where the standard form was not used the law was not so
clear. One possibility was that the condition might form part
of the deed, and be suspensively conditional, so that the plaintiff obligee was the party seeking to take advantage of it. Here
the plaintiff must declare on the condition and aver performance, at least if the condition was to be performed by him.[4]
Thus where the defendant was bound by obligation to pay the
plaintiff £10 if the plaintiff went to Rome, the plaintiff must
rehearse the condition and aver that he had gone to Rome, for
'. . . the duty commences on the condition'.[5] More tricky was a

[1] *Quaere* whether the replication was bad for duplicity if the breach of more than
one covenant was involved.

[2] 26 Hen. VIII, T. f. 5, pl. 25; and cf. 26 Hen. VIII, f. 1, pl. 6. Brooke (Condition 2) cites two other opinions in favour of the same view, and in Condition 180
notes that this was the mode of pleading in his day (i.e. *c.* 1550). Fitzherbert J.
states in 1535 that the general plea had only come into use in the previous few
years; I cannot understand this, since there seems to be abundant evidence that
it was in use in the fifteenth century. He was in a rage at the time when he made
this remark, and there is other evidence that Fitzherbert, when cross, was not too
careful in what he said.

[3] See 7 Hen. IV, M. f. 1, pl. 1; 28 Hen. VI, P. f. 7, pl. 8; 6 Edw. IV, M. f. 1,
pl. 3 (misreported, according to Brian C.J. in 13 Hen. VII, P. f. 18, pl. 1); 6 Hen.
VII, M. f. 12, pl. 11; H. f. 13, pl. 1a; 13 Hen. VII, P. f. 18, pl. 1; 16 Hen. VII, T.
f. 11, pl. 3.

[4] 3 Hen. VI, M. f. 6, pl. 6; 14 Hen. VII, T. f. 31, pl. 8; 15 Hen. VII, H. f. 1,
pl. 1.

[5] 9 Edw. IV, H. f. 48, pl. 3; 22 Edw. IV, H. f. 42, pl. 3; 15 Hen. VII, H. f. 1,
pl. 1; 3 Hen. VI, H. f. 33, pl. 26; 39 Hen. VI, M. f. 21, pl. 31.

involve a mere matter of fact, they must not afford the obligor an alternative, and
performance must not involve the act of anyone other than the obligor.

case where the condition formed part of the bond but performance was not exclusively in the plaintiff's control. The stock example was the grant of an annuity *pro consilio impendendo*; counsel claiming such an annuity could only give counsel if the defendant asked for it. Some thought it enough to aver readiness to give counsel, others that there was no need even to go this far.[1] Another possibility was an expressly suspensive condition not forming part of the bond; here it was probably prudent for the plaintiff to plead the condition and its performance, but perhaps not essential.[2] The sensible creditor avoided these difficulties by using the standard form of bond with its resolutive condition of defeasance.

The dispositive character of the bond

The common form of bond looks like a hybrid between an evidentiary and a dispositive document—it announces that the obligor is bound, and then goes on to bind him. But whatever the position may have been at an early period, the developed common law treated the instrument as dispositive—the instrument *was* the obligation—and at common law this position was rigorously maintained. Thus in an action taken on the bond the plaintiff creditor must show ('make profert') the instrument to the court, and a declaration which did not state that this had been done was defective. Hence if the creditor lost the bond, or it was defaced or the seal lost, the creditor's right was lost too. Until the decision in *Read* v. *Brookman* (1789)[3] there was no question at common law of proving the past existence of a lost deed by secondary evidence. A corollary was that a duty arising from a parole contract was consumed if an obligation was subsequently made for the same debt.[4] Hence a bond

---

[1] 26 Hen. VI, P. f. 1, pl. 5; 33 Hen. VI, H. f. 22, pl. 5; 39 Hen. VI, M. f. 21, pl. 31; 9 Edw. IV, H. f. 48, pl. 3, f. 53, pl. 17.

[2] 27 Hen. VI, T. f. 9, pl. 1. If a bond was conditioned upon the performance of covenants in an indenture and the defendant pleaded performance, it was the defendant's job to show the indenture; see 28 Hen. VI, P. f. 7, pl. 8; 6 Edw. IV, M. f. 1, pl. 4; 6 Hen. VII, M. f. 12, pl. 11; 7 Hen. IV, M. f. 1, pl. 1.

[3] (1789) 3 T.R. 151; *Doctor Leyfield's Case* (1611) 10 Co.Rep. 88a; and see Ames, 104–5; *H.E.L.* VII. 346.

[4] Brooke, *Contract* 29 (1537); and see 4 Hen. VI, P. f. 17, pl. 1; 3 Hen. IV, P. f. 17, pl. 14; 11 Hen. IV, T. f. 79, pl. 14. In the fourteenth century there was an exception where debt was brought for rent due on a lease; here the deed could be treated as purely evidentiary: see 44 Edw. III, f. 42; 10 Hen. VII, P. f. 24, pl. 32.

could not in general be used as evidence of a parole contract even if the obligee wished to so treat it. The dispositive character of the bond was accentuated by the general reluctance of the common law courts to allow anything in the nature of parole evidence of matters of fact to count as legally relevant to the modification or discharge of legal liabilities arising out of sealed instruments. The principle is difficult to formulate in modern terminology, for no close analogy exists in modern law. Bacon put it neatly this way:[1]

> 'The law will not couple and mingle matters of specialty which is of higher account with matters of averment, which is of inferior account in law.

Thus there was no question of calling parole evidence to vary the terms of a bond, or to show that an apparently single bond was subject to a parole condition. Nor was there any question at common law of any defence analogous to 'failure of consideration'. In the absence of an express condition in writing the courts were not prepared to investigate the real cause of the transaction. This was classically illustrated by a leading case in 1458.[2] One J.R. brought debt *sur obligation* against M.P. and J.B. citizens and aldermen of London. Choke for the defendants pointed out that the bonds had been entered into to secure payment for certain debts due to the plaintiff, which had been assigned to the defendants. The assignment was ineffective at law; the debts remained due to the plaintiff, and consequently the defendants neither had obtained nor would obtain anything in return for the money they had bound themselves to pay. Yet it was not so much as suggested that the bonds, because of these circumstances, were void or voidable at common law. Instead the defendants had taken their predicament to the Chancellor, who had, on the advice of the common law justices, ordered the plaintiff to release the defendants from the bonds, which he had refused to do, and was therefore committed to the Fleet prison in contempt, from whence he now sued on the bonds. The best Choke could do was to argue that the decree in Chanc-

---

[1] Bacon, *Maxims of the Law*, reg. 25.
[2] 37 Hen. VI, H. f. 13, pl. 3. The rule was the same in the case of annuities granted for a particular cause; see 21 Edw. III, H. f. 23, pl. 9; 41 Edw. III, H. f. 6, pl. 14; M. f. 19, pl. 3; 8 Hen. VI, H. f. 23, pl. 9; 7 Edw. IV, M. f. 16, pl. 10.

ery, though never complied with by the execution of a formal release, could be pleaded in bar to the common law action. This divided the court; Danby and Moyle JJ. taking the view that the bonds were void through the decree in chancery, whilst Prisot C.J. and Nedham J. thought that they could still be sued upon at law.

The principle Bacon stated is also illustrated by the refusal of the courts to treat mutual reciprocal obligations as dependent, in the absence of an express condition making them dependent. This applied both in debt and covenant, and the rule passed into assumpsit, though it came in the end to be modified. The clearest statement is to be found in a case in 1501,[1]

'Note by Fineux C.J.: if one covenants to serve me for a year, and I covenant with him to give him £20, if I do not say *for the same cause*, he will have an action for the twenty pounds although he has never served me; it will be otherwise if I say that he is to have £20 for the same cause. So if I covenant with a man that I am to marry his daughter, and he covenants with me that he will make an estate in tail special to me and his daughter, if I subsequently marry another woman, or his daughter marries another man, yet will I have an action of covenant against him to compel him to make an estate. But if the covenant was that he should make the estate to us for the same cause, then he is not to make an estate until we are married. And so was the opinion of the court. Rede J. said this was beyond doubt.'

The idea behind this refusal to go behind the express terms of the instrument was rational enough; if parties make one contract it is not the job of the court to make another. A case in 1505[2] illustrates the fact that there were then, as today, lawyers who were prepared to be more sympathetic in special cases. Three men were bound by penal bond to submit disputes to arbitration, the bonds being defeasible if they submitted. The arbitrator's award was that one should pay a sum of money to another, who was to execute a release of all actions; the question was, as we would say, whether payment and release were

---

[1] 15 Hen. VII, T. f. 10, pl. 17.
[2] 21 Hen. VII, T. f. 28, pl. 7.

concurrent conditions or not. Rede, by now Chief Justice, treated the two acts of performance as independent; each party was independently liable to forfeit the penalty if he did not perform. Kingsmill J. disagreed:

> 'He was of opinion that they were to be performed all at one time, so that the one was not bound to perform before the other had performed for his part.'

Serjeant Brudenell, however, agreed with Rede C.J.

The plea of 'non est factum'

Since the bond was dispositive, the most radical line of defence took the form of an attack upon the instrument. Thus the defendant could claim that the deed produced was not in law a deed at all—for example, because it was defective on its face through some material erasure or interlineation.[1] This raised an issue of law, and the proper course was to demur, so keeping the matter out of the notoriously unreliable 'mouths of the lay gents'. More simply the defendant could deny that the deed was *his* deed, pleading *non est factum meum*; the issue so raised was determinable by jury trial. The plea of *non est factum* was appropriate (obvious cases apart) where the instrument had never been delivered, or delivered as an escrow to a third party or even to the plaintiff until certain conditions were performed,[2] or where the person sealing totally lacked capacity, and therefore was incapable of an act (deed) in law; examples are a married woman during the coverture, or a monk professed.[3] It was also extended to cover a narrowly confined category of what we would call mistake. Commonly persons executing sealed instruments could be illiterate, and if so would have to rely upon hearing the terms of the bond read over to them by the scrivener or attorney. If the terms were incorrectly read, and the party sealed the deed in error, it could be said that the deed was not the party's deed at all. The 'will did not go with the deed'. In such cases a special form of the plea of *non est*

---

[1] See, e.g., 7 Hen. VI, f. 18, pl. 27; 14 Hen. VIII, P. f. 25, pl. 7; 14 Hen. IV, H. f. 30, pl. 38.
[2] The problem is discussed in 10 Hen. VI, M. f. 25, pl. 85; 9 Hen. VI, M. f. 37, pl. 12; 8 Hen. VI, H. f. 26, pl. 15.
[3] 14 Hen. IV, H. f. 30, pl. 39.

factum was allowed. This really constituted a concealed exception to the parole averment rule.[1]

The defence of duress

The other exception of general importance was the defence
of duress. Duress was regarded as making the deed voidable
rather than void;[2] hence it could only be raised in the form of
a special plea.[3] The standard cases were imprisonment or
threats of imprisonment by the plaintiff, or someone acting in
collaboration with him, or menace to life or limb[4]—duress by
imprisonment made Richard II's abdication a somewhat
delicate issue, since according to ordinary legal principle it was
voidable. Duress or menaces to a wife could be relied upon by
a husband, since husband and wife were one person, but not
duress to a child or friend.[5] Whether threats or menaces to
goods (burn your house down) counted was discussed in 1467,[6]
Danby C.J. Littleton and Moile JJ. inclining to a favourable
view; Choke J., a realist, gloomily observed that if this was law,

'Donques vous avoides plusors obligations en Angleterre.'

Choke's view prevailed.[7] Curiously enough a corporation could
plead duress.[8]

Neither mistake (except in the sense explained above) nor
fraud[9] affected the validity of a deed.

The principle that a deed must be met with a deed

The refusal of the courts of common law to allow a bond to
be met with a defence based on parole averment is exemplified
in many cases, but perhaps most strikingly by the case of *Donne*

[1] See Fifoot 232–3; 1 Hen. VI (S.S. Vol. 50) at p. 23; 3 Hen. VI, T. f. 52, pl.
19; 3 Hen. VI, H. f. 37, pl. 35.
[2] 1 Hen. VII, P. f. 14, pl. 2.
[3] On the anomalous nature of the defence, see Ames, 113.
[4] 39 Hen. VI, H. f. 50, pl. 16; 28 Hen. VI, T. f. 8, pl. 8; 43 Edw. III, H. f. 6,
pl. 15.
[5] 21 Edw. IV, M. f. 12, pl. 4; 39 Hen. VI, H. f. 50, pl. 16.
[6] 7 Edw. IV, M. f. 22, pl. 21.
[7] Perkins, op. cit., pl. 16–19.
[8] 39 Hen. VI, H. f. 50, pl. 16; 21 Edw. IV, P. f. 7, pl. 21; M. f. 12, pl. 4; P.
f. 27, pl. 22; M. f. 67, pl. 53.
[9] In *Anon.* (1506) Keilwey 154a it is suggested that fraud on the part of the
person who wrote out the bond might affect its validity where the fraudulent
person sought to rely upon the instrument.

v. *Cornewall* in 1485. Here the defendant owed money to the plaintiff by bond;[1] the money was paid and the bond handed back to the defendant, who foolishly failed to destroy it. The plaintiff tortiously took the bond back, and sued upon it, and the question for decision was whether the defendant's plea setting all this out was good or not. After a long discussion in the Exchequer Chamber and Common Pleas it was held that the plea was bad; as Brian C.J. put it,

> 'And as for the substance of the matter, it seems to me that the matter [in the plea] is not good, for I have never seen in any case in the world that a man can avoid a specialty by naked matter of fact concerning the same deed, if it so be that the deed was initially good.'

If a bond was neither void nor voidable then (if we leave on one side for the moment defences based upon conditions, or illegality or impossibility) the general principle was that a deed must be met with a deed. Hence a plea of payment, or of 'nothing owing' was not admissible; later we will see that the practical effect of this rule can easily be misunderstood. The debtor on payment should either ensure that the bond was cancelled or destroyed, or obtain an acquittance or release under seal,[2] and he need not pay unless the obligee on tender of the money offered one.[3] If the bond was sued upon and the creditor recovered, the court cancelled the bond.[4] The rationale of the general rule was clearly stated in *Waverley* v. *Cockerel* (1541)[5] in the argument of Stamford and Bromley,

> 'And although the truth be that the plaintiff is paid the money, yet it is better to suffer a mischief to one man than an inconvenience to many men, which would subvert a legal rule. For if a matter in writing were to be so easily

---

[1] 1 Hen. VII, P. f. 14, pl. 2. See also 43 Edw. III, P. f. 23, pl. 18; 11 Hen. VI, P. f. 27, pl. 7; 22 Hen. VI, P. f. 52, pl. 24; 5 Edw. IV, T. f. 4, pl. 10; 17 Edw. III, P. f. 24; *Waverley* v. *Cockerel* (1541) Dyer 51a; 20 Hen. VI, P. f. 28, pl. 21.

[2] 22 Hen. VI, P. f. 52, pl. 24; 37 Hen. VI, H. f. 14, pl. 3; 5 Edw. IV, T. f. 4, pl. 10; 22 Edw. IV, H. f. 51, pl. 8; 1 Hen. VII, P. f. 14, pl. 2; *Anon.* Dyer 25, pl. 60; *Nichol's Case* (1565) 5 Co.Rep. 43; Cro. Eliz. 455; *Cross* v. *Powel* (1585) Cro. Eliz. 483.

[3] 41 Edw. III, M. f. 25, pl. 19; 22 Edw. IV, P. f. 6, pl. 18.

[4] 11 Hen. IV, T. f. 73, pl. 12.

[5] Dyer 51a.

defeated and avoided by such a surmise and naked breath, a thing in writing would have no more authority than a matter of fact.'

Similarly accord and satisfaction was no plea,[1] nor was an agreement to submit to arbitration.[2]

The defence of performance of the condition where the bond was conditional

We must now introduce a very important qualification. If a bond was subject to a condition of defeasance the position was in practice rather different. The defendant would aver that the condition had been performed, and this plea would raise an issue of fact; all that was needed to sustain such a plea was the debtor's own assertion that he had performed, that is his naked parole averment. This issue was determinable by jury trial, either on the basis of the jurymen's local knowledge or on evidence submitted to the jury; it was up to them whether they accepted the defendant's assertion. Thus suppose Hugo is bound to Robert by common money bond in a sum of £200, the bond being conditioned so that it becomes void if Hugo pays £100 by the day. If Hugo is sued on the bond he cannot plead that he had paid £200; this is the sum due by deed, and a duty imposed by deed must be met by a deed. He can, however, aver payment of £100 as performance of the condition, and need produce no deed in proof. (In practice the normal procedure was for the bond to be destroyed on payment of £100, but if this was not done then the defendant debtor could still aver payment, though he ran the risk of not convincing the jury.) This plea of payment raised two questions—first, was there a condition, and second, if so, had the condition been performed? The condition must be proved by writing; its performance was an issue of fact for the jury. The same rule applied where the condition was for the performance of some act, such as building a house. Hugo need not indeed tender any *evidence* of performance at all. In medieval law nobody had to *prove* anything in the modern sense of adducing evidence to be submitted to the jury (or court) for evaluation. He must *plead* performance, or

---

[1] *Blake's Case* (1605) 6 Co.Rep. 43b; discussed Ames p. 111.
[2] 4 Hen. VI, P. f. 17, pl. 5; 3 Hen. IV, M. f. 1, pl. 5 (an action of covenant, where the rule was the same).

tender and refusal, and if the jury believed his naked parole averment, which they might well do from local knowledge, the defence might succeed. Hence, where the conditioned bond was employed, performance of what was in reality the substantial agreement, 'proved', if at all, by parole evidence,[1] counted as a good defence to the action.

The interpretation of conditions

The general principle was that conditions were to be strictly construed against the obligor; he must plead performance precisely in accordance with the terms of the condition.[2] A passage in Littleton's argument in a case in 1460[3] strongly reminiscent of passages discussing modern statutory interpretation of *acts*, that is *deeds*, of Parliament, illustrates this,

'. . . for [a condition] should be taken according to the words and their meaning, and not according to the intent. Thus it has been adjudged here that where a condition was that if the defendant did *not* pay to the plaintiff £10 by a certain day then the obligation for £100 should lose its force, and the defendant pleaded that he did *not* pay him £10, that for this non payment he should avoid the obligation for £100. And yet it seemed that this was not the plaintiff's intention, but according to how the words are, so ought judgment to be given accordance to the meaning of the words. And Prisot C.J. affirmed the said case, for he said that he was of counsel in the said matter when he was serjeant.'

The acceptance of this literal approach did not prevent the courts interpreting a condition sensibly when the meaning was not plain. Thus where the condition of an obligation was that

---

[1] 42 Edw. III, P. f. 13, pl. 25; 12 Hen. IV, T. f. 23, pl. 6; 35 Hen. VI, M. f. 15, pl. 25, at f. 16.

[2] See 20 Hen. VI, P. f. 23, pl. 2. If the condition was to be performed in a foreign country it was impossible to try the issue of performance, since a jury could not be summoned from the *locus in quo*; hence the condition was void and the bond unconditional; see Fitz., *Condition* 2 (10 Hen. VI); 22 Edw. IV, P. f. 6, pl. 17. Normally tender of performance and refusal was a full defence; see 27 Hen. VIII, P. f. 1. pl. 1; 15 Edw. IV, M. f. 5, pl. 9; 7 Hen. IV, f. 18, pl. 17. If, however, the condition involved the payment of a lesser sum in defeasance of an obligation for a greater sum, the defendant must also plead 'always ready to perform' (*tout temps prist*) and tender the money in court; see Statham, *Abridgement*, Barre, pl. 35 (M. 30 Hen. VI), *per* Fortescue; 14 Hen. VI, f. 23, pl. 68; 19 Hen. VIII, T. f. 12, pl. 8.

[3] 39 Hen. VI, M. f. 9, pl. 15.

the bond should be void if the Great Bell of Mildenhall should be carried to the defendant's house and there be weighed, it was held that although the condition did not say who was to weigh the bell it must be taken that the defendant was to weigh it, since he was a bell-founder and possessed the skill and cunning to perform this delicate task.[1]

Under a system of strict pleading, rules as to interpretation take the form of rules as to what must be pleaded in the way of performance of a condition, the terms of which must go into the plea. Since objections to the contents of a plea are demurrers and raise an issue of law, this means that the court handles problems of interpretation. This is the explanation of the modern doctrine, whereby questions of the interpretation of contracts are determined by the court, though by the light of nature one would expect that the interpretation of contracts should be a question of fact, not of law.

But in medieval times there was little law on such matters as directions to juries, what sort of evidence must be produced, or on such matters as the burden of proof. Once issue was joined on a plea the matter then became a jury question for the jury alone to decide; we pass into an area of no law. The strict pleading rules which determined the permissible contents of a plea of performance may well have been considerably softened in practice by the exercise of jury discretion; the lay gents may well have been prepared to treat substantial performance as good enough. The elaboration of special pleading in cases involving interpretation and questions of what counted as performance may well reflect the lawyers' fear of the consequences of jury discretion and irresponsibility, but in the nature of things there can be no evidence on what juries actually did.

The acceptance of a substitute for performance of a condition

A long line of cases, culminating in the famous or infamous decision in *Pinnel's Case* (1602)[2] and the less well-known case of *Peytoe* (1611)[3] deal with the legal effect of the acceptance by the obligee of some substitute for the performance of the condition

---

[1] 9 Edw. IV, P. f. 3, pl. 13.
[2] 5 Co.Rep. 117a; Moo. K.B. 677 (*sub nom. Penny* v. *Core*).
[3] 9 Co.Rep. 78.

of a defeasible bond. The subject is closely linked with the history of the doctrine of accord and satisfaction; indeed so close is the link that writers have commonly failed to distinguish the history of rules governing the acceptance by a creditor of some *substitute for a debt*, from the history of the rules governing the acceptance of some *substitute for the performance of a condition*.

Where a debt was due by informal contract, it was, according to a somewhat scanty medieval authority, a defence to show accord and satisfaction; the accord was the agreement to accept a substitute, and the satisfaction was the performance of the accord (which in effect varied the original contract).[1] A merely executory accord was no bar for the very good and indeed unanswerable reason that it was not itself actionable.[2] Where, however, a debt was due by bond, accord and satisfaction was no defence to an action for the debt; clearly, since full payment of a debt due by bond[3] was not a defence, the payment of a substitute could not possibly be pleaded in bar to an action of debt *sur obligation*; it never seems to have occurred to anyone to argue the contrary.

If, however, the bond was conditionally defeasible, the creditor might well accept some substitute for performance of the condition. Thus in *Pinnel's Case* the defendant Cole owed the plaintiff £16 on a bond; the bond was defeasible on payment of £8 10s. 0d. before 11 November 1600. Before the day Cole paid Pinnel £5 2s. 6d. in full satisfaction and Pinnel accepted this sum. The £5 2s 6d. was not a substitute for the debt of £16, but a substitute for £8 10s. 0d., which sum was never owed. The point is clearer where the case does not involve a money bond, as where John Doe is bound to Richard Roe in £500 unless he enfeoffs him of the Manor of Dale before a certain day, and before the day Richard Roe accepts £250 or a tomtit instead of the Manor of Dale. In such cases the court had to decide whether the debtor could plead substituted performance (with

---

[1] 47 Edw. III, M. f. 24, pl. 61; 12 Hen. IV, T. f. 23, pl. 6; 10 Hen. VII, M. f. 4, pl. 4.

[2] See Fitz., *Accorde*, pl. 5 (P. 30 Hen. VI); 6 Hen. VII, M. f. 11, pl. 8; 2 Ric. III, M. f. 22, pl. 52; 10 Hen. VII, M. f. 4, pl. 4.

[3] Strictly speaking, payment of the money was no plea in answer even to debt brought for a simple contract debt; the debtor must plead *nihil debet*, and give the fact of payment in evidence before a jury, or wage his law: see 40 Edw. III, P. f. 24, pl. 27; 1 Hen. V, T. f. 6, pl. 1.

consent) of the condition of defeasance. Though the problem is closely analogous to the problem of accord and satisfaction in actions of debt on parole contracts, it need not necessarily be solved in the same way.

In the case of a money bond a mere executory agreement to accept a substitute was never thought to provide a defence; a formal contract could only be varied formally. But payment of money to the obligee (though not to a third party) before the day fixed in the condition,[1] or payment at a different place with consent[2] counted as sufficient performance, although in effect this meant that a written condition had been varied by parole. Late payment, even if accepted, did not bar the obligee from suing for the penalty debt due on the bond.[3] In general any substitute for the money, if accepted before or at the time stipulated in the condition, counted as sufficient performance, and 'saved the bond' (i.e. the penalty); thus the delivery of a horse, or corn, or even the granting of a lease,[4] would suffice. Whether acceptance of a lesser sum of money on the day would be enough to save the bond was not very clearly settled. If one leaves on one side cases where the matter discussed is the payment of a lesser sum in satisfaction for a *debt due* by simple contract, the earliest authority on this precise point is Perkins, who says in 1532,[5]

> 'If a man be obliged in a hundred pounds to pay a hundred marks to the obligee etc., and the obligee accept £10 in satisfaction for the hundred marks, this is a good performance of the condition, and yet some have said the contrary, because £10 cannot be a satisfaction for a hundred marks, but this is not material because the obligee is content with this.'

The next direct authority is *Pinnel's Case* itself.[6] Here the court held that the defendant failed on a point of pleading, though on

---

[1] 9 Hen. VII, H. f. 17, pl. 11.

[2] 34 Hen. VI, M. f. 17, pl. 32.

[3] 46 Edw. III, M. f. 29, pl. 23; 22 Hen. VI, T. f. 57, pl. 7; 22 Hen. VI, H. f. 39, pl. 11.

[4] 12 Hen. IV, T. f. 23, pl. 6; 11 Hen. VII, P. f. 20, pl. 6; 2 Ric. III, M. f. 22, pl. 52.

[5] Perkins, *op. cit.*, pl. 789.

[6] (1602) 5 Co.Rep. 117a; Moo. K.B. 677. See also *Neal* v. *Sheffill* (1610) 1 Bulst. 66, Cro. Jac. 654. drawing the distinction between accord and satisfaction of the condition, and the bond itself.

the merits he should have succeeded, since the payment had been made early. The court also ruled that,

> '. . . payment of a lesser sum on the day in satisfaction for a greater cannot be any satisfaction for the whole, because it appears to the judges that by no possibility a lesser sum can be a satisfaction for a greater sum; but the gift of a horse, hawk or robe etc. in satisfaction is good . . . But when the whole sum is due, by no intendment can the acceptance of parcel be satisfaction to the plaintiff.'

In giving this ruling, which was strictly *obiter*, the court seems to have been influenced by earlier authorities on the payment of parcels of debts due by parole contracts;[1] indeed the last sentence in the passage quoted speaks of a sum *due*. This attitude is capable of two interpretations. One is that the court went wrong in its analysis—the lesser sum is not given in lieu of the sum due (in *Pinnel's Case*, as pointed out, the sum due was £16) but in lieu of the performance of the condition for payment of £8 10s. 0d.; hence the cases on parole contracts were irrelevant. Alternatively the court may have reasoned (with justification) that once the day of payment arrived and the express condition had not been performed the payment of the lesser sum could only be viewed as a substitute for the £16 (which was a debt due)—hence cases on parole contracts were relevant. In any event the doctrine in *Pinnel's Case*, though *obiter*, was subsequently accepted in a form which is familiar.

Where a condition of defeasance did not involve payment of money, but the performance of some act such as enfeoffing the obligee of land, which did not involve a third party, early performance, if accepted, sufficed.[2] But an agreed substitute for performance did not.[3] The rule seems extraordinarily harsh, and is not easy to understand; justifications attempted in the year-books do hardly more than state the rule. Legal rules, however, do not become established unless someone thinks

---

[1] 10 Hen. VII, M. f. 4, pl. 4; *Nota* (1561) Dalison 49, pl. 13; *contra, per* Danvers J. in 33 Hen. VI, M. f. 48, pl. 32.

[2] 9 Hen. VII, H. f. 17, pl. 11. In 10 Hen. VII, H. f. 14, pl. 11, it was said that early performance in favour of a stranger was also good.

[3] 12 Hen. IV, T. f. 23, pl. 6; 9 Hen. VII, H. f. 20, pl. 16; 10 Hen. VII, H. f. 14, pl. 11; Perkins, op. cit., pl. 789; *contra, per* Moile J. in 33 Hen. VI, M. f. 48, pl. 32; *Peytoe's Case* (1611) 9 Co.Rep. 78.

they are sensible, and a passage in *Peytoe's Case* (1611)[1] provides
a clue:

> '... a difference was taken between a condition in a deed to
> do a collateral act, as to be bound in a statute to make a
> feoffment, to yield a true account *et similia*, for there accord
> with execution for money or other thing, is no satisfaction
> to save the forfeiture of the condition; for the contract being
> made by writing to do such collateral act, can't without
> writing in such cases be altered ... But when the condition
> in a deed by the original contract of the parties is to pay
> money, there by accord amongst the parties, any other
> thing may be given in satisfaction of the money; for as the
> philosopher saith, *nummus est mensura rerum commutandum* ...'

Substituted performance of conditions, as this passage recognizes, varies a formal contract by mere parole agreement;
hence it was natural that the courts should in general refuse to
accept substituted performance, and admit exceptions grudg-
ingly.

Impossibility as a defence to actions on conditioned bonds

The institution of the conditioned bond inevitably shifted
the centre of gravity of the law of contract to conditions. Thus
a perennial problem of contract law is the effect of impossibility
upon contractual liability. In the world of the bond this problem is approached typically by asking whether an impossible
condition is void, and if so whether the effect is that the bond
becomes unconditional, or alternatively void also. Or take the
problem of the effect of a refusal by one party to accept a
tender of performance by the other: this problem too was
familiar to medieval lawyers, but they dealt with it largely in
connection with the performance of conditions. Inevitably a
mass of law grew up under the title 'Condition' which by the
light of nature one might expect to find under the heading
'Contract'.

If a bond was subject to a condition which was impossible of
performance from the outset, then the condition was void.
Just as more modern lawyers use rather fatuous examples of

[1] 9 Co.Rep. 78.

non-necessary goods ('spectacles for a blind man') so earlier lawyers give such examples as 'to go to Rome in a day, or to overthrow Westminster Hall with his finger'[1] when discussing impossibility. Some fifteenth-century lawyers drew the conclusion that the bond to· which such a condition was attached was void also, so that the obligor would be free from all liability.[2] But this view did not prevail;[3] hence the bond was treated as unconditional and the obligor must pay. An exception applied where the condition formed part of the deed itself; such a condition, if impossible, invalidated the deed. On the other hand an impossible *covenant* was void, so that if Hugo covenanted to go to Rome in a day he could not be sued for damages if he failed to go.

If, however, a condition became wholly impossible to perform through supervening impossibility, the general principle was that both condition and bond became void, so that the obligor was excused from all liability. The application of this principle was clear enough if the impossibility arose through act of God, such as death.[4] It was also clear that it did not apply if the impossibility arose through the act of the obligor. Thus in a case in 1488 an action was brought on a penal bond which was defeasible on condition that the obligor conveyed certain lands to a woman within three months of the death of his father; before his father died he married the woman, and it therefore became impossible for him to perform; it was held that he was still bound to pay the penalty.[5] Where the performance became impossible because of the act of the obligee the obligor was not liable on the bond,[6] but this was usually put on the ground that a tender of performance was sufficient rather than upon the ground of impossibility.

The precise scope of impossibility where no act of God was

---

[1] 2 Edw. IV, P. f. 2, pl. 2.

[2] e.g. Danby C.J. in 2 Edw. IV, P. f. 2, pl. 6. See also 8 Edw. IV, M. f. 14 pl. 15; 8 Edw. IV, M. f. 9, pl. 9; P. f. 1, pl. 1; M. f. 20, pl. 35.

[3] 19 Hen. VI, P. (f. 67, pl. 14; T. f. 73, pl. 1); T. f. 75 at 76; 41 Edw. III, f. 25, pl. 19; 4 Hen. VII, H. f. 3, pl. 7; 14 Hen. VIII, P. f. 25, pl. 7; *Laughter's Case* (1594) 5 Co.Rep. 21 (if one condition becomes impossible, and the conditions are disjunctive and alternative, the bond is void).

[4] 14 Hen. VII, T. f. 31, pl. 8; 15 Hen. VII, H. f. 1, pl. 1; 15 Hen. VII, H. f. 2, pl. 5; T. f. 13, pl. 24.

[5] 4 Hen. VII, H. f. 3, pl. 7.

[6] 33 Hen. VI, P. f. 16, pl. 7; 27 Hen. VIII, P. f. 1, pl. 1.

involved provoked considerable difficulty, especially in cases where the obligor was not in a position to bring about the performance of the condition, or was able to do so only with the co-operation of a third party. Thus suppose a bond was subject to a condition that the rain should rain, or that a tree should grow—some thought that such conditions were void since only God could control such things.[1] Cases involving conditions to be performed by strangers frequently came before the courts, and fell into two classes. The condition might be wholly outside the obligor's control—for example, Hugo could be bound to Robert in £200 unless Peter conveyed lands to Robert. Alternatively performance might require co-operation—for example, Hugo might be bound to Robert in £200 unless he, Hugo, married Alice, Alice of course having the feminine prerogative of saying no. In both types of case it could be argued that the condition was impossible unless the stranger co-operated; to put the point differently, it could be thought unreasonable to make the obligor pay the penalty when it was in no way his fault that the condition had not been performed. Nevertheless it was settled law that in both types of case the obligor could not excuse himself by showing that he had done his best. The principle was clearly laid down in a case in 1452:[2]

'Prisot C.J. to the contrary. For if I am obliged to you on condition to perform something which can lawfully be done, and is possible, then notwithstanding the fact that performance is refused by one who is a stranger to the condition, I shall be charged if he does not perform . . . which was conceded by the whole court.'

The rule was the same in covenant. As Illingworth put it,

'A man by his own act [*fait*] can bind himself to do something which he would not be compelled by the law.'[3]

Where a party thus bound himself strictly to the performance of a condition outside his control he was said to have 'undertaken' that the condition be performed, a fact which may

---

[1] 10 Hen. VII, P. f. 22, pl. 21; 11 Hen. VII, H. f. 16, pl. 13.
[2] 33 Hen. VI, P. f. 16, pl. 7. See also 8 Edw. IV, M. f. 9, pl. 9, f. 21, pl. 35; 4 Hen. VII, H. f. 3, pl. 7.
[3] 8 Edw. IV, M. f. 9, pl. 9.

throw some light upon the sense of the averment of an undertaking (assumpsit) in the action on the case.[1]

Illegal conditions were treated differently; in medieval law
an illegal condition was void and so too was the bond to which
it was attached;[2] the reason is explained by Littleton in a case
in 1468:[3]

> 'If the condition be against law all is void, as for example a
> condition to kill a man, or to beat him or deisseise him, and
> the cause that it is avoided, is so that no such deed be
> executed as emboldens a man to do something against the
> law.'

Medieval lawyers did not possess the categories corresponding
to the modern notions of immorality or public policy; something was either illegal or not. This is explicable in terms of their
general legal philosophy, according to which anything which
common reason would condemn was of necessity contrary to
law, since common reason was equivalent to common law. The
only sense in which the distinction between sin and crime would
have appealed to them would have been as a jurisdictional
distinction. Hence conditions in restraint of trade, for example,
were simply illegal.

However, in sixteenth and seventeenth-century law the
law governing illegality was elaborated. According to Coke in
his commentary upon Littleton,[4]

> 'it is commonly holden that if the condition of a bond, etc.,
> be against law, that the bond itself is void.'

He goes on, however, to argue that this is not entirely correct:

> 'But herein the law distinguisheth between a condition
> against law for the doing of any act which is *malum in se*,
> and a condition (that concerneth not anything that is *malum
> in se*) and therefore is against law because it is either repug-
> nant to the state [i.e. "estate"] or against some maxime or
> rule of law.'

---

[1] 33 Hen. VI, P. f. 16, pl. 7; 4 Hen. VI, M. f. 3, pl. 7.
[2] 2 Hen. IV, M. f. 9, pl. 44; 19 Hen. VI, P. f. 67, pl. 14; T. f. 73, pl. 1; T. f.
75 at 76; 14 Hen. VIII, P. f. 25, pl. 7; 2 Hen. V, f. 5.
[3] 8 Edw. IV, M. f. 20, pl. 35.
[4] Co. Litt. 206b.

Conditions of the second type, according to Coke, are not necessarily void when annexed to bonds, nor are the bonds to which they are attached necessarily void even if the condition is void. Now it is not at all easy to see quite what Coke meant by this. The examples he gives in illustration of his doctrine suggest that he was thinking of two types of condition. One comprised conditions which would be void on the ground of repugnancy if attached to the grant of a freehold estate, such as a condition against alienation attached to a grant in fee simple; such a condition was void and the grant absolute. Coke's point here is that a penal bond conditioned so as to be void if the grantee did not alienate was good. The other comprised a condition that something could be done which was against law only in the sense that it was legally impossible, such as a condition to enfeoff one's wife; here he thought the condition void but the bond good and absolute. So far as the distinction between *malum in se* and *malum prohibitum*[1] is concerned, there is no evidence that earlier authorities employed this distinction in dealing with bonds. However, Coke's doctrine was naturally influential in the seventeenth century.

In addition to this there also evolved a doctrine permitting severance of conditions which were partly lawful and partly unlawful. Thus in his report of *Henry Pigot's Case* (1611)[2] Coke claims that:

'It is unanimously agreed in 14 H.8. 25, 26[3] that if some of the covenants in an indenture, or of the conditions endorsed upon a bond, are against law, the covenants or conditions which are against law are void *ab initio*, and the others stand good.'

This is more or less correct, for, in the case referred to, three out of the four judges[4] do commit themselves to this view, though the point was not directly in issue in the case. However, in *Smith* v. *Colshill* (1595)[5] the court wholly rejected this view, with

---

[1] It is true that Coke does not contrast *malum prohibitum* with *malum in se*, and he presumably meant only that conditions which are merely *mala prohibita may* in some circumstances not invalidate the bond.

[2] 11 Co.Rep. 27a.

[3] 14 Hen. VIII, P. f. 25, pl. 9.

[4] Brudenell C.J., Brook and Pollard JJ. The fourth was Fitzherbert J.

[5] Two alternative reports are given in 2 And. at pp. 56 and 108, and a third in *Twyne's Case* 3 Co.Rep. 80b at 82b.

the consequence that if a bond was conditioned upon the performance of covenants in an indenture, and some were illegal, the bond was wholly void. *Smith* v. *Colshill*, however, concerned a case where the invalidity arose through a statutory provision, and was distinguished in *Norton* v. *Syms* (1614),[1] where it was held that severance was possible if the illegality arose through the operation of a common law as opposed to a statutory rule. This became the law of the seventeenth century; it is recorded of Hobart C.J.[2] that he expressed this doctrine by saying that,

> 'The statute[3] is like *a tyrant*; where he comes he makes all void; but the common law is like *a nursing father*, and makes void only that part where the fault is and preserves the rest.'

The flexibility of the conditioned bond as a contractual institution

The institution of the conditioned penal bond functions in what appears to us to be a peculiarly topsy-turvy way. Two parties reach an agreement, let us say for the sale of land; to make their agreement legally effective they execute conditioned bonds, which to our way of looking at the matter impose obligations to pay penal sums rather than obligations to convey the land and pay the price. Performance of what may be called the underlying agreement is not imposed as a duty; instead performance is only relevant as providing a defence to an action of debt for the penalty. Commonly the use of bonds will involve treating what is really a bilateral contract, say of sale, unilaterally; the bilateral contract is legally sanctioned by two independent unilateral debt contracts, with the odd result that all contracts become reduced to debtor–creditor form. The substantial agreement disappears beneath the legal form, which conceals the cause of the penal debt liability; each party is liable because he had executed a bond, not because he has agreed upon a sale. The institution has the merit of infinite flexibility; any agreement whatsoever which is lawful can be

[1] Moo. K.B. 856, Hob. 14.

[2] *Maleverer* v. *Redshaw* 1 Mod. 35, per Twisden J. See also *Collins* v. *Blantern* (1767) 2 Wils. 341, where the doctrine is repudiated.

[3] It is possible that the reference is meant to be confined to a particular statute, viz. 23 Hen. VI, c. 9.

accommodated by variations of the technique. If, for example, the parties wish to make their bonds mutually dependent there is nothing to prevent their doing so by the use of express conditions. The law governing bonds is tough law, inspired by the general philosophy that it is not the business of the courts to remake private contracts; having made their bed the contracting parties must lie in it. In the case of a bond to secure the performance of a complex agreement the system seems remarkably harsh; for any default in performance the whole penalty was forfeit. The common law made only slight concessions to paternalism. The formality required in contracting was sufficient to protect men from fraudulent claims, but not so onerous as to produce any practical difficulty which would produce commercial inconvenience; it was easy enough to execute a bond, and impossible to do so without meaning to do so. Granted that businessmen wish to know where they are, and that the basis upon which business is conducted is that bargains are there to be kept, the conditioned bond had obvious attractions. The widespread use of the conditioned bond, both in England and upon the Continent, is only explicable upon the ground that it provided what the commercial community wanted.

The penal character of the conditioned bond and the concept of usury

Clearly the conditioned bond could not be generally used today, for modern law objects to penalties; we shall see later on how the evolution of the modern rules governing penalties led to a decline in the use of bonds. These rules were not evolved in either the common law courts or the court of chancery until the late seventeenth century. Before their evolution the penalty fixed by private agreement and imposed by the bond was unobjectionable since *in theory its function was compensatory*, and it was this that saved the conditioned penal bond from being attacked as improper upon the only ground which would have occurred to a lawyer of the time, namely that such bonds were sinful and usurious.[1]

---

[1] The brief account of canonist thought which follows is based upon W. J. Ashley, *An Introduction to English Economic History and Theory*, Part II, esp. ch. VI and the authorities there cited, and J. T. Noonan, *The Scholastic Analysis of Usury*. See below, ch. ix. See also *H.E.L.* VIII. 99 et seq.

Any transaction which involved usury was clearly illegal in medieval common law; conversely, if conditioned penal bonds were not usurious, contemporaries could see no objection to them, for what other ground of objection could there be to such bonds freely entered into by persons of full capacity? At first sight, however, it seems odd that the conditioned money bond in particular, whereby the debtor bound himself to pay, say, £100 unless he paid £50 to the creditor by the day, was not thought to be usurious and therefore void for illegality. Now, although the concept of usury (which will be discussed more fully later in this book) was in some respects vague, flexible, and uncertain in late medieval thought, the paradigm case was that of a loan of money on such terms that the creditor was bound to receive payment for the use of the money; loans must be gratuitous. Canonist thought, however, distinguished between usury—payment for the use of money—and interest (*interesse*); a creditor could legitimately contract to receive compensation for loss suffered through the debtor's failure to repay the money on time. Such loss could be of two kinds— *damnum emergens* and *lucrum cessans*. Compensation for the former (broadly speaking, consequential loss excluding loss of potential profit) was regarded as permissible by Aquinas, but only where the creditor could actually prove that genuine consequential loss had occurred; later canonists, distinguishing Aquinas, came round to the view that compensation for *lucrum cessans* was also morally unobjectionable. The latter concept embraced such loss of profit as the creditor was bound to suffer through late payment, which deprived him of the opportunity to invest his money elsewhere in some legitimate manner. This was an important development, for whereas *damnum emergens* both could be proved and required proof, *lucrum cessans* was notional, and in the nature of things specific proof could not be required.

In conformity with this theory, the penal money bond did not involve usury, for the penalty, very commonly fixed at twice the sum lent (supposing the occasion to be loan), served to compensate the creditor in a legitimate manner for the loss of his *interesse*, and did not count as payment for the use of the money. An additional and distinct reason was that the debtor could in any event save the penalty by prompt payment; hence the lender was not certain to have back anything over and above the money lent. The common law accepted the canonist theory, as is illustrated by two cases. In the first, a case in the Eyre of Kent in 1313–14,[1] Passeley argued in the following terms against the validity of a money bond:

> 'This action of debt is based upon a penalty and savours of usury, of which the law will not permit you to have recovery. For example, if I say that I hold myself bound to you to pay you ten pounds upon such a day, and that if I do not pay them to you upon that day I am then bound to you in forty pounds. And if I fail to pay the ten pounds upon the appointed day the law will not allow you to recover, by way of usury, the forty pounds.'

Stanton J. rejected this argument:

> 'penalty and usury are only irrecoverable when they grow out of the sum in which the obligee is primarily bound.'

Stanton J.s idea was that only such a sum could be regarded as payment for use. Again in a case in 1352[2] an action was brought on a bond imposing a penalty of seventeen marks for failure to pay nine; Skipwith argued that the action sounded in usury, but the court rejected the argument. It is noticeable that in both cases the form of the bond was unusual. In general the lawfulness of the common money bond was so well settled that the cases do not contain any suggestion that usury was involved; indeed cases under the rubric 'Usury' are extremely rare in the year books. Brooke in his *Graunde Abridgement* could only note two cases, both dating from late in the reign of Henry VIII.[3]

These two cases, though not concerned with bonds, apply a doctrine derived from the canon law to the effect that a transaction was not usurious unless the creditor was certain to be owed some money in addition to the principal sum. The same doctrine is to be found in Coke's Reports in *Burton's Case* (1591),[4] and it provided an alternative theoretical basis for upholding the common money bond; the obligor could always save the penalty by prompt payment, and so the obligee was not as a result of the contract certain to gain it.

[1] S.S. Vol. 2, p. 27.
[2] Y.B. 27 Edw. III, M. f. 17, pl. 9.
[3] Brooke, *Usurie* 1 and 2.
[4] 5 Co.Rep. 69a.

Statutes of Usury

The Statutes of Usury passed in the late fifteenth and the sixteenth century did not attempt to invalidate the penal bond. Thus the Statute of 1487,[1] described on its repeal in 1495[2] as,

'so obscure derke and diffuse that the true entent of the makers thereof cannot perfitely be undrestond',

whatever it did achieve certainly did not touch the penal bond; the Act of 1495 has a clause,

'Savying lawful penalties for nounpayment of the same moneey lent.'

That of 1545,[3] which for the first time legalized interest, in the modern sense, of up to 10 per cent per annum, expressly excludes from its prohibitions penalties imposed by bond, and it escaped condemnation in the later legislation of Edward VI[4] Elizabeth I.[5] Thus it is clear that the legislature was consistently following the policy of the common law, which in its turn simply accepted the canonical view that penalties for non-payment of debts were not usurious or objectionable. Obviously the Chancery was bound to take the same view, and apparently did.

Granted the legality of the money bond, the legality of penal bonds for the performance of covenants followed *a fortiori*, and before the seventeenth century, so far as I am aware, it was never so much as suggested that there was anything objectionable about such bonds. If there was a theory I suppose it must have been that the penalty was compensatory, which seems a bit Irish; we may compare the non-punitive sanctions against Rhodesia.

Penal bonds could, however, furnish a cloak for usury. Suppose Robert lends Hugo £100 at 10 per cent per annum, a plain case of usury. He can do this by extracting a bond for £220 defeasible on payment of £110 within the year, actually handing over £100. Such a transaction was certainly unlawful

---

[1] 3 Hen. VII, c. 5.
[2] 11 Hen. VII, c. 8.
[3] 37 Hen. VIII, c. 9, which repealed all previous legislation.
[4] 5 and 6 Edw. VI, c. 20, held to apply retrospectively in *Anon.* (1554) Dalison 12.
[5] 27 Eliz. I, c. II; 29 Eliz. I, c. 5; 31 Eliz. I, c. 10; 35 Eliz. I, c. 7; 39 Eliz. I, c. 18. See too 21 Jac. I, c. 17, and 12 Car. II, c. 13.

and immoral, but it would be impossible at common law for the obligor to plead the usurious nature of the transaction.[1] For since it was impossible to plead that no money had been lent at all, it was *a fortiori* impossible to plead that only £100 had been lent; the cause of the transaction was irrelevant. The position here was altered by the Statute of Usury in 1545. This permitted interest of up to 10 per cent per annum; any interest in excess made the transaction wholly void. The statute allowed the usurious nature of the transaction to be raised by parole averment,[2] and the later statutes of usury continued the policy of allowing the substance to prevail over the form, though they amended the law in other respects which do not concern us here. But the legislation did not involve any prohibition of penalties which could be avoided by prompt payment.

The unpopularity of the action of covenant

A remarkable feature of the history of the common law of contract is the fact that, although agreements under seal could be sued upon by writ of covenant for damages, in practice the action of covenant was very rarely used; instead people preferred to sue the conditioned bond sanctioned by the action of debt *sur obligation* (or rely upon recognizances such as statutes merchant or staple). Plausible reasons for this are not difficult to suggest; there are obvious attractions from a creditor's point of view in contracts which fix a penalty in advance, especially when the alternative is assessment of damages by juries, but I suspect that there may be other reasons connected with the law of pleading and procedure. For example, a plaintiff who sued on a bond put the pleading onus on the defendant; he had to plead performance if he wished to escape forfeiture of the bond. In covenant the plaintiff had to plead breach of covenant. But whatever the explanation may be, it was certainly the case that covenant never ranked as an important contractual remedy, whilst the action of debt *sur obligation* certainly did.[3]

---

[1] The truth might, however, come to light; for an example see Statham, *Abridgement*, Dette, 17. The contention that the usurious nature of a transaction could not be raised depends upon the absence of any cases where it was raised, and the application of basic legal principle.

[2] *Burton's Case* (1591) 5 Co.Rep. 69a.

[3] See on this point S. F. C. Milsom, 'Reason in the Development of the Common Law' (1965) 81 L.Q.R. 496 at pp. 509–10, noticing particularly n. 26.

The decline of the bond

The primary factor which led to the decline of the conditioned penal bond was the evolution, originally in the Court of Chancery, of the practice of relieving defaulting obligors from forfeiture of the penalty due under bonds; this led eventually to the acceptance both in equity and at common law of the modern principle of contract law, according to which a distinction is drawn between a 'penalty' and 'liquidated damages'. In the words of Lord Dunedin,

> 'The essence of a penalty is a payment of money stipulated in terrorem of the offending party; the essence of liquidated damages is a genuine covenanted pre-estimate of damage.'[1]

So defined, a 'penalty' is irrecoverable.

The history of the evolution of relief against forfeiture has been very fully investigated by Turner and, more recently, by Yale.[2]

The three main areas in which the Court of Chancery came to grant relief against forfeiture were those of mortgages, leases, and bonds; though in the course of time the rules governing relief in these three areas tended to develop along independent lines, originally this was not the case. As early as the fifteenth century there are examples of the exercise of a jurisdiction to grant relief in a variety of circumstances. In addition to cases where there had been payment, but not formal acquittance or release,[3] the chancellors also from time to time were prepared to grant relief in cases of extreme hardship or oppression.[4] But there is no evidence of any common practice of interference before the reign of Elizabeth I, when petitions for relief become very common. The practice of the Court of Chancery by the beginning of the seventeenth century was summed up by Sir George Cary (more properly Carew) in a work based upon notes taken by William Lambard (d. 1601), who became a Master in Chancery in the year 1592, and although no doubt

---

[1] In *Dunlop Pneumatic Tyre Co. Ltd.* v. *New Garage and Motor Co. Ltd.* [1915] A.C. 79 at p. 86.

[2] See p. 88, n. 1, above.

[3] 9 Edw. IV, f. 25, pl. 34; 7 Hen. VII, f. 10, pl. 2; and see St. Germain, *Doctor and Student*, Dial. I, c. 22.

[4] *Bodenham* v. *Halle*, S.S. Vol. 10, p. 137; and see generally Turner, op. cit., pp. 22-4.

an investigation of the surviving records of the court (which I have not undertaken) would supplement Cary's bald account, I can see no reason to doubt its substantial accuracy. Cary (or Lambard) says this:[1]

'If a man be bound in a penalty to pay money at a day or place, by obligation, and intending to pay the same, is robbed by the way; or hath intreated by some other respite at the hands of the obligee, or cometh short of the place by any misfortune; and so failing of the payment, doth nevertheless provide and tender the money in short time after; in these, and many such like cases, the Chancery will compel the obligee to take his principal, with some reasonable consideration of his damages, (*quantum expediat*) for if this was not, men would do that by covenant which they now do by bond.'

He adds:[2]

'If the obligee have received the most part of the money, payable upon the obligation at the peremptory time and place, and will nevertheless extend the whole forfeiture, immediately refusing soone after the default, to accept of the residue tendered unto him, the obligor may find aid in Chancery.'

The Chancery also gave relief against forfeiture of ancient bonds sued upon long after default,[3] there being no statutory period of limitation introduced until 1833.[4] It is clear that the Chancery had not yet begun to grant relief against penalties simply upon the ground that they were penalties, and it is interesting to see how Cary explains the continued popularity of the bond as a consequence of the readiness of the Chancery to grant relief in cases of accident, extremity, or trifling default.[5]

In the course of the seventeenth century the scope of equitable intervention was extended. Thus in 1621 Norburie, in a letter

[1] Cary 1.
[2] Cary 2.
[3] See *Warcopp* v. *Culpepper* (1617) Bacon, *Cases*, p. 69; *Garfield* v. *Humble* (1618) Bacon *Cases*, p. 125; *Coles* v. *Emerson* (1634–35) 1 Ch.Rep. 78; *Geoffrey* v. *Thorn* (1634) 1 Ch.Rep. 88.
[4] 3 and 4 Will. VI, c. 42, s. 3. The common law followed equity in adopting the same practice: see *Willis' Case* (1707) Holt 123.
[5] Unless 'this' in the passage quoted means the practice of Chancery in requiring the payment of damages.

to Lord Keeper Williams,[1] said that Lord Ellesmere (who was Chancellor from 1596 to 1617),

> 'would not relieve any that forfeited a bond, unless it were in case of extremity, or that he could make appear that by some accidental means he was occasioned thereunto . . . whereas of late lenity has been used to all debtors, so that man, after four or five years suit and charges in this court, were glad to go away with their principal without costs or damages.'

The 'lenity' here mentioned was perhaps the ordering of a stay of execution at common law where the debtor seemed likely to pay money within a short time of the contractual date. After the Restoration it rapidly became established that the Chancery would grant relief against penalties due on money bonds on the payment of principal, interest, and costs, and against penalties due for failure to perform covenants on payment of costs and damages.[2] In the former case the Chancery would also order the refund of penalties paid; this jurisdiction is illustrated by the case of *Friend* v. *Burgh* (1679):[3]

> 'The plaintiff [i.e. in equity] was in execution on a judgment obtained on a bond, and being thus in execution the principal sum and interest and costs were tendered to the obligee, but he would not discharge him out of execution without paying the whole penalty of the bond.'

The obligor therefore paid the penalty, and exhibited a bill in Chancery to recover the excess over principal, interest, and costs; the court decreed accordingly. In the latter case the practice was for the Chancery to relieve against the penalty on condition that the defaulting party paid damages, the cause being remitted to a trial at law to assess the damages on a *quantum damnificatus*.[4] The basis of equitable intervention was

---

[1] Hargrave, *Law Tracts*, p. 431; cited by Turner, op. cit., p. 31.

[2] The cases are fully discussed by Yale, op. cit., pp. 7–30. See in particular *Hall* v. *Higham* (1663) 3 Ch.Rep. 3; *Wilson* v. *Barton* (1671–2) Nels. 148; *Hodkin* v. *Blackman & al.* (1674–5) 2 Ch.Rep. 103; *Duvall* v. *Terry* (1694) Show.P.C. 15. There must have been a transitional period; thus in *Wake* v. *Calley* (1661–2) 1 Ch.Rep. 201; *Dixon* v. *Read* (1668–9) 2 Ch.Rep. 21 and *Crisp* v. *Bluck* (1673–4) 2 Ch.Rep. 88 penalties as such seem to be unobjectionable, perhaps because of the special circumstances of these cases.

[3] Rep.T.F. 437.

[4] The name, not of a writ, but of an issue, which could be joined in an action on the case; alternatively a writ of covenant for damages could be used.

that the exaction of penalties was inequitable where it was possible to compensate the obligee for the loss suffered through default; hence where compensation was not thought to be possible, or damages could not be assessed, no relief would be given against the penalty. This limitation was suggested in the case of *Tall* v. *Ryland* (1670).[1] Two fishmongers who had adjacent shops had quarrelled and made friends again; one entered into a bond for £20 'conditioned to behave himself civilly, and like a good neighbour' and 'not to disparage his goods'. On the occasion of a sale of some flounders by his neighbour the obligor forgot himself, and opined that the fish stank. Sued on the bond he sought relief in equity, and one of the grounds upon which the suit was successfully resisted was that in such a case there could be no way to measure the damages; all that a court could do was to accept the penalty stipulated. The position reached by Lord Nottingham's time is neatly stated in Francis's *Maxims of Equity*:[2]

'Equity suffers not advantage to be taken of a penalty or forfeiture, where compensation can be made.'

Lord Nottingham himself in his *Prolegomena*[3] remarks on the effect of this development upon the usefulness of the penal bond for the performance of covenants:

'... a penal bond to secure the performance of covenants is not much better security than a mere covenant, as equity now orders the matter.'

The same observation could well have been made about the common money bond.

In opposition to the natural course of things the common law courts soon followed the example of the Chancery. Thus in *King* v. *Atkyns* (1670),[4] where an action was brought in the King's Bench on a bond for a penalty of £2,000 counsel argued that the default was trivial, costing the obligee no more than an attorney's fee; he suggested that the parties might be well advised to consent to determine the damage suffered by plead-

[1] 1 Ch.Ca. 183.
[2] Ed.princ. 1728.
[3] *Lord Nottingham's 'Manual of Chancery Practice' and 'Prolegomena of Chancery and Equity'*, ed. D. E. C. Yale (Camb., 1965), at p. 275.
[4] 1 Sid. 442.

ing to an issue of *quantum damnificatus* in an action on the case;
the point of this suggestion (which was not accepted) was no
doubt to save the costs involved in a suit for relief in Chancery.
In the case of money bonds the common law adopted the equitable principle by the mid 1670s;[1] the device employed was to
grant the defendant a perpetual imparlance[2] unless the plaintiff
would accept a tender of principal, interest, and costs. There is
some evidence that the common law courts also in effect gave
relief against penal bonds for the performance of covenants,
but it is not very convincing.[3] The position was eventually
regularized by statutes passed in 1696–97 and 1705.[4] The
first of these statutes permitted a plaintiff who sued for a penalty
due on a conditioned bond for the performance of covenants to
assign as many breaches as he wished. It was then the jury's
duty to assess the damage suffered for each breach. Judgment
could be entered for the whole penalty, but the plaintiff could
only recover the damages assessed, the action being stayed on
payment of these damages together with costs.[5] The Statute of
1705 authorized the court to discharge an obligor who brought
into court principal, interest, and costs due on a money bond;
it also reversed the ancient common law rule by allowing payment (without acquittance by deed) to be pleaded in bar to an
action on a bond. The effect of these two statutes was merely to
regularize the position which had already been achieved by
the combined efforts of the courts of common law and the Court
of Chancery, and although penal bonds continued to be used
as a contractual device (for lawyers are by nature reluctant to
abandon ancient forms) they were no longer penal in effect,
though the precise distinction between objectionable and
acceptable provisions continued to be highly[6] problematical.
Even after the Statutes of 1696–7 and 1705, an obligor still had
to seek relief in equity if he was unable to tender the principal
interests and costs at the time of action brought.

---

[1] Lord Nottingham, op. cit., p. 203.
[2] A licence to imparl (talk the matter over) stayed the proceedings.
[3] Turner, op. cit., takes this view, presumably relying upon the terms of the
Statute of 1705 (4 and 5 Anne, c. 3 or 16).
[4] 4 and 5 Anne, c. 3 (or 16). 8 and 9 Will. III c. 11.
[5] For subsequent breaches he could recover further damages.
[6] A short discussion of the later case law is to be found in H.E.L. XII 519, but
there is no full study of a complex development.

The establishment of the compensatory principle

This development involves a recognition of the notion that a contracting party should only be permitted to recover compensation for loss actually suffered through default, such compensation being assessed, broadly speaking, with a view to putting the innocent party into the position he would have achieved if the contract had been performed. Now it is a remarkable fact that this notion is not modern; it was accepted centuries before the modern law of penalties was evolved. As we have seen, the canonists were only prepared to accept the penal money bond upon the ground that the penalty served a compensatory function. What changed was not the theory of the matter, but the extent to which that theory was allowed to operate in hard practical terms; the courts came around to making a serious effort to apply the theory, asking in each case whether *this* penalty ought to be forfeit if the general aim of the law was to compensate rather than to punish.

Viewing the matter in this way it can be said that there existed for many centuries a divorce between contractual theory and contractual practice. This divorce can in its turn be understood if it is seen as reflecting a tension between two ideas. On the one hand we have the idea that the real function of contractual institutions is to make sure, so far as possible, that agreements are performed; the institution of the penal bond and the practice of the courts in upholding such bonds exemplified this idea. On the other hand we have the idea that it suffices for the law to provide compensation for loss suffered by failure to perform agreements. This second idea is not, of course, necessarily incompatible with the pursuit of the aim of encouraging contractual performance, but it is bound to impose a limitation upon the enthusiasm with which that aim is pursued, and there can well be contexts (for example, contracts for personal service) in which a positive value is attached to the right to break the contract so long as the defaulting party is made to pay compensation. Now if securing performance is the aim to be pursued, the use of penalties *in terrorem* of the party from whom performance is due is the natural and obvious technique. Thus today the decree of specific performance is given teeth by the threat of imprisonment for contempt, and in the criminal courts we are familiar with such institutions as the granting of bail and the entry into recognizances to keep the peace, which institutions, to those who are not over-impressed by labels, are nothing more than modern versions of the conditioned bond used to bind persons to the performance of contracts. What has happened is not that contracts *in terrorem* have been outlawed, or that the use of penal mechanisms no longer plays any part in contract law, but only that the courts have come to acquire a monopolistic control over the use of terror. It is today the courts which may do things which in former ages private citizens might do. Nobody who is familiar with the modern practice of hire-purchase, or other forms of usury could doubt that there is still a demand for private trafficking in penalties; the general trend is, however, to resist this demand.

In early law this demand is not resisted; hence the prevalence in more or less primitive communities of the use of the pledge or hostage, at least in the case of important contracts, as a device for securing performance; where men cannot trust each other, and the machinery of the law is weak, the contracting party must place some important stake at the mercy of the other party. The penal bond for securing performance was a sophisticated form of self-pledge, and Shylock's bond with its forfeit of a pound of flesh neatly illustrates the fact tht the best pledge of all is the body of the contractor, which in early law he could have used as security. The provision of security for performance is still a common practice today, but the general triumph of the compensatory principle has radically altered its character; so far as the law is concerned, security has come to be non-penal where the device is used by private persons. The decline in the use of the penal bond, and the corresponding shift in the centre of gravity of contract law from the law of debt *sur obligation* to the law of the action on the case upon an assumpsit represents a major step in social evolution.

It would be a mistake, however, to suppose either that the decline in the popularity of the bond was rapid, or that the granting of relief against penalties deprived it of all usefulness. Commercial and legal habits do not change overnight, and even if the law only permits contracting parties to stipulate for liquidated damages of a compensatory character there can still be advantages in adopting this course rather than leaving the question open to later settlement in litigation or negotiation —for example, in contracts where the determination of compensatory damages is necessarily speculative. Furthermore there can be exceptions to the general principle, and ways of getting round it. Thus even today the use of the penal bond is not wholly obsolete in private transactions.

Relationship between the history of bonds and the history of assumpsit

It is against the background of the decline of the penal bond that we must place the rise of the action of assumpsit, and statistics published by Dr. Kiralfy[1] make it very clear that we must guard against the notion that assumpsit triumphed as rapidly as is sometimes assumed. Thus in 1572 the roll of the Common Pleas for Trinity term contains 503 contested actions of debt *sur obligation*, and but three actions of assumpsit. We should also guard against the belief that the enforcement of informal contracts by parole was an unmixed blessing. Lord Ellesmere, for example, announced in 1603,

> 'that he nothing would help leases paroll in Chancery, and that it was good for the Commonwealth, if no lease paroll were allowed by law, nor promises to be proved by witnesses, considering the plenty of witnesses now a days, which be *testes diabolices qui magis fame quam fama moventur.*'[2]

Hence the attempt to put the clock back in 1677 by the Statute of Frauds and to restore some security by insisting on the use of written contracts in certain fields. Formality in one way or another has its part to play in any system of contract law which will satisfactorily cater for the needs of businessmen and others who make commercial contracts; the difficulty is to strike the right balance. In the development of assumpsit in the sixteenth and seventeenth centuries the common law courts were, as we shall see, not so much inspired by an enthusiasm for the encouragement of security in business as by an ethical attitude to the sanctity of promises. In consequence they were prepared to limit the scope of the actionable promise by that most moralistic of doctrines, the doctrine of consideration. In the

[1] Kiralfy, App. A.
[2] Cary 27.

conditions then prevailing in a litigious and disorderly society they might perhaps have done better to have paid a little more attention to practical realities and to have attached rather more importance to the value of formality in contract law.

B. RECOGNIZANCES

THE medieval creditor, instead of binding his debtor by a private contract under seal, and using the action of debt to recover the sum due by action in the event of default, could instead employ the institution of the recognizance, which was designed to cut out entirely that stage in the proceedings in an action of debt which was occupied by adjudication on the debtor's liability to pay. In essence a recognizance (of the type here discussed) involved a consensual transaction between creditor and debtor whereby the debtor's liability was established before a court, with the debtor's co-operation, before any dispute arose, and commonly before the occasion of indebtedness had arisen. In its simplest form this involved bringing the debtor to court, with his consent, to acknowledge (*recognoscere*) that he owed the sum of money agreed upon. This acknowledgement was then enrolled upon the record of the court, and was more or less the equivalent of a judgment in a contested action of debt; indeed the institution probably originated in the practice of obtaining such a judgment in an action with the debtor's acquiescence. In the event of default the creditor could then proceed at once to take steps to enforce execution. Recognizances of this type were in use throughout the medieval period.[1] They must be distinguished from the practice (which was also common) of enrolling contracts under seal in the royal archives (for example on the close rolls)[2] as a precaution against accidental loss and forgery; this practice facilitated the proof of debts but was not intended to allow the creditor to avoid the perils of litigation.

In Edward I's reign a more elaborate system for the enrolling and enforcement of recognizances was set up by the Statute of *Acton Burnell* in 1283[3] (also called the first Statute of Merchants)

---

[1] See in particular H. Hall, *Select Case in the Law Merchant*, S.S. Vols. 46 and 49.
[2] See Hall, S.S. Vol. 49, p. xiii.
[3] 11 Edw. I Extracts from the text in Fifoot at 239.

and the Statute of Merchants (1285)[1] which amended the earlier provision in the light of the experience of its working.[2] Both statutes were construed as a whole, and a reference to either in a medieval text is normally intended to refer to both. Recognizances introduced by this legislation were called 'statutes merchant'. They were supposed to be employed only by merchants, who formed a distinct class, and not by members of the public generally, though in practice this limitation was probably not very effectively enforced.[3] The debtor need not, however, be a merchant.

In order to execute a statute merchant the creditor and debtor had to appear before the Mayor of London or corresponding official in any other city or town designated by the King, or before two merchants specially appointed in a fair. The debtor would then acknowledge the debt, and this recognizance was enrolled by a clerk in duplicate on two rolls; the clerk kept one and the senior official the other. The clerk then wrote out an obligation for the debt, which was sealed both by the debtor and by the King's seal. In a fair the precautions were slightly more elaborate, two royal seals being used, each one kept in separate custody; the legal significance of the transaction also had to be explained to the debtor. Presumably the reason for this was that fairs, with their floating population and temporary accommodation gave better opportunities for fraudulent practices which would be more difficult to perpetrate in the more settled conditions of town life.

Once the debtor defaulted, the creditor could at once proceed to execution. The first step was to establish default and liability, and the whole purpose of the arrangements was to reduce this to little more than a formality. The creditor must produce his obligation, which could rapidly be compared with the two rolls and the official seal checked. No method of trial except this process of comparison was appointed, nor was there any need for the debtor either to be present or even to be notified of the

[1] 13 Edw. I, Extracts from the text in Fifoot at 239.
[2] This legislation is very fully discussed in Plucknett, *Legislation of Edward I*, Ch. VI.
[3] In 1311 by article XXXIII of the Ordinances of that year the rule that only merchants could use 'statutes' was expressly laid down by the Lords Ordainers. In 1322 this provision was enacted, but the enactment never got into circulation. See Plucknett, op. cit. 147, Hall, S.S. Vol. 46, p. xi.

proceedings. Presumably his seal need not be authenticated, and I suppose the point of attaching it was to enable the creditor to bring an ordinary action of debt on the bond if he wished to do so (which would be convenient if, say, creditor and debtor happened to be in London, and the rolls in York). The statutes make no provision for cancellation of the entries on the rolls if there had been payment or a compromise; what must have been envisaged was that the debtor in such circumstances would ensure that the creditor's obligation was destroyed or cancelled by defacement.

Once liability was established by inspection of the obligation and the rolls, the mayor must immediately set in motion steps to enforce payment. If he could be found, the debtor was at once imprisoned at his own cost; if not, a writ was obtainable from the Chancery to arrest him wherever he happened to be. After three months, if he had still not paid the debt, or reached a compromise, he was given a chance to raise the money himself from his lands and chattels. After a further three months all his lands and chattels, or a reasonable proportion of them, were to be delivered to the creditor, who could either use the proceeds to pay off the debt or retain them as security until he was satisfied.[1] This introduced a complication, for the debtor, still incarcerated, was now deprived of all means of support; consequently the statute makes a slight concession lest the debtor starve to death and requires the creditor to provide him with bread and water. The last avenue of escape was for the debtor to conspire with the gaoler to escape from prison, but this was provided for by making the gaoler liable to the creditor if he did so. 'Let the Keeper of the prison take heed,' the statute grimly observes, 'that he must answer for the body or for the debt.' This seemed to have more or less covered everything.

Statutes staple

The enthusiasm for making life easy for merchants inspired some opposition; in 1311 an Ordinance of the Lords Ordainers attempted to confine the use of statutes merchant to bona fide merchants, and to limit to twelve the number of towns operating the system. But reaction was short lived. In 1312 a somewhat similar system was set up in the staple towns, which was

[1] Redemption could be had by writ of *scire facias*.

extended and regularized by the Ordinance of the Staple in 1353.[1] Statutes staple differed from statutes merchant in a number of ways. The system of enrolment was somewhat simpler and the cost less, and statutes staple did not require the attachment of the debtor's seal. It is not clear whether the original intention in 1353 was to confine their use to merchants of the staple. A later enactment in 1357[2] was clearly designed to restrict any extension of jurisdiction by the mayors of the staple over debts which did not concern the staple traffick; it laid down, by way of implementing this policy, that the Ordinance of 1353 was to be strictly observed and this suggests that it was then thought that statutes staple should only be employed by merchants of the staple on staple business. In 1362[3] it was enacted that the *debtor* need not be a merchant of the staple, or indeed a merchant at all; that this needed saying indicates that there must then have been a feeling that the Ordinance of 1353 only applied when both parties were merchants of the staple. After 1362 therefore the strict position was that the creditor must be a stapler. However, it appears that in practice statutes staple came to be generally used and this was recognized in a statute in 1391.[4] Eventually in 1532[5] this practice, which was declared to have been always improper, was stopped. The popularity of statutes staple may have derived from the fact that, besides being cheaper and simpler to execute, the process of execution was even more rigorous than it was on a statute merchant, for the debtor was not permitted the three-month period of grace before his property could be taken and sold.

The Statute of 1532, though it restricted the use of statutes staple to merchants of the staple, established a new form of recognizance for general use; this was called a recognizance 'in the nature of a statute staple'. It was, however, only available in London, being enrolled before one of the Chief Justices in term and before the Recorder and Mayor of the Staple out of term. In effect such a recognizance did not differ from a statute staple. Though their popularity declined, the various forms of 'statute'

[1] 27 Edw. III, st. 2, c. 9., and see Hall, S.S. Vol. 49, p. xxvii.
[2] 31 Edw. III, st. 4, c. 9.
[3] 36 Edw. III, c. 7.
[4] 15 Ric. II, c. 9.
[5] 23 Hen. VIII, c. 17.

continued to be enrolled until 1774; indeed recognizances in the palatine court of Chester could still be enrolled until 1831.[1]

The introduction of adjudicative machinery

The enactments of the medieval period which established statutes merchant and staple made, as we have seen, only the most trivial arrangements for investigation into the debtor's liability; the system was designed to cut out litigation, and it was the absence of any formal 'trial' which was one of the attractions of the institution. No doubt it was thought that adequate safeguards against fraud or sharp practice had been built in, so that there was no need to give the debtor a right to raise objections to execution at a trial or to set up regular adjudicative procedure. In the great majority of cases this belief was no doubt justified, and the system worked fairly if harshly. But inevitably there arose cases where it was essential in the interests of justice to provide the debtor with some way of securing a hearing in situations involving gross frauds which had been perpetrated in spite of the statutory safeguards.

This need was satisfied by the invention in the early fourteenth century of a writ known as *audita querela*.[2] This writ could be issued to the justices of either the Common Pleas or King's Bench to require them to investigate the debtor's complaint. This example is given in the New Natura Brevium:[3]

'The King to the Justices of the Bench, greeting. We have received the complaint [querela] of C containing that A and B by collusion before had between them at W contriving craftily to delude our court, and to oppress the aforesaid C lately appearing before G mayor of our town of Southampton and R clerk, deputed to take recognizances of debts at Southampton asserted upon corporal oath that he the said C was present to perform this, by which he the said B under the name of the said C acknowledged himself to owe to the aforesaid A one hundred pounds, to be paid at a certain time now past before the said mayor and clerk, according to the form of the statute of merchants lately set forth at Acton Burnell, and afterwards him the said C because he paid not

---

[1] Hall, S.S. Vol. 46, p. xi.
[2] See Plucknett, *Legislation of Edward I*, 145.
[3] F.N.B. 103A.

the said hundred pounds to the said A at the time aforesaid, falsely and maliciously procured to be taken by the aforesaid mayor, and kept safely in our prison, until he should satisfy the said A of the said hundred pounds, to the great damage of him the said C and in manifest deceit of our court.'

The writ goes on to require the justices to investigate the matter and provide a fit remedy. The writ of *audita querela* was not confined to being used as a remedy in cases concerning statutes merchant and staple, though it was very commonly used for this purpose. It functioned not so much as a procedure for initiating review but rather as a procedure which ensured due process of law by providing the complainant with an opportunity to raise pleas which he was thought to be legally entitled to plead, but, through some fault in the arrangements he would otherwise never have a chance to raise. Hence *audita querela* could not be used to raise some point when the complainant had previously had a day in court where the point could have been taken in a regular plea.[1]

The origin of 'audita querela'

This is something of a mystery. The earliest unequivocal reference to the writ is in 1337-8,[2] and in 1338 the year-books contain a report of an action which may have been initiated by the writ.[3] Thereafter cases are common. In 1344[4] we have a confident statement by Pole, as counsel, that the action was introduced in Parliament in 1336, and never existed before. This could mean that there was a statute, or merely that its use began then in a case in Parliament; no statute has ever been traced. A year earlier Blaykeston had said that the writ was ordained by Parliament.[5] But in a case in 1339[6] the writ is expressly based upon the law and custom (*secundum legem et consuetudinem*) of the country, and this makes it improbable that the action had any statutory basis in an enactment just three years earlier, though it is just possible that the *lex* referred to is a statute or ordinance of some kind. In 1343 Stonor C.J. asserted

---

[1] See Keilwey 25a, 157a.
[2] 11-12 Edw. III (R.S.), 145.
[3] 12 Edw. I (R.S.), 463, and see 13 Edw. III (R.S.), 144.
[4] 18 Edw. III (R.S.), 308.
[5] 17 Edw. III (R.S.), 1343.
[6] 13 Edw. III (R.S.), 304.

that *audita querela* was given by 'equity' and not by 'common law'.[1] What this means is not very clear; perhaps Stonor was making the point that in allowing *audita querela* a concession was being made to the claims of fairness, although in strict law the debtor had no right to claim any such concession. But the remark is one which could never have been made if Stonor had known of any statute, and it is hardly conceivable that he would not have known.[2] Hence we can only interpret the mention of Parliament in 1343 and 1344 as a reference to a case in Parliament where an *audita querela* was heard, and perhaps some general principle enunciated.

There is indeed evidence which suggests that even before 1336 the Chancery had begun to issue writs which modified the strictness of the Statute of Merchants. Thus there is a case in 1306 where,[3] to the astonishment of counsel, the Chancery had issued some sort of writ releasing a debtor who had been imprisoned regularly on a statute merchant from prison. In 1332[4] there is another example: the Chancery issued a writ for the annulment of a statute merchant if it should be found that the debtor had entered into the recognizance when under age. This writ was issued to the King's Bench, where a *scire facias* was thereupon issued that the matter be investigated. The form of the chancery writ is not mentioned, but it was in all probability analogous at least to an *audita querela*—which would a few years later have been used for just this purpose. It appears therefore that there was some earlier precedent for whatever happened in 1336.

The scope of 'audita querela'

Audita querela provided a remedy in any situation in which there had been fraudulent or deceitful practice. The writ whose text has been set out illustrates such a fraud; eventually in the seventeenth century this particular trick was made felony by statute.[5] It was required for this purpose because the machinery set up by the Statute of Merchants proved not to be foolproof, and because of the absence of any arrangements for supervising

[1] 17 Edw. III (R.S.), 370.
[2] Stonor was a judge at the relevant time (i.e. in 1336).
[3] 34 Edw. I (R.S.), 127.
[4] 6 Edw. III, M. f. 39, pl. 14.
[5] 21 Jac. I, c. 28.

or reviewing the activities of the officials who enrolled and enforced recognizances. To this extent it could be said to provide machinery for review or supervision. But in addition *audita querela* came to be used to permit the debtor to raise for adjudication defences similar to those he could raise in an action of debt. This radically affected the scheme of things, for neither the Statute of Merchants nor the Ordinance of the Staple[1] provided the debtor with any opportunity to raise defences at all, or even gave him a right to be present at the summary hearing of the creditor's complaint of default. Albeit in a somewhat roundabout way, the debtor came to be able to insist upon litigation, which was the very thing that merchants wished to avoid then as they do at this day.

Thus, by bringing *audita querela*, the debtor (or recognizor) could object that he was under age when he entered into the recognizance.[2] It was an accepted principle of law that an infant could not bind himself by contract under seal to pay money, but the Statute of Merchants gave him no chance to take the point. No doubt in an ideal world the recognizance should never have been enrolled, but cases arose where it had been and required a remedy. After a long dispute it was in the end settled that he must take proceedings before attaining his majority in order to avoid the statute.[3] The reason given for this was somewhat peculiar. Age in *audita querela* was tried by inspection by the court; once the complainant was over 21 it was thought to be no longer possible (on logical grounds) for the court by inspection to make a finding of infancy retrospectively, for how could the court by looking at the man *now* tell what he looked like *then*? The defence of duress by imprisonment could also be raised;[4] that such a defence was needed is a striking comment on the conditions of medieval life.

[1] The Statute of 1532 mentions *audita querela*, but does not attempt to codify or regulate the practice which governed the action.

[2] In 6 Edw. III, M. f. 39, pl. 14 (1332) the point was raised in an action which may be an early form of *audita querela*. See for examples of *audita querela* on this point 13 Edw. III (R.S.), 304; 17 and 18 Edw. III (R.S.), 410, 500; 18 Edw. III (R.S.), 378, 380.

[3] *Harrison* v. *Worsley* (1564) Dyer 232b, *Note*, Keilwey 10b, in accordance with the early law in 17 and 18 Edw. III (R.S.), 410, 500; 18 Edw. III, H. f. 5, pl. 4.

[4] 20 Edw. III (R.S.), 92, where the point was taken that a matter of record ought not to be defeated by such an averment, but without success. See also 15 Edw. IV, M. f. 5, pl. 8.

The absence, in the Statute of Merchants, of any system for cancelling the enrolment of the recognizance caused particular difficulties which were solved in part by the use of *audita querela*. If the debt was paid, the creditor's obligation was normally defaced.[1] But the entry on the rolls remained uncancelled. A crafty creditor might then forge an obligation (which would tally with the rolls) and start proceedings again; if so the debtor must use *audita querela*.[2] Again the creditor might release the debt by instrument under seal, but retain the obligation, and by producing it (it would tally with the rolls) he would appear to have a cast-iron case; hence the debtor would be imprisoned in all good faith by the mayor, and he had no statutory right to a hearing where he could plead the release. Again his remedy was to use *audita querela*, where he could rely upon the settled common law principle that an obligation by record or under seal could be met by a release or acquittance under seal.[3]

Neither the Statute of Merchants nor the Ordinance of the Staple made any provision for dealing with conditionally defeasible recognizances; it does not seem to have been envisaged that statutes merchant or staple should be used to bind the recognizor to pay money unless he either paid a lesser sum (as in the common money bond) or performed some act (as in the bond for the performance of covenants). However, it was possible to employ statutes in the same way as private penal bonds, but the technique was somewhat different. Instead of endorsing a condition on the statute merchant itself, and enrolling the condition on the recognizance roll, it appears to have been the practice for the creditor to execute indentures of defeasance quite separately; by these the creditor granted to the debtor that the statute merchant (or staple) was to be null and void in certain eventualities; for example, in a case in 1347[4] the creditor granted that a statute merchant for £20 should be void if the debtor paid seven marks by a certain day. Such indentures could be executed at the same time as the recogniz-

---

[1] Without being able to produce a valid obligation he could not of course take any proceedings.

[2] Fitz. *Audita Querela*, pl. 10 (M.15 Edw. III).

[3] 13 Edw. III (R.S.), 52, 174; 17 Edw. III (R.S.), 516; 18 Edw. III (R.S.), 380; 18 and 19 Edw. III (R.S.), 358.

[4] 20 Lib. Ass. f. 70, pl. 7.

ance was entered into, or subsequently as the result of some form of compromise between the parties.[1] Though in substance such indentures produced the same result as a condition attached to a bond, the concept of a defeasance was distinguished from that of a condition;[2] the indentures did not make the originally unconditional recognizance conditional, but constituted an independent grant of a right of defeasance to the debtor. Why this technique was employed is not clear. One possible explanation is that it was not legally permissible to enrol a conditional statute merchant or staple, but there is no positive evidence that I know of in favour of this hypothesis. Alternatively the point may have been to give the debtor a right of action in covenant (as opposed to a defence) if the creditor broke his side of the agreement; a mere condition would not give him such a right of action, and since the enactments did not entitle the debtor even to a hearing a defence would appear valueless to him.[3] Once *audita querela* came into use the debtor, if proceeded against in breach of an indenture of defeasance, could obtain a remedy by using the action and complaining that the creditor had acted contrary to his own deed, just as he could do if he had been given a deed of release or acquittance.[4] If necessary the issue of fact which might arise in such proceedings could be tried by jury.[5] Whether *audita querela* lay on a condition, as opposed to a defeasance, does not appear to have been decided; the point may well have never arisen. The explanation for this could be that conditional statutory recognizances were legally impossible, or simply not in practice used.

[1] The case cited in the preceding note is an example.

[2] Hence 'Defeasance' is a separate title in the *Abridgements* from 'Condition'.

[3] In the case of a common law recognizance the recognizance could be conditional. If, however, it was not so enrolled, the debtor must have recourse to an action for damages on the defeasance, and could not use the defeasance as a bar to proceedings on the recognizance.

[4] 6 Edw. III, M. f. 53, pl. 53; 13 Edw. III (R.S.), 144; 17 Edw. III, H. f. 3, pl. 11; 20 Edw. III (R.S.), 268; 22 Edw. III, P. f. 5, pl. 13; 46 Edw. III, H. f. 4, pl. 9. Rastell, *Entries*, f. 98 et seq., gives precedents.

[5] 18 Edw. III (R.S.), 349. Similarly if an issue arose as to whether a deed of release was the creditor's deed, this could be tried by jury, 17 Edw. III (R.S.), 516.

III

DEBT ON INFORMAL CONTRACTS

In the absence of a record or recognizance, or a private bond, a plaintiff in debt could base his claim upon one of those informal transactions known as 'contracts'; this was the name given to such transactions as were recognized at law as giving rise to a debt. Typical contracts were sale of land or chattels, loans of money, agreements for services, and leases of land for years.

Methods of proof and trial

In debt *sur obligation* the party proof, which put the defendant to answer, was the profert of the deed.[1] In debt *sur contract* the party proof consisted in the production of suitors, who were originally witnesses to the transaction which generated liability. Their function was not the same as the function of witnesses in the modern action on a contract, for in medieval law witnesses called to substantiate the plaintiff's assertions, given in evidence on oath, were in no way essential to successful litigation. For in the first place the medieval plaintiff was not required to give evidence at all in the modern manner, or indeed permitted to do so; his opportunity to tell his tale was provided by the pleadings, which began with the count or declaration where he told his side of the story, or employed counsel to tell it for him. Under this system the function of suitors was to substantiate the plaintiff's count, not to corroborate his oral evidence. In the second place the production of suitors was an essential requirement; if no suit was tendered, the defendant need not answer the plaintiff's case at all. In the thirteenth century the production of suit was no mere formality; the suitors could be examined by the court to decide if there was a case which required an answer.[2] 'Fleta' thus explains the system as it worked in his time:

---

[1] On party proof see Thayer, *Preliminary Treatise on Evidence*, Ch. 1, esp. pp. 10 et seq.

[2] See 21 and 22 Edw. I (R.S.), 456. Thus in 2 and 3 Edw. III (S.S.), App. 1, 195, Bereford C.J. treats the examination of suitors as an alternative method of trial to wager of law or trial by jury.

'No free man is to be put to his law or placed on oath on a mere complaint without trustworthy witnesses brought for the purpose. But if the plaintiff produces suit, that is witnesses of law-abiding men who were present at the contract made between them, and if, after examination by a judge, they should be found in agreement, then the defendant may wage his law against the plaintiff and against the suit he has brought forward.[1]

But in the fourteenth century the practice of examining the suit fell out of use, and the offer to produce suitors became a mere formality. Thus in 1343 Mowbray was able to say 'Suit is tendered only as a part of the form of the count'.[2] Why so sensible a practice should fall out of favour is obscure, and the development provides a remarkable illustration of retrograde legal change. Though there may have been occasional efforts to revive the practice of examining suitors, it was generally true thereafter that the only check on the veracity of the plaintiff's count was the fact that counsel had been prepared to make it; in theory counsel were responsible for the truth of the pleadings.[3]

The method of trial *sur contract* was, as a general rule, at the defendant's option. He could either wage his law, or elect trial by jury. Wager law was possible if he pleaded the general issue (*nihil debet*), and if he made a special plea by way of special traverse or confession and avoidance,[4] though in actions in which wager of law was allowed special pleas of this type were discouraged.[5] In practice, however, wager on such special pleas as were permitted was uncommon, for if the defendant wanted to wage his law there was little point in pleading specially.[6]

Wager of law described

Compurgation, or wager of law, involved two stages. When sued, the defendant pleaded to the action (normally his plea

---

[1] Fleta II, c. 63 (S.S. Vol. 72, p. 211).

[2] 17 Edw. III (R.S.), 72.

[3] This is the original explanation of the surviving practice of signing the pleadings.

[4] 39 Edw. III, P. f. 9; 7 Hen. IV, H. f. 7, pl. 3.

[5] 8 Hen. VI, H. f. 5, pl. 5.

[6] The main point in traversing specially was to circumscribe an issue which was to be submitted to a jury.

would be the general issue, *nihil debet*) and offered to wage his law—in effect he offered to guarantee that he would successfully exculpate himself by an oath that he owed nothing. If his offer was accepted by the court, he was then given a day on which to appear and perform the oath, and he must find pledges for his appearance. On the appointed day he must then appear in his own person together with his oath-helpers (compurgators) and 'make his law'. The word 'law' here seems to be used in the sense of 'right'; thus to wage your law means to 'warrant your right', and to 'make your law' is 'to make good your right'. Normally[1] the number of compurgators required was eleven, and the defendant was said to make his law 'twelve-handed'. He must swear the oath with his hand upon the Bible, and kiss the Book, and his oath-helpers must go through the same procedure; if the ceremony was performed successfully the defendant won the action. The procedure could be modified to cater for a dumb person, and is thus described in a case in 1344:[2]

> 'Note that a man came in a *praecipe quod reddat* and waged his law for non summons by signs only. And now by signs he made his law, and the words were rehearsed to him, and he heard and put his hand upon the book, and kissed it, and so without a word performed the law. And Stone said to him, "Once forsworn, ever forlorn."'

If he perjured himself he would undoubtedly imperil his soul by falling into mortal sin, but he incurred no temporal penalty; the common law courts would not themselves entertain indictments for the spiritual offence of perjury, nor would they allow the courts christian to meddle in cases involving the debts of the laity. Even the Star Chamber held in 1587 that perjury in the course of compurgation was not a crime.[3] The compurgators were in the same case as the defendant, though the significance of their oath was different; they were said to swear *de credulitate* – that the defendants oath was good.

To a lawyer of the twentieth century, trial by wager of law

---

[1] In London thirty-six oath-helpers were required; see Thayer, op. cit. 27.
[2] 18 Edw. III, f. 53, pl. 64. cf. 21 Hen. VI, P. f. 42, pl. 15, where a Lombard who knew no English was allowed to wage his law in his own language.
[3] *Anon.* Goulds. 51, pl. 13.

seems slightly ridiculous; though oath-taking today is still a feature of legal procedure, and may add a useful note of solemnity to court proceedings (besides increasing the emoluments of commissioners for oaths), modern man, however religiously minded, does not believe in hell in the straightforward and vivid way in which men believed in it in the age of faith. But even today I suppose it would be difficult to collect eleven perjurers in order to resist an action for breach of contract; in the fifteenth century it must have been even more difficult, and the evidence shows that in a very considerable proportion of cases defendants opted for trial by jury.[1] Indeed, in one reported fifteenth-century[2] case (which does not involve an action of debt) one even finds the plaintiff trying to persuade the court to insist that the defendant should wage his law, whilst the defendant is trying to be allowed to leave the issue to a jury. It is there pointed out that, for a defendant, trial by jury has obvious advantages. It was quicker, and the jurors could be compelled to attend, whereas there was no way of compelling compurgators to turn up on the appointed day; furthermore, a person who was ill, or in prison, or one who was a recluse, could not make his law, for one could not make one's law by attorney. On the other hand, jurors could be challenged by the plaintiff whereas the compurgators who were selected by the defendant could not.

When compurgation is compared with trial by jury one must not of course have in mind jury trial as it exists today—fifteenth-century jury trial was not highly regarded by contemporaries, and was quite unlike modern trial by jury (obsolescent though it is in civil actions), with its elaborate production of evidence and judicial direction. A fifteenth-century jury was an oath-taking body which closely resembled a set of eleven compurgators, the main difference being the fact that its composition was not determined by the defendant. For honest defendants, compurgation may have seemed a valuable safeguard, and there is evidence that it was preferred by the commercial community to trial by jury.[3] A plaintiff in debt *sur contract* put forward

[1] See Hastings, *The Court of Common Pleas*, Ch. XIV, and S. F. C. Milsom, 'Sale of Goods in the Fifteenth Century', 77 L.Q.R. 257.
[2] 33 Hen. VI, f. 7, pl. 23.
[3] See Plucknett, *History*, 116, noting the statute of 38 Edw. III, st. 1, c. 5.

nothing beyond his own bare assertion that the debt was due, and did not produce the normal and business-like contractual bond; his claim merited suspicion. A defendant who could produce eleven compurgators prepared to swear that no debt was due deserved to win; *ceteris paribus* he would win today. It is difficult to tell how compurgation worked in practice, and how closely it was controlled by the court; examples of supervision are curiously late.[1] It is even more difficult to assess contemporary feeling on the subject;[2] thus, although there is plenty of evidence that plaintiffs attempted to restrict wager, this could be because it was easier for a dishonest plaintiff to corrupt jurymen than to suborn the defendant's compurgators. The best evidence that compurgation was felt to confer an unfair advantage on the defendant in actions of debt is the fact that the courts excluded wager in compulsory contracts, where the plaintiff was unable to insist upon a bond. But even here one must be cautious; the rational justification for compurgation was just that it did tip the scales in the defendant's favour in situations where he ought to be protected from ill-proved claims, and its exclusion in cases where the plaintiff could not have insisted on proper proof of the contract would be consistent with this rationale; in such cases it was fair that neither party should have any advantage.[3]

Situations where wager was excluded

There were a number of situations where wager was excluded. The most curious is the case of the compulsory contract. Under the provisions of the Statutes of Labourers,[4] common labourers[5]

---

[1] Thus in 22 Edw. IV, P. f. 2, pl. 8, there is an example of a defendant consulting the court as to whether he could in conscience wage his law; see also *Anon.* (1588) 2 Leon. 212, *Anon.* (1588) 4 Leon. 81, and *Sanderson* v. *Ekins* (1590) 3 Leon. 258, and for discussion Milsom, 416. On the institution in the 16th Century see now J. H. Baker in 1971 C.L.J. at 228.

[2] There is a evidence from Bereford C.J. in 2 and 3 Edw. II, (s.s.) App. I, 195, who thought that wager should be refused in cases where the facts were notorious.

[3] There is some evidence that originally the defendant who opted for wager of law in effect was made to stake a bet on the outcome, for if he waged law and failed to make his law the plaintiff recovered untaxed damages; see 21–2 Edw. I (R.S.), 60; 33–5 Edw. I. (R.S.), 396; 16 Edw. III (R.S.), 558. But in 18 Edw. III (R.S.), 622 this rule was changed.

[4] 23 Edw. III; 25 Edw. III, st. 11.; 34 Edw. III, cc. 9–11.

[5] They must be physically able to work, possess no land on which to live, be of the proper age, and not be retained by another.

could be compelled by law to enter into the service of anyone
who cared to retain them in the office of husbandman at the
rate of pay fixed by law. Such persons, if they sued in debt for
their salary, could not be met by wager of law.[1] The rationale
for this exception was that servants who were so compelled to
trust the master for their salary could not insist on the normal
recourse of the prudent creditor, which was to insist upon a
bond. The exception was extended to cover persons of any
occupation retained in husbandry, so that if a yeoman or cook
was so retained he could oust the master of wager although he
was not in the first instance compellable to serve—an extension
which was difficult to justify rationally.[2] The explanation may
be that there was an action for departure against the servant,
with trial by jury, and the claims of reciprocity were thought
to demand trial by jury when the servant sued. Attempts to
extend the exception still further failed. Thus in a case in 1460[3]
the defendant had retained the plaintiff to go to Rome to purchase a bull in return for a fixed remuneration; in an action of
debt the defendant tendered wager, and the plaintiff demurred
to this but lost on demurrer,

> 'Prisot C.J.: He will have his law perfectly well, for this
> retainer is at common law, and is not the same as the retainer
> of a servant in husbandry, which is given by statute in which
> case they are constrained to serve according to the statute,
> and because they are compelled to serve in spite of them-
> selves, this is the reason why their masters cannot wage their
> law against them.'

Nor could wager be excluded by the device of declaring that the
plaintiff had been retained in all manner of occupations.[4] The
exception also covered situations where the compulsion did not
derive from statute. Thus in 1449[5] the Warden of the Tower,
who was at this time thought to be bound to sell food to his
prisoners, sued in debt for the price of food supplied to a

---

[1] 2 Hen. IV, H. f. 14, pl. 12; 3 Hen. VI, H. f. 33, pl. 26; P. f. 42, pl. 13; 4 Hen
VI, f. 19, pl. 5; 11 Hen. VI, T. f. 48, pl. 5; 28 Hen. VI, M. f. 4 pl. 21; 8 Edw.
IV, H. f. 23, pl. 1; 15 Edw. IV, H. f. 16, pl. 3; 16 Edw. IV, H. f. 10, pl. 3.
[2] 38 Hen. VI, H. f. 22, pl. 4.
[3] 39 Hen. VI, M. f. 18, pl. 24.
[4] 38 Hen. VI, M. f. 13, pl. 30.
[5] 28 Hen. VI, M. f. 4, pl. 21.

traitor, and successfully maintained that wager was excluded·
The position of innkeepers and common victuallers was uncertain, since it was not clear that they were bound to sell on credit
(though they were certainly bound to sell).[1] The most remarkable and unnatural decisions were given in cases involving the
legal profession. An attorney of the common law courts could
resist wager, since he was compellable to serve.[2] In 1424,[3] an
attempt was made to apply the same reasoning to a member of
the bar, *without success*!

> 'Pole, Serjeant at law, brought a writ of debt, and declared
> how he was retained to be of counsel with the defendant for
> two years taking ten pounds for each year, and the defendant
> waged his law.'

It was held that wager was permissible, and the reporter adds
in shocked tones,

> 'Notwithstanding that it was shown to the justices that a
> serjeant of the law is compellable by law to be of counsel to
> anyone just as a servant is compellable to serve.'

Wager was also excluded where debt was brought on an account
found before auditors;[4] in consequence fictitious counts on
accounts were used by creditors who wished to oust the defendant of wager. In order to curb this practice the courts allowed
a special plea in such cases, the plea of *nul tiel account*.[5] Both the
device and the development of a counter to it indicate in a
characteristic way the two views it was possible to take of
wager—an abuse to be circumvented, or a valuable safeguard
against groundless claims.

In fifteenth-century law at least, wager was not possible where
arrears of rent was claimed from a tenant for years of land,[6]

---

[1] 19 Hen. VI, M. f. 10, pl. 25; 39 Hen. VI, M. f. 18, pl. 24; 10 Hen. VII, M. f. 7, pl. 14.

[2] 21 Hen. VI, M. f. 5, pl. 6.

[3] 21 Hen. VI, M. f. 4, pl. 6. The case is misplaced in the year-books, and in fact belongs to 3 Hen. VI, Paschal.

[4] 9 Hen. V, P. f. 3, pl. 9; 11 Hen. IV, H. f. 55, pl. 38.

[5] See Milsom, 77 L.Q.R. at 260. There was also a statutory power to examine the plaintiff on the truth of his count; this was introduced by 5 Hen. IV, c. 8. For an example of its operation see 8 Hen. VI, f. 15, pl. 36.

[6] 9 Edw. IV, P. f. 1, pl. 1; 10 Hen. VII, M. f. 4, pl. 4. In earlier law wager was allowed; see 50 Edw. III, T. f. 16, pl. 8, and cf. 49 Edw. III, H. f. 3, pl. 6.

though in the case of a lease of chattels the lessee could wage, a point established in a case involving a lease of sheep.[1]

Now in principle it was generally felt that wager of law should not be allowed in cases where the facts were in the nature of things notorious; as Prisot C.J. said in 1454,[2]

'All that which lies within the notice of the country shall be tried by the country.'

This was probably the reason why wager was excluded in actions for rent from leaseholders, but the principle was inconsistently applied. Thus where a boarder was sued for the price of commons, some thought that wager ought not to be allowed for such an arrangement could not in general remain private, but wager was nevertheless allowed.[3] The converse principle was that no one could be allowed to wage his law where in the nature of things he could not be certain of the facts, lest he be tempted to imperil his soul by taking a false oath. Thus wager should be excluded where the defendant was sued on the contract of a third party. The clearest case here was that of executors or administrators sued in a representative capacity on the contract of the deceased person; they were not able to wage their law on his behalf.[4] In consequence they could not be sued for a debt incurred by the deceased on a contract by parole, so that debts due by informal contract died with the debtor. There was no question here of trial by jury, for the deceased's informal contracts were not within the knowledge of the country; even if there was knowledge of the contract, the debt might have been paid. The immunity of executors and administrators was confined to cases where the deceased could have waged his law,[5] and some thought that the immunity

---

[1] 1 Hen. VI, M. f. 1, pl. 3. There was a general principle that wager was excluded in any action touching realty, and this made it worth recording that wager was possible on a sale of land by parole; see 22 Hen. VI, H. f. 43, pl. 28.

[2] 33 Hen. VI, H.f. 7, pl. 23.

[3] 19 Hen. VI, M. f. 10, pl. 25; 22 Hen. VI, M. f. 13, pl. 18; 39 Hen. VI, M. f. 18, pl. 24; 9 Edw. IV, P. f. 1, pl. 1.

[4] 41 Edw. III, T. f. 13, pl. 3; 2 Hen. IV, M. f. 14, pl. 12; 21 Hen. VI, H. f. 23 pl. 3. See generally below, ch. xi, for the eventual modification of this rule.

[5] Milsom, 77 L.Q.R. 265.

could be waived,[1] but this made little inroad upon the general rule.[2]

Jurisdictional limits upon the scope of the action of debt on a contract

The action of debt, as we have seen, could only be used to claim a sum certain. Its use was in addition limited by jurisdictional rules. Under provisions of the Statute of Gloucester (1278),[3] as interpreted, the sum claimed must be at least forty shillings. In practice this limitation seems to have been systematically evaded in the fifteenth century[4] by the use of fictitious counts, a fact which sheds some light on the popularity of litigation through the common law courts. The existence of the courts christian also of necessity imposed a restriction upon the jurisdiction of the courts of common law, for it was admitted that the common law courts must confine their activities to secular matters. But this left open some room for dispute as to quite what counted as a secular matter, especially as there was clearly some pressure from litigants for the extension of common law jurisdiction. But in general this pressure was resisted until after the Reformation had radically altered mens' conceptions of the proper relationship of Church and State.

Thus the general principle was that no action lay at common law to claim a legacy of personal property as such,[5] and this principle was maintained throughout the medieval period.[6] Again it was universally admitted that matrimony was a spiritual matter; hence (although there was some doubt on the point) it was never held that debt lay to recover marriage money (i.e.

---

[1] 10 Hen. VI, M. f. 24, pl. 84; 15 Edw. IV, P. f. 25, pl. 7; 41 Edw. III, T. f. 13, pl. 3.

[2] One could not wage law against the King; hence in *quominus* wager was excluded. See 20 Edw. III (R.S.), Vol. I, pl. 17, and see below, ch. xi. See also Co. Litt. 295a (Infants, outlaws, persons attaint).

[3] 6 Edw. I, c. 8.

[4] See Milsom, 77 L.Q.R. 257 at 258 et seq.

[5] 11 Hen. IV, M. f. 1, pl. 2; 37 Hen. VI, M. f. 8, pl. 18; 46 Edw. III, M. f. 32, pl. 37.

[6] The decision in 11 Hen. VI, T. f. 39, pl. 31 is not in conflict; there an executrix of one Andrew Urban sued one David Urban on an indenture whereby David conceded that he had in his possession some £40, being parcel of a legacy devised to the testator by one John Urban. The basis of the claim here was that the defendant was bailee of the money and had conceded as much by deed: the plaintiff did not sue on the devise.

dowries). Since the cause of such grants was spiritual the common law ought not to be concerned with them. The cases on this point are more fully discussed later in connection with the doctrine of *quid pro quo*.[1] But if marriage money was granted by deed, an action did lie at common law, since the cause of such a grant was irrelevant to its actionability. Cases involving tithes were a perpetual source of difficulty. Prima facie tithes were the concern of the ecclesiastical courts, since they were spiritual in nature, but there were numerous exceptions to the general rule. So far as the law of contract was concerned, the rule was that debt did lie on a contract for the sale of tithes, or on a lease of tithes, for the theory of the matter was that their nature was changed if they were made subject to commercial dealings.[2]

The common law courts, whilst keeping their own contractual jurisdiction within reasonable bounds, resisted firmly any attempt upon the part of the ecclesiastical courts to encroach upon the law of contract. The relationship between lay and ecclesiastical jurisdiction became critical where contracting parties took an oath or pledged their faith for the performance of a lay contract or covenant; back in Henry II's reign the Constitutions of Clarendon had reserved jurisdiction over debts to the lay courts even if faith was pledged. But in such cases it could be argued with some plausibility[3] that, although the principal action on the contract was clearly within the common law jurisdiction, nevertheless the ecclesiastical courts could properly entertain proceedings for perjury or *laesio fidei* as well, since these were clearly spiritual matters, and there is no doubt that such proceedings were entertained. But it was pointed out in a case in 1400[4] that to allow this would be to permit in effect the usurpation by the spiritual courts of contractual jurisdiction, for, on conviction for perjury, the perjurer was required to perform his oath in accordance with the general Christian practice of requiring the sinner to make amends for his sin. Hence such proceedings for perjury and *laesio fidei* could not be permitted. In 1459[5] the year-book contains a clear statement of the rule on the matter:

[1] See below, p. 156.
[2] 37 Hen. VI, M. f. 8, pl. 18.
[3] See 20 Edw. IV, M. f. 10, pl. 9.
[4] *Per* Hankford in 2 Hen. IV, M. f. 10, pl. 45.
[5] 38 Hen. VI, P. f. 29, pl. 11.

'Note that Fortescue said in the Exchequer Chamber before all the justices of both benches, that if a man binds himself by oath to pay another forty shillings at a day, and does not do so on the day, if the party sues him in the court christian for *laesio fidei* he will have a prohibition, since the court christian cannot entertain a plea about the principai matter. And the law is the same if he binds himself by oath to make a feoffment by a certain day . . . for the same reason: for this suit is in effect a compulsion to make the party perform an act which concerns the King's Court, and no other court. Hence it would be contrary to reason to punish the party for *laesio fidei* in a matter of which the cognisance appertains to the King's Court. Which was conceded by some and denied by none.'

Thus, unless the courts christian had jurisdiction over the principal (as, for example, in the case of an agreement concerning marriage), they had no jurisdiction over the accessory. But later in the fifteenth century some slight inroad was made into the rule, for it came to be admitted that although the courts christian could not punish for *laesio fidei* at the suit of the party, they could *ex officio*.[1]

The types of 'contract' on which debt lay

(a) INFORMAL LOANS

Perhaps the simplest of all transactions which give rise to a debt is the informal loan of money, which must, of course, be gratuitous to avoid the vice of usury. The creditor could, however, recover damages for the unlawful detention of the debt after the day of payment had passed. The award of such damages did not involve usury, since they did not constitute a payment for the use of the money, nor were they certain to be incurred; they merely compensated for loss of the *interesse* of the creditor in prompt payment.[2] Reported cases on informal loans are uncommon in the year books. Part of the explanation for this is that the informal loan is unlikely to throw up tricky legal questions which would interest a law reporter; in addition to this we must remember that prudent lenders of money (except

---

[1] See 22 Edw. IV, T. f. 20, pl. 47; 12 Hen. VII, T. f. 22, pl. 7. On the whole subject see Reeves, *History of English Law*, III, 103.

[2] See above, p. 114.

when dealing with borrowers whom they know they can trust) do not make informal loans. The absence of case law means that there is little evidence as to the legal theory of the loan, and it may be that the right of the lender to recover his money again is too obvious to require much in the way of legal theory. It is worth noticing that modern writers on contract never quite know what to do with the simple loan.

In Roman Law the contract of simple money loan (the *mutuum*) was distinguished by the fact that the transaction vested ownership in the coins in the borrower; Gaius tells us that the contract is called *mutuum* because what was *meum* becomes *tuum*.[1] The analysis was known to fourteenth-century lawyers[2] (though they did not necessarily derive it from Roman sources); the *mutuum* is regarded as a special form of bailment in which the property in the subject-matter is vested in the bailee. A loan of money is of course very closely analogous to a bailment of a chattel by way of deposit, and this sufficiently explains the fact that loans are sometimes called bailments in the year-books of the fourteenth century.[3] Loans were certainly 'contracts', but in fifteenth-century thought they may have been regarded as rather peculiar 'contracts'. Thus in a case in 1432[4] counsel seems to use the terms 'loan' and 'contract' alternatively, which may indicate a feeling that *mutuum* was *sui generis*. One reason for this could be the fact that the *mutuum* could not be fitted into the conception of a contract as a grant from debtor to creditor, for in *mutuum* the creditor is the grantor, which is the wrong way round. Nor could the creditor's right of action be justified by the fashionable notion of *quid pro quo*. The borrower, it is true, obtains the use of the money, but he gets this for nothing, and in no intelligible sense is the use given him *in return for* his duty to repay.

Where the informal loan was secured by an informal pledge the law seems to have been in a very uncertain state. If what was pledged was a chattel, to be retained by the creditor until the debt was paid, the debtor was reasonably protected. If he paid he could recover the chattel by writ of detinue. If sued he

---

[1] Gaius, *Institutes*, III. 90.
[2] See 41 Edw. III, P. f. 10, pl. 5.
[3] See 33 Edw. I (R.S.), 84; 33–5 Edw. I (R.S.), 454.
[4] 11 Hen. VI, T. f. 39, pl. 31.

could plead in bar to the action of debt that he was ready to pay on return of the pledge. Where, however, land was pledged informally there were difficulties which seem never to have been resolved, as appears from a long discussion in 1469.[1] Debt was brought on a loan; the defendant pleaded that after the loan there had been an agreement that he should enfeoff the plaintiff (the creditor) of land, and that the plaintiff should take the profits until the loan was paid. He had done so, and was ready to pay when the land was reconveyed to him. The defendant was in something of a predicament, for since he appears to have enfeoffed the creditor unconditionally he had no way of recovering his land directly by exercising a right of entry, nor could he bring covenant since there had been no covenant under seal for reconveyance.[2] The majority of the court appears after some vacillation to have inclined in favour of allowing the plea, but the case was adjourned without a decision.

(b) CONTRACTS OF SERVICE AND ANALOGOUS TRANSACTIONS

(i) *The scope of liability*
Where one person agreed informally to do something in return for some determinate reward or remuneration, the transaction involved was a covenant, and the rule established in the early fourteenth century was, as we have seen, that informal covenants were not actionable by writ of covenant at common law. Once this rule became settled there was clearly an objection to permitting an action of debt to be brought on such covenants for the agreed remuneration, for this would produce an anomalous state of affairs in which there was a common law action available to one contracting party, but no reciprocal common law action available to the other. Nevertheless in 1338,[3] debt was allowed on such a covenant.

'A writ of debt was brought against one, and he counted that the plaintiff, by covenant between him and the defendant,

---

[1] 9 Edw. IV, T. f. 25, pl. 34.

[2] Nor could he plead a condition attached to the contract of loan, since the loan was initially unconditional.

[3] 11 and 12 Edw. III (R.S.), 587, Fifoot 247. Earlier examples of actions of debt on covenants are 20 Edw. I (R.S.), 222, 487.

had been made his attorney for ten years, taking twenty shillings for every year, which were in arrear.'

Pole objected,

'He has shown nothing of the covenant.'

Sharshulle J. replied,

'If one were to count simply of a grant of a debt, he would not be received without a specialty, but here you have his service for his allowance, of which knowledge may be had, and you have *quid pro quo*.'

I understand Sharshulle's point to be this, that where such an agreement has actually been performed by the covenantor the absence of an action to compel performance does not matter; having got what he bargained for, the covenantee cannot rationally object to being sued by writ of debt upon the ground that he has no action to compel performance—he no longer needs an action. Sharshulle's remark, if translated, would end '. . . and you have reciprocity'. Much the same reasoning can be used to justify giving an action in modern law on a unilateral contract.

According to the view taken by Sharshulle J. in this case any agreement involving the doing of something in return for a fixed sum of money would be *actionable* by writ of debt when performed; Sharshulle J. does not advert to the distinct problem of deciding when the agreement would be *binding*. But not long after his decision the whole situation was altered by the passing in 1349 of the Ordinance of Labourers and the enactment of the various Statutes of Labourers. There evolved around this legislation, a comprehensive scheme of common law remedies to regulate and sanction contracts of service.[1] These remedies included, as we have seen, an action which lay at the suit of a master if his servant, retained in his service, departed out of his service without his leave. Where this action for departure was available there could be no sensible objection to permitting the servant to use debt to sue for his salary, and it was settled in fifteenth-century law that such an action was available. But even this position was not reached without some doubt and difficulty.

[1] 40 Edw. III, P. f. 24, pl. 27; 38 Hen. VI, H. f. 22, pl. 4.

The simplest case was where a common labourer, who could be compelled to serve against his will, sued for his salary. His right of action in debt could be regarded as based upon statute. The case of a retained servant who was not compellable was more dubious. Thus in a case in 1476,[1] debt was brought by a servant retained to do work on gowns. Catesby objected to the action,

> 'as to the remainder he asked judgement of the count, for this retainer is and sounds in covenant, and as I understand action of debt does not lie on a retainer except in the case of labourers, which is given by statute.'

But the court rejected the argument,

> '*Et non allocatur*, since it is a natural contract, for it well appears that the defendant has *quid pro quo*.'

What is noteworthy here is the fact that a skilled and experienced lawyer such as Catesby should regard the point as worth taking, so late in the fifteenth century as this. The courts had, though not without some doubt, extended the action for departure to cases where the servant was not compellable to serve,[2] and the mention of '*quid pro quo*' may be read as referring to the reciprocal remedy, or the fact that the defendant had received the benefit of the work, the latter interpretation being more probable.

Fifteenth-century authority generally favoured allowing an action of debt to lie where there was a retainer of the services of a skilled person, as for example, where a man was retained to be of counsel.[3] The authorities need, however, to be read with some care, for it is not always clear whether the action is thought to be available because the contracting party is compellable to serve, or whether this was irrelevant.

Where, however, the party could not be said to have been retained at all, the right to sue in debt was rather more dubious. The nearest we come to a direct authority in favour of liability

[1] 16 Edw. IV, H. f. 10, pl. 3; 11 Hen. VI, T. f. 48, pl. 5 (priest retained to chant mass) seems to assume liability. See also 3 Hen. VI, M. f. 21, pl. 16; 37 Hen. VI, M. f. 6, pl. 16 (per Moyle J) (Fifoot 249).
[2] See above, p. 49.
[3] 37 Hen. VI, M. f. 8, pl. 18; 9 Edw. IV, M. f. 36, pl. 4; 18 Edw. IV, T. f. 8, pl. 12.

is the case of the slaughterman, decided in 1424.[1] Here Rolf counted,

> 'that the plaintiff on such a day and year made a covenant with the same defendant in such a ward to be his slaughterman for the two years next ensuing, that is to say that he who is now plaintiff should slaughter his pigs and all other beasts and birds which he should bring to him, and that the plaintiff should find wood, fuel, and all other necessary things, taking a hundred shillings a year . . .'

The slaughterman averred performance and sued for his salary. Cottesmore, of counsel, objected to the count,

> 'You see how he has declared on a covenant of which he shows nothing.'

But the whole court held that this was a simple contract, of which he need show nothing. That this was worth saying and recording is significant of the uncertainty of the law. The report goes on to deal with the question of trial, there being at this date some uncertainty whether wager of law was available or not. This case, as pleaded, did not involve a retainer, though on the facts it looks as if a retainer of the services of the slaughterman (though not a retainer in service) could well have been averred. There could be cases where there was no question of a retainer in any sense, as in the case of a contract for a particular piece of work with an independent contractor. An example would be a contract with a carpenter to build a house for a sum certain. In all probability debt could be brought on such a contract, but there is a curious absence of clear authority.

The persistence of doubt upon the scope of debt on informal agreements for work is illustrated by a case reported in 1509,[2] where a manorial lord was sued on an agreement, reached informally, that the plaintiff should act as his court steward. Here the difficulty seems to have been caused by the fact that the job of steward, like such jobs as guardian of a park, was conceived of as an 'office' which lay in grant, belonging rather to property law than to contract. Nevertheless the court of King's Bench allowed the action:

[1] 3 Hen. VI, P. f. 42, pl. 12.
[2] *Anon.* Keilwey 158b, Dyer 248a.

'and although this be without any deed, if he holds the courts according to the retainer, he will have an action of debt for his salary against the lord, but he will not have a writ of annuity without writing [escript] of his office. And there can be retainer to be a steward, as well as a bailiff or servant without writing.'

(ii) *The theory of liability*

The general principle in all contracts of the class under discussion seems to have been that the party could certainly sue in debt (if he could sue at all) when there had been performance. Thus in a case in 1459 the plaintiff sued on a retainer for eight years in the office of husbandry, taking twenty shillings a year; the action was regarded as accruing at the end of the term.[1]

Confronted with cases where there had been performance, the fact that the defendant had received the benefit for which he had contracted was a powerful argument for allowing the action, and served to counter the argument that common law actions ought not be allowed on parole covenants. The defendant had *quid pro quo*. In certain types of contract the party might be regarded as having performed his side of the agreement although he had in fact done nothing. Thus Prisot C.J. explained in *Alice's Case* (1458),[2]

'Similarly one can have an action of debt on a retainer with a man to be of his counsel . . . but in this case I must declare in my account, that I was with him, or was otherwise ready to give counsel to him if he had demanded it.'

Here the agreement could be regarded as an agreement to give such counsel as was demanded, and this the plaintiff had done by holding himself available. From this it is a small step to allowing a party to sue if in any agreement for work he has held himself always ready and willing to perform, and it seems to have been the view of some lawyers that this was sufficient. Thus Newton C.J. said in 1442,[3]

[1] 38 Hen. VI, H. f. 22, pl. 4. See also *per* Thirning C.J. in 12 Hen. IV, H. f. 17, pl. 13 ('If money be promised to a man to make a release, and he makes the release, he will have a good action of debt on the matter').
[2] 37 Hen. VI, M. f. 8, pl. 18 (Fifoot 249).
[3] 21 Hen. VI, M. f. 6, pl. 16. See also 18 Edw. IV, H. f. 17, pl. 13.

'For let us suppose that one makes a covenant to serve me
for a certain salary, and afterwards he comes to me and
offers his service, and I will not accept him but refuse him,
if he is always ready in case I require him afterwards, I am
bound by law to give him his salary.'

According to this view then the contract is binding when made;
it becomes actionable only after it has been performed, or
after the time for performance has passed, provided that the
contracting party has always held himself ready to perform.

It follows, however, that no salary was due until the time for
performance was passed, a rule which must have been peculiarly
unsatisfactory in the case of a service contract involving a
retainer for a long term. Furthermore the duty was entire, and
could not be apportioned. Hence if the contract was discharged
by death during the term nothing whatever was due,[1] and it
was in all probability the law that if the contracting party
broke his contract[2] (as by departing from service within the
term) or even if he was discharged within the term with consent, he was entitled to nothing,[3] and the court would not make
any attempt to apportion his salary equitably to reward him
for the work he had done.

(c) CONTRACTS FOR THE BENEFIT OF THIRD PARTIES

In the context of agreements whereby money was to be paid
for services, or for the performance of an act, a doctrine of *quid
pro quo* seems to have been fairly generally accepted in fifteenth-
century law; the gist of the doctrine in this area was that a duty
to pay the debt certainly arose when the services had been
rendered or an act performed (as we have seen a duty might
arise even without performance, but we are not here concerned
with this possibility). The function of the doctrine was that it
provided a counter to the argument 'this sounds in covenant';
having received the thing he had bargained for the contracting
party should be compelled to pay for it. The receipt of a *quid
pro quo*, it must be noted, is thought to be relevant to the
actionability of the agreement, not to when it became binding.

[1] 27 Edw. III, f. 84.
[2] 49 Hen. VI, M. f. 18, pl. 23, and see 40 Edw. III, P. f. 24, pl. 27.
[3] 10 Hen. VI, M. f. 23, pl. 78 does not decide the point, but see Brooke's opinion
in Brooke, *Apportionment* 22, that the view stated in the text was the better view.

There might, however, arise cases where the performance of the agreement would benefit a third party, and not the person who had agreed to pay for performance. For example, A might promise B money if B, a doctor, cured a poor man; can B sue in debt for the money if he has performed the cure? In such a case B has performed his side of the agreement, and A has to this extent 'got' what he bargained for, but the beneficiary is the poor man, not the promisor. Cases involving third-party beneficiaries inevitably raised difficulties as to the precise scope of the doctrine of *quid pro quo*, and tempted lawyers who were in favour of imposing liability into extending the notion of benefit received in a somewhat artificial way. It would have been more natural, perhaps, to have justified liability, if it was to be imposed, by reference to the notion of induced reliance rather than by the notion of unjust enrichment, but it was not until the sixteenth century that this possibility was seriously canvassed.

The types of transaction which raised the problem may be broadly classified into three categories. Into the first can be placed informal agreements whereby A agrees to answer to C for the debt of D. An example would be a case of gratuitous parole guarantee—suppose D is buying bread from C, a baker, on credit, and A promises to pay the price if D defaults in the payment. Another example would be where D owe꞉ C a debt, and A promises to pay the debt if C releases D; C does so in reliance upon the promise. Here the mere fact that A had made a promise to pay the money was never thought to give rise to a duty to pay;[1] a debt must have a cause of some kind, and common lawyers, like the civilians, accepted the proposition that a nude (i.e. causeless) pact gave rise to no liability. The acceptance of this principle is illustrated by a case in 1431,[2] where Rolf, of counsel, maintained that if D was indebted to C in £20, and A bought a chattel from D for £20, and then A came to C and showed him the situation so that it was agreed that A should pay C, D being discharged, A was liable in debt to C on the contract. Cottesmore J. objected that this was *nudum pactum*.

'Rolf: I say that it is not *pactum nudum*, but *pactum vestitum*, for there was a contract between the person to whom I was

---

[1] See 5 Hen. VII, M. f. 1, pl. 1.
[2] 11 Hen. VI, P. f. 43, pl. 30.

debtor (D) and the other (C) and between me (A) and the person to whom I was debtor (D), and so this agreement between us is not *nudum pactum*. But when I grant to pay a certain sum to a man, or when I grant to pay the debt of another person to whom I am not indebted, these will be nude pacts, for in the first case there is no contract, and in the second case there is no contract or duty between me and the person to whom I grant to pay . . .'

But Cottesmore J. was not impressed:

'It is *nudum pactum* in the one case as much as in the other, for notwithstanding that all three are in agreement that he should pay this debt for the other, nevertheless the other is not discharged of his debt by anything at all. Which the whole court agreed.'

This discussion makes it clear that the references to nude and clothed pacts add little to the discussion, and the same may be said where agreements lacking a *quid pro quo* are categorized as 'naked'. Thus when Brooke, abridging the case in 1431, says,[1]

'Words or a promise to pay £10 without *quid pro quo* do not make a contract, for it is only *nudum pactum unde non oritur actio*.'

The latin tag adds little. Of the civilian learning which lay behind the maxim the common lawyers seem to have known something but perhaps not much. Common lawyers were, however, aware that their law and civil law alike rejected the idea that mere parole promises to pay were legally binding.

Thus in the case of a parole guarantee, or a promise in return for an executed release, liability, if it was to be imposed, had to be justified upon some ground other than the mere fact that there had been a promise. Further difficulty in the way of imposing liability was caused by the feeling that it was inappropriate to regard a guarantor of another person's debt as himself a debtor. By definition the guarantor promised to pay somebody else's debt, logically therefore *he* was not the debtor. Indeed, even where a guarantee was given under seal, the guarantor was liable in covenant and not in debt *sur obligation*.[2] It was hardly

---

[1] Brooke, *Contract*, pl. 33.
[2] See above, p. 17.

plausible to counter these difficulties by contending that the promisor had received a *quid pro quo*, for the benefit obviously accrued to the third party, and in the medieval period it seems clear that debt did not lie in such cases.[1] They were viewed as involving 'covenants' which were not under seal, and were therefore not actionable at common law, rather than as 'contracts' remediable by debt.

A second category of cases which caused difficulty comprised informal agreements to pay marriage dowries. The typical case is where a father agrees with a suitor to give him his daughter with a sum of money in marriage, and the suitor, having married the lady, sues for the marriage money. The leading case on this point is *Alice's Case* (1458);[2] the plaintiff had agreed to marry Alice, the defendant's daughter, and the defendant had agreed in return to pay him a hundred marks as marriage money. The marriage was celebrated, then the plaintiff sued for the dowry by writ of debt. The question of liability in such marriage agreements, which were of course normally made under seal,[3] was complicated by a jurisdictional problem, for marriage was a spiritual matter, and therefore primarily within the jurisdiction of the spiritual courts. Hence it was arguable that an agreement accessory to marriage should be within the jurisdiction of the courts which possessed jurisdiction over the principal matter. But quite apart from this objection, it was also not at all clear how such marriage agreements could be excluded from the class of parole covenants which were not, and ought not to be actionable at common law, for there was certainly no common law remedy to compel marriage, or give damages if the marriage never took place. To give a remedy in debt to one party when the other party had no remedy would seem to be unfair, for both parties should be treated equally. But if the marriage had been celebrated it could be argued that the absence of a reciprocal remedy no longer mattered; it could be

---

[1] 18 Edw. III (R.S.), 23; 44 Edw. III, T. f. 21, pl. 23. In the fifteenth century there is 9 Hen. V, M. f. 14, pl. 23 (a case of an executed release, where the promisor was held not liable because there was no *quid pro quo*; the reporter adds *ex nudo pacto non oritur actio*). There is a stronger case than a guarantee, for the original debtor is no longer liable. In 12 Hen. IV, H. f. 17, pl. 13, Thirning C.J. was in favour of liability in such a case.

[2] 37 Hen. VI, M. f. 8, pl. 18 (Fifoot 247).

[3] If under seal they were actionable at common law; 25 Edw. III, T. f. 24, pl. 30.

said that the promisor of the dowry received *quid pro quo*, in that he now had what he had bargained for. The trouble here was that the benefit appeared to accrue not to the father who promised the money, but rather to the daughter who was advanced by marriage.

No clear doctrine emerged in the medieval period, though the general trend of authority was unfavourable to liability. In 1348, before the doctrine of *quid pro quo* crystallized, Thorpe expressed himself in favour of the actionability of marriage contracts, and he drew an ingenious distinction which was designed to overcome the jurisdictional difficulty.[1] If a father promised his daughter *with* a sum of money in marriage the common law courts had no jurisdiction; if he promised money to a suitor *for* marrying the daughter then there was a contract actionable at common law. There is no decision on the point. In *Alice's Case* in 1458,[2] an inconclusive discussion showed Ashton and Danby JJ. against actionability, Moyle and Danvers JJ. in favour, and Prisot C.J. havering. Of these judges neither Ashton nor Danby based his view on the absence of *quid pro quo*—Ashton J. argued solely on jurisdictional grounds, and Danby J. thought that the case had not been properly pleaded.[3] Prisot C.J., who at first was opposed to liability, apparently took the view that there was no *quid pro quo*.[4] Both Moyle and Danvers JJ. were prepared to admit a benefit conferred on a third party as sufficient. Thus Moyle said,

'. . . though he had not got *quid pro quo*, he has the same in effect.'

Decisions against liability were given in 1475,[5] 1476,[6] and 1478[7] on jurisdictional grounds. To the decision in 1476 the reporter adds,

---

[1] 22 Lib. Ass. f. 101, pl. 70. Thorpe's distinction was picked up by the reporter in 14 Edw. IV, T. f. 6, pl. 3.
[2] 37 Hen. VI, M. f. 8, pl. 18 (Fifoot 247).
[3] The writ ran *concordatum est* and the plaintiff counted on an accord. Danby thought a 'concord' or 'accord' was a 'covenant' rather than a 'contract'.
[4] Prisot C.J. thought *quid pro quo* necessary except in a case of sale.
[5] 14 Edw. IV, T. f. 6, pl. 3.
[6] 15 Edw. IV, T. f. 32, pl. 13.
[7] 17 Edw. IV, f. 4, pl. 4, not strictly a decision, for Littleton and Choke JJ. were advising the Master of the Rolls. For another inconclusive discussion see 19 Edw. IV, H. f. 10, pl. 18, 20 Edw. IV, P. f. 3, pl. 17.

'the cause was that the defendant had no *quid pro quo*,'

which looks like an independent reason for the decision. But his idea was perhaps that if a temporal profit could be shown the case was a fit subject for temporal jurisdiction. The last of these three cases contains an interesting discussion of *quid pro quo*, in which it seems to be admitted that the requirement was satisfied so long as some sort of advantage accrued to the debtor from performance. Thus Townsend, arguing against liability on marriage contracts, said,

> '. . . if I promise you £20 to make your home anew, here no action lies for this, for he has no *quid pro quo*. And it is not the same as when I promise you 6s. each week for the commons of such a one, for then he has *quid pro quo*, and the law intends he is such a person that I, from his service, derive advantage.'

Rogers, and Suliard, arguing on the other side, contended that the defendant had *quid pro quo*,

> '. . . seeing that his daughter or friend is advanced by the marriage by intendment.'

By thus taking a loose view of what was to count as a benefit such cases could be accommodated in this way to orthodoxy.

A third category of case which was discussed involved promises of a charitable nature. The stock examples are such promises as a promise of money to a labourer who was to repair a highway, or to a surgeon who was to cure a poor man.[1] Here the promisor might derive a spiritual profit from the transaction, but the temporal advantage accrued to the third party. Again it was never settled in medieval law whether debt lay at the suit of the promisee if he performed the work requested. If, as some less orthodox lawyers thought, there could be contracts without a *quid pro quo*, such cases presented no difficulty;[2] if on the other hand *quid pro quo*, in some form, was essential, then it was dubious whether temporal courts should impose liability on the ground that the promisor had acquired, or might acquire, a purely spiritual advantage.

Uncertainty continued to prevail in the sixteenth century,

[1] 17 Edw. IV, f. 4, pl. 4.

[2] The most extreme statement of this view is by Callow in 20 Edw. IV, P. f. 3, pl. 17.

as to the status of all third party beneficiary contracts. In St. Germain's *Doctor and Student* (1530) we are told that some lawyers were prepared to allow an action,

'. . . if he to whom the promise is made have a charge by reason of the promise, which he hath also performed, then in that case he shall have an action for that thing that was promised, though he that made the promise have no worldly profit by it.'[1]

St. Germain's suggestion appears to have been limited to agreements to perform works of charity,[2] but here it must be noticed that promises of marriage money and transactions for the assistance of debtors could be regarded as falling within the conception of works of charity, as well as promises (for example) for the relief of the sick and the traveller. What is most significant in *Doctor and Student* is the appearance of an alternative to *quid pro quo*—the idea that there should be liability because there has been induced reliance upon the promise. Though St. Germain was in all probability[3] considering the action of debt[4] in the passage quoted, his 'charge' doctrine never in fact replaced or supplemented *quid pro quo* in the field *sur contract*; in *Jordan's Case* (1535),[5] where the idea could have been used, it was never mentioned. The plaintiff Jordan had released one Tatam from execution on a writ of debt upon the defendant's undertaking to pay the debt if Tatam failed to do so. Whether debt was available on these facts divided the court of King's Bench, but none of the judges discussed the 'charge' idea.

In the course of the sixteenth century, as we shall see, third party beneficiary contracts became remediable by assumpsit—indeed the fact that debt probably did not lie made it easier to justify the use of the action on the case. Only after this had

---

[1] Dial. II, c. 24 (Fifoot 326). The notion of charge is also used by Danvers J. in *Alice's Case* (1458): 'For the plaintiff is charged with the marriage of the daughter and by her espoused he is discharged, and so he has done the thing for which the sum is payable'. Danvers's point could be that the son was bound by the law of the church to marry; in the sense in which St. Germain uses the term being 'charged' cannot mean being liable.

[2] The doctrine is put forward as a compromise with the view that all charitable promises should be prima facie binding.

[3] *Sed quaere*; he may have been deliberately ignoring formulary distinctions.

[4] As opposed to assumpsit.

[5] 27 Hen VIII, M. f. 24, pl. 3 (Fifoot 353).

happened did the courts come round to saying that debt might also lie on marriage money contracts, and also on contracts for services or goods provided at request for the benefit of third parties. Thus in *Beresford* v. *Goodroufe* (1616)[1] the court accepted the distinction invented by Thorpe in the fourteenth century, and said that debt lay for money promised *for* a marriage; assumpsit had been available since *Joscelin* v. *Shelton* (1557)[2] if not earlier. In *Brett's Case* (1600)[3] it was accepted that a mother would be liable in debt for food provided at request for her son: other cases in the late sixteenth and in the seventeenth century adopt the same line.[4] As Ames pointed out,[5] these cases only allow debt against the promisor if the person receiving the benefit was himself not liable to pay for it, for they accepted a doctrine which had existed since year-book times whereby one contract could only give rise to one debt and one debtor. Thus where a servant's gown was embroidered at her mistress's request and the mistress promised to pay for the work, the embroiderer was only entitled to sue the mistress if unable to sue the servant.[6] The same principle necessarily excluded actions of debt on parole guarantees.

(*d*) CONTRACTS OF SALE

It was settled that debt lay for the price of chattels or land sold long before the doctrine of *quid pro quo* had achieved any kind of popularity. In the case of sale of chattels the common law courts possessed in the writs of debt and detinue the formulary machinery for enforcing the obligations of both buyer and seller, and in the fourteenth century there was no doubt but that both these actions could be brought without the plaintiff having to produce a specialty. In the case of sale of land the position was rather different, since the only action which the buyer could use was the writ of covenant, which only lay at common law on a deed; thus on a parole contract for the sale of

---

[1] 1 Rolle Rep. 433.

[2] 3 Leon. 4.

[3] Cro. Eliz. 755.

[4] *Applethwart* v. *Nortly* (1590) Cro. Eliz. 229 4 Leon. 56; *Stonehouse* v. *Bodville* (1674) 1 Keb. 439, T. Raymond 67; *Harris* v. *Finch* (1646) Aleyn 6.

[5] Ames, 94.

[6] *Lady Shandois* v. *Simpson* (1600) Cro. Eliz. 880, *Nelson's Case* (1587), unreported, being cited *contra*. See also *Hinson* v. *Burridge* Moo. K.B. 701.

land only the buyer's obligation to pay the price was at first enforceable. Parole contracts for the sale of land were therefore bound to throw up a problem of reciprocity of remedies, whilst sale of goods, on the other hand, was naturally provided with reciprocal remedies. Inevitably the law governing the two forms of sale developed somewhat differently.

(i) *Sale of goods: the seller's action for the price*[1]

In an action by the seller to recover the price, the plaintiff would normally aver that the price was payable on request, and base his claim to it on an averment that the defendant bought (*emisset*); he would not aver delivery of the goods. In fourteenth-century law it is possible, though by no means certain, that delivery was implied in *emisset*.[2] This would mean that in the absence of delivery (or, conversely, payment of the price) there would be no sale. If the case went to a jury on the general issue, then it would simply be a jury matter whether there had been a sale or not, and the jurymen would presumably attend to local customary practices—for example, the giving of earnest, on the handclasp. It was not possible to plead specially to raise the point, for the contract could not be traversed specially in an action in which the defendant could wage his law. In fifteenth-century law the position is much clearer; there was a good contract of sale binding the buyer to pay the price even if the goods had not been delivered. However, the buyer could, if he wished, plead a condition that delivery was to precede payment. Thus in a case in 1454[3] the defendant pleaded a condition that when the goods were delivered, *then* he would pay. The reporter notes:

'And so see that the plea was held good, and that a contract can commence on a condition. And not withstanding that the plaintiff alleged the contract generally, without any condition, yet the defendant can well allege that the contract commenced on a condition as above. But the defendant cannot traverse the contract when he can wage his law.'[4]

[1] The late medieval law of sale of goods has been very fully discussed by Milsom, 'Sale of Goods in the Fifteenth Century' 77 L.Q.R. 257
[2] Milsom, art. cit. 272.
[3] 33 Hen. VI, M. f. 43, pl. 23.
[4] What the reporter is pointing out to his students is that although the defendant cannot plead simply that 'he did not contract' (but must normally plead 'that he owes nothing') yet he can plead that he contracted on condition precedent, a

But in the absence of such a condition the buyer was bound to pay even if he had not received the goods;[1] he could not resist the seller's claim, but was put to his reciprocal action.

Some difficulty has been experienced in reconciling this state of affairs with the requirement of *quid pro quo*, for if the doctrine meant that the buyer, to be liable, must have actually received the goods, plainly sale of goods did not satisfy this requirement. But this was not what fifteenth-century lawyers meant. When they referred to *quid pro quo* in this context, their idea was that it would be unfair to say that the buyer was liable to pay (i.e. could be sued in debt) unless either he had actually received the goods or was going to receive them. Upon this view the doctrine would be satisfied if the buyer possessed an effective reciprocal remedy, so that he would, in the end, get what he had bargained for, or at least be able to sue for it. Commonly this view presented no great difficulty, for in a straightforward contract for the sale of specific goods, the buyer could take the goods from the seller, or bring an action of detinue (or debt). Since the buyer's action, whatever it was called, was conceived of as asserting a right to have the goods (which is after all the way buyers look at the matter to this day), the effect of the contract was to pass to the buyer a right to the possession of the goods, and this right was called 'property'. Since a contract of sale passed 'property' it could be, and was, regarded as a form of grant.

But this theory of sale could run into difficulties which fifteenth-century lawyers neither analysed nor solved in a satisfactory manner, since they did not very clearly distinguish between two distinct questions. The first is 'when, or in what circumstances, is a contract of sale binding?'.[2] The second is, 'when, and in what conditions is a contract of sale actionable?'. They tended to conflate these two questions, and to reason as if the answers given to the second question were answers to the

---

[1] 20 Hen. VI, T. f. 34, pl. 4; 37 Hen. VI, M. f. 8, pl. 18; 18 Edw. IV, f. 5, pl. 30 (and see H. f. 21, pl. 1, same case). Milsom, art. cit. 272.

[2] The word used to mean 'binding' in the late year-books is 'perfect'; this usage must derive from the civil law. Noticeably in the early fifteenth century there simply is no term at all to express the idea.

---

ruling which constitutes an exception to the ban on traversing the contract specially. Before this exception was recognized the correct plea would be the general issue, 'he owes nothing', and the condition could be given in evidence if the defendant opted for jury trial.

first. Thus the moment when 'property' passed ought to be the moment when the contract is actionable at the suit of the buyer, which need not necesarily be the same as the moment when the contract is made and becomes binding. Yet if there can be no contract at all without a *quid pro quo* and the *quid pro quo* is the passing of the property, this suggests that contracts must always be binding at the moment at which they become actionable.

Thus if 'property' must pass for there to be a contract *at all*, it was not at all clear how there could be contracts for the sale of future goods, for clearly nobody could have a present right to the possession of something which had not yet come into existence. This point thoroughly confused a court in 1442;[1] granted that a sale was not good unless property passed to the buyer, how could there be a sale at all if the vendor neither had the goods in his possession, nor was entitled to them? A similar difficulty was raised by a suspensively conditional contract; no right to possession passed to the buyer whilst the condition remained unperformed, so how could it be said that there was in any sense a contract before the condition was satisfied?[2] For if contracts required *quid pro quo*, and *quid pro quo* was to be satisfied by property passing, it appeared to follow that neither a sale of future goods, nor a conditional contract, could possibly rank as a contract at all.

The difficulties are classically illustrated by a case in 1488.[3] A husband seised of land in right of his wife sold 400 oaks for £20. The purchaser cut 100, and then the wife died; the husband then became tenant by the curtesy and had no right to allow the purchaser to cut any more. Consequently the purchaser's right to possession was gone; he nevertheless sued for the whole price.[4] Vavasour put the doctrine thus:

'It will be said to be contrary to reason to compel him to pay the money which is simply [i.e. unconditionally] payable where he had had nothing nor ever will have, for I take it to be a diversity that in all contracts or bargains, if the party has not *quid pro quo*, that the contract or bargain will be void. As

---

[1] 21 Hen. VI, P. f. 43, pl. 20.
[2] Hence it was worth noting that 'a contract can commence by condition'. In Roman Law very similar puzzles were raised.
[3] 18 Edw. IV, P. f. 5, pl. 30; H. f. 21, pl. 1.
[4] There was no question, as we have seen, of apportionment of a contract debt.

where I sell you a horse for £10, and I have no such horse *in rerum natura*, the contract or bargain is void.'[1]

Littleton J. seems at first to have been impressed by this, but his doubts grew as the discussion proceeded. Both he and Vavasour agreed that, if a stolen horse was sold, the contract was good and the buyer was prima facie liable to pay for it if the owner retook it after delivery; Littleton J. also thought that, if a horse sold died before delivery, the buyer remained liable in debt. The case actually before the court could be disposed of without raising these difficult theoretical issues, for the buyer had had a reasonable time to cut the oaks and it was perhaps his folly not to have cut them, but the discussion, though inconclusive, reveals that even a judge of Littleton's ability had no clear idea of the place of a doctrine of *quid pro quo* in the law of sale of goods. Indeed in *Alice's Case*[2] Prisot C.J. had contended that contracts of sale could only be viewed as exceptions to the rule that contracts require *quid pro quo*, and in *Mervyn* v. *Lyds* (1552) the doctrine is watered down to mean only that a sale requires a price.[3] Nor is this surprising, for the repetition of the dogma 'no *quid pro quo*, therefore no contract' was incapable of forming a satisfactory basis for dealing with the law of sale of goods.

(ii) *Sale of goods: the buyer's remedy*

In a sale of fungible goods the buyer's remedy was debt; where the goods were specific then there was some doubt as to whether his action was properly called debt or detinue. The prevailing view seems to have been that it was detinue, but the question was never settled in the medieval period; thus the author of *Natura Brevium*[4] firmly classifies the action as debt, although he must have been well aware of the existence of the contrary view, which had the support of lawyers as eminent as Fortescue and Brian C.JJ.

Here again we meet the doctrine that 'property' in specific goods sold passes to the buyer when the contract is made, a

[1] In 37 Hen. VI, M. f. 8, pl. 18 (Fifoot 249) Prisot C.J. contended that such a contract would be good, for *caveat emptor*; he was concerned to argue that contracts of sale did not require *quid pro quo*.

[2] See above, p. 157, n. 2.

[3] Dyer 90a.

[4] F.N.B. 119H, I. Milsom, art. cit. 257, takes this to apply to exchange.

doctrine explicitly stated in *Doige's Case* (1441-3)[1] by Fortescue C.J.:

> 'I would agree [or 'I am willing to prove'[2]] that if I buy a horse from you, now the property in the horse is in me, and, for this you shall have a writ of debt for the money and I shall have detinue for the horse on the bargain.'

In the context Fortescue is only making the point that in sale of goods, as contrasted with sale of land, there exist reciprocal common law remedies, for in the case of sale of land no right to possession[3] is acquired until delivery of seisin is made. He is not particularly concerned either with the question 'when is the contract binding' or 'when is it actionable', and in consequence no great significance can be read into his remark.[4] The position in his time appears to have been that a buyer could sue on a sale of goods for failure to deliver without averring payment of the price; the seller could, however, plead specially a condition that delivery was to precede payment.[5] This precisely mirrored the law governing the seller's right of action.

Behind this state of the law lies the view that so long as the seller can sue in debt there was no harm in letting him be sued. But the notion that a bird in the bush is as good as a bird in the hand is rather foolish. We all know that a right of action to recover a debt is not as valuable as hard cash on the nail, and in the later fifteenth century, opinion tended towards a more enthusiastic protection of sellers of goods. It came to be said that the seller, at least in cases where there was no express arrangement for credit (i.e. an agreed fixed future date for payment), had a right to retain the goods until he was paid.[6] In 1478,[7] Choke and Littleton JJ. were prepared to carry the

---

[1] 20 Hen. VI, f. 34, pl. 4, S.S. Vol. 51, p. 97 (Fifoot 347).

[2] These are variant readings, not variant translations. A variant translation would be 'I am willing to approve', which would make the sense the same in both texts.

[3] i.e. right of entry.

[4] In particular he is not attempting to rationalize the use of detinue by buyers of goods: there seems to be no evidence that this was felt to require rationalization. The rule which might have caused difficulty was that, action of detinue supposes possession precedent' (30 Edw. III, 25), but this was never followed.

[5] Milsom art. cit., 275, citing C.P. 40/521 m. 474, 8 Hen. VI, M. f. 10, pl. 24; 22 Hen. VI, M. f. 33, pl. 50.

[6] 5 Edw. IV, P. f. 2, pl. 20; 18 Edw. IV, H. f. 21, pl. 1.

[7] 17 Edw. IV, P. f. 1, pl. 2.

protection of the seller one stage further. If no right to possession
passed (i.e. no property passed) until payment then under the
dogma 'no *quid pro quo*, no contract' there could be no contract
at all in such a case until payment; thus a contract of sale was
not binding (in the absence of an express arrangement for
credit) unless there was immediate payment, and the seller
could at his option withdraw from the transaction. The
rationale of this is forcefully stated by Choke J.:

> 'For a contract cannot be perfect without the agreement of
> each party, for *dicitur de con quod est simul.* For if you ask me in
> Smithfield how much you will give me for my horse and I
> say so much, and you say you will have him and do not pay
> the money, do you believe that for all this it is my will that
> you should have him without paying the money? I say no;
> but I may at once sell him to another and you shall have no
> remedy against me. For otherwise I shall be compelled to
> keep my horse for ever against my will if the property is in
> you, and you would be able to take him when you pleased,
> which would be against reason.'

This appears paradoxical; the 'consensual' contract of sale[1]
is being rejected because of the explicit acceptance of a consensual theory of contract. In *Wheler's Case* (1522)[2] the same
approach is evident. The paradox is, however, unreal; Choke
and Littleton JJ. are not concerned to argue that there can
never be a perfect contract of sale before payment; it all depends
upon the intentions of the parties. Where they have not made
their intentions clear the law must put a reasonable construction
upon what they have done and said. Their view was in general
accepted in the late fifteenth and in the sixteenth century, and
it was in no way inconsistently held in *Wheler's Case* that if
earnest was given, or if a day for future payment was fixed (we
would say if there was an express agreement for credit), the
contract was perfect, that is 'binding' at once.[3] Once the contract was perfect the 'property'—meaning the right to posses-

---

[1] 'Consensual' can mean at least three things: (*a*) that the contract is binding
when the parties are agreed on thing sold and price, (*b*) that the contract is binding
without formality, (*c*) that the contract is binding when the parties agree to be
bound.
[2] 14 Hen. VIII, H. f. 15, pl. 1, f. 18, pl. 7 at f. 22.
[3] 14 Hen. VIII, H. f. 15, pl. 1, f. 18, pl. 7.

sion—passed to the buyer;[1] he could take the goods, sue for them in detinue, sue the seller by some form of action on the case, and perhaps sue a third party who meddled with them in trespass.[2] Where the goods were not specific no right to possession could pass until delivery, for it was at the pleasure of the seller to deliver any goods which conformed to the contractual description; the plaintiff's only remedy was to bring debt.[3] It should be noticed that according to this analysis the contract will normally become binding and actionable at the same time. It is also worth noticing that this view of sale confers upon the seller of goods a greater measure of protection than is enjoyed by the buyer; this may be explained by the fact that in the vast majority of cases the outstanding obligation in the sale of goods is the duty to pay the price, rather than the duty to deliver the goods.

(iii) *Chief Justice Brian's theory.* In opposition to the orthodox analysis was the theory put forward by Brian C.J. in 1478 and in the following year.[4] He thought that the contract was perfect even though there had been no payment (or giving of earnest or future date fixed for payment) ;[5] however, the seller had a right to retain the goods until payment or tender of payment, unless there was express agreement to the contrary, and conversely the seller could not sue for the price until he had delivered or tendered delivery. But Brian C.J. insisted that on perfection of the contract 'property' passed to the buyer, and it is this aspect of his theory of sale which is difficult to make intelligible. For he had to give 'property' some meaning which was distinct from 'right to possession'. He attempted to do so by means of an example.

'And yet I say that the property is in the defendant by the bargain in the case at bar, and in all your cases of the horses and the cloths, and yet it is not lawful for him who hath the property to take them without the other's leave . . . The case

[1] Cases referring to the 'property' doctrine are: 21 Hen. VI, P. f. 43, pl. 20; 21 Hen. VI, P. f. 55, pl. 12; 49 Hen. VI, S.S. Vol. 47, p. 163; 27 Hen. VIII, M. f. 14, pl. 6.
[2] 49 Hen. VI, S.S. Vol. 47 (Neilson), p. 163; 18 Edw. IV, P. f. 21, pl. 1.
[3] 20 Hen. VII, M. f. 8, pl. 18, Keilwey 69, 77 (Fifoot 351).
[4] 17 Edw. IV, P. f. 1, pl. 2; 18 Edw. IV, H. f. 21, pl. 1.
[5] This point is not discussed in the two cases.

is much the same as where the property remains all the time in me, and yet for a certain time I cannot take it; as where I bail certain sheep to a man to manure his fields for a certain time, here the property is in me, and yet during this time I cannot take them back.'

This is not a very satisfactory distinction when applied to sale of goods, and the truth is that his insistence that 'property' in some mysterious sense passes on perfection is an encumbrance on an otherwise simple and acceptable view of sale. What Brian C.J. was trying to say was that the contract became binding when wholly executory, though the right to possession and to payment only arose later; to explain what was meant by binding he should have concentrated upon the point that neither party could withdraw unilaterally after perfection, rather than the mysterious passing of 'property', and made this the consequence of perfection of the contract.

The reason why he attempted to link the moment when the contract became binding with the moment when the property passed was that he was unable to differentiate clearly between the idea of a contract being actionable, and its being binding on the parties. In order to say that the contract became binding when executory, he felt that he had to say that *in some sense* it became 'potentially' actionable by the writs of debt and detinue on perfection, and to explain this he maintained that the property passed—presumably to satisfy the doctrine of *quid pro quo*. The sense in which the contract was immediately actionable was this—if the buyer sued in detinue without having paid or tendered payment, he was entitled to recover *unless* the seller pleaded specially by way of defence the excuse that he was always willing to deliver on payment. This reasoning appears clearly in this passage:

'And yet I say that the property is in the defendant by the bargain in the case at bar, and in all your cases of the horses and the cloths; and yet it is not lawful for him who has the property to take them without the other's leave. And he shall have a writ of detinue, but the defendant will be excused by saying that he was ready to render them if the buyer had paid; and if he brings an action of debt he shall have the same plea.'

His point might have been better put by saying that on perfection the buyer obtains an ultimate right to possession, indefeasible without his consent, and called this right something other than 'property'.

Chief Justice Brian's analysis was not accepted in his own time or in the sixteenth century; eventually it was resurrected in the nineteenth century by Blackburn and passed into the law of sale of goods. Ever since then lawyers have been doing their inadequate best to make some sense of the doctrine. There must be a few areas of the law where the law student of the twentieth century is bemused by the faulty analysis of a fifteenth-century lawyer.[1]

(iv) *Sale of land*

Where the seller of land sued on contract by writ of debt the settled rule in the early fifteenth century (and perhaps in the fourteenth) was that there was no need to aver that the land had been conveyed.[2] But, as in the case of sale of goods, the purchaser could plead that the contract was subject to a condition that conveyance should precede payment, and such a plea, if accepted, would provide a defence to the action. Unless the vendor had covenanted under seal to convey the land, there was no question of the buyer using covenant as a reciprocal remedy; indeed even when the negotiations for the sale had been formally conducted there would normally be no such covenant. Instead the vendor would bind himself by bond to pay a penal sum to the purchaser, and the bond would be defeasible by condition subsequent if the land was conveyed by the day agreed upon in the negotiations. In practice, therefore, the remedy normally used by purchasers of land who sued at common law was debt, not covenant; viewed strictly, an obligation to convey land as such rarely if ever arose. Sellers of land were obliged to pay money, not convey land.

Until conveyance no 'property' in the land (i.e. right to enter) passed to the purchaser; this was so even where the

---

[1] Milsom has pointed out that the buyers commonly sued on a count averring that the seller before dealing was a bailee of the goods to the use of the buyer, a device which avoided the theoretical difficulties.

[2] See Milsom, art. cit. 272, and cases there cited, 19 Hen. VI, M. f. 23, pl. 47; 20 Hen. VI, T. f. 34, pl. 4; 22 Hen. VI, H. f. 43, pl. 28; 37 Hen. VI, f. 8, pl. 18.

purchaser had taken a penal bond as security for conveyance or the vendor had covenanted to convey. The purchaser's liability in debt could not be explained by any version of the doctrine of *quid pro quo*. If there was no condition he was liable although he had not received the land, and although he had no action to enforce a right to the seisin of the land. Naturally it was felt that he ought to have some sort of remedy; thus Newton C.J. said in *Doige's Case* (1441–3),[1]

> 'This will be marvellous law that a bargain will be perfect on which one party will be bound by writ of debt, and he will be without remedy against the other.'

This claim for reciprocity of remedy triumphed only to a limited extent; the purchaser obtained a right to sue in an action on the case for damages for deceit if the vendor conveyed the lands to a third party.[2] This, however, in no sense gave him a protected right to the seisin of the lands.

There is some slight evidence that in the later fifteenth century the vendor's right to sue in debt was restricted, so that he must aver conveyance before he could sue; Milsom has suggested that this indeed may have happened.[3] No doubt if the land had in fact been conveyed before the vendor sued for the price a prudent pleader would aver this, and the pleading precedents cited by Milsom may illustrate no more than this. More probably the theory of the matter was affected by the development of the doctrine that a bargain of land sales passed a 'use'[4] in the lands to the purchaser.[5] Once this doctrine became current in the early sixteenth century, the demands of reciprocity could be met by linking the liability of the purchaser in debt to his obtaining either the land or the use. Thus he would be liable either if there had been conveyance, or if there was a good bargain and sale to pass the use although the money had not been paid, which could only be the case if a future date for payment had been fixed.

---

[1] 20 Hen. VI, T. f. 34, pl. 4 (Fifoot 347).

[2] See below, p. 255.

[3] Milsom, art. cit., at 272.

[4] i.e. an equitable interest.

[5] See 21 Hen. VII, H. f. 6, pl. 4, where the link is made by Fineux C.J., and see also 21 Hen. VII, H. f. 18, pl. 30.

(e) LEASES

Debt lay to recover arrears of rent[1] due on a lease for years, such a lease being regarded as a 'contract', albeit a contract subject to somewhat special rules.[2] In strict theory the rent payable on a lease was not a payment for the use of the land analogous to the price payable for a chattel sold. Instead rent was viewed as a share of the profits of the subject-matter of the lease which the lessor reserved to himself (i.e. excluded from the grant) when he granted the lease; hence rent 'issued' out of the property demised during the term. The property indeed need not be land. Thus in 1422[3] a case is reported on the lease of a flock of sheep for a term of three years at an annual rental of four pence per sheep, fifteen pence being payable at the end of the term for any sheep missing; the lessor brought his action for a hundred shillings, which was made up partly out of rent in arrear and partly on account of certain sheep which had died. Such a flock, being capable of increase, could as well be made subject to a lease reserving rent as could land, and the practice is not extinct today. So also could certain incorporeal rights— for example, the profits of a rectory could be farmed.

In general a lease could be made by parole, and on a parole lease debt lay.[4] The action of debt for rent was, in two important respects, different from an ordinary action on a parole contract. The general rule was that a contract debt (or a debt by bond) was an 'entire thing', which could only be demanded *in toto*, and only when the whole sum fell due,[5] but this rule was not applied to rent due periodically.

'Debt on an obligation is an entire duty, and therefore it must be demanded entirely, although parcel is paid, but here the duty is in manner several, and for each term or each year he can have a writ of debt.'[6]

---

[1] Including rent due in kind. See 50 Edw. III, T. f. 16, pl. 8, where it is said that the writ must be 'in the detinet', and see *Lord Denny* v *Parrell* (1605) Rolle *Dett*, 591 pl. 1. On covenant at election see above, p. 70.

[2] See 7 Hen. VII, M. f. 4, pl. 5 and the note in Brooke, *Joinder* 90.

[3] 1 Hen. VI, M. f. 1, pl. 3.

[4] The right to sue for rent passed with the reversion, and the obligation to pay rent passed to an assignee of the land, see 9 Hen. VI, M. f. 52, pl. 35; 5 Hen. VII, P. f. 18, pl. 12.

[5] See above, p. 66.

[6] *Per* Strange, 7 Hen. VI, P. f. 24, pl. 4.

Hence in some circumstances the rent could be apportioned in time; thus if the lessor entered upon the lessee during the term liability to pay rent thereafter ceased.

The action also differed in the method of trial, for on a lease of land, or of land with beasts, wager of law was not permissible.[1] In fifteenth-century law the reason given for this rule was the notoriety of the transaction; a lease (which was only perfect on entry) lay within the knowledge of the country, and therefore gave rise to trial by jury. In sixteenth-century law the rationale for the rule changed;[2] it was said that wager was excluded upon the ground that a lease was concerned with the realty, and it was a general principle that wager was excluded in actions concerning realty. Had this been the theory of the matter in the fifteenth century, wager might have well been excluded in contracts for the sale of land, whereas in fact it was permitted.[3] The exclusion of wager in actions for rent gave rise to some difficulty in actions brought to recover money due for board and lodging, where the landlord (as in a case in 1469)[4] might aver in his count a lease of the lodger's chamber simply as a device to exclude wager. In order to counter this trick the defendant needed to be permitted to plead to the action in some way which protected his right to wage, but how quite he could do so was uncertain. One possibility was a special traverse of the lease coupled with a tender of wager in answer to the price for the price of board and lodging;[5] another possibility was a demurrer to the count as a whole.[6] The position was complicated by the fact that there seems to have been a current of authority in favour of excluding wager in contracts for board and lodging on the ground of notoriety, whether or not such contracts involved a lease of the lodger's chamber.

Though leases could in general be made by parole they were more commonly made by indentures under seal, and in an action for rent the lessor in such a case would normally base his

[1] 1 Hen. VI, M. f. 1, pl. 3; 9 Edw. IV, P. f. 1, pl. 1. In the fourteenth century wager may have been possible, see 50 Edw. III, T. f. 16, pl. 8.

[2] The change is apparent in Brooke, *Ley Gager*, pl. 97 (1542).

[3] 22 Hen. VI, H. f. 43, pl. 28.

[4] 9 Edw. IV, P. f. 1, pl. 1.

[5] This involved severing an entire count, which some thought objectionable: see 21 Edw. IV, P. f. 28, pl. 24.

[6] In the case in 1469 the count was arguably defective in form as originally tendered.

count upon the indenture and produce his part. But indentures of lease, unlike bonds, were not treated as dispositive documents which generated the liability, but as merely evidentiary. The distinction is clearly put by Rolf in a case in 1422,[1] though in another context,

'I put the case that I lend a man a horse by indenture, and I bring a writ of debt[2] [*sic*] on the loan without showing the indenture, will you have this plea—"that I have an indenture of the same contract, and are you to have an action without showing forth the indenture"? You will not ... But in the case which you put of an obligation I grant well, for the obligation and the contract are two separate contracts, and by the greater I am discharged from the lesser.'

Rolf's doctrine was applied to indentures of lease, with the consequence that, even if a lease was made by indenture, the lessee could answer the action in just the same way as he could if the lease was made by parole, by pleading defences (such as the defence that the sum in demand had been levied by distress) which were not based on some formal document but rested upon his mere parole averment. Thus the tenant could plead the general issue ('nothing owing') and substantiate this plea by giving in evidence to the jury the fact that he had paid the money due, without having to produce an acquittance under seal, which would have been essential had the indentures been regarded as dispositive documents.[3]

(f) ARBITREMENT AND ACCORD

It was a common practice in medieval England for disputes and quarrels to be submitted by the parties to the decision of

[1] 1 Hen. VI, M. f. 7, pl. 31.
[2] i.e. detinue.
[3] 44 Edw. III, M. f. 42, pl. 46; 45 Edw. III, H. f. 4, pl. 9; 33 Hen. VI, H. f. 3, pl. 12; 5 Edw. IV, T. f. 43 (Long Quinto); 10 Hen. VII, T. f. 24, pl. 32. 4 Hen. VI, P. f. 17, pl. 1. is contrary. The pleading rules in actions of debt for rent were complex. Since wager was normally excluded, a special traverse of the lease was good. It was much disputed whether a plea of payment which did not conclude 'and so nothing owing' was admissible where the action was brought in a county different from where the land was. See 34 Hen. VI, M. f. 17, pl. 32; 37 Hen. VI, M. f. 10, pl. 21; 22 Hen. VI, H. f. 36, pl. 1; 33 Hen. VI, H. f. 3, pl. 12; 28 Hen. VI, P. f. 6, pl. 2. After some doubt it was settled in 10 Hen. VII, M. f. 4, pl. 1, that accord and satisfaction was a good plea.

one or more arbitrators selected by the parties. Most commonly such a submission would be made binding upon the parties by private formal contract. The technique employed was for the parties to execute mutual conditioned bonds whereby they became obliged to pay penal sums unless they performed the arbitrator's award. The whole purpose of a submission to arbitration would be frustrated unless the parties were prevented from bringing actions in the courts based upon the disputes which they had submitted to arbitration, and there were two ways in which this problem could be handled. At the time of the submission they could both execute releases of all causes of action (or of those causes which were the subject of the submission), or alternatively the matter might be left to the arbitrator, who could, as part of his award, decide what actions ought to be released. Thus in a case in 1505,[1] three persons bound themselves mutually to submit to the award of arbitrators, who awarded that one should pay another a certain sum of money, and that the payee should release all manner of actions. In this case it was held that the payment of the money and the execution of the release were concurrently conditional; one need only pay (to avoid forfeiting his bond) if the other released, and vice versa. Hence if the two parties co-operated the money would be paid and the actions released, and if one or other failed to co-operate the penal sum imposed by the conditional bond which he had executed would be forfeit. But the actions would not be released, which might produce inconvenient results. So long, however, as the penal sums were large enough the parties would have a strong motive for co-operation.

A submission to arbitration could, however, be informal, the parties simply agreeing by parole to the arrangement. In such an event, if the arbitrator awarded that one should pay the other a sum of money, the action of debt lay to enforce this award.[2] But the method of trial in such an action was wager of law,[3] for the decision of the arbitrator was not treated as having the same status as the judgment of a court of record.

Besides being itself actionable by writ of debt, an informal

[1] 21 Hen. VII, f. 28, pl. 7.
[2] If debt was brought, the plaintiff must set out the cause and details of the award specially; see 5 Edw. IV, P. f. 1, pl. 5.
[3] 21 Hen. VI, H. f. 30, pl. 14; 4 Hen. VI, P. f. 17, pl. 3.

award could in certain circumstances be pleaded in bar to an action based upon a claim which had been made the subject of a submission to arbitration—typically 'arbitrement' was a good plea in answer to an action of trespass if trespasses had been submitted to arbitration. But there were certain actions to which 'arbitrement' was not a defence; for example, it was no plea to an action based upon a specialty, for the deed must be met with a deed, or to debt on account before auditors.[1] The broad principle was that the defence was permissible to actions based upon a mere parole averment of the plaintiff.

According to this principle one would expect to find that arbitrement was a good defence to an action of debt *sur contract* (but not to debt *sur obligation*). But this was not the precise position, for a claim to a debt could not, by itself, be made the subject-matter of an arbitration. This peculiar rule arose because it was not conceived to be the function of arbitration to replace regular adjudication on the existence of rights of action. The function was rather to settle a confused and uncertain state of accounts between disputants who admittedly had claims and counter claims, and who were prepared to settle their differences if only someone would tell them precisely what ought in justice to be done to sort out the mess. Consequently Hugo and Robert could not validly submit to arbitration Hugo's claim to a debt of £50 owed him by Robert; they must either agree between themselves or litigate regularly. They could, however, submit this claim and other trespasses to arbitration, and thus admit a confused state of affairs which was a suitable subject for arbitration. Hence it was reported in 1494:[2]

> 'Also it was agreed at another day that no manner of debt by itself lies in arbitrement, nor in concord, for arbitrement exists to reduce an uncertain thing to a certainty, and not one certainty into another. But it was agreed that debt, as well for arrears of a lease as on a contract, with trespasses, lies in concord or arbitrement.'

(The references to 'concord' will be explained in a moment.)

Subject to this qualification, 'arbitrement' was a good plea in actions of debt *sur contract*. If the award had actually been

[1] 4. Hen. VI, Pf. 17, pl. 3.
[2] 10 Hen. VII, M. f. 4, pl. 4. See also 4 Hen. VI, P. f. 17, pl. 3.

performed no further difficulty was involved. But suppose that the award had been made but still remained executory, so that the party pleading the defence had not yet done what was required of him. Since the award was itself actionable in debt (if what was required was payment of money), there was a case for saying that even an executory award should provide a defence. Although there was some doubt, a compromise position appears to have been adopted; the rule was that the party relying on the defence must not be in default.[1] Thus in order to rely on the plea of 'arbitrement' the party must have either performed the award or have been always ready and willing to perform (*tout temps prist*), or he must show that under the terms of the award the date for performance fixed by the arbitrator had not yet arrived.

We can now conveniently consider the analogous problems raised by a concord or accord, the names given to an agreement reached between parties to a dispute without the intervention of a third party as arbitrator. An informal accord might well take the form of an agreement that one party should pay the other a certain sum of money, but the rule was that on an accord as such no action of debt lay, although if the accord involved the performance of some act in return (such as the execution of a deed of release) the agreement might be binding upon the other party, once there had been performance, as a 'contract' which satisfied the doctrine of *quid pro quo*; on this point there is scant authority.[2]

Since an accord was not as such actionable, there was no question of pleading an executory accord in bar to an action. If, however, an accord that money was paid, or some chattel delivered, was executed by actual payment or delivery in satisfaction, then the fact that it had not been actionable ceased to matter. Hence 'accord and satisfaction' was a good plea in certain actions; again the typical example is trespass. Though there seems to have been some slight doubt on the point, debt *sur contract* was one such action.[3] There was, however, dispute as to whether a payment of a lesser sum than the

---

[1] See 19 Hen. VI, M. f. 36, pl. 90; 20 Hen. VI, M. f. 11, pl. 24; 20 Hen. VI, H. f. 18, pl. 12; 28 Hen. VI, T. f. 12, pl. 25; 33 Hen. VI, H. f. 2, pl. 8; 9 Edw. IV, M. f. 43, pl. 30; and see Brooke, *Arbitrement*, pl. 3.

[2] See above, p. 148.

[3] See 10 Hen. VII, M. f. 4, pl. 4.

debt could rank as a satisfaction at all, though it was admitted that the delivery of a chattel of uncertain value did so count.[1] But in all probability it did not much matter, for where a lesser sum had been accepted in satisfaction the debtor could get over the difficulty in one of two ways. He could plead that the accord concerned not only the debt but all other trespasses as well, or he could plead a fictional arbitrement concerned with both the debt and the other trespasses.[2] Either technique served equally well.

(g) DEBT TO RECOVER THE ARREARS OF AN ACCOUNT

In certain circumstances a person might be bound at law to render an account to another; for example, a bailiff of a manor had to account to the manorial lord for the profits of the manor. If such a person failed to render an account he could be compelled to do so in the action of account. In this action the court would decide whether the defendant owed a duty to account; if he did, auditors were then assigned to investigate the state of accounts and determine who owed what. Once this had been determined, a fixed sum of money became due at law, and if this money was not paid, an action of debt lay to recover the money. The auditors assigned by the court to take the accounts were regarded as possessing the status of judges of record, and in consequence in such an action of debt the defendant was not entitled to wage his law. The point which needs to be grasped is that it was not an action which lay to recover the money, or anything else. Its function was to compel the defendant to render an account. Once an account was rendered, the action had served its purpose; any money found to be due was recoverable by writ of debt. As a general rule, therefore, the action was not appropriate except in cases where the amount due was not determined at the outset by the transaction between the parties; where an initially liquidated sum was due (as in the case of a simple loan) there was no need to compel the defendant to render an account, and so account generally did not lie. Furthermore, if the defendant had rendered an account he had a complete answer to the action; there was no point in making him account if he had already done so, and it was wholly

---

[1] For a discussion of the cases see above, p. 105.
[2] See 10 Hen. VII, M. f. 4, pl. 4.

irrelevant that he had not settled the account by payment; the remedy for failure to pay was debt, not account.[1]

Very commonly a person who was accountable would voluntarily render an account, which he might do either to the principal himself (the accountee)[2] or to one or more auditors appointed (the technical expression is 'assigned') by the accountee;[3] by doing this he discharged his duty to account. Precisely what was involved in rendering an account is not at all clear; it seems to have been purely a jury matter on which no legal rules existed. But once an account was rendered voluntarily, whether before auditors or to the accountee himself,[4] an action of debt lay on the account to recover whatever arrears were due. It might happen that when the accounts were taken it appeared that there was a surplus due to the accountant; if so, this sum could in some circumstances be recovered by writ of debt.[5] The correct mode of trial in the action of debt depended upon the manner in which the account was taken. If taken before two or more auditors, wager was excluded upon the ground that the auditors were equivalent to judges of record, but where there was only one auditor, or the account was rendered to the plaintiff alone, wager was allowed. This encouraged plaintiffs into falsely declaring upon a fictional account before two auditors in order to oust the defendant of wager. To counter this, the defendant was allowed to tender wager and pray that the plaintiff's attorney be examined by the court on the veracity of his declaration; if it transpired that the declaration was false the defendant would then be admitted to wage his law.

The theoretical basis of liability in debt for the arrears of an account rendered voluntarily is a matter of some difficulty and obscurity. The general principle was, as Jackson put it, that

[1] For authorities see below, p. 179.
[2] See Rastell, *Entries*, 147b for a specimen count known as an *insimul computaverunt*.
[3] For an example see *Shymplyng* v. *Parly* 13 Ric. II (A.S.), 95.
[4] 45 Edw. III, M. f. 14, pl. 13; 13 Ric. II (A.S.), 20; 7 Hen. IV, P. f. 14, pl. 17; 34 Hen. VI, T. f. 34, pl. 4. The objection that the accountee was thereby made judge in his own cause was not accepted as a reason for denying liability.
[5] 7 Hen. IV, M. f. 3, pl. 18; 38 Hen. VI, M. f. 5, pl. 14. The right only existed if the accountant was a bailiff, since the two other categories of accountant (receivers and guardians in socage) had no right to claim expenses. This point is finally settled in the seventeenth century in *The Count of Suffolk v. Floyd*, 1 Rolle Abr. 599 pl. 15.

'Liability arose not from the pre-existing claims, nor from any promise, but *from the accounting itself*.'[1]

Hence the act of accounting discharged all prior liability, and gave rise to the duty to pay the arrears. In a case in 1406,[2] Thirning C.J. thus stated the principle:

'If a man once accounts before an auditor, or before the plaintiff, he is discharged from accounting for all time, because if there are any arrears, he will have a writ of debt for them, for by the account the action against him is put into another course.'

Suppose, however, that a person rendered an account when he was under no legal liability to do so—would he then be liable to pay the arrears simply because he had accounted voluntarily? Two fifteenth-century cases appear to say that he would be liable.

One is reported in 1401.[3] Debt was brought against a man and his wife. The wife was executrix of her late former husband, and she had herself accounted for certain receipts by her late husband, and had been found in arrear for a sum of 100s. She could not have been compelled to account, but since she had voluntarily done so she was put to answer the action. The reporter notes the principle:

'by the account she is chargeable, where she was not chargeable before.'

Again, in 1412,[4] a manorial bailiff voluntarily accounted to his lord before he was compellable to do so; he was held liable in debt upon the ground that he had charged himself by accounting early. Jackson[5] has, however, argued that if the defendant was not legally bound to account, but nevertheless did so, he could not be sued in debt for arrears found either on an account before auditors, or before the plaintiff himself, and cites two fifteenth-century authorities in favour of this view. But it seems doubtful whether these cases go so far. The first is a case in 1429.[6]

---

[1] Jackson, *Quasi-Contract*, 28.
[2] 7 Hen. IV, P. f. 14, pl. 17.
[3] 2 Hen. IV, H. f. 13, pl. 2.
[4] 13 Hen. IV, H. f. 12, pl. 3.
[5] Jackson does not appear to have considered these two cases.
[6] 8 Hen. VI, M. f. 10, pl. 25, f. 15, pl. 36.

Debt was brought and the plaintiff declared on an account before auditors. This count was apparently fictitious, and was designed to oust the defendant from his wager of law, for when the plaintiff was examined it transpired that the defendant owed the plaintiff for the price of goods which he had bought and that it was this sum which was the subject-matter of the account. The first report of the case suggests that the proper course was for the plaintiff to amend his declaration and declare on the contract, since a purchaser of goods was not legally liable to render an account. The second report, however, adopts a different solution—the plaintiff's declaration is allowed to stand, but the defendant is permitted to wage his law. The second case is in 1441;[1] debt was brought for the arrears of an account before auditors, and the defendant tendered wager of law and prayed examination. It appeared on examination that the defendant was lessee of a hostelry together with its equipment; he had not paid the rent and some of the chattels were wasted and some lost. Newton pointed out that this showed that the defendant was not liable to an action of account, but to debt for the rent and detinue for the goods, and said that he must bring these actions and not sue in debt on account. It is not clear from the case whether the defendant had in fact accounted or not.

The interpretation of these two cases is problematical. In both, the court is primarily concerned to prevent the plaintiff from ousting the defendant from his right to wager of law by declaring on an account taken before two auditors. One possible hypothesis is that in neither case did any such accounting in fact take place. On this assumption the first case merely holds that although the fictitious count is allowed to stand the defendant can wage; the second is that the plaintiff must begin all over again and bring two honest actions. Neither case, on this interpretation, is inconsistent with the view that where the defendant actually did account (either before auditors, or before the plaintiff himself) he could be sued in debt on the account although not compellable to account. An alternative view is that in both cases the defendant actually did account before auditors. The first case then holds that the defendant is thereby rendered liable, but can wage his law; the second that

[1] 20 Hen. VI, H. f. 16, pl. 2.

the accounting does not generate liability. Neither, however, deals with the case of a defendant who accounted to the plaintiff (where the question of ousting the defendant from wager of law would not arise). Of these two interpretations I prefer the first.

If I am right in supposing that a person who voluntarily accounted to the plaintiff (although not liable to account) could be sued in debt on the account, it becomes possible to understand the form of declaration known as an *insimul computaverunt*, which was used both in the action of debt and later in the actions of assumpsit. According to the form given by Rastell (which would be in use in the first half of the sixteenth century or earlier),[1] the plaintiff who used this form of declaration in an action of debt averred that the defendant, on a specified date and at a specified place,

> 'accounted [*computasset*] with the said C [the plaintiff] for diverse sums of money previously received of the said C by by said A [the defendant] to render an account thereof to him when required . . .'

and went on to aver that the defendant was found in arrears to the extent of the sum claimed. The declaration thus averred that the defendant was a 'receiver'—one of the categories of person liable to account and compellable by writ of account to do so.[2] On my interpretation of the fifteenth-century cases this averment was immaterial, and it would be no answer to the action to plead 'never receiver'. If this view is correct, an *insimul computaverunt* would be usable to claim the balance of any account settled voluntarily between merchants, even though the relationship between the parties was not one which gave rise to an obligation to account. For example, suppose Robert has bought wool in various parcels from Hugo to the value of £70, and Hugo has bought cattle from Robert on various occasions to the value of £40, then, so long as they account together, debt on an *insimul computaverunt* would lie to recover the balance due of £30. The utility of the action would, however, be limited by the fact that it was subject to wager of law.

Some support for this view is provided by the fact that a

---

[1] Rastell, *Entries*, 147b.
[2] The other categories are bailiff and guardian in socage.

seventeenth-century precedent for an *insimul computaverunt*
count in debt[1] drops the averment that the defendant was a
receiver; no attempt is made to show that the defendant was
compellable to account to the plaintiff. In the meanwhile, an
insimul computaverunt declaration had come to be used in the
action of assumpsit, which action was not subject to wager of
law.[2] In assumpsit the plaintiff averred an accounting together,
a sum found in arrears, and a promise by the defendant to pay
that sum,[3] supported by consideration in the form of the indebtedness arising from the rendering of the account. In assumpsit
there was certainly no need to show that the defendant was
compellable to account to the plaintiff;[4] all that mattered was
that he had in fact accounted and promised to pay the arrears.

'They accepting together and he promising to pay, was a
sufficient cause of the action.'[5]

(h) 'BAILMENTS' OF MONEY: THE BOUNDARY BETWEEN DEBT AND ACCOUNT

If money was bailed in a sealed box by way of deposit, the
transaction was treated as similar to a normal deposit of a
chattel; hence the bailor's remedy was detinue, not debt. In
such cases money was not treated as money, and this is understandable enough.

[1] 2 Brownl. and Goulds (1621).

[2] *Whorwood* v. *Gybbons* (1587) Goulds. 48, though cited by Jackson (op. cit)
104 and Lücke (81 L.Q.R. 547), is not an action of this type; the consideration
there was forbearance to sue. The development post-dates *Slade's Case* in 1602;
an early example is *Egles* v. *Vale* (1606) Cro. Jac. 69, which may indeed have
established this form of declaration.

[3] The averment of a promise suggested the modern rationale of actions on
'accounts stated'—the defendant is liable because he is supposed (through having
promised) to have admitted that he owes money. In debt on account no promise
was involved; hence liability was not based on any supposed admission or estoppel.
If there was a rationale it must have been that the operation of accounting rendered it certain what sum was due.

[4] Jackson, op. cit. 105 regards this as doubtful, but see *Bard* v. *Bard* (1616) Cro.
Jac. 602. Jackson's interpretation of *Milward* v. *Ingram* (1675) 2 Mod. 43 seems to
me to be incorrect. In that case the point made is that an accounting together
discharges any contract debts brought into account, and leaves only the obligation
to satisfy the account; hence one cannot sue for the debts in *indebitatus assumpsit*
on the contract, but one can only bring *insimul computaverunt* on the account. An
accounting certainly creates a debt, but the action to recover this debt is not called
indebitatus assumpsit.

[5] *Bard* v. *Bard* (1616) Cro. Jac. 602.

The legal position where there was a 'bailment' of money which was not in a sealed container was for long uncertain. Thus suppose Robert deposits £10 with Hugo to be safely guarded and returned on request; such a transaction is not a loan but a deposit: in Roman Law terminology it must be classified not as *mutuum* but as *depositum irregulare*, for it is not the intention that the transferee should have the use of the money. It was never really settled in medieval law whether in such a case Robert should use debt or account if Hugo failed to repay the money.[1] The point was still regarded as arguable in 1599, when it was held in *Bretton v. Barnet*[2] that the depositor could use debt. Probably he could also use account, but the point is unimportant since there would be no advantage in so doing. The availability of debt meant that *indebitatus assumpsit* could be used, once that form of assumpsit came to be established.

The suggestion that account was the proper remedy for a depositor of money seems peculiar, for the action of account seems an appropriate remedy only in situations where there is a need to take accounts to settle precisely what sum can properly be claimed by writ of debt. Thus, to take the example of a recalcitrant manorial bailiff, there must be two stages in bringing him to book. He must first be made to account, for until he does so his lord will not know how much he ought to pay; if he still proves awkward he must be made to pay the debt he has been found to owe. But in situations where there was no initial uncertainty account seems unnecessary, and in general it was not available in such cases. Thus if Robert lent Hugo £10, Hugo was not liable to account to Robert for this sum; he simply had to pay it back, and could be sued in debt if he failed to do so.

Nevertheless, there were certain other situations (apart from the case of deposit) where account was certainly the proper remedy, and excluded debt, although the situation was such that there would seem to be no point in taking accounts, the sum in issue being liquidated from the outset.

Thus suppose A transferred money to B to pay it over to C. Here the analogy to a chattel bailment to bail over or deliver

---

[1] See 4 Hen. VI, M. f. 2, pl. 4; 18 Hen. VI, M. f. 20, pl. 5; 6 Edw. IV, H. f. 61, pl. 6; 2 Ric. III, M. f. 14, pl. 39.
[2] Owen 86.

over is very close indeed; B is a mere intermediary; he is not to
have the use of the money (as in the case of a *mutuum*) at all, but
C is. Such a transaction could be described as a payment by A
to B 'to the use of' C. What are the remedies of A and C if the
intermediary, B, misbehaves himself by retaining the money?
It was settled in medieval law that C's remedy was by writ of
account:

> 'If I bail certain coins to you to bail to John, he will have a
> writ of account, because the property is in him as soon as
> you receive them from my hands, and he certainly cannot
> have an action by writ of debt.'[1]

C claimed that B was accountable because he had received the
money to C's use. Although some writers have maintained the
contrary,[2] there is no evidence in medieval law that C could
use debt as an alternative action.[3] The reason why debt was not
available is uncertain. Brooke,[4] writing in the middle of the
sixteenth century, seems to have thought that the difficulty was
the absence of 'privity'—the third party was a stranger to the
transaction. The passage quoted is from a case in 1367, and the
discussion in that case suggests a different explanation; debt
only lies against one who has 'property' in the coins (in the
sense that the specific coins are his), but a mere intermediary
(unlike a borrower) is not to use the coins himself but pass them
on to the third party. In sixteenth-century law it came to be
suggested that the third party could, if he wished, use debt or
account at his election,[5] and this was eventually settled in the

---

[1] *Per* Cavendish *arguendo* in 41 Edw. III, P. f. 10, pl. 5, F.N.B. 116 Q, *Core's Case* (1537) Dyer 20a at 21b *per* Luke J.

[2] See *H.E.L.* III. 326; Jackson, *Quasi-Contract*, 31, *dubitante*.

[3] Wangford in 36 Hen. VI, f. 7, pl. 4 at f. 9, properly understood, does not maintain the contrary. He says that if B owes A money, and at A's command pays this money to C , which discharges the debt, A can sue C in debt on account. This is not the case discussed in the text, and in any event Wangford's point is merely to say that C is liable one way or the other, it being irrelevant to his argument to say what the correct form of action is.

[4] See 11 Hen. VI, T. f. 39, pl. 31. Brooke, *Dette* pl. 130, which has the marginal note 'vers estranger sans privity'. Brooke here suggests that debt is available to the third party as well as account, and what strikes him as curious is that this should be possible in the absence of privity. See also *Account* pl. 61; both notes are based upon 36 Hen. VI, f 7, pl. 4. Luke J. in *Core's Case* also regarded the absence of a 'contract' between B and C as an objection to C's using debt.

[5] Brooke, *Dette* pl. 130, *Account* pl. 61, Dyer 152a *in margine contra*.

seventeenth century.[1] By then, to allow debt was to allow *indebitatus assumpsit*, and this, as Ames pointed out, is the origin of the count in *indebitatus assumpsit* for money had and received to the plaintiff's use.

A's remedy in medieval law, like C's, was account and not debt.[2] Presumably the reason for this was that in such a transaction it was not the intention that B should become A's debtor, for the money was to be paid to C and not to A. But it was held in *Core's Case* (1537)[3] that A could use debt at his election.

'And so it is if I bail £10 to you to give in alms for me, now you are accountable to me, for the property remains always in me until the alms be performed, and I can order you not to do the thing, and if you retain the £10 in your hands after, I shall have a good action of debt on this against you.'

In reaching this conclusion the court relied in part upon a curious case in 1367.[4] A purchaser of land sued a vendor in account; the vendor traversed the receipt, and it was found that £10 had been bailed to him on condition that if he enfeoffed the plaintiff of land he was to keep the money, and if not he was to rebail it to the plaintiff. It was said in this case that debt and account were alternative remedies. This case could have given rise to a general right of action in debt for (as we would say) money paid on a consideration which wholly failed, but in fact it does not appear to have been relied upon in medieval law, at least so far as the action of debt is concerned.[5]

The Medieval Conception of a Contract

These then were the more important situations in which the action of debt was available although the plaintiff could show no sealed instrument whereby the defendant had become his

[1] *Shaw* v. *Norwood* (1600) Moo. K.B. 667; *Clark's Case* (1614) Godbolt 210; *Greenvile* v. *Slaning* (1616) cited in *Harris* v. *de Bervoir* (1624) Cro. Jac. 687, 2 Rolle 440.
[2] 2 Hen. IV, M. f. 12, pl. 50; 21 Edw. IV, M. f. 38, pl. 5 at f. 42, and see generally Ames 119–20 and cases there cited.
[3] Dyer 20a.
[4] 41 Edw. III, P. f. 10, pl. 5.
[5] Disappointed purchasers could have averred a payment on condition as a fiction although there was in fact no such express condition.

debtor. The list is somewhat miscellaneous; it did not evolve as the expression of some general theory of debt liability. However, the medieval common lawyer could not fail to be aware of the fact that the debts which could be sued for in the action of debt *sur contract* normally arose as the consequence of some sort of voluntary transaction between debtor and creditor. The conception of 'contract' which he possessed certainly reflects this fact of legal and social life.

Now the history of legal doctrine is primarily concerned with the way in which people thought rather than the way in which they acted, and here, as elsewhere in the history of ideas, it is all too easy to suppose that because men of another age used a word which we use, their conception of the meaning of the word was the same as ours. It would be quite mistaken to suppose that a medieval lawyer meant precisely what we mean by the term 'contract'; so much is clear. But it is much more difficult to identify precisely what was meant by the term. This need not surprise us, for just as our modern notion of 'contract' is somewhat elusive and vague, so was his. Thus today some lawyers would call a deposit of a chattel a contract, and some would not. Similarly Brooke, in the sixteenth century, thought it worthwhile to make a special note of the fact that a lease for years was a contract,[1] and he could only have done so if there was some doubt as to whether it was or not.

Although in the early writers on English law some use is made of a general conception of contract, and we even find in *The Mirror of Justices* 'contract' defined as

'a discourse [*purparlance*] between persons that something that is not done shall be done,'[2]

the evolution of a native common law concept took a considerable period of time, and was beset by special difficulties. The common lawyers, like the Roman jurists, started life with a list of transactions which were actionable through the procedural forms within which they had to work, rather than with a general principle of actionability; it was settled, for example, that debt could be brought to recover informal loans, or the

[1] Brooke, *Joinder* pl. 90, based on 7 Hen. VII, M. f. 4, pl. 5. The source of the doubt is understandable: a lessee for years could be regarded as chargeable through his occupation of the land rather than as party to a consensual transaction.
[2] S.S. Vol. 7 (Whittaker and Maitland), p. 73.

price of chattels sold, long before any great progress had been made towards the evolution of a general conception of contract. Throughout the medieval period lawyers seem in general to have continued to think in terms of a catalogue of particular transactions. Indeed for most purposes it was not in the least necessary that they should do more. From time to time brave efforts were made to carry things further than this but these efforts were not attended by any conspicuous degree of success, and this perhaps is not surprising. For there was a radical difficulty in the way of the evolution of any general principles which would govern the actionability of informal agreements at common law: it was that such agreements were only partially covered by the common law forms of action.

It had been settled in the fourteenth century that the action of covenant, the remedy for failure to *do* something as agreed, did not lie at common law on a parole agreement; anomalously it was also settled that failure to pay a sum certain or hand over a chattel (but not land) as agreed was actionable at common law by writ of debt or detinue. The consequence was that the common law was only concerned with informal agreements to a limited extent, and the limit imposed was quite irrational. For example, in the case of an informal agreement for service in return for a sum certain by way of salary, one half of the agreement was enforceable at common law whilst the other half was not.[1] Against such a background it was hardly likely that any sophisticated generalizations about informal agreements would be developed. In the year-books the term 'contract' came to be earmarked for those informal agreements which could give rise to an action of debt (or occasionally detinue), for the good reason that only such agreements were the concern of the common law. But unfortunately the common law was only partially concerned with them.

'Contract' and 'Agreement'

Now the year-book term for an agreement was 'covenant'. It is sometimes said that the 'contract' of the medieval common law has little connection with the notion of agreement.[2] This

[1] See above, p. 148.
[2] See, for example, Jackson, 'The Scope of the Term Contract', 53 L.Q.R. 525.

is an exaggeration; the lawyers of the time were well aware of the fact that the standard debt contracts were the product of the agreement of the parties, at least as a general rule, so that there was a relationship between 'contract' and covenant. Thus Vampage, arguing in a case in 1428,[1] had this to say on the distinction between tortious and contractual liability:

'But it would be inconvenient to have an action of trespass and debt for one same thing, for they are entirely contrary. For one commences by contract and the assent of the parties, and the demand is for a duty, and the ground of action is a duty, and the other commences by tort, and without the assent of the parties, and the demand is to have the tort punished, which is prima facie an uncertain punishment . . .'

Even more emphatic statements of the relationship between 'contract' and 'agreement' are to be found in *Wheler's Case* (1522).[2] Thus Pollard J. there said,

'And to speak of bargains and sales, sir, all these depend upon the negotiations [communication] and words between the parties. For some bargains can take effect at once and others on a thing to be done afterwards, and they can be subject to condition and nevertheless be perfect, although there will be no *quid pro quo* immediately, and all this depends upon the negotiations between you and me. For example, if I am to have £20 for my horse, and I agree to this, now if you do not pay the money at once this is no bargain, for my agreement is for the £20, and if you do not pay them at once, now you do not act in conformity with my agreement.'

Brundenell C.J. made the same point,

'Sir, as has been said, bargains and sales are as concluded and agreed between the parties, however their intentions can be taken.'[3]

Other examples of the same sort of reasoning can be found in the year-books.[4]

[1] 7 Hen. VI, M. f. 5, pl. 9.
[2] 14 Hen. VIII, H. f. 15, pl. 1, f. 18, pl. 7, at f. 21 and 22.
[3] Both passages deal with the bargain and sale, the paradigm example of a contract.
[4] 21 Hen. VII, H. f. 6, pl. 4; 37 Hen. VI, M. f. 8, pl. 18, *per* Prisot C.J.

'Contract', however, was not synonymous with 'covenant'. Clearly only *certain* agreements bound a man to pay a debt, and thus ranked as 'contracts'. Furthermore, terminological usage tended to conceal the fact that many 'contracts' were 'covenants'; the term 'covenant' was most commonly used to refer to agreements which either were actionable by writ of covenant, or would be if only a specialty was available, whilst 'contract' was earmarked for transactions actionable by writ of debt. Only when in an analytical mood did medieval lawyers recognize that the categories overlapped. The compiler of Statham's *Abridgement* had this overlap[1] in mind when he tried to draw a conceptual distinction between 'covenants' and 'contracts', and he fastened upon the requirement that a contract must bind the contracting party to a *certain* sum; 'certainty' was the hallmark of 'contract'. He reports Yelverton J. as saying,

'I understand that a man may have a writ of debt for things which sound in covenant, for it is in certain, as is the case here. As if an indenture be made between us by such words, to wit, "So it is covenanted between us that J.C. shall pay to me twenty pounds at the end of Easter etc." that I shall have an action of debt. But it is other-wise as to a covenant which is not put in certain, for there a man cannot have any action but a writ of covenant.'

The compiler adds,

'And I think this is the reason, and not the other, that is the uncertainty. For a contract and a covenant are of much the same effect only for this reason. For a contract is as if two persons are drawn together, and a covenant is as if two persons come together, etc.'[2]

Thus 'contract' was in some respects a narrower category than 'covenant', for not all agreements were contracts.

Conversely there was some slight tendency to call all transactions which gave rise to an action of debt 'contracts', and, since debt liability could exist in the absence of agreement, the

---

[1] The overlap is recognized in 3 Hen. VI, P. f. 42, pl. 13; 7 Edw. IV, f. 12, pl. 2; and see also 37 Hen. VI, M. f. 8, pl. 18 *per* Moyle J.

[2] Statham, *Covenant*, pl. 9 (undated); the case abridged could be 22 Hen. VI, T. f. 57, pl. 7, *sed quaere*.

consequence was that in some respects 'contract' was a wider category than 'covenant'. The typical example here is the contract of record; where debt was brought to recover money adjudged due in an action the basis of liability was the record, and clearly the debtor's liability is in no sense based upon agreement. Nevertheless, the action of debt was occasionally said to be based upon 'contract'. Even here, however, the feeling that there was something peculiar in so divorcing the conception of 'contract' from agreement was reflected in terminology; such a 'contract' was a 'contract in law', and so differentiated from a 'contract in fact'.[1] The expression 'quasi-contract' reflects the same unease. It does not appear to have been current in the year-book period; the earliest use of the expression seems to be *Speake* v. *Richards* (1617).[2] In medieval times there seem to be few instances of the use of the term 'contract' in situations in which debt liability was imposed in the absence of any sort of consensual transaction; the predominant usage limited the term 'contract' to those informal agreements which were actionable by writ of debt. Thus the cases collected under the head 'contract' in the *Abridgements* of Statham, Fitzherbert, and Brooke are all concerned with informal consensual transactions.

The term 'simple contract' requires a special explanation. Today a simple contract means an informal contract, but what 'simple' ought to mean is 'unconditional', not 'informal', and in the old reports this is what it did normally mean.[3] This raises a conundrum—how did 'simple contract' come to mean 'contract not under seal'? Probably the explanation is that the normal contract under seal was conditioned and therefore not 'simple',[4] whilst the informal contract was usually unconditional, and could in addition be called 'simple' in the non-legal sense of 'unadorned'.[5]

[1] 11 Hen. VI, P. f. 35, pl. 30; 7 Hen. VI, M. f. 5, pl. 9.

[2] Hob. 209, where debt was brought against a sheriff who had levied a sum of £523 17s. 0d. by way of executors but refused to hand it over to the plaintiff. The court said that debt lay, 'For though there was no actual contract, yet there was a kind of contract in law, so it is *quasi ex contractu*.'

[3] See *Anon.* (1536) Dyer 29b, 9 Edw. IV, T. f. 25, pl. 34.

[4] Thus in 33 Hen. VI, M. f. 43, pl. 23, the reporter thinks it worth making a special note of the fact that a contract can commence by conditions (i.e. be suspensively conditional).

[5] 'Simple' is used in this sense in 3 Hen. VI, P. f. 42, pl. 13.

Contracts as 'grants'

Debts were specifically recoverable, and medieval lawyers tended to think that where something was specifically recoverable by a person that something must in some sense be his. If the basis for his claim was some form of consensual transaction which gave rise to a right to specific recovery then the transaction was, according to this way of looking at the matter, a grant. The most straightforward example of such a grant was a bond, which was viewed as a grant of a debt. But the same reasoning could be applied to a contract for the sale of chattels, and to other informal agreements. Thus in a case in 1442,[1] Yelverton, in the course of an argument designed to show that a sale of future goods was void, attempted to draw a distinction between a sale, when the seller must have property in the goods and must make the property pass by force of the sale, and a grant or lease, where the grantee or lessee will acquire a right to take the profits which are not in existence at the time of the transaction. But this failed to impress Paston J., who dismissed Yelverton's refined distinction by saying bluntly,

'All is one, for a sale is a grant in itself.'

This way of looking at 'contracts' was prevalent in the fifteenth and sixteenth centuries, and it possessed the attraction of identifying a characteristic of 'contracts' which would serve to differentiate them from covenants, promises, and agreements generally. A contract was a transaction which passed an immediate interest in a thing to the other contracting party; a covenant on the other hand was a transaction which bound the covenantor to performance in the future, but did not pass any immediate interest to the covenantee. Hence contracts presuppose private property, covenants personal freedom.

Now today we tend to think of contracts primarily as transactions which bind the parties to future performance; we think of contracts in the way in which the late medieval lawyers thought of covenants, though we recognize that contracts may incidentally operate as grants. Their analysis therefore appears topsy-turvy. Against the background of the forms of action it becomes more intelligible; they wished to limit the term 'contract' to transactions which were in a sense specifically enforce-

[1] 21 Hen. VI, P. f. 43, pl. 20.

able, which were those transactions which transferred rights to personal chattels or debts. When today we rather sloppily define a contract as an agreement *enforceable* at law we reflect the same idea; the difference is that we do not take such definitions seriously.

This theory could have practical effects, and this is illustrated in a very fully reported case in 1522, *Wheler's Case*.[1] A lessee for years purported to assign his interest to another by way of sale subject to conditions; the conditions were the favour of the head lessor should be obtained, and that the assignee should pay for the term a sum to be fixed by a third party. Before either condition was satisfied Wheler assigned the lease to a second person, and the question for decision was which of the two was entitled to the land.[2] Eventually it was held that the first assignee was entitled. The reasoning which led to this result was this. For the first assignee to succeed in his claim to the land it had to be shown that the first transaction was a perfect contract, effective by way of grant to pass an interest in the term to the first assignee before the second assignment took place. If the transaction fell short of being a perfect contract or grant, but was merely a 'promise', 'communication', or 'covenant' the first assignee might have an action of covenant (or action on the case) for failure to perform the agreement, but he would not be entitled to the land. Whether or not the transaction was a perfect contract turned upon the nature of the two unsatisfied conditions; if these were interpreted as conditions precedent, clearly there could be no perfect contract until they were performed, and the first assignee would lose the action, though he would be able to sue for breach of covenant or promise if they were eventually satisfied. Fitzherbert J. initially inclined to this view, arguing thus:

'Suppose I sell you my land for so much as John at Style says, now if I make a feoffment or estate to another before John at Style shows how much you are to pay, this is valid, and not withstanding that he [afterwards] says that the first

[1] 14 Hen. VIII, H. f. 15, pl. 1, f. 18, pl. 7.

[2] The plaintiff was the first assignee and he sued the second assignee, presumably in trespass, and declared on the first grant. The defendant justified, pleading the grant to him by way of confession and avoidance, and the plaintiff traversed the second grant by special traverse: issue was joined on this and a special verdict found.

vendee should pay a certain sum, yet he will not have the land, but is put to his action on the case if he has no specialty, and if he has specialty he will have his action of covenant. And so it is if I sell you my horse for as much as such a one says, and before he shows the certainty I sell him to another, now the first vendee will never have the horse, but is put to his action as above, and the reason is that these are contracts which take their perfection from a thing which is to be done afterwards, and they are not perfect until it is done. But if the horse remains in the seller's own possession, then the vendee will have this when the condition is performed.'

The majority, however, took the view that the conditions were to be treated as conditions subsequent, and Fitzherbert eventually came round to this view; the first assignee acquired an immediate interest defeasible by condition subsequent, and if the conditions had not been performed in a reasonable time Wheler would have been entitled to enter and defeat the interest which passed at once by the perfect contract.

Contract and the doctrine of 'quid pro quo'

In modern English law it is a well-settled doctrine that all contracts require good consideration. Understandably enough, legal historians have been interested in looking for some corresponding doctrine in the medieval law of informal contracts. The obvious candidate is the doctrine of *quid pro quo*; some mention has already been made of this doctrine. According to modern statements, the gist of it was that a duty to pay a debt if based upon some informal transaction (as opposed to a deed) only arose if it could be shown that the debtor had actually received a material benefit from the creditor; this benefit was the *quid* in return for which (*pro quo*) the defendant was saddled with liability in debt. If there was no *quid pro quo*, in the sense explained, there was no contract binding upon the defendant at all. Hence, it is said, medieval law only recognized *real* contracts, at least as a general rule. By 'real contract' is meant a contract which only becomes binding when one party has performed his side of the agreement.[1]

This theory has about it an air of attractive simplicity. It is

---

[1] See in particular Ames, Lect. VIII and Fifoot, Ch. 10.

commonly linked to the contention that the great change in contractual theory which came in with the rise of assumpsit in the sixteenth century was the recognition of bilateral contracts which were binding from the moment of mutual agreement, before either party had performed and therefore conferred a *quid pro quo* upon the other party.

Now it is certainly true that numerous cases in the fifteenth and sixteenth centuries mention the expression *quid pro quo*; furthermore statements to the effect that contracts require *quid pro quo*, or that *quid pro quo* is, as it is said in *Mervyn v. Lyds* (1533),[1]

'necessary to every contract',

are to be found in the reports. Thus it is clear that there existed a school of thought which maintained the proposition that contracts required *quid pro qou*.

What is not so clear is the significance of this contention. Modern writers have taken it to mean that contracts are only *binding* when performed on one side. But this interpretation seems to be wholly untenable, for in none of the cases in which *quid pro quo* is mentioned is the court concerned to fix the moment when the parties are unable to withdraw from the agreement unilaterally. Conversely, where this is the point under discussion, *quid pro quo* is not mentioned at all.[2] Indeed, we have seen that in the case of the two most important bilateral contracts—sale and hire of services—there does not appear to have been any rooted objection to treating contracts as binding before either party had performed. But it must be emphasized that medieval lawyers do not seem to have been as interested as we are in fixing the moment when contracts were binding; cases where the question is debated are not common.

Quid pro quo seems rather to have been regarded as relevant in cases where the point at issue is whether a particular transaction (for example, a marriage dowry contract) ought to be actionable by writ of debt at all. The presence of *quid pro quo* served to distinguish bare parole grants of debts, which were not actionable, from parole contracts, which could impose debt liability. *Alice's Case* (1458)[3] is a particularly clear example.

---

[1] Dyer 90a.
[2] See in particular 17 Edw. IV, P. f. 1, pl. 2 (Fifoot 252).
[3] 37 Hen. VI, M. f. 8, pl. 18 (Fifoot 249).

The case, as we have seen, concerned an action of debt brought
to recover a hundred marks which the defendant had agreed to
pay the plaintiff as a marriage gift if the plaintiff married Alice,
the defendant's daughter. The marriage had been solemnized.
Not one word of the discussion is concerned with the moment
at which this agreement is to be regarded as binding; the court
is solely concerned to decide whether the transaction is one
which properly gives rise to an action of debt at all.

Those who insisted upon *quid pro quo* as an essential element
in a debt contract seem to have thought that only such transactions as involved reciprocal exchange between the parties
should rank as 'contracts'; if one party was to be bound to pay
the other money then it was essential that the transaction which
gave rise to the liability was such that the debtor obtained something in return.[1] This idea is most clearly expressed by Vavasour
in 1488[2]

> 'It will be contrary to reason to compel him to pay the
> money which is merely paid where he has had nothing nor
> ever will have, for I take it to be a diversity that in all con-
> tracts or bargains, if the party has no *quid pro quo*, that the
> contract or bargain will be void. As if I sell you a horse for
> £10 and I have no such horse *in rerum natura*, the contract or
> bargain is void, or if I make an exchange with you, the
> exchange is void if each of us has no *quid pro quo*.'

The reciprocity of exchange upon which Vavasour insists could
as well be satisfied by the existence of a reciprocal remedy as by
actual performance of the other side of the bargain. But in
cases where no reciprocal remedy existed—for example in
Alice's case, there being no action to compel marriage—
Vavasour's theory would only be satisfied by actual performance
on one side. And if there had been performance of a reciprocal
bilateral agreement—if the defendant had actually received
what he had bargained for—there was naturally a strong
argument for holding him liable to pay the money he had
agreed to pay. Though it was a basic principle that a mere
unilateral grant of a debt was legally ineffective unless made

---

[1] We must exclude contracts of loan, which do not appear to have been discussed
in terms of *quid pro quo* at all.
[2] 18 Edw. IV, P. f. 5, pl. 30, discussed above.

under seal, justice appeared to require that if the grantor had actually received something in return for his grant she should be bound to fulfil it although it was not a grant by deed.

The doctrine of *quid pro quo* ran into particular difficulty, as we have seen, in the case of contracts for the benefit of third parties. Strictly speaking, such contracts do not involve anything in the nature of exchange between the parties, yet the grantor of the debt in such a case did in some sense obtain what he had bargained for. Hence the persistent doubts as to whether or not such transactions gave rise to debt liability at all.

Though the doctrine of *quid pro quo* certainly exercised some influence upon the law governing debt *sur contract* it never acquired either the status or clarity of the doctrine of consideration, and it has perhaps come to seem to historians rather more important than it was to contemporaries.

PART II
THE ACTION FOR
BREACH OF PROMISE

I

THE EMERGENCE OF THE
ACTION OF ASSUMPSIT[1]

Trespass on the case

MODERN English contract law grew up around the action of assumpsit, a special sub-species of the action on the case. It was not until the sixteenth century that lawyers began to treat assumpsit as an action with its own identity, its own distinct rules and theoretical doctrines; in the fifteenth century and before 'assumpsit' to contemporaries would mean no more than a word used in one of the many ways of pleading a trespass action.[2] But we can now trace the history of assumpsit back into the fourteenth century, since in retrospect we can detect the significance of changes in pleading forms where contemporaries could not.

This century saw a steady increase in the jurisdiction of the royal courts over actions for trespasses, or, as we would say, torts or wrongs.[3] The characteristic feature of these actions was that in them a plaintiff was allowed to claim damages by way of compensation for a wrong which had been done to him. In this respect trespass actions embodied a legal technique which was quite different from the technique of the ancient real actions, in which the claimant demanded the seisin of land, and quite different also from the technique of the ancient contractual actions of debt, detinue, and covenant, where the claimant demanded the specific recovery of the debt, the chattel or charter), or the actual performance of the covenant. Whereas

---

[1] On the subject-matter of this chapter the main secondary literature is the following: Ames, Lect. XIII, *H.E.L.* III. 428–34; Plucknett, 469–72, 637–9; Kiralfy, Chs. 1, 2, 11; Fifoot, Chs. 4 and 14, Milsom, Chs. 11 and 12.

[2] It is, of course, impossible to put a precise date on this, any more than it is possible to date precisely the recognition as a distinct form of such variants of case as the action for trover and conversion (*c.* 1550).

[3] On the early history of trespass see S. F. C. Milsom, 'Trespass from Henry III to Edward III' 74 L.Q.R., Part I, p. 195, Part II, p. 407, Part III, p. 561, and G. D. G. Hall, 'Some Early Writs of Trespass', 73 L.Q.R. 65. Milsom's articles have largely supplanted all earlier studies of the subject, and I have relied extensively upon them in the early part of this chapter.

these ancient writs were designed to put right a situation created by wrongdoing, the writs of trespass were designed to ensure that the wrongdoer should compensate in money for wrongdoing which could no longer be put right; they were actions for 'irrevocable wrongs'.

Representing as they did a newer conception of remedy, the trespass actions were initiated by a newer form of writ; in this the defendant was summoned to appear before the court to explain why (*ostenturus quare*) he had caused damage to the plaintiff by wrongdoing.[1] The summons to explain, which features as a sort of afterthought in the older writs of *praecipe*, becomes the central feature of the trespass writs. And since wrongdoing can take many forms, the clause in the writ which follows the words *ostenturus quare*, describing the wrongful action or inaction, had to be varied as the case required. Naturally, in the course of time, more or less standard forms were evolved to cover such obvious and common wrongs as assault,[2] false imprisonment,[3] the taking of chattels,[4] and so forth, and if an imaginative wrongdoer thought up some unusual form of wickedness[5] a suitable form could readily be evolved to cover the situation.

It could happen, however, that a bald recital of what the defendant had done or failed to do would not make it sufficiently clear that he had acted wrongfully. An example should make this clear. Suppose that a defendant is bound by a prescriptive duty to repair a sea-wall which is on his land, that he has failed to repair it, and that the resulting inundation has caused damage to the plaintiff's land or property. Here it will not be sufficient for the plaintiff to say merely that the defendant has not repaired the sea-wall, and that damage has resulted to the plaintiff. For why should the defendant repair the wall? The writ must include, in addition to a description of the defendant's wrongful inaction, an allegation that the defendant was under

---

[1] On the development in the diplomatic form of standard writs see generally R. C. Van Caenegem, *Royal Writs in England from the Conquest to Glanvill*, S.S. Vol. 77, and on the *ostenturus quare* forms see esp. pp. 244–8.

[2] Milsom 207.

[3] Milsom 209.

[4] Milsom 212.

[5] For judicial support for the possibility of inventing new forms of vice see the speech of Lord Simonds, *Shaw* v. *Director of Public Prosecutions* [1962] A.C. 220.

a prescriptive duty to repair.[1] Such a writ was called a special writ of trespass because it contains particular individual explanatory material in addition to the recital of the defendant's wrongdoing.[2]

This special matter was included in a clause introduced by the word *cum*, which may be translated as 'whereas'. The *cum*-clause preceded the description of the wrong and the allegation of damage, as can be seen from the following example, which dates from 1369,[3]

> 'Rex vicecomiti salutem. Si P fecerit te securum de clamore suo prosequendo, tunc summone per bonos summonitores D quod sit coram justitariis nostris apud Westmonasterium ... ostenturus quare cum idem D quendam digitum ipsius P casualiter laesum pro competenti salario in hac parte capiendo sanare apud London manucepisset idem D percepta magna parte salarii sui praedicti curam suam pro dicto digito sanando tam indiscrete negligenter aut maliciose fecit quod idem P magnam partem digiti sui praedicti amisit ad dampnum ipsius P £20.'

which reads like this in translation,

> 'The King to the sheriff, greetings! If P gives you security for pursuing his claim, then summon D by good summoners to be before our justices at Westminster ... to show why, whereas the said D took it in hand[4] in London, in return for a suitable remuneration to be taken on this account, to cure a certain finger of this same P which had been accidentally wounded, yet the said D, a major part of the said salary of his having been received, performed his cure in respect of the said finger which was to be cured so incautiously, negligently or maliciously that the said P lost a great part of his said finger, to his damage twenty pounds.'

It can be seen in this example that the *cum*-clause in the writ contains both some purely narrative matter, such as the

[1] Milsom 407.

[2] See generally Milsom 430 et seq. The special matter in the *cum*-clause could perform other functions than that discussed here.

[3] Taken from Kiralfy 224. For another example see Milsom 571.

[4] For the meaning of *manucepisset*, which has no modern English equivalent, see below, p. 212.

account of the wounding of the finger, as well as matter designed to show that the defendant ought to have performed the cure properly; the whole melancholy story is set out in particular detail in the writ. It was this feature of the special writs of trespass which gave rise to the expression 'on the case'.[1] 'Each action depended on its facts; and that is also the short explanation of the name.'[2] Expressions such as 'sur son cas', 'en cas especiel', 'sur le cas' are to be found in use early in the fourteenth century, where they express, quite untechnically, the idea that the writ had to be drawn up to fit the particular circumstances of the case. But by the end of the fourteenth century—the process begins in the 1370s or a little earlier—lawyers began to draw a technical distinction of some consequence between writs of general trespass and writs of the case. The former came to be characterized by the inclusion of an allegation of breach of the peace; the wrong, it was alleged, had been committed with force and arms, and against the peace of the lord King (*vi et armis, et contra pacem Domini Regis*).[3]

The function of this grave allegation in the early fourteenth century, and earlier, had been to justify the intervention of the royal courts by showing that the King had a special interest in the wrong, for at this period there was a feeling—one could almost call it a theory—that, in general, cases involving private wrongs should be determined in the local courts. An allegation of force and breach of the peace was not the only way of showing a royal interest, though it was the most usual, and it is clear that sometimes sham allegations of this kind were made by pleaders who were anxious, for some reason or other, to litigate in the royal courts.[4] In the course of the fourteenth century the jurisdictional questions raised by the use of trespass declined in importance, and the royal courts began to be quite open in exercising jurisdiction over trespass actions in which the Crown had no special interest.

[1] It is now no longer believed that the appearance of the action on the case has anything to do with c. 24 (*Consimili Casu*) of the Statute of Westminster II (1285). See T. F. Plucknett, 'Case and the Statute of Westminster II', 31 Col.L.R. 778, and Miss E. J. Dix, 'The Origins of the Action of Trespass on the Case', 46 Y.L.J. 1142.

[2] Milsom 587.

[3] Milsom 587. And see Milsom, 'Reason in the Development of the common-Law' (1965) 81 L.Q.R. 496

[4] Milsom 220, 572; Kiralfy 142.

This development made it unnecessary for writs to dissemble, alleging breach of the peace where there had in fact been none, and from about 1370 onwards the courts began to treat such sham allegations as not only unnecessary but as objectionable.[1] The insistence on the distinction may have been connected with a procedural matter—under a Statute of 1352 the process of *capias* and outlawry had been extended to personal actions generally, having been previously largely confined to trespass actions alleging a breach of the peace.[2] It may have been felt too harsh to apply such severe measures to mere private wrong-doers, a result only to be avoided if allegations of breach of the peace were excluded from actions on the case. In the class of trespass actions to which this rule was applied the common wrongful element of forcible breach of the peace was lacking. Instead of rehearsing what the defendant had done, and adding that he did it forcibly and against the peace, the plaintiff was required to substantiate his claim that the defendant was a wrongdoer by including in his writ special matter which showed that the defendant had done wrong. Thus the actions for private wrongs, private because the King had no special interest in them, came to be remedied by writs of special trespass formed according to the special circumstances of the case, or, more shortly, actions on the case. It is amongst this class of actions' that we find the first instances of actions in the nature of actions of assumpsit.

Actions on the case for breach of duty

Amongst the early actions on the case in the fourteenth-century reports and plea rolls there are a number in which plaintiffs sued to recover compensation for loss caused to them through incompetent or careless conduct on the part of the defendant, or through some default of his performing some duty which he was bound to discharge. One example has already been given: an action against a surgeon for failure to cure a finger.[3] Another which has been mentioned is an action for failure to repair a sea-wall.[4] Amongst this group of actions we

[1] Milsom 585 et seq. See in particular *Waldon v. Marshall* (1370) Y.B. 43 Edw. III, f. 33, pl. 38, *The Farrier's Case* (1373) Y.B. 46 Edw. III, f. 19, pl. 19.
[2] See Milsom 217. The Statute is 25 Edw. III, st. 5, c. 17.
[3] See above, p. 201.
[4] See above, p. 200. Milsom, at p. 430, gives a precedent for such an action

can also include suits against innkeepers for failing to look after their guests' property,[1] ferrymen whose incompetence killed animals entrusted to them,[2] doctors who were professionally negligent,[3] smiths who unskilfully lamed horses which they were shoeing,[4] and so forth. It was obvious enough that such persons, if the plaintiff was telling the truth, had done wrong and caused economic loss, and that their wrongdoing could most appropriately be described by using words like 'failure', 'default', or 'neglect'. For they, unlike those who beat or assaulted or imprisoned or maimed, had *not* done what they ought to have done. This way of analysing their wrongdoing, though never explicitly contrasted in the sources with its opposite—doing what ought not to be done[5]—is implicit in the language and thought of fourteenth-century law.[6] The contrast is neatly made in the words of the General Confession of the Anglican Book of Common Prayer: 'We have done those things which we ought not to have done and have left undone those things which we ought to have done, and there is no health in us.' Cases involving wrongdoing analysed in this way (not doing the right thing), raise the issue which modern lawyers call breach of duty; in jurisprudence the concept of duty is used in a wider sense than this, but that is another story.[7]

---

[1] (1368) 42 Lib. Ass. f. 260b, pl. 17, Kiralfy 150–1, *Reg.Omn.Brev.* f. 104. And see Milsom 434.

[2] (1348)22 Lib. Ass. pl. 41 (*The Case of the Humber Ferryman*). (See Appendix, Case No. 1.)

[3] See above, p. 201. Also Y.B. 48 Edw. III, H. f. 6, pl. 11 (*The Surgeon's Case*). The record is printed by Kiralfy, 225. And see Milsom 571–2. Statham (*Accions sur le Cas*, pl. 9) gives a report of the case which must derive from a different source from the printed year-book. See Appendix, Case No. 5.

[4] Y.B. 46 Edw. III, (1373) T. f. 19, pl. 19 (*The Farrier's Case*), Kiralfy 142, and see Milsom 220.

[5] The contrast is not identical with that between misfeasance and nonfeasance.

[6] Hence the recurrent use of the term default (*defectum*) in the language of the pleadings.

[7] The contrast is related to the contrast between rules which prohibit certain conduct, and rules which require certain conduct, but it is not precisely the same. The use of the concept of duty in relation to prohibition has spread into the law (duty not to . . .) probably through the influence of moralists and jurists, but a

---

dating from 1273–6, and other later examples. The earliest case in the year-books is in the courts from 1340–4; see 14–15 Edw. III (R.S.), 246; 15 Edw. III (R.S.), 86; 16 Edw. III (R.S.), Vol. I, 256; 18 Edw. III (R.S.), 231; Y.B. 18 Edw. III, T. f. 23, pl. 6; Kiralfy 208–9; *Public Works in Mediaeval Law*, S.S. Vol. 32; Milsom 431–2.

Fourteenth-century lawyers were perfectly familiar with this type of wrongdoing through the medium of the old contractual writs. Debt lay against those who *failed* to pay their debts (the concept of duty, *eo nomine*, was first confined to debts due), detinue lay against those who failed to perform certain agreements. Now when one man seeks to bring another to book for failing to do something for him, the general answer of the law is that no man is his brother's keeper; God and the law help those that help themselves. This at all times has been the general attitude of the law, with the consequence that some special ground or reason is required for saying that a person must either do something for another or be called a tortfeasor. In the old writs this special ground was normally some prior transaction between the parties, which might be a contract, a bailment, or an agreement. But there could, as we have seen, be other special grounds; for example, a claim in debt could be based on a custom, or a statutory duty, whilst detinue of charters might be brought by virtue of a title to land, which carried with it title to the charters relating to the land.[1]

Duty in actions on the case based upon transactions
Just as in the old contractual actions, so in the new actions on the case (where brought for failure or default) the law came to recognize a variety of ways in which the plaintiff could show that the defendant was under a duty to do something for him. Thus a man who suffered loss through another's failure to repair a sea-wall could establish the duty by setting up a prescriptive title; he who sued an innkeeper could rely upon a general custom of the realm which required innkeepers to look after their guests' goods. But amongst these early actions of special trespass we can distinguish a group in which the basis of liability is a prior *transaction* between the parties to the action, and it is in this group that the actions against ferrymen, doctors, horse-doctors, smiths, and no doubt others unremembered, belong. At the end of the fourteenth century it came to be established that such persons could be sued by action on the case for their misconduct, and their liability was based upon the

[1] See above, p. 56.

_____
glance at the index of legal books will substantiate the claim that lawyers generally still confine the use of the concept of duty in the way I suggest.

prior informal transaction which they had entered into with the plaintiff.

Status and contract

This concentration upon the transaction was destined to be very important, though contemporaries could not have known this; because of it the lawyers of the fifteenth and sixteenth centuries were able to develop an action on the case for breach of promise, and their successors eventually developed this action in its turn into an action for the breach of parole contracts generally. It could have happened differently, for if in these cases the basis of liability selected had not been the informal transaction it would not have been through the medium of the action of assumpsit that the medieval law of contract, based upon the old contractual writs, was superseded. Nor is it an idle speculation to suggest that another basis for liability could have been found; in the case of the innkeeper it was, with effects which are still with us in the twentieth century.[1] His liability was not based upon the informal transaction with his guest; instead it was based upon the law and custom of the realm, which made him liable both for his own default and for the defaults of his servants, who would normally not be parties to any transaction at all.[2] In modern parlance, the innkeeper's liability was based upon a general rule of law.[3] Indeed the plaintiff in an action against an innkeeper need never have visited the inn at all, for a master could sue for the loss of his goods in an inn which had been visited only by his servants.[4] The irrelevance of any voluntary transaction was still further accentuated by the rule that an innkeeper was in any case bound by law to receive guests whether he liked it or not.[5] The development in the fifteenth century and later of the doctrines associated with the common callings[6] indicates the way in which the earlier lawyers of the fourteenth century could have

[1] (1368) 42 Lib. Ass. f. 260b, pl. 17 (*The Innkeeper's Case*), *Reg.Omn.Brev.* f. 104, 105. 42 Edw. III, P. f. 11, pl. 13. See Kiralfy 151–3.
[2] 22 Hen. VI, H. f. 38, pl. 8.
[3] cf. the liability for escape of fire, also based upon 'common custom'.
[4] 2 Hen. IV, M. f. 7, pl. 31, and see *Anon.* (1553) Dalison 8, *Beadle* v. *Morris* (1609) Yelv. 162, Cro. Jac. 224.
[5] 39 Hen. VI, M. f. 18, pl. 24; 5 Edw. IV, P. f. 2, pl. 20; *Anon.* (1503) Keilwey 50a. There were, however, defences.
[6] See below, p. 229.

dealt with incompetent ferrymen, doctors, smiths, and the like by basing their liability not upon the transactions they had entered into, but upon their status; eventually something of the sort did happen, with the consequence in modern law that such persons are liable for negligence 'in both contract and tort', as we now put it.

What is important about the fourteenth-century cases which are traditionally and rightly regarded as the source of the action of assumpsit, and as the remote ancestors of our modern law of contract, is just the fact that in these cases liability *was* based upon informal voluntary transactions between the parties to the action, and that because of this the later development was made possible.

Covenant and trespass on the case

When a person betakes himself to his doctor, in the nature of things there is bound to be some sort of agreement, normally very informal (and sometimes, one suspects, not very voluntary), before the scalpel is produced; otherwise there will be a battery (we may ignore here refinements like the case of the unconscious patient, and similar tutorial fodder). If things go wrong subsequently, and the patient sues the doctor (the same reasoning will apply to smiths, etc.), the natural analysis of the situation is to say that the doctor's incompetent treatment is not what the patient agreed to submit himself to, or, more shortly, that the doctor has failed to perform his agreement. Now at first sight it would seem that the analysis of the situation which I have sketched would be an analysis which plaintiffs would want to use. But it was in fact defendants who advanced this analysis, and they did so as an argument for *not* allowing doctors to be sued by action on the case, for it was said that actions which were in substance actions for broken agreements—covenants— ought to be brought by action of covenant, and not by a trespass action. The common law had provided a perfectly good action for breach of covenant, so why not use it? This very point was made in a case in the Nottingham Eyre in 1329.[1]

An action was brought by bill against a doctor who, having

---

[1] Kiralfy, *Source Book*, 184, from Lincoln's Inn MS. Hale 137 (1) at f. 58 and B.M. MS. Egerton 2811, f. 218.

undertaken to cure the plaintiff's eye, put the eye out, and was very properly sued. Launde, arguing against the correctness of the way in which the action had been cast, said this,

> 'Sir you see very well that, as he supposes that he put himself under his medicines and cure, no trespass[1] can be found in him at that time, since he himself submitted to his cure. Hence, if he had any action at all it would naturally sound in covenant broken. So we ask judgment whether such a bill should be received.'

This argument was accepted, and Denom, the Justice in Eyre, added,

> 'I put it to you, that if a smith, who is a man of occupation,[2] drives a nail into your horse's hoof, so that you lose your horse, you will never have recovery against him, nor shall you here.'

And in consequence of these unpromising remarks, which suggested that even an action of covenant was impossible,[3] the plaintiff did not take his action any further.

The suggestion that actions of this kind should be brought by writ of covenant ran up against an obvious difficulty, which may explain Denom's extreme position; once it was settled that a deed had to be produced by anyone who sued in covenant in the royal courts, it was rather futile to recommend plaintiffs to bring that action in such petty cases.[4] For in the nature of things plaintiffs would never have a deed to proffer. To insist on the use of covenant would, in effect, exclude these cases entirely from the jurisdiction of the common law courts (whatever might be done about them elsewhere), and, for reasons which are still obscure, there seems to have been continuous pressure from litigants (or their counsel) in the fourteenth century to persuade the common law courts to accept jurisdiction over these

---

[1] 'Trespass' here means only 'wrong' or 'tort'; the point being made is that the defendant's interference with the plaintiff's eye was consented to, and therefore not itself wrongful.

[2] i.e. 'a professional'.

[3] Kiralfy (*Source Book* at p. 184), however, gives an example of a case in 1330 in the Bedford Eyre in which covenant was successfully brought against a negligent doctor.

[4] See above, p. 10.

petty cases. We must suspect that, inefficient though the central courts appear to us, contemporaries found some local courts worse. Where such pressure is exerted over a period of years it seems that sooner or later lawyers will find some way or other of bypassing the technical difficulties, for in the law the winds of change seem to blow in a direction favourable to plaintiffs. This in fact happened.

One device which was used was boldly fictional; a plaintiff who wished to sue a smith, say, for incompetently shoeing a horse which had subsequently died of septicaemia would bring a general writ of trespass and simply allege that the smith had killed his horse, period. Such a form of pleading would reveal nothing about the existence of any agreement; this might come out later in the course of the action, but at least the writ on its face was unobjectionable.[1] This method of pleading, however, fell into disrepute in the 1360s and 1370s, when the courts began to insist upon the use of honest writs; why this happened remains unexplained, though it is clear that it did happen, with the result that plaintiffs were forced into using special writs of trespass on the case.[2] Such writs, by revealing the circumstances which led up to the commission of the wrong inevitably revealed the fact that there had been a previous transaction, an agreement, between the parties.

But although honest writs were bound to reveal the transaction (thus incurring the risk that counsel would object to the use of trespass and not covenant), there was no need for the transaction to be described or handled in any particular way; something could still be done to play down the fact that there had been an agreement (that is a covenant) between the parties. This explains the most striking feature of these early cases, which is the fact that pleaders *never* call the transaction a covenant in either writ or count, notwithstanding the fact that the word covenant would have been the most natural word to choose to describe these informal transactions. The reason is obvious enough: to do so would have been to provide ammunition for defendant's counsel to use in arguing that a trespass writ was the wrong writ to use. Nevertheless, everybody was well aware that these transactions were covenants, and the word was

[1] See Milsom 220–4, and Kiralfy 142.
[2] See n. 1–4 to p. 204, above.

cheerfully bandied about in argument;[1] it is rare indeed for a court to be fooled by a trick of pleading. The best that could be achieved was that the record be kept straight, in the hope that the court would be sympathetic towards the attempt to bring these cases within the jurisdiction. This aim pleaders pursued by characterizing the informal agreement as something other than a covenant, and, since special writs of trespass were infinitely variable in their form, there was considerable scope for experiment; indeed it was some time before the allegation of an undertaking (*assumpsit*) became the common form of pleading.

The origin of actions alleging an assumpsit

These experiments can be traced in the cases. In *Bukton* v. *Townsend* (1348), traditionally known as *The Case of the Humber Ferryman*,[2] the plaintiff had entrusted his mare to the ferryman for transport over the Humber; the ferryman overloaded his boat and in some way or other the mare was killed.[3] On these facts one's instinct is to say that the proper action was detinue on a bailment, and the initial difficulty in understanding the case arises because the plaintiff not only did not sue in detinue, but nobody suggested that he ought to have done so. For this there must be some explanation, and it may be that the mare was not lost overboard in the Humber (as is normally assumed)

[1] See, for example, Cavendish C.J. in the *Surgeon's Case* (1375) 48 Edw. III, H. f. 6, pl. 11 (Fifoot 83): 'This action of covenant is of necessity maintained without specialty, since for every little thing a man cannot always have a clerk to make a specialty for him . . .'

[2] Reported in 22 Lib.Ass. f. 94, pl. 41. The record is printed by M. Hastings in Vol. XIII of the *Bulletin of the Institute of Historical Research* (1935), p. 36. The black-letter text is discussed by A. Kiralfy, 'The Humber Ferryman and the Action on the Case' (1953) Camb.L.J. 421. It is clear that the text ought to be amended at the point where Richmond says 'Judgement of the bill, which supposes no tort in us, but rather that he should have an action by writ by way of covenant or by way of trespass' to '*and not*'. Kiralfy gives two variant MS. readings—'et nemye per voie de trespass' and 'plus que per voie de trespass'. Mr. G. D. G. Hall has kindly drawn my attention to two other MS. reports Bodl. MS. 364, f. 90v) and (MS. Exeter College 134, f. lv) which have 'plus que per voie trespass' and 'et nemye per voie de Transgressio' respectively and to the fact that Fitzherbert in his *Abridgement* always had the case correctly. The full texts are printed from his transcription in the Appendix, Case. No. 1.

[3] The record alleges that the overloading was against the will of the plaintiff, and makes it clear (as does both Bodl. MS. 364 and MS. Exeter College 134) that the overloading was the cause of the perishing of the mare.

but was killed on the ferry, perhaps by being kicked or crushed by the other horses with which the ferryman overloaded his boat. If this speculation is correct then detinue would not have been a satisfactory action, for the plaintiff would want compensation for the death of his mare, and not the return of a corpse. Covenant no doubt was out of the question, since there would obviously be no specialty to produce, and so the plaintiff was left with only one possibility, a trespass action. This he brought. In the record of the case there is no allegation of an agreement, a promise, or an undertaking; the transaction is described by saying that the ferryman received (*recepit*) the mare to carry it safely (*ad salvo cariandum*) over the waters of the Humber. In the French of the Book of Assizes, where the case is is reported, this becomes 'avoit empris a carier sa jument', which looks like an allegation of an undertaking. But in view of the text of the record, we must translate 'had taken his mare in hand for carriage', and not 'had undertaken to carry his mare'.[1] Thus although the transaction in the case is treated as the basis of liability, the aspect of the transaction which is emphasized is what the ferryman did and the context in which he did it—he received the mare for safe carriage—rather than anything the ferryman agreed or undertook or promised to do. And this is a perfectly acceptable way of looking at the matter.

To say that the transaction was made the basis of liability only means that the recital of the transaction justified the assertion that the defendant had done something wrong, that he had committed a tort or trespass. In argument Richmond nevertheless objected to the action on the ground that no tort was shown in the defendant; his point here was that it had not been alleged that the defendant had killed the mare. To this argument Bankwell J. replied that it seemed that a wrong was committed when he, the ferryman, overloaded the boat with the other horses, against the wishes of the plaintiff; this was a wrong he had committed. It may be that his stress on this aspect of the story, which mirrored the way in which the story was told by the plaintiff's pleader, supports the suggestion that it was the

---

[1] On the meaning of 'empris' see 21 Edw. III, H. f. 46, pl. 65, where, in an action brought by the Master and Scholars of Merton against the Prior of St. Austin's in Oxford it was said that the Prior 'emprist le tenancy', which seems to mean 'took on the tenancy'.

behaviour of the other horses which was supposed to have directly precipitated the death of the mare. But the only reason why the ferryman's action in overloading the boat, which was probably his own boat anyway, could be plausibly treated as a wrong to the plaintiff, was the prior transaction between the parties, and it is in this sense that the transaction was the basis of liability. In the event the plaintiff succeeded.[1]

In *Waldon* v. *Marshall* (1370)[2] the transaction was handled rather differently. One William Waldon sued John, who was a Marshall,[3] and alleged in the writ.

'quod praedictus Johannes manucepit equum praediciti Willelmi de infirmitate,[4] et postea praedictus Johannes ita negligenter curam suam fecit quod equus suus interiit.'

The choice of the word *manucepit*, with the curious construction which follows it, is not at all easy so explain. *Manucepere* is a verb with a very specific legal meaning in the fourteenth century, developed in connection with the writ of mainprise (*de manu-captione*).[5] It must be translated with this in mind, so that the sense of the passage is probably something like this:

'that the aforesaid John took in hand and made himself responsible for the said William's horse so far as its illness is concerned, and afterwards the aforesaid John performed his cure so negligently that his horse died.'

This powerful assertion and the peculiar grammatical construction through which it is expressed is mirrored in the French of the year-book report, and this cannot be accidental. Thus Kirton says in argument,

'Because he has counted that he ought to have taken responsibility for the horse's malady . . . [*q. il. av. empris son cheval del malady* . . .]'

[1] For discussions of the case see Ames 130; *H.E.L.* III. 430; Plucknett 470; Fifoot 330.

[2] Y.B. 43 Edw. III, M. f. 33, pl. 38 (Fifoot 81). Note, however, that the text given by Mr. Fifoot is incomplete.

[3] John was the defendant's baptismal name, Marshall his occupation and name.

[4] Mr. Fifoot (p. 81) here inserts *curare*, which I think is a mistake. It is true that this makes the Latin construction less eccentric, but the view that the eccentric construction represents the original is indicated by the way in which the year-book report has the same construction in the French.

[5] See Elsa de Haas, *Antiquities of Bail*,77, F.N.B. 250.

and Thorp J. recalled,

> '. . . that he had seen how one M. was indicted, who had taken responsibility for a man's malady. [*q. av. empris un home d'un malady.*]'

It seems that the pleader was treating the informal transaction between the parties as an assumption of responsibility analogous to the assumption of responsibility by one who went bail for another, and who, by 'taking in hand' the prisoner, made himself answerable for the prisoner. Having thus tried to show that the burden of the horse's malady had been voluntarily transferred to the shoulders of the defendant, he alleges wrongdoing in the form of negligence or incompetence, just as the plaintiff did in the case of the Humber ferryman.

The propriety of the action was again challenged upon the ground that the proper writ was either covenant or general trespass *vi et armis*. To this Belknap, who was counsel for the plaintiff, replied by pointing out that he could not bring covenant, because he had no deed, nor general trespass, because the horse was not killed forcibly but died through default in the cure. In favour of his action he emphasized the fact that it was the wrongful conduct of the plaintiff which led to the death of the horse,

> '. . . this action is brought because you did your cure so negligently that the horse died.'

In the end the writ was held to be a good writ.[1]

The case of *Waldon v. Marshall* does not stand alone; at about the same time actions similarly conceived became possible against surgeons, doctors, and smiths who had caused injury or loss through incompetence. In such actions it seems to have been the practice to allege an assumption of responsibility through the taking of custody, using the word 'manucepit' (or 'manucepisset') as in *Waldon v. Marshall*; there is concrete evidence for this in two records which have been published by Dr. Kiralfy, one dating from 1369 and the other from 1373.[2] The latter is probably the record of the well-known *Surgeon's*

---

[1] The report then goes on to discuss the correct form of a special traverse denying negligence.

[2] Kiralfy 224 and 225.

Case in 1375.[1] But no rule required this term to be used; thus in 1374[2] there is an action against a glover, who ill-advisedly attempted some amateur surgery, with disastrous results, and here the plaintiff relied upon a *promise*. He alleged that the defendant,

'... fideliter promisisset quod ipse oculum ... bene et fideliter sanaret ...'

that is,

'... faithfully promised that he would well and faithfully cure the eye ...'

Here the word *fideliter* perhaps echoes the ecclesiastical view of breach of faith, *laesio fidei*.[3] Even here, although no assumption of responsibility was alleged, the defendant's pleader thought it worthwhile to be on the safe side and deny both a promise to cure and an assumption of responsibility,

'... absque hoc quod[4] idem Thomas Blythe promisit prefato Willemo seu manucepit ad oculum suum predictum sanandum.'
'... and the same Thomas Blythe did not promise the said William or make himself responsible for curing his eye aforesaid.'

The allegation of an 'assumpsit' is first found in 1373.[5] An early example is *Skyrne* v. *Butolf* (1387);[6] here an action on the case was brought against a leech to whom the plaintiff had come

[1] Y.B. 48 Edw. III, f. 6, pl. 11. The averment is that the defendant took in hand the plaintiff's wound to the end that it be cured.
[2] Kiralfy, 226.
[3] Milsom 571 prints a case in 1364 with the same allegation, that the defendant *fideliter promisisset*. On the jurisdiction over *laesio fidei* see above, p. 144.
[4] The expression *absque hoc quod* (with its French equivalent *sans ceo que*), which introduces the traverse in a special traverse, is completely untranslatable; the literal equivalent is 'without that which'.
[5] See Kiralfy 159. Kiralfy points out that in actions against bailees the form of pleading used in the *Humber Ferryman's Case*, where it was averred that the defendant received (*recepit*) the chattels, but not that he undertook (*assumpsit*), survived into the seventeenth century.
[6] Y.B. 11 Ric. II (A.S.), 223. The headnote to the case uses the expression 'le defendaunt garrantist de saver' and calls the transaction a 'covenant'; the words 'emprist' and 'covenant' appear in the report.

because he was suffering from ringworm. Here the pleader described the transaction by saying that the defendant,

> ... de quadam infirmitate qua detenebatur competenter curandam pro quadam pecunie summa pre manibus soluta apud London assumpsiset ...'

'... undertook, in London, in return for a certain sum of money previously paid into his hands, competently to cure [the plaintiff] of a certain infirmity by which he was confined ...'

Thereafter the word *assumpsit* came to be used commonly in such actions.[1] In legal contexts it had earlier been used in connection with entry into a religious order—one who did so *habitum religionis assumpsit*.[2]

The meaning of assumpsit

An 'assumpsit' is normally thought of as an undertaking, in the sense of an assurance, and for many purposes this is no doubt accurate enough to catch the sense of the word in the early cases. But simply to translate the word in this way, and leave the matter at that, fails to bring out the full range of the possible nuances of the word, for the modern word 'undertaking' does not carry with it the same overtones. It is of some importance to notice that the term was capable of bearing any of the following senses:

(*a*) It could be used to suggest that the defendant had made himself strictly responsible for bringing something to pass, with

---

[1] The compilers of manuscript Registers of Writs were not very interested in actions of assumpsit, and precedents for writs appear only infrequently in the section of the Register devoted to trespass actions; thus Harvard MS. 165 (temp. Ric. II) contains no assumpsit precedents. Harvard MS. 34 (begun in 1384) at f. 112b contains two variant forms (using the word 'assumpsisset') for actions against one who undertook to plough or sow the plaintiff's land at a seasonable time, but failed to do so, a situation referred to by Newton in 14 Hen. VI, f. 18, pl. 58. Harvard MS. 34 (probably begun in 1403) at f. 86a has a precedent for a writ against a smith ('assumpsit'), at f. 87b, another 'assumpsit' for negligent failure to protect crops from wild animals after an undertaking to do so. Harvard MS. 27 (begun in 1440) at f. xiiii has a 'manucepit' form for negligently performing a cure of a horse, an 'assumpsit' for negligence against the bailee of a horse, an 'assumpsit' for negligence for failure to cure the stone, and it has a writ similar to the one in Harvard MS. 26 at f. 87b, noted above.

[2] e.g. in 40 Edw. III, M. f. 37, pl. 11.

the consequence that he was still answerable even if it was not his fault that the event did not occur. It is in this sense that the term is used in fifteenth-century cases where a person by formal contract had bound himself to pay a penalty if a stranger failed to perform an act; clearly in such cases there could be no suggestion of fault if the stranger did not perform, but there was still liability to pay the penalty, and it was said that the defendant had made himself strictly responsible of performance. The word used to express this idea was 'assumpsit' or its French equivalent 'empris'.[1] The same idea was suggested by the word 'manucepit', for one who went mainprise was strictly liable if his charge escaped. This explains why, in some early cases, a defendant who has been sued for incompetence or negligence in an action of assumpsit thinks it worthwhile not only to plead that he used due care, but also to deny the *manucepit* or *assumpsit*. For if these words suggested strict liability, a mere denial of fault would be no answer to the claim.[2]

(*b*) It could be used to suggest only the idea that the defendant had made himself responsible or answerable, though not necessarily *strictly* responsible. This sense was emphasized when the expression *super se assumpsit*[3] came into vogue in the fifteenth century; it is of course intimately associated with sense (*a*), and is therefore as old as the action. A case which very clearly illustrates the underlying idea is reported in the year-books in Henry VIs reign;[4] the case is usually called *The Marshal's Case*. An action was brought against a horse-doctor, and in the course of the discussion Newton C. J. said,

'Suppose my horse is sick and I come to a marshal to have his counsel and he says that one of his own horses had a similar sickness, and that he applied a certain medicine to him, and so he will do to my horse. This he does, and my horse dies— shall the plaintiff have an action?

---

[1] 33 Hen. VI, P. f. 16, pl. 7; 4 Hen. VI, M. f. 3, pl. 7.

[2] See *Somerton's Case*, 11 Hen. VI, H. f. 18, pl. 10; P. f. 24, pl. 1; T. f. 55, pl. 26 (Fifoot 343); the discussion at f. 24 on the correct form of the Godred's plea illustrates some uncertainty whether an assumpsit entailed strict liability. In *Skyrne* v. *Butolf*, where the pleadings alleged an assumpsit, the headnote speaks of a guarantee. See 11 Ric. II (A.S.), 223.

[3] See, for example, *Watkin's Case*, 3 Hen. VI, H. f. 36, pl. 33 (Fifoot 341).

[4] Y.B. 19 Hen. VI, H. f. 49, pl. 5.

Why, no, unless he assumed [*assuma sur luy*] upon himself, etc.'[1]

(*c*) It could be used to suggest the idea that the defendant had made himself responsible in a particular way, viz. by taking something (or some person) into his custody or control. Lord Holt expressed this idea rather quaintly in *Coggs* v. *Bernard* (1703):[2]

> 'Assumpsit does not signify a future agreement, but in such a case as this it signifies an actual entry upon the thing, and taking the trust on himself.'

Manucepit (literally 'take in the hand') also suggests the same idea, and 'mainprise' could be used to mean 'undertake'[3]. In the early assumpsit cases the defendant has always taken the plaintiff's person or property into his custody, and *thereby* made himself responsible. The same notion appears in nineteenth-century criminal cases, and may appear in modern tort law in connection with the duty to rescue; perhaps if I take your children for a walk, I may thereby make myself responsible for them and be bound to attempt to rescue them if they disappear beneath the surface of a paddling pool.

(*d*) It could perhaps mean no more than 'he agreed', but here I suspect that we should be very cautious; if medieval lawyers wanted to talk about agreements they had perfectly straightforward words (*convencio, covenaunt*) which lay to hand,[4] and the inference is that when they used terms such as 'assumpsit' or 'emprist' they meant something rather different. Even in modern English to agree to do a thing is not quite the same as undertaking to do a thing, and is quite different from making oneself responsible if a thing is not done. 'Undertaking' to do something carries with it the suggestion that a job has to be done by somebody, and a burdensome job at that.[5] We may

---

[1] There is a certain similarity between the reasoning in this case and the reasoning adopted in modern law to justify actions for negligent misstatement.

[2] 2 Ld. Raym., 909. Perhaps, however, Lord Holt was thinking of the sense of 'undertake' where it means little more than begin.

[3] 11 Hen. VI, T. f. 48, pl. 5.

[4] Though as we have seen there were good reasons for avoiding the use of an averment of a covenant.

[5] And note how narrowly confined is the sense of the agent noun, undertaker.

agree to marry our girlfriends, or promise to marry them, but there is something slightly offensive about undertaking to marry them, whilst to make oneself responsible for marrying a young lady is plain rude.

It would be quite misleading to suggest that the choice of the word 'assumpsit' reflected any conscious lexicographical enthusiasm amongst medieval lawyers, or that pleaders used the word in a self-consciously precise manner; at the same time it is true that the selection of a legal term of art is never wholly accidental. Perhaps it was fortunate that the word assumpsit did carry various overtones, for this may have helped along the process whereby the action of assumpsit changed its character, whilst appearing not to do so; change in the law is always easier if it can be concealed. Perhaps the most useful latent defect in the allegation of an assumpsit is that it is systematically ambiguous between an allegation that the defendant *did* something and an allegation that he *said* something; but for this, the action of assumpsit could hardly have developed into an action for the breach of parole agreements.

The general character of assumpsit for negligent misfeasance

By 1400 the action of assumpsit was securely established, and it is worth pausing at this point in time to notice how restricted the scope of the action then was. The situations in which the action had been successfully brought shared certain common features. The plaintiff had entrusted his person or property (the property always being a living creature) to the defendant for some particular purpose; the defendant in all the cases is a person exercising some craft involving skill for its safe pursuit; he is either an artificer or else he has taken on work which is normally the business of artificers. The defendant, it is claimed, has been negligent; he has failed to use the skill he ought to have used, and his neglect has injured the plaintiff's property or person, or caused something closely analogous to a physical injury.[1] In all the cases the defendant has either been paid or is entitled to remuneration.[2] These characteristics define the scope

---

[1] The qualification is made necessary by *Skyrne* v. *Butolf* (1387) 11 Ric. II (A.S.), 223, where there was no injury, though there was a disability.

[2] For a discussion of this see below, p. 236.

of the action of assumpsit, and how far beyond this the judges are prepared to go is as yet uncertain.

From the point of view of the defendant, two important issues appear to have been settled. Liability in the action is not strict; the defendant may, by pleading a special traverse, deny the allegation of negligence. Thus in *Waldon* v. *Marshall* (1370)[1] the plea which the court accepts is that the defendant performed his cure as well as he knew how, *absque hoc* that the horse died through default in his cure. Some writers have doubted whether the allegation of negligence in medieval cases is to be understood in the modern sense of failure to do what is right and proper in the circumstances. The classic year-book discussion of what counts as negligent conduct is to be found in the *Parker's Case* (1465),[2] where an action by a parker claiming his annuity was resisted upon the ground that the plaintiff had been negligent in the performance of his duties in letting poachers kill beasts in the park: the discussion makes it clear that the medieval lawyers' conception of negligence was not radically different from the modern conception, consisting in failure to do what reason dictated as appropriate, bearing in mind such matters as the cost of precautions, the type of risk, etc. Later we shall see that the relevance of fault to liability in assumpsit was not finally settled; when the action became extended, the question came up again in a new context, and was answered differently.[3]

The second important point which had been settled was the method of trial of the issue; was the defendant allowed to wage his law, or must the issue be tried by a jury? Here the matter was settled in a curious way. In the *Surgeon's Case* (1375)[4] the defendant, by Gascoigne his counsel, offered to wage his law that he did not undertake to cure the plaintiff of his malady. Honnington, who was counsel for the defendant, took objection to this.

'This is an action of trespass, and concerns a matter which lies within the knowledge of the country, in which wager of

---

[1] Y.B. 43 Edw. III, f. 33, pl. 38 (Fifoot 81).
[2] 5 Edw. IV (Long Quinto), f. 24. S. C. 5 Edw. IV T. f. 5. pl. 22, below p. 624.
[3] See below, p. 528.
[4] Y.B. 48 Edw. III, H. f. 6, pl. 11 (for the record see Kiralfy 225), and for a variant report see Appendix, Case No. 5.

law is not allowed. Wherefore in default of an answer we demand judgment and pray our damages.'

Cavendish C. J. and the whole court held that wager was possible, upholding Gascoigne. This is the decision one would expect; in an action for what would appear to be a purely private tort, in whose outcome the Crown had no interest, the natural mode of trial would be wager. But for some reason or other the defendant then elected not to wage his law, but to accept trial by jury; and in spite of this precedent in favour of wager of law, in no later case was it so much as suggested that wager was possible, and trial was always trial by jury. It could be that the year-book report of the *Surgeon's Case* is incomplete, and the justices altered their opinion, requiring the defendant not to wage. But it seems more likely that judicial opinion on the question changed soon after 1375, and there is a case in Fitzherbert's *Abridgement* in 1382 which suggests this explanation, though the case is not directly in point.[1] But this does not explain why they changed their opinion; it could have been because the defendant's conduct in these cases, though not *vi et armis*, was still possibly criminal, as was suggested in *Waldon v. Marshall* (1370),[2] The point was of the first importance: had the action of assumpsit been saddled with wager of law it could never have been developed into the general contractual remedy of the common law. But matters which seem important in retrospect do not always seem important at the time.[3]

Assumpsit, covenant, and nonfeasance

We have already seen how lawyers realized from the very beginning that actions of the assumpsit type involved agreements or covenants, and how, because of this, it could well be

---

[1] Fitz. Ley, 41 (Trin. 7 Ric. II, otherwise unreported). 'Trespass on the case supposing that the defendant sold him a horse and warranted him to be good, safe and sufficient for all maladies of travel [*pour toutz maladies de traveler*], the defendant knowing the said horse to be full of maladies in the eyes and legs. Charlet: He did not bargain in the manner in which etc., ready to make our law. Pinch: This writ supposes he sold falsely and fraudulently etc., which sounds in disceit. Judgment. Fulthorpe to Charleton: Are you willing to demur? Charleton did not dare, but said that he did not bargain in the manner etc. Ready to have trial in the country.' On the nature of the action in this case see below, p. 240.

[2] 43 Edw. III, M. f. 33, pl. 38. The passage is omitted in Fifoot at p. 81.

[3] See also Co. Litt. 295a for a rationalisation.

argued that the proper action, to quote Richmond in the case of the *Humber Ferryman* (1348), was,

'by way of covenant and not by way of trespass'.[1]

This sort of argument was rejected in the fourteenth century, but at the very beginning of the fifteenth century the same problem of the relationship between (as we would say) tort and contract arose again in a rather more acute form. In *Watton* v. *Brinth* (1400)[2] an action was brought against a builder, and the writ was in this form,

'. . . quare cum idem Thomas [Brinth] ad quodam domos ipsius Laurentii [Watton] bene et fideliter infra certum tempus de novo construendo apud Grimesby assumpsisset praedictus tamen Thomas domos ipsius Laurentii infra tempus praedictum etc. construere non curavit[3] ad dampnum ipsius Laurentii decem librarum etc.'

. . . why, whereas the same Thomas Brinth undertook in Grimsby to reconstruct well and faithfully within a certain time certain houses of the same Lawrence Watton, yet the said Thomas took no care to construct the houses of the same Lawrence in the said time, etc., to the damage of the same Lawrence ten pounds etc . . .'

Here the plaintiff was suing for a straightforward failure to perform a covenant, which failure had resulted in economic loss, and the situation lacked the main feature of the earlier cases—the entrusting of the plaintiff's person or property to the defendant, negligent conduct, and injury to the plaintiff or his property—though there is a suggestion in the writ that the houses, which belonged to the plaintiff, were entrusted to the defendant for re-erection.[4] The plaintiff's serjeant, Gascoigne, could hardly expect to bamboozle the court by saying *assumpsisset* instead of *convenit*, and if he did have hopes he was at once disillusioned by Tirwhit, who said,

[1] See above, p. 210.
[2] Y.B. 2 Hen. IV, M. f. 3, pl. 9.
[3] Note the suggestion that the defendant has been careless, has taken no care.
[4] The houses may have been portable wooden constructions. The practice of prefabrication is referred to by Fifoot, n. 43, citing J. Harvey, *Gothic England*, 38.

'Sir, you see well how he has counted of a covenant, and of this shows nothing [i.e. proffers no deed]: judgment etc.'

The writ was abated, and Rickhill J. explained the reason with a brevity of which our modern judges seem incapable,

'Because you have counted on a covenant and shown nothing for it, you shall take nothing by your writ, but be in mercy.'

Precisely similar treatment was meted out nine years later when a similar action of assumpsit was brought against a carpenter who had failed to build a new house for the plaintiff within a time agreed; in this case there was no suggestion whatever of the entrusting of the plaintiff's property to the defendant. Giving his opinion as to why the action was misconceived Hill J. said,[1]

'Because therefore it seems to the court that this action, which is taken at common law,[2] is founded upon a thing which is a covenant in itself, of which nothing is shown, the court awards that you take nothing by your writ, but be in mercy.'

If actions in cases of this kind were to be refused, the refusal had, somehow or other, to be reconciled with the fact that it could equally be said that assumpsit actions for negligence were 'founded upon a thing which is a covenant in itself'. Not only could this be said; as we have seen, it was said. The distinction which was drawn in order to reconcile the decisions was the distinction between *misfeasance* and *nonfeasance*.

Misfeasance and nonfeasance

It came to be the orthodox legal doctrine of the fifteenth century that an action on the case based upon an assumpsit would not lie upon a nonfeasance; in order to succeed, a plaintiff must show that the defendant had done something wrong. Doing something, a misfeasance, was contrasted with doing nothing, a nonfeasance, so that it was not sufficient to show that the defendant had merely failed to do whatever he had agreed to do. The function of this distinction is easy enough

---

[1] Y.B. 11 Hen. IV, M. f. 33, pl. 60 (1409).
[2] Hill J. is contrasting the action with an action based upon the Statute of Labourers, which might have been available; see above, p. 48.

to understand. It served to demarcate the respective spheres of the action of covenant and the action on the case. For, as Martin J. explained in *Watkin's Case* (1425), without some sort of distinction it would inevitably soon become the law that,

'for every broken covenant in the world a man shall have an action of trespass.'[1]

The problem which Martin J. saw may not have been simply the problem of overlapping remedies, nor simply a problem of jurisdiction, involving the respective spheres of the royal and local courts. What he and other lawyers were perhaps concerned about was the danger involved in abandoning formality in the common law of contract, a danger which must have been very obvious at the time when the common law courts possessed only a rudimentary technique for establishing the truth by evidence, and a grossly unsatisfactory and as yet unidealized oracle, the jury, for deciding questions of fact. Had the defendant been protected from groundless claims by the right to wage his law, the feeling might have been different. But in the context of the fifteenth century common law there was perfectly good sense in resisting ingenious attempts to bring tort actions upon agreements without producing respectable proof that there had in truth been an agreement. Such attempts, if encouraged, would inevitably lead to the collapse of the whole structure of the medieval common law of contract (as indeed happened in the end), a prospect which was hardly likely to be viewed with enthusiasm by the legal profession as a whole.

What was really required was a doctrine which would enable petty agreements, where it was futile to insist upon a deed, to be sued upon by action of assumpsit so long as they could be reliably proved, for whilst it was sensible enough to require those who made important contracts to go through the formalities, it was quite another matter to require any formality at all from those who took their horses to be shod. In an oblique way the rule requiring a deed before covenant could be brought in the common law courts drew some such distinction in practice; petty cases were determined in the local courts, where actions of covenant lay without specialty, and the defendant was protected by wager, whilst serious business transactions were litigated

[1] Y.B. 3 Hen. VI, H. f. 36, pl. 33.

in the common law courts. In such cases respectable businessmen would in practice execute a deed, normally making their
contracts by the conditioned bond. The statutory provision
which excluded claims for less than forty shillings in the royal
courts was capable of producing the same sort of division. But
the fifteenth-century lawyers were faced not only by the fact
that the rule requiring a deed in covenant cases had already
been partially bypassed by the early assumpsit cases, but also by
the fact that the forty-shilling rule was systematically evaded,[1]
and the local courts, as ever, do not appear to have satisfied
litigants. It was somewhat unrealistic therefore to insist that
petty covenants should be reserved for the local courts. On the
other hand the common law judges were understandably
reluctant to undermine the importance rightly attached to
formality in contract law. The nonfeasance rule, which most of
them adopted as a general restriction upon the scope of the
action on the case for assumpsit, was an unhappy compromise,
because it enabled plaintiffs to sue on informal agreements in
the royal courts in big and little cases alike; it lacked apparent
rationality because it failed to differentiate between situations
where insistence on formality was sensible and situations where
it was not. In consequence the rule was bound to be constantly
under attack, for granted that a man may sue a carpenter on an
informal agreement for building badly, what sense can there be
in saying that the same carpenter is immune from suit if he fails
to build at all? The only defence which could have been made is
that where performance has been begun there exists satisfactory
evidence of the existence of an agreement, of which a jury may
have knowledge; this was to be the rationale three centuries
later of the equitable doctrine of part performance. This
rationale lies behind the argument of Newton in a case in
1436:[2]

> 'And the cause in all these cases [cases of misfeasance in the
> performance of parole covenants] is that there is an under-
> taking and a matter in fact [*matier en fait*] beyond that which
> sounds in covenant.'

---

[1] See Milsom, 'Sale of Goods in the Fifteenth Century'. 77 L.Q.R. 250 at
260.

[2] 14 Hen. VI, f. 18, pl. 58 (Fifoot 344).

The 'matter in fact' was something of which a jury might have knowledge.

The formulation of the nonfeasance rule

Nevertheless, the nonfeasance doctrine had a long innings; it appears in 1400, and it is found as the basis of a dissenting judgment in the King's Bench as late as 1533.[1] It may have restricted the action in a curious way, but it could be made to work, and it is obvious that some lawyers thought that it was rationally defensible. *Watton* v. *Brinth* (1400)[2] is the first case in which the doctrine is adumbrated; it is not there stated by either of the justices, but comes from Bryn, who, having agreed that 'this is merely a covenant', adds,

'and perhaps if he had counted, or in the writ mention had been made that the thing had been commenced and then by negligence[3] not done it would have been otherwise'.

Nine years later, in a similar case against a carpenter for failure to build a house, Norton, replying to the argument that 'this matter sounds in a manner of covenant, of which covenant he shows nothing', says,

'And we ask judgment sir, for if he should have made my house badly and should have destroyed my timber,[4] I should have an action sure enough on my case without a deed.'

To this Thirning C.J. replied,

'I grant well in your case, because he shall answer to the tort he has done, *quia negligenter fecit*. But if a man makes a covenant and shows nothing beyond the covenant, how shall you have your action against him without specialty?[5]

In 1425 in *Watkin's Case* the doctrine is rather more fully formulated by Martin J.:

'Suppose we put the case that a farrier makes a covenant with me to shoe my horse, and by his negligence he lames

---

[1] *Pickering* v. *Thoroughgood*, Spilman's MS. Reports, see Appendix, Case No. 6.
[2] Y.B. 2 Hen. IV, M. f. 3, pl. 9.
[3] i.e. neglect.
[4] The suggestion is that the plaintiff has provided the materials, and the defendant assumed custody of them.
[5] Y.B. 11 Hen. IV, M. f. 33, pl. 60.

my horse, on this matter shewn a good writ of trespass lies, for notwithstanding that in the rehearsal of the matter a covenant is supposed, I say that in as much as he has done badly what he covenanted to do, the covenant is thereby changed and made into a tort, for which a good writ of trespass lies.'[1]

This is the classic statement of the doctrine,[2] whose plausibility depends upon a contention that a total failure to perform an agreement cannot sensibly be treated as anything else but breach of covenant—not doing is no trespass, no tort, whatever else it may be.

The doctrine seems also to have been associated with the idea that doing nothing cannot bring about loss of a kind distinct from the mere loss of the bargain. This causal point lies behnd many of the illustrations used in fifteenth-century cases. Now the most obvious way in which a distinct form of loss (distinct, that is, from deprivation of expected advantage) can be caused is when physical damage is done to the plaintiff's property or person. Where a surgeon, who has agreed to cure the plaintiff's eye, negligently puts it out, the patient's complaint is not just that he has not been cured; his grumble is that the surgeon has not merely failed to improve the position but has actually made matters worse. Hence in cases where the nonfeasance rule was under attack there constantly recur hypothetical examples designed to show that doing nothing, just like doing something badly, *can* cause extra harm by making matters worse. Hence Babington C.J. in *Watkin's Case* puts this example,

'Put the case that one makes me a covenant to roof my hall or a certain house by a certain time, and within this time he does not roof it, *so that by default of the roofing the furniture of the house is all damaged by rain* . . .'

Cokayne J. in the same case similarly attacks the basis of the nonfeasance doctrine with this example,

---

[1] Y.B. 3 Hen. VI, H. f. 36, pl. 33.
[2] See also for references to the doctrine Y.B. 21 Hen. VI, P. f. 55, pl. 12 (*Tailbois v. Sherman*); 21 Edw. IV, P. f. 22, pl. 6; 2 Hen. VII, f. 11, pl. 9 (*The Shepherd's Case*); 3 Hen. VII, M. f. 14, pl. 20; *Anon.*, 18 Hen. VII, P. (Keilwey, f. 50, pl. 4). Cases in which the doctrine was under attack are discussed below, at pp. 248-264.

'Put the case that one makes a covenant to repair certain ditches on my land, and he does not do so, *so that by his default the water which should run into the ditches floods my land and destroys my corn* . . .'[1]

In a case in 1436 we find Paston J. devising an example with the same purpose in mind,

'And sir, if a farrier makes a covenant with me to shoe my horse and he does not do it, *and my horse is ruined for lack of shoes* . . .'[2]

These examples show that the nonfeasance doctrine gained its plausibility in part from the notion that doing nothing cannot make life worse; they also show that this notion was open to the obvious objection that doing nothing can do just that. This clearly is what the examples quoted are designed to show, for these examples were devised by lawyers who thought that the nonfeasance doctrine was irrational. Yet the idea that nonfeasance is distinguishable in the nature of things from misfeasance has a persistent appeal, which has diminished little through the centuries, and it is hardly surprising to find it figuring, sometimes in a crude form, amongst the irrational philosophical notions which have influenced the law's development in the past, and which still influence its development in our time.[3]

Assumpsit for misfeasance and legal theory

The lawyers of the fourteenth and fifteenth centuries, though they were not troubled by a purely theoretical dichotomy between tort and contract,[4] which for them had no significance, were nevertheless very soon faced with certain difficulties about the role which an allegation of an assumpsit played in these

---

[1] Y.B. 3 Hen. VI, H. f. 36, pl. 33.
[2] Y.B. 14 Hen. VI, f. 18, pl. 58.
[3] See Hart and Honoré, *Causation in the Law*, pp. 28 (esp. n. 2), 35–6, 121, 131–3, 329–32, 396–8 discussing continental theories. The difficulty which is felt about omissions is not likely to be felt so acutely in the context of an action which lies even where no physical injury to person or property is required, that is in an action where there is no need to show that the defendant produced a physical effect.
[4] Not, that is, in its modern form; they were, as we have seen, concerned with the problem of marking out the respective sphere of the actions of covenant and trespass actions.

actions on the case for misfeasance. For example, were there situations where an assumpsit need not be alleged at all? What was the relationship between an assumpsit and remuneration? In cases where an assumpsit must be alleged, was liability based upon the assumpsit, or on the negligent misfeasance? Such questions as these did not arise for determination in the abstract; they had to be answered only when they were relevant to the determination of some practical question of pleading or procedure, and views as to how they should be answered could and did develop and change.

The most radical question was whether an allegation of an assumpsit was necessary at all in actions for negligent misfeasance. Now, if we consider for a moment the modern common law as it applies, for example, to medical negligence, it is clear that a doctor's duty to use proper techniques and care is not necessarily explained in legal theory as the legal consequence of any agreement, undertaking, or transaction between doctor and patient. His duty *can* be so explained, for a doctor can be sued for breach of an express or implied term of contract, which binds him to use due care. But it need not be so explained; hence a doctor, when he operates on an unconscious patient who has never been party to any voluntary transaction, is just as clearly liable for negligence as one who has made a solemn contract before starting the treatment. In fourteenth-century law the choice between suing a doctor in contract and tort did not exist; our two modern forms of the action for medical negligence are both remote descendants of a tort action, the action on the case for negligent misfeasance. But there were two ways in which the basis for liability in this tort action could be put. One was for the plaintiff to rely upon the transaction, aver an assumpsit, and maintain that the doctor was liable for negligence because he had undertaken responsibility. The alternative was to play down the transaction, and maintain that there was some general rule of law which required doctors to use due care in treating their patients. The difference seems slight, and in most cases it will only represent two ways of looking at the same situation. But appearances here are deceptive: translated into pleading terms the difference may well be critical. For if it is the theory of the law that liability is based upon an undertaking, the assumpsit, certain consequences will follow. A writ which does not allege an assumpsit will be defective, a traverse of the assumpsit will be a good plea, and so forth. Legal theory here will be of direct practical importance.

In the early actions against surgeons, and others, for negligent misfeasance the plaintiff did emphasize the transaction; the forms used maintain that the defendant ought to have used proper care because he *recepit ad salvo cariandum, manucepit, assumpsisset.* The precise significance of these allegations was not canvassed, and for this reason, as we have seen, it is rather obscure. In the fifteenth century (there may be hints earlier) the idea developed that persons who exercised occupations which required skill and training, those who practised an art, craft, or mystery, were bound because of the nature of their calling to behave in a competent manner, so that in consequence some thought that such persons could be sued for negligence without an assumpsit being alleged. By the end of the medieval period the author of the book known as Fitzherbert's *New Natura Brevium* felt able to state it as a general principle that,

'It is the duty of every artificer to exercise his art rightly and truly as he ought.'[1]

What this meant was that in actions against artificers an assumpsit need not be averred. The steps which this view developed are not at all easy to follow. It involves a shift in emphasis from a theory of self-imposed liability for negligence to a theory that liability is imposed by law.

The common calling and the need to allege an assumpsit[2]

This shift has been thought by some writers to have been intimately connected with the controversial history of the 'common callings', for it has been supposed that there existed a

---

[1] F.N.B. 94D. This book was published in 1534 for the first time; Fitzherbert patronized the publication but was not the author of the text, which was an Inn of Chancery teaching manual in all probability.

[2] The main secondary literature is as follows: Holmes, *The Common Law*, 183–205; J. Beale, 'The History of the Carrier's Liability', *Select Essays in Anglo-American Legal History*, III. 148; E. G. M. Fletcher, *The Carrier's Liability*; P. Winfield, 'The History of Negligence in the law of Torts', 42 L.Q.R. 184; Fifoot 157–60; *H.E.L.* III. 385–6. The account given in the text differs considerably from that given by earlier historians.

set of general legal principles which governed all common callings, one of which imposed liability for negligence in the
absence of an assumpsit. This view seems mistaken, and to
show why I must digress.

The adjective 'common' as applied to such persons as hang-
men, prostitutes, informers, serjeants, labourers, attorneys,
innkeepers, carriers, originally[1] means no more than available
to or for the public, or generally available. Thus the common
hangman renders his disgusting services for the public generally,
and no doubt when he has become no more than a nasty
memory prostitutes will continue to make their services generally
available, thus being common prostitutes. Common innkeepers
are common because they keep a common inn, and not a private
inn like the Middle Temple.[2] This is the sense in which the word
is used in medieval cases, and it cannot be too strongly emphasized that the term is used without any technical overtones
whatsoever at this period; it is nowhere found as a legal term of
art. Once this is appreciated, it can be seen that attempts to
compile lists of persons who, *in law*, exercise common callings,
are quite radically misconceived; there were no such lists to
be discovered. What was or was not a common calling was
purely a question of fact, so that as soon as persons set up in
business as carriers of goods for the public generally there are
common carriers,[3] just as there are common attorneys[4] as soon
as persons begin to make an occupation of acting as attorneys for
the public generally.[5] There appear to be no common cooks,

---

[1] In the course of time the word has acquired special senses, as in the case of
'common prostitute'.

[2] See Y.B. 11 Hen. IV, H. f. 45, pl. 18.

[3] On medieval references to persons as common carriers see Fifoot 157–8; Mr.
Fifoot refers to a reference in 1459, and gives other examples. See too Plucknett
482, who notes a reference as early as 1392. To the reference given by Fifoot and
Plucknett there may be added the following order by the Keeper of the Town o
Beverley, issued in 1418, 'Recitata fuit antiqua ordinacio de portitoribus et Crelers
et aliis communibus cariatoribus . . .' S.S. Vol. 14, p. 22. This order suggests an
explanation of the relative infrequency of references to carriers—the term carrier
embraced a number of different medieval jobs, so that a man who was a carrier
would usually also be a porter, a hoyman, a creler, or whatever it was, and would
be so described and named. Hence there was no guild of carriers, though there
were guilds for porters. See also at p.57.

[4] See H. Cohen, *History of the English Bar and Attornatus to 1450* (1929). An attorney
basically is a person appointed, and hence an agent.

[5] We still appoint private attorneys by the grant of a power of attorney to a
friend. cf. the old contrast between an attorney at law and an attorney in fact.

not because a case says so, but because medieval cooks are found retained in private employment, and do not cook for all and sundry.

The second quite basic point about the conception of a common calling is that it was not restricted to persons who practised a skilled profession, that is to artificers; the two classes may overlap, but are nevertheless quite distinct. The clearest example of this is the common labourer, who was not an artificer,[1] but yet was consistently treated as 'common', and so described because he could be retained in service by any member of the public who cared to hire him.[2]

Since there is nothing in common between the common callings except the fact that they are common in the sense explained, it would be very surprising to find any general legal principles which applied to all who exercised such callings indiscriminately.[3] What in fact is found in the medieval cases is something which is both more complex and more intelligible: the courts treat the fact that a person exercises a common calling as relevant to his legal position in a variety of different ways. Thus the fact that a person was a common labourer brought him within the provisions of the Statutes of Labourers, so that he could be compelled to serve whoever offered to retain him,[4] and his wages were fixed by the Justices of Labourers.[5] A common hosteler was under a duty to look after the horses and goods of his guests, and was liable if they were lost through the default of himself or of his servants.[6] He must provide food at the market price.[7] He was also bound to receive guests and their horses, though whether this duty was enforceable by action on

[1] See Y.B. 47 Edw. III, M. f. 22, pl. 53; 11 Hen. IV, M. f. 33, pl. 60.

[2] See Putnam, *The Enforcement of the Statute of Labourers, passim* and see Y.B. 50 Edw. III, T. f. 13, pl. 3.

[3] Putative principles which could apply to all 'common callings' are (a) that those who exercise them are strictly liable, (b) that all are liable without proof of an assumpsit, (c) that all must show professional skill, (d) that all are liable for nonfeasance. But the sources do not support the idea that all common callings were covered by any one of these.

[4] 39 Edw. III, P. f. 6, pl. 12; 40 Edw. III, f. 39. Numerous cases discuss who is compellable to serve—e.g. 8 Edw. IV, H. f. 23, pl. 1; 38 Hen. VI, M. f. 13, pl. 30.

[5] Putnam, op. cit.

[6] See 42 Lib. Ass., pl. 17, f. 260 and 42 Edw. III, P. f. 11, pl. 13 and for discussion Kiralfy, Ch. 12.

[7] 39 Hen. VI, M. f. 18, pl. 24.

the case[1] or by criminal proceedings was uncertain.[2] His liabilities were balanced by the lien he enjoyed over guests' property to secure payment of his charges.[3] A common victualler must sell food in the market at the market price if offered ready money;[4] the food he sold must not be corrupt.[5] A common schoolmaster or a common surgeon enjoyed a special defence to an action for a wrongful retainer of another man's servant; if the servant's father took him to a schoolmaster to be taught, or to a surgeon to be cured of a broken leg, the master could not sue with success for wrongful retainer of the servant.[6] A gaoler who kept a common gaol was bound to receive certain classes of prisoner, must provide the prisoners with food and act as surety (subject to a very stringent liability) if a prisoner escaped from the gaol.[7] The decisions of the common law courts, laying down in detail the particular duties, responsibilities, and privileges of persons in various occupations are only a fragment of the multifarious rules and regulations which governed every aspect of medieval life, most of which were organized and enforced by agencies other than the common law courts. What is not to be found in the sources is any attempt to lay down general principles about those who exercised common callings—for example, that they are all liable for nonfeasance,[8] or that they are liable strictly[9]—and the reason for this is obvious

[1] Y.B. 39 Hen. VI, M. f. 18, pl. 24, *per* Moile and Danby C.J., but Prisot C.J. did not agree. The whole court held that action on the case lay in P. 18 Hen. VII (Keilwey 50a). See also Y.B. 14 Hen. VII, P. f. 22, pl. 4, *per* Higham. The same doctrine was thought by Paston J. to apply to smiths in Y.B. 21 Hen. VI, P. f. 55, pl. 12 and accepted in P. 18 Hen. VII (Keilwey 50a).

[2] Y.B. 5 Edw. IV, P. f. 2, pl. 20.

[3] Y.B. 5 Edw. IV, P. f. 2, pl. 20; the same doctrine was applied to tailors and sellers of goods, unless, in the latter case, a day for payment was fixed.

[4] Y.B. 39 Hen. VI, M. f. 18, pl. 24; Danby C.J. was responsible for the qualification that ready money must be offered.

[5] 9 Hen. VI, M. f. 53, pl. 37.

[6] Y.B. 9 Edw. IV, M. f. 31, pl. 4.

[7] See above, p. 128.

[8] Though some were; see *Anon.* (1503) Keilwey 50a.

[9] The two candidates for strict liability are the common carrier and the innkeeper. As for the first, there is little medieval authority, apart from a stray reference in Statham's *Abridgement* (Accompt pl. 56) in *c.* 1460 which suggests that a common carrier was not strictly liable where he was robbed. This is a note by the compiler. See also BM. MS. Harley 1624, f. 28b. The earliest discussion is in St. Germain, *Doctor and Student*, where it is quite clear that the carrier is only liable if he fails to exercise common prudence. The earliest reported case, *Anon.* (1553) Dalison 8, lays it down that a common carrier is not liable if goods are stolen from

enough once it is realized how wide and miscellaneous a category of occupations could be called common.[1]

The relevance of professional status to liability for negligence

When a person was sued by action on the case for negligence it was natural that his professional status would be treated as relevant by pleaders and the courts. Thus where a smith was sued for laming a horse by driving a nail into the quick, one way in which the plaintiff can show that he has misconducted himself is to emphasize the fact that he belongs to a skilled profession, and describe what he has done. For everybody knows that the one unforgivable sin in a smith is to drive the nail into the living flesh, an error which might be excused in an amateur but can never be excused in a professional. It is the medieval equivalent of leaving a swab in a patient. The professional status of the defendant can also be used to show in more general terms what standard of conduct is appropriate; thus in an action against a surgeon the defendant may be said to have undertaken to cure 'according to his calling'.[2] This makes it clear that the action is brought because the surgeon has fallen below the standards of his craft. But what was critical was not the mere fact that the defendant was in a common calling; this fact alone was compatible with his being wholly unskilled. What was important was that he was an artificer, a skilled professional.

The idea that artificers who pursued a common calling ought

[1] The adjective 'common' is found applied to the following occupations in the sources (no doubt an exhaustive search would produce other instances): marshal (Y.B. 19 Hen. VI, H. f. 49, pl. 5), schoolmaster, surgeon (Y.B. 9 Edw. IV, M. f. 31, pl. 4), hosteler (Y.B. 5 Edw. IV, P. f. 2, pl. 20), servant (Y.B. 3 Hen. VI, f. 42, pl. 13), attorney (see p. 230 n. 4, above), carrier (see p. 230, n. 3 above), labourer (11 Hen. VI, M. f. 33, pl. 62), laundress (11 Hen. IV, M. f. 1, pl. 2), tailor, (18 Hen. VI, pl. 5, f. 16). I have only given one reference in each instance.
[2] See Kiralfy 141.

him in a common hostelry, because the carrier can be compelled to carry goods. One who undertakes voluntarily to carry goods, however, is liable if they are lost in an inn, because he is not compelled to carry; he had his remedy over against an innkeeper. The two earliest pieces of evidence are therefore quite inconsistent with the theory of strict liability. As for the innkeeper, the restrictive rules as to the defences he could plead represent not an attempt to impose liability without fault, but rather an attempt to prevent slack or dishonest innkeepers from wriggling out of liability too easily.

to be answerable for negligence because of their status as members of a skilled profession suggested the view that it was unnecessary and immaterial to allege an assumpsit when suing them by action on the case for negligent misfeasance. This suggestion found some support in the fifteenth century, but medieval authority is scanty and deals only with farriers. The leading case[1] is the *Marshal's Case* (1441), where Paston J. says that a person will not be liable for negligent misconduct in attempting to cure a horse of a malady unless he is either a professional (i.e. a common marshal) or has expressly undertaken responsibility. It is not therefore clear that Fitzherbert's principle was justified by authority; it represented a possible analysis of liability for negligence, but not the only possible analysis. The whole history of liability for negligence, right up to our own time, reveals a constant interplay between the idea that liability for negligence can only be imposed if there is some previous *nexus*[2] between the parties and the idea that negligence alone is sufficient,[3] nor is there any indication that the conflict between these two ideas has been resolved in the course of the last five centuries.[4]

The basis of liability in assumpsit for misfeasance

In cases where an assumpsit was alleged, and such cases were the rule, there could still arise the difficulty of deciding the relative importance of the undertaking and the negligent misfeasance. Crudely stated, the problem could be stated in the form of a general question—was the basis of the action the undertaking or the negligence? The theory of liability could be relevant to the decision of various practical questions. Thus there was the problem of venue; supposing the undertaking was

---

[1] In Y.B. 19 Hen. VI, H. f. 49, pl. 5 (Fifoot 345). See also Kiralfy 139.

[2] 'Relationship' is the most commonly used term; I use the Latin term only because it has not been used in this branch of the law. The fantastic edifice of doctrine which has been built up around the concept of a duty of care in negligence, which now rivals in incomprehensibility the wilder doctrines of the old law of property, and possesses something of the same Gothic charm, stands witness to the powerful and persistent influence of this idea.

[3] The scope of liability being explained doctrinally upon other grounds.

[4] In medieval times, however, the relationship between the parties arose through a transaction, which was intelligible enough; in modern law the relationship is supposed to be shown to exist by asking and answering a series of questions of a boldly meaningless character.

given in one county and the misfeasance occurred in another, from which place should the jury come?[1] Or again, if the defendant wished to plead a general traverse, must he plead *non assumpsit*, and deny the transaction, or *non culpabilis*, and deny the misfeasance? Or if he wished to put forward a positive defence, and introduce new matter by means of a special traverse, must he conclude his plea by traversing the *assumpsit* in the *sans ceo* clause,[2] or should he instead deny that he killed the horse by negligence (or whatever it was)? These difficulties, which stem from the fact that in assumpsit a transaction is used to show that particular conduct is wrongful, are closely paralleled in the history of the action of detinue on a bailment, where their solution turned upon the relative importance attached to the transaction of bailment, and the wrongful act of detention; similar difficulties of course arise in modern law.

A modern lawyer would be tempted to say that the real question at issue here is whether assumpsit is a contractual or a tortious action, and the same might be said in relation to detinue. But from a historical point of view this is, first, anachronistic, because the 'contract–tort' distinction in its modern form[3] was then unknown, and, second, misleading because it suggests that the action could have been viewed as something other than an action in which damages were claimed for a wrong or tort. There was no such possibility; the question raised was internal to the law of wrongs, or torts.

The solutions given in the cases represent a compromise, for the courts refused to be driven into saying either that the transaction or that the negligence was the basis of liability. Both

[1] This is a version of a persistent legal problem, which is most familiar today in the field of conflict of laws. Lawyers forever are forced to ask 'where' questions, and to attribute location in contexts where the everyday concept of location provides no guidance.

[2] In a special traverse the defendant, instead of simply denying the story told by the plaintiff, set up as an affirmative case of his own. Thus suppose Smith sues Jones in detinue on a bailment, and in his count says that the goods were bailed to Jones to be safely kept and returned on request, and Jones wishes to defend himself by saying that they were bailed to him to bail over to Tompkins, which he has done. His course of action is to plead these facts, but his plea must conclude with a clause (introduced by the words *absque hoc* or *sans ceo*) which denies that the goods were bailed to him on the terms stated by the plaintiff.

[3] The distinction, though much used by modern writers, is by no means clearly analysed or consistently employed.

were equally relevant. Thus over the question of venue it was decided that the jury could be summoned either from the place where the undertaking was given, or from the place where the act of negligent misfeasance occurred.[1] The ruling here is similar to the ruling given in actions of covenant[2] and in actions based upon the Statute of Labourers for the departure of a retained servant from service, where the same problem arose.[3] Over questions of pleading the same approach was adopted; though in misfeasance actions it came to be settled that the form of the general issue was *non culpabilis*,[4] as in actions of general trespass, it was nevertheless possible to traverse the assumpsit in a special traverse.[5]

Assumpsit and remuneration

In actions of assumpsit whether for nonfeasance or misfeasance it was normal practice to allege either payment or an agreement for payment. The distinction is represented by standard pleading forms; the plaintiff either alleged that the defendant had undertaken 'in return for a certain sum of money previously paid into the hands of the defendant',[6] or that he had undertaken 'in return for suitable remuneration'.[7] The contrast between these two set forms is only explicable if the second form was appropriate where the money had not been paid. But sometimes, as in the case of the *Humber Ferryman* (1348),[8] there is no express mention of remuneration. But this is not perhaps of any significance; everybody would know that a ferryman was entitled to take toll, and so was not working for nothing. It is reasonable to suppose that pleaders would not have troubled to refer to remuneration unless there was a current of opinion that, at the least, it strengthened the plain-

---

[1] See Brooke, *Lieu*, pl. 37 (P. 11 Ric. II), *Accion sur le case*, pl. 107 (1543), and cf. 48 Edw. III, H. f. 6, pl. 11.

[2] 8 Hen. VI, H. f. 23, pl. 9.

[3] 41 Edw. III, f. 1, Brooke, *Lieu*, pl. 76 (26 Hen. VI).

[4] *Elrington* v. *Doshont* (1664) 1 Lev. 142, and see Brooke, *Accion sur le case*, pl. 77.

[5] *Waldon* v. *Marshal* (1370) 43 Edw. III, M. f. 33, pl. 38; *Marshal's Case* (1441) 19 Hen. VI, H. f. 49, pl. 4.

[6] *Pro quadam pecuniae summa prae manibus solutis*; for example, see the record of *Doige's Case* (1442) printed by Kiralfy 227.

[7] *Pro competente salario*; for example, see the precedent from 1374 printed by Kiralfy 226. cf. at p. 225 *pro rationabili mercede*. And see generally Kiralfy 180-1.

[8] 22 Lib. Ass. pl. 41. See above, p. 210.

tiff's case, but we cannot assume that the averment was essential simply from the fact that it was commonly made.

So far as actions for misfeasance are concerned, there is only one medieval case which is perhaps relevant to the matter. This is the *Marshal's Case* (1441),[1] where Newton C.J., in a peculiarly obscure passage, may have expressed an opinion about the relevance of remuneration in actions for misfeasance. The point under discussion in the case was this. A marshal was sued on an assumpsit in London to cure a horse; the plaintiff alleged that he had so negligently and improvidently applied medicines that the horse died. The defendant proposed to plead a special traverse, a plea introducing new matter by way of positive defence—he had undertaken in Oxford to cure the horse, and had done so. Such a plea had to traverse (deny) the gravamen of the plaintiff's averment in a clause beginning *absque hoc*, and the defendant's plea went on: *absque hoc* he had undertaken in London to cure the horse. The argument centred upon whether this plea was good as it stood, or whether the defendant ought to have denied that he had killed the horse by negligence in the *absque hoc*. On this point Newton C.J. said:

'It seems that the plea is good, for suppose that he assumed to cure the horse in Oxford, as is said, and he did so, and then in London your horse has the illness again, and he *de son bon gré* applied his medicines, and then your horse died— now for what he did *de son bon gré* you will not have an action.'

Here Newton's general point is clear enough; he is saying that the mere fact that the defendant killed the horse by negligence in London will not make him liable in the absence of an assumpsit in London; hence it need not be denied. But what is obscure is the contrast which Newton draws between an act done *de son bon gré* and an act done after an assumpsit—what does *de son bon gré* mean? According to one view it means *gratuitously*;[2] Newton C.J. is saying that the marshal will not be liable for what he does gratuitously even though he is guilty of negligent misfeasance.

---

[1] 19 Hen. VI, H. f. 49, pl. 5 (Fifoot 345).

[2] Fifoot 345, thus translates it. Ames 131, quotes the passage, but leaves the expression *de son bon gré* untranslated.

I doubt if this view is correct. The expression *de son bon gré* seems properly to mean 'voluntarily' or 'of his own free will' and there seems to be no linguistic warrant for translating it 'gratuitously'. This still leaves the contrast which Newton C.J. is drawing somewhat obscure—what sense can be made of a contrast between an act done 'of his own free will' and an act done after an undertaking? Perhaps Newton's idea could have been that a marshal who applied medicines after an undertaking was not acting 'of his own free will' in that he was under a duty to apply them; conversely if there was no prior undertaking the act was wholly voluntarily. If this is correct then the sense of the passage would be no different if for *de son bon gré* we read 'without a prior undertaking', and the case has nothing to do with the relevance of remuneration to actions for misfeasance. If this interpretation is correct the earliest authority on the point is *Powtuary* v. *Walton* (1598).[1] This case, decided after the doctrine of consideration had been invented, held that consideration was not necessary in actions of assumpsit for negligent misfeasance. We must resist the temptation to say dogmatically either that this restated what had always been the case[2] or that the law was changed. Alternatively the expression is equivalent to such expressions as 'of his mere motion', and is intended to indicate that the act was voluntary in proceeding from a *nuda voluntas*, a will lacking a cause. This would be an echo of civil or canon law long predating the later reception of doctrines of *causa promissionis*[3]

Remuneration and nonfeasance

As a general rule, as we have seen, actions for *nonfeasance* in assumpsit for broken agreements were not allowed in fifteenth-century law, and in consequence there was little call for any investigation into the relevance of remuneration in such cases.

There is, however, some slight discussion of the question in *Watkin's Case* (1425),[4] where an action was brought against a

---

[1] 1 Rolle Abr. f. 10, pl. 5. See also *Everard* v. *Hopkins* (1614) 1 Rolle Rep. 125, *Coggs* v. *Bernard* (1703) 2 Ld. Raym. 909.
[2] As Ames maintained: see Ames 130.
[3] See below ch. VI and VII.
[4] 3 Hen. VI, H. f. 49, pl. 5 (Fifoot 345).

mill-maker for failure to build a mill. The plaintiff did not state in either the writ or the count the agreed remuneration, and this unusual omission provoked some comment from the court. Both Babington C.J. and Cokayne J. thought that it was essential for there to be agreed remuneration; a gratuitous undertaking was not sufficient to impose liability. But they differed on the question of what must be expressively laid in the pleadings, for Cokayne J. did not think it essential for the plaintiff to aver an agreed price.

'For it is not to be supposed that he should make the mill for nothing, and it is all one as if he had expressly said so in his pleadings.'

Presumably, though he does not say so, Cokayne J. would have allowed a defendant to raise the question by a special plea. Neither judge seems to have attached any importance to pre-payment. *Watkin's Case*, it must be noted, was an action for nonfeasance, and the idea may have been that, because the action was for nonfeasance, remuneration had some *special* relevance. A case in 1441[1] certainly contains this idea. An action was brought for failure to convey land, and this provoked the standard discussion of the nonfeasance doctrine. The reporter notes at the conclusion of the report some interesting remarks by Brown, who was one of the clerks of the court,

'If a man prepays any sum of money that a house be built for him and he does not do it, he will have an action of trespass on his case because the defendant has *quid pro quo* and so the plaintiff is damaged.'

The reporter adds that this doctrine was privately denied, and there is indeed no evidence that it was ever acted upon at this time. Nevertheless Brown's remarks have a curiously prophetic ring about them; Frowicke C.J. was to argue in the same way in a great case of *Orwell* v. *Mortoft* (1506)[2] where he attacked the nonfeasance doctrine but insisted on prepayment as a pre-requisite of liability. Brooke, when he compiled his *Abridgement* in the mid-sixteenth century, when the nonfeasance doctrine had gone, explained away the fifteenth-century cases in which

[1] See Appendix, Case No. 3.
[2] Discussed below, p. 262.

actions for nonfeasance had been denied by suggesting that the plaintiff failed because there had been no remuneration.[1] The common sense behind Brown's theory was clear—the carpenter who had benefited ought to perform, and if he had the plaintiff's money in pocket it was rather foolish to suppose that the plaintiff had suffered no loss through the nonfeasance. In such a case nonfeasance certainly had caused loss. Reasoning of this kind eventually carried the day.

Remuneration or payment of money might be treated as relevant to an action not because of some general rule of law which denied binding force to gratuitous promises, but upon the more mundane ground that the parties had agreed that payment should precede the imposition of any actionable duty upon the promises, and their agreement should be respected. The proper course for a defendant who wished to take this point was to plead a condition specially. Thus in a case in 1475[2] an action of deceit on the case was brought against a vendor of land for enfeoffing a third party in breach of a bargain to enfeoff the plaintiff. The defendant pleaded a condition that the money should be prepaid, and said that it had not been paid, and issue was joined on this. This is as one would suppose; if the bargain was conditional there would be no liability if the condition was not performed, for the promisor is only liable if he has broken the agreement which he has made. But one cannot deduce from this case that he would not have been liable if there had been no condition.

The action for deceit for breach of warranty

At the same time as the courts were developing the action on the case for assumpsit they were also concerned with the evolution of another variety of the action on the case which came to be known as the action on the case in the nature of an action for deceit, or, more shortly, the action for deceit. The history of this variety of the action on the case is complicated by an acute difficulty of classification, which troubled contemporaries just as much as it troubles modern historians; the

---

[1] Brooke, *Accion sur le case*, pl. 7 *Watkin's Case* (Y.B. 3 Hen. VI, f. 36, pl. 33), 'and the reason seems to be that otherwise it is a nude pact from which arises no action, note, for if he undertakes for nothing he is not bound by this undertaking'. cf. pl. 40, where the reasoning is the same.

[2] Y.B. 16 Edw. IV, f. 9, pl. 7.

difficulty arises from the fact that actions for deceits, brought by writs in the *ostenturus quare* form, are so varied in their character that it is well-nigh impossible to detect any helpful organizing principle which can be used as a basis for classifying these actions.[1] The only common features are the use of an *ostenturus quare* writ, the fact that the plaintiff alleges deceit or fraud, and the claim for damages. Such actions could be and in fact were described and classified as actions for trespasses, since they were actions in which damages were claimed for a wrong or tort. Since deceit is a distinct kind of wrong or trespass these actions could be placed in a separate pigeon-hole, and so the compilers of the early abridgements, in their heroic attempts to impose order on the law, treated *Deceit* as a separate legal title,[2] and thus reflected and strengthened the tendency to regard actions for deceits as forming a separate and distinct class of action. Naturally enough, it was thought to be inappropriate to allege that deceits were committed *vi et armis et contra pacem*, and this, coupled with the fact that writs alleging deceits could be varied to suit the particular circumstances of the case, suggested the idea that at least some of these actions could be as well classified as actions on the case as writs of deceit. The difficulty of classification here gave rise to the use of compromise labels, such as 'action on the case in the nature of deceit', or 'action of deceit on the case'.[3] The only way to deal with these

---

[1] The author of Fitzherbert's *Natura Brevium* (1534) 217E attempted to state a general principle, which is discussed below, p. 254. However, although his principle works for many actions for deceit, it does not fit all cases, and in his book he obviously found difficulty in drawing any clear distinction between actions of trespass on the case and actions for deceits. His principle was this: 'This writ properly lieth where one man doth anything in the name of another, by which the other person is damnified and deceived.'

[2] The title is found in Statham's *Abridgement*, which was compiled *c.* 1460, and in the later *Abridgements* of Fitzherbert (1514–16) and Brooke (compiled *c.* 1550). It is also found in MS. *Abridgements* of the fifteenth century, such as BM. Add. MS. 25, 187 (*c.* 1450), Harvard Law Library MS. Dunn 41, Camb. Univ. Kk. v. 1.

[3] To illustrate the confusion: *Garrok v. Heytesbury* (1387) is describe in a headnote as 'a writ on his case' (*bref sur soun cas*) and as 'an action taken in the nature of deceit (*pris en nature de deceit*), in the report as 'a writ of trespass' (*bref de transgressioun*), 'an action taken on our case' (*pris sur nostre cas*), and 'an action of deceit' (*accion de desceit*). Statham classifies the case under *Accions sur le Case* (pl. 15), not under *Disceipte*, but under the latter heading he has a cross-reference, 'See as to deceit in the title action on the case, many matters'. He classifies Y.B. 9 Hen. VI, M. f. 53, pl. 37 under *Disceipte* (pl. 7); Fitzherbert (G.N.B. 94A) has the case under 'Writ of Trespass sur le Case', though he discusses warranties also under 'Writ of Disceit' at 98K.

problems of nomenclature and arrangement is to recognize that they existed, and not to worry about them.[1] Just as today an action in tort will not fail because a name cannot be given to the tort, so in medieval law an *ostenturus quare* writ was no worse off for having no brand on its buttock.

It was through the medium of the action for deceit that the common law courts in Richard II's reign extended jurisdiction to cover actions for breach of warranty which were accessory to contracts for the sale of goods, the first successful action being an anonymous case reported in 1383.[2] Primarily the common law actions on a sale of goods were debt and detinue, and through these actions the royal courts had long exercised jurisdiction over the contract of sale. But neither debt nor detinue could be used to provide a remedy where a buyer of goods had been induced to enter into a contract of sale by the seller's representations as to the quality of the thing sold and had later discovered that these representations were untrue. The consequence was that redress in situations of this kind had to be sought in the local courts. In an anonymous case in 1383, however, a successful attempt was made to develop a common law action, and the precedent established by this case was followed a few years later in *Garrok* v. *Heytesbery* (1387);[3] these two cases both established liability for breach of warranty on a sale of goods and quite permanently affected the treatment of contractual representations in the common law.

The form of the action

The first action is described in Fitzherbert's *Abridgement* as an action of trespass on the case. The plaintiff alleged that the defendant sold him a horse, warranted that the horse was good, safe, and sufficient, and knew that he was in fact full of maladies; these allegations were coupled with an allegation that the defendant had sold falsely and fraudulently.[4] In *Garrok* v. *Heytesbery* (1387) the allegations take the same form in their essential particulars. The plaintiff alleges a bargain to buy a horse at a great price induced by a warranty that the horse was

[1] Or, which is perhaps more important, not to attach too much importance to labels.

[2] *Anon.*, Trin. 7 Ric. II, reported only in Fitz., Ley 41.

[3] Y.B. 11 Ric. II, Trin. (A.S.), 4.

[4] The full text from Fitzherbert is given above at p. 220, n. 1.

sound, the horse being unsound to the knowledge of the seller, and further alleges that the defendant sold fraudulently. The use of the conception of a warranty, previously at home in the land law, is paralleled by its use in *Skyrne* v. *Butolf* (1387).[1] It serves to suggest an analogy between the position of the seller of goods and the grantor of lands; both ought to be answerable if the other party to the transaction fails to acquire what he expected to acquire, whether it be a sound and useful horse or the quiet and profitable enjoyment of land. But this analogy is nowhere expressly drawn in the cases, so that, although it may explain the choice of the term, it cannot be said that the law of warranty in chattel sales was directly influenced by the law of warranties real.

The use of a distinct action—distinct that is from the actions of debt and detinue which enforced the primary obligations of buyer and seller—to impose liability for breach of warranty in sale is the source of the curious way in which the common law even today continues to treat contractual warranties as collateral contracts, prising them apart from the agreement as if the giving of a warranty formed a separate transaction. Thus, to take an example: suppose that Robert promises to deliver a sound horse for money to Peter, and delivers an unsound horse. By the light of nature one would expect the law to say that Robert is under a single obligation—to deliver a sound horse—and to provide a single action if he fails to make his obligation good. This way of analysing the situation only became possible in the sixteenth century, when the courts came to allow actions for nonfeasance in assumpsit. Back in the fifteenth century and the late fourteenth century Robert's promise or agreement had to be split in two, and analysed differently. First, he had contracted to deliver a horse, and if he failed to do this his contractual obligation was enforceable by action of debt or detinue. Secondly, he had induced the buyer to contract by warranting the horse sound, and if the horse turned out to be unsound he could be sued by tort action, the action of deceit. This analysis came into the law in the late fourteenth century; it persists as an alternative to the present day, and is the source of much that is unintelligible in modern law.

[1] Discussed above at p. 214.

The action for deceit and covenant

Just as actions for assumpsit concerned covenants, and could be objected to upon the ground that covenant was the proper action, so too could actions taken on warranties. Thus in *Garrok* v. *Heytesbery* (1387) Lokton took exception to the action on this very ground.

'*Lokton*. Sir, you see well how he has counted on the sale of a horse which we ought to have warranted, which sounds as it were in covenant, upon which he ought to have a writ of covenant; judgment of the writ.

'*Rickhill*. And since this action is taken on our case, that is that we bought a horse with warranty, to which you give no answer, and since we cannot have an action of covenants without a deed, therefore etc.'[1]

The court rejected Lokton's argument, and therefore the action was safe from the objection 'this sounds in covenant'. In a fifteenth-century case, reported only in Statham's *Abridgement*,[2] a principle was invented to explain the relationship between the actions of deceit and covenant. An action was brought on a warranty given on a horse sale, the plaintiff alleging that the defendant sold him a horse at Southwark, knowing him to be infirm in body through various diseases, and warranting him to be sound. Objection was taken to the declaration on the ground that it was *double*,[3] or bad for duplicity. The rule against duplicity in pleading forbad a pleader to allege in his declaration two distinct matters, either of which would be sufficient to create liability. Here the argument for saying that the declaration is double is that it would be enough to allege *either* that the defendant sold a horse, knowing that it was infirm, *or* to allege that he warranted a horse to be sound, knowing it to be infirm. Consequently to allege both the sale and the

---

[1] 'Lokton, sire vous veiez bien coment il ad counte dun vendicion de un chivalle le quel nous duissoms garrauntir la quel gist en maner de covenaaunt de quel il duist avoir bref de covenaunt iugement de bref. Rikill, et del houre qe ceo accion est pris sur nostre cas saver que nous achatames un chivalle ove garraunty a quel vous ne respondez riens et accion de covenaunt nous ne poioms avoir sauns fait par qi etc.'

[2] M. 31 Hen. VI (1452), Statham, *Accions sur le Cas*, pl. 26.

[3] Statham in the same title, pl. 18, comments upon another warranty case that the writ was double.

warranty was objectionable.[1] This argument was rejected by the court:

'And it was challenged for duplicity, and it was adjudged good, for it was said that the action does not lie in this case unless there had been a warranty, also he cannot have an action on that warranty unless he shows the deceit. For upon the warranty by itself the action does not lie without a specialty, because it sounds in covenant, and therefore it is necessary that he show a deceit precedent.'

Put more fully, the reasoning of the court was that the defendant's liability did not arise simply because he had failed to make good a warranty; he was liable because he had fraudulently induced the plaintiff to make a contract of sale by giving a warranty which he knew to be false; this was the deceit which was essential to the cause of action. It was not necessary to show that the buyer had been tricked out of money, and thus not necessary to show that he had paid the price before action was brought. Nor did the deceit make the contract void; the seller retained the right to sue for the price.[2] It was this fact that Hussey C. J. in 1493 regarded as the justification for allowing an action of deceit.

The scope of liability

It is not possible to tell from the evidence precisely what words or expressions or conduct on the part of a seller counted in law as a warranty;[3] whether some rather formal statement had to be made or not is wholly uncertain. Not only is it impossible to tell what the law was on the subject, but it is highly probable that there was no law. Under the medieval system of common law, attention concentrated upon the pleadings, and the intricate body of rules as to what must be pleaded, and what must not, gave expression to principles of substantive law. But once the case passed beyond the pleading stage, and an issue

---

[1] I have reconstructed the argument; the note of the case assumes that the reader will take the point without explanation.

[2] See Y.B. 9 Hen. VII, H. f. 21, pl. 21, *per* Hussey C.J. *et tot.cur*. But there must be a price, for otherwise there was no *bargain*—no price, no sale. See Y.B. 7 Hen. VI, M. f. 1, pl. 3 (1428), and cf. Y.B. 37 Hen. VI, M. f. 8, pl. 18 (1468). The civil law started from the same principle.

[3] For the later law on this point see below, p. 536, and cf. the discussion of what counted as a promise, below, p. 407.

was submitted to a jury, we enter an area of no-law. There existed at this time no law of evidence—there could therefore be no legal rules as to what evidence could be used to show that a warranty had been given. Furthermore the idea that the jury ought to be directed was in its infancy. Hence it seems futile to attempt to discover what *counted* as a warranty; what counted as a warranty was simply a jury matter.[1] Indeed many attempts to trace back rules of law into medieval times are futile because of a failure to appreciate the fact that on many questions there were then no legal rules.[2] We can only discuss the scope of liability in terms of what had to be pleaded.

In all the early cases the plaintiff relied upon a warranty of quality which the vendor knew to be false, and the reasoning in the case in Statham's *Abridgement* (*Anon*, 1452) indicates that at that time the scope of the action was confined to such cases.[3] This at least was the prevalent view. There was, however, an exception in the case of the seller of corrupt victuals, who was liable even if he gave no warranty. The explanation of this exception was the fact that the sale of corrupt food was forbidden by statute, and for this reason it was thought to be unnecessary to allege a voluntary self-imposition of liability by warranty.[4] Here too the rule in the early fifteenth century appears to have been that the seller must know that the victuals were corrupt.[5] In the course of the fifteenth century there was a

---

[1] Hence all discussion of 'express' or 'implied' warranties in medieval law are misconceived; so too is any discussion of the supposed distinction between false warranties and false representations of fact (see *H.E.L.* III. 407–8).

[2] Typical of such futile inquiries is this: was negligence sufficient for liability in trespass in medieval law, or did you have to prove intent? The short answer is that you always pleaded as abusively as possible, and alleged not just that the trespass was intentional, but much worse than that. Nobody had to prove anything, and the idea that it would be a good plea to say that you wounded (or whatever it was) the plaintiff negligently, incompetently, unskilfully, etc. rather naturally never occurred to anyone; such a plea could only have been put forward as a joke.

[3] But the objection that the count was double would hardly have been put forward unless there was a feeling that the scope of the action was wider; this is what Statham himself thought. See above, p. 244, n. 3.

[4] Y.B. 9 Hen. VI, M. f. 53, pl. 37 (1430); 11 Edw. IV, T. f. 6, pl. 10 (1472); Keilwey 91a, F.N.B. 94C n. The same principle applied to a taverner.

[5] See Y.B. 7 Hen. IV, P. f. 14, pl. 19; 11 Hen. VI, H. pl. 10 at f. 18. There is some obscurity about the position of the seller of wine in bulk; he seems to have only been liable if he warranted. Perhaps this is explicable by the custom of tasting—one who neither tasted nor relied on a warranty had only himself to blame. See generally F.N.B. 94C.

tendency to extend the scope of the action of deceit, and impose a more stringent liability. Thus in 1507 Frowicke C.J. stated the law in the form of three propositions.[1] The seller of victuals was liable if he sold corrupt victuals whether he knew or not, and whether he warranted or not. Sellers of other chattels who knew that they were defective when the buyer did not were liable even if no warranty was given. Sellers of other chattels who warranted quality were liable irrespective of their knowledge of the defect. Of these three propositions the first and last probably represented current orthodoxy.[2] The second is problematical. There is nothing surprising in Frowicke C.J.'s view, for, as Professor Hamilton put it,

> '*Caveat emptor* is not to be found among the reputable ideas of the Middle Ages.'[3]

There is, however, no real evidence that the common law courts in practice gave effect to so paternalistic a doctrine.[4] There was never liability for patent defects, [5, 6] and whether there could be liability in a master for a warranty given by his servant was controverted.

> 'An action on the case does not lie against the servant on such warranty nor (as some held) against the master, for he did not warrant them.'[7]

[1] Keilwey, 91a pl. 16; this does not seem to be the report of a case, but a mere dictum, a fact to which contemporaries would have attached no importance.

[2] The evidence on the relevance of knowledge is not perfectly clear. In Y.B. 11 Edw. IV, T. f. 6, pl. 10 (1472) Brian C.J. seems to suggest that there could be no liability for breach of warranty in the absence of knowledge; however, I think that he was only saying that there could be no liability unless it is *possible* for the seller to know the truth. Liability can only therefore be incurred on warranties of existing facts, and this doctrine is agreed by Choke J. Littleton J. was certainly prepared to treat knowledge as irrelevant, but may have agreed with Choke J. and Brian C.J. that only existing facts could be the subject of a warranty.

[3] W. H. Hamilton, 'The Ancient Maxim Caveat Emptor', 40 Yale L.J. 1133 at 1136.

[4] Paston J. in *Doige's Case* (1442) Y.B. 20 Hen. VI, T. f. 34, pl. 4, took the same line as Frowicke C.J., and referred to an earlier case in the Common Pleas where he said the doctrine has been applied; the reporter noted that in fact there had been a warranty in the case which Paston J. relied on.

[5] This was assumed in Y.B. 13 Hen. IV, M. f. 1, pl. 4, where Thirning C.J. stated an exception; there could, he said, be liability for patent defects if the goods were not available for inspection at the time of the sale. See also on patent defects Y.B. 11 Edw. IV, T. (1472) f. 6, pl. 10, and F.N.B. 94C.

[6] As to defects in title see 42 Lib. Ass. (1367) pl. 8. As to the failure of goods sold to correspond with sample, see Y.B. 14 Hen. VI, f. 22, pl. 66 (1446).

[7] F.N.B. 94C note (*b*).

II

THE ACTION FOR
BREACH OF PROMISE

So long as the courts maintained the rule that assumpsit would not lie for a pure nonfeasance, it was impossible for litigants to use assumpsit as a complete substitute for the action of covenant, and thereby evade the rule which generally prevented litigation in the common law courts on agreements which were not made under seal. The nonfeasance doctrine, as we have seen, appeared in the law in 1400, and for well over a century it exercised a powerful restraining influence over the development of assumpsit.[1] But like all legal doctrines it was continually in danger of erosion; whilst it could never be ignored, it could be and was attacked, distinguished, reformulated, and by less timorous spirits flatly rejected,[2] with the consequence that a series of exceptions to the doctrine came to be recognized by the courts. Eventually the exceptions became dominant, so that it began to seem more comprehensible to reverse the rule and to say that assumpsit *did* lie for nonfeasance, and to explain the situations in which the action did not lie as *exceptions* to this new general principle. This stage was reached by about 1530, and thereafter it was no longer worthwhile for counsel to base an argument

[1] The doctrine is referred to in the following fifteenth- and early-sixteenth-century cases: *Watton* v. *Brinth* (1400) Y.B. 2 Hen. IV, M. f. 3, pl. 9; *Anon.* (1405) 7 Hen. IV, H. f. 8, pl. 10; *Anon.* (1409) 11 Hen. IV, M. f. 33, pl. 60; *Watkin's Case* (1425) 3 Hen. VI, H. f. 36, pl. 33; *Somerton's Case* (1433) 11 Hen. VI, H. f. 18, pl. 10, P. f. 25, pl. 1, T. f. 55, pl. 26; 14 Hen. VI f. 18, pl. 58, *The Marshal's Case* (1441) 19 Hen. VI, H. f. 49, pl. 5; *Doige's Case* (1442) 20 Hen. VI, T. f. 34, pl. 4 (and see S.S. Vol. 51, p. 97, and Kiralfy, *Source Book*, 192); *Tailbois* v. *Sherman* (1443) 21 Hen. VI, P. f. 55, pl. 12; *Anon.* (1443) 22 Hen. VI, H. f. 52, pl. 29; 37 Hen. VI, M. f. 8, pl. 18 (*Alice's Case*); *Anon.* (1482) 21 Edw. IV, P. f. 22, pl. 6; *Anon.* 2 Hen. VII (1486), H. f. 12. pl. 15; *The Shepherd's Case* (1486) 2 Hen. VII, f. 11, pl. 9; *Anon.* (1487) 3 Hen. VII, M. f. 14, pl. 20; *Anon.* (1502) Keilwey f. 50, pl. 4; *Nota* (1498) 21 Hen. VII, M. f. 41, pl. 66; *Orwell* v. *Mortoft* (1505) 20 Hen. VII, M. f. 8, pl. 18; and Keilwey, ff. 69, pl. 2 and 77, pl. 25 (see too Kiralfy, *Source Book*, 150). For the rule that where breach of duty was actionable the correct action was case see 12 Hen. IV, M. f. 3, pl. 4. I have printed in the Appendix (Cases Nos. 3 and 4) two previously unpublished cases on the doctrine from 1441 and 1443.

[2] As by Paston and Juyn JJ. in 14 Hen. VI f. 18 pl. 58.

upon the discarded proposition that the action of assumpsit did not lie for nonfeasance.

The traditional theory

Traditionally, however, it has been supposed that this radical change in legal doctrine was accomplished with remarkable rapidity; that the courts, having maintained the doctrine that assumpsit did not lie for nonfeasance in its full rigidity for over a century, suddenly abandoned the doctrine in the first few years of the sixteenth century.[1] Such legal revolutions are possible in the common law system; they have not, however, been common incidents in English legal development. In this particular instance the evidence for a sudden change is a case, *Orwell* v. *Mortoft*, reported in 1505,[2] and a note in the yearbook recording the opinion of Fineux C.J. expressed in the following year, 1506.[3] On the basis of this evidence it has been supposed that the change can be attributed with some precision to the years 1505–6. Before this time the nonfeasance doctrine can be found in the reports, the latest statement being in a note in Keilwey's *Reports* in 1502,

> 'where a carpenter makes a bargain to make me a house and does nothing, no action on the case lies, for it sounds in covenant. But if he makes the house improperly, the action on the case lies well.'[4]

This note, as Mr. Fifoot puts it, seems to be 'the last unashamed pronouncement of the old order',[5] for after 1505–6 there is no case in the printed law reports where the doctrine is mentioned, and it is particularly noticeable that in *Tatam's* or *Jordan's Case* (1535)[6] nobody thinks it worthwhile to refer to the doctrine, even as a preliminary to rejecting it. There is, therefore, some plausibility in the traditional account of the matter.

Nevertheless I do not think that the traditional account of the chronology is correct. Manuscript evidence indicates that the

---

[1] See Ames 141–2, *H.E.L.* III. 341 et seq., Fifoot, Ch. 14.
[2] Y.B. 20 Hen. VII, M. f. 8, pl. 18, Keilwey, ff. 69 and 77; and see Kiralfy, *Source Book*, 150.
[3] Y.B. 21 Hen. VII, M. f. 41, pl. 66.
[4] Keilwey, f. 50. pl. 4.
[5] Fifoot 337.
[6] Y.B. 27 Hen. VIII, M. f. 24, pl. 3.

nonfeasance doctrine did not disappear so suddenly, for as late as 1533 in the case of *Pickering* v. *Thoroughgood*[1] Portman J. justified a dissent from his colleagues in the King's Bench by reference to the doctrine; it still therefore retained some sparks of life a quarter of a century after it is supposed to have died. Moreover, the evidence provided by *Orwell* v. *Mortoft* (1505) and by the note of Fineux C.J.s opinion is not so straightforward as it appears at first sight. The note, though it is printed (along with other notes) in the year-book for 1506, does not in fact belong to that year; what has happened is that the owner of the manuscript which the printer used as copy economically filled up some blank space at the end of a term with jottings of opinions and cases which belong to earlier years. The majority of these addenda were individually dated, and the dates are reproduced in the printed text. The date given for the note on nonfeasance is 1498,[2] not 1506. The chronology here is important, for the note can now be seen to antedate the note in Keilwey by five years, and to antedate *Orwell* v. *Mortoft* by seven. It at once becomes clear that the change in the law was achieved by a more gradual process, and it is here worth remembering that the early years of the sixteenth century are peculiarly poorly covered by law reports, a fact which may tend to conceal from us the details of the transition. Nevertheless, the evidence which is available does, I suggest, indicate that the traditional theory is mistaken, and that the change in legal theory was not a sudden change. Indeed to understand how it came about we must begin our inquiry in the early years of the fifteenth century.

Nonfeasance in the early fifteenth century

The nonfeasance doctrine, as we have seen,[3] appeared first in two cases in Henry IV's reign, *Watton* v. *Brinth* in 1400 and an anonymous case in 1409. Both these cases concerned actions brought on building contracts made by parole. The doctrine, then new, can itself be viewed as an exception to a wider principle; actions on the case will lie on parole covenants, *except*

---

[1] See Appendix, Case No. 6.
[2] The other notes, from pleas 40 to 67 inclusive, come from the years 14, 15, 16, and 19 Henry VII.
[3] See above, p. 225.

where a pure nonfeasance is involved. As these two early cases themselves show—for they were both actions for *nonfeasance*, not *misfeasance*—there never was a time when this restriction on the scope of assumpsit was meekly accepted by the bar. Indeed in 1412, when perhaps the doctrine was not so firmly established as it later became, an action for pure nonfeasance seems to have succeeded. The case is reported in Fitzherbert's *Abridgement*.[1] An action was brought by a seller of hay against the buyer for failure to remove the hay from the meadow where it lay, thus depriving the seller of the use of the meadow. The very brief nature of the report does not reveal whether the plaintiff relied upon an assumpsit to establish the duty or not, nor does it reveal the outcome of the action. We are, however, told that issue was joined upon a plea which denied the sale; no objection in principle therefore was taken to the action. Perhaps the reason was that sales by parole were within the normal competence of the common law courts; sale did not obviously 'sound in covenant', for no action of covenant lay on a sale and so the source of the objection to actions for nonfeasance was absent. Nor was the action used here as a substitute for the primary actions on a sale—debt and detinue; the action on the case was here used to fill a gap in the scheme of remedies and to enforce an ancillary duty, rather in the same way as the action of deceit permitted for breach of warranty in no way poached on the preserves of debt and detinue. But all this is frankly speculative; we cannot certainly say that the action was grounded on an assumpsit, nor tell the story which lies behind the case.

This case in 1412, though perhaps not entirely isolated, was of little-lasting significance; it may be that it only became generally known to the profession in 1516, when Fitzherbert published his *Abridgement*. But even earlier than this, in 1401,[2] the year-books contain an anonymous case in which a pleader did succeed in devising a new way of framing an action on the case for breach of a parole covenant, and the technique which he adopted was destined to become of considerable importance in the subsequent history of the action.

---

[1] *Accion sur le cas*, pl. 48, H. 13 Hen. IV. For a specimen writ (*c.* 1406) of trespass on the case (not an 'assumpsit') for nonfeasance to enforce an ancillary term in a contract of sale see Appendix, Case No. 17.

[2] Y.B. 3 Hen. IV, M. f. 3, pl. 12.

Case was brought against one H, who was steward of a manor which belonged to one A. H had made a covenant with the plaintiff, agreeing to use his influence with the lord of the manor, A, to persuade A to grant to the plaintiff some of the manorial lands. In return the plaintiff had paid him five shillings. The defendant, in breach of this agreement, had caused A to enfeoff a third party of the same lands. Instead of framing his action as an action of assumpsit, the plaintiff's pleader alleged that the defendant had deceived him by causing A to make the conveyance.[1] The report contains no discussion of the propriety of this manner of pleading; instead the issue raised was one of venue—ought the action to be brought where the deceit commenced, which was where the manor was, or where the covenant was made, which was in London? Apparently the view taken by the court was that the basis of liability was the deceit, so that the action ought to be brought in the county where the conveyance took place.

In retrospect the importance of the case lies in the fact that it illustrated a method of pleading which served to blur the distinction between misfeasance and nonfeasance. For clearly, according to one way of looking at the matter, this was an action for nonfeasance; all that the plaintiff was really complaining about was the defendant's failure to perform his covenant. Alternatively it could be said that nonfeasance was not in issue here, for the defendant had done something: he had deceived the plaintiff by bringing about the conveyance of the land to the third party. The case illustrates the fact that it is usually possible, given some ingenuity, to characterize a course of conduct as either an act, or an omission, at will. In later cases lawyers, when confronted with the argument that actions framed in this way were in substance actions for nonfeasance, were able to reply that they were in truth actions for misfeasance; in consequence such actions could be permitted without in any way infringing the nonfeasance doctrine. It was this argument which prevailed in *Somerton's Case* in 1433,[2] where the relationship between actions for deceit and the nonfeasance doctrine was first aired on facts which were in all relevant respects the same

---

[1] This, and not the obtaining of the money, was the deceit.
[2] Y.B. 11 Hen. VI, H. f. 18, pl. 10; P. f. 25, pl. 1; T. f. 55, pl. 26. On the chronology of *Somerton's Case* see Plucknett 641.

as the facts in the anonymous case in 1401. A plausible theory of the matter, designed to justify allowing an action of deceit, was thus stated by Babington C.J.,

> 'For if I retain one to purchase a manor for me, and he does not do so, I shall not have any action against him without a deed . . . but if he becomes of counsel with another in this matter, then, because I have been deceived, I shall have action on my case, for he is bound to keep my counsel when he is retained by me.'

The background to 'Somerton's Case'

Both the anonymous case in 1401 and *Somerton's Case* (1433) itself concern deceits by agents who had been retained to acquire land from third parties; the legal rubric under which these cases belong is today called 'Principal and Agent'. The defendants in these cases had acted as agents or attorneys. Now the control of those who undertook legal business for others, whether they were professional attorneys or not, was a matter of very considerable concern to the medieval courts. Such persons could get up to all sorts of tricks and frauds, and their misdeeds, besides causing grave consequences to their principals, could also seriously embarrass and impede the administration of justice; it is notorious that only in modern times have attorneys become at all respectable.[1] For centuries the common law courts did their inadequate best to stamp out malpractices of various kinds, and one of the weapons which was used in the struggle was the action for damages brought against the attorney by the person who had been cheated. Such actions, brought by writs in the *ostenturus quare* form, or by informal bill, were available in medieval law in a wide variety of circumstances, and provided a remedy for those who had been cheated by persons who, with or without authority, had acted as their legal agents or attorneys. These actions were classified as actions for deceit.

Most actions for deceits which were in use in the fourteenth and fifteenth centuries involved misconduct associated with legal procedures;[2] they included actions against sheriffs who

---

[1] See M. Birks, *Gentlemen of the Law*, *passim*, but especially Chs. 2 and 3.
[2] See P. F. Winfield, *History of Conspiracy and the Abuse of Legal Procedure*, *passim*; Kiralfy, Ch. IV.

make false returns to writs,[1] persons who forge statutes merchant,[2] persons who purchase writs in the name of others without proper authority.[3] The intervention of the royal courts in such situations was obviously proper, for the wrongdoer had deceived not only his immediate victim but the court itself. As we have already seen, the common law courts, in Richard II's reign, had also begun to entertain actions for deceits which were incidental to purely private transactions, by allowing actions for breach of warranty inducing contracts for the sale of goods.[4] This represented a very considerable advance, for the only feature common to both groups of case was the fraud involved.[5] Actions for breach of warranty possess a special importance in that they involve actions for deceits which are connected not with litigation, but with private contracts. Against this background it was no great extension of the law to allow actions for deceit to lie against attorneys retained as agents for the purchase of land; indeed once the courts accepted jurisdiction over deceits in purely private transactions, the development looks almost inevitable.

Retrospectively the author of *The New Natura Brevium* was able to detect a principle behind the extension; the principle was that the action for deceit lay where one person acted in the name of another person in such a way that the other person suffered loss.[6] This was an ingenious formulation for it covered situations of the type involved in *Somerton's Case* and many of the deceits involved in legal procedures, such as the fraudulent purchasing of a writ in another's name without his authority. It could hardly be thought to cover the action for breach of warranty, and in any case the formulation of the principle cannot be found until 1534, long after the liability was firmly

---

[1] F.N.B. 97C; 38 Lib. Ass. f. 224, pl. 13; Y.B. 1 Hen. VI, M. f. 1, pl. 4; 8 Hen. VI, M. f. 1, pl. 3; and see Kiralfy 77.

[2] See F.N.B. 99A, 96B, 5 Edw. IV, M. (L.Q.) f. 126, Y.B. 19 Hen. VI, M. f. 44, pl. 92, and see Kiralfy 81.

[3] 7 Hen. VI, f. 43, pl. 19; 19 Hen. VI, M. f. 29, pl. 51, H. f. 50, pl. 7, P. f. 71, pl. 16. Kiralfy 74, describes this as 'perhaps the classical form of deceit'.

[4] See above, p. 240. The earliest action for 'deceit' in the sense of obtaining money by fraud is *Thompson* v. *Gardner* (1597) Moo. K.B. 538; see Kiralfy 82.

[5] Kiralfy 83, emphasizes the tenuous nature of the connection between such actions and the action for deceits associated with legal procedures.

[6] F.N.B. 95E.

established, though the text of the *New Natura Brevium* was earlier than this.

Somerton's Case (1433) is not an isolated decision. In 1435 an action on the case for deceit was allowed against an attorney retained to purchase land for his principal, who had fraudulently bought the land for himself.[1] In 1456 there is a report of an action in which, on any conceivable reasoning, the shadowy line between misfeance and nonfeasance was crossed.[2] A bill on the case was brought against John Ceveront, an official of the court, who had undertaken (*assumpsit super se*) in return for money paid to make an entry on the record of the court, but had failed to do so. No objection in principle was taken to this action; no doubt it was obvious enough that the court must provide a remedy for misconduct so closely connected with the litigation which came before it. Here was a clear exception to the nonfeasance doctrine in an action openly cast as an action of assumpsit, and it is apparent that the group of cases which establish the liability of deceitful attorneys can perfectly well be reinterpreted and used as support for the proposition that nonfeasance *is* actionable. For it could be said, and eventually it was said, that these cases showed that an attorney was liable if he did *not* execute his office; *ergo* 'not doing' was actionable.[3]

'Doige's Case' and the extension of actions for deceit

The pleading device which was used in 1401 and in *Somerton's Case* (1433) relied for its success upon the ingenious extension of existing authority. In *Doige's Case* (1442)[4] the development was taken one step further. The plaintiff had agreed to purchase

---

[1] Fitz. *Accion sur le cas*, pl. 44 (M. 16 Hen. VI, otherwise unreported). The doctrine in this case was referred to by Wangford, *arguendo* in *Doige's Case* (1442) S.S. Vol. 51 (Hemmant) at p. 98) as settled law. See also 20 Hen. VI P. f. 25 pl. 11 on the boundary between deceit and covenant.

[2] Y.B. 34 Hen. VI, M. f. 4, pl. 12. Another possible liability for nonfeasance is referred to by Stokes *arguendo* in *Doige's Case* as if the point was settled; he says that if counsel fails to appear in a case he is liable in deceit. cf. Y.B. 10 Edw. IV, P. f. 9, pl. 24, where a defence to an action of deceit for failure to enter a plea is discussed: the principle is that an attorney is not liable in deceit if he, on instructions, enters a plea which his conscience tells him ought not to be pleaded, but with the *caveat non fuit veraciter informatus*. cf. also Y.B. 8 Hen. VI, M. f. 7, pl. 16, at f. 8.

[3] *Per* Kingsmill J. in *Orwell* v. *Mortoft*; 20 Hen. VII, M. f. 8, pl. 18 (Fifoot 351).

[4] Y.B. 20 Hen. VI, T. f. 34, pl. 4, S.S. Vol. 51 (Hemmant), pl. 97. For the record see Kiralfy, *Source Book*, 192. Though the correct name of the case is *Shipton* v. *Dog*, the traditional name is more generally used.

land from the defendant, and had prepaid the purchase
price of £100; the defendant in his turn had agreed to enfeoff
the plaintiff of the land within fourteen days. He had not only
failed to do so, but he had enfeoffed a third party. The plaintiff
sued by bill,[1] rehearsing the bargain and the repayment of the
purchase money, and alleged that the defendant had committed
a deceit by making the conveyance to the third party.[2] The
defendant demurred to the bill upon the ground that covenant
was the proper action, and after prolonged argument, including
a full-dress disputation in the Exchequer Chamber, the plaintiff
had judgment on the demurrer.

What is remarkable about *Doige's Case*, and what distinguishes
it from *Somerton's Case* (1433), is that it extended the doctrine
previously applied to intermediaries or agents in land transactions to the vendor himself; it was the vendor's deceit which
was the ground of the action, and not the deceit of the purchaser's attorney. This was quite a new departure, though it
may have owed something to the earlier development of the
seller's liability for deceit in sale of goods; if the seller of goods
was chargeable for deceit, there was no very good reason why
the seller of land should not be chargeable. But though the
action in *Doige's Case* was framed as an action for a deceit, it
could only be by very strained reasoning that the deceit could
be distinguished from a mere failure to perform the agreement,
and of course the proper action for that was covenant; hence
the demurrer. Ascough J. indeed supported the demurrer on
the ground that in substance the action was an action for
breach of covenant.

'If a carpenter undertakes to make a house for me and he does
not do this I shall not have a writ of trespass but only an
action of covenant if I have specialty; but if he makes the
house and makes it badly then I shall have action on my case,
for by this misfeasance the cause of my action begins. So in
our case if the defendant had retained the land in his hand
without making enfeoffment to another, then the plaintiff
would only have a writ of covenant, and I think that it is all
the same case whether the defendant makes a feoffment to a

---

[1] This is of no substantive importance.
[2] Note that the deceit laid was not obtaining the money.

stranger or whether he retains the land in his own hand. Therefore the action does not lie.'

To counter this argument the other judges, who favoured the action, were forced into considerable flights of ingenuity, designed to show that the distinction between the deceit and the breach of covenant was no mere sophistry. Thus Paston J. gives this example,

'Suppose a man bargains to enfeoff me, as in our case here, and he afterwards enfeoffs another, and then he re-enters [i.e. on the first feoffee] and enfeoffs me, and the other ousts me. Now here the action of covenant may not be brought, because he has at last enfeoffed me according to his covenant, and yet the deceit remains upon which an action may be based. Wherefore it does not always follow that where there is a covenant the action of deceit will not lie.'

Paston J. in another passage drew an analogy with the law of sale of goods, where as we have seen actions for deceit for breach of warranty were by this time common form, the duty not to deceive the buyer and the duty to deliver the goods in performance of the bargain being kept distinct, and sanctioned by distinct forms of action.[1] Fray C. B.[2] and Westbury J.[3] gave examples designed to support the same argument.

Newton C.J.s doctrine of disablement

Newton C.J. was indeed prepared to adopt a more extreme position. As the Chief Justice pointed out, the law on parole sale of law was wholly anomalous, for whilst the vendor, if he conveyed the land, could recover the purchase price by writ of debt, the purchaser, even though he had paid, was unable to bring any action against a defaulting vendor—unless, of course, he was allowed to use deceit.[4] On the straightforward argument

---

[1] The development of Roman Law was in this respect similar. See A. M. Honoré 'The History of the Aedilician Actions from Roman to Roman–Dutch Law', *Studies in the Roman Law of Sale*, (ed. Daube) 132.

[2] Fray C.B.'s example was substantially the same as Paston J.'s.

[3] 'If a man after such a bargain as in our case but before the feoffment made a statute merchant [i.e. mortgaged the land] and then made feoffment, the party would have a writ of deceit.'

[4] 'This then would be remarkable law (*merveillous*) that there should be a bargain made whereby the one party will be bound by an action of debt and yet

that there should be reciprocity of actions he was prepared to allow the action.[1] From his reasoning it would seem to follow that the enfeoffment of the third party should be treated as irrelevant. But curiously enough Newton C.J. did not draw this conclusion. Instead he emphasized the fact that the vendor, by enfeoffing the third party, had *disabled* himself from ever performing his covenant—having lost the land, he never could convey it. This notion caught on; it is clear that after the decision in *Doige's Case* it was settled fifteenth-century law that deceit only lay against a vendor if he had so disabled himself; there is an express decision on the point in 1487.[2] This is a remarkable example of judicial timidity, and the rule at first sight appears to make very little sense. One possible explanation may be sought in the relationship between law and equity.

Sale of land in equity

The absence, before *Doige's Case*, of any action to protect the purchaser of land by parole contract may not have been a very serious defect in the law; properly conducted sales of land could be made enforceable by conditioned bond, and cases of genuine hardship must always have been rare, though there is an example of a common law action which failed in 1441, the year

---

[1] Prisot C.J. agreed with Newton C.J. that debt lay on a bargain and sale of lands without livery; see Y.B. 37 Hen. VI, Mich. f. 8, pl. 18. His views on the use of deceit by the purchaser are not known. Newton C.J.'s view on debt is also found in 19 Hen. VI, f. 24, pl. 47 and 22 Hen. VI, f. 43, pl. 28. Ames criticized this view (Ames 140 n.3) as idiosyncratic, but this may be unfair.

[2] *Anon.* Y.B. 2 Hen. VII, H. f. 12, pl. 15. cf. on the same doctrine 16 Edw. IV, P. f. 9, pl. 7; 3 Hen. VII, M. f. 14, pl. 20; 14 Hen. VIII, H. f. 15, pl. 1. Ames (141–2) discusses whether prepayment was needed in the cases. On this see above, p. 252, and see Y.B. 16 Edw. IV, f. 9, pl. 7, where a condition for prepayment was pleaded, and issue was joined upon the plea.

---

be without remedy against the other. Wherefore the action of deceit well lies.' There is a difficulty in following Newton's argument. In the vulgate text of the case Newton's point is that the state of the law on *parole* sales of land is anomalous. The text of the same speech given by M. Hemmant in S.S. Vol. 51 at p. 99 is radically different; Newton's point there is not concerned with parole sales, but with sales evidenced by specialty. It is that where a defendant has disabled himself from keeping the covenant, there is no purpose in suing him in covenant even if the contract is under seal (Newton presumably viewed covenant as an action for specific performance). Dr. Hemmant may be mistaken in treating *per fait* (line 34, p. 99) as two words (by deed) and not as one (perfect), and this would entirely alter the meaning of the passage, and conform to the vulgate text. Milsom's suggestion, discussed below, p. 259, would reconcile the apparent conflict.

before *Doige's Case*.[1] Where hardship did occur there was always the Chancellor, and there is some evidence that by 1442 a remedy, which would take the form of an order to convey sub-poena, was available in equity. Newton C.J. expressly mentions the fact that the plaintiff is entitled to have the land 'in conscience'. Later in the fifteenth century the doctrine was developed that a vendor of land on the perfection of the contract held to the use of the purchaser, and in the capacity of trustee he would be compellable to make an estate at the direction of the purchaser. Against this background the doctrine introduced by *Doige's Case*, and applied later in the fifteenth century, takes on a more rational appearance, for if the vendor had enfeoffed a stranger he clearly could not be compelled to make a conveyance to the purchaser; having disabled himself from performance he could not be compelled to perform, for *lex non cogit ad impossibilia*. The stranger might, of course, be compellable under the doctrine of notice, but the enforcement of equitable interests against third parties was at this time in its infancy, and in any case the stranger might well be a purchaser for value without notice. *Doige's Case* filled a gap in the scheme of legal and equitable remedies, rather than a gap in the scheme of legal remedies alone.

Disablement and the nature of covenant

An alternative explanation has been suggested by Professor Milsom.[2] He emphasizes Newton C.J.s rhetorical question:

'To what effect, then, is the plaintiff to have a writ of covenant, when the defendant cannot be held to any covenant with him even if he has a specialty? To no effect . . .'

There may, Milsom argues, have been a notion that an irremediable breach of covenant was not properly within the scope of the action of covenant, which envisaged actual performance as still possible, and this notion could, as he puts it,

'make colourable the use of trespass actions'.

But possibly Newton C.J. is here merely making the point that failing to perform an agreement, and disabling oneself

---

[1] See Appendix, Case No. 3.
[2] See Milsom in 81 L.Q.R. 476 at p. 510.

from ever performing an agreement, are two distinct things. I suspect that the year-book reporter may have telescoped two different arguments in his account of Newton C.J.'s speech.

Nonfeasance and bailment

Stathams *Abridgement* contains a curious case in 1449,[1] where case for assumpsit was brought against a bailee who had undertaken to keep some sacks of wool safely, and failed to do so. The action looks like an action for nonfeasance, but the point is not discussed in the abbreviated report, though the action did apparently succeed. This may be anomalous, but it illustrates the lack of consistency in the history of the nonfeasance doctrine, whilst throwing little light on its erosion.

Chief Justice Fineux and nonfeasance

The next landmark in the year-books is the note of Fineux's opinion, recorded in 1498,[2]

> 'Note, that if one makes a covenant to build me a house by a certain day, and he does nothing about it, I shall have action on my case on this nonfeasance as much as if he had been guilty of a misfeasance, for I am damaged by this, *per* Fineux C.J. And he said that it had been thus adjudged, and he held it to be law. And so it is if one makes a bargain with me that I shall have his land to me and my heirs for £20 and that he will convey the estate to me if I pay him the £20, that if he will not convey the estate to me according to the covenant, I shall have an action on my case, and I will not need to sue out a subpoena.'

This note hardly supports the view that Fineux C.J. was in favour of *generally* abandoning the nonfeasance doctrine. We know[3] that Fineux was of the opinion that case was a gap-filled remedy, which ought not to be allowed to overlap with the writ of debt, and the note is consistent with this. At the most he favoured case where debt did not lie. Furthermore, the two situations discussed in the note do not cover the whole ground;

---

[1] *Accions sur le Cas* 25, discussed by me in 75 L.Q.R. at 366.
[2] Y.B. 21 Hen. VII, M. f. 41, pl. 66.
[3] From his recorded view in *Orwell* v. *Mortoft*.

they involve special considerations, which might well be thought to justify the introduction of exceptions.

We may first consider the sale of land. It is not in the least clear that Fineux (as opposed to the reporter) said anything about sale of land, but even if he did favour assumpsit or deceit at the suit of the purchaser no very startling change in the law is involved. All that is to be abandoned is the requirement that that a third party must have been enfeoffed. At a practical level the change was unimportant; by this time purchasers were sufficiently protected in chancery, and there is no instance known in this period of a plaintiff acting on the advice given in the note, and suing at common law. Nor is there any reason to suppose that other lawyers accepted Fineux's opinion; in *Orwell* v. *Mortoft* in 1505,[1] and again in 1522,[2] the doctrine in *Doige's Case* is simply repeated without modification, though Frowicke C.J. in 1505 did agree with the note on this point, and said that the case had been adjudged.[3]

This leaves us with the action on a building contract, and there is no reason to doubt the accuracy of the note and the statement that the point had been decided. Dicta by Frowicke C.J. in *Orwell* v. *Mortoft* (1505) support Fineux C.J.'s opinion, though Frowicke insists upon prepayment as a necessary condition of liability; read as a whole, the note too perhaps envisages payment. The note clearly records an important development, for it shows that a major exception to the nonfeasance doctrine has been introduced into the law, and introduced just in the area in which the nonfeasance doctrine first appeared in the early fifteenth century.

But this does not mean that the general principle has yet been abandoned, and indeed if the decision to allow an action on a building contract is seen against the background of the medieval scheme of master–servant remedies it is clear that there were particularly good reasons for introducing an exception here. For since the fourteenth century, as we have seen, the common law courts had exercised jurisdiction over parole contracts of service, and so long as a master retained a servant in his service, whether to perform skilled work which was the business of

[1] Y.B. 20 Hen. VII, M. f. 8, pl. 18.
[2] Y.B. 14 Hen. VIII, H. f. 15, pl. 1 *per* Fitzherbert J., and cf. F.N.B. 98F.
[3] Keilwey 77.

artificers or to perform unskilled work, he had an action against the servant for departure from service within the term.[1]

In the mid-fifteenth century the courts insisted that there must be a genuine agreement to enter into service, and not merely to perform particular work as the occasion demanded. It may be—there is no clear evidence—that this change in policy prevented the use of the statutory action against independent contractors, and thus encouraged the use of assumpsit to fill the gap. For unless assumpsit was allowed, the resulting state of the law would be anomalous, the independent contractor being protected by action of debt, whilst his employer was remediless. The decision to allow assumpsit would only amount therefore to a decision to remedy a glaring anomaly, and Fineux C.J., as we know, was of the opinion that the action on the case was available to fill gaps in the law. If indeed actions on the Statute of Labourers were still used semi-fictionally in such cases, which is possible, though unlikely, the decision would only amount to saying that assumpsit rather than the statutory action ought to be used in such cases. Upon this interpretation the practical effect would be trivial, though the impact on legal theory would still be important.

'Orwell v. Mortoft'

In *Orwell* v. *Mortoft* (1505)[2] an action on the case was brought by a purchaser of twenty quarters of barley against a seller for failure to deliver; here the orthodox action would have been debt, and so the action on the case was being used not to fill a gap in the law, but as a substitute for an old contractual action. An earlier attempt to do this, in 1443, had failed.[3] The plaintiff's pleader drew up an ingenious declaration. He declared that he had bought the barley and paid the price, and left it with the seller for safe keeping for a fixed period.[4] He further

---

[1] See above, p. 48.

[2] Y.B. 20 Hen. VII, M. f. 8, pl. 18; Keilwey, ff. 69 and 72; Kiralfy, *Source Book* 150. For discussions of the case see Simpson, 'The Introduction of the Action on the Case for Conversion', 75 L.Q.R. 364; Milsom, 'Sale of Goods in the Fifteenth Century' 77 L.Q.R. 257.

[3] *Tailbois* v. *Sherman* Y.B. 21 Hen. VI, f. 55, pl. 58, see Appendix, Case No. 4 for a report probably of the same case.

[4] Thereby suggesting that the seller was in the position of a bailee, or so according to the report in Keilwey. The record as published by Kiralfy differs, the action being based on a promise, undertaking and covenant to deliver.

declared that the seller had undertaken (*super se assumpsit*) to keep the barley safely and deliver it on the day, but had converted the barley to his own use. The report shows that the argument mainly centred upon the propriety of allowing case in lieu of debt, and the majority of the court, Kingsmill, Fisher, and Vavasour JJ., as reported, took the view that case was inappropriate. The reporter notes that Fineux C.J.K.B. agreed with this. Frowicke C.J.C.P. dissented on this question. The judgment in *Orwell* v. *Mortoft* has not been found; Fitzjames C.J. in 1537 stated that the action was eventually allowed, but one cannot be certain that he was correct in saying this.[1] But the case also clearly raised the problem of nonfeasance, and it is with this aspect of the argument that we are concerned here.

The most interesting remarks come from Frowicke C.J. The general tenor of the Chief Justice's argument makes it plain that he was prepared, if not to abandon the doctrine entirely, at least to countenance very considerable inroads upon it. The actual examples of liability for nonfeasance which he mentions differ not at all from those mentioned by Fineux C.J.—sale of land and building contracts—and in both instances he emphasizes that there must be payment of money as a necessary condition of liability. His general contention seems to be that nonfeasance is actionable so long as the plaintiff can show that he has suffered damage through the deceit of the defendant, and to support this argument he relied considerably upon the doctrine laid down in *Doige's Case*; the seller, by converting the goods, had disabled himself from performance. Kingsmill J. also committed himself to the proposition that nonfeasance was actionable, but, read in context, all he is really saying is this: the mere fact that the action is brought for a nonfeasance is not an insuperable objection to the action, because *sometimes* nonfeasance is actionable. In support he refers not to some recent case, but to the early-fifteenth-century rule that an attorney was liable in deceit, and to the late-fourteenth-century action for the departure of a servant from service, and this makes it clear that he is reinterpreting the nonfeasance doctrine and the old cases which deal with it, and not wholly rejecting it. The significance of *Orwell* v. *Mortoft* (1505) is not then that the case

[1] See *Core's Case*, Dyer 20a and Kiralfy, *Source Book*, 150.

rejected the nonfeasance doctrine, but rather that the arguments of Frowicke C.J. and Kingsmill J. showed how earlier authorities, some of them quite ancient, could be more happily accommodated if it was recognized that there could well be exceptions to the nonfeasance doctrine where good grounds existed for making an exception. This way of looking at the matter could be linked with the idea that the action on the case was primarily a gap-filling remedy.

This link is most obvious in Kingsmill's reasoning, for he argued that there was no objection to actions for nonfeasance as such, but only an objection to such actions where a general action—here the action of debt—was available. Thus the nonfeasance doctrine could be viewed as a mere application of a wider principle, governing the function of the action on the case, to a particular type of case. This principle suggested that, where a general action was not available, case ought to lie for nonfeasance, so long as damage could be shown. This became the prevalent sixteenth-century doctrine. Kingsmill put the argument like this:

> 'And where a general action lies, a special action on the case does not lie, as where assize of nuisance lies, action on the case lies not. But for a nonfeasance, action on the case lies, as if an attorney does not execute his office or a labourer does not do his service in tending my land, for by this I am damaged, and no general action lies.'

On this basis it was permissible to allow assumpsit in any situation not covered by a general writ, so long, of course, as common sense showed that there had been a wrong, and arguments of justice or convenience militated in favour of granting a remedy.

The spread of actions for nonfeasance

The first half of the sixteenth century is peculiarly poorly covered by printed law reports and year-books, and although a number of manuscript reports have survived and can be used to supplement the printed sources, there remain, and perhaps will always remain, serious gaps in the evidence. The meagre handful of cases do nevertheless witness the spread of assumpsit for nonfeasance in the following fields:

(a) PAROLE GUARANTEE AND INDEMNITY

The leading case here is a decision of the King's Bench in 1521, *Cleymond* v. *Vincent*.[1] One Roger Penson was negotiating to buy goods from Cleymond, and Robert Penson was with him. In the negotiations preceding the sale the plaintiff said that he was in doubt as to the payment, and Robert Penson gratuitously and informally guaranteed the debt; it is important to note that the promise was gratuitous, for this is the first instance of the enforcement by assumpsit of a promise of this kind. Robert Penson died without having paid the debt, and the plaintiff, who was presumably unable to get the money from the purchaser, Roger, sued the executrix of Robert the guarantor, in an action of trespass and deceit based upon the promise. The King's Bench, with Fineux C.J. presiding, allowed the action to succeed, and the decision was justified on three grounds. The first was the absence of any other remedy; debt certainly did not lie against executors on a parole contract, and according to the view which was then prevalent, the guarantor would probably not even have been liable in his lifetime, more particularly since the guarantee was gratuitous and he had therefore received no *quid pro quo*. The second ground given was injurious reliance;[2] the plaintiff had suffered a prejudice in that he had delivered the goods (which he was entitled to have retained against payment) to Roger on the faith of the guarantee. The third was the possible peril to the soul of the deceased man if the money was not paid. This is the justification based upon the Christian conception of life after death; the protection of the soul of the deceased guarantor was an object of concern to the court.

Fitzherbert, as counsel, had appeared for the plaintiff in this case, and some years later as a judge he strongly criticized the decision in so far as it allowed an action against executors, for the ruling reversed in effect (though not in theory) the well-established doctrine that a debt due by a simple contract died with debtor.[3] But in so far as the case allowed an action of assumpsit on a gratuitous parole guarantee it was never

[1] *Anon.* Y.B. 12 Hen. VIII, f. 11, pl. 3, Kiralfy, *Source Book*, 198. See also *Norwood* v. *Read* (1558) Plowden 180, and see below, p. 565 for further discussion.

[2] On which see below, p. 429.

[3] *Nota* (1536) Y.B. 27 Hen. VIII, T. f. 23, pl. 21. The case must by then have been in print in a lost edition of the year-book of 12 Henry VIII.

subsequently doubted. In *Jordan's Case* (1535) it is noted by
Luke J. that in his time as a judge (that is between 1532 and
1535) a similar action against a living parole guarantor had been
allowed on a demurrer.[1] *Jordan's Case* itself concerned an action
against one Jordan, who had guaranteed the debt of Tatam,
who was in prison on a judgment debt. Jordan induced the
plaintiff to release the debtor from prison in reliance upon his
promise to pay the debt if Tatam failed to do so. Again the
action was allowed; the argument in the case centred upon
the problem of overlapping remedies, and on this the court
divided. It is noticeable that in *Jordan's Case* the question of
nonfeasance was not raised in argument. Not many years later,
in *Anon.* (1544),[2] an unpublished manuscript contains an
interesting case in which an action of assumpsit was brought
on a gratuitous parole guarantee of a debt due by obligation.
Montague C.J. and Cholmley J. were of the opinion that the
action lay.

So far as contracts of indemnity are concerned, the earliest
case which I have found is *Sukley* v. *Whyte* (1543),[3] which is
inconclusive. The litigation was connected with the well-known
case of George Ferrers, a landmark in constitutional history.[4]
The facts were that Sukley was a sheriff who was unwilling to
arrest Ferrers on a *capias*, since Ferrers was a burgess of Parliament for Plymouth and therefore privileged from arrest. The
defendant Whyte said to Sukley that if he did arrest Ferrers he
would indemnify him against any damage he suffered thereby.
Sukley did arrest Ferrers, and in consequence was imprisoned
in the Tower and lost his office; he therefore sued Whyte on the
agreement. The case was argued in the Common Pleas before
Shelley and Willoughby JJ.; Willoughby J. favoured liability
and Shelley J. was unwilling to commit himself. The discussion
is of particular interest for three reasons. The first is that the

---

[1] Y.B. 27 Hen. VIII, M. f. 24, pl. 3. For a note on the dating of the case see 74
L.Q.R. 384 n. 17. Brooke J. who appears in the case was dead by 1535, and in
any case he is in the wrong court. Either the reporter has made a mistake or, more
probably, the copyist mistook Luke for Brooke, perhaps writing to dictation. The
case is also reported in B.M. MS. Hargrave 388 at f. 140a.

[2] Library of Congress MS, Washington, D.C., 'A collection of MS. Yearbooks'
at f. 25v.

[3] See Appendix, Case No. 9 and for *Ferrer's Case* see O. Bridg. at p. 625.

[4] See *Tangswell-Langmead's English Constitutional History* (ed. Plucknett) 11th. ed
249.

nonfeasance doctrine was not mentioned. The second is that Willoughby J. in his argument said that he was able to show a reported case on similar facts in which liability had been imposed. The third is that the discussion reveals an anxiety lest the scope of promissory liability might be in danger of extending too widely; this aspect of the case is considered later in the course of this chapter.

(*b*) ACTIONS AGAINST BAILEES

There is a solitary case in the King's Bench; its date is probably 1527.[1] The plaintiff delivered an obligation or bond to John Stile to safely guard it, and the defendant bailee undertook (*assumpsit super se*) and promised to do so. Whilst the bond was in his custody the seal came off the bond, which was therefore rendered valueless. On these facts the court, Inglefield J. dissenting, allowed the action. The report is preoccupied with the possible overlap with detinue, but the nonfeasance point is also taken, and dealt with in this way:

'And it was said that the defendant had only committed a nonfeasance, for which he could not have an action on the case. To this they said that if the nonfeasance amounted only to a *nudum pactum* then this was a good objection—for example if I promise you to build you a house by a certain day, which is not done, this only is *nudum pactum* for which I will not have an action on the case, and I have suffered no wrong [*tort*] by this nonfeasance. But if he has suffered a wrong [*tort*] by this it is otherwise, as if I have a person bound in an obligation for a hundred pounds to pay twenty pounds by a certain day, and I deliver the obligation before the day,[2] and he does not pay before the day so that I have lost my obligation, then in this case for the nonfeasance I shall have an action on the case for he has done me a wrong [*tort*] in the law. If I give certain money to a person to make me a house by a certain day and he does not do it by the day, in that case this is a consideration why, for the nonfeasance I shall have an action on the case.'

---

[1] Spilman's MS. Reports, B.M. MS. Hargrave 388, f. 215b.
[2] i.e. in return for a promise to pay the debt.

(c) ACTIONS ON PROMISES BY EXECUTORS

No action lay at common law to recover a legacy.[1] An executor might, however, promise to pay a legacy, and accept a sum of money for such a promise; it was held in 1538 that if he did so he could be sued on the promise by action of assumpsit.[2] The distinction between such an action for damages for breach of a promise, and an action based upon the testament for the recovery of the legacy itself, is a fine one. But to refuse an action on the promise would simply encourage dishonesty by executors, allowing them to extract money upon promises which they had no intention of honouring. In practice the distinction would prove hard to maintain, and the action for breach of promise could easily develop into what was in effect an action for the legacy if juries were allowed to include the value of the legacy in the damages awarded; whether this was allowed in the earliest case cannot be told. There could be no problem over competing remedies in actions of this type, for clearly the writ of debt did not lie on promises to pay legacies; the obvious issue was one of jurisdiction, for primarily legacies were the concern of the spiritual courts, where an action to recover legacies was allowed. There seems to have been no remedy, however, in Chancery before 1538.[3]

(d) ASSUMPSIT IN LIEU OF DEBT[4]

There is some slight evidence that the courts allowed assumpsit, or some form of action on the case, to be brought against debtors in the fifteenth century.[5] The majority view in *Orwell* v. *Mortoft* (1505) frowned upon the general use of the action on the case as an alternative to debt, and Fineux C.J. agreed with this view. The earliest example of a court allowing assumpsit is the

---

[1] The legatee had no right even to take possession of a specific legacy; he must await delivery at the hands of the executor, or sue in the spiritual court. See Y.B. 44 Edw. III, f. 32; 2 Hen. VI, T. f. 15, pl. 17; 37 Hen. VI, M. f. 8, pl. 18; Brooke, Devise 30 in the case of a legacy of a specific or certain thing, the legatee could sue a third party in trespass for taking the thing. This was decided in Y.B. 27 Hen. VI, H. f. 8, pl. 6. The decision seems contrary to principle; Brooke thought it was 'marvellous'.

[2] Camb. Univ. Library MS. Gg. ll. 5, at f. 31a, B.M. Hargrave MS. 388, f. 151a.

[3] See *H.E.L.* III. 319.

[4] On this subject see the next chapter.

[5] See below, p. 287.

case of *Pickering* v. *Thoroughgood*, a decision of the King's Bench in 1533.[1] The use of assumpsit in lieu of debt raised special problems and difficulties over alternative remedies, which are discussed later in this book; by 1533 these questions probably seemed more important than any difficulty which was felt over nonfeasance. Nevertheless nonfeasance was discussed in *Pickering* v. *Thoroughgood*, and the case has a particular interest because it seems to be the last case where the point was treated as worth discussing in an action of assumpsit.

The action was brought on an undertaking and promise to deliver fungible goods which had been sold to the plaintiff; part of the price had been prepaid. The majority of the court— Fitzjames C.J. and Spilman and Coningsby JJ.— were in favour of allowing the action, and Spilman J. dealt with the objection that the action was taken on a nonfeasance in this way:

'And in some books a difference has been taken between nonfeasance and malfeasance; thus on the one an action of covenant lies, and on the other an action on the case lies. This is no distinction in reason, for if a carpenter for £100 covenants with me to make me a house, and does not make it before the day assigned, so that I am deprived of lodging, I shall have an action for this nonfeasance just as well as if he had made it badly . . .'

Spilman J. got over the difficulty over the giving of alternative remedies by emphasizing that the action on the case was an action for breach of a promise and undertaking which had caused damage, and thus was an action to remedy a tort; he pointed out that no other common law action was cast as an action for breach of promise, and concluded that no question of alternative remedies arose. This refined casuistry was all too much for Portman J. who took a plain man's view of the matter; Spilman reports his dissent in these terms,

'Master Portman, Justice, to the contrary, that this promise is part of the covenant, and all one, and no act done by the defendant, but solely the non-delivery of the malt, for which detinue lies.'

[1] See Appendix, Case No. 6.

Thus spoke the voice of common sense, but legal development does not always take place by heeding its promptings.

Squier v. *Barkley* (1533)[1] is a curious case where overlapping remedies were perhaps not involved. The defendant promised to pay for goods delivered to a third party, and on delivery was held liable on the promise. Perhaps this was not counted a sale to the defendant, who would not therefore have been liable in debt.

(e) BREACH OF PROMISE OF MARRIAGE

There is a case in 1504,[2] decided in the King's Bench before Fineux C.J., which might or might not be regarded as an action of nonfeasance.

> 'And the case was, a woman in London had given to the plaintiff flattering words equivalent (*aequipollentia*) to a promise of marriage, and by that means he delivered to her money and other things, and she had caused the plaintiff to retain counsel for her, and to travel about her suits in Chancery, and afterwards the woman refused to marry him, and married another, in deceit and fraud of the plaintiff.'

The plaintiff recovered, the jury apparently having found a special verdict to the effect that the woman had given flattering words equivalent to a promise of marriage.[3] It looks as though the King's Bench applied the doctrine in *Doige's Case* to agreements to marry by analogy, marrying a third party being a wrong not unlike enfeoffing a third party, polyandry being legally impossible. No report of the case survives, so that it is not possible to do more than guess at the theoretical justification of the decision; we cannot therefore be certain whether this was treated as a case of nonfeasance or misfeasance.[4]

---

[1] C.U.L. Gg. ll. 5, f. 31a.

[2] The note of the case, based on the record and not upon a report, is to be found in Cro. Eliz. at p. 79.

[3] This is one of the few cases which deals with what counts as a promise, discussed below at p. 407, and cf. the problem of what counts as a warranty.

[4] A somewhat similar set of facts provoked a petition in Chancery in 1438; see *Applegarth* v. *Sergeantson* 1 Cal. Ch. XLI. Conceivably Chancery may have provided a remedy in such cases where there was no formal marriage contract, but there is no clear evidence.

(*f*) MISCELLANEOUS CASES

There is also evidence of the use of assumpsit for non-feasance against persons who failed to perform services of one sort or another—an early case against a common carrier who promises to carry and fails to do so,[1] and against the steward of a manorial court who took money in return for a promise to make an entry in the rolls of the court. This latter action was brought by the heir of the promisee and it failed on the ground that an action for a personal tort dies with the person.[2] There was no objection in principle to the action, so far as can be told from a meagre report.

Nonfeasance and consideration

These cases probably represent no more than the visible fragment of the iceberg; yet they illustrate the way in which the nonfeasance doctrine disappeared from the intellectual apparatus of the common lawyers somewhere about the year 1530.[3] Thereafter the anxiety which lawyers felt over allowing the action of assumpsit to be used as a substitute for the action of covenant, shorn of the requirement of a sealed instrument, troubled the law no more. Sixteenth-century lawyers came to be concerned instead with two new problems. One was the propriety of allowing long-recognized liability, previously sanctioned by the action of debt, to be subsumed under the new and in some ways more satisfactory action of assumpsit. Another and more fundamental problem was that of defining the scope of the wholly new liability in the common law courts for the breach of those informal agreements with which the royal courts had hitherto not been concerned.[4] It was through the doctrine of consideration that the second problem was eventually tackled, and it is not surprising to find the first hints of that doctrine appearing not so very long after lawyers had come to recognize that the earlier limiting doctrine, the doctrine of nonfeasance, had been deprived of its practical significance.

We would not, however, expect a fully fledged doctrine of

---

[1] B.M. MS. Harley 1624, f. 28b (1491).

[2] B.M. Hargrave MS. 388, f. 43.

[3] See also J. H. Baker, *New Light on Slade's Case* [1971] C.L.J. 41 at p. 58 nn. 42-4 referring to King's Bench cases in 1520, 1530, and 1531 where assumpsit for nonfeasance was allowed.

[4] See below, Chs. iii and vii.

consideration to appear in the cases just at the very same time as the nonfeasance doctrine became extinct. The need to impose limits upon the new liability for breach of promise must be recognized before the doctrine is evolved to satisfy this need. One would expect there to be a period during which the courts were aware that there was a problem, but were uncertain as to how quite this problem ought to be tackled. Three of the cases which have already been mentioned as illustrations of the spread of liability for nonfeasance provide evidence that there was indeed such a period of uncertainty.

The first is *John Style's Case* (1527?);[1] the passage which has been quoted from the report very clearly reveals both judicial awareness of the problem of limiting liability for breach of promise, and an attempt to provide a solution. The majority of the court said that although nonfeasance was prima facie actionable in assumpsit, yet an action ought not to be allowed if the transaction was merely a *nudum pactum*. An attempt is then made to distinguish a 'nude' pact or promise from a promise which is actionable. At this point the reasoning becomes very difficult to follow; the court insists that only if the breach of promise amounts to a 'tort' is the promise something more than a nude promise or pact. One of the two examples given of an actionable promise is, however, easy to understand:

'If I give certain money to a person to make me a house by a certain day and he does not do it by the day, in that case this is a consideration [*sic*] why for the nonfeasance I shall have an action on the case.'

This, as we shall see, is the first hint of the notion that breach of promise is only actionable if there is a 'consideration' to charge the defendant, as well as a promise.

The second case is *Sukley* v. *Whyte* (1543).[2] Here there is no reference whatsoever to 'consideration', but the lawyers engaged in the case were clearly aware that there was some cause for concern over the scope of promissory liability. The agreement to indemnify the plaintiff, upon which action was brought, was gratuitous. Bromley, for the defendant, said this:

[1] B.M. MS. Hargrave 388, f. 215b.
[2] Appendix, Case No. 9.

'It seems to me that the action does not lie, and the reason is because this action is grounded upon a nude promise, and there is no specialty nor any money given in the agreement, but it is just solely a promise, on which promise he can have no action.'

Shelley J. put a more curious argument which, he thought, tended to show that the plaintiff had no cause to have an action. The arrest, he argued, was lawful prima facie; why should the sheriff be indemnified against damage suffered through performing a lawful act? Shelley J. was here groping towards an idea which was to become very influential in assumpsit cases—the idea that liability should only be imposed for breach of promise when there existed some reason apart from the promise for saying that what the defendant had promised to do ought to be done.

The third case is *Anon.* (1544)[1] where an action was brought on a gratuitous parole guarantee of a debt due by bond. Here Marvin objected to the action on the ground that there was no *quid pro quo* for the promise, and Rastell agreed that a specialty was essential to liability. Like *Sukley* v. *Whyte* the case is an indication of an awareness of the problem, but hardly provides a solution; again neither Montague C.J. nor Chomley J., who favoured liability, mention 'consideration'.

The change in the character of the action of assumpsit

By 1530 the character of the action had been changed; it had become an action[2] for the breach of informal agreements or covenants. This was reflected in pleading forms. The allegation of an assumpsit, which had been appropriate enough in the early days when defendants had been made liable for their negligent misconduct which had caused damage to persons or property which they had taken into their custody and control, was not a very appropriate allegation in actions for failure to perform agreements. Pleading conservatism ensured that it could not be dropped entirely; instead it is more and more

---

[1] Library of Congress MS., f. 25b.

[2] An action of case, not trespass, in accordance with the doctrine in *The Prior of Spalding's Case* Y.B. 12 Hen. VI, M. f. 3, pl. 4, that case lay where breach of duty was involved, since 'not doing is no trespass'.

commonly associated with the allegation of a promise.[1] We have seen how the allegation of a deceit in actions on the case came into the law, and served as ammunition in the battle against the nonfeasance doctrine; this too remained a standard allegation although it was no longer appropriate. The action of assumpsit had become an action for breach of promise. But the old action for negligent misfeasance survived alongside the new action for nonfeasance in breach of promise, and the boundary between the two actions was a continuous source of difficulty.[2] Rules worked out to delimit the scope of liability for breach of promise, and rules worked out to delimit the scope of liability for negligent misconduct, need to be kept apart; the peculiar history of assumpsit has made this task a difficult one, even today.

At the same time the recognition of an action for nonfeasance, though it involved a breach with the past, did not destroy all

---

[1] Allegations of a promise are to be found as early as the fourteenth century, but the first case in which serious emphasis is laid on the action being an action for breach of promise is *Pickering* v. *Thoroughgood* (1533).

[2] A clear indication that lawyers recognized that actions on the case for non-feasance (whether framed in assumpsit or for any other wrong involving failure to do what ought to be done) were distinct in principle from actions for misfeasance is the ruling that the plea of not guilty (*non culpabilis*), the gist of which is 'I didn't do it', can only be tendered in answer to an action for misfeasance This is laid down in 1541 (Brooke, *Accion sur le case*, pl. 109, and see also pl. 111). The position over pleading in assumpsit actions for misfeasance in medieval law is somewhat obscure. A common traverse of the assumpsit (i.e. a purely negative denial of the undertaking as alleged) appears to have been a good plea from the time of *The Surgeon's Case* onwards; presumably this only puts in issue the giving of the under-taking, but since there are no cases on what might be given in evidence under the plea we cannot tell. There is certainly no indication that the plea of *non assumpsit* was regarded as a 'general issue', and the conception of a general issue is in any case largely post-medieval, the old lawyers usually preferring to confine the opera-tion of pleas fairly narrowly. If the gist of defence did not consist in a straightfor-ward denial of the undertaking, they would plead specially. Thus a defence the gist of which was that the undertaking had been performed would be pleaded by special traverse, performance being averred in the inducement, and the under-taking traversed in the *absque hoc*. An example is the *Marshal's Case* (1441, Y.B. 19 Hen. VI, H. f. 49, pl. 5), but there the defendant did not admit the assumpsit as alleged; the discussion reveals considerable confusion. Probably if the defendant was prepared to admit the assumpsit exactly as alleged his proper course was to aver performance in the inducement and traverse the negligent misfeasance in the *absque hoc*. In *Skyrne* v. *Butolf* (1388, 11 Ric. II, Ames Series at p. 228) where the defendant finally put up a defence of performance, the plea does not include any traverse by way of *absque hoc* denying either the assumpsit or the negligence; he simply pleaded affirmatively that he performed his cure. In fifteenth-century law, however, such a plea would have been regarded as bad as a mere argumentative plea, and to be good would have had to include a denial by way of *absque hoc* either of the assumpsit or more probably the negligent misfeasance.

continuity. The action still remained an action for the recovery of damages by way of compensation for a wrong or tort. The change is only that the tort is now the wrong of breaking a promise.

Why did the courts of common law change their view?

It is natural to seek for some explanation of the demise of the nonfeasance doctrine in Henry VIII's reign; the courts changed their minds, and to say that 'it just happened' seems inadequate.[1] But unfortunately, satisfactory evidence for the 'real' reasons for changes in the doctrines of private law is hard to come by; indeed a cynic might sometimes suspect that there are writers who believe that any explanation for doctrinal change which can be supported by evidence must of necessity fail to come to grips with the 'real' causes of doctrinal change, a notion popularized by the American realist school of legal philosophers. The problem is easily illustrated by an example. We know that Fineux C.J. was in favour of permitting the action of assumpsit to lie against a carpenter who promised to build a house and did not do so; there is good evidence that he expressed this view in 1498, and evidence that other judges at about the same time agreed with him. But as to why Fineux C.J. took this view there is no direct evidence whatsoever, just as there is no direct evidence as to why Rickhill J. took the opposite view in 1400; it is idle to pretend the contrary. Hence any attempt at explanation must of necessity be speculative. We might as well accept that this is so, though it does not follow that an attempt to provide an explanation which is at least consistent with the evidence is wholly futile; there is a place for speculation, and a place too for different levels of historical explanation.

The view which perhaps most merits attention is that the common law courts were prompted to extend their jurisdiction over parole contracts by the activities of the Chancery. The essential basis for this explanation is supported by the evidence, which shows that the late medieval chancellors did exercise a considerable jurisdiction over contracts in situations where the common law courts did not provide a remedy.

[1] See S. F. C. Milsom, 'Reason in the Development of the Common Law' 81 L.Q.R. 496.

The enforcement of contract in equity

The scope of equitable jurisdiction in contract in the fifteenth century had been investigated by W. T. Barbour, and his essay on the subject, 'The History of Contract in Early English Equity', which was published in 1914,[1] has never been supplanted by any later writings, nor have the conclusions he reached been subjected to any serious criticism. Barbour himself, though he presented his conclusions with assurance, very frankly admitted the fact that many of these conclusions were themselves based upon inferences of a somewhat speculative nature. He relied in the main upon the evidence of surviving Chancery petitions. But unfortunately, as he explained, in the great majority of cases only the complainant's petition survives; there is no record of the defendant's answer to it, nor any record of the outcome of the petition. Further to this, the evidence of the practice of the Chancellors which is to be found in the yearbooks is extremely scanty, and there is no fifteenth-century evidence from text-writers. Confronted with these difficulties, Barbour took the view that he could nevertheless reach conclusions with a fair degree of certainty by making the assumption that:

> 'Where there are numerous petitions based upon the same or a similar state of facts . . . it can reasonably be inferred that relief sought was granted.'[2]

It is hard to see what else he could have done, but although one cannot reasonably quarrel with his method one can legitimately treat his conclusions with some reserve, for some of them rest upon very scanty evidence indeed. For example, he thought that the Chancellor would give relief, either in the form of a decree of specific performance, or by way of damages, on a parole building contract.[3] This may well be correct, and there is year-book evidence to support him,[4] but the evidence which Barbour himself relied upon consists of nothing more than two petitions asking for relief. These petitions by themselves certainly provide evidence of the absence of a common law

---

[1] As part of Volume IV of *Oxford Studies in Social and Legal History* edited by Vinogradoff.

[2] Barbour 70.

[3] Barbour 130.

[4] 21 Hen. VII, M. f. 41, pl. 66 (Fifoot 353).

remedy, but it is hard to see how they can be regarded as providing compelling evidence that the Chancellor gave relief.

Barbour did not confine himself to an attempt to reconstruct the practice of the Chancery; he attempted in addition to reconstruct the theory of contract upon which the Chancellor proceeded. Here he met even more severe difficulties. Only in the year-books do any accounts of the reasoning behind early decisions in equity survive, and the year-books do not contain many such accounts. But again Barbour quite explicitly recognized the uncertainty of his conclusions;[1] they could well be correct, but their tentative nature requires emphasis.

I do not propose to review all of Barbour's conclusions; clearly a summary account is no substitute for reading his essay in the original. I shall therefore confine attention to such of his conclusions as seem most significant to a history of the rise of the action of assumpsit.

Cases where no remedy is provided by the common law

Where the common law provided no remedy at all one would naturally expect pressure from petitioners for a remedy in Chancery. Barbour listed[2] a number of particular contracts which he thought were remediable in Chancery; those that chiefly concern us are:

(1) Parole contracts to convey land;
(2) Marriage contracts involving either the payment of marriage money or the conveyance of land;
(3) Parole contracts of indemnity and guarantee.

He did not regard his list as exhaustive, for he thought that the Chancery provided a general enforcement of parole covenants;[3] examples would be parole building contracts, or agreements to perform personal services. There is fairly strong evidence that the fifteenth-century chancellors provided a remedy in the three types of agreement instanced, and in the late fifteenth or early sixteenth centuries agreements to convey land in return for money, or on account of marriage, became absorbed into the law of uses. The evidence for the general

---

[1] Barbour 166.
[2] Barbour 55.
[3] Barbour 138.

enforcement of parole covenants is rather weaker, but not inconsiderable. He also showed that there was good evidence that the Chancery enforced simple contract debts against executors, so long as they had sufficient assets; generally the common law rule was that such debts died with the debtor.

If Barbour's conclusions here are, as seems probable, at least in general correct, they throw an interesting light upon the development of assumpsit. For assumpsit, as we shall see, was developed in the sixteenth century by the common law courts so as to provide a remedy in just those cases where the fifteenth-century Chancery had come to provide a remedy in equity. The rise of assumpsit can thus be viewed not as a development which provided a remedy where no remedy previously existed, but rather as transferring to the common law courts jurisdiction over cases previously within the province of the Chancery. And this interpretation naturally suggests the hypothesis that the common law courts, when they assumed jurisdiction over such cases, may perhaps have adopted at the same time the contractual theory, if there was one, upon which the late medieval chancellors proceeded in dealing with them.

The theory of contract in equity

But, for reasons which have been explained, it is extremely difficult to discover what theory of contract was acted upon in the Chancery to delimit the scope of actionable parole covenants, or indeed if there was a settled theory. The evidence simply does not admit of any definite conclusion. Barbour produces some slight evidence for the view that the Chancery may, in some cases, have based the defendant's liability upon his breach of faith (*laesio fidei*).[1] But in most petitions no breach of faith is averred, and for this reason it seems impossible to suppose that the Chancery confined its jurisdiction to agreements where the party pledged his faith. Generally the emphasis is not upon the defendant's breach of faith, but upon his breach of promise. As Barbour puts it,

'Emphasis is laid upon the promise as the indispensable part of the case.'[2]

---

[1] Barbour 163.
[2] Barbour 164.

This, as we shall see, was to become the basis of liability in the sixteenth-century action of assumpsit—the action for breach of promise. It is at least possible that in this respect the equitable theory of contract influenced the common law. The hypothesis cannot be proved or disproved; it is nevertheless not implausible.

The common law action for breach of promise came to be limited by the doctrine of consideration; not all promises are actionable, but only those given for good consideration. This doctrine, which came to be attached to the common law action for breach of promise from around 1550 onwards, appears, as we shall see, to have been closely connected with the doctrine of consideration associated in the first half of the sixteenth century with the law of uses, and its ultimate source may conceivably have been the canonist doctrine of *causa*. Now Barbour was inclined to think that the canonist doctrine of cause was adopted by the late medieval chancellors as the test of actionable promises; he was particularly impressed by the equitable enforcement of promises given on account of marriage, marriage being a clear instance of a good 'cause' for a promise.[1] But unhappily he was unable to produce any really convincing evidence for this thesis which must be regarded as conjectural only; it is discussed later in this book,[2] in the context of a rather different view which I put forward as to the basic theory underlying the practice of the late medieval chancellors.

Common law and Chancery in the early sixteenth century

Thus if Barbour's conclusions are in general correct, it would seem that, when the common law courts came to abandon the non-feasance doctrine, a shift in jurisdiction occurred; cases which would previously have been subject to royal jurisdiction only in the Chancery were transferred to the courts of common law. Thereafter the jurisdiction of Chancery in contract cases was confined to supplementing in detail the rules of the common law. It is, as we have seen, even possible that the common law took over not only the cases but the contractual theory with which they had been decided. There is some evidence that this shift was recognized at the time; in 1499[3] it is noted that the

---

[1] Barbour 164–5.
[2] See below, Cb. VI.
[3] 21 Hen. VII, M. f. 41, pl. 66 (Fifoot 353).

availability of assumpsit for nonfeasance removes the need to have recourse to Chancery.

The common law courts were in no position to control the activities of the Chancery; they had but two alternatives— either to acquiesce in Chancery jurisdiction over parole contracts, or render recourse to Chancery pointless by providing common law remedies.[1] For if it was conceded that a case lay outside common law jurisdiction, the common law courts could not object to the intervention of the Chancellor. There exist numerous examples of the readiness of the common law courts to adopt the second course, for though the doctrinal proposition is that equity follows the law, historically the tendency has frequently been the reverse. The reason for this need not be that the common law judges were fearful of losing lucrative business to a rival court. It is hard to believe that men like Frowicke C.J. or Fineux C.J., who favoured the extension of assumpsit, were likely to gain significantly by acquiring jurisdiction over a handful of trivial actions for breach of promise. But these and other judges could well have been influenced by the Chancery into accepting the view that the common law was defective, and that what reason and conscience dictated to the Chancellor, might well be agreeable to the reason of the common law. The reaction could also have been encouraged by a professional jealousy which was not solely the expression of sordid economic motives; particularly during the ascendancy of Wolsey (1516–29), there was certainly strong feeling on the relationship between the common law and the court of the Chancellor.

[1] See *H.E.L.* I. 459 et seq. for discussion.

III

THE RELATIONSHIP BETWEEN
ASSUMPSIT AND THE OLDER REMEDIES

ONCE the courts decided that the action of assumpsit for breach of promise could be brought on a pure nonfeasance, problems of the scope of the action were bound to arise; it had to be settled how extensive or how circumscribed promissory liability was to be. One aspect of these problems was presented to the lawyers of the time in terms of a series of demarcation disputes involving the relationship between the action of assumpsit and older remedies, in particular its relationship with the action of debt on a contract; difficulties also arose over the use of assumpsit in lieu of the action of covenant. These are the matters which are dealt with in this chapter.

Assumpsit against debtors

Until the nonfeasance doctrine was abandoned there was no question of assumpsit becoming a general remedy for the breach of parole contracts; a contractual remedy must of necessity lie where there has been no performance at all. But there was a further obstacle to be surmounted; assumpsit, if it was to become a general contractual remedy, must be permitted to usurp the sphere of the action of debt *sur contract*. For in a money economy the paradigm outstanding contractual obligation is obviously the obligation to pay a debt; the essential function of contract law is to permit credit, money-credit. The eclipse was achieved in the course of the sixteenth century, but not without considerable difficulty and controversy.

The lawyers who were responsible for this advance were not, of course, interested in the grand strategy of evolving a general contractual remedy. They no doubt were concerned only to remedy certain particular anomalies in the law, and do their best for their clients. The main criticism of the medieval law of parole contracts had been the lack of reciprocal remedies in certain cases, notably in the case of sale of land and the case of contracts for the performance of a service. Here one party to the transaction was protected by action of debt *sur contract*, whilst the other party did not have a common law remedy.[1] Another criticism was the failure to provide a remedy in the case of certain other important transactions when concluded informally, as in the case of contracts of guarantee and indemnity, and marriage contracts. Such criticisms could be met by the extension of assumpsit to fill the gaps. There was, however, a danger that this beneficial development of the law would produce a new anomaly, for the cost of patching up the medieval law with the action on the case was that the law of parole contracts was parcelled out between two actions, debt and assumpsit. These two actions reflected quite different conceptions of liability, and were governed by quite different legal rules.[2] The most serious divergence was over the mode of trial, which was in general wager of law in debt, as contrasted with trial by jury in assumpsit; it was clearly both inelegant and unfair that the reciprocal actions on, say, a building contract, should lead to quite different methods of trial, more particularly when one of these methods could degenerate into licensed perjury. The evolution of the jury from neighbours, answering a question on oath of their own knowledge, into a body proceeding by way of adjudication on evidence, no doubt heightened the contrast with compurgation. Another serious divergence was threatened in 1521, when the King's bench in *Cleymond* v. *Vincent*[3] allowed assumpsit to lie against executors. In one respect this was a valuable advance in the law, but unless it was to be matched by the supersession of debt the decision could lead to grave injustice. It was quite settled law that in general a debt due by simple contract died with the debtor,[4] and if assumpsit was to lie generally against executors the result would be that in a bilateral contract—say a contract to build a house—the obligation of one party to the agreement would be transmitted to his executors if he died before performance, whilst the

---

[1] See above, p. 148.

[2] A contract under seal could also give rise to two different reciprocal actions, debt and covenant, but the divergences between these two actions was not so serious. The use of conditioned bonds usually meant that both parties to a formal contract would use debt as a remedy.

[3] Y.B. 12 Hen. VIII, P. f. 11, pl. 3, discussed above, pl. 265.

[4] See below, p. 558, where the principle is discussed and the exceptions to it stated.

obligation of the other party would die with him. Lawyers who possessed any grasp of principle and who attached any importance to the rationality and consistency of the law which they administered could not fail to become aware of these and other consequences[1] of using new cloth to repair an old garment, and it lay in the logic of legal development that the action of assumpsit should eventually supersede the action of debt *sur contract*,[2] and thereby become the general contractual action of the common law. In response to the insistent pressure of litigants this legal revolution was indeed achieved in the sixteenth century, and consolidated in *Slade's Case* (1602), but throughout the sixteenth century the relationship between debt and assumpsit remained both controversial and unsettled.

The theoretical objection to the supersession of debt
    The chief obstacle to this development was the idea that the action on the case ought not to be allowed to do the job of one of the older actions, such as the assize of nuisance,[3] or the actions of detinue or debt.[4] We have already met this idea in discussing the relationship between the action on the case and the action of covenant, a matter which troubled the fifteenth-century lawyers. In a formulary system of law it is not surprising to find that lawyers attached importance to system and tidiness, with a place for everything and everything in its place; when Lord Raymond said,

'We must keep up the boundaries of actions, otherwise we shall introduce the utmost confusion.'[5]

he was expressing a point of view which in its context was both understandable and sensible. The forms of action provided the old lawyers with their categories, performing much the same

---

[1] For example, the doctrine of *quid pro quo* was thought to apply to debt, whilst in the sixteenth century the doctrine of consideration came to govern assumpsit.

[2] And, to some extent, detinue; when detinue was partly superseded by the action on the case for trover and conversion.

[3] For the relationship between the assize of nuisance and the action on the case for nuisance see Fifoot, Ch. 5. Here the King's Bench was prepared to allow election of remedies, and the Common Pleas was not. The view of the King's Bench prevailed in *Cantrel* v. *Church* (1601) Cro. Eliz. 845.

[4] For the relationship between the action of detinue and the action on the case see Milsom, 'Not Doing is No Trespass' (1954), Camb. L.J. 105, Simpson, 'The Introduction of the Action on the Case for Conversion', 75 L.Q.R. 364.

[5] *Reynolds* v. *Clarke* (1726) 1 Strange 634.

function as a modern code; categories which overlap fail to serve their primary function in systematizing the law. Order produces consistency, and consistency is required by justice.

The peculiar history of the common law, whereby different forms of action had been introduced at different times, introduced a complication, for to insist that the whole field of legal liability should be neatly portioned out between the forms in the Register would have been to compel some litigants to use archaic and unsatisfactory forms of action simply because their particular species of complaint had been provided with a remedy early in the history of the law. Conversely other litigants, more fortunate than they, would be allowed to use a more modern and satisfactory form of action simply because their complaint had been catered for later in the history of the common law. In order to avoid this, newer remedies were in fact allowed to supersede older ones in many branches of the law. Thus in the law of property the writ of right, the assize of novel disseisin, and the writs of entry both partially superseded each other, and in the end these old real actions were largely rendered obsolete by the evolution of the action of ejectment.[1] It was indeed vital that the older forms of action should be superseded by newer and better forms; only thus could the common law be preserved as a viable system of law. Milsom indeed has argued that the existence of the forms of action positively facilitated legal change.[2]

Case and the objection to overlapping remedies

Amongst the forms of action the action on the case was peculiar; it is a form of action which has no form.[3] The *ostenturus quare* writ with its *cum*-clause could be fashioned to cover any type of complaint which the courts were prepared to entertain, whereby a litigant sought to recover damages by way of compensation for a wrong. Such a formless form of action could readily get out of hand, and in response to the very natural feeling that it should be assigned a definite place in the scheme of things there emerged, as early as the fourteenth century, a

[1] See Simpson, *Introduction to the History of the Land Law*, Chs. II and VII.
[2] Milsom, 'Reason in the Development of the Common Law', 81 L.Q.R. 496.
[3] *In Slade's Case* (1602) 4 Co.Rep. 91a it was said that 'an action on the case on assumpsit is as well a formed action, and contained in the Register, as an action of debt, for there is its form'. This is a mere quibble on the meaning of 'formed'.

notion that the proper role of the action on the case was to provide a remedy for wrongs which were not remediable by any other means.[1] In its positive form this theory could be used to further the claim that if it could be shown that there was a lacuna in the scheme of remedies the action on the case ought to be allowed. Negatively the theory could be used to restrict the action on the case to this role. Throughout the fifteenth and sixteenth centuries these two facets of the theory persistently influenced the development of the law.

To claim, as some modern writers have done,[2] that the 'theory', 'doctrine', or 'principle' against overlapping remedies was capable of very precise formulation, or that all lawyers accepted it, or, if they did accept it, accepted it in the same form, would be to impose upon the evidence a simplicity which is not to be found in it. In its most straightforward form the doctrine could be stated by Pigot in 1504 like this,

'one can never have action on the case where one can have another action at common law.'[3]

This is the negative aspect of the doctrine; its positive aspect is illustrated by a remark of Brooke's in 1522,

'Action on the case lies where no other action is provided for such a wrong.'

Commonly the doctrine is linked to a contrast between 'general' actions and 'special' actions, as by Kingsmill J. in 1505:

'And where a general action lies, there a special action on the case does not lie',[4]

[1] See Kiralfy, pp. 14–15.
[2] e.g. J. H. Baker in [1971] C.L.J. at 219. Baker says that the objection was 'not to two different causes of action arising on the same facts, but to the same *cause* of action giving rise to two different *forms of action*', criticizing my formulation in 74 L.Q.R, at 382—'no single state of affairs should give rise to two separate causes of action'. His view seems to me to be mistaken in that the evidence does not permit of the precision claimed in supposing his formulation is 'correct', and also to involve the fallacy that 'causes of action' are natural facts.
[3] Y.B. 21 Hen. VII, M. f. 30, pl. 5; the context was nuisance and the court denied the doctrine. cf. 27 Hen. VIII, M. f. 24, pl. 3 (*Tatam's or Jordan's Case*) where Knightly advanced the doctrine in the same form, and it was rejected by the court. In both instances the objection is that the doctrine is being stated too widely, and in too crude a form.
[4] Y.B. 14 Hen. VIII, P. f. 31, pl. 8. (1522); *Orwell v. Mortoft* Y.B. 20 Hen. VII M. f. 8, pl. 18.

and sometimes between 'formed' actions in the Register and actions on the case.[1] In the second half of the sixteenth century the idea became current that the action on the case was related in some way to the *Consimili Casu* provision of the Statute of Westminster II (1285). This belief, though historically incorrect, nevertheless possessed some influence, and introduced a new twist to the doctrine, for it could be said that the action in the case was based upon statutory authority, and would only lie when no other action was available at common law, as the statute provided. This was said in *Wade* v. *Braunche* in 1596,[2] and there are earlier hints of the historical error which suggested this reformulation and lent it support.[3] But if lawyers found it difficult to agree both upon the existence and upon the formulation of the doctrine, they found it more difficult still to agree, when confronted with actual cases, upon how precisely the principle applied. A somewhat similar situation exists today in the law of torts. All but the most heretical lawyers agree that 'foresight' is extremely relevant in determining the scope of liability for negligence. It is nevertheless notorious that there is widespread disagreement both as to precisely what the relevance of the foresight principle is, and how it applies to real live cases.

The early sixteenth-century use of assumpsit in lieu of debt

The earliest suggestion that assumpsit lay in lieu of debt occurs in a note in Brooke's *Abridgement*, recording an otherwise unreported case heard in the Common Pleas in 1484.

---

[1] As in *Slade's Case* (1602) 4 Co. Rep. at 92b, where Dodderidge objected 'That the plaintiff upon this bargain might have ordinary remedy by action of debt, which is an action formed in the register, and therefore he should not have an action on the case, which is an extraordinary action, and not limited within any certain form in the register'. cf. *Mounteagle* v. *The Countess of Worcester* (1554) 2 Dyer 121, where it is said that 'where a man has an ordinary writ ready framed in the Register for his case, there he shall not sue out a new form of writ'.

[2] 2 And. 53.

[3] See *Anon.* (1553) Dalison 9, where it is said that the writ on the case in *Anon.* (1400) Y.B. 2 Hen. IV, M. f. 7, pl. 31 was framed by the chancery clerks under the power conferred by Westminster II. For a discussion see Kiralfy 29, and cf. Brooke, *Action sur le statute*, pl. 39, where in a cryptic note Brooke seems to deny the idea that case is a statutory action. cf. Baker, [1971] C.L.J. 219, who refers to William Lambard's MS. of Dalison's Reports, M.B. Harley 5141, f. 13, S.C. as above.

'Action on the case for that he undertook to pay £10 *to* the plaintiff for 5*s*. paid to him, and the defendant said that at another time the plaintiff brought debt for the same sum in which the defendant waged his law, by which the plaintiff was barred. Judgment if action, and a good plea by Brian C.J., contra Catesby Justice.'[1]

The note, laconic though it is, suggests that some encouragement may have been given to the use of assumpsit in lieu of debt even as early as this. The problem before the court was the secondary one of deciding whether a judgment in debt bars assumpsit for the same sum, a problem which is unlikely to arise before election of remedies has become a practical possibility; where, as in this case, a small sum of money was paid for an undertaking to pay a debt it could always be argued that to refuse case would be to allow a wrong to go unremedied, for the five shillings would not be recoverable in debt.[2] Catesby certainly must have favoured election. Indeed, if Coke is to be believed, actions of assumpsit in lieu of debt to recover the price of goods sold were commonly allowed in both Common Pleas and King's Bench from Henry VI's time onwards.[3] But Coke's story, which nobody has yet found evidence to support, is rather unlikely, for the first reported case in which the theoretical

---

[1] Brooke, *Accion sur le case* pl. 110, where there is a reference to 'An. 2 Ric. 3 fo 14'. In the printed year-book of 2 Ric. III, M. f. 14, pl. 39 there is a case dealing with an analogous point, but it is not the case abridged; presumably Brooke took the case from a MS. cf. *Action sur le case* pl. 105 (1542), where the King's Bench decided that assumpsit was a bar to debt for the same sum, and vice versa.

[2] cf. the reasoning of Statham, *Accions sur le cas*, pl. 25, where assumpsit was allowed against a bailee for failure to look after goods bailed, in lieu of detinue. Statham notes, 'And I believe that the reason the action lies is because the defendant took six shillings to look after them, which six shillings could not be recovered in a writ on detinue'. For a discussion of this case see 75 L.Q.R. 366–7.

[3] *Slade's Case* (1602) 4 Co.Rep. 92b at 93a, 'In respect of infinite precedents (which George Kemp, Esq., Secondary of the Prothonotaries of the King's Bench showed me) as well in the Court of Common Pleas as in the Court of King's Bench, in the reigns of King Hen. 6 E. 4 H. 7 and H. 8, by which it appears that the Plaintiffs declared that the Defendants, in consideration of a Sale to them of certain goods, promised to pay so much Money, etc., in which case the Plaintiffs had Judgement.' Now the reference to 'consideration' is anachronistic and *must* be wrong, and this throws doubt on the whole story. Dr. Kiralfy, 165–6, suggests that the cases may have been actions by purchasers in deceit for failure to deliver, but this is not what Coke says. Apart from deliberate dishonesty, either by Coke or Kemp, it seems just possible to interpret Coke's remarks as referring to actions of debt.

issues were discussed, *Orwell* v. *Mortoft* (1505), produced a majority of the court of Common Pleas opposed to allowing election between assumpsit and debt, and Fineux C.J.K.B. agreed with this view.[1] Only Frowicke C.J.C.P. favoured election, and if there had previously been cases in which election was allowed he would surely have referred to them. In spite, therefore, of the case in 1484 it is improbable that actions of assumpsit in lieu of debt were in general use in the fifteenth century.

The discussion in *Orwell* v. *Mortoft* (1505) was provoked by a curious hybrid form of action on the case. There had been a sale of sixty quarters of barley, and the seller had failed to deliver. Here the appropriate and traditional action was debt *sur contract*.[2] Instead the plaintiff's pleader experimented with case; he alleged that the price had been paid,[3] that the barley had been left with the seller to be safely guarded to the plaintiff's use,[4] and delivered on a certain day, and that the seller had undertaken (*super se assumpsit*) and promised to do all this. He further alleged that the seller, instead of performing his undertaking, had converted the barley to his own use, causing thereby damage to the plaintiff. To this declaration the defendant demurred, and notwithstanding the ingenuity with which it had been framed the majority of the court (as the case is reported) took the view that the action was misconceived, for since the plaintiff had no property (i.e. no right to the possession of any specific barley) in the barley at the time of the conversion he could not complain of its conversion. His proper remedy was debt.

Frowicke C.J. alone supported the action, and in his argument he laid particular stress on the fact that the purchase money had been prepaid. Now in an action of debt for the barley this money would not be recoverable, and it could therefore be said that the buyer had suffered loss which was distinct from the mere non-delivery of the barley, and that this

---

[1] Y.B. 20 Hen. VII, T. f. 8, pl. 18, Keilwey, f. 69a, pl. 2, f. 77a, pl. 25. For the record see Kiralfy, *Source Book*, pl. 150. Dr. Kiralfy has been unable to trace any judgment.

[2] Not detinue, since the goods were not specific.

[3] The prepaid price could not, in theory at least, be recovered in debt.

[4] The suggestion is that the seller is in the position of a bailee. The averment does not occur on the record; see Kiralfy, *Source Book*, 150.

loss would go unremedied unless an action on the case was allowed. Thus the action on the case would not be doing the same job as an action in debt for the barley; it would be filling a gap in the law. This reasoning is wholly specious, because if the buyer has an action to get the barley, there is no conceivable reason why he should get the price back as well; however, it is an illustration of the technique whereby strained reasoning could be employed to justify election of remedies in fact, whilst maintaining the integrity of the theory which forbade overlapping remedies; this pointed the way to things to come. No decision has been traced in *Orwell* v. *Mortoft*, and the probability is that the action was dropped by the plaintiff when it became clear that the court was against him, though over a quarter of a century later Fitzjames C.J. said that the action eventually succeeded.

In *Pickering* v. *Thoroughgood* (1533),[1] the facts were substantially the same; there was a sale of malt with part-payment of the price, and the seller failed to deliver. Here again the normal action would have been debt, but the plaintiff instead brought an action on the case on an assumpsit. The declaration was somewhat differently framed, the allegation of a conversion being dropped; instead the plaintiff alleged that the defendant had,

'bargained and sold to the plaintiff forty quarters of malt . . . and assumed and promised to deliver it accordingly.'

The action was thus not framed as an action to recover the malt, nor as an action for compensation for the conversion of the malt, but simply as an action for the damage which the plaintiff had suffered because the promise to deliver had been broken. The pleader emphasized that the loss which had been incurred through the seller's default was quite distinct from, and greater than, the value of the malt. He alleged that because of the non-delivery he had been forced to buy other malt, in order to maintain his business as a brewer, at a much greater price than the contract price; the price was £11 6s. 8d., but the damage suffered and claimed was £20. The defendant pleaded to the

---

[1] Spilman's MS. Reports, B.M. MS. Hargrave 388, f. 67b, Camb. Univ. Library MS. Gg. ll. 5, f. 30a. See Appendix, Case No. 6, and cf. *Squier* v. *Barkley* (1533), above, p. 270.

action and lost before a jury on the facts; he then raised the
issue of law by motion in arrest of judgment, moving that,

> 'this action did not lie, because an action of debt lay, and
> where a general action lies, there in the same case a special
> action on the case does not lie.'

This motion in arrest of judgment directly raised the theoretical issue, and the King's Bench, which allowed the action to
succeed, was forced into the position of having either to deny
the principle which forbade overlapping remedies, or to argue
that the principle was not infringed by its decision. Earlier
precedents for such actions in the King's Bench existed in cases
for which we have no reports.[1] The justices adopted the second
solution, arguing that the action of assumpsit was performing a
function which was distinct from the function performed by
debt. Thus Spilman J. said,

> 'And as for the fact that he could have an action of debt this
> makes no difference, for the action of debt is based on the
> debt and the detinue, but this action is based on the other's
> tort—that is on the breach of promise.'

Coningsby J. and Fitzjames C.J. agreed with this,

> 'It seems that the action lies, and it is at the election of the
> plaintiff to choose one action or the other, for they are based
> on different grounds, as Spilman has said.'

Only Portman J. thought that the distinction drawn was too
refined to be tolerable, and in consequence he dissented from
the decision.

In the King's Bench it seems that actions of assumpsit in lieu
of actions of debt were allowed from 1520 onwards, and it may
well be that *Pickering* v. *Thoroughgood* was the critical case in that
it first settled the issue of law involved. The last doubt upon the
question is found in 1521,[2] where the year-book reporter, who
was perhaps Serjeant Carrell,[3] regarded the question as
unsettled and says so in a note. Brooke in his *Abridgement*,

---

[1] See J. H. Baker in [1971] C.L.J. at p. 58, referring to cases in 1520, 1530, and
1531 which he has traced on the plea rolls.
[2] *Cleymond* v. *Vincent* Y.B. 12 Hen. VIII, P. f. 11, pl. 3.
[3] See 73 L.Q.R. pp. 89 et seq.

noting *Jordan's Case* (1536), remarks that assumpsit will lie in place of debt.[1] The case as reported hardly goes this far, for on one view of the facts debt would not have been available for want of a *quid pro quo*. Both Spilman and Port JJ. in *Jordan's Case* did hold that the debt was available, and were prepared nevertheless to allow assumpsit, and Brooke's note of the case may be prompted by the knowledge that it was their view which prevailed. A case in 1542, which Brooke abridges, makes it quite clear that by then assumpsit in lieu of debt was well established, for it lays down that a judgment in debt bars assumpsit for the same sum, and vice versa.[2] In pure theory such a decision was indefensible, for to allow a judgment in one action to be pleaded in bar to a suit in the other tacitly recognizes that the actions are in substance alternative to each other, and reveals the sophistry of the claim that the actions are taken on different points. But any other decision would have been intolerable in practice.

Brooke, in noting *Jordan's Case*, calls his readers' attention to the fact that the decision is in the King's Bench. This suggests that in his time the practice of the Common Pleas was different, assumpsit in lieu of debt not being allowed there. Brooke died in 1558,[3] and not very long after his death, probably by 1573,[4] the Common Pleas began to allow assumpsit against living debtors. It is a conjecture, though nothing more, that the reason why the court changed its practice was sordid self-interest; the judges were alarmed by the loss of business which the development of the law in the King's Bench was causing. There is no doubt that the state of business in the Common Pleas was depressed at the time of Elizabeth I's accession, and that for a short period the only Serjeant-at-Law in active

---

[1] Brooke, *Accion sur le case*, pl. 5, abridging Y.B. 27 Hen. VIII, M. f. 24, pl. 3. On the date of this case see 74 L.Q.R. at p. 384 n. 17. Mr. Lücke in 81 L.Q.R. at p. 549 n. 4 maintains that Brooke is saying 'the precise opposite', but the point Lücke is making is only that Brooke thought that the theoretical basis of liability in debt was different from the basis in assumpsit, and with this I should not disagree.

[2] Brooke, *Accion sur le case*, pl. 105.

[3] The *Abridgement* was a posthumous publication.

[4] *Edwards* v. *Burre* (1573) Dalison 104. This was an action against the executors of a debtor; the report indicates, however, that actions against living debtors were by then allowed. See also *Whorwood* v. *Gybbons* (1586) Goulds. 48, 1 Leon. 61.

practice was old father Bendlowes, whose family was rather proud of this distinction.[1]

Now in strict theory the Common Pleas had a monopoly of the action of debt and the old personal actions, but in practice actions of debt could be brought in both Common Pleas and King's Bench, and had been for many years. The King's Bench had acquired jurisdiction by a fiction. It was accepted that the court did possess jurisdiction when the defendant was in the Marshalsea, the court's prison, or when one of its ministers or officers was involved. In order to litigate in the King's Bench in debt it was only necessary to allege that the defendant was in custody of the marshal, and this was commonly done. The practice seems to have been established in Henry VII's time.[2] Thus the King's Bench did not acquire new contractual business by allowing assumpsit against debtors; they already possessed jurisdiction over debt cases. However, the development of assumpsit in the King's Bench must have increased still further the advantages of litigating in that court, whose procedure was in any case better; parties could be represented in banc by utter-barristers, so that there was no need to brief an expensive and often elderly Serjeant-at-Law. The obvious countermove on the part of the Common Pleas was to allow assumpsit too, for neither a general overhaul of procedure nor the ending of the Serjeant's monopoly of the right of audience was practical politics. The Common Pleas judges at this time had no power to control the decisions of their brothers in the King's Bench; they had perforce to copy them.

The ascendancy of the judges of the Common Pleas

In 1585, however, the relationship between the two courts was entirely changed by statute. Before that date, writs of error from the King's Bench went to Parliament, which at this period met infrequently, for Elizabeth summoned few Parliaments. This was felt to be unsatisfactory, and so the Statute of 1585[3]

---

[1] A MS. in the Bodleian Library, Rawl. C. 728, which appears to be the autograph MS. of Bendlowes's Reports, emphasizes this.

[2] See Coke, *4th Institute*, 72, Reeves, *History of English Law*, II. 602, III.752. And see 7 Hen. VI, T. f. 41, pl. 15; 9 Edw. IV, P. f. 2, pl. 4; 21 Hen. VII, M. f. 33, pl. 26.

[3] 27 Eliz. I, c. 8: 'An Act for Redress of erroneous Judgements in the Courte comonly called the Kinge's Bench.' The Act applied expressly to actions of Debt,

provided that writs of error could be taken before a new court of Exchequer Chamber, which was to be staffed by a minimum of six of the Justices of the Common Pleas and those Barons of the Exchequer who were Serjeants-at-Law. The effect of this statute was to put the justices of the Common Pleas in a dominant position, for at the time when the statute was passed it was usually only the Chief Baron who was a Serjeant. After 1585 the Queen adopted the practice of raising the puisne Barons to the degree of the coif, and so by the end of the sixteenth century the justices of the Common Pleas came to share their dominance with the Barons.[1] For some years after 1585 nothing of importance came of the new arrangement, but after 1595 the new court of Exchequer Chamber became active in the field of contract, and the reports contain a string of cases in which decisions of the King's Bench allowing assumpsit in lieu of debt were reversed on writs of error in the court.[2] The 'postponement of hostilities' until the mid 1590s has been plausibly connected with the death of Wray, Chief Justice of the King's Bench, in 1592 and the succession of Popham.[3]

This was a remarkable change of policy, and it is not easy to find an explanation for it. A possible one is that the judges of the Common Pleas hoped to regain some of their lost business from the King's Bench by this move, but this explanation is not really convincing. If it had been the case that the Common Pleas in practice enjoyed a monopoly over the action of debt, it is clear that they would have gained a great deal of business by suppressing the use of assumpsit in lieu of debt. But, as we

---

[1] In earlier times it was most unusual for Barons to be Serjeants-at-Law.

[2] *Paramour* v. *Payne* (1595) Moore 703; *Maylard* v. *Kester* (1598) Moore 711; *Turges* v. *Beacher* (1595) Moore 694. See also *Wade* v. *Braunche* (1596) 2 And. 53, a case in the Common Pleas where assumpsit was refused. And cf. *Hinson* v. *Burridge* (1593) where a King's Bench judgment was affirmed because debt was not available in the circumstances. See Moo. K. B. 701.

[3] See J. H. Baker in [1971] C.L.J. at 223.

Detinue, Covenant, Account, Action on the Case, Ejectment, and Trespass. The Act preserved the right to take a case from the new court to Parliament. In 1587 an amending Act, 31 Eliz. I, c. 1, was passed. This gave litigants a choice of bringing error to the new court or to Parliament, and made a number of procedural changes. See *Curriton* v. *Godbary* (1583) I Leon 275 'for it is hard as it was said by Wray to drive the party to a writ of error in Parliament, because Parliaments are not now so frequently holden as they have used to be holden'. And so the court altered its own judgment.

have seen, the King's Bench in practice was well able to hear actions of debt, and in consequence the only result of outlawing assumpsit would be that litigants would be forced to sue in debt, which they could do either in the Common Pleas or the King's Bench. Frequently they would have chosen the latter court, since its procedure was better and litigation there cheaper.

We must therefore look for some explanation other than mere economic self-interest. In the climate of legal thought which prevails today it is unfashionable to suggest that legal decisions of any general importance are ever explicable except in terms of some social policy, be that policy openly avowed or not. This somewhat naive dogma leads those who adhere to it to neglect to attach sufficient importance to the fact that common law judges, at all times in the history of the law, have conceived their primary function to be that of deciding cases in conformity with existing law, whether they approved of the existing law or not. This belief may or may not be rational; it is enough that it exists, for its existence has the consequence that many legal decisions are explicable only in terms of legal doctrine, and nothing else. It is quite possible that the decisions of the Exchequer Chamber in the late sixteenth century were motivated simply by the belief that to allow assumpsit to do the work of the action of debt was to infringe a basic legal principle, which principle, in one form or another, had been accepted for over two centuries. If this is the explanation, it conforms readily to the evidence, for the ground given as justifying the reversal of the decisions of the King's Bench was straightforward enough— on the circumstances disclosed by the record the action of debt *sur contract* lay, and, this being so, debt and not assumpsit was the correct form of action.[1] In so holding the Exchequer Chamber applied the principle which forbade overlapping remedies in all its rigour, taking the principle at its face value,

---

[1] The view expressed here rejects the idea that the dispute between the courts centred on the use of a fictional subsequent implied promise in the King's Bench. In 'The Place of Slade's Case in the History of Contract' 74 L.Q.R. 381, I have given reasons for rejecting this interpretation. On this question see below, p. 421. Some of the views I expressed in the article I now think are incorrect, and in particular I was wrong in thinking that *Slade's Case* involved an action of *indebitatus assumpsit*. See now H. K. Lücke, 'Slade's Case and the Origin of the Common Counts', 81 L.Q.R. 422, 539, 82 L.Q.R. 81, and J. H. Baker, New Light on Slade's Case, [1971] C.L.J. Pt. I, 51, Pt. II, 213.

and it is clear that if these decisions had been faithfully followed the action of assumpsit could never have developed into a general remedy for the breach of parole contracts; at most it would have supplemented the action of debt.

The conflict between the courts and its settlement in 'Slade's Case'

Somewhat astonishingly the court of King's Bench took no notice of these reversals,[1] and continued to allow the action of assumpsit to be used. In the context of the times this is not perhaps so very surprising, for in the late sixteenth century the only court which enjoyed sufficient status for its decisions to possess binding authority, or something approaching it, was the ancient informal gathering of the judges, assembled to settle by their collective wisdom some delicate legal issue. To this body, which was also called the Exchequer Chamber, belonged all the judges who were of the order of the coif, in whichever of the three courts they sat. After some years of unseemly conflict between the King's Bench and the statutory court of Exchequer Chamber, *Slade's Case* was brought before the ancient informal court of Exchequer Chamber in order that the question of legal principle could be authoritatively settled by the assembled judges.

In *Slade* v. *Morley* (1602), or *Slade's Case*,[2] an action of assumpsit was brought by John Slade against Humphrey Morley for breach of a promise to pay the price of goods bargained and sold to him. The way in which the action was pleaded, and form of the special verdict around which the discussion of the legal issues turned, give rise to a number of questions of interpretation which are discussed later in this chapter. The central issue in the case is, however, quite clear; on the facts there was no doubt but that the action of debt was available to the seller, and the central issue was whether this meant that an action of

---

[1] See *Lady Shandois* v. *Simson* (1602) Cro. Eliz. 881.

[2] Also reported *sub nom. Morgan* v. *Slade*. The case is reported in 4 Co. Rep. 92a, Yelv. 20, and twice in Moore at pp. 433 and 667. Coke's argument in banc is in Bodl. MS. Rawl. C 720, f. 42a (Rich. 43–4 Eliz., pl. 21) and in B.M. Add. MS. 25215, f. 2a. I am indebted to Mr. G. D. G. Hall for this last reference. For a reconstruction of the stages of the argument see 74 L.Q.R. at p. 390, and now J. H. Baker in [1971] C.L.J. 51 and 213. Baker prints Tanfield's and Bacon's arguments in the case, and catalogues other MS. reports of the case.

assumpsit might not be brought.[1] The point was raised by Dodderidge as his first objection to the action,

> 'That the plaintiff upon this bargain might have ordinary remedy by action of debt, which is an action formed in the Register, and therefore he should not have action on the case, which is an extraordinary action and not limited within any certain form in the Register.'

When, after prolonged argument, the judges resolved in favour of the plaintiff, they accepted the view that there was no objection in principle to the use of assumpsit as a remedy purely alternative to the writ of debt, holding,

> 'That altho' an action of debt lies upon the contract, yet the bargainor may have an action on the case or an action of debt at his election.'

This amounted to a complete rejection of a doctrine which in one form or other had been accepted by most lawyers for over two hundred years, and one which had been repeatedly acted upon by the statutory Exchequer Chamber. It is hardly surprising that contemporaries took the view that *Slade's Case* involved a deliberate judicial change in the law.[2]

It has recently, however, been argued by Mr. J. H. Baker[3] that *Slade's Case* as an Exchequer Chamber case was indecisive; the assembled judges and Barons failed to achieve either a consensus in favour of the action or even a firm majority in favour of allowing it. They remained more or less evenly divided, the King's Bench judges taking one view, the Common Pleas judges another, and the Barons of the Exchequer dividing, Consequently, the Exchequer Chamber conference petered out, and the King's Bench on its own allowed the action. Nevertheless, he contends, the controversy came to an end, the Common Pleas judges thereafter mysteriously acquiesced in the King's Bench view. Baker's argument turns on the fact that neither in print nor in manuscript does there survive any report of the assembled judges and Barons delivering seriatim their final

---

[1] This is made particularly clear by Coke's argument in banc.

[2] This was said by the judges in *Pinchon's Case* (1612) 9 Co.Rep. 86b.

[3] 'New Light on Slade's Case', [1971] C.L.J. 51, 236, esp. at 53–4 (Chronology of the arguments) and 231–2.

opinions. The case we know was in dispute for a prolonged period. It was first argued in the Exchequer Chamber in Michaelmas Term 1597—this was an open or public argument. In the following year, in Michaelmas Term again, it was argued at Serjeant's Inn. In October 1601 it was again argued in the Exchequer Chamber, and in May of 1602 we are back again for apparently the last time in Serjeant's Inn. Coke in his printed report notes one appearance in the Exchequer Chamber and one in Serjeant's Inn, and adds that there were several conferences between the judges and Barons. On 9 November 1602, Popham C.J. announced in the King's Bench that the case had been resolved, and that 'they were agreed', a view confirmed by the other King's Bench Justices. It seems plain that the 'they' referred to were the justices and Barons generally, not simply those of the King's Bench; this appears from the context and from the fact that the King's Bench view was long settled. Coke, whose report was published in print in 1604, also says that the case was resolved, and would hardly have done so if this was simply untrue. Hence it seems plain that between May and November 1602 some sort of agreement (whether unanimous or not) was reached; this may well have been reached privately, as happens today in (for example) the Court of Appeal. It may well be that in *Slade's Case*, as indeed in other important cases, the judges argued the points at issue and came to an agreement without ever publicly delivering opinions in support of the final view adopted—opinions, that is, corresponding to modern 'judgments'; the judicial utterances found in old law reports may take the form of arguments designed to convince other judges, or expositions of the reasons for decisions already reached by the court, either unanimously or by majority. Coke's report of the resolutions derives from his own argument, but since his argument was accepted there is nothing to complain about (in terms of the way the common law system then functioned) in his presenting a version of his argument as representing the view adopted by the Exchequer Chamber.

The importance of 'Slade's Case'

The general effect of *Slade's Case* was that the action of debt *sur contract* became obsolete, in so far as that action involved trial by wager of law. As we shall see, *Slade's Case* did not wholly supersede the action of debt, for the case recognized limitations to the use of assumpsit. After *Slade's Case* had settled the law, few litigants would choose to bring debt in any case where they ran the risk of being met by wager of law; they could now elect to bring assumpsit instead. In those exceptional cases where, even after *Slade's Case*, debt (and not assumpsit) still had to be used, wager of law was not allowable. Thus *Slade's Case* virtually abolished wager as an institution, and the judges who decided the case were very well aware of this consequence of their decision.[1] As the case is reported by Coke, considerable importance was attached to this aspect of the matter, and Coke himself is at pains to justify depriving defendants of their right to wage their law in answer to claims for debts due on parole contracts.

'I am surprised,' he observes rather primly, 'that in these days so little consideration is made of an oath, as I daily observe.'[2]

It is not easy to judge how beneficial the supersession of wager of law was. There is some evidence that in the late sixteenth century the courts made some attempt to exercise control over wager, only admitting defendants to wage after examining them and satisfying themselves that there was a just defence to the claim,[3] but it is also true that a tolerated system of providing professional wager-men as 'knights of the post' existed, run by court officials. What was critical was the readiness of defendants to forswear themselves, and when the court supervised the choice wager may not have been so very unsatisfactory. But even if the right to wage made it too easy for debtors to evade the payment of their just debts, its disappearance, which left the defendant at the mercy of the twelve good men and true, made it too easy for plaintiffs to recover unjust debts. For a plaintiff to arrange for perjured evidence to be submitted to a jury in support of his

---

[1] Wager was abolished in 1833 by the statute of 3 and 4 Will. IV, c. 42, st. 13.

[2] On the view that wager was an institution of peculiar value see Plucknett 116 647, Baker [1971] C.L.J. 228–3.

[3] *Sanderson* v. *Ekin* (1590) 3 Leon. 258, also reported as *Anon.* 3 Leon. 212: 'The defendant in debt, being ready at the bar to wage his law, was examined by the Court, upon the points of the declaration and the causes of the debt, upon which it appeared . . .' For other examples see Baker [1971] C.L.J. 230 n. 94, but cf his account of abuses at p. 228.

claim cannot have been particularly difficult, nor were the juries of the time renowned for their impartiality. Eventually the Statute of Frauds (1677) was passed in order to redress the balance of advantage in favour of defendants once more. It is a fact of human nature, and one which *Slade's Case* neglected, that a failure to obtain a prospective advantage is not regarded as so painful an experience as being deprived of something of value which one already possesses.

Limitations on the use of assumpsit in lieu of debt

After *Slade's Case* the action of assumpsit occupied almost the whole ground formerly covered by debt *sur contract* and detinue when brought on a sale of specific goods. This meant that until wager was abolished in 1833[1] assumpsit, either as a substitute or the older actions, or in its own right, became the sole remedy for those informal parole contracts which did not involve bailment. Where bailment was involved, it shared the ground with the action on the case for conversion, which by the end of the sixteenth century had in practice wholly superseded detinue *sur bailment*.[2]

Attempts had been made in the sixteenth century to extend the scope of assumpsit still further, and to allow the action to be used as an alternative to covenant, and to debt brought on contracts under seal, and in lieu of debt for rent. In the case of contracts under seal the King's Bench allowed assumpsit in *Ashbrooke* v. *Snape* (1591),[3] holding that all that was due on a bond could be recovered by way of damages,[4] and further that a judgment in assumpsit could be pleaded in bar to an action of debt on the bond. This decision, which would have completely confused the relationship between formal and informal contracts, was a momentary aberration; decisions of the same court a year earlier and a year later are quite inconsistent with it.[5]

---

[1] 3 and 4 Will. IV, c. 42, st. 13.

[2] See Fifoot, Ch. 6, Simpson, 'Introduction of the Action on the Case for Conversion', 75 L.Q.R. 364.

[3] Cro. Eliz. 240, discussed by Lücke, op. cit., at p. 558; *Pyers* v. *Turner* (1592) Cro. Eliz. 283 is similar, but the decision was reversed on a different point in the Exchequer Chamber.

[4] cf. the fourth resolution in *Slade's Case*, discussed below.

[5] *Reade* v. *Johnson* (1590) Cro. Eliz. 242, an action for three years' rent due on a seven-year lease, held unanimously that debt lay and not assumpsit. In *Anon.* (1592) Moore 340, an action of *indebitatus assumpsit*, it was held (Gawdy J.

In the case of assumpsit for rent not even the King's Bench ever allowed assumpsit for rent as such. The proper remedy for the recovery of rent, it was agreed, was debt (which did not involve wager), and assumpsit did not lie upon real as opposed personal contracts.[1] In *Symcock* v. *Payne* (1599),[2] however, the King's Bench attempted to bypass this rule. Land had been demised for a term of one year and the tenant had agreed to pay £20 at the year's end. The court allowed assumpsit to lie on a promise to pay this sum, reasoning that it was not rent at all, but a sum in gross—or, as modern lawyers would say, a fine. This decision was reversed in the Exchequer Chamber, and the reversal, which reflected the view of the judges of the Common Pleas, was accepted.[3] By the time of *Slade's Case* it was settled that assumpsit could not be used as an alternative to debt *sur obligation*, or in lieu of debt for rent, or in lieu of covenant on a specialty.[4] As far as rent was concerned, the rule was in time bypassed by later decisions,[5] which allowed what was in substance rent to be recovered in assumpsit if suitable pleading forms were used; but the rule itself was not subsequently questioned. There were, as we have seen, certain other situa-

---

[1] See *Gardiner* v. *Bellingham* (1612) 1 Rolle 24 pl. 1, Hob. 5.

[2] Cro. Eliz. 786.

[3] See *Clerk* v. *Palady* (1597) Cro. Eliz. 859 where it was held in the Common Pleas that assumpsit did not lie for rent.

[4] Hence in *Gardner* v. *Bellingham* (1612) 1 Rolle 24, Hob. 5, it was held in the Exchequer Chamber on error from the Common Pleas that in an action of assumpsit against a debtor the pleading must make it clear that the debt was not due on a specialty or for rent.

[5] See in particular *Acton* v. *Symon* (1634) K.B. Cro. Car. 414, Jones 364, where it was held by a majority of the court that assumpsit would lie on an express promise to pay rent when that promise formed part of an agreement to grant a lease; Croke J. dissented upon the ground that once the lease was granted and the agreement executed by devise, the personal promissory obligation to pay the rent, remediable in assumpsit, is consumed by the real contract of devise on which debt lies, and not assumpsit. The same reasoning could be applied where there was a contract by parole to lend money by bond. Assumpsit was also held to lie on an agreement whereby one was permitted to occupy land in return for money, such an agreement being distinguished somewhat inconvincingly from a lease. See *Dartnal* v. *Morgan* (1620) Cro. Jac. 598, *Brett* v. *Read* (1633) Cro. Car. 343. See also *Green* v. *Harrington* (1619) Hob. 284, 1 Brown. and Goulds. 14. A promise to pay rent, on money due in bond, in consideration of forbearance, was actionable in assumpsit; see *Brett* v. *Read* (1638) and *Mapes* v. *Sir Isaac Sidney* (1623) Cro. Jac. 683.

---

dissenting) that if defendant pleads *non assumpsit* the plaintiff cannot give in evidence specialties to prove the debt, but only matters of contract, such as a receipt without deed. And see *Holme* v. *Lucas* (1625) Cro. Car. 6.

tions where wager was excluded, for example, the compulsory contract. In principle assumpsit would be excluded in these cases, but there appears to be no authority.

The form of assumpsit against debtors

Until *Slade's Case* finally and decisively abrogated the double-remedy doctrine in 1602, pleaders who drew declarations in assumpsit were naturally anxious to avoid the risk of falling foul of the doctrine, and since actions on the case were flexible and invited experiment, quite a number of pleading forms were in use in the sixteenth century. All were contrived in a spirit of caution, to make the action look as different from a writ of debt as could be. Thus in one of the earliest cases, *Orwell* v. *Mortoft* (1505),[1] the pleader drew a declaration against a seller of fungible goods which relied on a quasi-bailment, an assumpsit to look after the goods, and a conversion to the use of the seller. This form was no doubt influenced by a desire to allege a positive act of misconduct, and thus avoid the nonfeasance doctrine, as well as by a desire to make the action look quite unlike an action to recover a debt. In *Pickering* v. *Thoroughgood* (1533)[2] the pleader, in a similar situation, frames the action differently; he recites prepayment of part of the price, and an assumpsit and promise to deliver. This did the trick, for the King's Bench thought that these allegations sufficiently distinguished the cause of action from debt—breaking a promise is not the same thing as detaining a debt. From the mid-sixteenth century onwards (there is one early example in the fifteenth) we find cases in which it is alleged that the plaintiff has paid a small sum for an undertaking and promise to pay a debt, or to deliver goods. The case of *Norwood* v. *Read* (1558)[3] is an illustration. There was a contract for the sale of fifty quarters of wheat, deliverable in two equal instalments; for each instalment £16 13s. 4d. was payable on delivery. It was alleged that forty shillings[4] had been paid for a promise and undertaking to deliver, and it was for breach of this promise that the action was

---

[1] Y.B. 20 Hen. VII, M. f. 8, pl. 18, Keilwey f. 69a, pl. 2, f. 77a, pl. 25, Kiralfy, *Source Book*, 150.

[2] See Appendix, Case No. 6.

[3] Plowden 180.

[4] Presumably forty shillings because of the rule that restricted the competence of the royal courts to actions for more than this sum.

brought. Dr. Kiralfy has found a number of other example son
the rolls;[1] for example, in 1566 there is a case where it is alleged
that five shillings was paid for a promise to repay a loan of
£130.[2] Such averments were fictional and could not be specially
traversed; nor need they be proved in evidence before the jury.[3]
The curious practice of averring these payments lingered on
even after *Slade's Case*. Yet another form, again designed to
make it clear that the action of assumpsit is being brought on a
transaction which is distinct from the contract on which debt
lies, makes play with a nearly fictional agreement not to sue.
The plaintiff alleges that the defendant was indebted to him in
a certain sum, and that in return for his undertaking not to sue
in debt, the defendant promised to pay the debt when required.[4]
Where there was an undertaking not to sue for a definite time
it could honestly be said that assumpsit was being brought on a
distinct transaction, or, in contemporary terminology, 'on a
collateral promise'. Actions were, however, allowed for a time
where it was alleged that the plaintiff had promised not to sue
for 'a little time', which, as Gawdy J. acidly pointed out in
Whorwood v. *Gybbons* (1587),[5] might mean three hours. At this
point such allegations become fictional; they function only as
pleading devices.[6]

---

[1] Kiralfy, 184. Dr. Kiralfy suggests that these small sums were paid to satisfy a
rule that consideration must be executed, but this seems dubious; the practice is
older than any such rule.

[2] K.B. roll Hil. 8 Eliz. 96.

[3] See *Anon.* (1567) Bodl. MS. Rawl. C. 112 at f. 262, Appendix, Case No. 10.

[4] Examples are *Gill* v. *Harewood* (1587) 1 Leon. 61, *Hog* v. *Black* (1589) Moore
685, *Sackford* v. *Phillips* (1594) Moore 689. Another device was to allege a promise to
pay in consideration that the plaintiff should give a day for payment; this was tried
in the King's Bench in *Anon.* (1582) Godbolt 13, but failed,the court holding that
the consideration must be executed. See also *Austin* v. *Bewley* (1620) Cro. Jac. 548,
where the distinction between pleading in this way on a collateral promise is distinguished clearly from pleading on a promise which 'sounds in a duty payable'—
i.e. amounts to a promise to pay a debt.

[5] *Lutwich* v. *Hussey* (1582) Cro. Eliz. 20; *Whorwood* v. *Gybbons* (1587) Goulds. 48,
1 Leon. 61.

[6] In *Sackford* v. *Phillips* (1594) Moore 689, the Exchequer Chamber held that a
definite time for forbearance must be averred, following the view taken by the
Common Pleas in *Lutwich* v. *Hussey*. However, in *Whorwood* v. *Gybbons* (1587) the
Common Pleas, in the absence of Anderson C.J., allowed an action where the
defendant, being indebted on arrears of account, in consideration that the plaintiff
differet diem solutionis debiti praedicti per parvum tempus ('should postpone the day of
payment of the aforesaid debt for a little time'), promised to pay. The case was
treated as raising a question of sufficiency of consideration, and the declaration

'Indebitatus assumpsit' as a pleading form

Out of this period of experiment emerged the distinct form of assumpsit which came to be called *indebitatus assumpsit*. This variety of the action, as it existed in the early nineteenth century, is thus described by Stephen in his *Treatise on Pleading*,

'Indebitatus Assumpsit is that species of the action of assumpsit in which the plaintiff first alleges a debt and then a promise in consideration of the debt. The promise so laid is generally an implied one only.'[1]

The action therefore took its name from the form of the declaration, in which the plaintiff alleged that the defendant, being indebted (*indebitatus*), undertook to pay (*assumpsit solvere*). An action of *indebitatus assumpsit* is thus an action pleaded in a particular way. In the period before *Slade's Case* there are occasional references to this method of pleading an action of assumpsit brought against a debtor, both in the King's Bench[2] and perhaps in the Common Pleas.[3]

The earliest example is an anonymous case in the King's Bench in 1572, where the plaintiff declared,

'quod cum defendens indebitatus fuisset al pl. pro duodecim denarijs solutis Assumpsit solvere . . .'[4]

In this example the declaration contains no considerations clause, and though the pleader might allege that the undertaking had been given 'in consideration of' the fact that the defendant was indebted to the plaintiff, this was not essential, and it appears to have been a common practice to declare without any words *in consideratione*.[5] There is one case—the case quoted in 1572—in which the King's Bench held it to be essen-

---

[1] Stephen, *Treatise on Pleading*, 2nd ed. p. 35 on 5.
[2] *Lord North's Case* (1588) 2 Leon. 179; *Anon.* (1582) Godbolt 13; *Anon.* (1592) Moore 340; *Mathew* v. *Mathew* (1594) Moore 702; *Turges* v. *Beacher* (1594) Moore 694. See also *Bagnal* v. *Sacheverell* (1592) Cro. Eliz. 292, *Rayne* v. *Orton* (1591) Cro. Eliz. 305.
[3] *Pulmant's Case* (1584) 4 Leon. 2 is perhaps an example. The reasoning in *Gill* v. *Harewood* (1587) 1 Leon. 61 suggests that the Common Pleas allowed the pleading form, but is indecisive. On the other hand *Anon.* (1586) Godbolt 98, a very obscure case, may indicate that *indebitatus assumpsit* counts were not allowed.
[4] *Anon.*, Dalison 84.
[5] *Whorwood* v. *Gybbons* (1586) Goulds. 48, 1 Leon. 61.

---

was upheld upon the ground that in actions against debtors words of consideration were not needed.

tial to declare expressly that the undertaking was given after the indebtedness arose. The declaration must say that the defendant, being indebted, *postea assumpsit*. This is the only case in which the point was insisted upon, but it is clear that this was the normal practice in the *indebitatus* count.[1] In actions of assumpsit against debtors when the *indebitatus* count was not used there was no such requirement; for example, in *Slade's Case* itself the promise was alleged to have been given at the moment of the debt contract—*adtunc et ibidem*.

The reason for the practice of alleging a subsequent promise in actions pleaded in the *indebitatus* form has provoked some discussion. The simplest explanation is that the insertion of the word *postea* did no more than make it plain that the defendant was indebted at the time when he made the promise, and thus served to emphasize the fact that the fact of indebtedness was the motivating reason (i.e. the consideration) for the promise: this it could not be unless the defendant was already indebted when he promised. Before the decision in *Slade's Case* the allegation would also assist the evasion of the double-remedy doctrine; a subsequent promise could more plausibly be regarded as a basis of liability distinct from the original contract which gave rise to the duty to pay the debt.[2]

The attraction to pleaders of the declaration on an *indebitatus assumpsit solvere* is lucidly stated in argument in *Manwood* v. *Burston* (1587).[3]

'As in an Action upon the Case: that whereas the defendant was indebted to the Plaintiff in divers summes of money, amounting to £40, the Defendant, in consideration thereof promised etc., the Plaintiff needs not to show any certainty of the Contract, or other circumstances, how, or in what manner the debt did accrue, or begin.'

Precisely the same point was made by Gawdy J. in *Hughes* v. *Rowbotham* (1592):[4]

[1] The doctrine is referred to by Manwood *arguendo* in *Manwood* v. *Burston* (1587) 2 Leon. 203, and in *Sidenham* v. *Worlington* (1585) 2 Leon. 224, where Periam J. says that to declare on a subsequent promise was the normal course.
[2] The question is discussed by Ames, and by Lücke, op. cit. 551–2. A subsequent promise might or might not be a fiction. For difficulties over the subsequent promise and the rule that consideration must not be past see below, p. 456.
[3] 2 Leon. 203.
[4] Popham 30.

'And therefore in an Action on the Case upon an Assumpsit, it sufficeth to say, that whereas the Defendant was indebted to the Plaintiff in divers summs of money amounting in all to a 100 l. The Defendant assumed to pay him the 100 l. at such a day, without saying how, or in what manner these debts accrued, or when, because the action is merely founded not upon the Debt but on the promise, and the Debts are but inducements to it: But if it were to recover the Debts themselves in an Action of Debt, there ought to be made a certainty thereof, to wit, when, and how it comes.'

It is for this reason that *indebitatus assumpsit* as a pleading form, as described by Gawdy J., was called 'general' as in the expression 'a general *indebitatus assumpsit solvere*'. The plaintiff need only say that the defendant was indebted *generally*, without stating *specifically* the cause of the debts or debts involved. If any dispute over the existence of the indebtedness arose the plaintiff would have to tender evidence before the jury and the matter would be fought out at that stage. But the less that had to be alleged in the pleadings, the more room there was for manoeuvre in the trial of the issue.[1]

'Indebitatus assumpsit' and special assumpsit

Legal historians have tended to apply the name *indebitatus assumpsit* indiscriminately to *all* actions of assumpsit brought in lieu of debt against debtors. This is an error, to which the author himself pleads guilty.[2] Not all such actions in lieu of debt are actions of *indebitatus assumpsit*, but only some; for an action to be an action of *indebitatus assumpsit* it must not only be an action in lieu of debt, but also an action pleaded in a peculiar and characteristic manner.

It needs to be emphasized that the feature which identifies an action of *indebitatus assumpsit* is the form of the declaration, where

---

[1] An additional advantage was that a single assumpsit count could be used although the debts involved arose from a number of different contractual transactions.

[2] In the article I wrote in 74 L.Q.R. 381 ('The Place of Slade's Case in the History of Contract') I made this mistake, and I can only plead in mitigation that I erred in good company. I am greatly indebted to Mr. G. D. G. Hall, who in a conversation expressed some doubt as to whether *Slade's Case* involved an action of *indebitatus assumpsit*, and thereby led me to rethink the whole matter. See now Lücke.

it is alleged that the defendant, being indebted to the plaintiff in a certain sum, promised or undertook to pay the debt. The straightforward alternative to this form of declaration was one in which the plaintiff, instead of just saying that the defendant was indebted to him, set out *in detail* the contractual transaction (a loan, for example, or a sale of goods) and alleged a promise to repay the money or pay the price, or whatever it was. An early example of a declaration of this kind is the declaration in *Edwards* v. *Burre* (1572), where the reporter notes that the plaintiff,

> 'Counted that the testator, in consideration that the plaintiff lent the testator 40*s*., the said testator undertook to pay him 40*s*..'[1]

An *indebitatus* count in *Edwards* v. *Burre* would have taken the following basic form,

> 'that the testator, being indebted to the plaintiff in a sum of 40*s*., in consideration thereof promised to pay the debt.'

A full version of a detailed count, as opposed to a general *indebitatus* count, would set out the place of the transaction, the date and subject-matter of the contract, and would allege that the promise or undertaking upon which action was brought was given in consideration of the counter promise of performance by the plaintiff. *Slade's Case* itself provides an example,

> '. . . the said Humphrey (the defendant), the aforesaid 8th. day of May, in the 37th. Year aforesaid, the said Wheat and Rye in Ears upon the close aforesaid then growing, at Halberton aforesaid, in consideration that the said John (the plaintiff) then and there, at the special instance and request of the said Humphrey had bargained and sold unto the said Humphrey to the use and behoof of the said Humphrey all the ears of Wheat and Corn which then did grow upon the said close, called Rack Park (the tithes thereof to the Rector of the Church of Halberton aforesaid due only excepted), did

---

[1] Dalison 104. Similar forms are given in Rastell's *Entries* (ed. 1566) at f. 4 et seq. under the heading 'Accion sur le case in lieu de dett' and 'Accion sur le case sur assumption de paier money', and in none of the early cases is the *indebitatus assumpsit* form used. Coke's *Entries* does not contain a single precedent for an action of *indebitatus assumpsit*.

assume, and then and there faithfully promised, that he the said Humphrey 16 1. of lawful Money of England to the aforesaid John, in the Feast of St. John the Baptist then next following, would well and truly content and pay . . .'[1]

Actions pleaded in this way were actions in lieu of debt, but they were not actions of *indebitatus assumpsit*, for the details of the transaction which gave rise to the debt (i.e. the contract) were pleaded specially, that is to say specifically or explicitly. They were therefore called actions of special assumpsit, the adjective 'special' referring *to the way in which the action was pleaded*. Actions of special assumpsit were also always used when assumpsit was not being used in lieu of debt—for example, for breach of a promise to deliver a specific thing sold, or to marry, or to perform services. They were also always used when assumpsit was brought on a promise which was incidental to a debt transaction—for example, on a promise to forbear from suing for a debt—such promises being called by contemporaries 'collateral' promises.[2] Just to make things even more confusing, the adjective 'collateral' is also used to describe all promises which are not in substance promises to pay debts.

The subdivisions of assumpsit can be set out like this:

A. *Actions in lieu of debt*
{
 (1) Pleaded as actions of *indebitatus assumpsit*

    OR

 (2) Pleaded as actions of special assumpsit.
}

B. *Actions not in lieu of debt*—Pleaded as actions of special (sometimes called assumpsit. actions on collateral promises)

'Slade's Case' and 'indebitatus assumpsit'

Slade's Case (1602) therefore did not directly concern *indebitatus assumpsit*. Indeed, so far from having established the action of *indebitatus assumpsit* in the common law, it appears from one report of the decision that the judges disapproved the use of the

[1] 4 Co. Rep. 91a.
[2] e.g. *Serle* v. *Rosse* (1595) Cro. Eliz. 459.

declaration on a general *indebitatus assumpsit solvere*. Serjeant Moore in reporting the case notes cryptically,

'But it is not so in the case of an *indebitatus assumpsit solvere*, for there the cause does not appear.'[1]

This is confirmed by Coke's own report of the *Case of the Marshalsea* (1612).[2] It has been argued[3] that this point was not aired in *Slade's Case* and was not 'settled' until *Woodford v. Deacon* (1608);[4] this may be so, but it is curious that both Moore and Coke seem to have thought that the issue was at least raised in *Slade's Case*. This becomes quite intelligible once it is seen that a decision to allow assumpsit in lieu of debt, when pleaded specially as in *Slade's Case*, does not in any way entail a decision to allow the general *indebitatus* count. The objection to such a count, as Moore says, was that it failed to reveal the cause of the debt. This could rank as objectionable because the defendant was not fully informed of the details of the debt or contract or contracts on which, in substance, he was being sued. It was this very feature of the count which made it attractive to plaintiffs, and at the same time rather unfair to defendants.

But, curiously enough, this was not the reason which came to be given for hostility to the general *indebitatus assumpsit* count. Instead the reason was that if the cause of the debt was not revealed the court could not tell whether the action was being brought in a situation in which wager was possible or not. The action might, for example, be for rent, and if this was the case assumpsit did not lie.[5] A consequence of the acceptance of this doctrine was, as we shall see, the revival of a modified less general form of *indebitatus assumpsit* after *Slade's Case*.[6] It was this new, modified *indebitatus assumpsit*, which was distinguished from the bad old *general indebitatus assumpsit*, which lasted until the nineteenth-century reforms in the law of pleading.

---

[1] *Morgan v. Slade*, Moore 667 at 668, 'Mes n'est issint d'un indebitat' assumpsit solvere, quia la le cause n'appiert'. Similarly *Pinchon's Case* (1612) disapproved the use of the *indebitatus* count in actions against executors. See the report (*sub nom. Sir Edward Puncheon v. Thomas Legate* in 2 Brownl. 137.

[2] 10 Co. Rep. 68b.

[3] Baker in [1971] C.L.J. 214.

[4] Cro. Jac. 206.

[5] *Bellingham v. Gardner* (1612) 1 Rolle 24, Hob. 5. See Lücke op. cit. 560.

[6] See below, Ch. xii.

Slade's Case and damages

Before *Slade's Case* the theory of the matter was that assumpsit actions in lieu of debt were allowed in order to redress a wrong, distinct from the mere failure to pay a debt; a conscientious application of this theory would have led the courts to allow a party to an agreement to bring the action of debt to recover the debt, and an action of assumpsit in which compensation would be recovered for the damage caused through the breach of promise. Nobody, however, took the theory as seriously as this; the reality of the matter was that assumpsit was being used as an alternative to debt, and in 1542 we find the inevitable decision that a judgment in one action is a bar to a suit by the other;[1] the same ruling was given in other branches of the law where the action on the case was used as an alternative to one of the older actions. The fact that it required a decision to say that assumpsit barred debt is an indication, however, of the hold which the theory of the matter had on the minds of lawyers. If assumpsit was to be a satisfactory alternative to debt it was essential for the courts to rule that in assumpsit the debt itself could form part of the sum recovered by way of damages, and hence we find that one of the resolutions of the Exchequer Chamber in *Slade's Case* was this,

'And it was resolved, that the plaintiff in this action on the case in assumpsit should not recover only damages for the special loss (if any be) which he had, but also for the whole debt, so that a recovery of bar in this action should be a good bar in an action of debt brought upon the same contract. So vice versa . . .'[2]

This did no more than approve what must have been the practice of the King's Bench for the previous sixty years.

Attempts to revive the general 'indebitatus' count

Notwithstanding the disapproval of the general *indebitatus* count in *Slade's Case* persistent attempts were made throughout the seventeenth century to use this form of pleading, and there

[1] Brooke, *Accion on the Case*, pl. 105, and cf. pl. 110 (1483) discussed above, at p. 291.

[2] Co. Rep. 94b. But assumpsit was no bar when the promise was merely collateral, that is not a promise to pay a definite sum of money or things certain. This was made clear in *Lee* v. *Mynne* (1605) Cro. Jac. 111.

are many cases in which the ruling is repeated.[1] By 1628 Prothonotary Moyle somewhat boldly stated:

'that a general indebitatus is now at peace, for it was ruled by all the justices in the Exchequer Chamber to be naught.'[2]

But the matter continued to be aired many years later.[3] The rationale of the rule was clearly stated in 1612[4] by Tanfield C.B.,

'the reason why a general indebitatus assumpsit is insufficient was given often when I was practising at the bar there [i.e. before 1606]. It was that in the case of a general indebitatus assumpsit it was possible that the debt was for rent, which is real . . .'

Assumpsit was only to be allowed where wager of law was possible; where wager was excluded, as in debt for rent, debt on a bond or recognizance, and debt on a judgment assumpsit was not to lie, and in order to carry this policy into effect it was essential to outlaw the general declaration, which did not reveal the cause of the debt. The restrictive doctrine was much insisted upon by Holt C.J. in *Shuttleworth* v. *Garnet* (1689).[5]

'It doth not follow that an indebitatus assumpsit lies because debt lies; where wager of law doth not lie, there an indebitatus assumpsit don't lie, and it is mischievous to extend it further than Slade's Case',

and caused difficulty in the development of quasi-contractual liability.

Granted this rationale there could be no objection to a declaration which revealed just sufficient to make it clear that the debt for which assumpsit was brought was not rent, or a debt due by bond or recognizance. The suggestion that a

---

[1] *Woodford* v. *Deacon* (1608) Cro. Jac. 206, in the Exchequer Chamber; *Buckingham* v. *Costendine* (1608) Cro. Jac. 213, *Woolaston* v. *Webb* (1611) Hob. 18, *Gardiner* v. *Bellingham* (1612) Hob. 5, (1614) 1 Rolle 24; *The Baker of Grays Inn* v. *Occould* (1612) Godbolt 186; *Austen* v. *Bewley* (1620) Cro. Jac. 548; *Davies* v. *Warner* (1620) Cro. Jac. 593; *Barker* v. *Barker* (1621) Palmer 170; *Mayor* v. *Harre* (1622) Cro. Jac. 642; *Holme* v. *Lucas* Cro. Car. 6; *Foster* v. *Smith* (1626) Cro. Car 3*v*; *Hern* v. *Stubs* (1627) Godbolt 400.
[2] Hetley 106, 113.
[3] *Cooke* v. *Samburne* (1664) 1 Sid. 182; *Wise* v. *Wise* (1675) 2 Lev. 152.
[4] *Gardiner* v. *Bellingham* Hob. 5.
[5] See Comb. 151. Holt C.J. was dissenting.

modified form of the *indebitatus* declaration might be permissible
was first made in *Woodford* v. *Deacon* (1608).[1] The plaintiff had
brought assumpsit on a general *indebitatus* in the King's Bench,
and had been allowed to recover. Error was brought in the
Exchequer Chamber.

> 'because the plaintiff . . . does not show for what cause the
> debt grew, viz. for rent, or by specialty, or by record, for if
> it was by any of those means a general assumpsit will not lie.
> And for this cause all the Judges and Barons held it to be
> error. But if it had been, that he, being indebted for divers
> wares sold, or for such like contract, assumed to pay, etc. it
> had been good enough (notwithstanding) the generality
> thereof.'

Precisely the same reasoning is to be found in *Buckingham* v.
Costendine,[2] another case in the Exchequer Chamber in the same
year.

These cases invited pleaders to employ a new form of
indebitatus assumpsit, and this invitation was accepted. The
earliest example is probably *Rock* v. *Rock* in 1609.[3] The new
approach was approved on a writ of error in *Gardiner* v. *Bellingham* in 1612[4] from the Common Pleas. Here the plaintiff,
suing in assumpsit, declared,

> 'that the defendant, in consideration that he was indebted
> unto the plaintiff in ten pounds four shillings and four pence,
> for agistment and feeding of certain beasts of his in the
> plaintiffs ground, and for wheat and *aliis mercimoniis per
> preadict. B habitus et receptis* [*sic*] did assume to pay the said
> debt.'

The defendant having traversed the assumpsit and lost, he
brought a writ of error, and assigned as error,

> 'that there must be some certain cause of the debt assigned'.

The Exchequer Chamber held the declaration sufficient. Here
the pleader indicated in general terms what the claim was
about, and the court took the view that the declaration was

---

[1] Cro. Jac. 206.
[2] Cro. Jac. 213.
[3] Yelv. 175.
[4] 1 Rolle 24.

sufficiently certain, since it made it clear that the debt was for personal things, and was neither a specialty debt nor a debt for rent. But the only certainty required by *Gardiner* v. *Bellingham* was directed to showing that the plaintiff was bringing the correct form of action. Yet such a method of pleading, though it satisfied the formulary requirement, did not satisfy another more radical objection to the general *indebitatus* declaration, which was that it failed to give the defendant proper notice of the cause of action. The case of *The Baker of Gray's Inn* v. *Occould* (1612),[1] decided in the Common Pleas, shows that there was some feeling that this was the real objection, and it was there said that the inconvenience of such pleading was that,

> 'the defendant should be driven to be ready to give an answer to the plaintiff to the generality.'

But this more rational view did not prevail.

In consequence *Slade's Case* only momentarily checked the evolution of *indebitatus assumpsit*. As Lücke puts it,[2]

> 'the plaintiff could continue to plead the debt generally in indebitatus assumpsit provided that he attached a label to his statement of the defendant's indebtedness which, while not giving any particulars as to its origin, yet characterised it as one arising from simple contract. This suggestion was generally accepted and became the immediate basis on which the Common Counts were built.'

The cases amply support Lücke's account of the matter.

A variety of laconic and non-committal standard forms of *indebitatus* count were evolved in the course of the century—the defendant might be said to be indebted 'for work and labour done',[3] 'for money lent',[4] 'for a certain salary',[5] 'for goods sold and delivered'[6]—and these evolved into the common counts which became the standard form of pleading. How uninformative one could be and still get away with it was inevitably the occasion for litigation—thus it was held in *Bucknall* v. *Thompson*

---

[1] Godbolt 186, and cf. *Mayor* v. *Harre* (1622) Cro. Jac. 642, where the same point is made.
[2] H. K. Lücke in 82 L.Q.R. at p. 91.
[3] *Rushden* v. *Collins* (1669) 1 Vent. 44, 1 Mod. 8, 1 Sid. 425, 2 Keb. 522.
[4] *Anon.* 1 Vent. 252.
[5] *Fowk* v. *Pinsacke* (1675) 2 Lev. 153.
[6] *Magdalen College's Case* (1673) 1 Mod. 163.

in 1673[1] that a count alleging indebtness 'for divers things' (one could hardly be more non-committal) would just not do, though 'for divers things and merchandise' would.[2]

'Indebitatus assumpsit' on an account

One variety of common count involved an allegation that the defendant had become indebted to the plaintiff as a consequence of an accounting together—here the allegation was that the parties had accounted together, the defendant had been found in arrears and was thereby indebted and promised to pay the sum due. The basis of this form of *indebitatus assumpsit* was that an accounting together was a transaction which could give rise to a debt. An example is provided by *Janson* v. *Colomore* (1616),[3]

'Janson brought an action on the case against Colomore, and counted that whereas the defendant was indebted to him on an account and he was found in arrears so much, and in consideration thereof the defendant then and there promised to pay the said moneys on a certain day then to come . . .'

This form of assumpsit (known as an *insimul computaverunt*) was in use before *Slade's Case*, an example being *Whorwood* v. *Gybbons* in 1587.[4] It was held in *Egles* v. *Vale* (1606)[5] in the Exchequer Chamber that an *indebitatus assumpsit* lay on such an account; the report by Croke says:

'(it was moved) there is not any consideration nor cause to ground such an action; for the being in arrear is not any cause to make a special promise; nor is there any thing done on the plaintiff's part whereupon this promise should be grounded, viz., the forbearing of the suit, or any such thing. Sed non allocatur; for the debt itself, without any other special cause, is sufficient to ground the action'.

Again in *Janson* v. *Colomore*[6] it was insisted that the debt arose on the finding of arrears, and would support a simultaneous or subsequent promise to pay.

[1] 1 Freeman 350.
[2] *Okington* v. *Thompson* (1673) 1 Freeman 357.
[3] Moo. K.B. 854, 1 Rolle 397, 3 Bulst. 208. See generally Lücke in 81 L.Q.R. at 547 and 82 L.Q.R. 89.
[4] Goulds. 48.
[5] Cro. Jac. 69, Yelv. 70.
[6] Moo. K.B. 854, 1 Rolle 397, 3 Bulst. 208.

Now it could be argued that in principle the plaintiff ought to set out the causes of the various items in the accounting, in case some involved (for example) rent due, in accordance with the doctrine which led to the rejection of the general *indebitatus* count, so that this form of assumpsit ought not to have survived *Slade's Case*. This point was indeed taken before the Exchequer Chamber in 1611 in *Brinsley* v. *Partridge*.[1] The plaintiff and defendant accounted together and the defendant was found £7 in arrears, and in consideration of this promised to pay. Error was assigned,

> 'that the consideration was not sufficient, because the plaintiff did not show whether the money upon the said account was due as for money received or lent, or for wares bought and sold'.

But the holding was that there was no need to specify, and this was followed in subsequent cases,[2] though with some doubt.[3] These decisions came near to a revival of a form of general *indebitatus* count; however, the accounting together was not a fiction, being specially traversable,[4] so that this form of assumpsit could not be used where no taking of accounts had in reality occurred. The promise to pay was, however, a fiction, in the sense that it was implied from the accounting together.[5]

Forbearance assumpsit[6]

Another way of formulating an action of assumpsit against a debtor was to allege that the defendant was indebted to the plaintiff, stating the sum involved, and then to allege that the defendant promised to pay the debt in consideration for the plaintiff creditor's forbearance to sue until the day fixed at the time of the promise. The promise to pay the debt and the fixing of a day for payment in such cases constituted a distinct and subsequent transaction to the original cause of the debt—which

---

[1] Hob. 88.

[2] *Bard* v. *Bard* (1620) Cro. Jac. 602, *Benson* v. *Sankeredge* (1628) Hetley 85, *Holmes* v. *Savill* (1628) Cro. Car. 116, *Goodwin* v. *Willoughby* (n.d.) Noy 81.

[3] *Anon.* (1628) Litt. 148.

[4] *Dalby* v. *Cooke* (1609) Cro. Jac. 234, Yelv. 171, 1 Bulst. 16.

[5] *Conye* v. *Lawes* (1655) Style 472.

[6] See generally Lücke 81 L.Q.R. 545, 82 L.Q.R. 88 et seq.

might, for example, have been a sale or informal loan. *Woolaston* v. *Webb* (1611)[1] illustrates this form of pleading:

'Henry Woolaston brought an assumpsit against Edmond Webb, and declared that whereas Webb did owe him 30 pounds, in consideration that the plaintiff the 28th day of August 1610 had given day to the defendant for payment of the same money until the 9th. of October following, that the defendant did assume to pay him the said 9th. day . . .'

It can be seen that the cause of the debt of £30 is not stated in this declaration, and it might therefore be thought that to allow such a form of pleading in effect amounted to permitting the general *indebitatus* declaration, albeit thinly disguised. Nevertheless it was held in *Woolaston* v. *Webb* and in a series of later cases[2] that the cause of the debt need not be shown. Hence it was possible to use this form of pleading where the debt arose for rent, or on a bond or record.[3] The rationale of this in the cases consisted primarily in an insistence that the action was brought in these cases upon an entirely different transaction— as it is put in *Green* v. *Harrison* 'a special promise on a collateral cause'. It is clear that the promise to pay on the day fixed was no fictional implied promise, but an actual promise,[4] and some stress was laid upon the argument that,

'the taking of a day certain to pay the same, this proves the verity and certainty of the duty'.[5]

The express promise was conceived of as constituting an express acknowledgement that the debt was due, given on a separate occasion. In *indebitatus* actions on the common counts the promise was implied in the sense that no distinct promisory transaction over and above the transaction giving rise to the debt had to be found by the jury.[6]

[1] Hob. 18.
[2] *Dean* v. *Newby* (1611) 1 Bulst. 153; *Papworth* v. *Johnson* (1613) 2 Bulst. 91 *Thorne* v. *Fuller* (1616) 1 Rolle 379; *Linghen* v. *Broughton* (1616) Moo. K.B. 853, 3 Bulst. 206; *Austin* v. *Bewley* (1620) Cro. Jac. 548; *Davies* v. *Warner* (1621) Cro Jac. 593; *Barker* v. *Barker* (1621) Palmer 170; *Brett* v. *Read* (1633) Cro. Car. 343.
[3] *Green* v. *Harrinton* (1619) 1 Brownl. and Goulds. 14,
[4] This is plain from *Woolaston* v. *Webb* (1611) Hob. 18.
[5] *Dean* v. *Newby* (1611) 1 Bulst. 153.
[6] See e.g. *Acton* v. *Symon* (1634) Cro. Car. 415.

IV

THE DOCTRINE OF CONSIDERATION
—INTRODUCTION

THE long-drawn-out struggle to supersede the action of debt *sur contract* by assumpsit, which culminated in *Slade's Case* in 1602, did not involve any extension of liability on informal agreements. The question at issue in the cases was not whether a debt was owed, but by what procedure the debtor's liability should be enforced. Nor did the evolution of the action of *indebitatus assumpsit* and the common counts entail any extension, though an incidental result was that the scope of liability increased, notably in the case of executors' liability and the field of law known now as quasi-contract. But where no debt was involved, since the promisor was not a debtor, the rise of assumpsit did involve the recognition by the common law courts of a new liability. Promises to marry, for example, to build houses or to return lost dogs do not involve any obligation to pay a fixed sum of money, and promises to guarantee debts or pay marriage dowries did not give rise to debts according to the principles of the medieval law, although definite sums of money were involved. The extension of promissory liability into areas previously outside the scope of the common law generated a need for a new set of boundary markers. It was natural that in a doctrinal system of law there should be a place for a new body of doctrine, whose function was to define which promises should be actionable, and which should not give rise to legal liability. Such a corpus of doctrine was evolved in the sixteenth century, and one part of it is the doctrine of consideration, which delimits the actionability of informal promises *by reference to the circumstances in which the promise in question is made.*

It is important to notice in passing that other limiting doctrines are both conceivable and have in some cases been adopted by the common law. Thus one possibility is to insist upon some measure of formality such as writing, or the formal words once insisted upon in the stipulation of Roman Law. But until the passing of the Statute of Frauds in 1677 formality was in general treated as irrelevant in assumpsit. Other restrictions were imposed. Some promises, because of their content or subject-matter, fell outside the jurisdiction of the common law courts; this was so in the case of promises to marry, which until the mid-seventeenth century were regarded as wholly spiritual in nature. Other promises might be illegal, or contrary to public policy, or impossible to perform, or induced by fraud or duress; consideration is and always has been only one of the pre-requisites of promissory liability. In modern law consideration is also intimately linked to the doctrine of offer and acceptance, and paralleled by the requirement of an intention to create legal relations; consequently the requirements for what we call 'formation of contract' are complex. Neither doctrine is to be found in the period with which we are concerned, so that consideration was the characteristic doctrine of the action for breach of promise to a more striking degree than today.

It is hardly surprising that the history of consideration has given rise to an extensive literature, some of it unfortunately produced as ammunition with which to mow down writers on the modern law whose views are supposed to exhibit dangerous and heretical tendencies, and some written without the least regard for the contemporary evidence. I do not propose to review these writings in any detail.[1] Instead I shall in this introductory chapter first of all establish briefly the time at which the action of assumpsit became associated with the doc-trine of consideration, and then set out in very broad outline the essential features of the doctrine in the sixteenth and seven-teenth centuries without at this stage setting out the evidence for what is said.[2] In subsequent chapters I shall give an account of the antecedents of the doctrine, which are to be sought primarily in the law of uses. This will be followed by a detailed account of the minutiae of consideration in the first century or so of its evolution, and in this account I shall refer to theories as

---

[1] The main discussions are those of *H.E.L.* VIII. 2–48; Holmes, *The Common Law*, Lect. VII; Ames, Lect. XIII; Salmond, *Essays in Jurisprudence and Legal History*, pp. 187 et seq.; Fifoot, Ch. 16; Kiralfy, Ch. 16; Milsom, pp. 309 et seq.; Milsom, 'Not Doing is No Trespass', [1954] Camb. L.J. 105; J. L. Barton, 'The Early History of Consideration' (1969) 85 L.Q.R. 372.

[2] The view I have come to hold corresponds most closely to the hypothesis put forward by Sir John Salmond.

to the origin of the doctrine of consideration which other writers
have advanced, whenever this is relevant.

The chronology

The doctrine of consideration came to be associated with the
action of assumpsit for breach of promise in the second half of
the sixteenth century. The earliest example of a case in which
there is an express averment of consideration is *Newman* v.
Gylbert (1549).[1] The plaintiff declared on a payment of five
shillings and also averred that the defendant *pro diversis aliis
rationalibus causis et considerationibus ipsum Edwardum adtunc et
ibidem moventibus super se assumpsit* (for divers other reasonable
causes and considerations the said Edward then and there
moving took upon himself . . .). The earliest case in published
law reports which mentions consideration in assumpsit is
Joscelin v. *Shelton* (1557),[2] where the consideration was a future
marriage, the plaintiff averring that,

> 'the defendant, in consideration that the son of the plaintiff
> would marry the daughter of the defendant, assumed and
> promised to pay 400 marks in seven years next ensuing . . .'

At this date, however, it was not the invariable practice of
pleaders to refer *eo nomine* to consideration. Thus in *Pecke* v.
Redman (1555)[3] there is no such reference, and in Rastell's *Book
of Entries*, published in 1566, the specimen declarations in
assumpsit,[4] which date back for some considerable period, do
not use the words 'cause' or 'consideration', though they include
explanatory material which would soon be called 'consideration'. Again it is noticeable that Brooke (who died in 1558), in
commenting upon certain fifteenth-century cases in his *Abridgement*, explains the failure of the plaintiff to recover in terms of
the maxim *ex nudo pacto non oritur actio*, but makes no express
mention of consideration.[5] It was around the 1560s that pleaders
came usually to include a considerations clause. The first
reported cases in which the actionablity of agreements is clearly
related to the presence or absence of considerations are *Sharring-*

---

[1] Kiralfy, 176. K.B. Roll Mich. 3 Edw. VI, m. 135, Devon.
[2] 3 Leon. 4, Benloe 57, Moo. K.B. 51, Brooke, *Accion sur le case*, pl. 108. There is
an express averment in *Norwood* v. *Read* (1558) Plowden 180.
[3] Dyer 113a.
[4] Rastell died in 1562.
[5] Brooke, *Accion sur le case*, pl. 7 and pl. 40.

ton v. *Strotton* (1566),[1] *Lord Grey's Case* (1567),[2] and *Hunt* v. *Bate* (1568).[3] Soon after this the reports contain many cases which discuss and develop an intricate body of doctrine about the relevance of consideration in actions of assumpsit. By 1586 Egerton, arguing as Solicitor-General in *Golding's Case*,[4] was able to state the position in the form of a clear general principle,

'In every action upon the case upon a promise, there are three things considerable: consideration, promise and breach of promise.'

Subject indeed to a few exceptions,[5] this had been the position for some years; and by the end of the sixteenth century there were indeed few possible problems which had not been raised and determined one way or the other.

Once established so rapidly, the requirement of consideration in contracts by parole stayed with the law. Over the course of the centuries there have been both changes in detail and shifts in emphasis and analysis. Indeed it has survived one very radical change in the way in which the law of parole agreements is conceived—the shift from a world in which actions lie for the breach of promises (a promise being essentially *unilateral*) to a world in which actions lie for the breach of contracts (a contract being essentially *bilateral*), and the related reception of the doctrine of offer and acceptance, a nineteenth-century development. Yet in modern times the doctrine of consideration can still be regarded as the central feature of the common law of contracts by parole, sharing the field uneasily with 'offer and acceptance', 'intent to create legal relations', and an ill-analysed notion of 'consensus'.

The function of consideration in the pleadings

The gravamen of an action of assumpsit lay in the averment in the declaration of a promise and a breach of promise; the

[1] Plowden, 298, a case on uses.

[2] Appendix, Case No. 10.

[3] Dyer 272a. One may contrast *Reniger* v. *Fogossa* (1548) Plowden 1, where an elaborate discussion of the concept of an agreement includes no mention of consideration.

[4] 2 Leon. 72.

[5] Actions against debtors, actions for negligent misfeasance, and actions on collateral warranties; I do not here discuss the details of these exceptions, which are complicated.

consideration or considerations for the promise appeared in that part of the declaration which contained 'matter of inducement' (matter which 'led in'). Stephen explains the inducement as:

> 'matter brought forward only by way of explanatory introduction to the main allegations'.[1]

'Matter of inducement' was also called 'matter of conveyance'— again in the sense of something 'leading in'. The matter of inducement in pleadings more or less corresponded to the recitals in a conveyance, and since the inducement did not comprise the substance of the declaration it was not necessary to set out the matter with such particularity. It was also generally true that matter of inducement could not be made the subject of a traverse, though there were numerous exceptions to this rule, particularly where the matter of inducement was essential.[2] The function of the averment of consideration is clear from (for example) the declaration in *Slade's Case*, where the pleader sets out by way of inducement the circumstances which led up to the making of the promise by Humphrey Morley, the defendant:

> 'the said Humphrey ... in consideration that the said John (Slade) then and there at the special instance and request of the said Humphrey had bargained and sold unto the said Humphrey to the use and behoof of the said Humphrey all the ears of wheat and corn which then did grow upon the said close called Rack Park ...'

Having thus set the scene, the pleader then goes on to aver the promise,

> '... did assume and then and there faithfully promised ...'

Averments of consideration in other legal documents performed the same function of explanation; we may, for example, compare the recitals in the letters patent appointing Francis Bacon as King's Counsel in 1604.[3] They are as follows:

> 'KNOW THAT WE,
> Both in consideration of the good, faithful and acceptable service performed and carried out by our chosen servant

---

[1] Stephen, *Pleading*, 243.
[2] See e.g., *Kimersely* v. *Cooper* (1588) Cro. Eliz. 168.
[3] *H.E.L.* VI. 678. Original in Latin.

Francis Bacon, as for other various causes and considerations . . .'

Rules and doctrines about consideration in assumpsit are therefore rules and doctrines concerned with the circumstances in which promises must be made if they are to give rise to legal liability.

The meaning of 'consideration'

Pleadings in assumpsit had always included matters of inducement. For example, in the pleadings against a negligent surgeon in 1369[1] the pleader explained the circumstances in which the surgeon undertook to look after an injured finger—the declaration stated that the middle finger of the plaintiff's right hand had been accidentally injured, and that the surgeon had been paid a proper fee of 6s. 8d. The development in the 1560s of the settled practice of setting out not any. circumstances, but circumstances known as 'the considerations', or 'the causes and considerations', entails the acceptance of some general contractual theory, and the first step towards understanding this theory is to identify what was then meant by 'considerations'. The consideration, or considerations, for a promise meant the factors which the promisor considered when he promised, and which moved or motivated his promising. Although not a precise equivalent, 'motive' is perhaps about as near as one can get by way of synonym. The essence of the doctrine of consideration, then, is the adoption by the common law of the idea that the legal effect of a promise should depend upon the factor or factors which motivated the promise. To decide whether a promise to do X is binding, you need to know why the promise was made. This basic idea can be elaborated in various ways— for example, one might or might not accept love of charity, or a future marriage, or a past payment, as sufficient in law to impose promissory liability. Whatever decisions are made about such matters as these can be fitted into the basic analysis.

Consideration and the will

The recognition by the common law that a promise, to give rise to legal liability in assumpsit, must be 'supported' by good,

[1] Kiralfy, 224.

sufficient, or adequate consideration, entails the idea that a promise on its own, an unsupported promise, is not sufficient to impose liability. Now in contemporary thought a promise was conceived of as an expression of will, and the effect of the doctrine was therefore that of depriving a bare or naked expression of will, the *nuda voluntas*, of legal significance; looked at from the point of view of a promisee, it deprived a mere volunteer (i.e. one whose claim depended solely upon the will of another) of an actionable claim. As we shall see, this reluctance to permit a mere or naked expression of will to have legal significance—to rank as an act in the law—first achieved prominence in the law of property in connection with uses and testamentary dispositions ('wills'). In the context of contract law it is first clearly set out in the second part of St. Germain's *Doctor and Student*, published in 1530, the essential principle being stated by the Doctor in this passage, where, after dealing with promises made to God, the Doctor says:[1]

> 'And of other promises made to a man upon a certain consideration, if the promise be not against the law, as if A promise to give B £20 because he hath made him such an house or hath lent him such a thing or other such like, I think him bound to keep his promise. *But if his promise be so naked that there is no manner of consideration why it should be made, then I think him not bound to perform it:* for it is to suppose that there were some error in the making of the promise'.

The naked promises excluded by this theory were so called, as the Student of the common law explains,

> '... because there is nothing assigned why they should be made'.

In modern terms one can see the plausibility of the theory—a promise which lacks any adequate motive cannot have been serious, and therefore ought not to be taken seriously.

Promises reinforcing existing obligations

Granted this analysis it is plain that a promise to do something which one is already under an obligation to do, the promise being made in consideration of the circumstance giving

[1] Dial. II, c. 24.

rise to the obligation, is the paradigm or central case of a
binding promise. For example, suppose A owes B a debt of £10,
and because of this (in consideration . . .) promises to pay B £10.
According to the theory the mere promise to pay £10 is not
enough—it must be supported or bolstered up by an adequate
motivating circumstance. What better circumstance than a
pre-existing obligation to pay £10? Or again take an illustration
used by St. Germain. My father is cold and needs a gown to
keep him warm—I ought, of course, as his son to give him a
gown, I have a natural duty to do so. If I now *promise* to give
him a gown then the promise is binding. Hence in the early
history of consideration it must be appreciated that what has
come to be called pre-existing 'moral' obligation—today
associated with Lord Mansfield's activities in the eighteenth
century—was not some curious aberration; it logically lay at the
heart of the doctrine. It is only by realizing this that sense can
be made of the classic definition of consideration,

> 'A consideration is a cause or meritorious occasion, *requiring*
> a mutual recompense in fact or law',[1]

or of apparent curiosities such as the fact that in *Mountford* v.
Catesby (1572).[2] Serjeant Lovelace thought it worthwhile to
insist in argument that a person might by word or covenant
bind himself to do that which he is not bound by law. Today
this seems so utterly obvious that one would suspect counsel of
wandering if the point were made, but in the early history of
assumpsit this needed saying. It is perhaps worth noticing in this
connection that in everyday life promises are frequently used not
so much to impose but to reinforce, or render more precise
previously existing duties and obligations, the archetype here
being the child's promise to be good, with such variants as the
promise to tell the truth.[3]

Alternative contractual theories

Plainly the idea of relating promissory liability to an analysis
of the motives for the promise is only one of a number of possible
theories which share a reluctance to base liability simply upon

---

[1] *Calthorpe's Case* (1574), Dyer 334b at 336b.
[2] 3 Leon. 43, one of the earliest reported cases involving an averment of consideration.
[3] St. Germain, Dial. II, c. xxiv, on which see below.

the making of the promise alone. Where, for example, the promisor has been paid or recompensed for his promise, one might justify holding him to performance in order to prevent his being unjustly enriched, a rationale which has nothing to do with the inspection of the promisor's motive. Or one might conceive of such a promise as being a trick or deceit, and hold the promisor to it in accordance with the idea that people ought not to be allowed to profit from their wrongs. Such contractual theories as these will be found lurking in modern case law as they are to be found in old cases, there being in this field nothing new under the sun. Now one such rationale for the enforcement of promises is the notion (variously formulated) of induced reliance. Promises do not simply give rise to expectations, they also serve to induce promisees to act in reliance upon them, changing their situation or circumstances in ways which they otherwise would not have done. Where there has been such induced reliance it seems fair to hold the promisor to the promise (or at least require him to compensate). Such a theory of contract with its significantly different implications is to be found in St. Germain as well as the theory of consideration. The context, more fully discussed later, is a discussion of the binding nature of promises made with a spiritual motive or consideration, such promises being charitable in nature. An example is a promise of money to a surgeon to heal a poor man, and the problem for the common law over an analysis of such promises in terms of motive is that the motive is spiritual and a lay court, it could be argued, should not be concerned with spiritual matters. So in the dialogue between the Doctor and the Student an *alternative* contractual theory is put forward:

> 'And therefore, after divers that be learned in the laws of the realm, *all* promises shall be taken in this manner: that is to say, if he to whom the promise is made have a charge by reason of the promise, which he hath also performed, then in that case he shall have an action for that thing that was promised, though he that made the promise have no worldly profit by it'.

This notion was to find a confused expression in detriment consideration, and the confusion arises in this way. The detriment suffered in reliance upon the promise—in our example the work done by the surgeon—is induced by the promise; it is not the motive for the promise. Consequently it is only by a perversion of both the meaning and the basic idea involved in the doctrine of consideration that 'detriment to the promisee' could be portrayed as a form of consideration. In a tidy and more intelligible scheme of thought, induced injurious reliance as a ground for actionability would have been presented not as an aspect of the doctrine of consideration but as an alternative to it. But there has always in the common law been a tendency towards a sort of doctrinal monism—there must be *one* test for the formation of contract (offer and acceptance), *one* principle governing possession, *one* test for the actionability of promises. Hence the adoption of good consideration as *the* requirement for *all* promises, which necessitated a mystifying twisting of the meaning of the term. And even to this day the principle of induced reliance leads an uneasy existence somewhere on the borderline of contract, property, tort, and evidence, notoriously in cases now barbarously referred to as cases of equitable estoppel. The same point can be made, though less importantly, in relation to benefit consideration—put at its simplest the idea that a promisor who has been paid for his promise should perform it can be regarded as independent and alternative to, or supplementary to any *recherché* analysis of promissory motives. But benefit to the promisor was to become another aspect of the sole doctrine—consideration. Since orthodoxy required that all contracts by parole should be supported by consideration, whilst underlying common sense recognized a variety of justifications for holding men to promises, it was bound to happen that the doctrine of consideration became something of a dog's breakfast. The position in modern tort law is similar—since all questions about liability for negligence are supposed to turn on the doctrine of the duty of care, one must expect the duty of care to be something of a dog's breakfast too. It is.

Theories of consideration

With the exception of Sir John Salmond (with whose approach I am broadly in agreement), historians who have sought to produce explanations of the origin of the doctrine of consideration seem to me to have generally missed the point of what has to be explained. What is curious about the common law is not that it enforces business agreements (a somewhat ill-defined category), or that it holds binding promises which have been paid for—it would be extraordinary if it did not. The curiosity is that the actionability of informal promises is made to turn upon an analysis of the motivating reasons which induced the promisor to make the promise—the consideration or considerations for the promise. It is idle to look for *this idea* in the doctrine of *quid pro quo*, or in the rule (which never existed anyway) that in an action on the case the plaintiff must show damage, and to fail to see this involves a quite fundamental mistake, which vitiates any attempt at a historical understanding of the doctrine. A similar and related mistake is to suppose that definitions of what considerations will do—classically the analysis into benefit and detriment—are to be identified with the core of the doctrine. Such definitions are secondary, for before you come to evolve rules of thumb for telling what considerations will suffice, you have first to have got around to worrying about considerations at all. Once that initial step has been taken, the contents of the doctrine may well reflect ideas previously current in the law—for example, the idea that people who have accepted payment for doing things should do them—but it is the initial step which is critical to the structure of the law of informal promises.

V

CONSIDERATION IN THE LAW OF USES

THE equitable doctrine of consideration applied in the law of uses of land must surely have a strong claim upon the attention of anyone who sets out to investigate the history of the contractual doctrine, for it was fully and elaborately developed before there was any doctrine of consideration in assumpsit. If a lawyer of Henry VIII's time had been sat down in an examination and asked to 'Write an account of the doctrine of consideration and discuss its merits' it is the equitable doctrine he would have written about, concerning himself with the law of uses and not the law of assumpsit.

Equity, conscience, and common lawyers

A preliminary point of nomenclature is really of wider importance. The doctrine which concerns the law of uses is traditionally called the 'equitable' doctrine of consideration and for convenience I retain this title. But it is a title which is not to be found in use in the sixteenth century and could be seriously misleading. It suggests that the doctrine was worked out in the Chancery, where 'equity' was applied. So far as I am aware there is no evidence that this was the case. It is a striking fact that in all the reported discussions and decisions which deal with the doctrine in its evolving years it is the common lawyers who are concerned to formulate rules and principles about consideration and indeed about the law of uses generally; it must always be remembered that the common law courts possessed an extensive jurisdiction over uses long before the passing of the Statute of Uses in 1535.[1] Nowhere is there any suggestion that the common lawyers conceived it to be their function simply to discover and apply doctrines already formulated elsewhere, or indeed any suggestion that such doctrines existed, though there

---

[1] Particularly under the statute of 1 Rich. III, c. 1, which allowed *cestui que use* to convey the legal estate by feoffment. See generally Simpson, *An Introduction to the History of the Land Law*, pp. 172–4 and D. E. C. Yale, 'The Revival of Equitable Estates in the Seventeenth Century,' [1957] Camb. L.J. 72.

is a possibility that their thinking was influenced by the canon law, as we shall see. It is, of course, true that the Chancery would give a remedy by subpoena in situations where the common law courts either would not do so, or could not do so, and that the Chancery possessed a settled practice in some matters; it is quite another matter to suppose that this practice was based upon or justified by reference to a body of legal theory called 'equity'. In fact the chancellors of the period with which we are concerned applied 'conscience', not 'equity', and there is, as we shall see, considerable difficulty in demonstrating the pedigree of the principles on which they acted, or even saying what they were. It is also true that in certain instances there was a definite conflict between the views of common lawyers and the view taken in the Chancery as to the propriety of providing remedies by subpoena in certain cases; except, however, in one instance[1] the development of rules governing the law of uses does not exhibit any serious tension, and well before the Statute of Uses the common lawyers had not only fully accepted the protection of uses in the Chancery, and were busily protecting uses themselves, but they had even come around to the view that the use was recognized at common law and was in no way incompatible with sound common law principles.[2] To common lawyers who seriously believed that law was itself simply the expression of reason, there could be no contradiction admitted between their system of rules and some other system of superior wisdom which was the private possession of the chancellors; at the most there could only be an area of disagreement as to what was the course which reason dictated in particular circumstances. Once they had been brought to admit that the use was justified by reason, there was no other course intellectually possible but to accept the use of lands, and to work out rationally in their traditional manner the principles which ought to govern the institution, and which were therefore 'the law'; it was in this spirit that the equitable doctrine of consideration was built up

---

[1] The enforcement of uses against the heir of the feoffee to uses, discussed later in this article; even here the common lawyers had accepted Chancery practice well before the end of the fifteenth century.

[2] See Y.B. 14 Hen. VIII, M. pl. 5, f. 4, and 27 Hen. VIII, P. pl. 22, f. 7, where views were expressed not unlike those of Jessel M.R. in *Walsh* v. *Lonsdale* (1882) 21 Ch. D. 9, a case decided at a time when the 'fusion of law and equity' was momentarily taken seriously.

by the common lawyers. The remoter origins of the ideas which they applied are discussed in the next chapter.

The meaning of the word 'Consideration'

Any study of the doctrine of consideration must begin by fixing the ordinary meaning of the word; a legal concept evolves through the progressive refinement of a concept which is not in origin specifically legal.[1] In the late fifteenth and early sixteenth centuries the word 'consideration' was very familiar to lawyers, and although it had not yet acquired a special legal meaning (and indeed was not to do so during the period under discussion) it had already begun to develop legal associations. Most commonly it was used in statutes. It was then the general practice to include in a statute an elaborate and often lengthy exposition of the circumstances which had inspired the legislation. Thus the celebrated Henrician statute[2] providing for the boiling of the Bishop of Rochester's cook rehearsed the whole grisly story of the murder which inspired this dramatic application of the deterrent theory of punishment, telling us how,

'. . . in the xviiith. day of Februarye in the xii. yere of his most victorious reygn one Richard Roose late of Rouchester in the Countie of Kente coke, otherwyse called Richard Coke, of his moste wyked and dampnable dysposicyon dyd caste a certeyne venym or pyson into a vessell replenyshed with yeste or balme stonding in the Kechyn of the Reverend Father in God John Bysshopp of Rochester at his place in Lamehyth Marshe with whych yeste or Barme and other thynges convenyent porrage or gruell was forthwyth made for his famylye there beyng, whereby nat only the nombre of xvii persons of his said famylie wych dyd eate of that porrage were mortally enfected and poysoned and one of them that is to say Bennett Curwen gentylman thereof ys decessed, but also certeyne pore people which resorted to the sayde Bysshops place and were there charytably fedde with the remayne of

---

[1] See Simpson, *The Analysis of Legal Concepts*, 80 L.Q.R 535 for a theoretical discussion.

[4] 22 Hen. VIII, c. 9, 'An Acte for poysonyng'. L. Radzinowicz, *A History of English Criminal Law*, Vol. I, p. 238, n. 24, records that the sentence was in fact carried out. The statute also made poisoning high treason; for a cook to poison food which he had prepared could well be accounted a crime against nature, and this may explain the legislation.

the said porrage and other vytayles, were in lyke wyse infected, and one pore woman of them that is to saye Alyce Typpyt wydowe is also thereof deceased. . . .'

In the statutes of Henry VI it became common for the draftsman, after he had rehearsed the circumstances, to introduce the enacting part with a clause in the following (or similar) form: 'The King, considering the premisses, of the Assent and Request aforesaid, hath ordained and established. . . .'[1] The original text of a statute at this time would normally be in French,[2] and the examples I give are therefore translations of a literal kind. There was no set model which had to be followed, and so various variants were possible. Thus a clause in a statute in 1429 is introduced in this way: 'ITEM, Our Sovereign Lord the King, considering certain articles ensuing, to be conceived and desired, as well for the profit and wealth of him and his realm universal. . . .'[3] There are many other instances in the legislation of Henry VI.[4] The noun 'consideration' appears in 1429 in the phrase 'by consideration'[5], and in 1430 in the phrase 'through consideration of which mischiefs',[6] The word is here being used to mean the act of considering, and in this sense the word is to this day quite commonly used, as when we say that we have devoted a great deal of consideration to the history of consideration. In the early fifteenth century the noun form is not very generally used in legal contexts.[7]

In the course of time the matters which were considered, and to which consideration was given, came themselves to be called 'the considerations'. The earliest example I have noted is in 1483–4,[8] when a statute of Richard III for the annulment of letters patent begins, 'For certain great causes and considerations, touching as well the surety of the most Royal person of the King. . . .' In the statutes of Henry VII the use of the noun in this sense becomes very common, and the word continues to

[1] 2 Hen. VI, c. 2 (1423).
[2] '*le Roy considere les premisses.*'
[3] 8 Hen. VI, c. 18, '*le Roy considerant certeins articles ensuonts*'.
[4] 8 Hen. VI, c. 10, c. 11, c. 14, c. 21, c. 27; 9 Hen. VI, c. 1, c. 3; 10 Hen. VI. c. 7; 11 Hen. VI, c. 4, c. 6, c. 15; 14 Hen. VI, c. 3, c. 5, c. 7, c. 8; 23 Hen. VI, c. 17; 27 Hen. VI, c. 1, c. 5 (in Latin); 3 Edw. IV, c. 2.
[5] 8 Hen. VI, c. 26, '*per consideracion qil est ordine*'.
[6] Hen. VI, c. 7, '*per consideracion des queux mischiefs ordine est.*'
[7] There is an example in 1449 in 28 Hen. VI, c. 1, '*et surcest consideracion*'.
[8] 1 Ric. III, c. 15, '*item pur certeins graundes causes & consideracions*'.

be used in the older sense as well, as the following examples
show:

'upon many and great considerations and lamentable com-
plaints . . .' [1485][1]
'in consideration of the hurt likely to grow of and by the
premisses . . .' [1487][2]
'that where upon consideration of the marriage betwixt the
said viscount and the said Dame Cecill, it was promised . . .'
[1491][3]
'the Kinge oure Sovereign Lord for certeyn considerations
him moeving . . .' [1495][4]
'for dyvers and many resonable consideracions and causes the
Kingis Highnes moeving . . .' [1496-97][5]

Thus when used of the object of consideration, the considerations were the matters considered; they were the factors which
Parliament or the King was supposed to have had in mind in
legislating, and which moved or motivated the enactment.[6]
Loosely the word could be treated as synonymous with 'cause',
and both in statutes and elsewhere causes and considerations
were often mentioned in the same breath. But 'cause' does not
mean exactly the same as 'consideration'; it lacks the suggestion
of what was in the mind, what was considered, what motivated.
Nor is the word 'reason' a precise equivalent, for an explanation
of the reasons for an action need not be confined to an account
of conscious motives; in the sixteenth century 'reason' possessed
all sorts of special connotations, and the word is not usually
found in company with causes and considerations, except in St.
Germain's *Doctor and Student* (1530),[7] though causes and considerations may be called 'reasonable'. There is indeed no

---

[1] 1 Hen. VII, c. 9, '*sur plusours et graundes consideraciouns & lamentablez complaintz*'.
[2] 3 Hen. VII, c. 9, '*en consideracioun del Dammage semblable accresser de & pur les
Premisses*'.
[3] 7 Hen. VII, c. 17 (original in English).
[4] 11 Hen. VII, c. 49.
[5] 12 Hen. VII, c. 3.
[6] For other examples see 1 Ric. III, c. 13; 4 Hen. VII, c. 23; 7 Hen. VII, c. 14,
c. 15; 11 Hen. VII, c. 6, c. 9, c. 11, c. 26, c. 39, c. 40, c. 55, c. 62; 12 Hen. VII,
c. 1, c. 3, c. 10; 23 Hen. VII, c. 30; 25 Hen. VIII, c. 32, c. 33; 32 Hen. VIII, c.
24, c. 28, c. 43. The considerations are said to 'move' in many statutes; the idea
survives enshrined in the tag 'consideration must move from the promisee'.
[7] See Dial. II, cc. 23 and 24.

other word which does the job of the word 'consideration' as well as it does itself.

The word is also found in private conveyances[1] and royal charters[2] in the fifteenth century, and it also turns up occasionally in chancery proceedings,[3] and in the year-books. One early example is *Brandon's Case* (1460),[4] where 'The Duke of Norfolk came into the King's Bench and Thomas Boucher with him, and showed how for divers causes and considerations he had ousted J. Brandon of his office of Marshal in the same place.' The earliest example I have noted is almost a century earlier.[5] It is used also in St. Germain's *Doctor and Student* in a discussion of contractual theory, where it is treated as being roughly synonymous with 'cause' and 'reason'. Its meaning can also be illustrated from two cases in Dyer's Reports. In the first, a case in 1536, the facts were that a man gave certain goods with his daughter in marriage, and the daughter was divorced; the question was whether the daughter should have the goods back, and Dyer notes, 'And by Fitzherbert and Baldwin it seemed reasonable that she should have them, inasmuch as the cause and consideration of the gift is now defeated; for the goods were given in advancement of her marriage, and *cessante causa* etc.'[6] Here it is obvious enough what the word means; the marriage is the consideration of the gift because it motivated the gift. The word is used in the same sense a few years later in the case of *Lyte* v. *Peny* (1541);[7] the case is discussed and the relevant passage quoted later.[8]

[1] See 27 E.H.R. 323 where Miss C. L. Scofield published a conveyance executed in 1461 which contains the phrase 'And the consideracioun for the makyng of the foreseyde estate was. . . .' So far as I have been able to judge, the term was very uncommon in private conveyances; it is not, for example, used in the precedents in *Carta Feodi* (ed. princ. late 15th century) or in Phaer's *Book of Presidents* (ed. princ. 1543). Kiralfy, p. 179, has also reached this conclusion.

[2] See Kiralfy, p. 177, citing an example from the Charter Rolls in 1419.

[3] See *Kymburley* v. *John Goldsmith*, temp Hen. VI, *Calendar of Proceedings in Chancery in the Reign of Elizabeth*, Vol. I, p. xx, 'like it your noble grace through consideracion of rightwise & justice', 'in consideracon thereof, it may please your seyd grace the premissis considered'.

[4] 39 Hen. VI, M. f. 32, pl. 45. See also 10 Hen. VII, M. f. 4, pl. 4, 13 Hen. VII H.f. 13, pl. 14.

[5] 41 Edw. III, M.f. 19, pl. 3, discussed below p. 403.

[6] Dyer 13a. The complete maxim is *Cessante causa cessat effectus*.

[7] Dyer 49a.

[8] Other incidental uses are to be found in *Anon*. (1536) Dyer 31b; *Bold* v. *Molineux* (1536) Dyer 14b at 17b; Y.B. 20 Hen. VII, f. 11, pl. 20; 27 Hen. VIII.

The protection of uses

During the fifteenth century, by 1446 if not earlier, it came to be the practice for the medieval chancellors to protect the use of lands.[1] In a straightforward case a use would arise by express creation on a conveyance,[2] as where Hugo enfeoffed feoffees of Blackacre in fee simple, and declared his intention at the time of the feoffment that he himself, or some party, was to be allowed to take the profits of the land. Here the Chancellor would ensure that the wishes of Hugo were respected, and he did this by compelling the feoffees to hold the legal estate for the benefit either of Hugo or of the third party, as the case might be. The beneficiary came to be called the *cestui que use* or 'pernor of the profits'. The protection extended by the Chancery could take various forms; thus in addition to being bound to allow the *cestui que use* to take the profits the feoffees were also bound to make such conveyances of their legal estate as the *cestui que use* directed.[3] By making a practice of protecting the *cestui que use* in this and other ways even against third parties the chancellors conferred upon him a form of property interest; in simple terms he was treated as owner in equity, whilst the feoffees were treated as owners at law.[4] The modern equivalent of the use is the trust, though there are many differences in detail; perhaps a more useful analogy might be sought in those many arrangements in modern society which have not become legally institutionalized and which involve the separation of legal title from beneficial ownership. We are all familiar, for example, with the car which the firm owns, in which the managing director takes out his secretary, or his wife does the shopping. It is notorious that many other tax-evading devices involve uses of one form or another which are only partially recognized by the law, and then only incidentally. There can be respectable uses

---

[1] See *Myrfyn v. Fallan, Cal. Proc. in Chancery,* Vol. II, p. xxi (Record Commission 1827–32), and see generally Simpson, *Land Law,* Chap. viii.

[2] Normally a feoffment with livery of seisin to joint feoffees.

[3] See Y.B. 37 Hen. VI, T. f. 35, pl. 23; 2 Edw. IV, P. f. 2, pl. 6; 16 Edw. IV, T. f. 4, pl. 1; and on the feoffees' duty to defend actions see 7 Edw. IV, H. f. 29, pl. 15.

[4] See Y.B. 4 Edw. IV, P. f. 8, pl. 9; 5 Hen. VII, M. f. 5, pl. 11; 15 Hen. VII, H. f. 2, pl. 4, T. f. 12, pl. 23; 10 Hen. VII, P. f. 20, pl. 13.

M. f. 26, pl. 16. Employment of the term in connection with uses is very common under Henry VIII, and the relevant cases are discussed in this chapter.

too—an example is the right of a wife in the matrimonial home when the home is owned by the husband alone, and here the English courts have come some little way towards protecting the wife's use.

The will of lands put in use

It is in connection with the revocation of uses that we first meet with references to causes and considerations.

In protecting the *cestui que use* the Chancellor most commonly proceeded by giving effect to the wishes, intentions, or will (*volunt*) of the feoffor or settlor. His wishes might be declared either informally by parole, or they might be expressed formally either in a writing or by a deed, such declarations being made on the occasion of the feoffment. Alternatively the uses might be declared subsequently; the validity of such a subsequent declaration was apparently accepted by 1452, though not without a hint of doubt.[1] We would talk here of the reservation of a power of appointment, but this conceptual compartment had not been invented in the fifteenth century, or indeed before the Statute of Uses was passed in 1535.

One of the commonest reasons for putting lands in use was that a landowner wished to secure what amounted to a power of devise over his lands; he could do this by making a conveyance to feoffees to the use of his will, or to the use of his last will, or to the use that a certain person should have the lands after his death. Such a transaction was originally not thought to be analogous to a devise, or to raise any issue different in principle from that raised by a feoffment to uses designed to create a settlement *inter vivos*, as where feoffees were enfeoffed and the feoffor declared his will that the feoffees should be seised at once to the use of his son in tail; the basic policy was that the wishes and intentions of the settlor, whatever they were, should be respected. In consequence there is no talk in the earlier cases of a landowner devising a use; he merely declared his will, necessarily in his lifetime, and his will was made effective. With the rise of the idea that a use was a property interest, to which was attached by statute many of the liabilities of normal legal

---

[1] Statham, *Conscience*, pl. 1—'*Ardern*: if I enfeoff a man I cannot declare my will to him subsequently—which was denied.' On the same point see Y.B. 5 Edw. IV, M. f. 8, pl. 20.

landownership and, after 1484, the legal right of alienation by feoffment, ideas were bound to change. It came to be settled, as we shall see, that a last will (*darrein volunt*) would revoke an earlier, and in Henry VIII's time it came to be said that a declaration of will only became effective upon death, and would be ambulatory in its operation. In consequence lawyers had to admit that there was no difference in substance between a declaration of will to feoffees which took effect on the death of the settlor and a devise of landed property, so that it was said that a use, conceived as a property interest, was devisable.[1] Just before the Statute of Uses (1535) this did not pass without question; and in the case of *Lord Dacre of the South*,[2] just before the Statute of Uses was passed, the validity of such devises was argued before all the justices except Englefield J. and the Chief Baron, and before Sir Thomas Audley[3] and Thomas Cromwell. The division of opinion is thus reported by Spilman J.:

'And to this question the said Chancellor, the said Secretary,[4] Lyster the Chief Baron, Baldwin the Chief Justice of the Common Bench and Luke, Justice of the King's Bench, were of opinion that such a will was of no effect but void for no land is devisable by will except by a custom, for it is contrary to the nature of land to pass in such a manner. Another reason was given [*fait*] because the land was in the feoffees for all purposes [*a toutz intentz*] and it is contrary to reason that *cestui que use* who in effect has nothing should make a will and by this give the land to another, to whoever he pleases. And Spilman, Justice of the King's Bench, Shelley and Fitzherbert, Justices of the Common Bench, and Fitzjames

---

[1] Y.B. 10 Hen. VII, P. f. 26, pl. 4, is a clear example—*cestui que use* devises his use by testament (i.e. by the same document by which he deals with his personality). See also 14 Hen. VII, H. f. 14, pl. 4, and 15 Hen. VII, T. f. 1, pl. 10, f. 11, pl. 22, dealing with trusts and powers of sale conferred by testament.

[2] *Lord Dacre's Case* is reported in the year-books, in 27 Hen. VIII, P. f. 7, pl. 22, but the year book does not contain any account of the decision of the justices. The case is also reported in Spilman's MS. Reports (B.M. Hargrave 388) at f. 96a, from which the text given is an extract; I have only quoted so much of the report as deals with the abstract question—Are uses devisable by will? See also E. W. Ives, The Genesis of the Statute of Uses, LXXXII E.H.R. 673.

[3] Thomas Audley became Lord Chancellor in 1533; he had been trained as a common lawyer at the Inner Temple, where he had been a reader.

[4] i.e. Cromwell.

Chief Justice of the King's Bench, were of the contrary opinion, that such a will is a declaration of the trust and a showing to the feoffee of his intent how the feoffment shall be, and the feoffee is obliged in conscience to perform this. And the devisee [?] has no remedy by the law to compell him to perform the will. And he[1] gives nothing in the land by his will, but only his use, and the estate of the feoffee is not impaired in any way by this, but by this the use is changed out of *cestui que use* to him to whom he has given this by the will [and] he can enter and make a feoffment by the Statute of Richard III.[2] And Port, another Justice of the King's Bench, was of the same opinion. But he spoke so low that the said Chancellor and Secretary understood him to be of the contrary opinion. And because of this they thought that the greater number of the Justices were of opinion with them. And therefore all the Justices were commanded to appear before the King. And he ordered them to assemble to agree in opinion. And those who were of opinion that the will was void should have of the King good thanks [*avoent de roy bon thanke*]. And then the Justices reassembled before the said Chancellor and Secretary and debated this question and Fitzjames, Fitzherbert and Spilman came round to the opinion of the Chancellor, Secretary and the other Justices, who were men of great reason and the number of them was greater, and they conformed themselves to their opinion. But Shelley was not there because he was ill, and Englefield was in Wales.'

It is not a pretty story, for in 1528 the justices had given the opposite opinion,[3] and it sheds a curious light both on the subservience of the Henrician judges and on the passing of the Statute of Uses, for the consequence of this decision was that the statute could not be said to abolish the power of devise at all. This must have deprived those who opposed it of their best point, which was all very convenient. It is also noticeable that those judges who were prepared to uphold wills of land only did so upon the basis that such wills, properly construed, operated as delayed declarations of trust.

[1] The settlor.
[2] 1 Ric. III, c. 1.
[3] Noted by York *arguendo* in the year-book report at f. 8.

The revocation of uses

The development of the law governing wills of land was intimately connected with the evolution of rules as to when a settlor of lands in use could change his mind, and revoke a prior declaration of uses effectively. This question was first discussed in a case in the Exchequer Chamber in 1452,[1] and it was in this connection that lawyers first came to investigate causes and considerations in the law of uses. The case is reported fully in Statham's *Abridgement*:

> 'In the Exchequer Chamber Kirkeby, Clerk of the Rolls, rehearsed a matter which was in the Chancery, how one had made a feoffment in trust [*de trust*] and declared his will [*volunte*] to the feoffee after the feoffment, that after his decease one of his daughters should have the land. And then he came to the same feoffee and said that she who was to have the land was not willing to be married off by him, nor be well governed, and for this he said that he revoked his will, and that he wished that the other daughter should have the same land after his death. And then he dies. And which of the two daughters should have the land—this is the case.'

In arguing in favour of the ungovernable daughter Lacon treated the 'will' as operating as an immediate grant, and took his stand on vested rights:

> 'When he declared his will the daughter at once had an interest in the land which he could not after defeat, anymore than when a man enfeoffs me to enfeoff another who is stranger to the blood, he cannot revoke it afterwards.'

Prisot C.J. agreed with him. In opposing this view, Illingworth[2] and Fortescue[3] did not make what would seem to us to be the obvious point—that a will is ineffective until death—and this itself makes it clear that at this period a 'will' was not thought to be testamentary. Instead they developed an argument couched in terms of 'cause', reasoning that only by investigating why the

---

[1] Statham, *Conscience*, pl. 1. The discussion probably was influenced by civilian ideas: in the civil law gifts could be revoked for ingratitude. Justinian, *Institutes* 2.7.3. *Codex* 8.56.10.

[2] Illingworth subsequently became Chief Baron of the Exchequer.

[3] Fortescue at this time was Chief Justice of the King's Bench.

original declaration of will was made, and why it was revoked, could one determine the validity of revocation. Thus Illingworth said:

'... to the contrary, for he does not show that the feoffment ought to have been made [*duist etre fait*][1] to [the use of] the daughter for any cause [*cause*], as that the feoffor had *quid pro quo*, so there is no bargain, but [it is] of his mere will [*miere volunt*],[2] which he may change by conscience perfectly well.'

What is to count as a good cause here is a prior duty (there is no point at this date in differentiating moral and legal duty), a notion which notoriously persists throughout the history of consideration. He goes on to illustrate the possible 'causes' of revocation:

'And I put the case that after he has declared his will he himself had been in poverty and for this cause he wished and required the feoffee to re-enfeoffs him—is it not conscience that the feoffee should re-enfeoff him? As it were he answered "Yes".'

Fortescue took the same line:

'We are not to argue the law in this case but conscience, for it seems to me that he can change his will for a special cause, but otherwise not. And I put the case that I have issue one daughter and I am sick, and I enfeoff a man and say to him that my daughter is to have my land after my death. And then I get better, and I have issue a son—now it is conscience that the son shall have the land for he is my heir, for if I had a son at the time etc. I should not have made such a will. And the law is the same if I wish that one of my sons should have the land, and he becomes a robber.'

---

[1] One could translate 'that there was a duty to make the feoffment'.
[2] The curious expression in modern law 'a voluntary conveyance' (cf. 'a volunteer') derives from this usage. A conveyance is voluntary because the person who makes it has no cause to make it—he makes it voluntarily, of his own will. A volunteer is one whose only claim to the property is the mere will of another. The contrast involved is the contrast between doing something just because you want to, and doing something because you ought to. Cf. in *Lyte* v. *Peny* (1541), Dyer 49a, 'For when a man makes such sort of conditional gift of his mere will and pleasure', and the expression 'of his mere motion', used in *Doctor and Student*, Dial. II, c. 22.

The issues raised in the case and the type of argument used have a curiously modern ring; there appear to be only a limited number of questions of basic legal principle, and a limited number of arguments to be deployed. Unfortunately no decision is recorded.

Now it must always have been accepted that where a settlor conveyed lands to feoffees to his own use in fee simple,[1] he could in such circumstances change his wishes and direct the feoffees to hold the lands to some other use; no third party being involved or prejudiced the rule is obvious, and it is admitted in a case in 1465[2] where the year-book reporter attempted to enunciate principles which would deal with both this and other more complex problems of change of will. He starts by saying:

'If a man enfeoffs another without expressing his intent [*sans limit entent*], and he makes a will later, the last will shall be observed.'

This seems to imply that a later will will always revoke an earlier, so long as the earlier will is not declared at the time of the feoffment. He goes on,

'But if a feoffment has been made to a *certain* intent, this alone shall be observed without variation. . . .'[3]

Thus a will declared in certain at the time of a feoffment is irrevocable by a last will. This general rule is then qualified,

'unless the intent should be to the use of the feoffor and his heirs, he can vary and express a new will, because no stranger has a prior interest.'

Clearly this implies that a will declared on a feoffment is thought to operate at once, and not on the death of the settlor. A further qualification is then introduced,

'But it is otherwise if the feoffment is made to the intent that he [i.e. the feoffor] should take an estate tail, there he cannot vary, for it is not the same as an estate general.'

This reflects the idea that in some sense or other the issue in tail of the settlor obtain an immediate interest in an entail, and

---

[1] Where an entail was involved the position was different.
[2] Y.B. 5 Edw. IV, M. f. 8, pl. 20.
[3] My italics.

that it would be unfair to allow the settlor to deprive his issue of their expectancy by allowing variance or revocation; it must be remembered that at this time an entail was not thought to be a barrable estate. The note makes no reference to 'cause' or 'consideration'.

The next case in point of time is that of *The Duke of Buckingham's Case* argued but not decided in 1504 before the justices assembled at the Church of St. Bride's.[1] The Duke, in order to encourage a marriage which was in contemplation between his younger brother and a lady, *le Dame de Wiltshire*, covenanted with Sir Reginald Bray and others that certain manors should, after his death, be held to the use of the lady in tail special on the body of her intended husband. The marriage was celebrated, but the Duke changed his mind and purported to revoke the declaration of uses; in place of the entail he declared uses in favour of the brother and the lady jointly for life, and suffered a recovery of the manors to this use. The argument centred around two questions. The first was whether the first covenant[2] was effective to pass a use; the second was whether the Duke was entitled to change his mind and revoke the declaration of the use in tail. These two questions were regarded by counsel on both sides as interrelated, for it was assumed that if the effect of the covenant had been to vest some interest or right at once in the lady (giving a present right to the use in tail on the Duke's death) then revocation was impossible.[3] Whether or not such a right or interest did vest at once was thought in its turn to depend upon the cause or consideration (or absence of cause or consideration) for the covenant. Thus counsel on the one side, arguing that the revocation was effective, said:

> 'But perchance if in this case there had been any bargain between the Duke and the Lord [the younger brother] or other consideration, then the grant would change the use and it would be executed in the grantee at once, but all wills which are not to take effect until after death are executory

[1] Y.B. 20 Hen. VII, M. f. 10, pl. 20.

[2] The case does not concern a covenant to stand seised to uses; the idea of such a covenant, designed to make it clear that the covenant was to be effective at once, had not yet been thought up.

[3] The facts are a little obscure; probably the agreement was expressly that the lady should have the entail after the death of the Duke, and I have so construed the case. A different interpretation is possible.

and not executed, and therefore he can change his will . . . so because there is no bargain or consideration for the grant the use is not changed. . . . So it is reasonable that the Duke can change the grant.'

Counsel on the other side attempted to reply to this by saying that there was good consideration, prior obligation,

'For it was made on good consideration, for the older brother is bound by the law of nature to aid and comfort his younger brother.'

The Duke of Buckingham's Case is of peculiar importance for the history of the equitable doctrine of consideration. It is, in the first place, the earliest case in which the term 'consideration' is used in this context. In the second place it shows how legal thought has developed since 1452, when an investigation into 'cause' is thought to provide an alternative method of solving questions of revocation, alternative, that is, to investigating whether the person affected adversely by revocation has acquired a vested right or interest. By 1504 lawyers have come round to thinking that the way in which one decides whether an interest has vested is by examining the cause or consideration which motivated the declaration of will—here the first covenant. Once this prior question is settled, the question of revocation solves itself. Thus there emerges the principle, fundamental to the equitable doctrine of consideration, that to pass a use consideration is necessary. Viewed in terms of revocability, the principle is that only such declarations of intention or will as are motivated by good considerations are binding and preclude a change of mind. It is important here not to be confused by labels. The first transaction which the Duke went through could be called or categorized as a promise, a covenant, a grant, a declaration of intent, a 'will' in the sense of a testament effective only on death, or a 'will' in a neutral sense; the problem of deciding whether it was binding (which here means effective to pass an interest and *therefore* irrevocable) remains the same.

This same problem was discussed in a reported moot case which, though undated, may perhaps be assigned to the 1480s.[1]

---

[1] Keilwey 120a, pl. 69. On the dating of this case see S. E. Thorne, 'Readings and Moots at the Inns of Court,' Vol. I, S.S. Vol. 71 at p. xlvii, n. 2.

A bought lands, and told the vendor to enfeoff feoffees to the use of himself and his wife jointly in fee; he then changed his mind and told the feoffees to hold to the use of himself and his wife in tail. Could the wife, who was prejudiced if the change of mind was effective, claim that it was nugatory? On one side it was argued that the use had vested in the wife, making revocation impossible. On the other it was argued that it depended whether the settlor husband had a *quid pro quo* (marriage being included in this concept); thus the cause of the transaction here is treated as an alternative basis for solving the problem of revocation.

In Henry VIII's reign a quite different approach gained favour. It came to be thought that a 'will' just meant a declaration of intention which only became effective on death and could be revoked at any time before death; what was required was only some way of telling whether a declaration (to use a neutral word) was a 'will' or not. In 1527 Brudenell C.J. and Fitzherbert and Englefield JJ. attempted to state a principle.[1] They ruled that where a feoffment was made to the use of the feoffor's will, then whether his will was declared at once or subsequently he was always entitled to change it, and his last will would be effective at his death. On the other hand where uses were declared on a feoffment, and the feoffment was not declared to be to the use of the settlor's will, no subsequent revocation was possible. A note in Brooke's *Abridgement* to a case in 1539[2] follows the same line of thought,

> 'If a man makes a feoffment and annexes a schedule to the deed containing the use, he cannot change the use afterwards, and the law is the same if he expresses the use in the deed of feoffment. But the contrary is the law where he declares the use by words of will, such as "I will that my feoffee shall be seised to such a use"—there he can change this use because by "will" etc.'

The problem is thus solved by a formalistic test—if the word 'will' is used then a right to revoke is reserved; otherwise

---

[1] Y.B. 19 Hen. VIII, T. f. 11, pl. 5. Apparently the same case is reported in Spilman's MS. Reports at f. 41a; a feoffment had been made and the words in the charter were 'to the use and intent to perform the last will next following.'

[2] Brooke, *Feoffments al Uses*, pl. 47.

revocation is impossible. The emphasis has thus shifted away from an investigation into motives towards an investigation of the intention of the settlor to reserve a right to change his mind, and this intention is determined by the words used.[1]

Curiously enough the older line of thought was resurrected in *Lyte* v. *Peny* (1541),[2] a case involving a use of money (or one could say an imperfect gift of money). A man had bailed money to another to the use of a woman, to be delivered to her on the day of her marriage; before the marriage he purported to countermand his instructions and revoke the gift. Was this revocation effective? In the course of an inconclusive discussion Shelley J. revived the old reasoning,

'And there is a difference, when a man makes a gift or bailment to give to a stranger upon a consideration or former duty. As if I say that J.S. has enfeoffed me of certain land, and in recompense thereof I give him this money, and bail it to a stranger to give it over, I cannot countermand it, because the gift does not take effect as a pure gift, but as a satisfaction. And the law is the same when a thing is delivered in consideration, satisfaction or recompense of another thing, there he cannot countermand. And so here, if the case had been that the bailor had been bound by covenant in consideration of a marriage precedent to pay such a sum then could he never revoke it; for this alters the property. But it is otherwise of a mere gift without any cause precedent.'

This is strikingly like the reasoning of Illingworth and Fortescue back in 1452, and may well be derivative.

The early case law on revocation of uses shows how the courts, in groping towards a solution of the difficult question of deciding when a man may go back on his word, made play with four basic ideas. The first is that he cannot fairly do so to the prejudice of vested rights. The second is the idea that a man's declaration ought particularly to bind him if he can be shown to have had some sort of prior obligation to make the declaration of his intention which he did in fact make. The third is the

---

[1] Spilman's MS. Reports at f. 175a contain an interesting note dated 1530, 'Note by Fizherbert that if a man by his deed makes a will that I shall have all his land, if after the will is executed he purchases the manor of Dale and dies I will have this manor by reason of the will, for it is not a will until his death.'

[2] Dyer 49a.

idea that a man may fairly go back on his word when he has some good reason for doing so. The fourth is the idea that a man may, by the form in which he expresses himself, reserve a right to go back on his word.

Implied uses

Where uses were not expressly declared on a feoffment, or where it was said at the time that they were to be declared subsequently, rules had to be worked out to determine who was to have the use of the lands after the legal conveyance of the seisin had taken effect; once you invent a property interest the law must determine how it is to be transferred from one person to another. Under these rules, as common sense would suggest, it was important to investigate the circumstances surrounding the feoffment, and the reason why it was made. Thus if Hugo enfeoffed Robert on account of a sale it was right that Robert should hold the land to his own use; he would therefore obtain both the legal estate (and seisin) because of the feoffment, and the beneficial ownership because of the sale. But if there had been no sale, and the feoffment had been expressed to be to the use of Hugo's last will, no will being declared on the feoffment, by implication Robert would hold the lands to the use of Hugo. In practice Hugo would stay on the land, and everyone would know that this was the intention and that this was what was normally done when lands were put in use with the intent to declare a will. Here it could be said that although the legal estate and seisin passed, the use remained where it was and did not pass, for there was no reason why it should be altered. In later jargon there was a 'resulting use' to the grantor, but the term is a little misleading; it suggests that the use comes back to Hugo from Robert. It is simpler to think as the early lawyers did, and say that the use never leaves Hugo at all.[1]

Commonsensical rules of this kind were worked out before any theoretical or doctrinal explanation of these rules was current, just as actions for negligence have been entertained for centuries before anyone was moved to invent such mysteries as the duty of care, and the reasonable man, to explain how this

---

[1] The doctrine is adumbrated in Littleton's *Tenures*, ss. 462–4, but without reference to cause or consideration. Littleton wrote *c.* 1480. And see *Abbot of Bury* v. *Bokenham* (1536) Dyer 7b.

could be. But sixteenth-century lawyers, like their twentieth-century successors, had great fondness for metaphysical theories, and just as these now run riot in the law of tort (and elsewhere), at an earlier period they reached their fullest perfection of extravagance in the law of property; perhaps the best-known example is the doctrine of the *scintilla iuris*,[1] and those who are provoked to merriment by it would do well to reflect upon the possibility that future generations will probably find some contemporary discussions of 'foresight' just as comical. The equitable doctrine of consideration which was evolved in the early sixteenth century both to rationalize past decisions, and to provide a chart for future development, has this merit, that it never become detached from common sense.

The basis of the theory was straightforward enough. When a feoffor to uses had not declared his wishes and intentions expressly, the circumstances surrounding the feoffment became important in determining what ought to be done about the use; in particular, what had induced, motivated, or caused the feoffment was treated as critical. The motivating circumstances, which the feoffor was thought to have considered when he made the feoffment, were called the considerations.[2] Thus where a feoffment was made on account of a bargain and sale, the bargain and sale was the consideration for the feoffment, and the bargain and sale was viewed as a good reason or 'consideration' why the use as well as the seisin would pass to the purchaser. Alternatively the payment of the money price, or just the fact that a money price was payable, and recoverable by writ of debt, could be called the consideration which passed the use. Again, if there was a gratuitous feoffment it would normally be the case that the use was not intended to pass; this could be explained doctrinally by saying that there was no bargain and sale or other good consideration for the grant, and thus no consideration to pass the use to the feoffee.[3] Thus the general

---

[1] *Brent's Case* (1575) Dyer 340, *Chudleigh's Case* (1595) 1 Co. Rep. 113b; for discussion see Simpson, *Land Law*, pp. 205 et seq.

[2] The earliest use of the term in connection with uses seems to be in 1504, Y.B. 20 Hen. VII, M. f. 10, pl. 20.

[3] The first full statement is in Y.B. 14 Hen. VIII, M. f. 4, pl. 5. For the retrospective application of the doctrine to earlier cases see Brooke, *Feoffments al Uses*, pl. 37 and pl. 32, abridging Y.B. 7 Edw. IV, H. f. 29, pl. 15, and Y.B. 5 Edw. IV, M. f. 17 pl. 16. For the rule that a feoffee, in the absence of an express declaration that he was to hold to his own use, must show 'money paid, or other special matter'

principle was that consideration was needed to pass a use, except where uses were expressly declared on a feoffment,[1] and it is clear that this general principle had achieved some currency by 1504, for in *The Duke of Buckingham's Case*[2] in that year both counsel seem to be familiar with the idea.

Implied uses arising without transmutation of possession

(a) THE BARGAIN AND SALE

So far we have only considered uses arising on a feoffment; the problem involved is the fate of the use where the seisin has been transferred by a common law conveyance. In Henry VII's time, however, it was suggested that a use might pass from one person to another even when there had been no common law conveyance; as the old lawyers put it, it was argued that uses might be raised and passed without transmutation of possession. The idea was first mooted in the case of a bargain and sale of lands.

In the fifteenth century it seems to have been common practice in the Chancery to enforce contracts to convey land specifically, at least when the vendor still had the land and was able to convey.[3] If he had parted with the land, wrongly enfeoffing a third party, the purchaser was put to his action of deceit at common law under the doctrine in *Doige's Case* (1442) which was probably evolved to fill in a gap in the scheme of remedies.[4] It may sometimes have been the practice for the purchaser not to take a conveyance from the vendor, but to treat the vendor instead as a feoffee to uses—this would be convenient if the purchaser wanted to make a will of the lands, for it would obviate the need for a subsequent conveyance to uses. Against this background it was no great step to hold that a purchaser before conveyance was in the position of a *cestui que use*, to be treated as owner in equity; it must be remembered

[1] See Brooke, *Feoffments al Uses*, pl. 46, and *Doctor and Student*, Dial. II, c. 22.
[2] Y.B. 20 Hen. VII, M. f. 10, pl. 20.
[3] See Barbour, pp. 116–23.
[4] Y.B. 20 Hen. VI, f. 34, pl. 4.

if he claimed beneficial ownership see pl. 40 (1532), *Anon.* (1535) Benloe 16, and cf. *Audley's Case* (1558) Dyer 166a, 324b, Dalison 88, 2 Leon. 159.

that in the case of a straightforward feoffment to uses the most important right of the *cestui que use* was his right to insist upon specific enforcement of the trust in a suit against the feoffees (and, after hesitation, against certain third parties who acquired the land). Thus early in the sixteenth century it came to be established that a bargain and sale of lands would pass the use to the purchaser, the rule in fact being settled before it was explained by reference to a doctrine of consideration.[1] As contemporaries realized, there was a close analogy between this rule and the common law of chattel sales, whereby a perfect contract passed the property in the goods to the purchaser before delivery;[2] the source of this common law doctrine in its turn was the right of a purchaser of chattels specifically to enforce the contract by writ of detinue.[3]

A bargain and sale of lands, like a bargain and sale of chattels, could be good though by parole only;[4] formality only became necessary as a general rule after the Statute of Enrolments in 1535.[5] The rules governing perfection of the contract were also the same in both branches of the law, so that a purely executory contract for the sale of land would pass a use so long as a day of payment was fixed in the future.[6] No doubt contracts under

[1] Y.B. 20 Hen. VII, M. f. 10, pl. 20, f. 8, pl. 18; 21 Hen. VII, f. 6, pl. 4, f. 18, pl. 30, *Robert Marshal's Case* (1506) Keilwey 84b. The doctrine was also applied to the sale of a use; thus Spilman's MS. Reports contain this note (at f. 176a) dated 1524—'Note by Brooke Justice and all others, that if *cestui que use* bargains all his interest to a stranger, after which bargain the bargainor enters and makes a feoffment or other assurance by livery and seisin that there is a disseisin, for at once after the bargain concluded the feoffees are seised to the use of the bargainee, and therefore since the use is out of the bargainor, he by the statute [i.e. 1 Ric. III, c. 1] cannot make a feoffment. . . .' cf. 27 Hen. VIII, P. f. 5, pl. 15, where it is noted that although words of limitation are now used, the bargainee will obtain a use in fee simple.

[2] 20 Hen. VII, M. f. 8, pl. 18.

[3] See generally Milsom, 'Sale of Goods in the Fifteenth Century', 77 L.Q.R. 257; Fifoot, pp. 227 et seq.

[4] This view was taken in *Chibborne's Case* (1563) Dyer 229a, where it was held that the Statute of Enrolments did not apply to lands in London, which therefore would pass on a parole bargain and sale. There is no evidence that formality was required before the Statute of Uses.

[5] 27 Hen. VIII, c. 16.

[6] On sale of land and future payment see Y.B. 21 Hen. VII, f. 6, pl. 4, and Brooke's note in *Feoffments al Uses*, pl. 15 (and see pl. 54), *Sharrington v. Strotton* (1566) Plowden 298 at 301, *Mervyn v. Lyds* (1553) Dyer 90a at 90b, *Calthorpe's Case* (1574) Dyer 334b at 337a, *Smith v. Lane* (1587) 1 Leon. 170. Spilman's MS. Reports at f. 31a and f. 174b contain two cases. In the first, dated 1523, Norwich C.J.C.P. is reported as saying that so long as there is a fixed date for payment in

seal, with either prepayment or payment secured by bond, were normal in practice, for informality has never been a characteristic of well-conducted business transactions of an important sort. The recognition of the bargain and sale meant that contracts for the sale of land came closely to resemble conveyances, more particularly as the statute of 1483[1] conferred on *cestui que use* the power of alienating by feoffment (or other grant), thus giving him one of the chief attributes of ownership. The effect of the Statutes of Uses and Enrolments (1535)[2] was to complete the assimilation; a bargain and sale of lands once enrolled became equivalent to a feoffment with livery of seisin at common law.

In terms of consideration the doctrine of the bargain and sale could be explained by saying that a bargain and sale was a consideration to pass a use.

(b) COVENANTS

At the same time as the courts were coming to recognize a bargain and sale as effective to pass a use it was also suggested that other agreements or covenants might have the same effect. The type of covenant involved was normally one entered into between two families on the occasion of a marriage, or some other family arrangement.[3] An example of such a covenant, taken from a case in Henry VIII's reign, is this:

'One covenants with me that I should marry my son to his daughter, for which marriage he will give me £100, and for which I covenant with him that I shall leave my son all my lands and that all will descend to him after my death. . . .'[4]

Such an agreement, though involving a recompense in money, could not be regarded as a sale of the lands; it was more like the sale of a marriage, though the analogy is misconceived. Family covenants concerning land were at this period socially and economically important, and just as the courts in the sixteenth

---

[1] 1 Ric. III, c. 1.
[2] 27 Hen. VIII, c. 10, c. 16.
[3] For a discussion of the enforceability of such covenants in the fifteenth-century Chancery see Barbour, pp. 123–7.
[4] Spilman's MS. Reports, f. 230b., undated.

---

the future the use will pass. In the other, which is undated, it is said that the use will pass if there has been part payment, with a fixed date for payment of the balance; however, it is also noted that the passing of the right to have the land can be made conditional upon payment.

century came to allow assumpsit for marriage money,[1] so also they came to extend the doctrine of the bargain and sale to the family covenant concerning land.

This extension was beset by a theoretical difficulty. To allow that a covenant would change or pass a use would make a covenant tantamount to an immediate grant of an interest in property, and to a well-schooled common lawyer this seemed a very curious thing. For common lawyers had been brought up to think of a covenant as essentially an agreement to do something in the future, and they had also been trained to recoil in horror from the notion of a grant which takes effect in the future. Their inhibitions here had no precise counterpart in the case of sales, for there was in the case of the sale of goods a long tradition of thinking of a sale as a grant; indeed the medieval concept of a 'contract' at common law was of a transaction which passed an immediate interest, in sharp distinction to a covenant which bound the covenantor to performance in the future.[2] Thus although we would think of sales as a sub-class of covenant (i.e. agreement), sixteenth-century lawyers tended to draw a somewhat uncertain line between the two types of transaction. If Hugo sold lands to Robert, this was thought just to mean 'sell now' (linguistically), whereas if Hugo covenanted with Robert, this just meant covenant for the future, and this line of division could be backed up by the fact that covenants were in practice normally expressed in the future tense, while bargains and sales were not. The distinction is one which is no more and no less intelligible than the distinction between a sale and an agreement to sell, or the distinction between a lease and an agreement to lease—both of which must seem pretty silly to the man on the Clapham omnibus, if he gives his attention to these matters, nor, so far as I know, has any lawyer attempted to explain what sense there is in them.

---

[1] *Joscelin* v. *Shelton* (1557) 3 Leon. 4, Brooke, *Accion sur le case*, pl. 108, Benloe 57, Moo. K.B. 13, seems the first case. The earliest case which suggests that debt lay is *Applethwart* v. *Nortly* (1590) Cro. Eliz. 229; before this the availability of debt was a standard moot question, much disputed but unsettled. Promises on account of marriage must be clearly distinguished from promises to marry, which have a different history.

[2] See Y.B. 22 Hen. VI, T. pl. 7, f. 57; 19 Hen. VI, P. f. 62, pl. 1; 27 Hen. VIII, M. pl. 6, f. 14, pl. 16, f. 28. cf. the argument advanced in 37 Hen. VI, f. 9, pl. 20 and 22 Edw. IV, M. f. 22, pl. 1, that a promise of payment cannot give rise to a debt, since a promise is not a grant.

The question was first raised in *The Duke of Buckingham's Case* (1504),[1] counsel suggesting that a covenant for good consideration might operate as a grant of a use:

'But perchance if in this case there had been any bargain between the Duke and the Lord, or other consideration, then the grant[2] would change the use and it would be executed in the grantee at once, but all wills which are not to take effect until after death are executory and not executed. . . .'

Counsel on the other side replied by arguing that there was good consideration—brotherly love—but there was no decision. In the following year Rede J. discusses the point more fully in a case involving covenants entered into on account of marriage:

'And then as for the other matter, which is whether this covenant will change a use at once, or not at all, it seems to me that it will not. But for the sake of argument I am willing to agree that where one is seised to his own use, if he sells the land, by force of this sale he shall be called feoffee to the use of him who buys the land. But here it is not as a bargain and sale is, seeing that it is merely in covenant, and that which sounds in covenant cannot change a use. And a use cannot be changed here for several causes. One is, it is in the future time that he is to have it, which does not give him any immediate interest, seeing that it must be interpreted in conformity with his words of covenant.'[3]

Rede J. cited in support a decision in *Sir John Mordant's Case* (no date), where it had apparently been held that a covenant could not pass a use. It is not really clear whether he thought that a covenant could never pass a use, or only that a covenant which purported to grant an immediate interest would pass one. His colleague Tremaile J. would not even accept the bargain and sale, and found the idea that such a bargain would pass an interest in land extremely shocking.

The earliest clear decision in favour of covenants concerns a covenant in consideration of marriage; it is the case of *Assaby* v.

---

[1] Y.B. 20 Hen. VII, M. f. 10, pl. 20.
[2] It is noticeable that counsel describes an agreement which does pass a use as a 'grant' rather than a covenant.
[3] Y.B. 21 Hen. VII, H. f. 18, pl. 30.

Lady Manners,[1] decided in 1516 by Fineux C.J. and Thomas More,[2] after discussion in the Exchequer Chamber.[3] The facts were that:

'A was seised of land in fee, and in consideration of a marriage to be had between his daughter and heir apparent and B, son and heir apparent of C, he covenanted and agreed by indenture with C that he himself would have, hold and retain the land to himself, and the profits of it, during his life, *and that after his decease the said son and daughter should have the land to them and to the heirs of their two bodies lawfully begotten, and that all persons then or afterwards seised of the land should stand and be seised immediately after the marriage solemnized to the use of the said A for the term of his life, and after his death to the use of the said son and daughter in tail. . . .'*

The marriage took place, and it was held that the use was changed in accordance with the terms of the indenture. The propriety of this decision was still in doubt in 1540, when a writ of error was brought, but the judgment was never reversed. The terms of the indenture make it clear that the use was to change in the future, after the marriage was solemnized; thus in upholding the covenant the court was allowing what was in effect a grant to take effect *in futuro*. Whether or not the settlor could have revoked before the marriage is not clear; probably he could.

There is other evidence of the dubious state of the law in Henry VIII's reign. Thus a case (or perhaps a mere note) in 1530 seems to reject totally the power to pass a use by covenant.

'Note, that if I covenant by indenture that in consideration of my marriage to be executed, I shall leave all my land after my death to my son in tail, this is only a covenant, and no use is changed by it, though the marriage is executed. But if estate is made according to the covenant by a feoffment, then after my decease they [i.e. the feoffees] are seised to the use of my son in tail.[4]

¹ Dyer 235a.
² Acting as Justice of Assize; at the time Thomas More was a Serjeant-at-Law.
³ The record was moved into the Common Pleas, and it is clear that the point was regarded as of great importance.
⁴ Spilman's MS. Reports at f. 180a. For examples of covenants followed by conveyances to feoffees to the uses expressed in the covenant see *Audley's Case*

In 1532, however, it was held that although a covenant expressed for the future was ineffective, yet if it could be construed as purporting to grant an immediate interest the use would pass; the example given is this:

> 'But if he says that he and all other persons who shall be seised of the same land shall afterwards be seised to this same use, it shall be otherwise'

and this form of covenant is contrasted with one where

> 'A man makes a covenant in consideration of marriage that the lands should descend to his issue after his death.'[1]

Brooke in his *Abridgement* also notes that in *Mantel's Case* (1542) a covenant in consideration of £100 and a marriage whereby the covenantor covenanted to stand seised (apparently at once) to the use of his wife for life, and thereafter to the use of his issue in tail, was held to pass a use.[2] An undated note in Spilman's Reports goes further than this, upholding a covenant as effective even though expressed for for the future:

> 'note if one covenants with me that I should marry my son to his daughter, for which marriage he will give £100 and for which I covenant with him that I will leave my son all my lands and that all will descend to him after my death that now the use of the lands is changed, and for this if I alienate my land he has a remedy, yet this bargain is in the future time. But I believe it good policy to put in the indenture and say, "for which sum he bargains and covenants".'[3]

By 1566, when *Sharington* v. *Strotton* was decided, it had come to be admitted that not only a bargain and sale but also a covenant would pass a use but this was not quite settled by the end of Henry VIII's reign, as appears from *Lord Burgh's Case* in 1543,[4] and it seems impossible to date the evolution precisely.

---

[1] Spilman's MS. Reports at f. 76b.
[2] Brooke, *Feoffments al Uses*, pl. 16.
[3] Spilman's MS. Reports, f. 230b.
[4] Dyer 54b. cf. *Bainton* v. *The Queen* (1553) Dyer 96a. However, the covenant must purport to grant an immediate interest. See *Anon.* (1561) Benloe 121 and cf. *Anon.* (1556) Dalison 18, drawing a somewhat artificial distinction between

(1558) Dyer 166a, 324b, Dalison 88, pl. 3, 2 Leon. 159, *Lady Wingfield* v. *Littleton* (1557) Dyer 162a.

In the cases decided before and shortly after the Statute of Uses there is no discussion as to whether the covenant must be by deed, or at least in writing,[1] in order to be effective to pass a use; on principle it is difficult to see any reason why a parole covenant should not be as effective as a covenant formally executed. No doubt the question was not likely to arise frequently. It appears, however, from the report of *Collard* v. *Collard* (1593)[2] that in 1553 it was held by all the justices that a parole covenant in consideration of marriage was effective, and in *Collard* v. *Collard* itself Popham C.J. and Fenner J. in the King's Bench took the same view, the other members of the court concurring with their decision upon another ground; the Exchequer Chamber, however, reversed the King's Bench on this ground. The question also arose in *Page* v. *Moulton* (1570)[3] on a covenant in consideration of marriage, and it was there held that no use passed: 'By the opinion of all the four Justices of the Bench, without open argument, the use is not altered by such naked promise.' The ground for the decision is, however, uncertain; it may have turned upon the absence of valuable consideration, or upon the fact that the covenant was expressed to take effect *in futuro*. *Corbin* v. *Corbin* (1594)[4] also indicates that at the end of the sixteenth century there was some judicial support for the view that a parole covenant was good to pass a use. Eventually the Statute of Frauds (1677) required writing.

Covenants and considerations

The recognition that a covenant could pass a use must have seemed to some lawyers to have carried enthusiasm for informality and solicitude for the will of landowners somewhat

---

[1] What precisely counted as a deed in sixteenth-century law is not very clear: for some purposes at least a signed instrument may have been treated as the equivalent of a sealed instrument. See Y.B. 7 Hen. VII, T. f. 14, pl. 1, *Anon.* (1536) Dyer 19a, *Core's Case* (1536) Dyer 19b at 22b, *Penson* v. *Hodges* (1598) Cro. Eliz. 737.

[2] Popham 47, Cro. Eliz. 344, Moo. K.B. 688, 2 And. 64.

[3] Dyer 296b. The facts were that a father in consideration of a marriage contemplated by his son promised the friends of the wife to be that after his death and the death of his wife the son would have his lands in fee. And see Cro. Eliz. 344.

[4] 2 Rolle Abr. 784, pl. 4, Moo. K.B. 544.

---

instruments which purported to be grants, and were therefore ineffective without livery, and covenants, which were effective to pass a use and therefore the seisin under the Statute of Uses (1535).

too far, particularly if it was the case that such covenants need not be executed by deed. The position had nearly been reached in which any mere unilateral declaration of will by a landowner would be capable of passing a use to another—for example, a promise to a friend that he would have a manor after the promisor's death, made out of gratitude for past favours; there is obviously an analogy here between the problem which confronted the courts in property law and the problem which confronted them in the law of contract. The danger was in part averted by distinguishing the law governing the transfer of uses *in esse* (i.e. separated from the seisin before the transfer) from the law governing the simultaneous creation and transfer of uses by a landowner seised to his own use.

Where a use was *in esse* (suppose A had enfeoffed B to the use of C) the *cestui que use* C could transfer or assign his use to a stranger by a mere declaration of will, his *nuda voluntas* being effective even though unsupported by consideration or a deed. The rule here is clearly stated in *Doctor and Student* (*c.* 1530),

> 'When a use is *in esse*, he that hath the use may of his mere motion give it away, if he will, without recompense, as he might the land if he had it in possession.'[1]

The analogy drawn here and in another passage with the legal right of alienation is somewhat misleading, for although it is true that at common law a feoffment by way of gift was effective to pass the legal estate, such a feoffment must be accompanied by livery of seisin; a mere declaration 'I give you my lands' would have no effect at law. A use *in esse* would also pass out of the *cestui que use* even without an express declaration of will where there was sale, and the two situations were treated as analogous in *Lord Dacre's Case* (1535) by York *arguendo*:

> 'For I say that there is no doubt but that if I sell you my use, at once on the sale the use is changed into you out of my person; therefore I think that if I say to you, "I give you my use in these lands" by these words you have the use, for the use does not pass as the land passes, for land cannot pass without livery, but a use by nude paroles.'[2]

[1] Dial. II, cc. 22 and 23.
[2] Y.B. 27 Hen. VIII, P. f. 7, pl. 22; the same doctrine was stated by Brooke J. and others in 1524, Spilman MS. Reports, f. 176a.

This was not denied. An incidental effect of the Statute of Uses was to reintroduce formality here, for such nude grants of a use *in esse* became impossible; since a use would be executed by the statute (*cestui que use* acquiring the legal estate and seisin), it became impossible for him to transfer his interest in the property by a bare declaration of will, a bare or naked grant; either a bargain and sale enrolled, or a feoffment, or other common law conveyance became necessary. To perfect an assignment of the beneficial interest before 1536, so as to bind the feoffees to uses, notice would have to be given to them, but the point is hardly touched upon in the cases; an early case in 1458 suggests that unless the notice was given personally it must be by deed, an idea which Brooke found incredible.[1] The problem involved here is similar to the problem involved in modern law where there is an assignment of a contractual chose in action.

Where a use was not *in esse* at the time of the transfer (i.e. when the transferor was seised to his own use) then a use had both to be 'raised' and to be 'passed', and the rules were different. We must distinguish two situations.

(*a*) USES RAISED ON A COMMON LAW CONVEYANCE PASSING THE SEISIN

Where uses were expressly declared on a feoffment, or other common law conveyance, neither consideration nor a deed was necessary.[2] This at least was one way of putting the matter. Some lawyers, however, preferred to suppose that consideration was *always* needed to pass a use, and fitted in the case of uses declared on a conveyance by the old legal device of 'deeming' or 'implying'—thus it was sometimes said that a grant implies consideration.[3]

Consideration did become relevant where there was no express declaration, as we have seen. Thus if a feoffment had been made for value, the feoffee would hold to his own use.

Consideration was also relevant where an express declaration to uses was made which was regarded as repugnant to the nature of the common law grant. Thus if a feoffment was made to

---

[1] Y.B. 37 Hen. VI, T. f. 35, pl. 23 abridged by Brooke, *Conscience*, pl. 5.
[2] Brooke, *Feoffments al Uses*, pl. 46.
[3] See Y.B. 14 Hen. VIII, M. f. 4, pl. 5, where Brudenell C.J. took this line, and cf. *Sharrington* v. *Strotton* (1566) Plowden 298, discussed in detail below.

Hugo in tail to the use of Robert for life, the use in favour of Robert was void, and Hugo held to his own use; the same rule applied to any conveyance which created a tenure between grantor and grantee, such as a gift of a life interest or perhaps a term of years. This was explained in terms of consideration by saying that the tenure created was a consideration why the grantee or donee should hold to his own use.[1] Similarly, if Robert conveyed lands to Hugo on account of a sale, Hugo would hold to his own use irrespective of any express declaration of a use by Robert in favour of some third party. Here the consideration—the bargain and sale or the recompense had— was a consideration why the use should pass to the bargainee and nobody else. Thus in some situations the invalidity of an express declaration of a use on a conveyance was explained theoretically by reference to the doctrine of consideration.[2] However, in *Andrews* v. *Blunt* (1571)[3] it was held that an express declaration of a use in writing or by indenture would be good even if it was contrary to a consideration implied by law, so that on a gift in tail, or a grant by fine, a use could be declared in writing in favour of a third party.

(b) USES RAISED WHERE THERE WAS NO CONVEYANCE OF THE SEISIN AT LAW

Where no use was in existence, and there was no conveyance passing the seisin at law, consideration was essential if a use was to be 'raised' and 'passed'. The doctrine on this point was clearly stated in *Doctor and Student*.

'*Doctor:* And what if a man, being seised of land in fee, grant to another of his mere motion, without bargain or recompense, that he from henceforth shall be seised to the use of another: is not that grant good?

[1] Y.B. 14 Hen. VIII, M. f. 4, pl. 5, 27 Hen. VIII, P. f. 7, pl. 22, noting a recent decision that a tenant in tail could not be seized to the use of another, Brooke, *Feoffments al Uses*, pl. 24, 40 (1533), *Abbot of Bury* v. *Bokenham* Dyer 8b at 10a, Perkins, *Profitable Book*, pl. 529, 533.

[2] Brooke, *Feoffments al Uses*, pl. 40 (1533), pl. 54 (1544), *Villers* v. *Beaumont* (1556) Dyer 146a. And cf. 14 Hen. VIII, M. f. 4, pl. 5. The real point at issue in *Tyrrel's Case* (1557) Dyer 155a, Benloe 61, 1 And. 37, was the scope of the doctrine that an express declaration of uses repugnant to the consideration was void. The contractual analogy to the rule in *Tyrrel's Case* is the rule that consideration must move from the promisee.

[3] Dyer 311a at 312a.

Student: I suppose that it is not good, for as I take the law, a man cannot commence an use but by livery of seisin, or upon a bargain, or some other recompense.[1]

The student's statement of the law is only incomplete in that he fails to mention the possibility of other forms of consideration in addition to a bargain or other recompense, and in particular marriage.

The result of insisting upon consideration was that, as the Doctor put it, 'if a man seised of lands makes a gift thereof by a nude or naked promise' the use remained where it was, and the promise was ineffective. The well-known discussion of nude or naked promises in *Doctor and Student* and the discussion of *cause* in relation to contractual liability follows immediately after the discussion of the effect of such promises in the law of uses; having made the point that naked promises are ineffective as grants St. Germain goes on to make the point that they are also ineffective as contracts as well.[2]

Uses and third parties

The institution of the use began life as a personal trust or confidence reposed in a feoffee to uses by the feoffor, and the primary manner in which the Chancery sanctioned the institution was by allowing a subpoena to lie against a feoffee who misbehaved himself and broke the trust reposed in him. Very frequently the feoffor and the *cestui que use* would be the same person, and it may be that in the earliest instances where protection was given the subpoena was brought by the feoffor in his capacity as feoffor, and not as beneficiary, his right to sue depending upon the fact that he was privy to the fiduciary transaction. There is some slight suggestion of this idea in the case in 1452[3] in Statham's *Abridgement* which has already been discussed in connection with the revocation of uses, and clearly the recognition of the third-party beneficiaries' right to sue is intimately bound up with the problem of the feoffor's right to revoke the trust. From the mid-fifteenth century onwards it is clear, however, that title to sue by subpoena depends upon the

---

[1] Dial. II, c. 22.
[2] Dial. II, c. 24.
[3] Statham, *Conscience*, pl. 1.

petitioner being *cestui que use*, not upon his being the feoffor, and this continued to be the guiding principle.

The evolution of rules under which persons other than the original feoffee or feoffees could be bound by the use took longer, and the rules themselves were more complex. Perhaps at first only the original feoffee or feoffees could be sued. But by 1452, the date of the earliest reported case on the subject, it was recognized that the feoffee to uses could transmit his obligation to another person so as to render him liable,

> 'If I enfeoff a man to perform my last will, and he enfeoffs another, I cannot have a subpoena against the second, because he is a stranger. But I shall have a subpoena against my feoffee and recover in damages for the value of the land, according to Yelverton and Wilby, Clerks of the Rolls, who said that if my feoffee in confidence enfeoffs another in confidence of the same land, that I shall have subpoena against the second. It is otherwise where he [i.e. the feoffee] enfeoffs in good faith, for there I am without remedy, and so it was adjudged in the case of the Cardinal of Winchester.'[1]

Again, it was originally the law that the heir of a feoffee was not bound, at least as a general rule. This may not have worked much injustice, for it was normally the practice when putting lands in use to enfeoff a number of feoffees, and the *ius acrescendi* would exclude descent to an heir. By 1482, however, it had come to be the practice in the Chancery to hold the heir bound.

> 'The Chancellor said, that it is the common course in the Chancery to grant [subpoena] against an obligation, and also on a feoffment in trust, where the heir of the feoffee is in by descent or otherwise, for we find records in the Chancery of such subpoenas.'[2]

Chief Justice Hussey found this peculiarly shocking and quite contrary to reason; it meant that the rights of the heir, the darling of the common law, could be upset by a purely informal declaration of a use proved only by the word of two witnesses,

---

[1] Fitzherbert, *Sub pena*, pl. 19.

[2] Y.B. 22 Edw. IV, P. f. 4, pl. 18; see also Y.B. 8 Edw. IV, T. f. 6, pl. 1, Fitzherbert, *Sub pena*, pl. 14 (Mich. 14 Edw. IV).

and he must have thought, with some justification, that such a rule would endanger all security in property. Somewhere about 1460 it had indeed been adjudged, probably at a conference in the Exchequer Chamber, that the heir took free of the use, but the ruling cannot have been respected. Thus it came about that the rights of a *cestui que use*, though originally perhaps contractual in character, became by degrees proprietary. The development can be followed in the cases.

(*a*) NOTICE AND CONSIDERATION: PERSONS ACQUIRING TITLE THROUGH THE ACT OF THE FEOFFEES TO USES

Consider first the position of one who took the land by conveyance from the original feoffee to uses—when will he be seised to his own use, and when will he be seised to the old use, so that the interest of *cestui que use* is not divested by the conveyance? Here it will normally be the case that the conveyance by the original feoffee is a wrong, tort, or deceit to the *cestui que use*, and if the alienee is privy to the tort and has knowledge (*conusance*) or notice (*notice*) of the use this will be a good ground for holding him bound by the use.[1] The principle here is stated clearly in a case in 1467.[2] One J.S. had been enfeoffed to the use of a woman, who then took a husband. The husband sold the property to a stranger, who paid the purchase price to the wife; husband and wife then instructed the feoffee, J.S., to convey the property to the purchaser, which he did. The husband died, and the wife brought a subpoena against the purchaser. The case was rehearsed before the Chancellor and all the justices in the Exchequer Chamber, where it was agreed that the sale had in fact been solely the act of the husband; presumably she had been a good medieval wife and did as her husband told her. At common law, if she had held a legal estate in the property, she would have been able to recover the property in a *cui in vita*, and it was agreed that equity should here follow the law. It was therefore held that the purchaser could be sued by subpoena, provided only that he had 'knowledge of the deceit and tort done to the wife'. Two years earlier a somewhat similar principle was stated in a note, where it was said that if J enfeoffs A

---

[1] In the early cases the two notions are not confused—one has notice if notified, but knowledge can come in other ways.

[2] Y.B. 7 Edw. IV, T. f. 14, pl. 8; cf. Y.B. 33 Hen. VI, p.f. 14, pl. 6.

to his own use, and A enfeoffs R, R will hold to J's use if J gives notice to R of the intent of the feoffment, and this will be so even if the land has been sold to R.[1] Presumably the notice here would have to be given before the feoffment, though the note does not say this; the reporter seems to be primarily interested in emphasizing the fact that even a purchaser for value will be bound. This suggests that before 1466 there had been some feeling that such a purchaser (even with notice or knowledge) would not be bound to hold to the old use.[2]

Although the question must frequently have arisen in practice we have to wait until 1522[3] for another reported discussion of any importance.[4] In the intervening period the doctrine had developed that the presence or absence of consideration (which is not referred to *eo nomine* in the early cases) was a factor which determined whether or not a transaction passed a use, and it is a justifiable speculation that there had been decisions involving third parties where consideration had been treated as the determining factor. As the case in 1522 itself makes clear, there was still some considerable degree of uncertainty over the precise relationship of 'notice' or 'knowledge' and consideration; everyone by then knew that both could be important, but the task of saying precisely how one affected the other caused some difficulty. The point for decision in the case was this: suppose feoffees to a use grant a rent charge for life gratuitously to a stranger without authority from *cestui que use*, does the stranger hold the rent charge to his own use, or to the use of *cestui que use*? The question was a delicate one. No difficulty would by then have been felt if the feoffees had simply granted their estate in fee simple of the lands to a stranger without consideration; he would then have held to the original use, stepping, as it were, into the shoes of the original feoffees. The complexity was that the original feoffees had never been seised of the rent charge to anyone's use, for the simple reason that until they made the grant no rent charge had been in existence; how then could the stranger be seised to a use to which the feoffees had never been seised themselves? How could the conscience of the grantee of

---

[1] Y.B. 5 Edw. IV, M. f. 7, pl. 16.
[2] Y.B. 11 Edw. IV, T. f. 8, pl. 13, applies the same principle to one who is not notified, but takes with knowledge.
[3] Y.B. 14 Hen. VIII, M. f. 4, pl. 5.
[4] Note also *Robert Marshal's Case* (1506) Keilwey 84b.

the rent charge be more heavily burdened than the conscience of the feoffees to uses? This issue divided the court of Common Pleas, Brudenell C.J. taking the view that the grantee was seised to his own use, and Fitzherbert, Brooke, and Pollard JJ. opposing him; Brooke J. indeed somewhat unkindly suggested that Brudenell was simply arguing the opposite view for fun, which I suspect was true. The argument did, however, force the judges who formed the majority to examine the fundamental principles involved, and in the course of it Pollard J. achieved the distinction of being the first lawyer on record to state clearly the relationship between notice and consideration:

> 'If the feoffees enfeoff one without consideration, this is to the first use, even if it is without notice: but on consideration without notice the use is changed. But on notice with consideration the first use remains, and this is the difference.'

In effect Pollard J.'s statement of the law was accepted by the court, except perhaps by Brudenell C.J.; it was not disputed during the period leading up to the Statute of Uses (1535) in any reported case, and the statute made the doctrine largely obsolete.[1] When the trust was revived, the old rules, which made the beneficiaries' immunity from the divesting of their interest depend partly upon notice and partly upon consideration, were given a new lease of life, and in a refurbished form they inspired the doctrine of purchaser for value without notice, the basis for the distinction between legal and equitable ownership to this day.

---

[1] The same rules are stated in an undated note in Spilman's MS. Reports at f. 177b attributed to Hales and Hasket, perhaps in a reading: 'Note that if a man has feoffees to his use, and the feoffees make a feoffment over to others who are strangers, without any consideration, now are they seised as the feoffees are before according to the first use. But if the second feoffment was made for a certain consideration then if the second feoffees have no knowledge of the first use and that *cestui que use* will suffer a wrong and lose his use then they will be seised to their own use, and not according to the first use. But if they have knowledge of the first use and are parties to the wrong done to *cestui que use* at the time of the feoffment made to them, notwithstanding such considerations they will be seised according to the first use. And this matter—whether they had knowledge or not—lies in averment and shall be tried. Which note by Hasket and Hales. The reason why they will be seised to the first use if they have knowledge of this is that the last feoffees are privy to the first wrong, and therefore they will not obtain advantage of this but be seised to the prior use.' See also *Abbot of Bury* v. *Bokenham* (1536) Dyer 7b.

(b) PERSONS ACQUIRING TITLE THROUGH OPERATION OF LAW

Notice and consideration were only relevant when the person acquiring the land was in some sense a party to a wrongful act by the feoffee to uses. Thus if the alienation was lawful,[1] or if title was acquired through operation of law and not through an act of the feoffee, the position was different.

The simplest case is that of the heir taking by descent; surprisingly enough he was treated exceptionally, and from about 1480 onwards, as we have seen, he was held bound by the use. The general rule was otherwise, so that a widow taking in right of dower, or a lord taking by escheat,[2] took the property to their own use even with notice. The heir may have been singled out because of the feeling that he represented his ancestor in an intimate sense, succeeding both to his liabilities and his rights. This would distinguish his position clearly from that of wrongdoers, such as disseissors, who took free of the use, and more obviously those who took by title paramount.[3]

The suggested basis for the special treatment of the heir finds some support in a case reported in the Exchequer Chamber in 1456, when the rules on the subject were in their infancy.[4] A tenant in tail had, by tortious feoffment in fee simple, enfeoffed certain persons to perform his will, and he then made his will and directed the feoffees to retain the lands after his death, and accumulate the profits until they had raised a sum of two hundred marks for the marriage of his daughter. After the death of tenant in tail, her father, the daughter brought a subpoena against the feoffees and the heir in tail, her brother (who had wrongfully gone into possession), to know why the money had not been raised; no defence could be offered, and it was ordered that the feoffees should retain the lands and raise the money,

---

[1] See Brooke, *Feoffments al Uses*, pl. 56 and 57, noting a curious example attributed to Fitzherbert J. Feoffees to the use of another in tail (being seised to their own use in fee simple in reversion) sell the land to a purchaser with notice; the purchaser holds to his own use; since the feoffees have the fee simple they are entitled to sell it, and the sale is therefore a lawful act. The act being lawful, the bargainee cannot be privy to any tort, and therefore notice is irrelevant.

[2] Y.B. 14 Hen. VIII, M. f. 4, pl. 5. cf. Spilman MS. Reports, f. 175b, mentioning tenant by the curtesy.

[3] Y.B. 27 Hen. VIII, M. f. 29, pl. 21, *Abbot of Bury* v. *Bokenham* (1536) Dyer 7b at 12b.

[4] Fitzherbert, *Sub pena*, pl. 22.

and that when the money was raised they should enfeoff the heir in tail. In defiance of this direction the heir entered and took the profits, so that the money could not be raised; the daughter therefore brought a second subpoena against the brother, and the question was whether the action lay against him. It was held that it did. In argument it was agreed that if a stranger had wrongfully entered the lands he would not have been bound; the brother was not, however, a stranger, for in his capacity as heir he was privy to the acts of his father, and bound to perform his father's will. He was not therefore to be treated in the same way as a mere stranger, and for this reason he was bound by the use. Had the brother recovered the land by writ of formedon in the descender (as he was entitled to do), and thus entered rightfully by a title paramount to the title of the feoffees, the decision would have been different.

The distinction between those who took the property free of the use, irrespective of notice or consideration, and those who took subject to the use, either if they had notice, or if they took without consideration, came to be stated in the sixteenth century in terms of a distinction between those who came *in the per* and those who came *in the post*. In modern terminology one who comes *in the per* is one who derives title through another who is seised to a use, such as an heir or an alienee of the feoffee to uses; one who comes *in the post*, such as a lord taking by escheat, a disseisor, or one taking by title paramount is one who does not rank as a successor in title. The rule then is that only a person who in some intimate sense represents a person who is seised to the use of another, or is a party to a wrong done by him, can be affected by the use. The distinction was not followed out in the modern law of trusts.[1]

The types of consideration

Payment of money or some other recompense seems always to have been accepted as good consideration; this comes in with the bargain and sale, and the analogy responsible is the doctrine of *quid pro quo*.[2] The performance of services was recog-

[1] On devices for barring uses in tail see Brooke, *Feoffments al Uses*, pl. 7, 48, and 56. The question was complicated by a doubt as to whether uses in tail, as opposed to uses in fee conditional, were possible, since the Statute *De Donis Conditionalibus* did not obviously deal with uses at all.
[2] Y.B. 20 Hen. VII, M. f. 10, pl. 20, f. 8, pl. 18, 21 Hen. VII, f. 6, pl. 4.

nized as a possible consideration in 1556.[1] Marriage was accepted as good consideration in *Assaby* v. *Lady Anne Manners* (1516);[2] the down-to-earth explanation here is the prevalence of property transactions on account of marriage, and the desire to give legal effect to a well-established social institution. At a more technical level it is possible to argue that marriage is a benefit, and run the analogy with *quid pro quo*;[3] alternatively marriage can be accounted a good consideration in its own right, without inquiry as to whether it is beneficial or indeed detrimental. Long before the evolution of the equitable doctrine of consideration lawyers were very familiar with the idea that marriage could count as a *cause of a gift*; marriage was so treated both in connection with gifts in frank marriage and in connection with the writ *Causa Matrimonii Praelocuti*, which lay to recover land granted on account of marriage when the marriage did not take place—we would call this a writ to recover land granted on a consideration which has wholly failed.[4]

Natural love and affection within a family, as distinct from marriage, seem to have been recognized as a good consideration before 1529. Spilman reports this case:

> 'Note by Broke, that where a man makes feoffees to his use and to his heirs, and dies, his heir being in ward, and at full age the feoffees sue an ousterlemain (and not the heir who has the use, for he cannot do so when a man has feoffees in trust), and [the heir] makes a will that his feoffees should make an estate to one John at Stile, his cousin, in fee, and dies, and John at Stile enters and makes a feoffment in fee; it seemed to all the court, except Fitzherbert, that the use is in John at Stile at once after the death of the testator, for there appears a consideration in the will—that the said John at Stile was his cousin—whereby the use should be to him. And it should not be taken for a feoffment in trust[5] because

---

[1] *Anon.* Dalison 19.

[2] Dyer 235a; see also Brooke, *Feoffments al Uses*, pl. 40 (1532), *Lyte* v. *Peny* (1531) Dyer 49a, *Bold* v. *Molineux* (1536) Dyer 14b, *Lord Burgh's Case* (1543) Dyer 54b, *Anon.* (1556) Dalison 19.

[3] *Anon.* Keilwey 120a (a moot case).

[4] Y.B. 27 Hen. VIII, f. 7, pl. 22, *Villers* v. *Beaumont* (1557) Dyer 146a, *Sharrington* v. *Strotton* (1566) Plowden 298.

[5] What is meant is that the testator's intention was not that on the feoffment to John at Stile there should be a resulting use to him—John at Stile was not intended to be a feoffee to uses, but to take beneficially.

seeing that it appears by his will that he [i.e. John at Stile] should have the land to himself to his own use, therefore the use should be in him before any estate made. For where on consideration it appears that an estate ought to be made, now before any estate be made the use shall be adjudged in him. Therefore his feoffment by force of the statute of Richard III shall be said to be good, and no disseisin.'[1]

The leading case, however, is *Sharrington* v. *Strotton* in 1566,[2] which clearly accepted the doctrine. The idea was indeed hinted at in *The Duke of Buckingham's Case* in 1504[3] in the course of a discussion of the revocability of uses, counsel suggesting, 'It seems that he cannot change the grant, for it was made on good consideration, for the elder brother is bound by the law of nature to aid and comfort his younger brother.' To a modern lawyer who has come to link the conception of 'consideration' to the conception of exchange, it is difficult to see how a prior natural or moral obligation could be accounted a good consideration; when 'consideration' meant no more than 'reason' or 'motive' what better consideration could there be?

The creation of a tenure was accepted as a good consideration as early as 1522 to rebut the presumption of a resulting use when lands were granted gratuitously in tail, or for life.[4] Furthermore, even if there was an express declaration to the contrary a donee in tail, or for life, held to his own use, so that here the consideration would override the will of the donor. One explanation for this may be the fact that gifts in tail, or for life, were normally incidental to family settlements, in which the intention was to make a gift of the beneficial interest to the donee.[5] Another possible explanation is the fact that very commonly

[1] Spilman's MS. Reports, f. 179a. The case is undated. If the Brooke mentioned is Richard Brooke the judge, the case must be earlier than 1529, for he died in that year. Fitzherbert became a judge in 1522 and died in 1538. The case must be earlier than the Statute of Uses in 1535.

[2] Plowden 298. See also *Wingfield* v. *Littleton* (1557) Dyer 162a.

[3] Y.B. 20 Hen. VII, M. f. 10, pl. 20. The advancement of a member of the family could be treated as an advantage, and therefore a *quid pro quo*—see *Abbot of Bury* v. *Bockenham* (1536) Dyer 7b at 8b.

[4] Y.B. 14 Hen. VIII, M. f. 4, pl. 5, Brooke, *Feoffments al Uses*, pl. 40 (1532), Y.B. 27 Hen. VIII, P. f. 7, pl. 22, Perkins, *Profitable Book*, pl. 53, *Abbot of Bury* v. *Bokenham* (1536) Dyer 7b at 10a.

[5] For the doctrine that a devise implies consideration, so that a devisee will hold to his own use, see Y.B. 14 Hen. VIII, M. f. 4, pl. 5 (Brooke, *Feoffments al Uses*, pl. 10).

the donee and the original settlor would be the same person, as where Hugo, being seised in fee simple, enfeoffed Robert in fee on the understanding that Robert would re-enfeoff him in tail; the re-enfeoffment here would be gratuitous, and it would be unfair to allow Robert to declare uses on it. To say that the creation of a tenure on a gift in tail, or for life, is a reason why the donee should be seised to his own use may be to give a theoretical justification rather than a real explanation, though it could have been seriously thought that the duty of a lord to look after his tenant, and warrant his title, was incompatible with the limitation of uses on the gift. Grantees of terms of years also held to their own use, at least as a general rule; usually a tenant for years would pay rent, and in such a case it was obviously fair that the tenant should hold to his own use, but there was some difficulty here over the correct explanation of the rule. If the tenure was the consideration (and there was authority for saying that a lease for years produced a tenure), then even a gratuitous lessee for years would hold to his own use. If the consideration was the rent, then uses could be declared on a gratuitous lease for years. Both views had some support in Henry VIII's time, and the latter view eventually prevailed after the Statute of Uses, thus allowing the creation of trusts of leasehold which were not executed by the Statute of Uses.[1]

One would expect that motives of piety or charity would have counted as good consideration to rebut the presumption of a resulting use when lands were granted gratuitously to ecclesiastical or educational bodies for godly and charitable purposes, and this doctrine is suggested by Brooke J. in 1522,[2] when he says,

'And so if I give land in tail, here is a consideration, whereby unless the use is expressed he [i.e. the grantor] will not have a use: and so it is if one gives land to an Abbot or Prior. Yet if the use is expressed it is good.'

A case in 1532, however, adopted a different line of reasoning, dealing with the question in terms of capacity. It was said that a charitable foundation only possessed capacity to take pro-

---

[1] Brooke, *Feoffments al Uses*, pl. 40 (1532).
[2] Y.B. 14 Hen. VIII, M. f. 4, pl. 5.

perty to the use of the purpose for which it enjoyed corporate status; in consequence such corporations could only take land to their own use, and not to the use of another, whatever the grantor said. Thus if land was conveyed to a monastic foundation out of motives of piety there was no need to invoke the doctrine of consideration to explain the absence of a resulting use, and thus no need to recognize charity as a good consideration.[1] It is sometimes said that a corporation, like the King, could not be seised to the use of another, but this is not quite accurate; the rule was only that a corporation could not *take* to the use of another. Thus if a monastic foundation under its common seal bargained and sold lands in fee, the bargain and sale would pass a use.[2]

It is an interesting speculation, though nothing more, whether if a charitable motive had been accepted as good consideration to pass a use, the same rule would have passed into the law of assumpsit.

The analysis of consideration by time

In addition to deciding what types of consideration were good, the courts also had to decide the time at which the consideration was effective. In the case of the bargain and sale of land the rules were derived from the law of sale of goods; the contract was perfect and effective to pass a use if the money was paid at once, or was payable at a fixed date in the future.[3] In the case of marriage covenants the agreement would usually be entered into in consideration of a marriage to be celebrated in the future, and though at first it may have been the rule that the consideration was only effective when the marriage had been executed,[4] by the end of Henry VIII's reign it seems to have been the law that a future marriage counted as good

[1] Brooke, *Feoffments al Uses*, pl. 40 (1532).

[2] So held by Brooke J. and Brudenell C.J. in 1523, Spilman's MS. Reports at f. 175a.

[3] See above, p. 347, n. 6.

[4] *Assaby* v. *Lady Anne Manners* (1516) Dyer 235a, is not clear on the question. In accordance with ordinary principle, a declaration of will subject to condition precedent would be ineffective if the condition remained unperformed. Thus Spilman has this note: 'If I make my will that if a certain person does a certain thing, as pay certain money or something else, on condition that then my feoffees shall be seised to his use, or if I bargain with a man on condition that he should do something, now in both cases if any part of the condition remains unperformed then the use is not changed, which note,' B.M. Hargrave 388, f. 174a.

consideration.[1] The problem of past consideration was first discussed in a reported case in 1542:

> 'And according to Hales a man cannot change a use by a covenant which is executed before, as in the case of a covenant to be seised to the use of W.S. because W.S. is his cousin, or because W.S. has previously given him £20 unless the £20 was given in order to have the same land. But the contrary is the case of a present or future consideration for the same purpose, as for £100 paid for the land at the time of the agreement, or to be paid at a future day, or to marry his son, or something of that sort. Many held against him in the first year of Mary, and [held] that this could be good for a consideration past.[2]

The difficulty of past consideration was one of the obstacles to holding natural love and affection good consideration, and when the courts did so hold (the decision in the first year of Mary's reign may have dealt with this or perhaps with a past marriage) the analysis of considerations by time was refined by distinguishing between a past consideration—something which was over and done with in the past—and a continuous consideration which was some continuous state of affairs which at any time furnished a good reason for a covenant to pass a use. Thus in *Calthorpe's Case* (1573) in Dyer's very abbreviated notes of his own judgment we find this:

> 'Also the mode of giving *ad faciendum tale quid* or *ut faceret tale* or *ad intentionem*, or *ea intentione ut* etc. *ad effectum*: condition, consideration, executory, future and continual, and considerations executed present, done and determined on one part.'[3]

The division of considerations into past or executed, present, continual, future, or executory passed into the common learning of assumpsit, where the earliest appearance of the analysis by time is *Hunt* v. *Bate* (1568),[4] where Dyer's report includes a report of an anonymous case in the same year:

[1] Brooke, *Feoffments al Uses*, pl. 54 (1542).
[2] Brooke, *Feoffments al Uses*, pl. 54. The problem is discussed in *Doctor and Student*, Dial. II, c. 24.
[3] Dyer 334b, and cf. *Anon.* (1569) Dyer 286b.
[4] Dyer 272a.

'But in another like action on the case brought upon a promise made to the plaintiff by the defendant in consideration that the plaintiff, at the special instance of the said defendant, had taken to wife the cousin of the defendant, that was good cause, although the marriage was executed and past before the undertaking and promise, because the marriage ensued the request of the defendant. And land may also be given in frankmarriage with the cousin of the donor as well after the marriage as before, because the marriage may be intended the cause.'

Whether before 1568 a past marriage was sufficient consideration to support a covenant to stand seised to uses is uncertain, though what little evidence there is tends to the view that it was.[1]

The rejection of the doctrine that a deed imports consideration

It had never been necessary to aver consideration in actions of covenant brought on covenants under seal, or actions of debt on an obligation. In the period under discussion—that is, the first half of the sixteenth century—examination of the consideration for covenants (whether under seal or not) was only embarked upon when such a covenant was relied on as passing a use, not when an action for damages was brought on a covenant. It is in this context that the theory was advanced, *and rejected*, that 'a seal imports consideration'. It has commonly been supposed that this tag has something to do with the application of the doctrine of consideration in assumpsit, albeit fictionally, to actions for damages for the breach of sealed covenants; that the statement 'a seal imports consideration' is a way of saying that covenants under seal are deemed to be given for consideration, and that is why they are actionable without proof of consideration. This idea has achieved currency

---

[1] See the decision in 1553 noted in Brooke, *Feoffments al Uses*, pl. 54, which may refer to a past marriage. cf. also *Sharrington* v. *Strotton* (1566) Plowden 298 as explained by Moore *arguendo* in *Lord Buckhurst's Case* (1595) Moo. K.B. 488 at 505. For a hint of the doctrine that the court will not inquire into adequacy of consideration see *Wilkes* v. *Leuson* (1558) Dyer 169a. For a discussion of whether, where there is an express consideration in a deed, the court may treat as consideration some circumstance not expressed, as consideration by the party, see *Villers* v. *Beaumont* (1556) Dyer 146a, and cf. *Thomas* v. *Thomas* (1842) 2 Q.B. 851.

because of a quite fundamental misunderstanding of certain passages in *Sharrington* v. *Strotton* (1566)[1]

Sharrington v. *Strotton* was a case in which the court was concerned to determine whether a covenant by indenture executed by one Andrew Baynton, whereby he covenanted to stand seised to certain uses, was effective to pass these uses in accordance with the terms of the indenture. This question was treated as depending primarily upon whether or not there was good consideration for the uses to pass. Bromley and Plowden, arguing in favour of the contention that the uses had passed, based their argument mainly[2] upon the orthodox contention that the considerations which had motivated the execution of the indenture were good considerations to pass the uses. These considerations were elaborately analysed in their argument; for present purposes it is enough to note that they included marriage, natural love and affection for kinsmen, and family pride. But as an alternative and more radical argument Bromley and Plowden contended that Baynton's deliberate expression of his wishes or will, his *nuda voluntas*, the deliberation being evidenced by the execution of a document under seal, was in itself a sufficient consideration or reason why the uses should pass.[3] This contention was expressed in this passage:

> 'So that where it is by deed, the cause or consideration is not enquirable, nor is it to be weighed, but the party ought only to answer to the deed, and if he confesses it he is bound, for every deed imports in itself a consideration, viz. the will of him that made it, and therefore where the agreement is by deed, it shall never be called *nudum pactum*.'

Put into modern terms the celebrated remark that 'every deed imports in itself a consideration, viz., the will of him that made it' means in the context something like this:

---

[1] Plowden 298.

[2] See at p. 303 the division of Plowden's argument into two points: 'First, whether the grant and agreement upon these considerations (admitting it had been without deed or writing) had been sufficient to raise the uses according to the agreement or not. Secondly, admitting the considerations to be insufficient if they had been without deed, or admitting that there were no considerations at all, if nevertheless the uses shall be raised here as the agreement thereunto is by deed.'

[3] The argument on this point begins on p. 308. The covenant, as Plowden pointed out, was one which purported to grant an immediate interest (see p. 303). Since the covenantor did not agree to do anything in the future it was not actionable contractually by writ of covenant.

'The execution of a deed is by itself a reason for passing the uses, for the fact that it has been executed is conclusive evidence of the wishes of the person whose deed it is, and the deliberate expression of the will of the person executing the deed is a sufficient reason for holding that the uses have passed.'[1]

This argument could be supported and made plausible, as it was by drawing analogies from many branches of the law where a deed was a dispositive document.[2] It could also be supported by arguing that the doctrine in earlier cases which required 'consideration' to pass a use was designed to ensure that only deliberately expressed intentions should be legally effective; the argument here rests in part upon a typically Elizabethan play on the word 'consideration', which could mean 'deliberation', as for example in the phrase 'on great consideration'.[3] Nor were Bromley and Plowden the first lawyers to argue along these lines. Thus in a case in 1522[4] one A was seised to the use of B, and A granted a rent by deed gratuitously to X for life, and the question was whether X held the rent to his own use, or to the use of B. Amongst other arguments for saying that X was seised to his own use was the argument that every grant implied consideration—that is to say that where there is a grant by deed this alone is a sufficient reason for saying that the uses pass. Viewed in another way, this type of argument purports to apply the doctrine of consideration to grants by deed, but in substance treats such grants as exceptions to the

[1] cf. at p. 308, '. . . and if his land be subject to his will, then is his will a sufficient consideration for which the land will go as his will is.'

[2] Most strikingly in the case of a grant of a chattel by deed, referred to at p. 308. cf. at p. 309, 'So that where it is by deed, the cause or consideration is not enquirable nor is it to be weighed, but the party ought only to answer to the deed, and if he confesses it he is bound.'

[3] 'And because words are oftentimes spoken by men unadvisedly and without deliberation, the law has provided that a contract by words shall not bind without consideration.'

[4] Y.B. 14 Hen. VIII, M. f. 4, pl. 5 at f. 9, 'Car premierement le fait del grant est al contrary, car chescun grant implie consideration.' The same idea may perhaps lie behind the rule that upon a conveyance by fine the alienee held to his own use, even if no other consideration was evident. And cf. *Anon.* (1535) Benloe 16, pl. 20, holding that when land is conveyed by feoffment expressed to be to the use of the feoffee, the feoffee obtains the use 'because the use was limited to him by the deed, which was a good consideration', although no other consideration existed for the feoffment or was expressed in the deed.

rule that consideration is needed to pass a use; 'implying', 'importing', 'deeming', and 'conclusively presuming' are ways in which lawyers dress up exceptions to look as though they are not exceptions.

If the argument had been accepted, it would have become the law that any interest in land could be transferred by deed, the deed passing the use and the Statute of Uses executing it, and there would have been no need to enrol the deed under the provisions of the Statute of Enrolments[1]—an anticipation by some centuries of the rule introduced in English law by the Real Property Act of 1845[2] The court rejected the invitation to so radical a step, and held that the deed was effective to pass the uses because it was supported by good consideration in the form of natural love and affection, not because the mere execution of a deed was by itself a sufficient consideration.[3] Thus *Sharrington* v. *Strotton* rejected the doctrine that a deed imports consideration. In 1566, when *Sharrington* v. *Strotton* was decided, the doctrine of consideration in assumpsit must have been in its infancy; indeed, *Sharrington* v. *Strotton* is the earliest reported case in which it is suggested in argument that the doctrine of consideration as developed in the law of uses, applied to *assumpsit*. Neither the court nor the counsel who argued the case were concerned with the actionability of assumpsits and covenants under seal except by way of analogy; it was with the law of uses that they were concerned, and the doctrine that a sealed instrument 'imports consideration' was advanced and rejected as a doctrine about uses.

The relationship between the equitable doctrine of consideration and the action of assumpsit

Once it is realized that since Richard III's reign the common lawyers had been continually concerned with the law of uses, and that since Henry VII's reign they had in this field formu-

[1] 27 Hen. VIII, c. 10, c. 16.

[2] 8 and 9 Vict., c. 106. However, conveyances of corporeal hereditaments by deed (apart from the bargain and sale enrolled) in effect became possible with the evolution of the bargain and sale with lease and release operating under the Statute of Uses. See Simpson, *Land Law*, pp. 177–9.

[3] The considerations actually held effective were 'the affection of the said Andrew for the provision of the heirs male which he should beget, and his desire that the land should continue in the blood and name of Baynton, and the brotherly love which he bare to his brothers.'

lated and consistently applied the 'equitable' doctrine of consideration, and further that this doctrine had been very fully worked out before there was any discussion of consideration in actions of assumpsit, it seems difficult to doubt that the doctrine of consideration in assumpsit was originally intimately associated with the doctrine of consideration in the law of uses. In many questions of detail the lawyers in dealing with assumpsit simply applied the same rules as they were used to applying in questions concerning uses—for example, marriage was held to be a good consideration in both instances, and so was money paid, or other recompense, as also was a future consideration. In some instances the two doctrines, though alike in some respects, tended to diverge; typically this happened over natural love and affection as consideration, which was eventually not so fully recognized in assumpsit as in the law of uses. Again, though the details may have come to differ, the same ideas feature in both doctrines; thus we have seen how the idea that a prior obligation might be a good consideration, and the idea that considerations could be analysed into types by time, appear in both. Furthermore, in some of the early discussions of consideration as relevant to assumpsit in cases, most strikingly in *Sharrington* v. *Strotton* (1566) and *Hunt* v. *Bate* (1568)[1] the reasoning of contemporary lawyers makes it clear that they at least thought that there was a close relationship between the rules governing uses and the rules governing agreements generally, as well they might when it is remembered that the cases on uses were concerned with the effect in law of agreements; it would hardly have made sense to say, for example, that a covenant in consideration of marriage was good to pass a use, but not actionable in assumpsit. But a comparison in detail is not perhaps so important as a comparison between the fundamental principle which is expressed in the two doctrines. The basis of the doctrine of consideration in assumpsit is the idea that the factor which motivated the promise should be treated as determining the legal effect of the promise. The basis of the doctrine in the law of uses is the idea that the factor which motivated a transaction—be it a contract, a conveyance, or a covenant—should be treated as determining the legal effect of the transaction. Both doctrines serve to deprive a naked

[1] Plowden 298, Dyer 272a.

expression of will of legal significance; only an expression of will supported by good consideration will pass a use, or make a promise binding. Thus, just as the consideration for the expression of will in the law of uses becomes the consideration to pass the use, so the consideration for the promise becomes the consideration which will charge the defendant in assumpsit. It is this broad similarity in legal analysis which is the best argument in favour of the view that there is historical continuity between the two doctrines, and the similarities in detail serve only to strengthen an argument which would still be persuasive even if these similarities in detail were less obvious than they are.

VI

CONSIDERATION AND THE CANON LAW[1]

THE close connection between the doctrine of consideration in assumpsit and the doctrine of consideration as applied to the law of uses is clear enough, and the relative chronology of the two doctrines, or the two aspects of the same doctrine, justifies the conclusion that the equitable doctrine was in a sense the direct source of the contractual doctrine. An alternative way of stating the connection would be to say that the equitable doctrine was applied to assumpsit and in the process modified. What is much less easy to determine is the remoter ancestry of the doctrine of consideration, and in particular its connection with ideas developed in the medieval canon law, which was, in its turn, intimately connected with the civil law of Rome, as interpreted by medieval lawyers. That there was some connection is hardly open to doubt, but it is inherently impossible to give any very precise account of the connection. There are a variety of reasons for this. One is the absence of direct evidence. For example, in a case in 1476[2] Genney in argument states the proposition,

'for by our law words without reason [*parols sans reason*] bind no one',

and it seems to me to be a reasonable assumption that the reference to 'our law' indicates a context in which either the canon or civil law had been mentioned and contrasted with common law, though this does not appear in the report, and further that his remark reflects some knowledge of doctrines of *causa* in other systems. But it is quite impossible to tell the course of Genney's knowledge, or its extent, and the same is true when reference is made to such alien notions as *nuda pacta* and *pacta*

---

[1] See in particular Vinogradoff, 'Reason and Conscience in Sixteenth Century Jurisprudence', 24 L.Q.R. 273, and J. L. Barton, 'The Early History of Consideration', 85 L.Q.R. 372.

[2] 16 Edw. IV, M. f. 8, pl. 5, the proposition being related to the doctrine of *quid pro quo* and accord with satisfaction.

vestita.[1] A second difficulty is that there was anyway no settled doctrine of *causa* in either the civil or canon law, but a variety of views (what they were being controversial). And furthermore, even if the common law doctrine of consideration reflects, or echoes, ideas to be found in canonical or civilian authors, it does not certainly follow either that the ideas are in any straight-forward way derived from these authors, or if they are that the common lawyers were not capable of developing them in their own individual way. Sixteenth-century Serjeants-at-Law were quite as good at working out and refining legal doctrines as were lawyers of other systems; the very prevalent belief that the home product was really rather second-rate is based merely upon ignorance.

St. Germain's 'Doctor and Student'

The starting-point for any investigation into the relationship between the common and canon law in this field must be Christopher St. Germain's *Doctor and Student*. St. Germain, or German,[2] was a lawyer of the Inner Temple; he may have spent some time at Exeter College, Oxford, though this has not been confirmed by recent research. Not a great deal is known about his life, though he is said to have had an extensive practice and to have possessed a library greater than that of any other lawyer. He is remembered partly as a theological controversialist but mainly for his *Doctor and Student*. This comprises two dialogues between a Doctor of Divinity and a Student of the Common Law, and is a discursive critical work of a speculative character in which, as Winfield put it, 'legal rules are put in the witness box and cross-examined to credit'. The dialogues contain a considerable body of material derived from the canon law. The first dialogue appeared in an edition by John Rastell in 1528 in Latin under the title, *Dialogus de Fundamentis Legum Anglie et de Conscientia.*[3] It was translated into English and republished by Robert Wyer in 1531; the evidence for a first edition of 1523 is unsatisfactory.[4] The second dialogue, which contains the dis-

---

[1] e.g. in 11 Hen. VI, P. f. 43, pl. 30.
[2] See the article in the *D.N.B.* by Pollock, and Winfield, *Chief Sources*, 321 et seq. See now the introduction by J. L. Barton to S.S. Vol. 91, the new edition of the Dialogues by Barton and the late T.F.T. Plucknett.
[3] S.T.C. 21559.
[4] See Dibdin, *Typographical Antiquities*, III. 86–7. The description seems to fit the

cussion of contract law, appeared first in English in 1530[1] in an edition by Peter Treveris. *Doctor and Student*, as it came to be called, was a very popular book and was frequently republished; indeed a second edition of the second dialogue with additions appeared within a year of the first. This popularity is hardly surprising, since no other critical legal work *about* the law then existed, nor indeed was anything remotely comparable to appear until the seventeenth century. There can be no doubt that it was a very influential work, and, so far as the action of assumpsit is concerned, its publication precedes[2] by some years the appearance of a doctrine of consideration. However, it is plain that the doctrine of consideration as applied to uses, which is discussed in *Doctor and Student* at some length, was well established long before 1530, so that St. Germain's book cannot have been the decisive influence here. We are indeed confronted with a triangular problem as to the relationship between *Doctor and Student* and the two aspects of the doctrine of consideration, a problem which possesses a chicken-and-the-egg quality, and it is certainly not possible to say with any confidence that the influence of the canon law on the law of assumpsit (assuming for the moment that there was an influence) *simply* derived from *Doctor and Student*. So tidy a solution does not fit the chronology.

St. Germain's sources

The immediate sources of St. Germain's statements of the view of the Doctors on the moral status of promises, which are put into the mouth of the Doctor of Divinity, can be identified as the *Summa Angelica* and the *Summa Rosella* (or *Baptistiniana*).[3] The practice of sacramental confession in the Western Church gave rise, after the Lateran Council of 1215, to a form of literature which supplanted the earlier *Penitentials*; it took the form of comprehensive manuals for confessors, the *Summae Confessorum*, and many such works were produced during the later

[1] S.T.C. 21561.
[2] See above, p. 318.
[3] See Vinogradoff in 24 L.Q.R. at 378. The amount of borrowing from John Gerson's *Regulae Morales* is very small.

edition of 1528, and it may be that a colophon with the date MVCXXVIII was misread as MVCXXIII. No copy of the edition of 1523 has ever been traced, nor is there satisfactory evidence that Herbert owned one.

medieval period,[1] and have continued to be written ever since. They were the work of casuists, and provided a sort of *vademecum* for priests, providing analysis, answers, and information on a wide variety of 'cases' with which a priest might be concerned in his professional life. In them one could look up such matters as usury, whether nocturnal pollutions constituted a sin, when absolution must be conditional, whether gifts might be revoked for ingratitude, or what rules governed matrimony; the range of subjects covered was very considerable. Such works were primarily concerned with moral theology, which was what interested confessors; hence their main concern was sin and conscience. Their interest in law, whether civil or canon (or indeed anything else), is peripheral, though because of the extreme legalism of the Western Church, and the influence of Roman Law conceptions and analyses, questions which we would conceive in terms of moral philosophy are discussed in what seems to be an excessively legalistic manner. Furthermore what they provide by way of solutions to cases consists of a somewhat bizarre hodge-podge of Roman Law, canon law, moral theology, and common sense, much of it presented as derived from or supported by earlier writers of authority and Holy Writ. In a sense the *Summae* were practical works, designed to be *used*; they were, however, very much the product of speculation in the medieval equivalent of the armchair.

The *Summa Rosella* was probably the first of these two works to be compiled and certainly the earliest to be printed. It was completed in 1483 and printed in 1484. The author, about whom very little seems to be known, was a Franciscan, Brother Baptista de Salis, also known by his family name Baptista Trovamala or Troamala.[2] He came from what is now La Salle, near Aosta, and completed the work in the convent at Levante which is on the Italian Riviera. It is not known when he was born or when he died, though he was alive in 1494.[3] The first

---

[1] For example, the *Summa Astesana* (ed. princ. 1468), the *Summa Pacifica* (ed. pr. 1479), the *Summa Tabiena* (ed. pr. 1517), the *Summa Sylvestrina* (ed. pr. 1516), the *Summa Margarita* (ed. 1526).

[2] He was also called Joannes Baptista, Baptista Salvis, etc. He is not to be confused with the later saint of the same name.

[3] Information is derived either from the early editions or from L. Waddingus, *Scriptores Ordinis Minorum* (1650), 47, R. Stintzing, *Geschichte der populären Litteratur des römisch-kanonishien Rechts* (1687), 533 et seq., and *The New Catholic Dictionary*.

edition of his work was called *Summa Casuum Utilissima*: so too was that of 1488. though the name *Baptistiniana* is then given as an alternative. In 1489 the name Rosella is first associated with it, and by 1516 it has become *Summa Rosella de Casibus Conscientiae*. The name became attached to the work because it was a collection of the most elegant conclusions (that is determinations) which could be compared to a garland of sweet-smelling roses which Baptista had gathered together. The *Summa* is indeed an encyclopedia, with the material arranged under alphabetical headings, in the manner of an encyclopedia, and not by books. It was a very successful work, and was reprinted twice in 1488, and again in 1489, 1495, 1499, and 1516.[1]

The *Summa Angelica* was a somewhat larger work of exactly the same character compiled by another Franciscan, the Blessed Angelus Carletus, or Angelus de Clavassio.[2] He too was born in Piedmont in what is now Chivasso, near Turin, in 1411, and he died on 11 April 1495.[3] He was a doctor of both laws (i.e. canon and civil) of the University of Bologna, and achieved considerable distinction, being several times Cismontane Vicar-General of his order (1472–5, 1478–81, 1484–7, 1490–3). He must, of course, have known Brother Baptista well, but there is no direct evidence so far as I know that this was so. The *Summa Angelica* was first printed in 1486, and was even more successful than the *Summa Rosella*, probably partly because it was fuller, and partly because its compiler was a more important man. The British Museum lists editions in 1488, 1489 (2), 1490, 1491, 1492 (2), 1495 (2), 1497, 1498, 1499, 1500, 1504, 1509, 1512, 1513, 1523, 1534, and 1698.[4] It was therefore something of a best seller in a curious field of literature which was clearly in great demand at the very close of the Middle Ages. The date of compilation (the work may, of course, have taken many years) cannot be established, but writing was still in progress in 1479, since the text includes a papal bull of that year (*Et si dominici gregis* . . .). Angelus explains that his *Summa* is mainly intended

---

[1] Editions in the British Museum, catalogued under Trovamala. I have used the edition of 1499 in the Bodleian (Auct. 1.Q.VI.63). There is no English edition.

[2] Numerous variants will be found, such as de Chivassio.

[3] Sources of information as above, but include A. Vacant et E. Mangerot, *Dictionnaire de theologie catholique* (1903), and J. Moorman, *A History of the Franciscan Order*, 539.

[4] I have used an edition of 1500 printed in Lyons; there is no English Edition.

to make life simpler for poor and simple confessors who have no skill in laws, and are confused by too many cases of conscience in the extensive literature. He also thinks his *Summa de casibus conscientie* will be useful to scholars of both laws (civil and canon), and to all who wish to live a godly, right, and civil life.

The *Summa Angelica* is in general based upon a work known as the *Summa Pisana* or *Pisanella*, whose compiler was one Bartholomeus de Santocordio (or de Pisa), a Dominican; this was yet another best seller, being many times reprinted after a first edition in 1473.[1] The *Summa Pisana*, though, of course, not printed before the fifteenth century, was a much earlier work, the author dying in 1347.[2] It is not, however, the source of the discussion of promises and contracts in the *Summa Angelica*, which is in fact virtually identical (so far as the matters here under discussion are concerned) with the earlier *Summa Rosella*, from which it is probably copied (with some slight modifications in the arrangement)[3] in the cheerful plagiaristic spirit of the times. Virtually exact copies of the *Summa Rosella* and *Angelica* are to be found in the *Summa Tabiena* (also called the *Summa Summarum*) which was compiled by a Dominican, Brother John de Thabia, and completed in first draft in 1512 (printed 1517),[4] and in the *Summa Sylvestrina* (ed. princ. 1516) by Sylvestre de Priero, another Dominican.[5] In all probability Angelus copied from Baptista, who in his turn relied on earlier sources. One such source can be identified—the *Summa Astesana*. This was a massive compilation in eight books by an obscure fourteenth-century Franciscan, John Astexanus, who is known to have died about 1330 and to have come from the same area as Baptista and Angelus, his home town being Asti in Piedmont.[6] It was one of the earliest books to be printed, the first edition being undated but attributed to 1468; there were later editions in 1478 and

---

[1] The Bodleian has editions of 1473, 1474, 1475 (2), 1481, 1492, one early un dated edition, and one of 1601.

[2] See Vacant et Mangerot, op. cit.

[3] In the *Summa Rosella* the principal title is *Promissio*, whereas in the *Angelica* the principal title is *Pactum*. St. Germain's *Advow* relates to *Votum*.

[4] The compiler, also known as Joannes Cagnazzo, died in 1521. The British Museum has editions of 1517, 1520, and 1580. I have used that of 1517, which is in the Bodleian.

[5] The compiler, also known as Sylvester Mazolinus, died in 1523. I have used the edition of 1518 in the Bodleian; the British Museum has the first edition.

[6] Near Turin.

1479.[1] Considerable portions of the *Summa Rosella* on pacts and promises are copied from Astexanus, and it is clear that Baptista used it as a major source, whilst adopting a different and better scheme of arrangement. The title of the work is *Opus de casibus forum anime. Seu conscientie concernentibus*—'A work about cases concerning the forum of the soul or conscience.'[2]

The theory of contract in the 'Summae'

The theory of contract set out in the *Summa Rosella* and the *Summa Angelica* is a complicated one. The basic question with which both are concerned is whether a man is obliged by a nude pact or a mere promise:

'Utrum ex nudo pacto sive ex sola promissione homo obligetur',[3]

and the discussion of this question in the *Summae* must be read in the context of the canonical distinction between what was appropriate *in foro externo* and what was appropriate *in foro interno* (sometimes called *in foro animo* or *conscientie*, as in the *Summa Astesana*). In deciding cases in the internal forum, as was appropriate in giving individual moral advice, or in connection with the confessional, the Church was concerned with the individual's spiritual health, and the avoidance of sin; different principles applied when the Church was concerned with the external forum, in particular in the determination of causes in the ecclesiastical courts, for there the concern was with the welfare of the Church and its members generally. In *foro interno* the rightly directed conscience was the guide to the avoidance of sin, and the *Summae* were primarily concerned with the *forum internum*; hence the *Summae* were not so much concerned with the formulation of rules to be applied in courts, but with the rules which rightly ought to direct the conscience of a good Christian. The 'obligation' under discussion is therefore in modern terms a personal moral obligation.

In order to answer the question posed, the *Summae* assume it is first essential to be clear what is meant by a 'nude pact' or a

---

[1] The Bodleian has the first two editions.

[2] A 'case of conscience' strictly means a situation which uninstructed conscience finds puzzling, since alternative courses of action seem equally right, Cf. the borderline case of the common lawyer.

[3] The question is central also in the *Summa Astesana*, Book III, Tit. 6, *De Pactis*.

'mere promise'. So it is explained that there is a distinction between a *pactum*, a *pollicitatio*, a *conventio*, a *stipulatio*, and a *promissio*. A *pactum* is an agreement of two or more people to do or give something expressed in words in such a way that the words come from the promisor; this distinguishes a pact from a stipulation, when the words come from the promisee or person who is to receive the thing. A *pollicitatio* is a promise which has not been either requested or alternatively accepted by the promisee (cf. the modern 'offer'), and can thus be differentiated from a *promissio*; and *conventio* is just a rather general term for agreements.

Granted this initial analysis, it is clear that there is no real difference between a pact and a promise (in the sense defined), and that the distinction between a *stipulatio* and a pact or promise, though a real one, is totally unworkable in terms of real life except in a world in which some sort of formal question and answer are actually used to make agreements, as was once the case in Rome,[1] and is still the case in (for example) the marriage service. Nothing of the sort happened in medieval Europe, except perhaps in ceremonies of betrothal where set forms were in use in England at least, and one must therefore bear in mind the fact that the analysis of agreements given in the *Summae* is of an extremely academic character, and needs to be taken with a grain of salt. In terms of the basic question under discussion there is no real point in differentiating between pacts, promises, and stipulations; one could as well simply ask 'when are promises binding in conscience?' They were, however, conventional categories, and as such were the inevitable stock-in-trade of canonists such as Baptista and Angelus; the source is Astexanus. The lumping together of the discussion of bare pacts and mere promises represents a cautious awareness that in a sense there is no difference; the exclusion of the *stipulatio* is explicable easily enough in terms of the distinction between *nuda pacta* and *vestimenta pacta*, for a *stipulatio* was 'clothed', and was not therefore in doubt as a source of obligation.

A *nudum pactum* was one which was not clothed (*vestita*), and the *Summae* explain that there were six ways in which a pact could be clothed: *re, verbis, litteris, consensu, coherentie contractus,*

---

[1] Those unfamiliar with civilian terminology will find a clear account in Barry Nicholas, *Introduction to Roman Law*.

and *interventio rei*.[1] The first four categories correspond to the *real, verbal, literal, and consensual* contracts of Roman Law, the second category comprising the stipulation (which for the reason given was an empty category in terms of real life). The literal contract could be assimilated to the contract under seal, and the real and consensual contracts fitted easily enough into the live world, since these categories included such contracts as loan, sale, and hire. The fifth category corresponded to the *pacta adiecta* of Roman Law, and the *Summa Angelica* gives this example:

'for example if I have sold you a house with the pact that I should remain in that house for a year.'

Here the pact is accessory to a consensual contract, the contract of sale. The last category reflects the principle of induced reliance or change of circumstances:

'I have promised you to give you something that you should do or give something. Then at once when I have given you what I have promised the pact is clothed from my part.'

Only pacts which are not clothed in one or other of these ways counted as *nuda pacta*.

Plainly not much is left, when all vested pacts are admitted to be obligatory, and one cannot but feel that the question whether nude pacts were binding was not an enormously important one. Angelus somewhat desperately gives this example:

'as for example I have promised to give you a hundred [*sic*] without any precedent question [*stipulatio*] or cyrograph [*litteris*] or whatever.'

If we confine attention to *nude pacts* the field of inquiry is rather thinly populated. One might, by the light of nature, imagine that *mere promises* were less rare animals. But this is not the case, for no independent definition of a 'mere promise' is given. Hence although the basic question under discussion is about *two concepts*—nude pacts *and* mere promises—the discussion proceeds as if dealing with one only.

[1] This all comes from the *Summa Astesana*, III. 6.

The doctrine of 'causa'

So far, the obligatory quality of pacts and promises has been discussed in terms of a distinction between those that are naked and those that are clothed by one or other of the six types of 'vestment'. The waters are now muddied by the introduction of a rather different criterion—the presence or absence of a *causa*. The doctrine of *causa promissionis* has a long and complex history, and so far as concerns us here it involves the idea that an informal undertaking (to use a neutral term) does not oblige if it lacks a good cause. The *Summae* do not apply this doctrine of cause simply to promises (e.g. saying that naked pacts on the one hand do not bind because they are naked and causeless promises on the other do not bind because they lack a cause). Instead they proceed to conflate the *nuda/vestimenta* contrast with the *causa/sine causa* contrast, by saying that nude pacts are not clothed *because they lack a cause*. Now from this one would expect that a 'cause' would be the same as a 'vestment', but the *Summae*, in a completely inconsistent and confusing way, proceed thereafter to develop a theory of *causae promissionis* which is in reality quite distinct from the theory of the vestments of pacts. This conflation of two doctrines comes directly from the *Summa Astesana*:

'Nuda sunt illa qua non continent causam',

and the ineffectiveness of a *pactum sine causa* is explained by reference to the civil law doctrine that a delivery was ineffective to pass title if it lacked a cause,

'For a *traditio sine causa* has no efficacy and causeless pacts have no efficacy for bringing an action or imposing an obligation, granted that they may be effective as giving rise to a defence.'

According to this theory, which is then set out,[1] one starts from the proposition that a naked pact or mere promise does oblige in canon law or in conscience or *sub pena* mortal sin, so long as it has a cause. The only example given of a causeless

---

[1] The development and elaboration of the doctrine of *causa* is not in the *Summa Astesana*, nor is the doctrine that a causeless promise must have been given in error. I have not made any exhaustive attempt to trace the history of *causa* in the canon law; it may be that other direct borrowings could be traced.

promise is a promise on account of a past sale or loan. 'I promise you something because you *had* sold me such a thing, or lent me such a thing, and so on.' The explanation as to why such a causeless promise does not oblige even in conscience, the *ratio* of the rule, is that it is presumed to have been made in error. However, a promise to give money, or a promise to a holy place, is not without a cause, since in the first place a *causa donandi* is presumed from the generosity of the promisor (*liberalitas pro-missionis*) and in the second instance the promisor is presumed to have promised on account of a pious cause, so that error is not to be presumed. So in the event it turns out that the require-ment of cause merely excludes promises on account of something past—in modern terminology, promises for past consideration.

The compilers of the *Summae* had indeed reached the position of saying, as the natural lawyers later maintained, that in prin-ciple all pacts and promises were binding, and the doctrine of cause relates to an *exception* to this general principle, the excep-tion being related in its turn to a doctrine of error. This basic line of thought, reproduced in the *Summae Angelica* and *Rosella*, is derived from earlier canonists, in particular Astexanus, who says,

> 'In short, note that every pact is to be kept if it be such that it can be kept without harm to the soul or the safety of the body . . . so long as it is lawful, honest, and possible.'

Such other rules as were accepted were conceived to be merely *limitations* to this general principle. In the canon law, as con-trasted with the civil law, a man might be morally obliged and (subject to limitations) sued on a nude pact on simple words, because one who went against his simple word sinned mortally, and, so far as the *Summae Confessorum*, are concerned, this intensely moral view is natural enough, for the confessor is concerned with the avoidance of personal sin and not with the ordering of litigation.

The cause of the promise was also relevant in two other ways. The first of these involves change of circumstances. If a condi-tion or cause of the promise fails, or does not eventuate, or a cause arises whereby the promise ought not to be performed, then the promise ceases to be obligatory. The second relates to the requirement of an *animus obligandi*; the *Summae* as a general rule require such an intention, but there is an exception if there exists a cause binding the promisee by previous necessity to do the thing promised. The example given here is of a promise by a son to his father to give him a cloak because he is dying of cold. Here Angelus and Baptista do not require an intention to be bound as a requirement of the promise being binding in conscience.

Other prerequisites of the binding promise

To count as a promise at all the promise must be either requested (when it will also be a stipulation and thus a clothed pact) or accepted, and furthermore if it is acted upon it becomes clothed *interventu rei*, though it is not clear how far this notion was extended. This leaves but a small area for the promise *simpliciter*, the mere promise, and this makes more intelligible the curious doctrine that an *animus obligandi*, except in the prior obligation case which I have just mentioned, was regarded as essential. This notion was related to the persistent idea that a man who breaks his promise is some sort of liar, and to the further idea that if he never intended to be bound, or never intended to perform, he has not been involved in any sort of lying. For example, in the *Summa Pisana* in the title *Promissio* it is noted that a promisor who never intends to perform is not a liar, but failure to perform, Bartholomeus of Pisa says, means that he seems to have acted unfaithfully, because he has changed his mind. This is taken verbatim from Aquinas's *Summa Theologica*, and the analysis turns upon the notion that a promise is a statement of intention, and breach of promise a sort of retrospective act of falsification. If the promisor never intended to perform, failure to perform tells the truth about his intention.[1] The association between the obligation to tell the truth and the obligation to perform promises coupled with the idea that promising involves some sort of reporting of one's intention, persists in various forms to this day.

In addition the promise, to be binding, must be honest, lawful, and possible,[2] ideas not developed in these texts, and it

---

[1] Q.CX Art. 3. Aquinas admitted two defences or excuses for breach of promise— the unlawfulness of the promise, and change of circumstances, the latter being based on the incident when St. Paul broke his promise to return to Corinth, on which see II Corinthians Ch. I and II.

[2] This comes from the *Summa Astesana*.

follows from the doctrine of *causa* that a promise made in error is not binding, though this too is left undeveloped.

The 'Pollicitatio'

The *pollicitatio* (the promise neither requested nor accepted) was an even more miserable creature than the mere promise or bare pact; one would not expect it therefore to be binding at all. But both Baptista and Angelus held a *pollicitatio* binding in two situations. The first was if it was made to a university, a city, the clergy, the Church, or to the poor of some place with a cause, for example, to the honour of God or something similar. This is the charitable promise (though not so described in the *Summae*). The second situation is when the person making the *pollicitatio* takes something on account of it.[1]

St. Germain's Dialogue: the preliminary statement by the Student[2]

St. Germain presents his discussion of promissory obligation in the form of a dialogue between the Doctor of Divinity and the Student of the Common Law. The question which is discussed is lifted from the *Summae*, but placed in a new and alien context —the common law:

'What is a nude contract or a naked promise *after the laws of England?* [my italics] And whether any action will lie there upon?'

But, as we shall see, the discussion is not limited to the purely legal question; the question in conscience is also discussed. The Student opens the bowling by an attempt to define his terms, in imitation of the *Summae* with their list of different contractual conceptions, and his attempt is not a happy one. He first of all defines a *contract*, which he conceives to be a transaction involving transfer of property,

'For when all things were in common, it needed not to have contracts, but after property was brought in, they were right expedient for all people, for that a man might have of his

---

[1] For discussion of the Digest Title *De Pollicitationibus* see Buckland *A Textbook of Roman Law*, 458.
[2] All quotations are from the edition of 1531, with spelling and punctuation modernized. The relevant chapter is the 23rd.

neighbour that he had not of his own, and that could not be lawfully but by his gift, by way of lending, concord, or by some lease, bargain or sale. And such bargains and sales be called contracts, and be made by assent of the parties upon agreement between them of goods or lands or for other recompense.'

He then distinguished a *concord* as,

'an agreement between the parties with divers articles therein, some rising on the one part and some on the other',

and gives an example in the lease of a room with board;[1] he then has to explain that this is also a contract and an action lies on it, and at this point rather gives up, saying that,

'. . . it is not much argued in the laws of England what diversity is between a contract, a concord, a promise, a gift, a loan, or a pledge, a bargain, a covenant or such other, for the intent of the law is to have the effect of the matter argued and not the terms.'

The Student then moves on to define a *nude contract*, and a *nude* or naked *promise*. The former is

'where a man maketh a bargain or a sale of his goods or lands without any recompense appointed for it'

—that is to say a sale without a price fixed. Such a nude contract is, says the Student, void in both law and conscience. A naked promise is defined as one which lacks a cause,

'where a man promiseth another to give him certain money such a day or to build him an house or to do him certain service, and nothing is assigned for the money, for the building, nor for the service; these be called naked promises because there is nothing assigned why they should be made'.

Unless performed, no action lies; the qualification is introduced to cater for the liability of a bailee who loses or impairs goods by negligent keeping. He is not liable on a promise to receive the goods, but if he does accept them then he will be liable for negligence.

---

[1] e.g. 22 Hen. VI, H. f. 43, pl. 28, discussed above, at p. 143.

The Doctor's statement of the position in conscience

The Doctor now asks what common lawyers think about the status of naked promises *in conscience*, and the Student explains that they have said little on the subject, which he will save up until he has heard the view of the doctors. The question is indeed a somewhat bizarre one, since it is hard to see why common lawyers should have any interesting views on the question of sin and conscience. The Doctor then sets out a curiously modified version of the *Summa Rosella* and *Summa Angelica*. He first deals with the *advow*, the promise made to God; this binds in conscience even if made secretly in the heart so long as it is made with a deliberate heart. This is the doctrine governing the *Votum* (not to be confused with oaths or pledges of faith) of the *Summae*, unmodified. We then pass on to the promise, and the departure from the *Summae* begins.

> 'And of other promises made to man upon a certain consideration, if the promise be not against the law, as if A promise to B £20 because he hath made him such a house or hath lent him such a thing or such other like I think him bound to keep his promise, but if his promise be so naked that there is no manner of consideration why it should be made, then I think him not bound to perform it, for it is to suppose that there was some error in the making of the promise.'

This passage equates *causa*, which *is* mentioned in the *Summae*, with 'consideration' which is not, and states the doctrine of the *Summae* that a promise with a cause/consideration, so long as it is lawful, is binding in conscience. St. Germain then makes the Doctor give an example (which is in fact taken from the *Summae*) of a promise lacking a cause (the cause being past) which the *Summae* say is *not* binding, and uses it as an example of one which *is* binding; I take this to be merely a misunderstanding by St. Germain. He follows the *Summae*, however, in relating the doctrine of *causa promissionis* to a presumption of error in the case of promises lacking a cause. There is then a curious departure from the canonists, for he misses out entirely the passages in the *Summae* which allow a presumption of *causa donandi* where there is a promise to make a gift; no English lawyer whose knowledge of canon law derived from reading *Doctor and Student* would realize that 'the doctors' held a promise of a gift binding, any more than they would realize that the doctors held a promise for a past cause not binding.

The pollicitatio and the charitable promise

St. Germain's Doctor then proceeds to misreport the *Summae* on the status of promises made 'to an university, to a city, to the church, to the clergy and to the honour of God or such other cause like as for the maintenance of learning of the commonwealth, of the service of God, or in relief of poverty or such other'. Such promises, says the Doctor, bind in conscience although

> 'there be no consideration of worldly profit that the grantor hath had or intendeth to have for it'.

This departs from the *Summae* in two respects. The first is that they discussed these examples in relation not to the question of whether a *promissio* binds, but whether a *pollicitatio* binds. Yet no hint of this appears in St. Germain, who never mentions the distinction between *promissiones* and *pollicitationes*. Second, the *Summae* were not concerned in the least with worrying about the absence of worldly profit, which is not mentioned as an issue in them. Here again St. Germain, either by mistake or deliberately, distorts his sources.

St. Germain's Doctor then follows the *Summae* with no serious departures over the requirement that there must be an intention to be bound (except in the case or prior obligation, giving the example of the father who is cold), over change of circumstances and the rule that the promise must be honest, lawful, and possible. The only departure is that the Doctor insists that the promisor needs to anticipate no worldly profit to be bound by a promise, but merely a spiritual profit. The *Summae* wholly lack any interest in profits, spiritual or otherwise.

The Student on problems of proof

Having listened to the Doctor's exposition, the Student takes exception to the requirement of an intention to be bound,

> 'For it is secret in his own conscience whether he intended for to be bound or nay, and of the intent inward of the heart man's law cannot judge; and that is one of the causes why

the law of God is very necessary, that is to say, to judge inward things.'

No action, whether at common or canon law, ought therefore to be governed by a rule requiring one to judge what could not be judged. Here the Student is relying upon a commonplace of fifteenth-century legal thought.[1] The Student then goes on in a confused passage to set out a doctrine which he attributes to 'divers that be learned in the laws of the realm'—which I take to mean 'a certain school of thought'; this is that,

'. . . all promises shall be taken in this manner, that is to say, if to whom the promise is made, have a charge by reason of the promise, which he hath also performed, then in that case he shall have an action for that thing that was promised though he that made the promise have no worldly profit by it.'

In this context this doctrine is clearly offered as an alternative to allowing the actionability of promises to turn on the *animus obligandi*, and an alternative (though this is not clear) to requiring a cause or consideration. It is also put forward as a secular theory, appropriate to secular law, where spiritual profits ought not to be relevant. The character of the doctrine comes out in the examples,

'As if a man say to another "heal such a poor man of his disease" or "make such an highway" and I shall give thee thus much. And if he do it I think an action lieth at the common law. And moreover though the thing that he shall do be all spiritual, yet if he perform it I think an action lieth at the common law. As if a man say to another "Fast for me all next Lent and I shall give thee etc." and he performeth it I think an action lieth at the common law. And in like wise if a man say to another "marry my daughter and I will give thee £20" . . .'

He goes on, inconsistently, to attribute the actionability of a promise of a marriage dowry to *quid pro quo*—the benefit the

---

[1] Normally associated with Brian C.J.'s remark in 17 Edw. IV, P. f. 2, pl. 2, 'for it is common learning that the intent of a man shall not be tried, for the Devil has no knowledge of a man's intent'. See also Statham, *Abridgement*, Duress, pl. 5, for an earlier illustration.

father receives through the preferment of his daughter.[1] He also cites the instances of promises made to universities et cetera for pious causes, and says that actionability turns (according to the doctrine under discussion) on whether the promisee has a new 'charge' on account of the promise.

This doctrine is a version of the basic idea of induced reliance brought about by the promise; the promisee 'has a charge' in the sense of a burdensome commission which he has been induced to accept by the promisor, who ought therefore to be held to his promise once the burden is discharged. Although some of the illustrations used derive from the year-books,[2] the doctrine itself is not, so far as I know, to be found stated explicitly in any common law source earlier than *Doctor and Student*, with the exception of the case of *Cleymond* v. *Vincent* in 1523 which laconically refers to 'prejudice' as a ground for promissory liability. Its source could be this or some other contemporary common law argument, of which reports no longer survive. It is also possible, though no more, that St. Germain is here adapting from the *Summae* the notion that a nude pact could be clothed, and thus rendered actionable, *interventu rei*:

'I have promised[3] you to give you something that you should do or give something. Then at once when I have given you what I have promised the pact is clothed from my part'.

The 'intervention' here, however, comes from the promisor, not the promisee. The relationship between the doctrine of 'charge' to questions of proof is obvious enough—in common law terms the jury can have cognizance of the promisee's action of performance, which is a 'matter of fact' and thus triable.

The Student also takes the opportunity to hold forth on the moral relevance of *animus obligandi* and the identity of the promisee. Breaking promises to the Church, the clergy, et cetera is in his view no worse than breaking promises to common people, and the relevance of *animus obligandi* (treated as being the same as an intention to perform) is only this: a promisor who does not intend to be bound offends merely for his dissimulation—

---

[1] This comes from the year-books; see 37 Hen. VI, M. f. 8, pl. 18.
[2] See above, p. 158.
[3] Note that there has been acceptance, for otherwise there would be only a *pollicitatio*.

he lies to the other by deeds. If he intends to be bound, but does not perform, then he proves himself instead to be a liar. Here St. Germain is giving a very muddled version of Aquinas;[1] he grasps the fact of the distinction between the two cases, but misunderstands it. Aquinas in *Summa Theologia* said, 'A man does not lie, so long as he has a mind to do what he promises, because he does not speak contrary to what he has in mind; but if he does not keep his promise, he seems to act without faith in changing his mind.'

The Student on past consideration or cause

The Doctor then asks the Student two questions. The first is 'What hold they if the promise be made for a thing past, as I promise thee £5 for that thou hast builded me such a house. Lieth an action there?'

The Student replies that no action lies, though the promise is binding in conscience if the promisor intended to perform (the Student seeing no harm in the requirement of *animus* in matters of conscience, where proof does not matter, rather than law). This departs inexplicably from the *Summae*, which, as we have seen, St. Germain misunderstood on past cause anyway, and it is hardly conceivable that the explanation is that the matter by this date had been settled in common law litigation. The Doctor's next question is,

'And if a man promise to give another £5 in recompense for such a trespass that he hath done him, lieth an action there?'

The Student says that no action lies, and this was settled common law at the time.[2] It is plain that in the context the Student thinks such a promise binding in conscience so long as there is an intention to be bound, as in the prior case. He then provides a theoretical explanation in terms of categories which is not to be found elsewhere,

'For a contract is properly where a man for his money shall have by assent of the other party certain goods or some other profit at the time of the contract or after. But if the thing he

---

[1] *Dissimulatio* is a technical term meaning to lie by deeds and not by words. For Aquinas see *Summa Theologia*, Q. 110 Art. 3.
[2] See above, p. 176.

promised for a cause that is past by way of recompense then it is rather an accord than a contract.'

And he then explains that it is the law that an accord, to be effective, must be accompanied by a satisfaction, for no action lies on an accord;[1] the reasoning is, of course, circular. Here the combination between the ideas derived from the *Summae* and the current common law is intimate; St. Germain, through his Student, states common law, but in doing so introduces notions of *causa* which must come from Angelus and Baptista.

The Student on prior obligation

The Doctor then points out that in the case of the trespass the promisor was under an existing obligation to make recompense when he made the promise. Therefore, he argues, he will be bound in conscience to perform his promise even though he did not intend to be bound. This reproduces the doctrine in the *Summae*, which is illustrated by the example of the promise to give one's father a cloak to keep out the cold, which is binding even if not intended to be binding. The Student does not agree with the Doctor in the case of the trespass, and gives this reason for saying that the promisor is his own judge as to whether the promise is to bind him or not:

'Yet he was not bounden to no sum certain but by his promise, and because that same may be too much or too little, and not equal to the trespass, and that the party to whom the trespass was done notwithstanding the promise is at liberty to take his action of trespass if he will . . .'

He then adds that

'if it were a debt, then they hold that he is bound to perform his promise in conscience'.

The discussion then turns to other matters.

The relationship between 'Doctor and Student' and the common law

The mere date of *Doctor and Student*'s publication—in the case of the second dialogue, 1530—makes it impossible to claim that St. Germain through its publication introduced the common

---

[1] See above, p. 158.

lawyers to the notion of attaching legal significance to 'considerations' so that the contractual doctrine was derived through St. Germain. For in the context of the law of uses common lawyers had already, as we have seen, developed a doctrine of consideration. However, it may be that St. Germain did suggest or encourage the idea of applying a similar doctrine to promises, by giving wide publicity to the notion of *causa promissionis* (which he assimilated to the common law's 'consideration') as a possible tool of legal analysis, and by portraying the problem of the naked promise as related to the problem of the naked expression of will in the law of property. For the essence of the doctrine of consideration in assumpsit is to be found in the exposition of the Doctor before it can be found in any common law case dealing with promissory liability—I mean by the essence the basic idea that a promise is binding if it has a cause or consideration. It is further possible that certain notions passed into the thinking of common lawyers from St. Germain, though the treatment of them by the common law did not precisely follow his treatment. For example, the treatment of prior obligation in *Doctor and Student* is echoed, though not followed, in the common law. The Student says that a promise to pay a pre-existing debt binds *in conscience*, whereas the common law was to say that it bound *in law*. Again the relevance of prior obligation in the *Summae* was to *animus obligandi* with which the common law was not to be concerned until very recent times when 'intention to create legal relations' was to become a fashionable contractual doctrine. Again, over past cause or consideration, the influence of *Doctor and Student* may have been to pose and categorize the problem, rather than to provide the solution adopted in *Hunt* v. *Bate* (1568) and *Lampleigh* v. *Braithwaite* (1616).[1]

It is clear, however, that *Doctor and Student* provides no support for a simple view that St. Germain reproduced 'the Canon Law of Contract' and the common lawyers simply applied it. St. Germain's sources were, as we have seen, primarily concerned with the obligations of conscience which were relevant *in foro interno*, not with laying down rules for society to be applied in courts, whether ecclesiastical or lay; common lawyers were concerned to deal with secular litigation, and in

[1] Dyer, 272a; Hob. 105.

so far as they used the ideas of the canonists they were injecting moral notions into secular law, as they did when they lifted the requirement of a guilty mind from the penitentials and used it in the criminal law. No straight copying of canon law could in principle occur. Furthermore St. Germain's account of the canon law, as derived from the *Summae*, was itself distorted, and there were also important omissions, for example in the case of the *pollicitatio*. Not until the nineteenth century did the distinction between the *promissio* and *pollicitatio* pass into the common law, through the influence of Pothier, in the form of the doctrine of offer and acceptance, and it is an interesting speculation that had St. Germain mentioned it we should have had that doctrine four centuries earlier. It is also important to notice that only certain ideas to be found in the dialogue reappear (modified or not) in the early law of assumpsit. For example, the notion of *animus obligandi* was not used by the common lawyers, nor was the idea that a promise *sine causa* was void on account of error, nor the idea that a change of circumstances discharges a promisor from liability. In sum although there was in all probability *some* canon law influence through *Doctor and Student*, and perhaps a critical influence, if St. Germain popularized the idea that is central to the doctrine of consideration, it would be a mistake to suppose that the doctrine of consideration in assumpsit was received *in toto* from the jurisprudence of the two Franciscans, and indirectly from more remote sources in continental law.

Other sources of canon law influence: the Chancery

If *Doctor and Student* came too late to introduce common lawyers to the thought of canonists, there remains the possibility that a familiarity with casuistic thought, and indeed with ideas developed in civil and canon law generally, came about in other ways. That common lawyers knew *something* about canon and civil law cannot be sensibly doubted; how much they knew, and what sources were used by them cannot be established. One possibility, however, is that the late medieval chancellors, who undoubtedly exercised a jurisdiction in contractual matters, applied a doctrine of *causa promissionis* derived from the canon law; presumably the application of a doctrine of consideration to uses, which preceded the application to assumpsit, would need also to be derived from the canon law to make such a theory complete, though Barbour, who advanced this view in relation to contract, did not suggest such a refinement.[1] There is, however, an air of plausibility in Barbour's basic point, which is thus stated,

> 'The chancellor was an ecclesiastic, and probably carried with him into the chancery the principles and theories of the ecclesiastical court.'[2]

Now the principles upon which the fifteenth-century chancellors proceeded in providing remedies are inherently difficult to determine because of the relative rarity of reports of Chancery proceedings. The task is not, however, hopeless, for we do have numerous petitions and quite a number of year-book reports, which make it clear that the primary principle of decision involved in the activities of the fifteenth- and early-sixteenth-century court of Chancery was *Conscience*. Somewhat less important was the appeal to 'faith', 'right', and 'reason'.[3] Hence petitioners would appeal to the Chancellor to do,

> 'as right and good conscience requiren; For the love of God and in way of charyte' (*c.* 1464),

or

> 'as gude faith and conscens requyer' (1460–5),

or

> 'after the lawe of consciens, whiche ys lawe executory [i.e. to be applied] in this courte' (1456).[4]

The court is called a court of Conscience,[5] and in the year-book cases the argument is directed to deciding what conscience requires.[6] Hence the Chancellor in 1469[7] (Bishop Stillington of

[1] Barbour, 163 et seq.
[2] Barbour, 163.
[3] G. Spence, *Equitable Jurisdiction of the Court of Chancery*, I. 339, adds 'honesty', but this seems hard to support in the period under discussion. See W. P. Baildon, S.S. Vol. 10, pp. xxix et seq.
[4] S.S. Vol. 10, 153, 151, 146. For other examples see Barbour, 172, 176, 180, 181, 185, 188 etc.
[5] S.S. Vol. 10, case 123 (n.d.); Y.B. 38 Hen. VI, M. f. 26, pl. 36 (1461).
[6] 37 Hen. VI, H. f. 13, pl. 3; 39 Hen. VI, M. f. 26, pl. 36; 5. Edw. IV, M. f. 7, pl. 17; 9 Edw. IV, M. f. 41, pl. 26; P. f. 2, pl. 5; 11 Edw. IV, T. f. 8, pl. 13; 18 Edw. IV, f. 11, pl. 4; 4 Hen. VII, H. f. 4, pl. 8; 7 Hen. VII, P. f. 10, pl. 2.
[7] 9 Edw. IV, T. f. 14, pl. 8.

Bath and Wells) states that he is to judge *secundum conscientiam* and describes himself in the previous year[1] as possessing two capacities—those of a temporal judge and a 'judge of conscience'. Again the rubric under which cases in the Chancery are to be found is not Equity, but either *Subpena* (a procedural category) or *Conscience*.[2] If one had inquired of a late-fifteenth-century lawyer the appropriate title for a book on what went on before the court of Chancery, he would without doubt have said 'Conscience', *not* 'Equity'. Now it is at first sight a curious fact, which has frequently been noted, that references to any early connection between the Chancery and 'Equity' are extremely uncommon. It is also very significant. For 'Conscience' was at the time a term of art; and as Spence[3] says:

'The term Conscience, as denoting a principle of judicial decision, appears to have been a term of clerical invention.'

He goes on (in my view wrongly),

'it seems to have embraced the obligations which resulted from a person being placed in any situation as regards another that gave the one a right to expect, on the part of the other, the exercise of good faith towards him, and nearly resembled the *bona fides* of the Praetorian Code . . .'

For to a fifteenth-century ecclesiastic, sitting as a judge of conscience, in a court of conscience, to apply the law of conscience 'for the love of God and in way of charity', 'conscience' did not connote, though it included, some principle of injurious reliance or good faith. It connoted what we now call the moral law *as it applied to particular individuals for the avoidance of peril to the soul through mortal sin*. The fact that the late medieval chancellors proceeded to apply the law of conscience produced a most curious conception of the function of their adjudications. Although there is no doubt that the intervention of the Chancellor was in part governed and influenced by other considerations—for example, by solicitude for petitioners who lacked a remedy—as a judge of conscience, his primary function and concern was not with the petitioner but with the respondent

[1] 8 Edw. IV, T. f. 1, pl. 1.
[2] In Statham's, Brooke's, Fitzherbert's, and all early *Abridgements* and indices.
[3] Spence, op. cit. 411.

and of the good of his soul, that is with the wrongdoer. It is at first extremely difficult to adapt to this way of thought, in which a remedy is given to a petitioner not primarily to look after his interests, but rather to look after the losing party who has done wrong or proposes to do wrong. Indirectly, of course, this does look after the petitioner, for the avoidance of sin usually does benefit others, but this effect is incidental: hence arises the principle that equity acts in *personam*. This too is the explanation for the insistence upon specific performance, which compels the sinner to put matters to rights, which he must do if his soul is to be saved. Thus it is that in a case in 1491[1] before the Chancellor one executor had wrongly released a debt, due to the testator, without the assent of his co-executors. The question at issue was whether the Chancellor would remedy this by subpoena, brought against the executor and the debtor. The consequence of the release was that the will of the testator could not be performed. The Chancellor favoured a remedy, and one reason he gave was *Nullus recedat a Curia Cancellarie sine remedio* (the person needing the remedy being, it must be noted, the deceased testator). The other ground was that unless something was done by the executor to make restitution or amends

'he will be damned in Hell, and to grant a remedy in such a case, as I understand it, is to do well in accordance with conscience'.

This argument was in reply to Fineux C.J.'s claim that the matter was one simply between a man and his confessor, and the Chancellor's point is that he is *in foro conscientie*; he proceeds upon the same principles as a confessor. Another striking example of the fact that the Chancellor, as a judge of conscience, was essentially interested in souls, not secular matters, is provided by a case in 1468.[2] Genney in argument has contended that the Chancery should not intervene to protect people who have behaved foolishly by failing to observe formalities necessary to ensure a common law remedy; to this the Chancellor replies,

'And so you could say that if I enfeoff a man in trust, *etcetera*, and if he is not willing to perform my will, I shall, according

[1] 7 Hen. VII, P. f. 10, pl. 2.
[2] 8 Edw. IV, P. f. 4, pl. 11.

to you have no remedy, for it is my folly to have enfeoffed such a person who is unwilling to perform my will *etcetera*. But he will have a remedy in this court, for *Deus est procurator futurorum*[1] [God is the defender of the departed].'

The point being made is that the feoffor is dead by the time his folly comes to light, but God looks after the departed, and the Chancellor, being charged to do God's will, must act appropriately and make sure that the will is performed for the good of the soul of the departed. Now the conception of Equity, which modifies the rigour of the rules of positive law by providing exceptions in particular cases in accordance with the spirit, but not the letter of the law, is quite distinct from the conception of Conscience, and found its home originally and appropriately, in connection with the interpretation of written laws, finding its expression in common law in the interpretation of statutes. The distinction between the two conceptions (which distinction came in time to be blurred) is neatly put by Lord Ellesmere,[2]

'The Office of the Chancellor is to correct men's consciences for frauds, breaches of trusts, wrongs and oppressions, of whatever nature soever they be *and* [my italics] to soften and modify the extremity of the law.'

The first function involves Conscience, the second Equity, and in the early history of the court of Chancery, Equity had little part to play.[3]

Now it is hardly conceivable, if the identity and careers of fifteenth- and early-sixteenth-century chancellors are borne in mind, that as judges in conscience they could avoid deriving ideas from the canon and civil law.[4] Most were Oxford men,

---

[1] This is normally amended to *Deus est procurator fatuorum* ('God looks after fools'), following Vinogradoff in 24 L.Q.R. 330, but there is no warrant for this. The expression *procurator futurorum* echoes the term *procurator animarum*, used of advocates in courts christian.

[2] *The Earl of Oxford's Case* (1615) 1 Ch. Rep. 4.

[3] The most striking reference is in 1467, when the King in giving Robert Kirkcham, Master of the Rolls, custody of the Great Seal said, 'The King commandeth that all matters in his Court of Chancery shall be directed and determined according to equity and conscience and to the old course and custom, so that if difficulty or question arises he take the advice of the justices, so that right and justice be ministered to everyone'. *Cal. Close Rolls* (1467) p. 457. Early references to equity commonly refer to problems of interpretation of statutes.

[4] Biographical details are from A. B. Emden, *A Biographical Dictionary of the University of Oxford before 1500*, and E. Foss, *The Judges of England*.

and nearly all were law graduates. Thus John Stafford (1432),[1]
Bishop of Bath and Wells, and later Archbishop of Canterbury,
was a Doctor of Civil Law from Oxford; he had practised as a
lawyer in the ecclesiastical courts. His successor, John Kemp
(1450), Archbishop of York and of Canterbury, and later
Cardinal, had taken his M.A., B.C.L., and D.C.L. at Oxford
and had also practised as a lawyer. Thomas Bourchier (1455),
Archbishop of Canterbury, was an M.A. from Oxford, but had
graduated in the school of Theology, William Waynflete
(1456–60), Bishop of Winchester and Founder of Magdalen
College, was an Oxford Doctor of both Canon and Civil Law.
His successor, George Nevill (1460), Archbishop of York, was
another graduate of Oxford, being an M.A. of Balliol. Robert
Stillington (1467), Bishop of Bath and Wells, was a D.C.L. of
Oxford; he is known to have owned a canon law library.
Lawrence Booth (1473) was, exceptionally, a Cambridge
graduate. Thomas Rotheram (1474), Bishop of Lincoln, and
later Archbishop of York, held a doctorate in Theology from
Oxford and his extensive library included canon law books.
John Russell (1483), Bishop of Lincoln, was an Oxford Bachelor
in both Canon and Civil Law, and a Doctor of Canon Law.
Robert Morton (1486) was another Oxford Bachelor in both
laws, and a D.C.L. He had practised as a proctor in the Chancellor's Court in Oxford, which applied civil law, and he is
known to have owned canon law books. And Archbishop
William Warham (1501), who preceded Wolsey, was a Doctor
of both Civil and Canon Law who again had practised as a
lawyer in the ecclesiastical courts, and who owned an extensive
library of canon law books, including the *Summa Sylvestrina*.
Plainly ecclesiastics such as these men, given their education
and general background, must have been perfectly familiar with
the work of the casuists, and in so far as they required guidance
in deciding cases in accordance with conscience, which was their
accepted function, it is very likely that they would turn to the
obvious books on the subject—the *Summae de Casibus Conscientie*.
But direct proof of this is not available; hence specific connec-
tions cannot be established. It is, for example, virtually certain
that informal promises of marriage dowries were regarded as
binding in Chancery. Probably this is related to the orthodox

[1] The date is that of first assuming the office.

teaching of the *Summae* that a father was indeed under a duty to endow his daughter, if he could, so that such a promise merely reinforced and rendered specific a prior moral obligation. But there is no definite proof that the *Summae* influenced the Chancery here, though it is highly likely that the influence existed. Similarly the doctrine of *causa promissionis* in canon law must have been perfectly familiar to fifteenth- and early-sixteenth-century chancellors—in the case of Archbishop Warham we know that he owned a book which contains, in the title *De Pactis*, the same passages as are in the *Summae Rosella* and *Angelica* and passages taken from the *Summa Astesana*.

'Causa' in fifteenth-century common law

That some knowledge of civil and canon law notions had filtered into the common law world in the fifteenth century is clear from cases which refer to the contrast between *pacta nuda* and *pacta vestita*, and there is also evidence of the use of the notion of *causa* in connection with the revocation of gifts and in connection with grants of annuities. So far as the pacts are concerned there is, however, some difficulty in relating the use of the distinction by common lawyers to civilian or canonist sources. Thus in a case of 1432[1] Rolf argues that if A owes B £20, and C buys goods worth £20 from A and then shows B this and says that he will pay B direct, who will discharge A, this agreement is a contract binding on C. Cottesmore claims it is a nude pact; Rolf replies that it is a *pactum vestitum*,

'because this accord is based on contract'.

Presumably the argument is that it is *vestitum* as a pact accessory to a contract, but this is by no means clear, as the argument is not filled out. Similarly a reference to *nuda pacta* by the year-book reporter in 1421[2] takes this form,

'Parole ou promise de paier xli. sans quid pro quo ne fait contract car nisi nudum pactum unde non oritur actio.'

So laconic a note may amount to little more than tag-dropping. Cases on the revocation of gifts, in particular the case in

---

[1] 11 Hen. VI, P. f. 43, pl. 30.
[2] 9 Hen. V, M. f. 14, pl. 23.

Statham's *Abridgement* in 1452[1] (discussed as a case in *Conscience*), reveal a more sophisticated use of the concept of *causa*, and so do cases involving annuities. The principle here was that if an annuity was granted for some service, or for performing the duties of an office, then a failure to perform the service or discharge the duties of the office extinguished the annuity;[2] in modern terms the annuity ceased if the consideration was not performed or at least tendered. The principle gave rise to discussions in terms of the cause of the annuity and the maxim *cessante causa cessat effectus*, as in the case of the *Prior of St. Faith* v. *Abbot of Langley* (1469),[3] where an annuity had been granted in exchange for tithes, and the question was whether the annuity determined if the defendant's enjoyment of the tithe was interfered with. The argument proceeded in terms of the maxim, and the doctrine which emerged is that if the cause was executory then the maxim applied, whereas if it was not then it had no application. Where the cause was the grant of the tithes, and the grant had been executed, disturbance in their enjoyment might give rise to an action but did not extinguish the annuity. There is indeed a case in 1367 which uses the very word consideration as a synonym for the cause of an annuity,[4] and this is the earliest use of the terms as interchangeable which I have found. The notion of cause also turns up in connection with actions of covenant, for example in this statement of the law by Fineux C.J. in 1499,[5]

'If one covenant to serve me for a year, and if I covenant with him to give him £20, if I do not say "for the same cause" he will have an action against me for the £20 even though he does not ever serve me; it is otherwise if I say "for the same cause".'

Some sort of reference to the notion of *causa promissionis* also must lurk behind Genney's remark in 1476,[6] to which reference has already been made,

[1] *Conscience* pl. 1 discussed above, p. 337.
[2] See 21 Edw. III, H. f. 7, pl. 20; 8 Hen. VI, H. f. 23, pl. 9; 39 Hen. VI, M. f. 21, pl. 31.
[3] 9 Edw. IV, T. f. 19, pl. 22; 15 Edw. IV, M. f. 2, pl. 5. See also 14 Hen. VII, T. f. 31, pl. 8 and 5 Edw. IV, H. f. 8 pl. 1.
[4] 41 Edw. III, M. f. 19, pl. 3.
[5] 15 Hen. VII, T. f. 10, pl. 17.
[6] 16 Edw. IV, M. f. 8, pl. 5.

'I think the same, for by an accord between two parties it is necessary to have a satisfaction, or otherwise it is ineffective, for by our law words without a reason bind no-one, for if I say to you that I will give or pay you £20 by a certain day nothing is achieved by these words. And so it is (in the case of the plea) of submission to arbitration, or accord, and especially in accord, which is nothing but a speaking between the parties . . .'

though the abbreviated nature of the report makes it impossible to say how specific the reference is. A reference to payment of money as a 'cause' of an action on the case occurs in Frowicke C.J.'s argument in *Orwell* v. *Mortoft* (1505),[1] and in *John Style's Case* (1527) before *Doctor and Student* was published there is a discussion of liability for nonfeasance which relates the concept of *nudum pactum* to a requirement that promises were only actionable if there was a consideration why they should be actionable.[2] The tantalizing hints in the year-books are, of course, no more than the tip of the iceberg of fifteenth-century legal argument; they seem to suggest no more than a somewhat sketchy acquaintanceship with civilian and canonist notions such as might be acquired without serious study in the course of conversation and legal practice.

The pedigree of the doctrine of consideration

It has already been remarked that the detailed working out of the equitable doctrine of consideration appears to be the unaided work of the common lawyers, and, as we shall see when the details of the doctrine of consideration in assumpsit are examined, there is again little direct evidence that common lawyers were consciously borrowing *ab extra*. It is no doubt futile to attempt to quantify in an area such as this, but the end product—the doctrine developed in the course of the sixteenth century, becomes specifically a peculiarity of the common law, just as the modern doctrine of offer and acceptance, though ultimately resting upon notions first derived in a tortuous way from Roman Law, is not simply the product of a reception. We can sum up the pedigree of the doctrine of

---

[1] *Orwell* v. *Mortoft* (1505) Keilwey 77 at 78a where Frowicke C.J. refers to payment of money as the cause of an action—see below p. 413.

[2] Appendix, Case No. 8. See also 27 Hen. VIII, M. f. 28, pl. 16.

consideration in assumpsit by saying that the basic idea of allowing the consideration for a promise to determine its binding quality was probably received into the common law by extension from the law of uses, where the consideration for a transaction was similarly allowed to determine its legal effect, and that in this process of extension not simply the basic idea, but to some degree the details of the equitable doctrine were applied in a new area. This extension may have been encouraged by the publication of St. Germain's *Doctor and Student*. St. Germain's book also helped to familiarize common lawyers with canonist theories of promissory liability, worked out by late medieval casuists in the *Summae Confessorum*, and the doctrine of consideration in assumpsit came to echo and reflect ideas of alien origin. It is also probable, though not capable of strict proof, that the chancellors in the fifteenth and sixteenth centuries, in exercising a jurisdiction *in conscience*, applied notions set out in what were then the relevant manuals, the *Summae de Casibus Conscientie* or *Summae Confessorum*, and that common lawyers through their involvement in Chancery cases became familiarized with the ideas of the casuists and adapted them for home consumption. Finally it is probably a mistake to over-emphasize the 'insularity' of common lawyers in the relatively tiny world of late medieval London; they cannot have been wholly ignorant of the intellectual ideas generally current in Western Christendom at the time, more particularly those with which they must have come into direct contact in the confessional, though it is only incidentally (as through a library list) that direct evidence is available.[1]

---

[1] See E. W. Ives, 'A Lawyer's Library of 1500), (1969) 85 L.Q.R. 104, discussing the library of Thomas Kebell, a Serjeant-at-Law who died in 1500.

VII

ASSUMPSIT AND THE
DOCTRINE OF CONSIDERATION

IT was in the 1560s, as we have seen, that there was established
a firm association between the action of assumpsit and the
need to aver consideration in the pleadings, which culminated
in the principle stated in *Golding's Case* (1586):[1]

> 'In every action upon the case upon a promise, there are
> three things considerable, consideration, promise and breach
> of promise.'

The importance of the consideration was emphasized by the
fact that at no time was any particular form of words required
to count as a promise. The unilateral parole contract of the
civil law, the *stipulatio*, originally required the use of formal
question and answer before a contract could be concluded, only
six set forms being recognized, and certain relics of the original
verbal nature of the contract survived long after these forms
had passed out of use and stipulations were commonly written—
for example, deaf and dumb persons could not stipulate.[2]
Nothing of the sort is to be found in the common law, and the
position is summed up thus in the seventeenth century,

> 'As to the manner of the words of a contract, or promise,
> that it matters not in what form of words the assumpsit is
> made, so the sense be certain and clear ... Nor is the party
> that is to sue on the contract to declare in the very words of
> the contract, but to take up the substance and sense thereto,
> and the same to put into a formal way of pleading'.[3]

One had to aver a promise; thus in *Weeks* v. *Tybald* (1604)[4] a
declaration which failed to do this, but merely averred that the

---

[1] 2 Leon. 72.
[2] See Watson, *The Law of Obligations in the Later Roman Republic*, 1965,
Ch. 1, Nicholas, 'The Stipulation in Roman Law', 69 L.Q.R. 63.
[3] Sheppard, 84.
[4] Noy 11. See also *Wilson* v. *Bradshaw* (1623) 2 Rolle 463 where an averment that
the defendant *solvere vellet* was bad in the majority view, since God alone knew the

defendant asserted and published (*asseruit et publicavit*), was bad. The absence of verbal formalism here was probably the consequence of jury trial, it being purely a jury matter, once a promise had been averred, to decide whether there had been one.[1] As a jury matter it was one upon which there was no law. It is also possible that except in the case of engagements to marry there was no widespread use of traditional verbal forms in the contemporary life of the market. Just as there is no hint of a requirement of verbal formality, so there is no suggestion that any form of acceptance of a promise was necessary, the common law not receiving the distinction between promises and pollicitations; liability was placed solely upon the unilateral promise, and of this no particular evidence need be produced, the mere 'naked averment' of the plaintiff in his pleading being in all probability sufficient, though there is one case, *Wiver* v. *Lawson* (1626)[2] which suggests the emergence of a rule that at least one witness was essential. Hence the doctrine of consideration was the only restraining conception which confronted the plaintiff *in limine*, and although the matter is not anywhere discussed in the case law it could well be that in a sense Lord Mansfield's conception of consideration as 'evidence'[3] is historically correct, if the idea is given a somewhat extended sense along the following lines. The jury, before holding the defendant liable, need something more to go on than merely a parole promise, inadequately perhaps proved, but if they find that there was a good reason for the making of the promise which is also a good reason for holding the defendant liable then they can with more confidence award damages for breach, the consideration making it more plausible to say both that there was a promise and that it was seriously intended. But it must be emphasized that no such rationalization is to be found in the cases.

---

will: there must be words of assumpsit, as *dixit, asseruit, contractum fuit, agreatum fuit*. On the same point is *Buckler* v. *Angel* (1665) 1 Lev. 164.

[1] Cases purporting to report what was actually said are rare, but see *Anon.* (1484) Cro. Eliz. 79; 12 Hen. VIII, P. f. 11, pl. 13; 27 Hen. VIII, M. f. 24, pl. 3 for early examples.

[2] Litt. 33, Hetley 14, 15.

[3] Set out in *Pillans* v. *Van Mierop* (1765) 3 Burrow 1663.

Situations where consideration need not be averred

The requirement of averring a consideration was subject to certain exceptions:

(1) ACTIONS AGAINST DEBTORS

Where assumpsit was brought against a debtor, it was not essential or usual to plead a considerations clause, as we are told in *Whorwood* v. *Gybbons* (1587).[1] This did not mean that in such cases the doctrine of consideration did not apply; all that was in issue was a pure pleading point. There are two possible explanations for the rule. The first is that actions of assumpsit in lieu of debt were well established before the use of express consideration clauses became customary, and that the old pleading forms were retained unaltered, and held good out of respect for continuity of practice. The second is that in such actions it was realized that an old-established liability, based on the doctrine of *quid pro quo*, was being enforced by a new action, and therefore it was hardly important to worry about the limitation of the scope of assumpsit. Of these two explanations the first seems the more likely.

(2) ACTIONS AGAINST BAILEES FOR NEGLIGENCE

A second exception to the general principle appears in a case in Rolle's *Abridgement, Powtuary* v. *Walton* (1598).[2] Here an action on the case for negligent misfeasance was brought against a veterinary surgeon who had undertaken to cure the plaintiff's horse, and who had killed the horse through his negligence. It was held that,

'Action on the case lies on this matter without alleging any consideration, for his negligence is the cause of the action, and not the assumpsit.'

Unfortunately this decision is not fully reported, and there seem to be no other sixteenth- or seventeenth-century decisions upon the question; it is therefore difficult to know quite what to make of the decision.

When bailees,[3] or finders,[4] were sued by action on the case

---

[1] Goulds. 48.

[2] 1 Rolle Abr. f. 10, pl. 5.

[3] *Fooly* v. *Preston* (1585) 1 Leon. 297, *Taylor's Case* (1583) 4 Leon. 708, *Byne* v. *Playne* (1589) 1 Leon. 220, *Bigg* v. *Clark* (1589) 2 Leon. 104.

[4] An example of an assumpsit against the finder of a lost dog is *Ireland* v. *Higgins*

instead of by action of detinue, the action would be framed either as an action for conversion or as an action of assumpsit;[1] put either way it was clear that the action on the case was not being based upon the same ground as the action of detinue.[2] This satisfied the double-remedy doctrine, though, of course, the distinction between alleging that the defendant detained the goods and alleging that the defendant had broken a promise and undertaking to redeliver the goods was somewhat fine and artificial. An action on the case cast in the assumpsit form offered an alternative to the action on the case for conversion, and was used quite commonly in the sixteenth century when the gist of the plaintiff's complaint was that the bailee or finder had failed to return the goods; its attractiveness may have owed something to the theoretical difficulties involved in saying that failure to return (a not-doing) amounted to the wrong of conversion (which was viewed as a misfeasance).[3] An action of assumpsit for failure to perform a promise to return was clearly an action for nonfeasance, and in such actions, in accordance with ordinary principle, consideration in sixteenth-century law was regarded as necessary.[4]

[1] The forms represent two different ways of looking at the position; the action for conversion emphasizes the idea that the defendant has violated a property right of the plaintiff, the assumpsit form emphasizes the idea that the defendant has failed to perform an agreement. The assumpsit form was more natural where the defendant had broken a special term of the bailment, where by agreement he had subjected himself to a duty which was not imposed upon him by the general law. But the forms could be used as pure alternatives.

[2] This, Kiralfy (161) suggests is the explanation of the ruling in *Mosley* v. *Fosset* (1596) Moore 543, where the Justices of the King's Bench agreed that in an action against a paid bailee of a gelding for agistment, the gelding having been lost by negligence, being taken by persons unknown, a special assumpsit to guard safely was required. *Sed quaere*; the ruling may rest on the view that a bailee in such a case was not liable under the general law since he could have no remedy over (cf. *Southcote* v. *Bennet* (1601) Cro. Eliz. 815, 4 Rep. 83b) and that to impose an additional liability an assumpsit was essential. cf. *Taylor's Case* (1583) 4 Leon. 708, where it was held that 'act of God' was no plea in assumpsit against a bailee, though it was a defence in an action against a bailee in the absence of an assumpsit.

[3] See Fifoot, Ch. 6; there was also difficulty in viewing negligent keeping as a misfeasance; *Isaack* v. *Clark* (1614) 2 Bulst. 306 held that case for conversion did not lie for negligent keeping.

[4] *Fooly* v. *Preston* (1585) 1 Leon. 297; *Bind* v. *Playne* (1590) Cro. Eliz. 218; *Ireland* v. *Higgins* (1587) Owen 93; the idea that consideration was needed in such cases survived *Powtuary* v. *Walton*. See *Riches* v. *Brigges* (1602) Yelv. 4; *Pickas* v.

(1587) Owen 93. The more usual practice would be to sue in an action on the case for trover and conversion. Cro. Eliz 125, 3 Leon. 219 S.C.

The practice of alleging consideration in such actions of assumpsit for failure to deliver probably suggested the idea that where a bailee (or by a parity of reasoning a finder) was sued in assumpsit for negligently damaging the goods, as opposed to failing to return them, an allegation of consideration was similarly needed.[1] However, the liability of bailees for negligently damaging goods (which was viewed as misfeasance) had been established even in the case of a gratuitous bailment[2] long before the doctrine of consideration had been thought of, bailees being held liable just as doctors were held liable in actions of assumpsit for negligent misfeasance, and the decision in *Powtuary* v. *Walton* appears to represent a refusal to apply the doctrine of consideration retrospectively to this class of action. The decision has subsequently been taken as settling the law. It continued to be permissible in such actions, and still is permissible, to allege an agreement supported by good consideration to take good care; this, however, is not necessary.

However, there are certain respects in which both the basis of the decision in *Powtuary* v. *Walton* and the scope of the rule laid down there are uncertain. In the first place it is not clear whether the fact that the defendant was exercising a public calling was treated as relevant; if so it would follow that the decision would not apply to all actions for negligent misfeasance, even where such actions were brought against bailees or those who had custody of the plaintiff's person, such as surgeons. In the second place it is not clear whether the court held that the assumpsit was a wholly immaterial allegation, or merely held that the gravamen of the plaintiff's action was the allegation of negligence.[3] In the third place the distinction between an

---

[1] After *Isaack* v. *Clark* (1614) held that negligent keeping was a mere nonfeasance, it was in accordance with principle to take the view that in an action on the case for negligent keeping consideration must be shown; this view was adopted in *Coggs* v. *Bernard* (1703) 2 Ld. Raym. 909.

[2] See above, p. 238, and cf. *Anon.* (1510) Keilwey 160, where Serjeant More says, 'If I bail goods to a man to keep safely, and he undertakes to do it for reward or without reward, and the goods perish by his default, I shall have in such a case an action on the case'. For a discussion of the question see Kiralfy, pp. 161 et seq.

[3] It is possible that the court took the view that the plaintiff need only show negligence and damage. The first case to establish liability for negligence in the

---

Guile (1608) Yelv. 128; *Wheatley* v. *Low* (1623) Cro. Jac. 668; *Symons* v. *Darknoll* (1628) Palm. 523.

action against a bailee for negligently damaging the chattel, where consideration need not be alleged, and an action for failure to return in which the failure to return is the result of negligent damage or loss, where it was thought that consideration need be alleged, is somewhat artificial, and it is not at all clear whether the ruling in *Powtuary* v. *Walton* was supposed to apply to both classes of case or not.

(3) ACTIONS FOR DECEIT

In *Kirby* v. *Eccles* (1588)[1] the King's Bench, by a majority, held that consideration was immaterial in an action on a collateral warranty. The plaintiff declared that,

'*cum quaedam communicatio fuissett* betwixt the plaintiff and one Cowper, that Cowper should mast certain hogs for the plaintiff, the defendant did promise that in consideration that the plaintiff promised to give unto [Cowper] 3/4 for the fatting of each hog, that the hogs should be redelivered to him well fatted'.

On the strength of this warranty the plaintiff delivered 150 hogs to Cowper, who only returned 100 hogs to him. Objection was taken to the action upon the ground that there was no consideration to charge the defendant, he having received no benefit. The court, Gawdy J. dissenting, took the view that consideration was irrelevant; the basis of liability was the deceit—the defendant had tricked the plaintiff into contracting—and it was enough to show that the promise, which was made at the time of the contract, had induced the plaintiff to contract with Cowper.

The other possible ground for the decision in *Kirby* v. *Eccles* would have been to say that the plaintiff, in making the contract with Cowper, had suffered a detriment, or incurred a

---

[1] 1 Leon. 186, Cro. Eliz. 137 (*sub nom. Kirkby* v. *Coles*).

absence of a custom or a transaction was *Anon.* (1582) Cro. Eliz. 10. I take it that this case would be an example of what some moderns call, weirdly, negligence in the air, *sed quaere*. The facts were that J.S. at the door of his house took a shot at a bird, and in doing so set his own house and the house of his neighbour on fire; held an action lay, and that the plaintiff was correct not to declare on the custom of the realm, presumably because the custom only applied to a domestic fire, and not one started by mischance.

charge—a somewhat artificial way of satisfying the require-ment. But the action for deceit for breach of warranty had been established, as we have seen, long before the doctrine of consideration had been invented, and it is understandable that the court refused to treat consideration as relevant to such actions. The decision in *Kirby* v. *Eccles* is in conformity with other sixteenth-century cases dealing with actions for deceit for breach of warranty, where it appears that consideration was not alleged.[1] The liability of the defendant was based simply upon the notion of injurious reliance, which served as a sufficient justification in law, and for that matter in common sense, for holding the defendant liable. It is commonly said that consideration was not needed in these actions because they were tortious rather than contractual, but this is hardly illuminating unless these terms are further defined. Actions for deceit were tortious only in the same sense in which all actions of assumpsit were actions for wrongs or torts. They were contractual in the sense that liability was based upon a voluntary transaction between the parties, which transaction had induced a contract in the old sense of contract—for example, a sale. They were non-contractual, in the old sense of contractual, in that the action was not taken upon the contract, but on the warranty and deceit, and they were non-contractual in the modern sense because consideration need not be shown.

With these exceptions it was necessary to aver consideration in an action on the case for an assumpsit, and by degrees the courts evolved rules as to what considerations were good and sufficient to charge a defendant in the action, and what con-siderations were insufficient.

The types of consideration

(a) PAYMENT OF MONEY, OR SOME OTHER RECOMPENSE

The rule that assumpsit would lie for breach of promise where there had been payment of money is first suggested by Brown, second clerk of the King's Bench, in 1441,[2]

---

[1] Thus in *Andrews* v. *Boughey* (1552) 1 Dyer 75a there was no averment of con-sideration, and it is said that the deceit is 'the effect and substance of the matter'. For example of cases on warranty of title see *Kenrick* v. *Burges* (1583) Moore 126; *Dale's Case* (1585) Cro. Eliz. 44; on warranty of quality see *Gravenor* v. *Mete* (1600) Cro. Eliz. 885; *Chandelor* v. *Lopus* (1603) Cro. Jac. 4.

[2] Appendix, Case No. 3.

'If a man prepays any sum of money that a house be built for him, *etcetera*, and he does not do it, now he will have an action of trespass on his case because the defendant has *quid pro quo* [i.e. something in return] and so the plaintiff is damaged. But this was privately denied to him'.

The notion then surfaces in Chief Justice Frowicke's argument in *Orwell* v. *Mortoft* (1505),[1] where it is linked to a notion of cause,

'And if I covenant with a carpenter to make me a house, and pay him £20 for the house to be made by a certain day, and he does not make the house by the day, now I shall have a good action on my case because of [*per cause de*] the payment of the money, and yet it only sounds in covenant, and without payment of the money in this case no remedy ... and it seems to me that in the case at the bar the payment of the money is the cause of the action on the case without any alteration in the property'.

Frowicke C.J. was here dissenting, and his insistence upon payment (the money paid being irrecoverable) is probably directed mainly to the common-sense argument that in such a case there is a good reason for making an exception to the general rule that nonfeasance is not actionable, lest the defendant get away with the money and do nothing in return. The use of the word 'cause' may or may not indicate some civilian or canonist influence, or be linked to its use in connection with actions of annuity. In *John Style's Case* (c. 1527)[2] the absence of payment is linked to the notion of a nude pact; the Justices of the King's Bench, having agreed that such a pact to build a house is not actionable, differentiate such a pact from one which has been paid for.

'If I give certain money to a person to make me a house by a certain day and he does not do it by the day in that case this is a consideration why for the nonfeasance I shall have an action on the case'.

[1] In Keilwey 88a at 78a. See also Keilwey 82b, where Frowicke C.J. in another context says 'For it seems to me that the promise to pay money is only a void matter in itself, for if I grant you to pay £20, this is only a void matter, and an action of debt does not lie on this grant. for *ex nudo pacto non oritur actio*'.
[2] Appendix, Case No. 8.

This, the first use of 'consideration' in the context of assumpsit, indicates some kind of conceptual linking of the relevance of payment to the notion that a nude pact was a pact lacking a cause, but the reference is too laconic to be really intelligible. Brooke also in his *Abridgement*[1] explains the absence of a remedy in early nonfeasance cases to lack of payment, so that mere *nuda pacta* were involved. In *Doctor and Student*[2] and later in *Sharrington* v. *Strotton* (1566),[3] and in the following year in *Lord Grey's Case*[4] nude promises (or nude words) are promises unsupported by good consideration, the usual example being past consideration.[5] There appears therefore to be a definite link between the acceptance of payment as consideration and an analysis in terms of the distinction between nude and vested pacts, the former being those which lacked a cause, and, as we have seen, the canonists conflated the idea of *causa promissionis* and the idea of *nuda pacta*. Payment of money was accepted in the law of uses as a good consideration to pass a use as an off-shoot of the doctrine that a bargain and sale passed a use.[6] In the case of actions against debtors the payment of money as consideration for a promise to pay the debt possessed an additional significance as a justification for allowing the use of assumpsit in lieu of debt. This is illustrated by *Lord Grey's Case* in 1567,[7] where Lord Grey was sued for a debt due by his father, the consideration averred being the indebtedness and a payment of two shillings for the promise to pay. Gawdy wanted to traverse the payment specially, and Dyer replied,

'No, for this is only alleged as a matter of course . . .'

which makes clear that the averment was fictional only.

---

[1] Brooke, *Accion sur le case*, pl. 7 and 40.

[2] Dial. II, c. 24.

[3] Plowden 298.

[4] App., Case no. 6.

[5] See *Sidnam* v. *Worthington* (1588) Cro. Eliz. 42 ('Anderson said that if I promise one that hath served me, it is *nudum pactum*') and *Lampleigh* v. *Braithwaite* (1616) Hob. 105. In *West* v. *Stowel* (1577) 2 Leon. 154 *nudum pactum* means a promise without consideration. See also *Onely* v. *Earl of Kent* (1576) Dyer 355b and *Estrigge* v. *Owles* (1587) 3 Leon. 201.

[6] *Villers* v. *Beaumont* (1556) Dyer 146a. Deinshil in an argument in 27 Hen. VIII, f. 16, pl. 28, links the idea of a nude covenant with consideration.

[7] Appendix, Case. No. 11. See also e.g. *Fetherston* v. *Hutchinson* (1587) 3 Leon. 208, 222.

The recognition of payment of money (or some other recompense) as consideration naturally persisted, and Frowicke C.J.'s statement was frequently quoted.[1] Whether or not the origin of payment as a ground for allowing an action for nonfeasance is essentially related to theories of *causa promissionis*, or whether it was relevant merely as a common-sense justification for allowing such an action, turns upon the interpretation of Frowicke's remarks in *Orwell* v. *Mortoft*; probably a number of notions—reciprocity, the prevention of unjust enrichment, the conception of *quid pro quo* as benefit conferred—coincided here. Once the idea was accepted that only those promises should be actionable which had been motivated by a legally sufficient reason or consideration, the rule that payment of money or some other recompense was a ground for assumpsit could readily be fitted into this analysis. Payment now comes to be relevant because it motivated the promise; thus what happens is that payment is looked at in a new and more sophisticated way. This change is only a change in the theory of the matter; the substance remains as before. This development may have been encouraged by *Doctor and Student*:

'And a nude contract is where a man maketh a bargain or a sale of his goods or lands without any recompense appointed for it ... And a nude or naked promise is where a man promiseth another to give him certain money such a day, or to build him an house, or to do him such certain service, and nothing is assigned for the money, for the building or for the service. These be called naked promises because there is nothing assigned *why they should be made*.'[2]

The link is more clearly established in *Sharrington* v. *Strotton* (1566)[3] in this passage in counsel's argument,

'For if upon consideration that you are my familiar friend or acquaintance, or my brother, I promise to pay you £20 at such a day, you shall not have an action on the case, or an action of debt for it, for it is but a nude and barren contract, *et ex nudo pacto non oritur actio*, and there is no sufficient cause for the payment ...'

---

[1] See E. Rabel, 'The Statute of Frauds and Comparative Legal History', 63 L.Q.R. at 180, citing Sheppard and Rolle.
[2] Dial. II, c. 24.
[3] Plowden, 298 at 302.

But a more obvious source of this new way of looking at payment as relevant because it had motivated the promise, that is because it was the consideration which had moved the promisor to promise, is the law of uses, where payment of money or other recompense as a consideration for a grant or covenant had long been regarded as a good consideration to pass a use.[1] For here assumpsit simply inherited the same rule. There is even a precise counterpart in the law of uses to the nude pact—the nude grant,[2] a grant which is made without good consideration and is therefore ineffective.

Payment or recompense distinguished from benefit

By recognizing the rule that a promise was enforceable if given in return for payment or some other recompense the common law came to enforce *bargains*—two-sided agreements in which performance by one party is paid for by the other party, and vice versa. In such bargains things of value are *exchanged*—land for money, chattels for money, services for money, and so forth. In developed societies bargains normally involve a money price, though they need not do so; if there is an agreement that chattels should be exchanged for chattels the principle behind legal enforcement remains the same. The paradigm case of a bargain is the contract of sale, and in the sixteenth century only a sale was called a bargain;[3] sale most typically involves the element of reciprocal exchange, with performance by one side viewed as a remuneration or recompense for performance by the other, which is the characteristic feature of a bargain. This is neatly brought out by Plowden,

> 'And a bargain and sale is, when a recompense is given by both the parties, as if a man bargains his land for money, here the land is a recompense to the one for the money, and the money is recompense to the other for the land, and this is properly a bargain and sale.'[4]

Though contemporaries did not call an agreement to build a house for money (for example) a bargain, but a covenant, the

---

[1] See above, p. 363, n. 2.
[2] Dial. II, c. 23.
[3] The conception of a bargain was not identical with the conception of a contract—a loan, for example, was a contract but not a bargain.
[4] *Sharrington* v. *Strotton* (1566) Plowden 298 at 303.

same analysis will fit such a transaction. Thus by accepting recompense as good consideration in assumpsit the courts brought bargains within the scope of the action. Throughout the sixteenth century, however, the enforcement of bargains was shared somewhat uneasily by assumpsit and the old contractual action of debt, though eventually the newer action became the only weapon for the enforcement of parole bargains.

By recognizing types of consideration other than payment or recompense as good consideration in assumpsit—and we shall see that other types of consideration were accepted—the courts extended assumpsit to situations which were not bargains in the sense explained, or, to put the same point in a different way, to agreements and promises which can only be called bargains if we are anxious to extend the meaning of the term bargain so that it simply means any sort of agreement, and is thus deprived of all analytical significance. I can see no advantage in doing this. It leads to a forced analysis of actionable agreements, designed to make such agreements look analogous to sales when the analogy is faint and unilluminating; it leads to a strained emphasis upon the commercial element in contract law (for not all important contracts are commercial), and it misrepresents the way in which the law of assumpsit developed. For in recognizing other forms of consideration in addition to payment or recompense contemporaries were not influenced, as I read the sources, by the notion that all that needed enforcement were agreements closely analogous to the bargain and sale. If they were we should expect them somewhere to say so.[1]

In particular it is important to notice that the principle that something of *benefit* to the promisor will be a good consideration for the promise is a wider principle than the recognition merely of recompense or payment, though, of course, it *includes* payment or recompense; only by forced reasoning can benefit be made to look the same as recompense. A simple illustration of

---

[1] Fifoot, p. 398, argues that a system of contract law can be based 'upon the principle either of promise or of bargain', and claims that the Elizabethan judges, being commercially minded, preferred the latter alternative. K. O. Shatwell, 'The Place of Consideration in The Modern Law', 1 Sydney L.R., p. 289, adopts much the same position. Neither writer seems to me to relate his argument at all closely to historical evidence, nor does either make it very clear what he means by a 'bargain'. In the tradition of Holmes, they link their theories about the modern law to their account of the history of the subject, always a methodological error for a legal historian.

this is provided by the gratuitous loan of money. Here the receipt of the money by the borrower is certainly a benefit to him, and as such will provide a consideration for a promise to repay the money, but to view the handing over of the money as a *payment for*, or *recompense for* the promise to return it is absurd. Nor does such a gratuitous loan involve any element of exchange. It is simply not a bargain at all. The evolution of the wider principle of benefit as consideration seems historically to be connected not so much with payment or recompense, but with marriage as consideration, and, as we shall see, benefit consideration enabled assumpsit to be used in situations where gratuitous contracts were involved.

(b) MARRIAGE GIFTS OR DOWRIES

Agreements to make gifts of land, money, or other property, entered into on account of marriage, and conveyance of property on account of marriage, were a normal feature of family life in medieval times and for many centuries later amongst persons of property. Indeed there was thought to be an obligation upon a father to endow his daughter. It is only in very modern times with the decline in the importance of the family (for better or for worse) that substantial endowment has become uncommon. In fifteenth-century law it was a great question whether or not an action of debt lay at common law to recover money promised by parole agreement on account of marriage.[1] Such agreements could take various forms, but the standard case was a promise made by a father of his daughter with money (a dowry) in marriage to a suitor. One difficulty which was felt in such cases was jurisdictional; marriage was the concern of the courts christian, and so questions involving marriage should be litigated there. Another problem involved the doctrine of *quid pro quo*; if the suitor married the girl it was clear that she received a benefit, but she was not being sued. The common-sense view was that the arrangement was beneficial to the daughter, but costly to the father. On one or other of these grounds the prevailing view in the fifteenth century was that

[1] In 1348 Thorpe expressed the opinion that debt lay in the Royal Court (22 Lib. Ass. pl. 70). The fifteenth-century cases are 11 Hen. IV, T. f. 83, pl. 32; 7 Hen. VI, M. f. 1, pl. 3; *Alice's Case* (1458) Y.B. 37 Hen. VI, M. f. 8, pl. 18; 14 Edw. IV, T. f. 6, pl. 3; 15 Edw. IV, f. 32, pl. 14; 17 Edw. IV, f. 4, pl. 4; T. f. 32, pl. 13; (1480) 19 Edw. IV, H. f. 10, pl. 18, (1481) f. 3, pl. 17.

the action did not lie. But the arguments in favour of saying that there ought to be a remedy in such cases were strong. The simplest was that the suitor, by marrying the daughter, had performed his side of the agreement, so the father ought to perform his. This was advanced by Danvers J. in 1458, in *Alice's Case*,

> 'For the plaintiff was charged with the marriage of the daughter, and by her espousal he is discharged, and so he has done the thing for which the sum is payable.'

A more sophisticated argument is hinted at by Moyle J. in the same case, and developed later, though unsuccessfully, by Rogers and Suliard in 1478, where they treated the problem as analogous to the general problem of charitable promises, as where a promise was made, for example, to a surgeon to pay him for curing a poor man. To provide for the marriage of a daughter or servant or a poor maid was in contemporary thought a work of charity, from which the promisor would derive if not a worldly yet a spiritual benefit. When it became possible to bring actions of assumpsit for nonfeasance, promises given on account of marriage were an obvious area in which the new action for nonfeasance could be used; the fact that debt did not lie for marriage money was an asset, for there could be no difficulty over alternative remedies, and assumpsit was not encumbered with the doctrine of *quid pro quo*. Though there is no record of the technical reasoning by which the development was achieved, it was established by 1557,[1] and probably earlier than this, that a promise to pay money on account of marriage was actionable in assumpsit. Indeed the first case which makes this clear is *Joscelin* v. *Shelton* (1557), and this is also the first reported action of assumpsit in the old printed reports to mention consideration. Again one of the two cases reported under the name *Hunt* v. *Bate* (1568),[2] where there is the first discussion of consideration, involves marriage as consideration.

Before there is any record of assumpsit actions on promises given on account of marriage, or of the treatment of marriage as a consideration to support a promise, marriage had been

---

[1] 3 Leon. 4, Brooke, *Accion sur le case*, pl. 108, Benloe 57, Moore 51. The case was not fought on whether marriage was a good consideration or not, which suggests that the point was by then settled.

[2] Dyer 272.

recognized in 1516 in *Assaby* v. *Lady Manners* as a good consideration to support a covenant which would pass a use;[1] here again there seems to be a close connection between the equitable doctrine of consideration and the doctrine of consideration in assumpsit.[2] At a common-sense level the recognition of marriage as good consideration in both fields serves much the same purpose. If a marriage agreement says that the new family is to have land, then the doctrine that marriage is a consideration to pass a use ensures that the family does get the land; if the agreement provides that the family is to get money, then the doctrine that marriage is a good consideration in assumpsit ensures that the money is paid over. Again at a common-sense level, what better reason for an agreement could there be than a marriage? Common sense apart, there is little doubt that informal promises of marriage gifts had been enforced in the Chancery in the fifteenth century, and the Chancellor may have seen such promises as examples of prior obligation in conscience, there being in general a duty to endow in the eyes of the canonists. Here there may have been a close link between the practice of Chancery and the development of a remedy at common law.[3]

Lawyers, then as now, were not content simply to say that marriage was a good consideration; they liked to go further and explain theoretically *why* marriage was a good consideration. Here there were two different lines of approach. The first was to explain the rule by saying that (in the standard case of a father's promise on his daughter's marriage) the father derived a benefit or some gain or advantage, from the marriage. This line of reasoning is developed in the argument for the plaintiff in *Sharrington* v. *Strotton* (1566):

'So in the case of a covenant upon consideration, as if I promise to another that if he will marry my daughter, he shall have my land from henceforth, and he does so, there he shall have a use in my land, and I shall be seised to his use, because a thing is done whereby I have benefit, viz. the other has married my daughter, whose advancement in the

---
[1] Dyer 235a.
[2] For the relationship between marriage as a consideration in equity and the analysis of consideration by time see below, p. 455, and above, p. 367.
[3] See Barbour, 123.

world is a satisfaction and comfort to me, and therefore this is a good consideration to make him have a use of my land.'[1]

The reasoning is not in this passage linked in any way to payment or recompense as consideration, nor could it be without artificiality; the parent's satisfaction and comfort is not the price paid by the other party, nor is it in the least analogous to a price. On the part of the defendants Plowden, who was concerned to argue in favour of the view that natural parental or family love and affection was a sufficient consideration, does not stress this idea of benefit;[2] why marriage is a good consideration in the eyes of the law is because nature instils into man a desire to look after his blood, and so marriage as good consideration is not an example of a wider principle about benefit, but instead an example of a wider principle which recognizes natural love and affection as good consideration.[3] Both these approaches were influential in later law, and it is probably to the attempt to explain marriage in terms of benefit to the promisor in *Sharrington* v. *Strotton* (1566) that we owe the formulation of the doctrine of consideration (or rather one half of it) in terms of benefit to the promisor, which is to be found in the cases in the 1580s, after Plowden's *Commentaries* had been published and become the staple food of lawyers.[4]

(c) BENEFIT

The rule that something of benefit to the promisor will be a good consideration is recognized in numerous cases in Elizabeth's reign,[5] and from the frequency with which the argument

---

[1] Plowden 298 at 301, the argument of Fleetwood and Wray. Later in Fleetwood's and Wray's argument (p. 302) an attempt is made to assimilate 'gain or advantage' with recompense; the reasoning is that for a use to pass in the lands the person seised must obtain in return some gain or advantage to recompense him for the loss of the use.

[2] 'But here there is no such bargain and sale, nor such recompense given on both sides' (p. 303). And cf. at 307 where Plowden argues that marriage and natural love and affection are 'greater than any money or matter of recompense'.

[3] Plowden 305. Plowden's treatment of marriage emphasizes the gratuitous nature of agreements on account of marriage. cf. *Villers* v. *Beaumont* (1556) Dyer 146a at 148a where the gratuitous character of marriage gifts is stressed.

[4] It must be remembered that when Plowden's *Commentaries* were first published in 1571 and 1579 no other sizeable collection of modern cases was in print.

[5] The rule is associated with the benefit or detriment doctrine in *Richards* v. *Bartlett* (1584) 1 Leon. 19, and in *Stone* v. *Wythipol* (1588) Cro. Eliz. 126, 1 Leon. 113, Owen 94. For other cases see the next note.

that only a consideration which involved benefit to the promisor was good in assumpsit it is clear that there was a strong current of opinion in favour of such a rule. But this argument was consistently rejected by the courts, who refused to limit the conception of good consideration so narrowly, and the series of cases which establish this point provide a short and conclusive answer to any attempt to establish the doctrine of *quid pro quo* as the single ancestor of the doctrine of consideration in assumpsit.[1]

The treatment of benefit as consideration in gratuitous contracts which lacked any element of remuneration is illustrated in a number of cases. Thus in *Fooly* v. *Preston* (1585)[2] the plaintiff bailed a writing obligatory to the defendant, and declared that,

'the defendant in consideration that the plaintiff should deliver to him the said writing promised to deliver the same again to the plaintiff within six days, or to pay him £1000.'

It was held that the consideration was good and sufficient. In *Byne* v. *Playne* (1589)[3] it was held that the delivery of goods to a bailee by one who had possession of them was a sufficient consideration to ground a promise to redeliver, or pay money, irrespective of whether the bailor had property in them, and the reason given by Periam J. was that,

'the defendant hath benefit by the use of them'.

Thus it was that under the wing of benefit consideration gratuitous contracts of bailment and loan could be treated as actionable in assumpsit. Behind this development lies the fact

---

[1] *Webb's Case* (1576) 4 Leon. 110, *Gill* v. *Harewood* (1586) 1 Leon. 61; *Preston* v. *Tooley* (1587) Cro. Eliz. 74; *Foster* v. *Scarlett* (1587) Cro. Eliz. 70; *Baxter* v. *Read* Dyer 272a *in margine*; *Wichals* v. *Johns* (1599) Cro. Eliz. 703; *Howel* v. *Trivanian's Case* 1 Leon. 93. cf. also as illustrations of the acceptance of benefit consideration *Greenliff* v. *Baker* (1589) 1 Leon. 238, Cro. Eliz. 193; *Smith* v. *Smith* (1538) 3 Leon. 88; *Reynolds* v. *Purchowe* (1585) Moore 412, Cro. Eliz. 429; *Lane* v. *Mallory* (1624) 1 Rolle 26. Similarly these cases provide an answer to Ames's attempt to argue that in the sixteenth century there were *two* forms of consideration only—detriment and precedent debt. See Ames, Lect. XIII. Ames, I suspect, was reluctant to attach importance to benefit consideration because he thought this would force him into admitting *quid pro quo* as the ancestor of consideration; hence he was led to throwing out the baby with the bath water.

[2] 1 Leon. 297.

[3] 1 Leon. 220, Cro. Eliz. 218.

that such gratuitous contracts had long been treated as actionable; nevertheless it is important to notice how easily the doctrine of consideration could be applied to them. The reason why the doctrine of consideration could be fitted to gratuitous contracts of loan and bailment is apparent so long as the meaning of the word consideration is not forgotten; in common sense the delivery of money on loan or the delivery of a chattel bailed is both a good reason ('consideration') why the borrower or bailee should promise to refund the loan or repay the money, and a good reason ('consideration') why such promises, made by a person who has benefited by the receipt, should be held binding.

The widest application of the conception of benefit as good consideration is in the case of a gratuitous deposit. In *Riches* v. *Brigges* (1602)[1] the plaintiff sued a depositee of wheat on a promise to redeliver, and obtained judgment in the King's Bench; Popham C.J. supported the decision by saying that,

> 'the very possession of so much wheat might be a credit and good countenance to the defendant, to be esteemed a rich farmer in the country . . .'

But this decision was reversed in the Exchequer Chamber, upon the ground that there was no sufficient consideration. A few years later in *Game* v. *Harvie* (1605)[2] the King's Bench allowed a plaintiff to sue in assumpsit on a loan of money on the ground that the defendant, not being liable to return the identical coins, had a benefit by the use of the money, and distinguished such a case from a deposit of money in a bag. Commenting upon the decision of the Exchequer Chamber in *Riches* v. *Brigges* the court maintained that the reversal had been erroneous, for in the earlier case similarly there had been no obligation to return the identical wheat, but this looks like an afterthought. The law was settled in conformity with this reasoning in *Pickas* v. *Guile* (1608).[3] Later, in *Wheatley* v. *Low*

[1] Yelv. 4, 6, Cro. Eliz. 833.
[2] Yelv. 50. cf. *Anon.* (1610) 2 Brownl. and Goulds. 40 and *Anon.* (1689) 2 Vent. 45.
[3] Yelv. 128. See also *Gellye* v. *Clark* (1606) Noy 126, distinguishing between a promise by an innkeeper depositee to keep hats safe (no benefit) and a horse (a benefit, since the horse ate food for which the innkeeper could charge). Cro. Jac. 188.

(1623),[1] it was held that the bare receipt of money was good consideration for a promise to pay the money over to a third party. Thus in the law of bailment it is clear that the doctrine of consideration does not serve to differentiate between gratuitous bailments and loans[2], and bailments and loans where there is remuneration or a commercial element.

Benefit consideration and 'quid pro quo'

Benefit as consideration, which embraces payment or recompense, looks as if it ought to be connected with the old doctrine of *quid pro quo* in the action of debt *sur contract*. There is a sense in which there is a connection. The doctrine of *quid pro quo* expresses in a technical legal form the idea that a party to a bilateral agreement who has received something of value in performance of the agreement ought not in the name of reciprocity to be allowed to get away with not performing his side of the agreement; it is fair to hold him to performance because he has received something in return, a *quid pro quo*. The doctrine that a benefit to the promisor is a good consideration in assumpsit also expresses the same idea in a technical legal form, though that form is different, and so there is a connection between the old and the new doctrine at this level; both reflect the same common-sense view of what is fair and just.

When it is claimed that there is a closer and direct connection between the two technical doctrines, the argument becomes weaker. The doctrine of *quid pro quo* was not very elaborately developed in medieval law; indeed it hardly merits the name of a doctrine.[3] It was not even applied with any great enthusiasm to the paradigm case of a bargain—the contract of sale—which was recognized as binding though executory in spite of the doctrine of *quid pro quo* rather than because of it. In addition there is a quite basic difference between the two doctrines, for there is nothing in the doctrine of *quid pro quo* to suggest the idea that the benefit received is relevant to liability *because it motivated a promise*; the benefit received was not thought of as a consideration. Thus even if it were true that the doctrine of

---

[1] Cro. Jac. 668, Palm. 281.

[2] It must be remembered that the original theory was that all loans were supposed to be gratuitous, because of the prohibition of usury.

[3] See above, p. 193.

quid pro quo suggested the rule that benefit should be a good consideration, we should have to look elsewhere for an answer to the question, 'why analyse liability in terms of considerations at all?'

Turning from these general arguments to the cases themselves it is a striking fact that there is very little reference to the doctrine of *quid pro quo* in assumpsit cases. One explanation of this is that the basis of the generalization that a benefit to the promisor is a good consideration is the recognition of marriage and payment or other recompense as consideration; neither marriage nor payment of money has been treated as a *quid pro quo* in debt. Where it is perhaps most surprising to find no reference to the doctrine of *quid pro quo* is in actions against simple contract debtors. Here one explanation is that no one who was anxious to encourage such actions would be likely to say that the consideration for the promise was the receipt of a *quid pro quo*, for if *quid pro quo* was the basis of liability surely the proper action was debt? Thus the payment of small sums of money for promises by parties to debt contracts was designed, for example, to make it clear that the payment of the money and not the *quid pro quo* in the contract was the basis of liability.[1] Actions of assumpsit against debtors were fitted into the law either by saying that consideration did not matter very much in such actions, or by saying that the fact that there was a debt owed was a sufficient consideration for a promise—i.e. a good reason for making a promise, and a good reason for enforcing such a promise. They were never explained by saying that the promise was supported by the *quid pro quo*.

Though there are few assumpsit cases in which there is explicit reference to the doctrine of *quid pro quo*,[2] there are cases in which the doctrine must clearly have been in the mind of the court,[3] and it is significant that in such cases the court

[1] See above, p. 301.
[2] I have only noted references in *Brett's Case* (1600) Cro. Eliz. 755; *Baxter* v. *Read* (1588) Dyer 272b (but *quare* if the original report included it), and *Anon.* (1588) Appendix, Case No. 13; in the last case the reference is related to an incidental point, the court holding that purported assignment of an interest in property by one who has no interest is not to be counted as performance of a promise to assign, because the assignee can derive no benefit from it. *Jordan's* or *Tatam's Case* (1535) Y.B. 27 Hen. VIII, M. f. 24, pl. 3 is an early example.
[3] This must surely be true of some of the cases cited on p. 422, n. 1, above, though it is impossible to prove this.

seems to have been anxious to deny the idea that assumpsit was to be restricted in its application to contracts supported by *quid pro quo*; on the contrary the theory of the matter was that assumpsit lay just in those cases where there was no debt contract. This is perhaps most clearly illustrated by the case of *Hinson* v. *Burridge* (1593).[1] Here the plaintiff had sold 200 hog-lambs[2] to one Dowling, the defendant's factor, to the use of the defendant. He sued the defendant in assumpsit on a promise to pay for the lambs the price agreed between the plaintiff and Dowling, the promise being laid in consideration of the sale to Dowling to the use of the defendant. In the King's Bench the plaintiff recovered, and error was brought in the Exchequer Chamber on the ground that debt lay against the defendant, and therefore assumpsit did not lie. The Exchequer Chamber rejected this argument; the sale was to Dowling, and *he* could have been sued in debt, but not the defendant. But the fact that the sale was to the use of the defendant was a sufficient ground for allowing him to be sued in assumpsit, notwithstanding the fact that the property in the lambs passed to Dowling, and not to the defendant. Thus here Dowling obtained the *quid pro quo*, though the benefit was to come to the defendant. Here therefore the decision turns on the distinction between the *quid pro quo* in debt and the consideration in assumpsit; in conformity with general theory debt and assumpsit were distinct remedies for distinct causes of action, and in consequence assumpsit could hardly be closely associated with the doctrine of *quid pro quo*.

(*d*) DETRIMENT, TRAVAIL, OR CHARGE

The rule that some service performed for the promisor would be a good consideration was clearly recognized in cases in the 1570s. Thus in *Rogers* v. *Snow* (1572)[3] we first meet in the context of assumpsit the famous case of the man who goes to York; it is said by Gawdy J. that a trip to York about the business of the promisor will be good consideration for a promise of pay-

---

[1] Moore 701.
[2] Lambs are still called 'hoggs' in the north of England.
[3] Dalison 94. See also *Onely* v. *Earl of Kent* (1576) Dyer 355b; *Webb's Case* (1577) 4 Leon. 110; *West* v. *Stowell* (1578) 2 Leon. 154, *Baxter* v. *Read* (1583) Dyer 272 *in margine*.

ment in return.[1] Though performance of some act or service in return or exchange for a promise is not *quite* the same thing as payment or recompense, the distinction is both legally and in common sense unimportant, and no decision was ever required to establish the rule. In the 1580s we meet in *Richards and Bartlett's Case* (1584)[2] and in *Stone* v. *Wythipol* (1588)[3] the familiar doctrine that a consideration can be either a benefit to the promisor or something of detriment to the promisee. Unlinked to the benefit–detriment analysis the rule that a detriment can be a good consideration is clearly formulated in *Manwood* v. *Burston* (1586).[4]

Now in very many situations the consideration for a promise can be viewed both as a benefit to the promisor and as a detriment to the promisee; thus if Smith performs work for Jones, and Jones promises money in return, the labour of Smith is both detrimental to him and beneficial to Jones. To cover situations of this type there is no purpose in having a rule allowing detriment as consideration, in addition to benefit, for the detriment rule would be simply redundant. It is easy enough, however, to construct situations in which there has been detriment to Smith but no benefit to Jones.[5] Thus Smith may perform the work requested, but this may not bring any benefit to Jones; for example, he may have been requested to go to London and try to obtain a pardon for Jones, and he may have done so without success, so that no benefit comes to Jones from his efforts.[6] Or he may have been requested to perform some work which brings benefit to a third party, but

---

[1] The example has degenerated since Gawdy's time; he at least tells us why the man is to go to York. Versions are common in medieval law in connection with conditions, usually using Rome as the terminal. In modern times Paris has been used by Dr. Goodhart.

[2] 1 Leon. 19.

[3] Cro. Eliz. 126, 1 Leon. 113, Owen 94.
'Every consideration that doth charge the defendant in an assumpsit must be to the benefit of the defendant or charge of the plaintiff, and no case can be put out of this rule'
per Coke *arguendo*. Possibly derived from *Onely* v. *Earl of Kent* (1577) Dyer 355b.

[4] 2 Leon. 203.

[5] It is difficult to find cases where there has been a benefit consideration but no detriment; this is the basis of the argument that benefit is unimportant. Gratuitous deposit is a possible example.

[6] For example see *Lampleigh* v. *Braithwaite* (1616) Hob. 105. Moore 866, 1 Brownl. and Goulds. 7.

not Jones—for example, to cure a poor man of a disease. Clearly in such situations a rule expressed in terms of detriment will cover the case, whilst a rule expressed in terms of benefit will not.

There seems to be no example in the early-sixteenth-century law of uses of an induced detriment being treated as consideration to pass a use; detriment consideration is peculiar to assumpsit, and in assumpsit *as consideration for a promise* features in the cases from the 1570s onwards. But the rule that there can be an action of assumpsit where there has been injurious reliance upon the promise at the inducement of the promisor can be traced back long before it was expressed in terms of consideration. Indeed the story really begins in the fifteenth century.

In the fifteenth-century year-books there had been some discussion of what the legal position was if a man procured another to perform some work of charity upon his behalf, and promised to pay for the work involved.[1] The problem is discussed in terms of standard examples: a promise to pay a schoolmaster to teach the promisor's son, a promise to a surgeon to pay for the curing of a poor man, a promise to a labourer to pay him for mending a highway. Clearly in such cases the promisor was neither recompensed for his promise nor did he acquire any worldly benefit from the performance of the promise, so that if he were to be held liable to an action of debt for the payment, his liability could not be based in a secular court upon the receipt of a benefit. Cases of this kind were thought to be closely analogous to promises given on account of marriage, the stock example being a promise by a father to a suitor of money if the suitor married the promisor's daughter. But the analogy was not precise, for in the case of marriage it could be argued, though the argument is rather forced, that the father did obtain a worldly benefit—pleasure at the advancement of his daughter—and this argument could be used to distinguish promises on account of marriage from other charitable promises.[2] The reason why some lawyers thought that the analogy was strong was presumably the fact that mak-

[1] See *Alice's Case* (1458) 37 Hen. VI, M. f. 8, pl. 18, where the example of the surgeon and the poor man is put by Moyle J., and Y.B. 17 Edw. IV, (1478) f. 4, pl. 4; this latter case is obviously the source of the examples put in *Doctor and Student*.

[2] The Student argues in this way in *Doctor and Student*.

ing provision for the marriage of a poor maid or servant was just as much a charitable undertaking (and a spiritual matter) as healing the sick, providing for education, aiding the poor, and helping the traveller.

It was never settled in medieval law that the action of debt lay in such cases. There was, however, a school of thought which maintained that some action ought to be allowed, and St. Germain stated its theory in this form:

> 'And therefore after divers that be learned in the laws of the realm, all promises shall be taken in this manner, that is to say, if he to whom the promise is made have a charge by reason of the promise, which he hath also performed, then in that case he shall have an action for that thing that was promised though he that made the promise have no worldly profit by it.'[1]

If we are to take 'all promises' seriously, this doctrine is advanced as an alternative to a doctrine of *causa promissionis*, for the cause of such a promise (love of charity on expectation of spiritual benefit) was not the sort of cause which a secular common lawyer could regard as relevant in a lay court. By emphasizing the charge performed, it would serve to justify an extension of liability to the category of case discussed, whilst still referring all liability to a single principle. As far as charitable promises were concerned, the new doctrine, if accepted, would lead to a compromise whereby only a limited number of charitable promises were made actionable, where the injurious reliance upon the promise by the person who directly performed the work of charity provided a special reason for allowing a remedy, especially as it may have been thought that once payment was promised the promisee was morally bound to perform the act.[2]

---

[1] *Doctor and Student*. Dial. II, c. 24. The examples given in *Doctor and Student* are a promise for healing a poor man, making a highway, fasting all Lent, marrying the promisor's daughter.

[2] The use of the conception of 'charge' in *Doctor and Student* is difficult to understand. In one passage the Student seems to be suggesting that the Surgeon who is promised payment for healing a poor man (etc.) is in some way obliged to perform the cure through the promise of payment. Perhaps the idea is that in the examples given the Surgeon, once promised payment, is *morally* bound to perform the work of charity: in some sense he is no longer a free agent, for to refuse to perform the cure would be spiritually dangerous. *Sed quaere.*

This doctrine was never established in medieval law; the earliest case in which it was held that debt, as opposed to assumpsit, lay where the benefit had been conferred on a third party at the defendant's request is *Lady Shandois* v. *Simson* (1602).[1] However, it was mooted at just the right time to be incorporated into the learning of assumpsit. Thus in *Cleymond* v. *Vincent* (1521),[2] where the King's Bench allowed an action against the executors of a parole guarantor of a debt due on a contract of sale, the doctrine later stated by St. Germain is laconically referred to by Fineux C.J. as one justification for the decision, to allow an action on a gratuitous parole guarantee of a debt:

'he [the creditor] by the promise is to have a prejudice.'

It was acted upon, though not in terms referred to, in *Jordan's* or *Tatam's Case* (1535).[3] Here the facts were that Jordan had Tatam imprisoned in the Counter for a debt, and the defendant undertook to pay the debt if Tatam were discharged from prison. Jordan discharged the debtor Tatam, and successfully sued the defendant on his promise. In *Jordan's Case* Luke J. mentions a similar decision adjudged in favour of the plaintiff a few years earlier, where,

'a stranger came with a man to a Baker of London and said to the Baker, "Give this man as much bread as he wants and if he does not pay you I will," and the Baker delivered certain bread to the man, who did not pay him, and the Baker brought his action on the case on the special matter against the stranger, and the stranger demurred in law, and it was adjudged clearly that the action lay, and the Baker recovered.'

Tatam's Case was expressly approved by Dyer C.J. in *Lord Grey's Case* (1567),[4] where the principle of injurious reliance was expressly married to the newly formulated doctrine that a

---

[1] Cro. Eliz. 880. The doctrine was not, however, justified by reference to the 'charge' or 'detriment' doctrine. *Nelson's Case* (unrep.) in 1585 holds the contrary. The ingenious explanation of apparently conflicting cases by Ames (94) is not to be found expressed in Elizabethan cases.

[2] Y.B. 12 Hen. VIII, P. f. 11, pl. 13.

[3] Y.B. 27 Hen. VIII, M. f. 24, pl. 3.

[4] Appendix, Case No. 10.

good consideration was necessary to charge a defendant in assumpsit,

> 'And so it is that if a man is in execution at your suit, and I say "Discharge him, and if he does not pay I am willing to do so", this is a good consideration, if you discharge him, to charge me in an action on the case, for there because of my promise you discharged the execution as in *Tatam's Case* in twenty seven Henry VIII.'

The discussion in the inconclusive case of *Sukley* v. *Wyte* (1543),[1] where action was brought on a promise to save harmless a sheriff in arresting a burgess of Parliament makes it clear that contempoary lawyers were well aware of the gratuitous character of the promises involved in transactions of this kind, and some at least did not think that this alone constituted an insuperable objection to imposing liability.

Now it is true that in none of these cases—except possibly *Cleymond* v. *Vincent*[2]—is there any explicit reference to the charitable nature of the promise. Nevertheless it is not improbable that these early decisions which favoured the use of assumpsit for the breach of gratuitous promises—and it must be emphasized that the cases all concern gratuitous promises— were influenced by the charitable nature of the transaction; to aid the debtor, to release the prisoner, and to feed the poor were all charitable and godly activities. In the context of contemporary thought the demands of Christian charity may well have influenced the courts as strongly as the demands of commerce, and this may explain how it was that gratuitous promises came to be actionable in assumpsit in certain specially defined circumstances.[3] But this does not mean that in later-sixteenth-century law detriment consideration was associated with the enforcement of charitable promises; induced detri-

---

[1] Appendix, Case No. 9.

[2] Fineux C.J. also gives as a reason peril to the soul of the deceased guarantor. The soul may be in danger not simply because the debt is unpaid, but because the work of charity has been frustrated.

[3] For later references to charitable promises see *Sharrington* v. *Strotton* (1566) Plowden 298 at 305 (commentary upon Y.B. 17 Edw. IV, f. 4, pl. 4), *Onely* v. *Earl of Kent* (1576), 'and Dyer thought the consideration above good and legal and charitable, so to aid and ease a feme sole in her widowhood in her affairs'.

ment could be found in cases involving no charitable purpose whatsoever, and *Sukley* v. *Wyte* (1543) is such a case.[1]

The charge or detriment which was discussed in *Doctor and Student*, and incorporated into the law of assumpsit in these early cases, was not spoken of as the cause or consideration for the promise. Indeed in *Doctor and Student* the charge or detriment theory is apparently put forward as an *alternative* to an analysis in terms of consideration or cause; the Student, in putting the theory forward, is in effect saying that it is possible to ignore the charitable motive, or the motive of obtaining spiritual merit, which is the consideration which explains why the promise was made, and possible to base liability upon injurious reliance alone. Indeed it would have been possible, and perhaps preferable, to build up a law of parole contracts solely around the injurious reliance principle, just as it would have been possible to reject it entirely in favour of the notion of cause. But instead of doing so, the Elizabethan lawyers married the notion of injurious reliance to the analysis in terms of reasons for promises. But they did not work out the consequences of this uneasy alliance with perfect consistency. The logical consequence ought to have been to hold that a plaintiff who relied upon a detriment as consideration should be required to show that the promise had been made with the purpose of inducing the detrimental act or omission, for only thus could the detriment be the consideration in the original sense of motivating aim. In general this did become the rule, with the curious exception of past consideration furnished at request, which this rule could not be made to fit. But the natural requirement derived from a theory of injurious reliance is that the detriment must be induced by the promisor, not that it should be the motive for the promise, and the difference, though nice, is not always unimportant.

Indeed some writers, impressed by the fact that a rule stated in terms of detriment will, if coupled to the insistence that consideration must move from the promisee, always include situations which would fall under a rule stated in terms of

---

[1] In *Manwood* v. *Burston* (1586) 2 Leon. 203 the doctrine is still linked to the example of a charitable promise, 'where he to whom the promise is made is damnified by doing any thing, or spends his labour at the instance of the promiser, although no benefit cometh to the promiser; as I agree with a surgeon to cure a poor man (who is a stranger unto me) of a sore'.

benefit, have drawn the conclusion that benefit consideration is accidental and unimportant. But this is to confuse systematics with writing history. Perhaps sixteenth-century lawyers might have developed the doctrine of consideration around detriment to the promisee only, and perhaps the law would have been simpler if they had done so, and more elegant; it seems a pity to have a number of rules if one rule will do the same job. But for better or for worse they did not in fact do this,[1] though there is evidence that the idea was acceptable to some. The strongest statement is in *Chapman* v. *Barnaby* (1615),[2]

'for the matter considerable in such actions upon the case for promises made is not whether the party, which doth thus assume, hath, or is to have any benefit thereby but only whether the other, to whom the promise is thus made, hath any manner of prejudice by it.'

But this may be limited by its context to action against an executor on a promise in consideration of forbearance.

Detriment consideration has been explained in two other ways. According to one theory, the source is the rule that in an action on the case the plaintiff must show damage.[3] According to the other, which is in fact a more refined version of the first, the source is the fact that assumpsit is an action for a deceitful wrong,[4] or at least began life as such. Both theories claim that a requirement which originated when assumpsit was a *tortious* action came to be viewed differently when the action became *contractual*. These theories both depend upon certain preconceptions about the history of the theory of damage in assumpsit actions, the most important being that assumpsit began life as an action for restitution, and at some point changed its

---

[1] The argument is typically put forward by Holdsworth, *H.E.L.* VIII. 3–11; also by Street, *Foundations of Legal Liability*, III. 68, accepting the argument of Langdell, Contracts S 68. And see E. H. Bennett, 'Is Mere Gain to Promisor a Good Consideration?', 10 H.L.R. 257.

[2] 2 Bulst. 278. For other illustrations of the constant repetition of the rule that a detriment sufficed see *Lane* v. *Mallory* (1614) 1 Rolle 26; *Freeman* v. *Freeman* (1614) 1 Rolle Rep. 61; *Covill* v. *Geffery* (1619) 2 Rolle 96; *March* v. *Culpeper* (1626) Cro. Car. 70; *Kirby* v. *Towerson* (1680) 2 Show 95.

[3] Hare, *Contracts*, Chs. VII and VIII, *H.E.L.* VIII 10.

[4] This was Ames's view; see Lect. XIII. It has been championed in modern times by Milsom, 'Not Doing is No Trespass', (1954) Camb. L.J. 105, though in a modified form.

character and became an action in which a plaintiff recovered a substitute for performance; I shall discuss these assumptions in connection with the history of damages.

(e) NATURAL LOVE AND AFFECTION

Friendship between persons who were not blood relations, or related by marriage, was held not to be a good consideration in *Hunt* v. *Bate* (1568),[1] and this was not subsequently questioned, though only a year earlier Dyer C.J. in *Lord Grey's Case* (1567)[2] had argued that,

'And therefore if my brother, cousin or friend is indebted to you, and I say to you "If he does not pay you I shall", here if you forbear because of this to sue and charge my friend, this is a good consideration to charge me, *for what you did in ease of and for the benefit of my friend is to my ease and benefit also.*'

This would link friendship to benefit consideration, but the idea was not followed. The position over natural love and affection 'within the family' is not quite so straightforward, and one reason for this is the fact that it was recognized in the law of uses as good consideration to pass a use. However, the general principle, which was established by the decision in *Harford* v. *Gardiner* (1587),[3] was that natural love and affection was not a good consideration in assumpsit. Here the plaintiff declared

'that the defendant, in consideration that the father of the plaintiff had imployed his service about the business of the testator of the defendant, to the great profit of the testator, and in consideration of love and affection that the testator bore to the plaintiff, promised to give unto him £100'.

The court ruled that,

'Love is not a consideration upon which an action can be grounded: the like of friendship'.

Quite why the courts adopted this general principle is nowhere stated, and, in view of the adoption of the opposite principle in the law of uses, there is an apparent inconsistency. However,

[1] Dyer 272.
[2] Appendix, Case No. 10.
[3] 2 Leon. 31.

the inconsistency is not so glaring as appears at first sight. The practical consequence of the rule that 'natural love and affection' was a consideration to pass a use was that it enabled the courts to give effect to family settlements of landed property, usually though not exclusively executed in connection with a marriage. Where marriage was the cause of an agreement, the courts, as we shall see, introduced an exception to the general rule that natural love and affection was irrelevant in assumpsit, and in consequence most family agreements involving payment of money were as effectively sanctioned by assumpsit as were family agreements involving land.

We have seen that marriage was accepted as a good consideration in assumpsit just as in the law of uses. This rule could be related to a principle stated in terms of benefit (a father derives a benefit from the advancement of his daughter) or it could be related to a principle stated in terms of natural love and affection (a father is liable upon a promise given on account of the marriage of his daughter because the consideration for such a promise is parental love and affection) or prior obligation in natural law. In the main it mattered little which theory one adopted; the end product would be the same. However, in *Hunt* v. *Bate* (1568)[1] the common law adopted in assumpsit the doctrine that a consideration past at the moment of promising was bad, and the adoption of this doctrine gave rise to some difficulty over family agreements. For suppose a father, instead of promising a dowry before or at the time of marriage, promises it a few days later; such a promise will be given for a past consideration, and will therefore be unenforceable. This struck contemporaries as silly, perhaps because a covenant to stand seised to uses in the same circumstances would be effective, the parental love then being a good consideration to pass the use. If effective for land, why not for money?

The problem could be evaded in many cases by the doctrine of precedent request, whereby a past act was good consideration if it had been requested or induced by the promisor, and this doctrine could be applied to marriage.[2] But what was to

---

[1] Dyer 272.

[2] For example, in the anonymous case in 1568, reported with *Hunt* v. *Bate*, Dyer 272a.

happen if the marriage had not been previously requested by the father? This problem came before the judges in the great case of *Marsh* v. *Rainsford* (1586).[1] Marsh had been negotiating with Rainsford with a view to marrying Rainsford's daughter, but negotiations broke down, whereupon Marsh took the bit between his teeth and eloped with the lady, marrying her without the knowledge or consent of her father. However, in the way parents do, Rainsford accepted this *fait accompli*, and subsequently promised Marsh £200 in consideration that he had married his daughter. Of this promise Rainsford must have repented, for he failed to pay the money, and was therefore sued upon it by Marsh. The action was allowed, upon the ground that the father's natural love and affection for the daughter continued, and provided a good consideration for the father's promise; thus although the marriage was past, the natural love and affection of a father for his daughter continued all the time, and thus could never be past, but was always a present consideration.[2] In modern parlance, parental love for a child is at all times a very good reason for making a promise for the advancement of the child. This reasoning is linked in all probability to the idea that marriage as consideration is good because of a wider principle that natural love and affection is a good consideration.[3]

The court of King's Bench which decided this case had recently, in *Style* v. *Smith* held that a promise by a father of payment to a surgeon who had treated the defendant's son without his request was actionable; there is no surviving report but presumably the doctrine applied was the same. Thus although natural love and affection was not by itself a good consideration in assumpsit, nevertheless a promise given in consideration of natural love and affection and in consideration of a past act (which would be a good consideration if not

[1] 2 Leon. 112, Cro. Eliz. 59 (*sub nom Marsh* v. *Kaverford*) Dyer 272b *in margine.* A better report is printed from a MS. in the Appendix, Case No. 11.

[2] The doctrine in the case was denied by Clench J. in *Pearle* v. *Edwards* (1586) 1 Leon. 102. It was first stated in *Sidenham* v. *Worlington* (1584) 1 Leon. 324 by Anderson C.J. ('for marriage is always a present consideration') and accepted in *Halifax* v. *Barker* (1598) by Walmesley J. in the Common Pleas. See Dyer 271b.n.

[3] Thus it is hinted, but not decided, in *Browne* v. *Garborough* (1587) Cro. Eliz. 64 that marriage would only be a good consideration to support a promise by a relative, and not by a stranger.

past, or if requested) was actionable.[1] Natural love and affection was relevant therefore in that it was the basis for an exception to the general invalidity of past consideration. A modified version of the same doctrine, which avoided allowing natural love and affection as consideration at all was simply to say that marriage (a continuous state) was always a continuous consideration.

(f) THE EXISTENCE OF A DEBT

In an action of assumpsit against a debtor it was not strictly necessary to aver consideration as such;[2] the theory of the matter was not that consideration in such cases was irrelevant, but rather that there was no need to state the obvious, which was that the debt, or perhaps more accurately the state of indebtedness, was the consideration for the promise.[3] It became the practice, however, to allege consideration in such actions, and where the action was pleaded as an action of *indebitatus assumpsit* the consideration alleged was the precedent debt. The doctrine that a precedent debt was a good consideration is first clearly stated in *Manwood* v. *Burston* (1587).[4] A clear illustration of the principle is the case of *Egles* v. *Vale* (1603)[5] decided in the Exchequer Chamber. The plaintiff declared on an account taken upon which the defendant had been found in arrears to the extent of £10, and upon a promise to pay the sum. It was moved,

'there is not any consideration nor cause to ground such an action, for the being found in arrears is not any cause to make a special promise, nor is there any thing done on the plaintiff's part whereupon this promise should be grounded, viz. the forbearing of the suit or any such thing. *Sed non allocantur*, for the debt itself without other special cause is sufficient to ground the action'.

[1] See *Brett's Case* (1600) Cro. Eliz. 755 (promise by mother in consideration of natural love and affection for her son and, in part, a past consideration, held good).

[2] See above, p. 408.

[3] *Gill* v. *Harewood* (1586) 1 Leon. 61; *Anon.* (1581) Godbolt 13; *Smith* v. *Johnson* (1600) Moore 601.

[4] 2 Leon. 203.

[5] Cro. Jac. 69.

When in the seventeenth century the modified *indebitatus assumpsit* form became the usual mode of declaration in actions against debtors, a debt precedent became one of the most typical forms of consideration.[1] Actions against debtors were of course established, in the King's Bench at least, well before the scope of assumpsit became limited by a doctrine of consideration, so that the application of the doctrine to this class of case was retrospective. The theory of the matter seems to have been straightforward; the fact that a debt is owed is a good reason for a promise by the debtor to pay, and a good reason for holding him liable to pay. There is no link in the cases with the doctrine of *quid pro quo*.[2] Before the doctrine of consideration was attached to assumpsit it was at least a common practice to allege payment of a small sum of money for a promise to pay the debt, such allegations being often fictional;[3] with the rise of the idea that a promise given for good reason was actionable, this subterfuge became unnecessary. The consideration averred in special assumpsit against a debtor would be a benefit conferred to or to be conferred, not a precedent debt. The existence of a debt could not, however, be a consideration for a promise to do anything other than pay the debt in money. In *Godwin* v. *Batkin* (1652)[4] the defendant, in consideration of a debt of £20, promised to deliver certain cattle; this was held to be *nudum pactum*. No clearer paradigm example of the basic idea of consideration could be found—the consideration shows what ought to be done, and the promise merely reinforces an existing duty.

(g) THE POSSESSION OF PROPERTY BELONGING TO THE PROMISEE

One who found or in some other way came into possession of property belonging to the plaintiff was liable to be sued in detinue *sur trover* for its wrongful detention, or in an action on

---

[1] The decision in *Hodge* v. *Vavisour* (1616) 3 Bulst. 222, 1 Rolle 413, got over the difficulty of past consideration. See also *Jeremy* v. *Goochman* (1595) Cro. Eliz. 442; *Rampston* v. *Bowman* (1584) 3 Leon. 98 (consideration past).

[2] Ames, Lect. XIII at p. 129 does not distinguish between the recognition of assumpsit against debtors, and the application of the doctrine of consideration to this class of action.

[3] See above, p. 301 and *Lord Grey's Case* (1567) Appendix, Case No. 9. Another example is *Smith* v. *Johnson* Moo. K.B. 601.

[4] Style 330.

the case for trover and conversion for wrongful conversion, or indeed if he had not taken possession to look after the thing to the use of the owner he could in theory be sued in trespass *de bonis asportatis*. Threatened with this formidable battery of remedies one might have thought enough was enough, but in *Ireland* v. *Higgins* (1587)[1] assumpsit was brought against the finder of a lost greyhound upon a promise to return the dog to its owner. The defendant demurred to the declaration on the ground that a dog was *ferae naturae* and once out of possession property was lost, and this provoked an amusing discussion of the legal status of dogs, it being argued that the law recognized four types of dog—mastiffs, hounds, spaniels, and tumblers—in which property could be had. Since the action was taken on the promise the relevance of 'property' is not at once apparent—it is that if the dog belonged to the plaintiff then the defendant had a very good reason for promising to return it, and the court a good reason for holding the promise actionable, since the defendant had promised to do what it is his duty to do anyway. If on the other hand the dog was a *res nullius* the promise would be a mere voluntary promise, and thus not actionable. According to William Sheppard, the promise in such a case could be implied,

'So where one findeth my goods, hee is chargeable to mee for them, by reason of his possession, by the Law in this Action, upon the implicite assumpsit'.[2]

(h) THE POSSESSION OF ASSETS BY EXECUTORS AND ADMINISTRATORS

Closely analogous was the position of personal representatives, who might be liable upon promises made in consideration of their possession of the assets of the deceased.

The liability of personal representatives in a representative capacity, where judgment would be against the goods of the testator (*de bonis testatoribus*) is discussed later;[3] after very considerable controversy it came to be settled that they could be sued for simple contract debts, this being settled in *Pinchon's*

---

[1] Cro. Eliz. 125, Owen 93, Hetley 50.
[2] Sheppard 24.
[3] See below, p. 567.

Case (1611).[1] It was a point of controversy whether the plaintiff in such an action had to aver that the executor had sufficient assets to pay debts and legacies, but it was settled in the end that no such averment was needed. The possession of assets here did not rank as a consideration, but merely as a precondition for any enforceable liability, since execution could only be against the assets of the deceased.

Rather different questions arose when personal representatives were sued in their personal capacity on their own promise to discharge some liability incurred by the testator, or pay legacies willed by a testator. The background to the practice of making such promises was that a personal representative who had discharged some liability due by the deceased was entitled to recoup himself from the estate, and furthermore that in the absence of a residuary legatee he was in any event entitled to the balance of the estate. Now special promises by representatives, in accordance with ordinary principle, had to be supported by consideration. This might take a variety of forms. Sometimes the plaintiff would rely upon a payment of money to the personal representative for the promise. Or he might rely upon a forbearance to sue the personal representatives. Or finally he might rely for consideration upon the fact of the duty owed to him (to pay the debt or legacy) coupled with the fact that the defendant had sufficient assets to satisfy it. Put simply the argument here was that the duty, and the possession of assets, added up to a good reason for the promise, and a good reason why such a promise should be binding. The law on this subject was controversial for a very long period, and came to a head in the eighteenth century in the well-known decisions of Lord Mansfield's court in *Rann* v. *Hughes* (1778)[2] and *Hawkes* v. *Saunders* (1782)[3] and the controversy associated with these and other decisions of Lord Mansfield. I shall first consider the status of promises to pay legacies.

The basic principle was that no action lay at common law to compel the payment of a legacy, since matters testamentary were the concern of the ecclesiastical courts.[4] At some uncertain

---

[1] 9 Co.Rep. 86b.
[2] 7 T.R. 350 n.a. 4 Brown P.C. 27.
[3] 1 Cowp. 289.
[4] 10 Hen. IV, M. f. 1, pl. 2. There was long dispute as to whether one was

period the Chancery also acquired a jurisdiction.[1] The earliest attempt to bring an action on the case seems to be in 1538, where the plaintiff alleged that the testator had left him a legacy of £20, and after his death the plaintiff paid his executor one shilling for a promise to pay the legacy; this had not been performed, and the plaintiff had in consequence lost credit with others to whom he owed money. The action succeeded,[2] but the decision does not infringe the general principle, which appears to have been maintained until the Commonwealth[3] when the common law courts allowed actions for legacies on the ground that the ecclesiastical courts were not sitting.[4] In *Smith* v. *Jones* (1610)[5] there was a decision to the effect that an action did not lie on an executor's promise to pay a legacy in consideration of forbearance to sue him for the legacy, he having assets to pay; the basic ground was jurisdictional, in that the executor was not liable at common law and therefore forbearance to sue when he could not be sued could be no consideration for his promise. Contrary decisions were given in *Bothe* v. *Crampton* (1622)[6] and *Davis* v. *Reyner* (1671)[7] and it was further held in these cases that an averment of assets was not necessary. The rationale of these decisions may have been that forbearance to present a suit in Chancery was a good consideration, as a detriment to the promisor and benefit to promisee. There is also a statement in argument in *Eeles* v. *Lambert* (1671)[8] that an action lies on a promise to pay a legacy, but no decision to this effect. These are the only relevant authorities[9] and they do not entail the view that an action lay

[1] See Gareth Jones, *History of the Law of Charity*, pp. 5 et seq.
[2] Spilman's MS. Reports, C.U.L. MS. Gg. ll. 5, f. 31.
[3] See *Lloyd* v. *Maddox* (1616) Moo. K.B. 917. Difficulties arose, however, over legacies payable out of the proceeds of sale of land under trust for sale, on which see *Paschall* v. *Keterich* (1557) Dyer 151b, Benloe 60; *Anon.* (1568) Dyer 264b; *Love* v. *Naplesden* (1611) Cro. Jac. 279, and cf. *Edwards* v. *Graves* (1619) Hob. 265.
[4] *Butler* v. *Butler* (1657) 2 Sid. 21; *Nicholson* v. *Sherman* (1661) 1 Sid. 45, T. Raymond 23 after the Restoration holds that no action lies.
[5] Yelv. 184, Cro. Jac. 257, 1 Bulst. 44.
[6] Cro. Jac. 613.
[7] 2 Lev. 3, 1 Vent. 120.
[8] Style 54.
[9] The other authorities relied upon by Buller and Mansfield are irrelevant to the *precise point at issue*.

entitled to take a chattel left by will, or await delivery by the executors. See 37 Hen. VI, f. 30, pl. 11.

to recover a legacy in consideration of assets, though the forbearance consideration might well be virtually fictional.
There appears therefore to be no direct justification for the
claim put forward in argument by Buller in *Atkins* v. *Hill*
(1775)[1] and accepted by the King's Bench in that case and in
Rann v. *Hughes* and *Hawkes* v. *Saunders*[2] that at common law an
action lay on a promise to pay a legacy in consideration of
assets (rather than in consideration of forbearance), so far as
early authority is concerned, though there is some authority
for this in eighteenth-century law. However, the authorities
come very near to allowing such an action, and the contention
of Mansfield and Buller is based upon a generalization from the
case of promises to pay debts—a perfectly respectable form of
legal reasoning in the common law system.

Promises by executors or administrators to pay simple
contract debts due by the testator raised somewhat similar
problems. For until the decision in *Pinchon's Case* in 1611 it
was a matter of controversy whether they were liable even in
their representative capacity, and if they were not (as some
thought) then a special promise to pay a debt was in the same
case as a special promise to pay a legacy, being a promise to
discharge a liability which was not in itself legally enforceable
even in the courts christian, though it was not doubted that
there existed a moral duty on executors to pay debts. Attempts
to bring actions against executors and administrators personally, with the consequence that judgment would be a general
judgment or a judgment *de bonis propriis*, take two forms. In the
first the plaintiff sues on a promise by the representative in
consideration of forbearance to sue him in his representative
capacity.[3] Here the leading case is *Sir William Bane's Case*
(1611),[4] where it was held that the declaration in such an
action did not need to aver that the defendant had assets

---

[1] 1 Cowp. 284.

[2] 7 T.R. 350 n.a., 1 Cowp. 289.

[3] For earlier examples see *Stone* v. *Wythipol* (1588) Owen 94, 1 Leon. 113,
Latch 21, Cro. Eliz. 126; *Estrigge* v. *Owles* (1587) 3 Leon. 201; *Trewinion* v.
Howell (1589) Cro. Eliz. 91, 1 Leon. 94.

[4] 9 Co.Rep. 93b, Cro. Jac. 273, following *Cottingham* v. *Hulett* (1586) Cro.
Eliz. 59; *Lingmill* v. *Broughton* (1616) Moo. K.B. 853 followed *Bane's Case*. See
also *Bigg* v. *Malin* (1618) Hutton 27; *Bothe* v. *Crampton* (1621) Cro. Jac.
613; *Davies* v. *Warner* (1620), Cro. Jac. 593; *Evans* v. *Warren* (1620) Cro. Jac.
604.

sufficient to satisfy the debt. The defendant's counsel had objected to the declaration,

> 'for if she [the executrix] does not have assets then this is *nudum pactum*, for there is no consideration to charge her or bind her to her promise . . .'

The Exchequer Chamber held as a pleading point that an averment of assets was not needed on the ground that it should be presumed prima facie that she had assets; the theory of the action was, however, that the forbearance of suit *and* and the possession of assets were the consideration for the promise. Later decisions went beyond this by holding that the possession of assets was quite irrelevant,[1] so that the forbearance alone was the ground of the action. In conformity with this it was held in *Hume* v. *Hinton* (1651) that the defendant was liable in assumpsit even if he was not an executor at all, but this remained questionable law.[2] Forbearance might be little more than fiction. *Bane's Case* settled a controversy between the Common Pleas and the King's Bench,[3] the former court having disapproved of such actions and overruled decisions of the King's Bench in the Exchequer Chamber. The Common Pleas view was that, since a simple contract debt was not recoverable against executors anyway, a forbearance to sue for such a debt could not be regarded as a sufficient consideration for a promise to pay, and once the Common Pleas lost the battle in *Pinchon's Case* over actions against representatives in their representative capacity the decision in *Bane's Case* logically followed; hence Coke reports the cases side by side in his Reports.

A more radical line of development may be traced from *Lord Grey's Case* in 1567[4] to the decision in *Rann* v. *Hughes* (1778). In the former case a son was sued for the debt of his deceased father, in consideration of a nominal payment of two shillings (this being admittedly fictional); Dyer C.J. and Weston

---

[1] See Style 304 and *Hayward* v. *Ducket* 1653 at p. 405.
[2] *Spade* v. *Barker* (1627) Palm. 522, *Davis* v. *Reyner* (1671) 1 Leon. 3, 1 Vent. 20 (dealing with a legacy).
[3] See *Mathew* v. *Mathew* (1595) Moo. K.B. 702 (Exch. Ch.) and *Fisher* v. *Richardson* (1603) Cro. Jac. 47 (Q.B.).
[4] Appendix, Case No. 10, and see *per* Egerton S.G. in *Stone* v. *Wythipol* (1588) Owen 94.

J. seem to have inclined to allow the action, and, according to what Egerton said in 1588, did so,

> 'where the Lord Grey, being heir to the former Lord Grey, although he was not bound to pay the debts of his father upon simple contract, yet in regard he did assume to pay them, he was made chargeable. And in 15 and 16 Eliz.[1] it is a good consideration where an administrator undertakes to pay debts upon a simple contract.'

A note, which is in the same year, and probably refers to the same case,[2] states particularly clearly the doctrine of prior obligation,

> 'If a man makes a simple contract and dies, and has no goods, but he has lands which descend to his heir, yet his heir is not chargeable. But if his heir assumes upon himself to pay this duty a good action lies against him, for there is a privity between the son and the father notwithstanding the fact that before [i.e. before the promise] he was not chargeable, but now he has made himself chargeable'.

The rationale of this view was restated by Chief Justice Dyer in these terms in another case in the same year,[3]

> 'Also the Lord Dyer said that although an action does not lie against executors on an assumpsit given by the testator, if the executor himself undertakes to pay this debt an action . well lies against him, for he is charged in conscience to pay this'.

Charged in conscience means in our terms both 'morally obliged' and 'liable in Chancery', and the same notion is used by Egerton in *Stone* v. *Wythipol* (1588)[4] to justify an action based on forbearance,

> 'but admitting the Executor be not chargeable by law, yet in equity and conscience he is chargeable in Chancery; and when he promiseth in consideration that the Plaintiff will not sue him, that is a good consideration'.

[1] Not traced.
[2] Bodl. MS. Rawl. C. 113, f. 262.
[3] Bodl. MS. Rawl. C. 113, f. 261.
[4] Owen 94.

The linking between what comes to be called the doctrine of moral obligation and the liability in Chancery is inevitable, granted the conception of the Chancery as a court of Conscience (i.e. in our terms a court of morals). After Dyer's death in 1582 the Common Pleas seems to have turned against imposing liability in such cases, and in 1587 it is noted that there had recently been a decision in the Common Pleas to this effect.[1] Wray C.J., who became Chief Justice of the Queen's Bench in 1574, seems to have been more sympathetic,[2] and in his court the doctrine was applied in *Trewinian* v. *Howell* (1587),[3] on a writ of error. The plaintiff alleged a promise by the defendant, executor to his brother, to pay a debt if he had goods sufficient, and coupled this with an averment that he had goods sufficient.

'The principal error assigned was that there is no sufficient consideration alleged, for the having of goods is no consideration. But in consideration he would forbear to sue etc., this had been a good consideration. But it was said of the other party, that he being executor, his promise (he having assets) doth bind him, for it is his duty to pay.'

The court upheld the action, and it appears from the report that similar decisions had been given in *Hudson's Case* and *Sir William Cook's Case*; the judgment in such case should be *de bonis propriis*.[4] The doctrine in *Trewinian's Case* was revived by Buller and Mansfield[5] in the eighteenth century, Buller probably being the moving spirit, and generalized, being applied both to cases involving debts and to cases involving legacies, as we have seen. The reason for the absence of cases illustrating the doctrine after *Trewinian* v. *Howell* is probably that averment of forbearance as consideration for such promises became the standard form.

Adequacy of consideration

In modern law it is well established that the courts will not investigate what is called the *adequacy* of consideration; if I am

---

[1] Noted by Gawdy J. in Owen at p. 95.
[2] See *Chapman* v. *Barnaby* (1614) 2 Bulst. 279.
[3] Cro. Eliz. 91. See also *Hodgson* v. *Maynard* (1576) 3 Leon. 67.
[4] See also *Wheeler* v. *Collier* (1594) Cro. Eliz. 406.
[5] *Atkins* v. *Hill* (1775) 1 Cowp. 284; *Rann* v. *Hughes* (1778) 7 T.R. 350 n.a.; *Hawkes* v. *Saunders* (1782) 1 Cowp. 289.

foolish enough to sell my Renoir for sixpence, the inadequacy of the price is no defence to an action for failure to deliver. Furthermore there is no objection to *nominal* consideration (the peppercorn rent, for example), which is a slightly different rule. The law was in principle the same in the sixteenth and seventeenth centuries, and Sheppard[1] points out that,

> 'the value and proportion of this consideration is not considerable; for a penny is as much obliging in a promise as £100. But there it is probable the jury will give damage according to the loss'.

Now a doctrine about adequacy can only be applied to agreements involving exchange or remuneration of some kind, for one cannot discuss disparity of value in connection with promises in consideration of marriage, or promises whose actionability involves injurious reliance (such as parole guarantee). But one would expect there to be some discussion of the matter in appropriate contexts, for everyone in the sixteenth century must have known about the doctrine of the just price.[2] Yet in fact there do not seem to be any cases discussing disparity or lack of proportion, where it is argued that a promise is not binding because the consideration (viewed, I suppose, as the price) was inadequate. For this there are perhaps two explanations. The first is that no such defence had ever been recognized at common law in medieval times—for example, in connection with sale—in spite of the fact that then most market prices were controlled.[3] The second is that the conception of consideration was not that of a price for a promise, but a reason for a promise.

So conceived, the natural question to ask is whether there is or is not a good reason for the promise, and the cases usually cited as dealing with *adequacy* in fact deal with the distinct question—is there any consideration at all? Thus, for example, in *Sturlyn* v. *Albany* (1587)[4] the plaintiff had leased land at a rent to J.S. for life, and J.S., the rent being behind, assigned his interest to Albany. Sturlyn demanded the rent from Albany, who promised to pay if Sturlyn would show him an indenture

[1] *Action on the Case*, pp. 18, 21.
[2] See generally Tawney, *Religion and the Rise of Capitalism*.
[3] The market sale would not, except in unusual circumstances, come before the common law courts at all.
[4] Cro. Eliz. 67, 150, 1 Leon. 171.

proving that the rent was due. This Sturlyn did. It was moved that the showing of a deed could not be consideration for the promise.

> 'But it was adjudged for the plaintiff: for when a thing is to be done, be it never so small, this is a sufficient consideration to ground an action; and here the shewing of the deed is a cause to avoid suit . . .'

The court here was only concerned with the question 'Is there consideration which ought to be sufficient to impose liability in assumpsit, or not?' The admission of trivial or nominal acts of consideration in such cases as these was in all probability encouraged by the fact that the liability of the defendant in such a case was well established anyway—the rent here was due. Trivial consideration performed the function of permitting assumpsit to be used rather than some older remedy, and where the court did not wish to sanction the supersession of an older remedy the consideration would be held insufficient. Hence 'showing a bond' would not support a promise to pay the sum due—to hold the contrary would be tantamount to allowing assumpsit in lieu of debt *sur obligation*.[1] There is no suggestion in this or other cases of any argument cast in terms of disparity of value, nor are the cases which lay down the same principle cases involving payment, remuneration, or benefit as consideration. They are cases where induced detriment is relied upon as consideration, and the question involved is whether the performance of some trivial act is any consideration at all.

Where disparity of value *is* treated as legally significant is in agreements in which a precise monetary value could be placed upon the promise and the consideration. This arose in *Richards* v. *Bartlett*[2] (1584), where an executory agreement to take 3s. 4d. in the pound was pleaded in bar to an action of assumpsit for £10, the price of goods sold and delivered. One ground for the decision that this was no bar was that there was no consideration for the agreement to accept the lesser sum in satisfaction for £10; clearly there was neither benefit to the creditor nor detriment to the debtor. But the basis for the decision is absence of consideration, not inadequacy; the disparity of value is only

---

[1] So held in *Sturlyn* v. *Albany*.
[2] 1 Leon. 19.

relevant because it shows that there is no consideration at all. The other branch of the law in which disparity in value was significant was in the law governing the award of damages. Thus in a case in 1588[1] an action was brought for breach of conditional promise to pay £100, and the consideration alleged was the payment of a French crown. The case clearly involved a bet and the question raised was whether damages should be given for £100, or for the French crown. On ordinary principle the damages ought to be the value of performance, but it was moved and perhaps accepted that the damages here should be restitutionary only; the reporter notes that this had been the decision in a similar Chancery case involving a bet.[2] This represents a different approach to the problem; instead of treating the promise as not binding at all through absence of consideration, the manifest disparity of value is allowed relevance at the later stage when damages were assessed. But this idea does not seem to have applied overtly except in cases involving a money payment on both sides; juries of course may well have done a certain amount on the quiet to deal justly with extortionate bargains.

The recognition of nominal consideration is usually linked by modern writers to the doctrine that the courts will not inquire into adequacy of consideration, but this is a confusion. A system of law could very well refuse to hold inadequacy of price in, say, a sale a defence, yet insist upon something more than a mere derisory price; this would involve an insistence that there really was a sale. This Roman jurists did, for they were anxious to distinguish gifts from other contracts. Common lawyers do not seem to have been much interested in distinguishing gift transactions from other transactions, or gratuitous transactions from non-gratuitous transactions, and no doctrine about derisory considerations ever developed; it is indeed notorious that modern contract law has inherited from the past a body of doctrine under which it is well-nigh impossible to differentiate promises of conditional gifts from contracts. Nominal consideration confuses categories.

[1] *Anon.* Owen 34.
[2] cf. *Colman's Case* (1595) Moo. K.B. 419. Defendant promised to pay £10 damages in consideration of a payment of 4*d.*; held the damages should be the £10, not 4*d.* Here there was a prior liability to pay the damages.

Where something like nominal consideration features in sixteenth-century cases is in actions where this is its function. Typically it arises in actions against debtors, where a trivial or small sum is paid to a debtor for a promise to pay a debt.[1] Here the function of the payment is not to create a legal obligation, but to make that obligation enforceable by assumpsit instead of by action of debt. There seem to be no instances in the cases of the use which can properly be called a 'nominal' consideration—a peppercorn or a tomtit—to create a legal obligation. Where modern lawyers would use a nominal consideration sixteenth-century lawyers instead alleged the payment of a small but not derisory sum of money, such allegations being fictional but not on their face ludicrous.

The borderline between sufficient consideration and no consideration

An enormous body of uninteresting case law developed on the borderline between holding that there was consideration and that there was none, though the principle itself was clear. A classic application of it is the decision in *Stone* v. *Wythipol* (1588).[2] Here an action was brought against Dorothy Wythipol, the executrix of her husband, and the plaintiff declared that the deceased was indebted to him for the price of goods sold and delivered, and that he came to Dorothy Wythipol and demanded the debt, and she promised to pay it in consideration that he would forbear from suing for it until Michaelmas. The defendant pleaded in bar that her husband was an infant at the time of the sale, and the plaintiff demurred to this plea. The court held that the promise was not actionable for want of consideration. The infant's contract, it was held, was void,[3] and in consequence the executrix was not liable to an action; it followed that the plaintiff's forbearance to sue was no good consideration for the promise of the executrix. The court accepted Coke's argument for the defendant,

'That is no consideration, for every consideration that doth charge the defendant in an assumpsit must be to the benefit

[1] e.g. See (1595) Moo. K.B. 419; *Featherstone* v. *Hutchinson* (1587) 3 Leon. 208, 222, Cro. Eliz. 199; *Norwood* v. *Read* (1558) Plowden 180.
[2] 1 Leon. 113, Cro. Eliz. 126, Owen 94, Latch 21.
[3] Egerton had argued that it was voidable.

of the defendant or the charge of the plaintiff, and no case can be put out of this rule. And this contract by the infant was void; and staying of suit is no benefit to the defendant, nor any charge to the plaintiff more than before'.

A long line of cases illustrate and follow this decision;[1] if it appeared on the face of the pleadings that the claim was invalid in law a forbearance to sue was no consideration.

A more sophisticated application of the principle is illustrated by the decision in *Smith* v. *Smith* (1583).[2] Thomas Smith, lying sick of a mortal sickness, was concerned for the future of his children, and reached an arrangement whereby one John Smith, in consideration that he should be given the custody of the children and Thomas Smith's property during the minority of the children with a view to their education, promised in return to procure the assurance of certain copyhold land to one of the children. Lambert Smith, Thomas's executor, sued for breach of this promise. Now it is obvious from the terms of this disagreeable arrangement that John Smith expected to make some profit from having the custody of the children and the property. Nevertheless it was moved that there was no consideration for the promise, and (the realist Gawdy J. dissenting) this view was upheld,

'it was said by Wray C.J. that here is not any benefit to the defendant, that should be a consideration in law, to induce him to make the promise; for the consideration is no other but to have the disposition of the goods of the testator for the education of the children, for all the disposition is for the profit of the children. And notwithstanding that such overseers commonly make gain of such disposition, yet the same is against the intendment of the law, which presumes every man to be true and faithful if the contrary be not shewed; and therefore the law shall intend that the defendant hath not made any private gain to himself . . .'

On the facts this may have been ostrich-like, but the legal principle is clearly illustrated.

---

[1] e.g. *Estrigge* v. *Owles* (1587) 3 Leon. 201; *Filcock* v. *Holt* (1589) 1 Leon. 240; *Tooley* v. *Windham* (1590) Cro. Eliz. 207, 2 Leon. 105; *Mathew* v. *Mathew* (1595), Moo. K.B. 702; *Pecke* v. *Lovedon* (1602) Cro. Eliz. 804; *Rosyer* v. *Langdale* (1650) Style 248. See Ames, pp. 325 et seq.

[2] 3 Leon. 88.

An area in which endless difficulty was caused was where there was averred as consideration a forbearance to sue for a short period of time—a ludicrous example is *Lutwich* v. *Hussey* (1583)[1] where there was a conditional promise to pay two debts if the plaintiff should forbear for a little time, which, it was pointed out, might mean a quarter of an hour or less. Forbearance for a 'reasonable' time was upheld in *Treford* v. *Holmes* (1628).[2] Great difficulty was caused by arrangements with no time limit (even reasonableness) fixed, as in *Mapes* v. *Sir Isaac Sidney* (1621),[3] where the consideration averred was future forbearance (not a promise to forbear) for a great time. Here the debt was due by bond,[4] and the court held that the action lay, the plaintiff averring a forbearance for a great time,

'this difference was taken, when the promise[5] appear to be such that it shall not be any benefit to the party in whose behalf it was requested, as forbearance for an hour, then it is not good, but where it is general and not limited to any time, that shall be a total forbearance, or at least a forbearance for a convenient time, and that ought to be alleged for such a time which the Court shall adjudge a convenient time'.

Another source of difficulty arose in cases where what was averred as consideration was performance of what was already due either on a contract with a third party or under general law. Here the courts tended to accept such performance as good consideration. Thus in *Bagge* v. *Slade* (1616)[6] the parties were both severally liable on bonds as sureties for a debt, and they agreed that, if the plaintiff paid the whole debt, the defendant would contribute half. The promise was held binding on the curious ground that there was a 'charge' to the plaintiff, and what this meant was not that he paid the debt, but that the arrangement was one in which he became, as between himself and his co-surety, responsible for paying it. *Mackerney* v.

[1] Cro. Eliz. 19. See also *Sackford* v. *Phillips* (1595) Cro. Eliz. 455, Owen 109, *May* v. *Alvares* (1594) Cro. Eliz. 387. See Baker in 1971 C.L.J. at 220.
[2] Hutton 108, *Lingen* v. *Broughton* (1618) 3 Bulst. 207, 1 Rolle 379.
[3] Hutton 46, Cro. Jac. 683. And see *Cowlin* v. *Cook* (1625?) Noy 83, Latch 158.
[4] The bond was not discharged, but there was in the view of the court an actionable implied promise not to sue on it.
[5] A reporter's mistake—it is an 'act'.
[6] 3 Bulst. 162, 1 Rolle Rep. 354.

Erwin (1628)[1] involves a duty under general law—returning the property of the defendant—but the court found on the facts that the consideration involved more than what the law required, and on this ground the consideration was sufficient. A stronger case is *Johnson* v. *Astell* (1666),[2] though again there is a suggestion that the plaintiff had gone beyond his general legal duty.

The analysis of considerations by time

The analysis of considerations by time first appears in *Doctor and Student*; it then features in the law of uses, and it first appears in connection with assumpsit in 1568 in *Hunt* v. *Bate*.[3] In Elizabethan law it was recognized that the consideration which had motivated a promise might be some occurrence which was over and done with before the promise was made; this was called a 'past' or 'executed' consideration, since the consideration was past or executed at the time of the promise. Alternatively a promise might be motivated by some continuous state of affairs, which had come into existence before the promise, but which still existed when the promise was made; this was a 'continuous' consideration, and natural love and affection is an example. A third alternative was that a promise might be given because of some act or occurrence which was (quibbling apart) contemporaneous with the promise; this was called a 'present' consideration. The fourth possibility was that a promise might be given in consideration of some future act or occurrence, as in the case of a promise given in consideration of a marriage to take place in the future. This was a 'future' or 'executory' consideration. The terms 'executed' and 'executory' are really self-explanatory; a consideration is 'executed' if it has happened or occurred, 'executory' if it has not.[4] It is clear that this analysis by time cuts across an analysis by type—thus marriage can be past, present, or future.

(a) THE REJECTION OF PAST CONSIDERATION

The general principle established by *Hunt* v. *Bate* (1568), and never subsequently abrogated, was that a consideration

---

[1] Hutton 100, 1 Danv. 67.
[2] 1 Lev. 198, 2 Keb. 155.
[3] Dyer 272a.
[4] This analysis is different from the modern one.

which was *past*, that is executed and bygone *at the time of the promise*, was insufficient to charge a defendant in assumpsit. The doctrine first appears in *Doctor and Student*, though its roots lie in the canon law, as we have seen.

> '*Doctor:* But what say they [learned common lawyers] if the promise be made for a thing past, as I promise thee £5 for that thou hast builded me such a house, lieth an action here?
> '*Student:* They suppose nay, but he shall be bound in conscience to perform it after his intent, as is before said.'

The Doctor goes on to ask what the legal position is if a promise is made in response for a past trespass; the Student gives the same answer, and supports his view with this reason:

> '... and the cause is for that such promises be no perfect contracts, for a contract is properly where a man for his money shall have by assent of the other party certain goods or some other profit at the time of the contract or after. But if the thing be promised for a cause which is past by way of recompense then it is rather an accord than a contract, but the law is that upon such an accord the thing that is promised in recompense must be paid or delivered in hand, for upon an accord lieth no action'.[1]

The gist of the Student's argument then is that a past consideration is bad because the law only enforces as contracts agreements involving immediate or future mutual exchange, and this is ingeniously linked to the common law doctrine governing accord and satisfaction.

The next discussion of past consideration is in a case concerning uses in 1542,[2]

> '... and according to Hales[3] a man cannot change a use by a covenant which is executed before, as to covenant to be seised to the use of W.S. because W.S. is his cousin, or because W.S. previously gave him twenty pounds unless the twenty pounds were given in order to have the land'.

Brooke notes that many took the contrary view in Mary's reign, holding a covenant good for a past consideration; this

---

[1] Dial. II, c. 24; see above, p. 393.
[2] Brooke, *Feoffments al Uses*, pl. 54.
[3] Probably the Serjeant, James Hales.

may refer to covenants in consideration of past marriages. The doctrine is also referred to in *Sharrington* v. *Strotton* (1566)[1] in argument, where it is linked in a somewhat obscure argument to the idea that whatever is to count as good consideration for a covenant must be given in return for or in exchange for what is given by the other party and to the idea that a consideration must be induced by the covenant to be good. Two years later it appears in assumpsit in *Hunt* v. *Bate* (1568).[2]

In *Hunt* v. *Bate*, Bate's servant had been imprisoned on a writ of trespass; two of Bate's friends, Hunt and another, went bail for the servant, in effect becoming sureties for the debt owed by the servant (i.e. the quantified damages). When Bate heard of this he promised as a friendly act (*pur le dit amicable consideration*) Hunt to save him harmless against any liability he might incur. Hunt subsequently became liable to pay thirty-one pounds, and when Bate refused to indemnify him he sued him on the promise. On a motion in arrest of judgment it was held that the action did not lie,

> '. . . because there is no consideration wherefore the defend-
> ant should be charged for the debt of his servant, unless the
> master had first promised to discharge the plaintiff before
> the enlargement and mainprize[3] made of his servant, for
> the master did never make request to the plaintiff to do so
> much, but he did it off his own head'.

It should be noted that the rule that a past consideration, viewed as a charge or detriment to the promisee, is good if furnished at the request of the defendant or induced by him is not an *exception* to the principle laid down in the case; it is an integral part of the principle. The report of *Hunt* v. *Bate* in fact includes a report of another earlier case where a marriage gift had been promised to a man in consideration that he had married the cousin of the promisor at his special instance and request. The marriage was held 'a good cause', though past. What the case does is to introduce a curious twist to the doctrine of consideration in assumpsit; it is not enough to show that a promise was motivated by a sensible reason or consideration,

---

[1] Plowden 298. at 302.
[2] Dyer 272a.
[3] 'release and giving bail'.

for in addition the plaintiff must show that he was induced to furnish the consideration at the defendant's instance. Thus the idea that only such promises should be actionable when motivated by a good reason is married to the idea that only such promisees shall sue who can show that they have been induced by the promisor to act to their own detriment. From this stems the principle in the developed law whereby a plaintiff needs to aver not only promise, consideration, and breach, but in addition in all cases a *request*,[1] and this was the regular mode of pleading. The doctrine introduced in *Hunt* v. *Bate* was restated in the case of *Lampleigh* v. *Braithwaite* (1616),[2] in a famous but singularly obscure passage,

'First it was agreed, that a meer voluntary curtesie will not have a consideration to uphold an assumpsit. But if that curtesie were moved by a suit or request of the party that gives the assumpsit, it will bind, for the promise, though it follows, is not naked, but couples itself with the suit before and the merits of the party procured by that suit, which is the difference'.

From this it is clear that the rule was found to be easier to state than to explain.[3]

In the course of the sixteenth century a number of cases made inroads into the doctrine. Thus in *Marsh* v. *Rainsford* (1586)[4] it was held that a past marriage celebrated after an elopement without the consent of the bride's father could be a good consideration for a subsequent promise of money by the father to the son; plainly there was here no request. This was fitted into the law by saying that the consideration for the promise was really the natural love and affection of the father, and this

---

[1] In most cases the request will be implied by law; the requirement is only a way of saying that the consideration must be related to the promise.
[2] Hob. 105, 1 Brownl. and Golds. 7, Moo. K.B. 866.
[3] The doctrine in *Hunt* v. *Bate* was followed in many cases; see *Sydenham* v. *Worlington* (1584) Godbolt 31, 2 Leon. 224; *Moore* v. *Williams* (1574) Moo. K.B. 220; *Pearl* v. *Unger* (1587) Cro. Eliz. 94; *Jeremy* v. *Goochman* (1594) Cro. Eliz. 442; *Rigges* v. *Bullingham* (1598) Cro. Eliz. 715; *Bosden* v. *Thinne* (1603) Yelv. 41; *Jones* v. *Clarke* (1613) 2 Bulst. 73; *Cotton* v. *Westcott* (1616) 3 Bulst. 187; *Townsend* v. *Hunt* (1635) Cro. Car. 409; and see cases *in margine* in Dyer at 272a. *Franklin* v. *Bradell* (1627) Hutton 84 looks like a case where the rule is not followed, but may be misreported; so also *Docket* v. *Voyel* (1601) Owen 144, Cro. Eliz. 885.
[4] Appendix, Case No. 11 and Cro. Eliz. 59, 2 Leon. 112.

always *continued*.[1] A continuous consideration was always a present and not a past consideration, and thus good. This conception of a continuous consideration also served to explain why a debt precedent could be a good consideration for a subsequent promise to pay the debt.[2] It was also held that a subsequent promise was good if in substance it formed part of an earlier transaction. Thus where money had been paid for land, and an action was brought on a subsequent promise to make an assurance of the land, the action was allowed although the payment and promise were not contemporaneous.[3] Another isolated but interesting exception to the general doctrine was accepted in *Style* v. *Smith* (*c.* 1585), which is unfortunately not fully reported.[4] It was there held that,

> 'if a physician, who is my friend, hearing that my son is sick goeth to him in my absence and helps and recovers him, and I being informed thereof promise him in consideration etc. *ut supra* to give him £20, an action will lie for the money'.

It is not at all easy to see in the cases any clear indications of the reasoning which led sixteenth-century lawyers to accept the doctrine of past consideration and the exceptions to it, and it is only too tempting to read into the cases modern ideas which are simply not to be found there. In *Hunt* v. *Bate* itself the court seems to have approached the problem for decision by asking whether there was a good reason for making the master answerable for the debt of his servant—this would have been the substantial effect of a decision for the plaintiff. The answer given was that there was no good reason, since the master had not undertaken to be answerable before the servant was bailed nor had he induced the plaintiff to procure the release in some other way. Now this line of reasoning brushes aside as irrelevant to the issue the most obvious ground for making the defendant

[1] See *Halifax* v. *Barker* (1598) Cro. Eliz. 741; *Pearle* v. *Edwards* (1588) 1 Leon. 102; *Sidenham* v. *Worlington* (1584) 2 Leon. 224, Cro. Eliz. 42, Godbolt 31, but cf. *Harford* v. *Gardiner* (1587) 2 Leon. 31.

[2] *Hodge* v. *Vavisour* (1616) 3 Bulst. 222, 1 Rolle Rep. 413. The notion of a continuous consideration was also applied where there had been a request—see *Beaucamp* v. *Neggin* (1591) Cro. Eliz. 282.

[3] *Warcop* v. *Morse* (1588) Cro. Eliz. 138.

[4] Referred to in *Marsh* v. *Rainsford*; it is not clear if this is the correct name of the case.

liable—the fact that he had *promised* to save the plaintiff harmless. It is this feature of the reasoning which requires explanation, and I think the explanation is this and is central to the theory of consideration: the court is not prepared to hold the defendant liable for breaking a promise to do something unless it can find some reason for imposing liability over and above the mere fact that a promise has been given. To put the point in a slightly different way: a promise to do X is only actionable if it can be said, somewhat loosely no doubt, that the promisor ought to have done X anyway. Thus in *Hunt* v. *Bate*, if the defendant had induced the plaintiff to go bail for his servant, then everyday morality would say that he ought to save the plaintiff harmless; *ergo* a promise to do so would be actionable. One must resist the temptation to ask at this point the question 'Ought legally?' or 'Ought morally?'. To contemporaries, who believed the law consisted in the main of a set of rationally defensible principles of conduct, the question would have made no sense, so the answer is 'Just ought'.

We have already met this idea in another area, but it is perhaps in the context of the doctrine of past consideration that it has been most influential. Thus the explanation for the decision in *Style* v. *Smith* (*c.* 1585) is surely the everyday notion that fathers ought to pay doctors for their children when they are ill; in consequence a promise to pay is actionable. Again the reference in *Lampleigh* v. *Braithwaite* to 'the merits of the party procured by that suit' in the statement of the reason for the doctrine only means this: if a person performs a service at request he deserves or merits payment, and since he ought to be paid a promise to pay him is actionable. Hence it is that in later law it could be said that a past consideration would only support a subsequent express promise in circumstances in which the promisor would be liable in any case on an implied promise.[1] The germs of this idea are to be found in sixteenth-century law, though not specially linked to the doctrine of past consideration. Thus in *Fooly* v. *Preston* (1585)[2] it was said by Anderson C.J. that on the bailment of an obligation an assumpsit for failure to return would lie even in the absence of an express promise—

[1] See *Kennedy* v. *Brown* (1863) 13 C.B. (N.S.) 677, *Re Casey's Patents* [1892] 1 Ch. 104.
[2] 1 Leon. 297.

the law will imply a promise to do what the defendant ought to do in any event. *A fortiori* an express promise in consideration of the delivery was actionable—the reason for implying a promise is the same as the consideration for an express promise.[1]

(*b*) THE RECOGNITION OF FUTURE CONSIDERATION

It seems never to have been doubted that a promise might be made in consideration of some act which was to be performed in the future, after the promise had been made. Perhaps the typical example of such a future consideration is a marriage; obviously most marriage agreements are going to be made in advance of the wedding day, and if the law is going to give effect to such agreements it must accept future consideration, which it did both in the law of uses[2] and in the law of assumpsit. An early example in assumpsit is the case of *Joscelin* v. *Shelton* (1557),[3] which is the earliest printed reported case to include an averment of consideration,

> 'In an action upon the case, the plaintiff declared, that the defendant in consideration that the son of the plaintiff would marry the daughter of the defendant, assumed and promised to pay to him 400 marks in seven years next ensuing, by such portions.'

It must be noticed that nothing is said about any *promise* of marriage, which would in any event not be actionable at common law; the consideration averred is the future marriage, not a present promise of marriage.[4] There are numerous other examples of the averment of such *future* or *executory* consideration[5] in the reports, and it is important to distinguish such cases from cases in which a promise was averred as consideration.

Where such a future consideration was averred, the plaintiff must also aver performance. This was clearly laid down in

---

[1] See below, p. 490.

[2] *Assaby* v. *Lady Anne Manners* (1516) Dyer 235b; *Marmaduke Constable's Case* (1553) Dyer 101b, *Villers* v. *Beaumont* (1556) Dyer 146; *Calthorpe's Case* (1573) Dyer 334b, Moo. K.B. 101.

[3] 2 Leon. 4.

[4] So too in *Pecke* v. *Redman* 2 Dyer 113a.

[5] e.g. *Simmes* v. *Westcott* (1588) 1 Leon. 299 (future marriage); *Applethwaite* v. *Nertley* (1590) 4 Leon. 56 (future marriage); *Rogers* v. *Snow* (1572) Dalison 94 (delivery of bond).

Rogers v. *Snow* (1572).[1] Here the consideration averred was that the plaintiff should take a bond and should not sue for a debt for a fixed term. Gawdy moved that the count was defective in that performance was not averred,

> 'as if I promise a man 20s. if he should go to York on my business, in an action on the case on such a promise it is obligatory to surmise performance on his part'.

This was agreed by the court, and on a motion in arrest of judgment the count was held to be defective. The same principle was applied in *Anon.* (1581),[2]

> 'An action upon the case upon a promise was: the consideration was, that in consideration that the plaintiff *daret diem solutionem*, the defendant *super se assumpsit*; and because he doth not say *in facto*, that he had given day, it was adjudged that no sufficient consideration was alleged: but if the consideration were *quod cum indebitatus* etc, the same had been a good consideration without any more, for that implies a consideration in itself'.

The rule that the plaintiff must aver performance if the consideration was executory (that is executory at the time of promising) was balanced by the rule that the defendant could traverse the consideration specially if it was executory—that is he could plead that there had been no performance, and thus offer to join issue on this limited point. This was an exception to the general pleading principle in assumpsit which forbade special traverses of the consideration; where a past or present consideration was pleaded the defendant must plead the general issue, *non assumpsit*, and give in evidence before the jury matters tending to show that there was in fact no consideration for the promise.[3]

(*c*) THE RECOGNITION OF A PROMISE AS
CONSIDERATION

The first case in which it is clear that a promise, as distinct from a future act, was averred as consideration is *West* v.

---

[1] Dalison 94.
[2] Godbolt 13.
[3] *Smith* v. *Hitchcock* (1590) Cro. Eliz. 201; *Anon.* (1591) Cro. Eliz. 250; *Alderton* v. *Man* (1592) Moore 595; *Babington* v. *Lambert* (1616) Moo. K.B. 854; *Lampleigh* v. *Braithwaite* (1616) Hob. 106. See Lücke in 81 L.Q.R. 441 et seq.

Stowel in 1577,[1] which concerns a bet on an aristocratic archery match. The plaintiff declared that,

> 'the defendant, in consideration that the plaintiff promised to the defendant, that if the defendant shall win a certain match at shooting, made between the Lord of Effingham and the defendant, then the plaintiff should pay to the defendant £10, promised to the plaintiff, and if the said Lord of Effingham shall win the same match of the defendant, that then the defendant would pay to the plaintiff £10 . . .'

His lordship won, and an action was brought on the promise. It was moved that there was no consideration for the promise, and the ground for this objection was not that a promise was averred as consideration, nor yet that the promise had not been performed (which on the facts would have been absurd); it is that the plaintiff's promise was not actionable. Now this suggests that it was already accepted that a promise could count as a good consideration, so long as that promise was actionable. On this motion Mounson J. and Manwood J. disagreed. Mounson J. thought the consideration good,

> 'Mounson, Justice, conceived, that here the consideration is sufficient, for here this counter promise is a reciprocal promise, and so a good consideration, for all the communication ought to be taken to-gether'.

Manwood J. disagreed,

> 'Such a reciprocal promise betwixt the parties themselves at the match is sufficient; for there is consideration enough to each, as the preparing of the bows and arrows, the riding or coming to the place appointed to shoot, the labour in shooting, the travail in going up and down between the marks: but for the bettors by, there is not any consideration, if the bettor does not give aim'.

The case is inconclusive, no decision being reported. The next clear evidence is the note of *Strangeborough* v. *Warner* in 1589:

---

[1] 2 Leon. 154. At this period there was no objection to allowing actions on bets— see *Baynton* v. *Cheek* (1652) Style 353. And generally see Lücke in 81 L.Q.R. at 539 et seq.

'Note, that a promise against a promise will maintain an action on the case, as in consideration that you do [promise to] give to me £10 on such a day, I promise to give you £10 the day after.'

Thereafter a number of cases reflect the rule, and make as little fuss about it,[1] but it is clear that it was already accepted long before this.

What seems remarkable to a modern lawyer is the way in which the doctrine that a promise can count as a good consideration comes into the law in this quiet and unobtrusive way; contemporaries clearly did not think that *this* required much explanation or justification. There may be a very simple explanation. A very large number of promises are as a matter of fact motivated by promises given in return, and if an action was brought on such a promise it seems never to have entered anyone's head to suggest that there was some fundamental objection to telling the truth and saying that what motivated the promise sued on (i.e. was the consideration) was the counter-promise. What did seem to them to be at least worth discussing was whether a plaintiff who alleged a promise as consideration ought in addition to be required to aver performance of the promise before he was allowed to sue for breach. Thus the cases do not really deal with the question 'Is a counter-promise a good consideration for a promise?'. Instead they are concerned with the slightly more complicated question. 'Is a counter-promise, granted it has not been performed, a good consideration to charge the defendant in an action of assumpsit brought before performance?'.

The answer which was given to this question in a series of cases was that it was not necessary to aver performance. Thus in *Gower* v. *Capper* (1596)[2] the plaintiff alleged, as consideration for the defendant's promise, his own promise to deliver a bill

---

[1] 4 Leon. 3 *Sackford* v. *Phillips* (1593) Owen 109, Moo. K.B. 690; *Gower* v. *Capper* (1596) Cro. Eliz. 543; *Medcalfe's Case* (1597) Moo. K.B. 549, *Wichals* v. *Johns* (1599) Cro. Eliz. 703, Moo. K.B. 574; *Lea* v. *Exelby* (1602) Cro. Eliz. 888, *Bettisworth* v. *Campion* (1609) Yelv. 133; *Nichols* v. *Rainbred* (1615) Hob. 88; *Spanish Ambassador* v. *Gifford* 1 Rolle Rep. 336; *Lampleigh* v. *Braithwaite* (1616) Hob. 105; *Harleton* v. *Webb* (1626) Benloe 150; *Browne* v. *Downing* (1620) 2 Rolle 194; *Bibble* v. *Cunningham* (1628) Hetley 89; *Shann* v. *Bilby* (1651) Style 280; *Ernely* v. *Lord Falkland* (1655) Hard. 103; *Bennett* v. *Astell* (1660) 1 Lev. 20; *Anon.* (1662) 1 Lev. 87; *Peters* v. *Opie* (1671) 1 Vent. 177; *Smith* v. *Shilbury* (1675) Freeman 165.

[2] Cro. Eliz. 543 and cases in n. 1, above, *passim*.

obligatory to the defendant, and further alleged that he had delivered the bill. The defendant pleaded a special traverse, that the plaintiff had not delivered the bill, and to this plea the plaintiff demurred. It was held that the defendant's plea was bad,

> 'for the alleging that he had delivered the bill was but surplusage; for the consideration was the promise to deliver it; and therefore he needed not to have alleged that he delivered it. But a promise against a promise is a sufficient ground for an action'.

Thus where a promise was averred as consideration the rule was that the plaintiff need not aver performance, and it was not a defence for the plaintiff either to plead specially or give in evidence on the general issue that the promise had not been performed; in short performance was totally irrelevant.

In this way a sharp distinction was drawn between cases where a future act was averred as consideration, and cases where a contemporaneous promise was the consideration. The theory of the distinction is clear enough. When the consideration averred was a future act—say a marriage to be celebrated—then there was no consideration for the promise until the act was performed. In insisting upon an averment of performance in such cases the court was only applying the rule that in assumpsit for nonfeasance there must be consideration for the promise (in addition to promise and breach). Where, however, a contemporaneous promise was averred as consideration (and the promises had to be made at the same moment) there was not the same basis for the argument that performance must be averred—the *promise* was the consideration averred, and the plaintiff had averred that the promise had been given. Thus a promise was not conceived to be a future consideration, or an executory consideration within the rule which allowed executory considerations to be specially traversed; instead a promise was a present consideration.[1] To have insisted upon

---

[1] See *Nichols* v. *Rainbred* (1615), 'Note here the promises must be at one instant, for else they will be both nude pacts.' The same idea is, of course, involved in the rule in *Lampleigh* v. *Braithwaite*. The case of *Cooke* v. *Oxley* (1790) 3 T.R. 653, which modern lawyers find difficult, turns on this rule, which disappeared with the rise of the doctrine of offer and acceptance; it is of course only appropriate to parole contracts *inter praesentes*.

an averment of performance where a promise was the consideration would therefore have involved imposing upon the plaintiff an additional requirement over and above the need to show promise, consideration, and breach, and this the courts consistently declined to do.

The refusal to do so was justified in part by insisting that, where a promise was averred as consideration, it was the *promise* and not the performance which was the consideration averred; by thus calling attention to the state of the pleadings the court was in effect saying to counsel for the defendant—'Why should performance be averred; the plaintiff has satisfied the requirements in assumpsit by showing promise, consideration, and breach—what else is needed?'. It was also justified, more convincingly, by saying that the averment of a promise by the plaintiff showed that the defendant in his turn could sue the plaintiff in assumpsit if breach occurred.[1] Thus in *West* v. *Stowel* (1577)[2] Mounson J. refers to the reciprocal promises of the parties and the possibility of reciprocal actions. In *Wichals* v. *Johns* (1599)[3] the defendant had promised to pay £120 to the plaintiff in consideration of the plaintiff's promise to pay £120 to one Rogers, to whom the defendant was indebted. Popham C.J. and Clench J., holding the consideration good, used the same idea,

'and Popham and Clench held it to be well enough; for there is a mutual promise, the one to the other; so that if the plaintiff doth not pay it to Rogers, the defendant may have his action against him: and so also the defendant shall be charged as to him; and a promise against a promise is a good consideration'.

The same idea is found in other cases, and is the only justification employed to show that the rule was fair, as, for example, in *Fuller's Case* (1588)[4]. It explains the distinction between a future act and a present promise quite neatly. If the plaintiff alleges a future act as consideration (and not a promise to perform the act) it is only fair to require him to show performance,

---

[1] *Bettisworth* v. *Campion* (1609) Yelv. 133 is an exception.
[2] 2 Leon. 154.
[3] Cro. Eliz. 703.
[4] Appendix, Case No. 12, and see also *Everard* v. *Hopkins* (1614) 2 Bulst. 332 and *Spanish Ambassador* v. *Gifford* (1615) 1 Rolle Rep. 336.

because it does not appear from the declaration that the defendant can sue if the act is not performed. If he avers a promise it is clear that the defendant *can* sue, and so there is no need to insist on performance before allowing an action. Precisely the same principle was applied in relation to reciprocal covenants under seal,[1] and in both branches of the law performance only had to be averred if the covenant or promise was made conditional upon performance, that is if the covenants were mutually dependent. Thus in *Lea* v. *Exelby* (1602)[2] the plaintiff sued on a breach of a promise to surrender a lease, and averred as consideration his own promise to pay a sum of money. The precise terms of the defendant's promise were that he promised to surrender the lease *on the plaintiff's payment* of the money. It was held that the plaintiff must aver actual payment, or tender and refusal,

> 'But all the Court held, that if the promise had been in consideration he [i.e. the plaintiff] assumed to pay such a sum, that the defendant had assumed to surrender, that had been sufficient; for then he is to make his surrender, and he ought to take his remedy against the other for the non-performance of his promise: but here it is, that he assumed to pay, and the other assumed to surrender it upon the payment, so as he would not trust to his promise, but when he had paid, he would then surrender it. And in the first case, he needed not allege the performance of the promise; but here in this he ought'.

This principle is clear enough, but its application to real-life situations is bound to be pretty arbitrary. In formal contracts under seal the text of the deed can be used to determine whether a covenant is conditional or not, and the decision will turn on the precise words used; rulings on the use of certain expressions will enable those who draw deeds to know in advance whether or not the use of these expressions makes the covenant conditional. In the informal agreement reached by parole it will seldom be at all clear whether the promises are mutually dependent or not. Not only will it usually be difficult to find out

[1] See 15 Hen. VII, f. 10, pl. 17, *Brocas' Case* (1587) 3 Leon. 219; *Ware* v. *Chappel* (1649) Style 186.
[2] Cro. Eliz. 888.

both what the parties said and what the parties intended; very frequently there will be no intention on the matter one way or the other; hence the distinctions which the law seeks to draw here make little sense when applied to many informal agreements. This is a very common phenomenon in the law—a so-called 'test' requires lawyers to search for intentions, wishes, states of mind, and the like which unfortunately are only rarely to be come across, and in any event inherently difficult to prove. The consequence is that the problem which is supposed to be solved by prying into the minds of the parties is in fact solved by a set of more or less arbitrary rules, or the decision is left to the court and not determined by rules at all. The former technique was adopted to solve problems concerning the dependence of mutual promises—the *locus classicus* being the case of *Pordage* v. *Cole* (1669),[1] and the notes to that decision, where an attempt is made to explain when a promise may be sued upon without the plaintiff having to aver that he has either performed, or been ready and willing to perform his side of the agreement. The modern tendency is to abandon this technique in favour of giving up the idea that the problem should be solved by rules at all.

Promises as consideration and contractual theory

The cases which accepted the doctrine that a promise could count as a good consideration for the promise sued upon are commonly thought to represent a dramatic step forward in the history of the law of contract, which is somewhat variously described as the recognition in the common law of 'consensual', 'wholly executory', or 'bilateral' contracts.[2] It is not always very clear what this is supposed to mean. There are two possibilities. The first is that the great step forward was the acceptance of the rule that mutual promises were to be treated as *independent*, notwithstanding the fact that the promises were given in exchange for each other, so that one party could sue

---

[1] 1 Wms. Saund. 319, and see the notes to *Cutter* v. *Powell* (1795) 6 T.R. 320, and the notes in Smith's *Leading Cases*. I have not set out the rules in the text.

[2] The 'promise against a promise' doctrine had little to do with the recognition of the standard consensual contracts of sale and hire, where the remedy was usually *indebitatus assumpsit* in any event. The recognition of the basic contracts long precedes the rise of assumpsit.

for breach of his promise without showing that he had performed, or was ready to perform his own. This is what some of the cases referred to on the 'promise against a promise' doctrine do in fact support. But clearly this rule has nothing whatever to do with the recognition of 'consensual' or 'bilateral' contracts, and would only be relevant to the recognition of 'executory' contracts if an executory contract means an agreement which can be sued on by one party without alleging performance, which is not I think what is meant. Furthermore the law seems to have taken a number of steps backward since the sixteenth century, for it is no longer the general rule that mutual promises are independent. The second possibility is that the great step forward was the recognition that an agreement involving mutual promises became *binding* when the promises were made, and this I think is what is meant.

Unfortunately, however, the sixteenth-century cases do not concern themselves with the question 'When is a promise binding?' but only with the question 'When is a breach of promise actionable?'. What is meant by saying that a promise is 'binding' is that the promisor cannot revoke his promise with impunity without at the least the consent of the other party. Now in modern contract law the moment when a promise becomes binding is determined by reference to the doctrine of offer and acceptance. This doctrine was entirely unknown in the sixteenth and seventeenth centuries. Originally there was no requirement that the plaintiff must show that a *contract* had been made, and therefore no room for a doctrine designed to assist in determining whether a contract had been made, and when, and where. Instead the plaintiff was required to show that a *promise* had been made for good consideration and broken. The doctrine of the independence of promises indeed emphasized that there was no further requirement—granted that the plaintiff satisfied the three requirements there was no need to show performance *as well*. In this context there can be no room for a doctrine designed to determine when a contract is made, and it would have been futile to have had a doctrine about when a *promise* is made; the only possible answer is 'when it is made, of course'. Once the plaintiff in assumpsit satisfied the three basic requirements, by showing promise, consideration, and breach, it became the defendant's move in the litigation, and if he wished to rely upon special defences, whilst confessing the promise, consideration, and breach, he must either plead specially or raise the matter in evidence to the jury upon the general issue. Thus by way of special plea in confession and avoidance he could plead that the plaintiff discharged him of the promise before the time for performance, or he could plead accord and satisfaction after breach.[1] Whether or not he could revoke his own promise unilaterally before breach, and plead this revocation in bar to the action, could only fall to be decided in a case where such a plea was tendered, and pleaded in bar to an action. No sixteenth-century case so far as I know involves such a plea, or discusses the matter. In consequence it is quite impossible to say when promises became binding in sixteenth-century law, and all talk about the recognition of 'wholly executory', 'bilateral', or 'consensual' contracts in that century is wholly misconceived.

The first case in which the point was raised is *Hurford* v. *Pile* (1616).[2] One J.S. was in execution for a debt of £40 owed to the plaintiff, and the defendant said to the plaintiff, 'Deliver J.S. out of execution, and what it costs you I will repay.' The plaintiff did so, and sued the defendant on the promise. The defendant pleaded that,

> 'after the assumpsit, and before the plaintiff had done anything in that business, he forbade him to meddle therein, and that he would not stand to his promise'.

To this plea the plaintiff demurred, and this provoked a difference of judicial opinion,

> 'Houghton Justice said, that a man may discharge a promise made to himself, but he cannot discharge an assumpsit made by himself. But another day the defendant's counsel moved, that it was a good plea, and that as long as nothing was done, it was but an executory promise.

> 'Dodderidge. If I promise to J.S. that if he build an house upon my land before Michealmas, I will pay him a hundred pounds, and I countermand it before he hath done anything concerning the house, it is a good countermand.

[1] See below, pp. 578 et seq
[2] Cro. Jac. 483.

'Houghton *e contra*; but he said, that may be considered in damages.'

Eventually the plea was held bad on demurrer, Dodderidge J. probably dissenting. It is clear that the point appeared to the court to be a novel one, and an arguable one. Two years later the same question arose again in *Winter* v. *Foweracres* (1618),[1] where the facts were similar, an action being brought on a promise to pay to the plaintiff the cost of discharging the defendant's son of a judgment. The defendant pleaded a countermand of his promise before discharge, but the plaintiff nevertheless discharged the son, and sued on the promise. On the first hearing we again find Dodderidge J. in favour of the plea,

'And it was said at the bar, *quo ligatur eo dissolvitur*, and Mr. Justice Dodderidge put this case. A man assumes to build me a house, for which I promise him such a sum, then I can countermand before he does anything in this'.

At the second hearing it was held that the revocation was invalid. Thus Houghton J. said,

'A contract by parole on good consideration is as binding [*fort*] as a covenant by deed, and no-one would say that if a covenant by deed was to do a thing, that he could countermand'.

Croke J. agreed,

'If I say to you build me a house and I will be willing to give you £10, and before you have provided materials, or have been to any charge, I wish to revoke my promise and countermand my precedent agreement, this is not valid, *car meum est promittere et non dimmittere*'.

And even Dodderidge J. was persuaded, on the ground that in contracts both parties have an interest in the contract.[2] The

---

[1] 2 Rolle Rep. 19, 39.

[2] The right to revoke a promise was treated as closely analogous to the right to countermand a bailment to bail over, on which see *Lyte* v. *Peny* (1541) Dyer 49a and *Bridget Clark's Case* (1586) 2 Leon. 89, 30, where the matter turned upon whether the instruction to bail or deliver over was voluntary or supported by consideration.

reasoning in *Hurford* v. *Pile* and *Winter* v. *Foweracres* does not turn upon any distinction between unilateral and bilateral contracts, a sophistication which had yet to be dreamt up; the point at issue is simply whether a promise can be unilaterally revoked before it has been relied upon, and the decision is that it cannot.

Winter v. *Foweracres* did not, however, conclude the question. In two cases decided in 1685 opinion swung back in favour of allowing unilateral revocation, so long as no action had been taken in reliance upon the promise. Thus in *The Mayor, Aldermen and Burgesses of Scarborough* v. *Butler*[1] the whole court agreed that,

'on a promise merely executory of both parts, as the cases cited before are, any thing may be discharged by parole; as if I promise you 5s. if you go to Pauls, before you go I may discharge you from the going, and thereby the other shall be discharged from paying the 5s'.

Here it is clear that the court is thinking of an agreement involving promise for promise, and the theory is that one party, by discharging the other, indirectly discharges himself. In *Howe* v. *Beeche*[2] in the same year the defendant promised to pay the plaintiff 100 [£100?]

'in consideration that the plaintiff would solicit a business which the defendant had with Gillingham, and put an end thereto'.[3]

The plaintiff began to solicit (whatever that involved) but had not put an end to the business when the defendant countermanded the promise. It was argued that such employment was always countermandable, though the promisee could have an action on a *quantum meruit* for what work he had performed. But this view was rejected. It was ruled in the Exchequer Chamber,

'That though the employment was countermandable, yet if after part of the business done the defendant countermands it, the plaintiff shall have his action for the whole',

---

[1] 3 Lev. 237.
[2] 3 Lev. 244.
[3] i.e. clinch the deal.

but the court agreed that the countermand could be considered in assessing damages. Now although this case involves a unilateral contract (in modern terms), nothing turns on this; the doctrine is that unilateral revocation is possible before there had been reliance upon the promise. So far as unilateral contracts are concerned, this may well be still the law. The point has, however, given rise to considerable theoretical difficulty because of the ridiculous application of the doctrine of offer and acceptance to this class of contract, and because of the evolution of the idea that the presence of consideration should be the test of whether a promise is binding (i.e. not unilaterally revocable) instead of simply a requirement of actionability.

The doctrine of consideration and the discharge of contracts

Whereas a countermand of a promise is the act of the promisor, discharge primarily involved the act of the promisee.[1] It was held in *Coniers* v. *Holland* (1588)[2] that it was a good plea in answer to an action that the plaintiff had discharged or exonerated the promisor of his promise, and this according to Wray C.J. had been often ruled, as in the case of the Lord Chief Baron; this may be a reference to *Manwood* v. *Burston* (1587),[3] where some reference is made to the doctrine of accord and satisfaction, or to some other unreported decision. A long line of cases[4] applied this rule but limited it to cases where the discharge was before breach of promise and before any debt fell due. The doctrine was based upon the principle *eodem modo quo oritur, eodem modo dissolvitur*—'an action grounded upon a promise by words, it may be discharged by words'.[5] In *Treswaller* v. *Keyne* (1621)[6] it was argued that a discharge was not effective as a bar unless supported by consideration. The parties had agreed that the defendant should pay the plaintiff

---

[1] Holdsworth (*H.E.L.* VIII. 82 et seq.) confuses the two.

[2] 2 Leon. 214.

[3] 2 Leon. 203.

[4] *Wolverton* v. *Davies* (1610) 1 Bulst. 38; *Hurford* v. *Pile* (1616) Cro. Jac. 483; *Treswaller* v. *Keyne* (1621) Cro. Jac. 620; *Langden* v. *Stokes* (1634) Cro. Car. 383; *Fortescue* v. *Brograve* (1646) Style 8; *Knight* v. *Chaplen* (1656) 2 Sid. 77; *Cook* v. *Newcomb* (1661) T. Raymond 42, 1 Keb. 158; *Milward* v. *Ingram* (1675) 1 Mod. 205, 2 Mod. 43, 1 Freeman 195; *Edwards* v. *Weeks* (1677) 1 Mod. 262, 2 Mod. 259.

[5] See Cro. Car. 383.

[6] Cro. Jac. 620.

£4 for going to London to search for a will; as pleaded by the plaintiff this was a case of a promise for a future act (going to London). Before any preparation had been made for the journey the parties agreed that the arrangement was off, the plaintiff discharging the defendant of his promise to pay £4 and the defendant discharging the plaintiff of his journey; this is raised in a plea in confession and avoidance in which the arrangement is portrayed as promise for promise. One objection to the plea was that,

'where a promise begins on consideration, it cannot be discharged by words only, without some other consideration'.

This assumes that there was no consideration, and of the Justices Houghton J. held that consideration was not needed (the other judges appear to have said nothing on the point, the case going off on another ground). It is clear therefore that originally this rule was not connected with the doctrine of consideration.

Different principles were applied when either a debt had arisen, or a promise had been broken so that a claim for damages existed—the former situation would exist when there was a promise to pay an existing debt sued on typically by some form of *indebitatus assumpsit*. A release under seal would operate as a discharge in such a case, a deed being of a higher nature than mere words.[1] A mere parole discharge was not effective,[2] there must be an accord or concord (which just means an agreement) to take something in satisfaction, and this accord must be executed, that is to say carried out, before it became effective to discharge the defendant promisor from liability. Such an accord with satisfaction was held effective in assumpsit in *Andrews* v. *Boughey* (1552)[3] under the general principle of medieval law that in cases where 'nothing but amends is to be recovered in damages, there a concord carried into execution is a good plea'. In origin this doctrine has nothing whatever to do with the doctrine of consideration, which it long pre-dates; in *Andrews* v. *Boughey* there is no reference to consideration

[1] See *Fortescu* v. *Brograve* (1646) Style 8; *Milward* v. *Ingram* (1675) 1 Mod. 205, 2 Mod. 43.
[2] See cases cited in n. 2, p. 104, above.
[3] Dyer 75a, and see *Onely* v. *Earl of Kent* (1577) Dyer 355b, where again there is no reference to consideration.

as being in any way relevant. The satisfaction, so Manwood and Dyer argued in *Onely* v. *Earl of Kent*,[1] must be

> 'Some charge to the one party, and commodious and profitable to the other (Else as good never a whit, as never the better)',

and this may well be the source of the 'benefit–detriment' analysis later applied to consideration. The rationale of the insistence that the satisfaction must be paid was that in medieval law no action lay upon an executory accord, so that it would be unfair to allow an accord without satisfaction to operate as a bar.[2] It has been pointed[1] out that once mutual promises came to be held as consideration for each other it would have been logical to have altered the rule, for an executory accord was now actionable. Holdsworth indeed thought that this step was taken in *Goring* v. *Goring* (1602),[4] but this is incorrect. In that case one H. Goring owed Smith, deceased, £205 on simple contract. His executor was J. Goring. H. Goring and J. Goring agreed that H. Goring was to pay £150 in annual instalments, and he was sued by the executor J. Goring on this promise. It was objected that there was no consideration for his promise, for the plaintiff had not averred that the debt of £205 had been discharged; hence even if he paid the £150 he might still be sued. The court agreed that the debt had not been discharged, but held that there was consideration since the law would imply a promise by the plaintiff not to sue for the £205, which promise was actionable by H. Goring if broken. Thus though the debt was not discharged by the accord without satisfaction,[5] it provided a counter remedy—presumably the damages for breach would be £55. This same doctrine was generally applied to cases of promises in consideration of forbearance to sue for debts.[6] Later in the century in *Case* v. *Barber* (1681)[7] it was

---

[1] Dyer 355b. For the record see Benloe 297.

[2] See above, p. 104.

[3] See *H.E.L.* VIII. 83.

[4] Yelv. 11.

[5] Since £150 could not be satisfaction for £205, and in any event had never been paid.

[6] See *Mapes* v. *Sidney* (1623) Cro. Jac. 683; *Thorne* v. *Fuller* (1614) Cro. Jac. 396.

[7] T. Raymond, 450. See also *Wickham* v. *Taylor* (1681) Jones 168, which suggests that an accord without satisfaction was a bar if immediately actionable. *Parsloe* v. *Bailey* (1704), 1 Salkeld 76, 2 Ld. Raym. 1039, dealing with executory awards of arbitrations to deliver chattels is consistent.

suggested, and agreed, that an executory accord should be a bar in *indebitatus assumpsit* now that mutual promises were actionable, but the case went off on another point.

Whether or not an accord had to be executed to operate as a bar, it must be an accord which involved a satisfaction, and in general anything would serve as a satisfaction. The curious doctrine in *Peytoe's Case* (1611),[1] which dealt with substitutes for the performance of conditions, did not apply, so that money could be a satisfaction for a thing, or an act, or vice versa in the sense that a broken promise could be met with whatever amends the parties agreed upon. There was, however, one limitation; it had come to be accepted, after some hesitation, that a lesser sum of money could not be a satisfaction for a greater, a doctrine normally known as the rule in *Pinnel's Case*,[2] and it was bound to be a question whether this doctrine, which originated in connection with actions of debt and actions on conditioned bonds, should be transferred to the action of assumpsit.[3] Now in strict principle there is no doubt but that it should not have been, for when an accord and satisfaction (paid or payable) is pleaded in bar to an action of assumpsit, the satisfaction is for unliquidated damages, an uncertain sum, and not for a debt. On the other hand it can well be argued that actions of assumpsit in lieu of debt (normally *indebitatus assumpsit* on the common counts) are merely actions of debt under a new name, and should therefore be subject to the same doctrine of accord and satisfaction as the action of debt; this was eventually decided in *Cumber* v. *Wane* (1721)[4] and followed in *Foakes* v. *Beer* (1884).[5] The position before *Cumber* v. *Wane* is not very clear. There is, however, authority going back to *Richards* v. *Bartlett* (1584)[6] for the view that the efficacy of an accord as a bar should be determined by applying the doctrine of consideration. In that case there was an executory accord to take 3s. 4d. in the pound, and this was pleaded in bar to an action of assumpsit for the price of goods sold. The court, relying upon dicta by Dyer and

[1] (1611) 9 Co.Rep. 78. See above, p. 106.
[2] (1602) 5 Co.Rep. 117, Moo. K.B. 677. See above, p. 105.
[3] Its application to debts is recognized, for example, in *Goring* v. *Goring* (1602) Yelv. 11.
[4] 1 Strange 426.
[5] 9 App. Cas. 605.
[6] 1 Leon. 19.

Manwood in *Onely* v. *Earl of Kent* (1577),[1] gave as one ground[2] for the decision that this accord did not bar the action the want of consideration, using the benefit–detriment analysis derived from the earlier case; the accord was of no benefit to the plaintiff, and no detriment to the defendant. Again Coke in *Peytoe's Case* (1611)[3] clearly thought that the doctrine of consideration applied to accords (though the rule in *Pinnel's Case* was not in issue),

'But if a man by contract or assumpsit (without a deed) is to deliver a horse, or build a house, or do any other collateral thing, there money can be paid in satisfaction of such a contract, for just as a contract on consideration can begin by words, so by accord by parole for any valuable consideration it can be dissolved'.

Covill v. *Geffery* (1619),[4] a case where an accord with satisfaction was pleaded in bar to an action for slander, takes the same line. Now once it is thought that this is the correct approach there is much force in the argument that an agreement to pay a lesser sum in satisfaction of a greater is no bar for want of consideration, and (consistently) that such an accord is not itself actionable (and vice versa). *Woodward* v. *Rigby* (1677)[5] held that one could not sue on an agreement to take £220 in satisfaction for £250, and this plainly entails the view that such an agreement would not bar *indebitatus assumpsit* for the full sum.

There is, however, an argument on the other side, which relies upon the principle that a bird in the hand is worth more than a rather grander fowl in the bush. Hence in *Reynolds* v. *Pinhowe* (1594)[6] a promise in consideration of actual payment of £4 out of a debt of £5 was held actionable, and it would have been consistent with the rationale of such cases—that actual payment of less is an improvement upon the possible alternative

---

[1] Dyer 355b.
[2] The other was that the accord was executory.
[3] 9 Co.Rep. 78.
[4] 2 Rolle Rep. 96.
[5] Jones T. 87.
[6] Cro. Eliz. 429, Moore 412. See also *Anon*, 1 Rolle Abr. 27, pl. 53; *Cook* v. *Hunt* (1582) 1 Leon. 238, Cro. Eliz. 194; *Anon.* Hutton 101; *Flight* v. *Crasden* (1625) Cro. Car. 8, Hutton 76; *Anon.* (1675) 1 Vent. 258. It must be noted, however, that these cases deal with promises to do what the promisor ought in any event to do, typically deliver up a bond in return for payment.

of litigation—to permit an executed accord involving payment of less to operate as a bar, but there are no decisions to this effect, and in the end some degree of reconciliation was achieved by accepting early payment of less as good—an idea hinted at in one of the reports of *Reynolds* v. *Pinhowe*. Whether it was right or wrong to reinterpret the doctrine of accord and satisfaction in terms of the doctrine of consideration, and further to hold that payment of a lesser sum was insufficient consideration, is hardly a real question; historically, however, it is clear that the idea of doing so was current from Elizabethan times onward.[1]

Who is entitled to sue for breach of promise?

The solution of this question in particular cases is today determined by the doctrine of privity of contract,[2] but unfortunately the doctrine of privity of contract is itself obscure, particularly in its relationship to the doctrine of consideration. According to one school of thought the doctrine is that no one may sue (or be sued) upon a contract to which he is not a party, except in some exceptional situations. This school of thought admits that there is another legal principle which lays down that 'consideration must move from the promisee', but this is a distinct principle which is quite independent of the doctrine of privity. According to the rival school, the principle that only a party to a contract may sue upon it is only another way of putting the rule that 'consideration must move from the promisee'. Controversy does not stop at this point, however, for the learned disagree over the merits of the doctrine (whatever it is), and whilst those who like it claim it is of great antiquity, those who dislike it opine that it is a modern and new-fangled departure from the wisdom of our ancestors. In the course of all this some pretty wild remarks are made.[3]

The early history of the attempts of the courts to work out principles which would determine who was entitled to sue for breach of promise is complicated; as might be expected, it took some time before any consistent principles emerged; then, as

---

[1] For discussion see Ames, 330 et seq., Fifoot 412.
[2] The leading modern case is *Beswick* v. *Beswick* [1968] A.C. 58.
[3] Of the modern literature see in particular M.P. Furmston, 'Return to *Dunlop* v. *Selfridge*', 23 M.L.R. 383, though not for wildness.

now, there was disagreement as to what the rules should be. By way of clearing the ground two preliminary observations may be made. The first is that all talk of 'privity' in the context of assumpsit, and talk of a rule which provides that only 'parties to a contract' can sue upon it, is obviously modern; lawyers in the sixteenth and seventeenth centuries simply did not think of the action of assumpsit as an action between parties to a contract, except when the action was being brought in lieu of the old contractual actions, it was instead an action for breach of a promise. The second is that the proposition 'consideration must move from the promisee', although it looks likely to be more ancient, is not in fact to be found in cases before the nineteenth century.[1] Somewhat similar expressions are to be found in seventeenth-century cases; thus in *De la Bar* v. *Gold* (1661),[2] Windham J. speaks of consideration 'moving':

'If the promise had been to J. S. from whom the consideration moved . . .'

and so indeed does counsel in *Crow* v. *Rogers* (1724),[3] but similarity here must not be confused with identity. The proposition that 'consideration must move from the promisee' really suggests two limitations upon the use of assumpsit—first the plaintiff must be the promisee, and secondly he must 'furnish'[4] consideration, or in contemporary terms be 'within' or 'not a stranger' to the consideration. In seventeenth-century law this amalgamation of the two limitations had not taken place, and it would be wrong to be misled by the appearance of something like the modern principle into confusing the propositions that only the promisee can sue with the distinct proposition that the plaintiff must be within the consideration. It is quite incorrect to suppose that the nineteenth-century principle is contained, as is often said, in *Bourne* v. *Mason* (1670). It takes some time to evolve sophistications like a

---

[1] *Price* v. *Easton* (1833) 4 B. & Ad. 433; *Thomas* v. *Thomas* (1842) 2 Q.B. 851.

[2] 1 Keb. 44, 63. See also *Fountain* v. *Smith* (1658) 2 Sid. 127; *Bourne* v. *Mason* (1670) 1 Vent. 6, 2 Keb. 457, 527.

[3] 1 Stra. 592, where counsel 'insisted, that there was no consideration moving from the plaintiff to support the promise'.

[4] This term reflects the modern idea that consideration is something provided 'in exchange' for the promise.

doctrine of privity of contract, or to sum up the law in so haunting and melancholy a phrase as 'consideration must move from the promisee'.

There are indeed many cases in the sixteenth and seventeenth centuries in which the courts wrestled with the problem of the third-party beneficiary, and one simple approach to transactions intended to benefit a third party is to allow the third party to sue if he does not obtain the intended benefit. In a number of cases the courts simply proceeded upon the footing that the intended beneficiary should be allowed to sue. A common form of agreement which gave rise to the problem was the marriage agreement, where the fathers of the prospective bride and groom reached an agreement over the endowment of the young couple, but the agreement was not performed; could the bridegroom sue, or must his father bring the action? Such a case was *Lever* v. *Heys* (1598),[1]

> 'In the King's Bench, the father of a girl promised the father of a boy that if he would be willing to give his consent to the marriage and assure forty pounds worth of land to the son, he, the father of the girl, would pay £200 to the son in marriage. And the question was if the son himself or his father should have the action on the case on assumpsit against the girl's father if he did not pay the £200. Popham and Fenner thought that the son should have the action. Clench to the contrary, Gawdy being absent'.

After considerable doubt it was held that the son must sue and not the father, though this continued to be controversial.[2] A more elaborate illustration of the same principle is found in the curious case of *Rippon* v. *Norton* (1601).[3] The defendant, for good consideration, promised that his son Richard would not make a nuisance of himself either to the plaintiff or to the plaintiff's son Walter. Richard, however, beat and wounded Walter, and the plaintiff sued. The action was supported by an averment that the plaintiff had lost the services of the son, and incurred medical expenses. The court held that the son was the

[1] Moo. K.B. 550, Cro. Eliz. 619, 652.
[2] Followed in *Provender* v. *Wood* (1627) Hetley, 30, not followed in *Archdale* v. *Barnard* (1607) 1 Rolle Ab. 30; *Cardinal* v. *Lewis* (n.d.) cited Hetley 176; *Bayfield* v. *Collard* (1646) 1 Rolle Ab. 31.
[3] Cro. Eliz. 849.

proper person to sue, not the father, because the father had suffered no recoverable damage through the wounding: he had not shown that the son was his servant, and the payments for medical expenses were voluntary. In so deciding the court was following *Lever* v. *Heys*; the son was to benefit by the performance of the promise, and he therefore was the one who lost if it was broken. The son sued in a second action and recovered.[1] The link in the reasoning in *Rippon* v. *Norton* between the right of action and the incidence of loss upon non-performance can be related to the idea that the person with an interest in performance should be allowed to sue, an idea mooted in the inconclusive case of *Hadves* v. *Levitt* (1630),[2] dealing with a marriage contract; here Richardson C.J. and Hutton J. inclined to favour the son's right of action:

'This action should have been more properly brought by the son, for he is the person in whom the interest is.'

But although there was quite a respectable line of authority in favour of the view that the person intended to benefit should have the right of action,[3] there were difficulties in accepting so simple a solution.

The first difficulty was a consequence of the fact that assumpsit was an action for breach of promise; inevitably this suggested the idea that the proper person to sue was the person to whom the promise had been made. Thus in *Taylor* v. *Foster* (1600)[4] the defendant, in consideration that the plaintiff would marry his daughter, undertook to pay £100 in two instalments to one J.S. to whom the plaintiff was indebted. On a motion in arrest of judgment it was held that the plaintiff was the proper person to sue, and not J.S.,

'although the £100 had been to be paid to a stranger, and not to himself; because the promise is unto him'.

The same principle was applied in *Jordan* v. *Jordan* (1594).[5]

---

[1] Cro. Eliz. 881, Yelv. 1.
[2] Hetley 176.
[3] See also *Rookwood's Case* (1589) 1 Leon. 193, Cro. Eliz. 164; *Manwood* v. *Burston* (1587) 2 Leon. 203; *Oldham* v. *Bateman* (1637) 1 Rolle Ab. 31.
[4] Cro. Eliz. 776, 807.
[5] Cro. Eliz. 369, 849. See also *Anon.* Hetley 12 and cf. *Weeks* v. *Tybald* (1604) Noy 11.

This principle, if accepted, will of course only exclude *some* third-party beneficiaries from a right of action; it will also encounter the difficulty of saying quite what is meant by a 'promisee'. However, it had its adherents.

A second and distinct difficulty was created by the doctrine of consideration. Although there are a number of cases in which the problem of the third-party beneficiary is discussed without any reference to consideration, there is another line of cases which reflect the idea that the real difficulty in the face of his suing was not so much the fact that he was often not the promisee, but rather that he was unable to show that the consideration which motivated the promise was a consideration or reason why *he* should be the lucky man with the right of action. Thus in *Lever* v. *Heys*[1] counsel, arguing in favour of the view that in a marriage agreement the father, not the son, should have the action, said,

> 'that the promise is only made with the father, and all the considerations arise on his part, and the son is a stranger thereto'.

In conformity with this view it could be argued that so long as a plaintiff could get over the difficulty about consideration, he ought to be allowed to sue even if he was not the promisee. This line of reasoning is well illustrated in the two leading cases of *Bourne* v. *Mason* (1670)[2] and *Dutton* v. *Poole* (1677).[3]

In *Bourne* v. *Mason* the facts were that one Parry was indebted to both Bourne and Mason,[4] and one Chaunter was indebted to Parry. In consideration that Parry would let Mason sue Chaunter, Mason promised to pay to Bourne part of the sum owed to him by Parry. The action was objected to on the ground that the plaintiff was not the person entitled to sue.[5] The decision of the court, which was against the plaintiff, turned on consideration; the court held that,

---

[1] Cro. Eliz. 619.

[2] 1 Vent. 6, 2 Keb. 457, 527.

[3] 3 Keb. 786, 814, 830, 836, Jones T. 102, 1 Vent. 318, 332, 2 Lev. 210, Sir T. Raymond 302. On the relevance of the decision to actions on deeds see *Gilbey* v. *Copley* (1683) 3 Lev. 138.

[4] And a co-defendant Robinson.

[5] It appears that the plaintiff was the promisee, though Kelyng C.J. (see 2 Keb. 527) seems to have thought he was not.

'here the plaintiff is a stranger, and no meritorious cause moves from him . . .'

or, as it is put in another report,

'But here the plaintiff did nothing of trouble to himself or benefit to the defendant, but is a mere stranger to the consideration'.

Thus the plaintiff was not allowed to sue because the consideration for the promise was not such as to show that *he* deserved to be allowed the right of action; the reason for the promise was not a reason why he should sue on it. The court considered that the case was similar to *De le Bar* v. *Gold* (1661),[1] an earlier case in which an action had been brought on a promise supported by a consideration moving from a third party; no decision is recorded, and the case provoked a bewildering diversity of opinion. A clear earlier precedent for the decision is *Ritler* v. *Dennet* (1606).[2] There C owed money to Ritler, and Dennett owned money to N. C at the request of Dennett paid the money he owed to N, and appointed Dennett to pay what he owed to Ritler for him. In consideration of all this Dennett promised to pay the money due to Ritler, who sued him on the promise. It was held that he could not do so,

'for he is a stranger to this and there is no consideration for any promise to him'.

In *Bourne* v. *Mason* the court approved two earlier decisions which might at first sight seem difficult to reconcile. In one, *Sprat* v. *Agar* (1658),[3] the father of a girl promised the father of a boy to settle land on the boy in consideration of marriage with his daughter, and it was held that the son, though not the promisee, could sue. This decision was approved because it was the son who 'did the meritorious act' by marrying the daughter. In the second a promise was made to a physician that if he performed a cure the promisor would pay a sum of money to the physician's daughter. This decision was approved because the preferment of the daughter was a benefit *to the*

---

[1] 1 Keb. 44, 63.
[2] 1 Rolle Ab. 30.
[3] 2 Sid. 115, but as there reported the case is quite irrelevant; the report must be erroneous.

physician; normally, of course, benefit to the *promisor* is relevant. This is a somewhat curious reason; the idea perhaps is that the stranger is entitled to sue if his (or her) suing will bring a benefit to the person who has furnished consideration. Thus on the facts of the case the court, in allowing the daughter to sue, was not depriving the physician of a benefit to which he, since he had performed the cure, was primarily entitled, but was conferring a benefit on him. It was also approved on the ground that 'the nearness of the relation gives the daughter the benefit of the consideration performed by her father'.

The line of reasoning adopted in *Bourne* v. *Mason*, which made the right to sue turn on consideration rather than upon the question 'Is the plaintiff the promisee?', was carried further in *Dutton* v. *Poole* (1677). There the defendant, Nevil Poole, in consideration that his father[1] Sir Edward Poole would refrain from cutting down certain timber trees (which he was proposing to sell to raise money to pay portions to his children), promised to pay to Sir Edward's daughter Grizil, his sister, £1,000. On this promise Grizil (as Mrs. Dutton) sued, with her husband Sir Ralph Dutton as co-plaintiff. The promise upon which the action was brought had been made to Sir Edward, and not to Grizil, who had not been present when the promise was made. It was held that the action could be maintained, though not without considerable doubt, and this judgment was affirmed in the Exchequer Comber. The ground for the decision is not very easy to appreciate, but it is perhaps most clearly stated in the following two passages, which are taken from different reports of the case:

'And now Scroggs C.J. said: That there was such apparent consideration of affection from the father to his children, for whom nature obliges him to provide, that the consideration and promise to the father may well extend to the children'.

'The Court said, it might be another case, if the money had been to have been paid to a stranger, but there is such a nearness of relation between the father and the child, and 'tis a kind of debt to the child to be provided for, that the plaintiff is plainly concerned.'

[1] To whom he was heir apparent at law. The father was tenant for life without impeachment of waste, and was therefore legally entitled to cut the timber trees

The reasoning of the court seems to have been something like this: the objection to allowing the daughter to sue is that the daughter is a 'stranger' to the consideration and promise. What this means is that it was her father who gave something up when the trees were not cut down, not the daughter; furthermore the promise was not made to her. She therefore has no legitimate interest in the performance of the promise; she did not deserve to be allowed to sue. To this the court replies that the daughter had an interest in the consideration. As Sir Edward's child she had a moral right to be provided for, and the timber trees were going to be cut down in order to raise money to pay her a portion. Sir Edward's giving up his right to cut down the trees (which was the consideration) meant that she lost her portion, and the defendant's promise to pay money was in lieu of a portion. She was therefore interested in the consideration. Just as she was morally entitled to the portion, so she is morally entitled to sue on the promise given in lieu, and therefore has a legitimate interest in the enforcement of the promise. Furthermore the agreement was clearly ('apparent') motivated by natural love and affection for Grizil, and thus Grizil can show that the consideration for the agreement is a consideration why she should be allowed to sue. Reasoning of this kind, with its emphasis on the plaintiff's moral right, appears little short of weird to a twentieth-century lawyer; this is because we tend to forget the fact that the original reason why the presence of consideration for a promise provided an argument for allowing that promise to be sued upon was that some principle of common-sense morality suggested that the consideration provided a special ground for saying that the promise ought to be performed. This reasoning came to be built into the law; *Dutton v. Poole* (1677) dates from a period when the building was going on, and therefore the references to moral principle are explicit. When law is being made it has to be justified by reference to extra-legal principles; once it has been made such justification ceases to be necessary.

Somewhat special problems were raised over who could sue in assumpsit when the action was being used to replace the older medieval contractual actions. In the cases we have considered so far the right to sue was (except in cases turning solely upon the benefit text) determined by reference to who was the promisee, or by reference to the consideration for the promise. In the medieval contractual actions such as debt and account such ideas had no place, and when assumpsit came to be used to do the work of the older actions there was some difficulty in fitting old-established rights of action into the new mould. This is well illustrated by the history of the right of action of C when money has been paid by A to B to be paid over to him.[1]

In medieval law if money or property was delivered to B to be handed over or paid over to C, C had a right of action. For property he could bring detinue, the delivery to the intermediary altering the property in his favour; in the case of money he could bring account, and, after some doubt debt, though this was still to some extent disputed throughout the sixteenth century.[2] In so far as there was any theory as to why the beneficiary could sue although he was not a party to the contract (and there was precious little), it was that a trust was created by the delivery 'to the use' of the third party, which the law would enforce. In sixteenth-century law it became settled too that if the payment to C was to be in performance of some precedent duty owed by A to C, or was supported by consideration, A could not countermand his instructions and get the money back.[3] This provided an additional reason why C should be allowed a right of action.

In *Howlet* v. *Osbourn* (1595)[4] an attempt was made to bring assumpsit, the plaintiff suing on an express promise by the defendant intermediary to pay the money—there was no difficulty therefore over the plaintiff not being a promisee. Nevertheless the action failed, apparently because it was thought that there was no consideration for the promise. A second attempt in *Gilbert* v. *Ruddeard* (1607)[5] succeeded. Here one Tempest had delivered money to the defendant to deliver it to the plaintiff in discharge of a prior liability. Popham C.J. justified the decision in this way,

---

[1] On this subject see Jackson, *History of Quasi-Contract*, pp. 30–1, 93–103.

[2] See *Core's Case* (1536) Dyer 20a, Brooke, *Dette* pl. 129; *Whorewood* v. *Shaw* (1602) Yelv. 25, Moo. K.B. 667, Cro. Eliz. 729, Owen 127; *Clark's Case* (1614) Godbolt 210; *Harris* v. *De Bervoir* (1625) Cro. Jac. 687.

[3] *Lyte* v *Peny* (1541) Dyer 49a; *Clark's Case* (1588) 2 Leon. 30.

[4] Cro. Eliz. 380. See also Keilwey 77 for an early suggestion that case lay on account.

[5] Dyer 272b *in margine*.

'When Tempest delivered the money to the defendant to deliver to the plaintiff, there was included an agreement of the defendant to deliver it to the plaintiff, which agreement will charge him in assumpsit to him who ought to have the money'.

Popham's implied agreement may have been designed to get over the difficulty that the plaintiff was not a promisee, but this is not clear. Tanfield agreed, subject to a qualification,

'when there is any precedent matter which caused the delivery, as in our case by a debt, then the delivery cannot be countermanded'.

Both judges apparently thought that there ought to be some consideration for the implied agreement (more particularly Tanfield J.) and that this requirement was satisfied by the precedent duty to pay the money, though whether the reference is to Tempest's duty or the defendant's is not clear. *Gilbert* v. *Ruddeard* (1607) was following in *Beckington and Lambert* v. *Vaughan* (1616),[1] when it was held that *indebitatus assumpsit* lay, and in other cases.[2] There was no difficulty over consideration; the receipt of the money to the plaintiff's use was treated as consideration. The form of action in later seventeenth-century law was an action of *indebitatus assumpsit* for money had and received to the plaintiff's use.[3]

However, as Jackson points out,[4] there is a theoretical difficulty if one accepts a doctrine of privity in justifying the beneficiaries' right of action,

'If the trust concept is eliminated, it is not easy to distinguish the principle of these cases from that of allowing a third person to sue on a contract to which he was not a party'.

Thus in the nineteenth century, beginning with the case of *Williams* v. *Everett* in 1811,[5] the idea gained ground that some

---

[1] 1 Rolle Rep. 391, Moo. K.B. 854.
[2] *Oldham* v. *Bateman* (1637) 1 Rolle Ab. 31, *Disborne* v. *Denobie* (1649) 1 Rolle Ab. 31, *Starkey* v. *Milne* (1651) 1 Rolle Ab. 32.
[3] *Brown* v. *London* (1670) 1 Mod. 285, 1 Vent. 152.
[4] op. cit., p. 97.
[5] 14 East. 582.

sort of relationship or 'privity' must exist between beneficiary and intermediary. The consequence was a tendency to restrict the beneficiaries' right of action, exemplified in a tangled body of case law.

General principles and the doctrine of consideration

The doctrine of consideration developed piecemeal in the typical manner of common law doctrines, and the evolution of succinct statements of the requirement was retrospective; furthermore there were, during our period, no institutional works of any quality dealing with the doctrine, so that the orthodox learning was never tidied up, and had to be gleaned from what was recorded in the disorderly law reports of the sixteenth and seventeenth centuries. Basically a consideration meant, as we have seen, what Periam J. called,

'a moving cause or consideration precedent, for which cause or consideration the promise was made'.[1]

Sheppard, in his rambling work on actions on the case published in 1663, includes such definitions as

'the material cause of the Contract, without the which the same is not binding'.[2]

Throughout the whole of our period this is what consideration 'meant', but a lawyer wants to know more than this; he needs to know what sort of consideration will serve to impose liability. One line of approach to this need is reflected in definitions of consideration of the type found in *Calthorpe's Case* (1573),[3]

'a cause or occasion meritorious, requiring a mutual recompense in fact or law'.

'Meritorious' consideration, consideration that is of desert, persists throughout our period, and the underlying idea is not a surprising one—a promise to do what one ought to do, to render to another his due, given in consideration of the circumstances giving rise to the prior obligation, or simply in

---

[1] *Sidenham* v. *Worthington* 2 Leon. 224, Cro. Eliz. 224.
[2] Sheppard, 19.
[3] Dyer 334b.

consideration of it, should surely in commonsense be performed.[1] Promises to return lost dogs, observe the award of
arbitrators, pay debts, make marriage gifts to one's children,
pay for services requested—these are all illustrations of the
notion.

Another popular approach involved analysing all good
considerations in terms of benefit to the promisor or detriment
to the promisee. The emphasis upon benefit in the analysis
reflects the idea that promises should be binding if the promisor
has been paid, or has received (or will receive) something in
return; in modern terms consideration is 'the price of the
promise'. This idea in its turn came to be muddled up with the
old notion of *quid pro quo*—Sheppard,[2] for example, says,

> 'Some contracts also are clad with a consideration, and have
> *quid pro quo* in them (that is to say) where there is something
> in the agreement that is a recompense in deed or in law, and
> is the material cause of the engagement, by which it is made
> obligatory . . .'

and there is much more to the same effect. The insistence upon
benefit indeed provokes the numerous cases where it has to be
pointed out that it is not the only form of good consideration.[3]
Detriment, the other half of the analysis, reflects the notion of
induced reliance which as we have seen fits uneasily into a
doctrine cast in the form of rules about the reasons for promises,
and at times is presented as the only test of consideration, as in
Chapman v. *Barnaby* (1615),[4] in certain types of case,

> 'for the matter considerable in such actions upon the case
> for promises made is not whether the party which doth thus
> assume, hath or is to have any benefit thereby, but only
> whether the other, to whom the promise is thus made, hath
> any manner of prejudice by it'.

The benefit–detriment analysis originally appears in connection
with the discharge of promissory liability in *Richards* v. *Bartlett*

---

[1] See *Stone* v. *Wythipol* (1588) Cro. Eliz. 126, etc.; *Bosden* v. *Sir John Thinn*
(1603) Cro. Jac. 18; *Flight* v. *Crasden* (1624) Cro. Car. 8; *Lampleigh* v. *Braithwaite*
(1616) Hob. 105, *Dutton* v. *Poole* (1677) Sir T. Raymond 302, etc.

[2] Sheppard, 18.

[3] e.g. *Freeman* v. *Freeman* (1615) 2 Bulst. 261, 1 Rolle Rep. 269.

[4] 2 Bulst. 278. The context is consideration of forbearance.

(1587),[1] and is derived from earlier cases dealing with the doctrine of accord and satisfaction, in particular *Onely* v. *Earl of Kent* (1577).[2] It is first applied to the creation of promissory liability by Coke, arguing in *Stone* v. *Wythipol* (1588)[3] thus,

'. . . every consideration that doth charge the defendant in an assumpsit must be to the benefit of the defendant or charge of the plaintiff, and no case can be put out of this rule'.

But Coke's rule, though often repeated, was probably originally intended as a formulation of the idea of sufficiency or adequacy of consideration (not then distinguished as terms of art), and it can only be applied to cases involving, for example, marriage, or precedent debt, as consideration by very artificial reasoning. A more helpful way of looking at the decisions is to see benefit consideration, detriment consideration, and meritorious consideration as three different categories.[4]

It is natural to seek, behind the rules of law, for some general explanation in terms of contemporary social conditions or ideas, and this is right. Hence it has been suggested, notably by Mr. Fifoot, that the evolution of the doctrine of consideration reflects the idea that the courts should only hold commercial agreements actionable, and concern themselves with the bargains of businessmen.[5] Fifoot argued that a law of contract must be based upon either the principle of bargain or the principle of promise, an antithesis I should not accept as inevitable. Direct evidence for his view is not to be found, and indirect evidence hardly supports it; it hardly seems to be the sort of idea which sixteenth-century men would find appealing. The courts dealt with cases involving commerce, though the contractual instrument of the commercial world was the bond, not the informal promise. But family agreements, obligations to return lost dogs, bets, gratuitous guarantees, and a host of petty transactions which had little to do with big

[1] I Leon. 19.
[2] Dyer 355b.
[3] Cro. Eliz. 126, 1 Leon. 113, Owen 94, Latch 21.
[4] As in *Reynolds* v. *Prosser* (1656) Har. 71.
[5] Fifoot, 395 *et seq* P.S. Aliyah in *Consideration in Contracts, A Fundamental Restatement*, Australian National University Press, Canberra 1971 has from a non-historical viewpoint questioned the bargain theory.

business were held actionable too. Nor was there any general principle denying actionability to gratuitous undertakings or promises of gifts, the most important gift being the marriage gift. Assumpsit was developed around a compromise, according to which not *all* promises were actionable, but only those supported by consideration. More radically, the view that the law of contract is the handmaid of commerce seems to me to be mistaken if it is opposed to the view that the law of contract expresses, in a form thought appropriate (bearing in mind the practicalities of litigation), moral ideas. For commerce, like other areas of life, must be conducted morally if the general good is to be furthered, and there is no special set of principles of commercial morality. The doctrine of consideration is indeed intensely moralistic, and we may disagree with some of its judgments; what is mistaken is to fail to see that a good law of contract has as its function in relation to the commercial world the imposition of decent moral standards.

VIII

IMPLIED PROMISES AND
QUASI-CONTRACT

THE sixteenth and seventeenth centuries saw the beginnings of the evolution of the branch of the law which came to be known as *quasi-contract*, though this branch of the law mainly developed in Lord Holt's time and after. The term itself comes from the civil law, in which institutional writers distinguished between obligations which arose *ex contractu* and obligations which arose *ex delicto*. Confronted with certain obligations which did not happily fit into either category the scheme was modified to include quasi-contractual and quasi-delictual obligations. An example of a quasi-contractual obligation is the obligation to return money paid in error to a person to whom it is not owed. The civilian conception of a quasi-contract was the product of analytical systematization: that is to say it was evolved *ex post facto* in an attempt to provide a rational set of categories in terms of which the law could be expounded. The term 'quasi-contract' was known to common lawyers, and borrowed by them as a label to describe situations where liability for breach of promise was imposed and made remediable by action of assumpsit although the promise sued upon was in some sense implied or fictional, or at least need not be proved by the plaintiff. The use of a civilian term does not, however, mean that the contents of the common law category of quasi-contracts or implied contracts are derived from the civil law, and in typical common law fashion the evolution of this branch of the law proceeded piecemeal. In particular it is not possible to unify the case law in terms of the principle against unjust enrichment; first, because there is no contemporary evidence of the conscious adoption of such a principle, and second, because some of the situations in which a promise was implied by law—for example, implied mutual promises to perform the award of arbitrators—are not explicable in terms of such a principle.

The basic reason for the development of implied assumpsit

was the desire to use a convenient form of action to remedy certain duties or obligations recognized either directly by law or by common sense or justice. For example, the law said that debts should be paid, but if the action of assumpsit was to be used to ensure that this was done there had to be a promise; if in fact there had been no promise in reality then the solution (if one wanted to permit assumpsit) was to engage in some deeming. Or again when money is paid under a mistake the right thing to do is to return it, and if the obligation to do this is to be sanctioned by assumpsit then a fictional promise will normally be required to keep the record straight. There is no natural limit to the extension of an action for breach of promise by this technique; it would be perfectly conceivable for the liability to pay damages for negligence in a running down case to be based upon an implied promise, and anyone who supposes the technique to be obsolete should reflect upon the conceptual devices employed in modern case law to justify the action for negligent mis-statement. How far the conception of an implied promise is extended will depend upon complex factors, prominent amongst them being the readiness of the courts to manipulate the law to fill gaps in its scheme of remedies, and the availability of other techniques and procedures.

Two factors particularly encouraged the use of the implied promise in the common law. The first is that a system of parole contract law which does not insist upon the use of formal expressions, or contractual ceremonies (such as the hand clasp), is bound to encounter some difficulty in drawing a dividing line between situations in which there has genuinely been a promise or agreement and situations where there has not, though the circumstances are such that an obligation ought to be imposed. At one end of the scale there can be an express verbal promise, as when the promisor actually says 'I promise to go to York'. More common is the case when the promise has to be deduced or 'implied' from conduct or less formal language, or some combination of the two, as when one says 'Here we are then' to the girl at the cash desk in the supermarket, pointing to the contents of a wire basket. At the other end of the scale is, for example, the obligation, imposed by law, to return money paid under mistake of fact, where any talk of an implied promise at the moment of receipt or indeed later may be purely fictional.

The blurring of the distinction between the categories was in one way very beneficial, since it enabled the action of assumpsit to be used to sanction duties which might otherwise have been difficult to accommodate within the scheme of common law actions, though the price paid for this was a considerable degree of conceptual confusion.

The second was the influence of the doctrine of consideration. Latent in this doctrine, as we have seen, was the notion that the strongest case for the imposition of promissory liability was where the promisor undertook to do something which (for one reason or another) he was bound to do anyway. From this it is no great step to say that the law will imply a promise (where none had been given) to perform the pre-existing duty. Thus why should not the law imply a promise to pay for services rendered at request, or to pay a debt, or return goods found to their owner? To take such a step involves treating the consideration as the ultimate basis of liability, rather than the promise, which becomes a mere fiction required by the particular form of action employed to sanction the duty.

Implied promises to pay debts[1]

The device of the implied promisor to perform an existing duty first achieved prominence in actions of assumpsit brought, for procedural reasons, in lieu of debt, and in this context the confusion between promises implied from the circumstances (promises 'in fact') and fictional implied promises (promises 'implied in law') is very obvious.

Actions of assumpsit against debtors originally had to be squared, however speciously, with the dogma which disapproved of overlapping remedies. At least until *Slade's Case* (1602)[2] it was said that the promise, upon which assumpsit was brought, was something different from the debt contract, on which the older action lay, and in so far as the theory of the matter was to be taken seriously, it followed that there ought to be two transactions—a contract and a promise—between the parties. Sometimes, as Lücke[3] has pointed out, theory and real life would readily coincide, for it is common enough for those

---

[1] See above, Ch. III.
[2] 4 Co.Rep. 91a.
[3] In 81 L.Q.R. at 549.

who owe debts to promise to pay them, promises being quite commonly used to reinforce existing obligations. There was indeed a school of thought which insisted upon an averment of a subsequent promise to pay a debt as an essential to the use of assumpsit against simple contract debtors. Thus in a case in 1572[1] Manwood argued that,

> 'he ought to have said *quod postea assumpsit*, for if he assumes at the time of the contract then debt lies on this and not assumpsit, but if he assumes after the contract, then an action lies on the assumpsit, and otherwise not'.

The court of King's Bench agreed. But this view does not seem to have prevailed, though the practice of declaring on a subsequent promise was revived in the seventeenth century as a possible form of pleading.

Where no reliance was placed upon a subsequent promise it was only by some form of doctrinal fiction that one transaction—say a sale of goods—could be viewed as two transactions—a sale and a promise. The court of King's Bench, being sympathetic to the use of assumpsit, adopted the doctrine that, where there was a debt contract and the debt was still owing, the law would imply a promise to pay the debt. Every contract executory imports or implies an assumpsit.[2] This must be understood in terms of directing jurymen; they may be told not to trouble their heads looking for two transactions; all they need to decide was whether a debt was owed, and, if one was, the law would supply the promise. In *Edwards* v. *Burre* (1573)[3] this is very clearly put by Wray C.J. Assumpsit had been brought on a promise to repay a loan; the plaintiff gave in evidence that he had lent the sum, thus providing evidence of the contract of loan. But what about the promise?

> 'Wray, Justice, said to the jury that if it was true that the plaintiff lent the said sum, then you ought to find for the plaintiff, for the debt is an assumption in law'.

In the Common Pleas during the period in the sixteenth century when that court was allowing assumpsit in lieu of debt it appears

---

[1] Dalison 84.
[2] First suggested in *Norwood* v. *Read* (1558) Plowden 180; *Estrigge* v. *Owles* (1588) 3 Leon. 201.
[3] Dalison 104, and see *Anon.* (1586) Godbolt 98.

that juries were told that they must find for the defendant unless they were satisfied that the plaintiff had proved a promise as well as a debt, though whether jurymen would make much of such a curious direction is doubtful. In *Slade's Case* itself the jury, no doubt coached, found a special verdict designed to raise the double-remedy doctrine with the precision of a moot case. To this end it was essential that there should be no suggestion of there having been two transactions between the parties; what was sought was an unequivocal decision that debt and assumpsit were purely alternative remedies on the same single transaction. Thus the plaintiff did not aver a subsequent promise, but one given at the moment of sale. The jury found that the sale took place as averred, but added,

'that betwixt the said J. Slade and the said H. Morley there was no promise or taking upon himself besides the said bargain aforesaid'.

The resolution of the Exchequer Chamber was that,

'Every contract executory imports in itself an assumpsit, for when one agrees to pay money, or to deliver any thing, thereby he assumes or promises to pay or deliver it . . .'

This resolution canonized the doctrinal fiction of the King's Bench (though whether this was intended seems to me obscure). Hence in seventeenth-century law, actions of assumpsit against debtors tended to be viewed as based upon promises implied in law, that is on fictional promises, even though debts would normally result from genuine consensual transactions. This somewhat perverse state of affairs inevitably confused the distinction between fictional and non-fictional promises.

The common 'indebitatus' counts

The confusion was inevitably encouraged by the evolution, after the decision in *Slade's Case* (and the disapproval of the action on a general *indebitatus assumpsit solvere*) of the new form of *indebitatus assumpsit*, in which standard or common forms of count were evolved for debts arising (for example) for the price of goods sold and delivered, goods bargained and sold, money lent, work and services performed. In all these cases the plaintiff averred a debt and a promise to pay the debt, and the promise was an implied one in the sense that there was no need for the jury to find that any actual promise had been made by the debtor. In general, however, the liability involved arose consensually, but there was no reason in principle why *indebitatus* counts could not be evolved to enforce liability which did not originate in a consensual transaction between the parties. So long as the situation was one in which a debt fell due, an action could be maintained upon an implied promise to pay it, and debts could perfectly well arise by operation of law, or in consequence upon some transaction to which the plaintiff was not a party. In this way quasi-contractual liability could be remedied by action of assumpsit. The development of the law here led to the evolution of *indebitatus assumpsit* for money had and received to the plaintiff's use, for money paid to the defendant's use at the request of the plaintiff, and to the employment of *indebitatus assumpsit* to recover a variety of debts, such as customary dues, which fell due by operation of law quite independently of any consensual transaction, implied trust, or principle of unjust enrichment. It also gave rise to the action for a *quantum meruit* and *quantum valebant*, which has, as we shall see, a distinct history.

'Indebitatus assumpsit' for money had and received to the plaintiff's use

The source of this form of pleading was the situation where A paid money to B to transmit to C.[1] In medieval law[2] it was settled that C could sue by action of account. In the course of the sixteenth century debt came to be an alternative remedy to account, though this was long treated as arguable.[3] The theory of the matter was that the transaction gave rise to what we should call a trust, and this trust could be enforced at the suit of the intended beneficiary. Granted that a debt was due, attempts were made to use assumpsit in place of the older action. The first case was *Howlett* v. *Osbourn* (1595)[4] where the attempt failed. In 1610 *indebitatus assumpsit* was allowed in

---

[1] See Jackson, *Quasi-Contract*, pp. 30–1 and 93; *H.E.L.* VIII. 88 et seq.
[2] See above, p. 184.
[3] See *Core's Case* (1536) Dyer 19b; the point was still arguable in *Harris* v. *De Bervoir* (1624) Cro. Jac. 687.
[4] Cro. Eliz. 380.

Rooke v. *Rooke* and again in 1616 in *Beckington and Lambert* v. *Vaughan*.[1] *Rooke* v. *Rooke* also involved a claim to recover money paid to a third party at the defendant's request. The same development lies behind the use of this form of action to recover money paid under a mistake. Account lay to recover money paid under mistake in late-sixteenth-century law,[2] though the precise scope of this liability is left very uncertain in the cases; debt becomes concurrent with account, and therefore *indebitatus assumpsit* lies, the earliest case being *Bonnel* v. *Fowke* in 1657.[3] The extension of the action to recover money paid upon a consideration that has wholly failed lies outside our period, but the germ of the idea is perhaps again traceable back to the law of account, where money had to be received without consideration to be accountable. The liability of a usurper of an office and for interception of rents also derives from account.[4] The action for money had and received was inherently capable of further extension to situations in which previously no action lay, but in origin all that was involved was a change in the procedure for enforcing admitted liability: it was not until the late seventeenth century that the potentialities of the action began to be appreciated.

'Indebitatus' for money paid at request

There is very little early authority on the right to recover for money paid by the plaintiff to a third party at the defendant's request.[5] In principle there cannot have been any objection to special assumpsit in such a situation; the problem turns on the theoretical availability of debt, a prerequisite to *indebitatus assumpsit*. The liability here was probably originally developed by analogy with the liability to pay for services rendered to a third party at the defendant's request. In *Lady Shandois* v. *Simson* (1600)[6] it was held that either debt or assumpsit lay to

[1] Cro. Jac. 245, 1 Rolle Rep. 391, Moo. K.B. 854. See also *Gilbert* v. *Ruddeard* (1607) Dyer 272 *in margine*, which was not an *indebitatus assumpsit*.
[2] *Framson* v. *Delamere* (1595) Cro. Eliz. 458; *Hewer* v. *Bartholomew* (1598) Cro. Eliz. 614. See Jackson, op. cit., 6.
[3] 2 Sid. 4, a very obscure decision.
[4] See *Woodward* v. *Aston* (1672) 2 Mod. 95, 1 Vent. 296, 1 Freeman 429; *Arris* v. *Stukeley* (1677) 2 Mod. 260, discussed by Jackson, op. cit., 61 et seq.
[5] See Jackson, op. cit., pp. 30 and 46.
[6] Cro. Eliz. 880; see above, p. 430. And see *Bret* v. *J.S.* (1600) Cro. Eliz. 756.

recover the agreed remuneration for embroidering a third party's gown; this settled a long-standing controversy as to whether the conferring of a benefit upon a third party constituted a *quid pro quo* to support debt. It followed that *indebitatus assumpsit* would lie. It may have been felt that by analogy a payment of money to a third party at request would give rise to a debt due to the person who had requested the payment, and to whose use the payment might be said to have been made, but I know of no authority. In *Rooke* v. *Rooke* (1610)[1] an action was brought for breach of a promise given in consideration that the promisor was indebted for

> 'forty pounds, viz. *pro diversis denariorum summis ei praestitis, ac pro diversis denariorum summis de eodem Richardo receptis et habitis, et pro quadam pecuniae summa,* by the plaintiff at the request to one John Amias paid for diet . . .'

The declaration was objected to on a motion in arrest of judgment on two grounds, one being that it was too general (and thus infringed the ban on a general *indebitatus*), but though it failed it did not fail for this reason. Nor was there any objection to the averment of a debt for money paid at request. We must conclude that it was by then admitted that in principle *indebitatus assumpsit* was available in such a case, and the promise, as in other actions of *indebitatus assumpsit,* came to be a mere fiction. This is the earliest example of which I know.[2] The later extension of the action was encouraged by the implication of a request, an innovation outside our period.

Actions for a 'quantum meruit' or 'quantum valebant'

A debt was by definition a certain sum due; hence in medieval law there was no question of any form of declaration in the action of debt which involved claiming a *quantum meruit* or *quantum valebant,* though there was no objection in principle to a claim in debt for a definite sum whose quantification depended upon some rule of law and not the agreement of the parties.[3]

---

[1] Cro. Jac. 245; this case was not noted by Jackson.

[2] For the special problem raised by cases where A supplied goods to B at C's request, see Jackson, op. cit. 47, and Ames, 94. If the payment on delivery to the third party made *him* the debtor then the defendant could not also be a debtor; hence he must be liable if at all in special assumpsit.

[3] See above, p. 46.

This continued to be the position in the sixteenth century, and it must be noted that debt was excluded even where the plaintiff declared upon an agreement to pay a reasonable sum coupled with an averment of a precise sum as being that reasonable sum; such a declaration certainly *claimed* a sum certain, but this was not thought to render the declaration unobjectionable.[1] For what was involved was a rule of substantive law—an agreement to pay a reasonable sum for services or a reasonable price for goods did not in law give rise to a debt. So long as this remained so, actions of *indebitatus assumpsit* could plainly not be brought on such transactions, and this opened the way for the use of assumpsit, which was well established in the late sixteenth century. Amongst the earliest examples is the case of *Floyd* v. *Irish*, decided in the King's Bench in 1587.[2] By 1600 the action was well established in the Common Pleas as well.

The evolution of this form of assumpsit has been much misunderstood. The early cases do not appear to be connected with fictional implied promises to pay reasonable remuneration. The plaintiff declares on a promise to pay 'a reasonable sum', or a variant such as 'as much as will content him'. To this is coupled an averment specifying what is a reasonable sum. Thus in *Floyd* v. *Irish*:

'A doth promise to pay B for his reasonable board, for such time as he shall be with him'.

The report continues,

'B sets forth in his declaration that he was with him ten months, and that five shillings a month is reasonable, amounting in all to fifty shillings'.

Similarly the declaration in *Delaby* v. *Hassel* (1587)[3] was

'that the defendant in consideration that he had retained the plaintiff to go from London to Paris to merchandise divers goods to the profit of the defendant, promised to give him so much as would content him, and also to give him all

---

[1] *Young* v. *Ashburnam* (1587) 3 Leon. 161.
[2] Sheppard 71; *Mery* v. *Lewes* (1587) 2 Leon. 53; *Delaby* v. *Hassel* (1587) 1 Leon. 123; *Anon.* (1588) Godbolt 145; *Royle* v. *Bagshaw* (1590) Cro. Eliz. 149.
[3] 1 Leon. 123.

and every sum of money that he would expend there in his affairs, and further declared that he was contented to have £20 for his labour'.

In the seventeenth century the practice of declaring upon a promise to pay what was deserved, *quantum meruit*, coupled with an averment saying what was deserved, was upheld as not infringing the general rule that a promise to be sued upon must be certain; similarly declarations in the *quantum valebant* form for goods supplied were upheld.[1] Hence arose what were called the common counts upon a *quantum meruit* or *quantum valebant*. The most remarkable example of the action is perhaps *Gardiner* v. *Fulforde* (1667) where a *quantum meruit* was brought for supplying 'four painted whores'[2] the pleader's Latin being defective.

Originally the promise sued upon in *quantum meruit* actions appears to have been implied from conduct, rather than to have been fictional, though the distinction is inevitably rather shadowy; the jury could always find a promise from the conduct of the defendant and did not ever have to find that formal promissory expressions were used. The distinction largely turns upon how the matter was put to a jury, on which there is no clear contemporary evidence, though such as there is suggests that juries were positively encouraged to find a promise whenever services or goods were supplied at request.[3] It is possible, though by no means clear, that the implication of a promise was a matter of law when the plaintiff was bound to provide the service, as in the case of a common carrier or innkeeper.

In the course of the seventeenth century there developed a tenuous chain of authority[4] in favour of allowing debt to lie on a *quantum meruit*. There is nothing particularly surprising in

---

[1] *Rogers* v. *Head* (1610) Cro. Jac. 262; *Shepherd* v. *Edwards* (1613) Cro. Jac. 370; *Hall* v. *Lallard* (1621) Cro. Jac. 618; *Ive* v. *Chester* (1620) Cro. Jac. 560; *Rolt* v. *Sharpe* (1626) Cro. Car. 77. See also *Warbrook* v. *Griffin* (1607) 2 Brownl. 254, Moo. K.B. 876.

[2] 1 Lev. 204.

[3] See *Warbrook* v. *Griffin* (1609) 2 Brownl. 254, Moo. K.B. 876, relied on by Ames as showing that an implied *quantum meruit* was actionable; the case is really inconclusive.

[4] *The Six Carpenters Case* (1610) 8 Co.Rep. 147a; *Waring* v. *Perkins* (1619) Cro. Jac. 626; *contra Mason* v. *Welland* (1688) Skin. 238, 242.

this; the plaintiff claimed a sum certain, quantified by reason or desert. If a debt could be said to arise then it followed that *indebitatus assumpsit* also lay. Eventually this came to be settled law,[1] with the consequence that the common counts on a *quantum meruit* and *valebant* became otiose; the plaintiff gained no advantage by declaring upon them in preference to common *indebitatus* counts for goods sold or services rendered. But this development largely lay outside our period; the ill-reported case of *King* v. *Locke* (1663)[2] and the case of *Tate* v. *Lewen* (1672)[3] are the earliest examples of the use of *indebitatus* counts on a *quantum meruit*.

Actions on account stated

Probably the action of debt lay in medieval law upon any informal accounting together, whether or not the defendant was legally compellable to account.[4] Whether or not this was so, there developed in the seventeenth century a form of assumpsit known as *insimul computasset*, and later as the action on an account stated, in which the plaintiff relied upon an averment that the parties had accounted together—that is to say, stated accounts to each other—and that the defendant had promised to pay the sum for he was found to be in arrears.[5] The earliest example is *Egles* v. *Vale* (1605)[6] where the plaintiff declared on an accounting together, a finding that the defendant was in arrears £10 and a promise to pay the arrears. It was moved,

'there is not any consideration nor cause to ground such an action, for the being found in arrearages is not any cause to make a special promise, nor is there any thing done on the plaintiff's part whereupon the promise should be grounded, viz. the forbearing of the suit or any such thing. *Sed non allocantur*; for the Debt itself without any other special cause, is sufficient to ground the action'.

---

[1] See Bullen and Leake, *Pleading*, 3rd ed., 35, Chitty, *Pleading*, 7th ed., 351, and see 2 Wms. Saund. 122, n. 2.

[2] 1 Keb. 422.

[3] 2 Wms. Saund. 371. On these cases see Fifoot 360 et seq.

[4] See above, p. 178.

[5] See S. Stoljar, 'What is Account Stated?', 4 Sydney L.R. 373, Jackson, *Quasi-Contract*, 105.

[6] Cro. Jac. 69, Yelv. 70. *Whorwood* v. *Gybbons* (1587) Gould. 48 is cited by Jackson, but is not an example: the promise there was in consideration of forbearance.

The theory of the action changed, in that the accounting together came to be regarded as the consideration; this was said in *Dalby* v. *Cooke* (1609)[1] and *Bard* v. *Bard* (1620):[2]

> 'they accompting together, and he promising to pay, was a sufficient cause of his action'.

Any difficulty over the rule against past consideration was got round by an averment that the promise was made at the moment of the finding in arrears.[3] It was not necessary to set out the grounds of the various items of the account, so that they might include debts for rent, and legacies[4]—debts that is not remediable directly by *indebitatus assumpsit*. Thus in *Brinsley* v. *Partridge* (1611)[5] it was moved for error that

> 'the consideration was not sufficient, because the plaintiff did not show whether the money upon the said account was due as for money received or lent or for wares bought and sold',

but the court rejected this argument. This meant that the action came near to constituting a revival of the old general *indebitatus* count, disapproved in *Slade's Case*, in substance if not in form.[6]

In the early cases the promise sued upon was probably genuine, though here again the distinction between a genuine and a fictitious promise is hard to draw where there has in fact been a mutual statement of accounts. It came to be said, however, that the promise would be implied by law:

> 'le ley fait un promise a ceo paier'.

The earliest evidence is *Vigerous* v. *Drake* (1649).[7] The development can have meant little more than a change in emphasis in the way the matter was put to the jury. Much later, in the

---

[1] Cro. Jac. 234, 1 Bulst. 16, Yelv. 171.

[2] Cro. Jac. 602.

[3] *Janson* v. *Colemore* (1616) 1 Rolle 397, 3 Bulst. 208, Moo. K.B. 854.

[4] As in *Bard* v. *Bard*.

[5] Hob. 88.

[6] See also *Goodwin* v. *Willoughby* (n.d.) Noy 81; *Benson* v. *Sankoredge* (1628) Hetley 85; *Holmes* v. *Savill* (1628) Cro. Car. 116; *Ayre* v. *Sils* (1648) Style 131, and see generally Lücke in 82 L.Q.R. 89 et seq. There was a difficulty if the items included a debt due by bond, since the accounting did not discharge the bond; see *Anon.* (1626) Litt. 148.

[7] 1 Rolle Ab. f. 22, *Conye* v. *Lawes* (1655) Style 472, Sheppard 24.

early nineteenth century, the scope of the action was extended
by making the accounting fictional; the mere acknowledgement
of a sum due (which could be a single item) was treated
as evidence of an accounting together.[1] This development,
however, lies well outside our period; as Jackson[2] points out,
the reason was to allow the recovery of sums where recovery
based on the original transaction was barred by the Statute of
Frauds.

The action on an account stated was not an *indebitatus
assumpsit*. There was no averment of indebtedness involved in
the standard form of pleading. Jackson has suggested that the
action on an account stated was evolved to cover cases where
the accounting did not create a debt, so that an *indebitatus* was
not available and some other form of pleading had to be
evolved. His authority for this is *Milward* v. *Ingram* (1675),[3]
where North C.J. says,

> 'If A sell his horse to B for ten pounds, and there being
> divers other dealings between them, they come to an account
> upon the whole, and B is found in arrear five pounds, A
> must bring his *insimul computasset*; for he can never recover
> upon an *indebitatus assumpsit*'.

Jackson takes this to mean that on the facts stated the defendant
B was not liable to account; the voluntary account did not
therefore create a true debt, and so *indebitatus assumpsit* did not
lie for the £5, but only *insimul computasset*, as it were as a gap
filler. This is, however, a misunderstanding; North C.J.'s
point is that the accounting together discharges the debt of £10,
and such other debts as may have arisen from the 'other
dealings', leaving only an obligation to pay £5; hence *indebitatus
assumpsit* does not lie for the £10. This leaves open the question
why one should not bring an *indebitatus* for the £5, upon the
principle that the accounting created a debt. The explanation
I suspect is that one could, but that there was no advantage in
doing so rather than declaring, as was customary, on the
account.

[1] *Knowles* v. *Michel* (1811) 13 East 249; *Highmore* v. *Primrose* (1816) 5 M. &
Sel. 54.
[2] op. cit. 107 et seq.
[3] 2 Mod. at 44; 1 Mod. 205, Freeman 195.

Submission to arbitration[1]

Closely analogous to the action on account stated is the action on a promise to perform the award of arbitrators. Debt lay to enforce the award of an arbitrator on a parole submission, but no other action, and because of a peculiar doctrine whereby an award must be mutual it was not possible to have a valid award to the effect that one party should pay money, and the other execute a release. It is said that Chief Baron Manwood used to get over this difficulty by making the party who was to release pay money if he failed to release, thus satisfying the requirement. Once it came to be settled the assumpsit lay on mutual promises there was no reason why assumpsit could not be brought reciprocally on promises by both parties to perform the award of arbitrators to whom their suits and controversies had been submitted; the earliest clear recognition of this is *Penruddock* v. *Mounteagle* (1612),[2] and Sheppard indeed refers to an earlier unreported case in 1595, *Neale's Case*.[3] Common sense would suggest that a promise to perform the award would be implied from the fact of submission to the award, and according to Sheppard this was held to be so as a matter of law in *Neale's Case* and in *Broom's Case* (1620),[4]

'If two refer matters in difference between them to arbitrators to end it, albeit they do make no promises each to other, to abide and perform their award, yet the law doth supply this, and make up this by implication, and each of them may have this action against the other for not performing it; upon this bare submission to an award without any express promise'.

But for a long time it seems that there was uncertainty about this; thus in *Read* v. *Palmer* (1648)[5] it was argued that,

'every submission to an award implies a promise to perform it'

---

[1] See above, p. 173 and Ames, *Lectures*, 159. For a short account of the history of arbitration see *H.E.L.* XIV. 187 et seq. and for the mutuality doctrine see at p. 194. Holdsworth's account is based on S. Kyd, *Treatise on the Law of Awards*, Dublin, 1791.

[2] 1 Rolle Ab. f. 7, pl. 3. In *Samon's Case* (1593) 5 Co. Rep. 77b there was a nominal payment for a promise to perform an award; see also *Browne* v. *Downing* (1620) 2 Rolle Rep. 194.

[3] Sheppard 24.

[4] Both unreported.

[5] Aleyn 69.

but held that,

> 'though a submission to an award be good evidence to induce a jury to find a promise to perform it, yet in judgement of law the promise is collateral to the submission and not implyed in it'.

Not until Holt's time did it become settled that Sheppard's statement of the law was correct.[1] The distinction is little more than a quibble except again that two different forms of direction to a jury are involved.

Implied promises in forbearance assumpsit

It was common in the sixteenth and seventeenth centuries for actions of assumpsit to be brought on promises to pay money in consideration of forbearance from suing either the promisor or some third party for a debt. Such actions might simply involve the use of assumpsit in lieu of debt against a debtor—for example, if D owed P £10 on a simple contract P might sue on a promise to pay the £10 by a certain date in consideration of forbearance until that day. Alternatively suretyship was included, so that there might be forbearance to sue some third party; for example, D might promise to pay P £10 in consideration for P's forbearance to sue a third party, J.S., for £10 due to P on a bond.[2] Many possible variations and permutations were possible, but in all such cases there was a difficulty over holding the promise actionable—the risk of permitting the plaintiff to recover twice. Thus in the first example suppose P does forbear until the day fixed, and then sues in assumpsit on the promise; it is obviously quite unfair that he should then be permitted to recover the debt in an action of debt. In the second illustration the same problem arises in an even more acute form, since there is no question of the bond being discharged. *Smith's Case* (1585)[3] turned on this difficulty. Smith promised that if the plaintiff should forbear to sue one J.N. on a bond for £40 and if the money was not paid by a certain day he would pay it. The plaintiff sued Smith

---

[1] See *Tifford* v. *French* (1663) 1 Sid. 160, 1 Lev. 113, 1 Keb. 599; *Anon.* (1670) Style 101; *Squire* v. *Grevell* (1703) 6 Mod. 34.

[2] See above, p. 314, and Lücke in 81 L.Q.R. pp. 423 and 545.

[3] Owen 29. See also *Goring* v. *Goring* (1602) Yelv. 11.

'and it was moved by Kingsmill that he could not have this action until J.N. be dead, for as long as he lives he hath time to implead him . . . he cannot sue unless he shews he hath discharged the other of the obligation.

'*Clench J.* It is implied that he will never implead him.

'*Shuttleworth J.* Not so, for if hereafter he sue him contrary to his promise, then the other who made the assumpsit shall have his action on the case, and recover to the value of the sum in the bond'.

In the event the problem was solved by the surrender of the bond in court. Later cases picked up the suggestion of an implied promise not to sue. Thus in *Thorne* v. *Fuller* (1614),[1] a suretyship case, it was objected that a declaration stating as consideration that the plaintiff 'agreed and was content' not to prosecute a suit was insufficient,

'for he may forbear one day and prosecute again the day following. *Sed non allocatur*; for it is a promise for an absolute forbearance of the prosecution; for that is implied'.

The same doctrine was accepted by the majority of the court in *Mapes* v. *Sidney* (1623).[2]

Assumpsit and liability wholly imposed by law

All the examples of implied assumpsits which have been considered so far involve liability more or less closely associated with a consensual transaction. Liability came, however, to be sanctioned by actions of assumpsit upon wholly fictional promises to satisfy a liability imposed by law. Now debts, as we have seen, could be due quite irrespective of the debtor's assent, and this, coupled with the implication of a promise to pay the debt opened the way for the use of actions of *indebitatus assumpsit* to sanction a variety of obligations to pay quantified sums of money. For example, suppose P pays D £10 under the misapprehension that this sum is owing to him. So long as the courts are prepared to hold that the result of this transaction is to create a debt due from D to P, and imply a fictional promise to pay this debt, it will be possible for P to recover in some form of *indebitatus assumpsit*.

[1] Cro. Jac. 396.
[2] Cro. Jac. 683.

The first sign of development here is *Lord North's Case* in 1588,[1] where the facts were,

'The Queen granted unto Lord North and his heirs the fines *pro licentia concordanti*, and one would not pay him the fine, for which cause the Lord North brought an action on the case against him, and declared upon *indebitatus assumpsit*'.

The argument in the case (which is obscurely reported) centres upon whether debt lay, for if it did not the declaration was plainly bad on its face. The prevailing view seems to have been that it did, and therefore *indebitatus assumpsit* lay.

Considerably later, in *Mayor of London* v. *Gould* (1667)[2] and in the more important case of *Mayor of London* v. *Gcree* (1676)[3] an action of *indebitatus assumpsit* was allowed on a purely fictitious promise to pay customary dues—water-bailage, scavage, or weighage. This was considered to be analogous to allowing an *indebitatus assumpsit* on a bill of exchange[4] and for an insurance premium.[5] This was followed in similar cases involving, for example, money forfeit under a by-law and due to a chartered corporation.[6] The rationale of these cases was simply that since debt lay, *a fortiori indebitatus assumpsit* lay on an implied promise. But these cases in reality represented a considerable extension of the scope of assumpsit and went far beyond the decision in *Slade's Case*, for there was no contract between the parties, and later in the seventeenth century Holt C.J. vehemently attacked these decisions.[7]

---

[1] 2 Leon. 179, discussed in Jackson, *Quasi-Contract*, 41. The other cases mentioned by Jackson are inconclusive.

[2] 2 Keb. 295.

[3] 3 Keb. 677, 2 Lev. 174, 1 Vent. 298, Freeman 433; Keble refers to earlier decisions.

[4] *Vanheath* v. *Turner* (1622) Winch 24; see generally J. M. Holden, *The History of Negotiable Instruments in English Law*, Ch. III.

[5] Allowed apparently in the early seventeenth century.

[6] *Barber Surgeons* v. *Pelson* (1679) 2 Lev. 252; *Mayor of London* v. *Hunt* (1681) 3 Lev. 37; *Shuttleworth* v. *Garrett* (1688) Comb. 151; *Duppa* v. *Gerard* (1689) 1 Show. 78.

[7] *H.E.L.* VIII. 90–1.

IX

THE PROMISE AND ITS VALIDITY

LEAVING on one side questions of capacity, it is obvious that there will evolve rules of law dealing with possible grounds upon which promises, though supported by consideration, will not be actionable. In the sixteenth and seventeenth centuries these rules appear to have been less fully developed than a modern common lawyer would expect, and there are two basic reasons for this. The first is that many questions which would now figure in law reports as questions of law, or at least discussed questions of fact, were then regarded as purely jury matters. The second basic reason is that the existence of the doctrine of consideration excluded certain defences as independent grounds of invalidity.

St. Germain's Doctor of Divinity says that a promise, to be binding in conscience, must be 'honest, lawful and possible'.[1] A little over a century later Sheppard,[2] attempting to impose some order upon the development of assumpsit in the intervening years, sets out five requirements:

'As to the matter of the contract, or promise itself, this is to be known. That to make it such as upon which this action may be raised, it must have these things in it.

1. The thing promised or undertaken must be lawful.
2. It must be possible to be done.
3. It must be clear and certain.
4. It must be co-hering, and agreeing in itself, and with the consideration.
6. It must be serious and weighty.'

These requirements, or possible sources of invalidity, can be conveniently considered in this order.

[1] *Doctor and Student*, Dial. II, c. 24.
[2] Sheppard 84.

1. Illegality

In the medieval law of formal contracts it was recognized that illegality in the contract was a ground for holding the contract void.[1] The simplest case would be a covenant to perform an illegal act, but since the conditioned bond was the usual contractual instrument the problem, in so far as it arose at all, turned upon the effect of an illegal condition. The effect of such a condition in medieval law was to render not only the condition, but also the bond itself void, for a reason explained by Littleton,[2]

'and the cause that it is avoided, is so that no deed be executed as emboldens a man to do something against the law'.

There was some suggestion in sixteenth-century law that a condition which was merely *malum prohibitum* should be differently treated, but little came of this.[3] There was also some authority for the view that common law illegality should be treated differently from statutory illegality, severance being possible in the former case but not in the latter.[4] The practical importance of the defence of illegality in the case of formal contracts was very much reduced by the rule that the illegality must appear on the face of the instrument, and could not be established by parole evidence; the principle was stated in *Brook* v. *King* (1588),[5]

'And it was argued by the whole court that when the condition of an obligation shall be said against the law, and therefore the obligation void, the same ought to be intended when the condition is expressly against the law in express

[1] See above, p. 110.
[2] 8 Edw. IV, M. f. 20, pl. 35. For a curious case of a condition originally illegal becoming legal see y.B.12 Hen. VIII T.f.5 pl.4 — a condition to marry a deceased husband's brother legalised by dispensation. No decision given.
[3] *Browning* v. *Beston* (1554) Plowden 131, Co. Litt. 206b.
[4] *Norton* v. *Simmes* (1614) Hob. 12; *Maleverer* v. *Redshaw* (1669) 1 Mod. 35; *Pearson* v. *Humes* (1671) Carter 229. The authority for a general power of severance is not satisfactory. In 14 Hen. VIII, P. f. 25, pl. 7, relied upon by Coke in his report of *Pigot's Case* (1615) (11 Co.Rep. f. 27b.), illegality was not in issue; what was involved was severance of covenants in a plea of *non est factum* by an illiterate, who had executed a bond to perform covenants in an indenture, some of which were never read over to him. See Moo. K.B. 856 for a suggestion that negative covenants were severable:
[5] 1 Leon. 73, and see *Macrowe's Case* (1585) Godbolt 29, *Jones' Case* (1588) 1 Leon. 203, *Olbury* v. *Gregory* (1598) Moo. K. B. 564.

words, and *in terminis terminantibus,* and not for matter outside the condition'.

This remained generally so until the decision in *Collins* v. *Blantern* (1667)[1] at law,[2] and followed from ordinary principle. A bond, itself innocuous, conditioned on a covenant void for illegality was itself void.[3] In one important area, however, there was a statutory exception; from 1545 onwards the usurious nature of a transaction could be gathered from parole averment, and there are many examples in the reports of the court investigating the usurious story behind the headlines.[4]

The rise of the action of assumpsit opened up a considerably greater scope for the defence of illegality, since the nature of the action necessarily involved the reception of parole evidence, and the cause or consideration of the promise, so far from being beyond any investigation (unless appearing on the face of the specialty) formed an essential element in the cause of action. Consequently, although the general principles governing illegality are the same in formal and informal contracts, the latter class of agreement more commonly failed upon this ground.

TYPES OF ILLEGALITY

Modern systematic writers divide the various types of illegality or unlawfulness into categories—contracts to commit crimes, contracts contrary to public policy, contracts rendered void by statute, and so forth—and these categories, besides being convenient for exposition, are also reflected to some degree in the thinking of the courts. In the sixteenth and early seventeenth centuries there was no systematic writing on illegality in contract, and the case law consists merely in an unsystematic application of the general principle that a promise ought not to be actionable if it, or the consideration for it, was in a loose sense unlawful. 'And so generally whatsoever for the matter of it in the consideration will make the assumpsit void, the same is the promise will make it void.'[5] The unlawful character of the

---

[1] 2 Wils. 341. On the whole subject see Ames 107–8.
[2] Relief in equity was possible; see Tothill 26.
[3] *Caponhurst* v. *Caponhurst* (1661) 1 Lev. 45.
[4] See *Burton's Case* (1591) 5 Co.Rep. 69a.
[5] Sheppard 85.

promise could arise in various ways. It could derive from statute; thus by statute usurious contracts were made unlawful,[1] though here the statute affirmed a common law principle.[2] Alternatively the source of illegality might be the common law. A familiar example here is the common law principle against contracts in restraint of trade. Illegality at common law was in fact fairly widely extended. Thus simoniacal contracts were covered, although the offence here was spiritual and might be regarded as outside lay jurisdiction.[3] So too were fraudulent or covinous agreements, or agreements involving sexual immorality. *Collins* v. *Willes* (1598)[4] is a curious example of a transaction of a 'covinous' nature. Willes had been a suitor for the hand of the co-defendant, who was by the time of the action his wife. She was the plaintiff's daughter, and the plaintiff had been willing to give her in marriage with a dowry of £80. But Willes had held out for £90, and Miss Collins, fearing no doubt a complete breakdown in the negotiations, secretly promised to return £10 to her father if he gave her in marriage with £90; presumably she hoped to save this from the housekeeping. The promise was never performed, and the father Collins sued his son-in-law Willes and daughter, now Mrs. Willes. The action failed—'this was an insufficient and unlawful consideration to ground an action, and made only in deceit of the defendant, her husband'. The category of sexual immorality is illustrated by the bizarre and unfair case of *Gardner* v. *Fulforde* (1667).[5] Here the plaintiff, an upholsterer, had made hangings for the defendant, and sued him on a *quantum meruit*. In the pleadings, however, the hangings were called *quatuor pictas pellices*, *Anglice* 'gilt skins', and Levinz for the defendant pointed out

'That *quatuor pictas pellices*, is four painted whores (and *pelles* is the word for skins) and the providing of them for the defendant is unlawful'.

[1] 3 Hen. VII, c. 5; 11 Hen. VII, c. 8; 37 Hen. VIII, c. 9; 5 and 6 Edw. VI, c. 20; 27 Eliz. I, c. 11; 29 Eliz. I, c. 5; 31 Eliz. I, c. 10; 35 Eliz. I, c. 7; 39 Eliz. I, c. 18; 21 Jac. I, c. 17; 12 Car. II, c. 13.
[2] See above, p. 115, and cases there cited, Hawkins, *Pleas of the Crown*, Vol. I, Ch. 82.
[3] *Mackwaller* v. *Todderick* (1633) Cro. Car. 337, 353, 361.
[4] Moo. K.B. 537, Cro. Eliz. 774, Owen 93.
[5] 1 Lev. 204, 2 Keb. 154, 172.

For this judgment was stayed 'for *pellex* signifieth a harlot'. The main body of case law, however, deals with usurious contracts and contracts in restraint of trade, two topics which provoke a very considerable body of litigation.

Usury[1]

Medieval Christian thought, as we have seen, condemned usury, which at its simplest involved payment for the use of money or fungibles lent, and the taking of usury was forbidden to laymen from the time of the first Council of Carthage in 345; indeed from the time of the Council of Vienne in 1311 it was heresy to maintain the lawfulness of usury. The Reformation did not in the least bring about any weakening of the extreme vehemence with which the sin of usury was condemned; as Bishop Jewel put it

'It is filthy gains, and work of darkness. It is a monster in nature . . . it is theft, it is the murdering of our brethren, it is the curse of God and the curse of the people'.[2]

Such denunciation was typical of sixteenth- and seventeenth-century economic thought. A variety of objections were levelled against the practice; the most ingenious was perhaps that used by St. Thomas Aquinas.[3] St. Thomas argued that in the case of a *mutuum*, a loan of fungibles for consumption, the use of the thing cannot be distinguished from the thing itself as it can in the case, for example, of land. This is so because the use destroys the thing. The usurer who contracts both for the return of an equivalent and for extra for the use is obtaining in effect double payment, for the equivalent is to be viewed as the price for the thing itself, and the extra payment is for the use, which has no independent existence. The usurer is really selling something which does not exist at all, a plainly unnatural and improper proceeding. Other arguments[4] were that the usurer

---

[1] The leading study is J. T. Noonan, *The Scholastic Analysis of Usury* (Camb. Mass., 1957). See also J. W. Baldwin, 'The Mediaeval Theories of the Just Price', Transactions of the American Philosophical Society, Vol. 49 Pt. 4 (1959), J. W. Ashley, *An Introduction to English Economic History and Theory*, Vol. 1 (London, 1893).

[2] *Works of Bishop Jewel*, II (Parker Society, Camb. 1847), p. 851.

[3] *Summa Theologica* IIa IIae Qq. 78 aa. 1–4.

[4] Many arguments stem from an anonymous fifth-century work known as the *palea Ejiciens*; Noonan, op. cit. 81.

sells time, which belongs to God alone, that money is by nature fruitless and so the usurer is unnaturally getting something which does not really exist, that money does not deteriorate (so that payment for use is no form of compensation), and that fungible goods possess by nature a definite intrinsic value, being worth exactly the same as an equivalent quantity of the same goods. From this characteristic Joannes Andreae (1270–1348), a distinguished professor of canon law at Bologna, the greatest of the medieval law schools, argued that to attempt to get back more than one loaned on a *mutuum* was no more than a device to make goods worth more than their natural price, a sinful proceeding.

The paradigm case of usury—payment for use on a loan for consumption—was straightforward, but the canonists became involved in endless controversy as to the proper extension of the conception of usury and the exceptions which ought to be recognized. As we have seen, it came to be admitted that the creditor was entitled to compensation for his interest in prompt payment, so that penalties were unobjectionable if the debtor could avoid incurring them by paying up on time. Some curious exceptions came to be recognized—thus, for example, since it was lawful in some circumstances to kill one's enemy it was *a fortiori* permissible to take usury of him.[1] This could hardly have been a common case; there were, however, two major exceptions whose recognition by the canonists let in the modern notion of investment. Investment of money in a partnership by contract of *societas* was permissible upon the ground that a risk was involved, and usury essentially involved the idea of a certainty of return of principal with payment for use as well; the same element of risk made insurance contracts lawful. Also permissible was the contract known as a *census*,[2] a common form of Italian investment whereby the investor purchased an obligation to pay an annual return charged upon fruitful property; the common law equivalent is the rent charge or annuity.

It was by a combination between the contract of *societas* and the contract of insurance that there developed the most bizarre and controversial exception to the ban on usury, the so-called

[1] See generally Noonan, op. cit. 100 et seq.
[2] Ashley, op. cit. 406 et seq.

triple contract (*contractus trinus*) or 'contract of five per cent'. Granted that one could invest in a partnership because of the element of risk, and granted that one could lawfully insure against loss, why should not these two activities be combined so that one invested in a partnership whilst insuring against any risk? This basic idea was popularized by Angelus de Carletus in the *Summa Angelica*,[1] and developed by John Eck, Professor of Theology at Ingolstadt, and the theory of the matter was that one entered into a contract of partnership to gain or lose (the first contract), insured the capital invested with one's partner, the premium or price being the giving up of possible future gain above a fixed percentage return (the second contract), and finally insured against possible low future gains by the same agreement to take a lower fixed return (the third contract). In effect one invested capital for a fixed rate of interest, and the division into three contracts was conceptual only; the theoretical argument was that since one could lawfully make each one of the three contracts with three different people, why was there any harm in making all three contracts with one's partner? John Eck[2] defended the *contractus trinus* in a celebrated five-hour-long dispute before the Faculty at Bologna in 1515, and in his *Tractatus de Contractu de centum*. Although the Roman Pontiff rejected the argument in the Bull *Detestabilis* (1586), the tendency both in the Roman and in the Reformed Churches was increasingly sympathetic towards the recognition of legitimate business investment so long as the rate of return was modest and the contract lacked oppressive characteristics. The matter remained, however, highly controversial in the sixteenth and seventeenth centuries,[3] the view of the established Church being fairly uniformly opposed to usury; the Church of England inherited and continued to insist upon the commercial ethics of the medieval canonists. But the views of Anglicans and of the civilians engaged in the enforcement of religious discipline came increasingly into open conflict with the views of the business community, and the rise

[1] See above, p. 379.

[2] John Eck's view was supported by the celebrated John Major (*c.* 1469–1549), Professor of Theology at the University of Paris and Professor elect at Cardinal College, Oxford at the fall of Wolsey.

[3] See generally R. H. Tawney, *Religion and the Rise of Capitalism* (1926), for a classic account of the development. See also *H.E.L.* VIII. 100 et seq.

of puritanism led to the progressive weakening of the opposition to usury.

The legislative history of the ban and restriction on usury is understandably rather confused. By Statute of 1545[1] usury at the rate of 10 per cent per annum was in effect permitted. The statute, however, is designated *An Acte against Usurye*, which it described as 'a thinge unlawful', and technically what it permitted was compensation for loss of interest, not usury *stricto sensu*. Ten per cent might be stipulated 'for the forbearinge or givinge daye of payment', so that the theory of the matter was that the debtor must be *in mora*. If excessive interest was charged there was to be treble forfeiture of the interest at the suit of a common informer, who would share the penalty with Crown; and the usurer could suffer fine and imprisonment. In 1552 this statute was repealed by *A Byll against Usurie*,[2] which complained that people had misunderstood the Henrician Statute, which had never been intended to permit usury. For the future, however, 'any manner of Usurie encrease lucre gayne or interest' was forbidden in uncompromising terms, and the usurer was to forfeit both capital and interest, half going to the Crown and the other half to the common informer; the usurer was also to be imprisoned until he ransomed himself. This statute remained in force until 1571, when yet another statute was passed repealing the Edwardian Statute and reviving the Statute of 1545. This new *Acte Against Usurie*[3] introduced a peculiar compromise, which has been sometimes misunderstood.[4] It made contracts involving interest (in either the old or the modern sense) of over 10 per cent per annum completely void; in such a case the treble penalty of the Henrician Statute and the provision for fine and imprisonment was to be applied; further to this, the usurer was to be amenable to the discipline of the ecclesiastical courts a well as to the common law courts. Contracts involving interest of under 10 per cent

---

[1] 37 Hen. VIII, c. 9, repealing all previous legislation. For an earlier plan see *Letters and Papers of Henry VIII*, IX. ii. 725.

[2] 5 and 6 Edw. VI, c. 20.

[3] 13 Eliz. I, c. 8, originally in force only for five years but made perpetual by 39 Eliz. I, c. 18.

[4] Ashley, op. cit., p. 488, n. 268, suggested that the text of cl. 4 is incorrect, but this is a mistake. Tawney, op. cit., p. 159 incorrectly states that the Act expressly authorized loans at interest, but this again is an error.

were not, however, void, but since 'all usurie being forbydden by the law of God is synne and detestable' anything paid over the principal was to be forfeitable.

This Act plainly did not make usury lawful; it merely made contracts involving usury at a rate of less than 10 per cent valid, though the interest was forfeitable, and indeed was more severe to usurers than was the Act of 1545. However, the provision for forfeiture appears always to have been a dead letter,[1] though it is not immediately obvious why this should have happened. The solution may lie in the precise wording of clause 4, which allows recovery not of interest *eo nomine* but only of 'so muche as shall be reserved *by way of Usurie*'; it is possible that the courts construed amounts of less than 10 per cent as constituting 'interest' in the old sense and not 'usury'.

The theoretical status of usury brought about by the Act of 1571 was discussed in *Sanderson* v. *Warner* (1622),[2] where action was brought on a promise to pay a debt 'and interest due' in consideration for a promise to forbear a debt. There were two points at issue—could a promise to pay interest be a good consideration, and did the common law recognize interest at all? No decision was given, since the court did not wish to create a precedent in so delicate a matter. Yelverton on one side argued that usury of under 10 per cent was unlawful but tolerated; Noy that usury was always unlawful. The court divided. Ley C.J. and Houghton and Chamberlain JJ, thinking that

'usury which is allowed by statute has obtained such strength by usage, that it would be a great impediment to traffic and commerce if it should be impeached'.

Ley C.J. explained that the usury which the common law condemned

'fuit un common trade de biting usury',

not respectable and moderate investment; if anyone wished to endanger his conscience by charging 10 per cent the law would

---

[1] See *H.E.L.* VIII, 100, Tawney, op. cit. 180. Half the sum forfeited went to the Crown. The effectiveness of the legislation may have been reduced by the rule that even if the informer was a third party the borrower could not himself give evidence, since he would then be *testis in propria causa*. See Co. Litt. 6b, citing an unreported case in 1611, *Smithe's Case*.

[2] Palmer 291, 2 Rolle Rep. 239.

not impede him. Dodderidge, on the other hand, took the view that all usury was unlawful both by statute and common law and the law of God; even the heathen, he thought, reached this conclusion by natural reason. The only thing that was permissible was damages for loss of *interesse* through non-payment. Coke's view also was that,

'it is also enacted by Parliament, that all usury is unlawful, that is to say against the lawes of the realm'.[1]

In *Oliver* v. *Oliver*,[2] two years after *Sanderson* v. *Warner*, Dodderidge J. was supported by Whitlock J. in holding that

'a cest jour use de money nest bon consideration, quia encounter ley natural, car come Herle dit,[3] est monstrous que argent produce argent, et ad estre defame per touts, estatutes, come horrible, damnable etc.'[4]

and it is noted that the Bishops would only agree to the passing of the Statute of Usury of 1623[5] on condition that there be added to it a clause denouncing usury; clause 4 of the statute consists of a proviso to the effect that the statute, which lowered the tolerated rate of interest to 8 per cent,[6] was not to be expounded as making usury permissible in religion or conscience. Houghton J., however, pointed out that usury must be differentiated from *interesse*, whether *interesse lucri* or *interesse damni*. *Harris* v. *Richards* (1632)[7] held that interest at the permitted rate would rank as a good consideration, but as late as 1673 in *Wilson* v. *Dove*[8] Chief Justice Vaughan was of the opinion that assumpsit could not be brought to recover interest money even at the permitted rate, though the majority of the court of King's Bench opposed this view.

The conception of usury at common law was derivative of

[1] Inst. III, cap. lxx.
[2] 2 Rolle. Rep. 469.
[3] The reference has not been traced; William de Herle (ob. 1347) was Chief Justice of the Common Pleas several times in Edward III's reign.
[4] In cases on usury reference is frequently made to 26 Edw. III, M. f. 17, pl. 9 using an incorrect reference to f. 71; the source of the error is Fleetwood's index to the year-books.
[5] 21 Jac. I, c. 17.
[6] Again reduced to 6% in 1660 by 12 Car. II, c. 13.
[7] Cro. Car. 273.
[8] 3 Keb. 183, 1 Freeman K.B. 114. See also 2 Rolle Ab. 782.

the canon law, and in its developed form was thus stated by Hawkins in its strict sense:

> 'a contract upon a loan of money to give the lender a certain profit for the use of it, upon all events, whether the borrower make any advantage of it, or the lender suffer any prejudice for the want of it, or whether it be repaid on the day appointed, or not.'[1]

Coke less helpfully says,

> 'Usury is a contract upon a loan of money, or giving days for forbearing of money, debt or duty, by way of lone, chivisance shifts, sales of wares or other things whatsoever'.[2]

Hence whether a contract was a corrupt and usurious contract or not turned upon the real intention of the parties, not upon the form. Hence in *Button* v. *Downham* (1598)[3] a bond to pay £10 for forbearance of £20 *if the son of the obligee be then alive* was usurious if the condition was inserted merely with the intention of evading the statute by introducing a risk, 'and it is the intent which makes it so', although a bona fide wager on an uncertain event was not usurious. The principle was critical in cases involving annuities. Following canon law, the purchase of an annuity was a legitimate investment, even though the rate of return was high, but only so long as the intention was not that the purchaser was to receive back his capital payment, an arrangement which removed the element of risk. Thus in *Dr. Good's Case* (1576) Popham and Plowden 'held'[4]

> 'that if a man giveth £100 for an annuity of £20 p.a. this is not usury, for he shall never have his stock again',

and this principle was followed, as in *Fuller's Case*[5] where £300 was paid for an annuity of £50 per annum assured for a hundred years if the annuitant, his wife, and four of his children should so long live,

---

[1] Hawkins, *Pleas of the Crown*, Bk. I, Ch. 82.
[2] Coke, Inst. III, cap. lxx. It was essential that there be a loan.
[3] Cro. Eliz. 643.
[4] See Cro. Eliz. 27; possibly they so held as Commissioners of Assize.
[5] 4 Leon. 208 in the King's Bench; also *Tanfield* v. *Finch* (1583) Cro. Eliz. 27, *Fountain* v. *Grymes* (1609) Cro. Jac. 252, 1 Bulst. 36.

'but care is to be taken that there be no communication of borrowing of any money before'.

Again a contract for an excessive rate of interest was good if the usurer as it were repented and took not a penny.[1] Insistence on the substance rather than the form failed, however, to triumph in *Dowman* v. *Button* (1598),[2] which upheld the following device. The borrower binds himself jointly with X to return a loan with excessive interest; the creditor sues X (who can be his accomplice), and X does not plead usury as a defence, but sues the real borrower on a separate contract of indemnity. This contract is upheld as not usurious. Glanvil J. dissented and observed cynically, 'that that judgment will be quickly conveyed to Cheapside'.

The basic conception of usury involved, therefore, the idea of *certain* gain; hence if the borrower could avoid payment of the interest by prompt payment then there was no 'gain certain', and therefore no usury.[3] The notion of certainty let in various forms of contract of a somewhat speculative nature involving hazards of one kind or another. Thus in *Bedingfield* v. *Ashley* (1600)[4] £100 was paid for an agreement to return £80 to each of the party's daughters alive after ten years; a manor was mortgaged as security for this and there were five daughters living when the agreement was made. Viewed as a loan the lender might receive back (or rather his daughters) at best £400. But the transaction was not usurious, for there was involved 'a great hazard', and nothing might be repaid at all. Another illustration is *Sharpley* v. *Hurrel* (1608),[5] a case involving a bottomry bond, a speculative contract for financing a voyage. Fifty pounds was given to the defendant, who was to return £60 at the end of a voyage to Newfoundland on return of the vessel to Dartmouth. The voyage could be completed in eight months. If the vessel did not return to Dartmouth, then

---

[1] *Mallory* v. *Bird* (1577) Cro. Eliz. 20. A sort of doctrine of severance; cf. *Pollard* v. *Scholy* (1581) Cro. Eliz. 20, where a non-usurious contact was not itself vitiated by a subsequent agreement for usury.

[2] Noy 73, not apparently the same case as *Button* v. *Downham*, Cro. Eliz. 643 and 2 And. 121, and perhaps a 'put up' case. The device is reminiscent of the *contractus trinus*.

[3] See Brooke, *Usurie*, pl. 1 (1537) and pl. 2 (1538).

[4] Cro. Eliz. 741.

[5] Cro. Jac. 209.

only £50 was to be repaid; if the vessel was lost, then nothing. Here although the lender might receive more than the permitted rate of 10 per cent per annum, he might lose all; the contract was therefore good. The exemption of bottomry bonds from the taint of usury was continued by *Sayer* v. *Gleam* (1661),[1] one justification being commercial usage. The doctrine let in speculative agreements amounting to little more than wagers, which were, of course, at the time unobjectionable as such,[2] and there was an obvious risk that a contract might be made conditional upon some hazard which was in reality quite unlikely to happen simply as a device to evade the usury laws. Dodderidge J. in *Roberts* v. *Tremayne* (1618)[3] attempted to refine the doctrine exempting contracts of hazard from the ban on usury. He asserted that if there was a contract in which only the interest was at risk then the contract would be usurious unless the borrower could by his act avoid becoming liable to pay. If the principal and interest were both at risk then the contract was not usurious. The doctrine appears to have been accepted seventeenth-century law.

Contracts in restraint of trade

The history of contracts in restraint of trade and the legal doctrine evolved in this branch of the law have been recently investigated by Professor J. D. Heydon,[4] and his conclusions seem to me to be in general correct. The earliest case dealing with the matter is *John Dyer's Case* (1414).[5] Here John Dyer[6] sued on a bond; the defendant pleaded that the bond was defeasible by a condition contained in an indenture that he should not exercise his art as a dyer in a certain town (where the plaintiff was in business)[7] for half a year, and offered to aver performance. Issue was joined on whether he had or had not done so, the plaintiff claiming that he had for one week during

[1] 1 Lev. 54. See also *Mason* v *Abdy* (1687) 1 Show. 8, 3 Salk, 390, Comb 125, Carth. 67, Holt 738, referring to a modified form of bond where the principal was not at risk.
[2] See *Reynolds* v. *Clayton* (1595) Moo. K.B. 397.
[3] Cro. Jac. 509, 2 Rolle Rep. 47.
[4] J. D. Heydon, *The Restraint of Trade Doctrine* London, (1971).
[5] 2 Hen. V, f. 5, pl. 26.
[6] i.e. John, who was a dyer.
[7] This expands the text of the year-book.

the half year. In the course of settling the pleadings Hull J. (or Hill J.) said,

'In my opinion you could have demurred on it, that the obligation is void, because the condition is contrary to common law, and by God if the plaintiff were here, he would go to prison until he had made an end [i.e. paid a fine] with the King'.

This outburst had a very considerable effect on the law, and the reasoning behind Hull's opinion has provoked considerable speculation.[1] It seems to me probable that the objection to the bond, and indeed to any contract restraining a man from exercising *his own* trade, followed more or less inevitably from basic axioms of medieval thought.

It was then believed that every member of society had his appropriate estate or degree which God had ordained for him, and that it was his duty to serve God in the estate or degree in which he found himself. Not only was this view applied to what we would now call class distinctions in a broad sense, but it was also extended so as to justify a system of economic regulation in which everyone had his own job to do and no other, and in fourteenth-century England this pigeon-holeα view of society was encouraged by the growth of the guild system, and by the labour legislation provoked by the aftermath of the Black Death. It was combined with the legislative recognition of a duty to work, itself based upon Christian ideals. This duty was first imposed upon unskilled labourers in husbandry by the Ordinance of Labourers of 1349,[2] and was extended to artificers in the Statute of 1351.[3] But the most extreme legislative expression of the ideas involved is to be found in the State of Diet and Apparel of 1363,[4] which set out to regulate in extraordinary detail the appropriate life style of the different sorts of people. This statute made it a criminal offence punishable by imprisonment for an artificer to practise more than one craft or mystery,

'It is ordained that artificers and men of mystery [*gentz de meistere*] hold them every one to one mystery'.

[1] Discussed by Heydon, op. cit., pp. 8 et seq.
[2] 23 Edw. III.   [3] 25 Edw. III, st. 2, c. 4.
[4] 37 Edw. III, c. 6.

Any notion of what is now called job mobility was anathema to medieval thought, and medieval thought on this and other economic matters was the thought of the Church, developed by the schoolmen and the canonists; there was no other system of economic thought and ethics. Had not St. Thomas Aquinas himself said in his *Summa Contra Gentiles*[1] that the divisions of work were necessary, and the consequence of divine providence? And the very year before Hull J.'s outburst, the Statute of Additions[2] had given further expression to these ideas by providing that in future writs should state the appropriate 'addition to a name, signifying the party's estate, degree, or mystery. A story which was told of Chief Justice Gascoigne[3] peculiarly well illustrates the thinking of a great fifteenth-century judge on these matters.

> 'in the time of Henry IV, when Gascoigne was the Chief Justice in this Court, I have heard that there was a vintner, who used to sell wine, and also to keep suppers and dinners in his house, and in this way sell victuals. And for this he was indicted and fined. The vintner consulted with other vintners, and said to them that if they would give £5 to Gascoigne then all would be well. And that Gascoigne, having intelligence of this, caused him to be indicted for this also, and he was fined for this too.'

The record of this case, so Sir James Ley (who told the story) said, still remains in the court, and it has now in part been printed by Dr. Sayles.[4]

Granted this rigid system and the recognition of a duty to work in the particular activity into which a man had been placed as a child (and very frequently the work would be what his father's had been) it necessarily follows that any form of contract which restrains a man from working at his trade must be regarded as highly improper, for such a contract enforces

---

[1] *Summa Contra Gentiles*, III, c. 134.

[2] 1 Hen. V, c. 5.

[3] William Gascoigne (ob. 1419) was Chief Justice of the King's Bench from 1400 to 1413; he was removed from office by Henry V on his accession, a fact which lends support to the well-known story about Prince Hal. The story mentioned here is told by Sir James Ley, Chief Justice of the King's Bench, in 1624, more than two centuries after the death of Gascoigne. See 2 Rolle. Rep. 392.

[4] S.S. Vol. 88 (Sayles), pp. 176 et seq., which prints the presentment of the vintner, one Thomas Nightingale, a thoroughly undesirable character.

idleness and poverty, and because of the guild system, under which geographical mobility was severely hampered, a merely local restraint was almost as much to be deplored as a general restraint. The guilds were vigorously opposed to 'strangers', and for this and other reasons it would usually be quite impracticable for an artificer who was bound not to work in Oxford to move to Wallingford and set up shop there. Indeed the law's objection to contracts in restraint of trade, viewed as a rejection of freedom of contract, is but the corollary of its objection to mobility of labour through private contract, another aspect of the rejection of freedom of contract. We are concerned with a period where the move from status to contract has not progressed far.

The medieval ideas survived into the sixteenth century. Thus Thomas Bacon, chaplain to Archbishop Cranmer, stated the basic principle in his catechism,[1]

'The subject is called to God to obey, and to be in subjection to his superiors, and every one of them is bound by the commandment of God to live in their vocation. The lawyer in pleading and defending poor men's causes, the shoemaker in making shoes, the tailor in making garments . . . and so forth in all persons, in whatsoever state God hath called them. Every man in his vocation ought to labour, and by no means be idle',

and in a sermon on St. Andrew's day Hugh Latimer said, 'Let us labour everyone in that estate wherein God hath set him'.[2] To prevent work was akin to theft; it was to withold the labourer's wages, a grave sin.[3] It is understandable therefore that in the late sixteenth and early seventeenth centuries contracts restraining a man from exercising a lawful trade were held bad in a well-known trilogy of cases. The earliest is *Anon.* (1578)[4] where an apprentice bound himself not to exercise the craft of mercer in Nottingham for four years; this was an attempt to extend the restrictive period of apprenticeship, and the brief report cites only *Dyer's Case* in support of the decision. *Anon.*

---

[1] Thomas Bacon, *Catechism* (Parker Society, 1833).
[2] Hugh Latimer, *Sermons and Remains.* II (Parker Society, 1845), p. 43.
[3] *The Decades of Henry Bullinger*, 3rd Decade, Sermon I (Parker Society, 1850).
[4] Moo. K.B. 115. On the relevance of apprenticeship see Heydon, op. cit. 9–10.

(1587)[1] involved a bond entered into between two black-smiths in Southmins, one of whom bound himself not to exercise his art and mystery in the town. The bond was held void as being,

'encounter le necessity del commonwealth'.

There may in fact have been an apprenticeship arrangement involved, but the report does not reveal this. The third case is *Colgate* v. *Bacheler* (1602)[2] where the defendant bound himself to pay the plaintiff £20 if he used the trade of haberdasher as journeyman servant, apprentice, or master in Rochester or Canterbury for four years. This was struck down as being against the benefit of the commonwealth, Anderson C.J. adding that a man

'might as well bind himself that he would not go to Church'.

Thus the objection rested upon the notion of a duty, in accordance with earlier theories.

The earliest case to depart from this rigorous view was *Rogers* v. *Parrey* (1614),[3] and this was also the earliest action of assumpsit on such a contract. The facts are somewhat obscure, but apparently the plaintiff agreed to lease property to the defendant for a twenty-one year term in consideration for a promise that the defendant would not exercise or permit the exercise of the trade of joiner in adjacent property which he owned; a payment of £10 was made for this promise. It is possible that the property concerned was that leased. The defendant sub-leased to a joiner, and assumpsit was brought for breach of this promise, and the action was allowed. Croke J. in the course of argument said,

'The doubt which at the first troubled me, was for the binding of one that he would not use and exercise his trade, being his livelihood'.

Coke C. J. replied,

'This is not so, being but for a time certain and in a place certain, but no general restraint there is here'.

---

[1] Moo. K.B. 242, 2 Leon. 210.
[2] Cro. Eliz. 872, Owen 143.
[3] 2 Bulst. 136, Cro. Jac. 326.

This view was adopted. Clearly the case is quite different from the earlier authorities, involving as it does merely a restriction upon the use of particular property. Coke's distinction between general and partial restraints was, however, to be taken out of context, and became extremely influential in later case law. It has been suggested that the decision in *Rogers* v. *Parrey* was influenced by the decision in the *Ipswich Tailors Case*[1] in which the King's Bench held unlawful an ordinance of the Corporation penalizing anyone who exercised a trade without the approval of the relevant guild, and laid down in strong terms a general principle to the effect that,

> 'at the common law, no man could be prohibited from working in any lawful trade . . .'

Although there is plainly some connection between the common law attack on the powers of the guilds and the extension of freedom of contract into contracts in restraint of trade, it is dubious whether the connection between the two cases is as direct as this, for the *Ipswich Tailor's Case* seems to have been decided *after Rogers* v. *Parrey*, and the latter case is in any event concerned with somewhat special facts. The critical decision was not *Rogers* v. *Parrey*, but *Broad* v. *Jollyfe* in 1621,[2] which went to the Exchequer Chamber.

Here a contract was made between two mercers in Newport. The defendant, who had been in business for some time, possessed a quantity of old stock which he sold to the plaintiff at considerably above its real value, who agreed to pay an inflated price in consideration for a promise by the defendant not to trade as a mercer in Newport. The defendant broke this promise and set up in competition, and the plaintiff sued in assumpsit. The action succeeded and the decision was affirmed on error; the decision was justified upon a variety of grounds— the promise was voluntary, it was given for a valuable consideration, it involved only a restriction upon trading in one place, such agreements were customary, the defendant benefited from

---

[1] 11 Co.Rep. 53a. The suggestion is made by Heydon, op. cit., but *Rogers* v. *Parrey* is reported by Bulstrode as being entered in Trinity 11 James I and decided in Michaelmas 11 James I; so too in Croke's Reports. The *Ipswich Tailors Case* was entered in Trinity 11 James I and decided in Michaelmas 12 James I.

[2] Reported under various names in Cro. Jac. 596, Noy 98, 2 Rolle Rep. 201, Jones 13.

the arrangement. The only dissenting voice was that of Hough-ton J. A similar decision was given in *Bragge* v. *Stanner* (1621),[1] which was decided whilst *Broad* v. *Jollyfe* was *en route* for the Exchequer Chamber. Later cases followed the distinction between partial and total restraints of trade which survived in the law until the *Nordenfelt Case* in 1894,[2] and it is a curious fact that the very term 'restraint' came to be associated with this branch of the law as signifying something partial. A doctrine was also developed which differentiated restraints imposed by bond and restraints imposed by promises actionable only in assumpsit. The former were bad, whether general or not, whereas the latter were good if limited in scope.[3] The rationale of this distinction turned upon two factors. The first was that an assumpsit, unlike a promise under seal, was only good if supported by consideration, and more favour should be extended to an undertaking so supported. The second was that in the case of a conditioned bond the plaintiff could recover the whole penalty irrespective of the loss actually suffered, whereas in an action upon an assumpsit the jury need only give damages to the extent of the actual loss suffered. Eventually in *Mitchel* v. *Reynolds* (1711),[4] outside our period, Parker C.J. systematized the earlier cases and based his exposition of the law governing voluntary restraints upon two contrasts—that between general and partial restraints, and that between restraints supported by consideration, and those not so supported. From this decision the modern law developed.

THE CONSEQUENCES OF ILLEGALITY

The general principle was that a contract tainted with illegality was void, whether the illegality affected the promise or the consideration for the promise.[5] Where two considerations were alleged, one being good and the other idle and vain, the good consideration was allowed to stand.[6] But if one con-

---

[1] Palm. 172.

[2] *Nordenfelt* v. *Maxim Nordenfelt Guns & Ammunition Co. Ltd.* [1894] A.C. 535.

[3] See *Hall* v. *Hawes* (1633), cited 2 Keb. 377; *Anon.* (1614) March 77; *Barrow* v. *Wood* (1642) March 191; *Prugnell* v. *Anne Gosse* (1649) Aleyn 67; *Hunlocke* v. *Blacklowe* (1670) 2 Wms. Saund. 156, 1 Mod. 64, 1 Sid. 464, 2 Keb. 674; *Clerk* v. *Taylors of Exeter* (1684) 2 Show. 345, 2 Lev. 241, 3 Lev. 243.

[4] 1 P. Wms. 181, on which see Heydon, op. cit. 11 et seq.

[5] Sheppard, 86–7.

[6] *Crisp* v. *Gamel* (1605) Cro. Jac. 128.

sideration was bad then it affected the other consideration as well.[1] If a promise could become lawful then the promisor would be liable for its breach according to the general notion that promissory liability was strict;[2] the promisor had undertaken to perform. The position of the innocent party was considered in *Fletcher* v. *Harcot* (1622); he could sue if the consideration was on its face apparently lawful.[3] The first case to deal with the recovery of money paid on an illegal contract is *Tomkins* v. *Bernet* (1693) outside our period.[4]

1. The promise must be possible

William Sheppard's second requirement is that the thing promised must be possible to be done, and cases on this subject are in the nature of things very uncommon. The medieval law as applied to formal contracts was that both an impossible condition and an impossible covenant were void, with the consequence that in the former situation a conditioned bond became absolute.[5] So far as formal contracts are concerned, the medieval law was maintained in the sixteenth and seventeenth centuries, and there was even a case in 1638, *Streete* v. *Danyell*,[6] involving a legal impossibility—the assignment of a commission of bankrupts. There appear to be no assumpsit cases, though it is clear that it was felt that the same principles applied. The rationale is not obvious, but presumably it was thought to be absurd that the law should recognize an impossible promise. There is, however, one case where the consideration for a promise was legally impossible; this was *Harvey* v. *Gibbons* (1676),[7] where the consideration was the release of a debt due to the promisee's master. A servant could not release such a debt, and so the performance would be impossible, but the ground given is illegality. Probably what was meant was legal impossibility.

Supervening impossibility raises issues which are at once more interesting and more likely to occur in practice. Here the

---

[1] *Bridge* v. *Cage* (1605) Cro. Jac. 103; *Best* v. *Jolly* (1660) 1 Sid. 38.
[2] *Howard* v. *Approbert* (1628) Litt. 85.
[3] *Fletcher* v. *Harcot* (1622) Hutton 55.
[4] 1 Salk. 22.
[5] See above, p. 107.
[6] 1 Rolle Ab. 419. See also *Graham* v. *Crawshaw* (1682) 3 Lev. 74.
[7] 2 Lev. 161.

medieval law was complex, as we have seen, but the general rule was that supervening impossibility rendered a contract void so long as the impossibility arose through an act of God or the law, but not if the impossibility arose through the act of a stranger. This principle was refined in a series of cases in the sixteenth century, the leading decision being *Laughter's Case* (1594).[1] The case law is predominantly concerned with conditions attached to bonds, but the principle of law involved seems to have been regarded as general in application, and in substantive terms involves the recognition of a contractual defence of act of God, which must be differentiated from the mere contention by a defendant that he was not at fault.[2] The sixteenth and seventeenth centuries produced an interesting body of case law on the possible extension of the conception of supervening impossibility, which culminated in the well-known case of *Paradine* v. *Jane* (1648).[3] The story begins with *Doctor and Student*.

The principal discussion of liability without fault in *Doctor and Student*[4] is in the context of the law of waste; the topic discussed is the liability of tenants for life, in dower, and by the curtesy, for waste done without their privity by a stranger. The Student points out that they are liable on the fictional theory of self-imposed strict liability,[5]

'they have wilfully taken upon them the charge to see that no waste be done',

The Doctor notes that there is no liability,

'if houses of these tenants be destroyed with sudden tempest or with strange enemies',

and opines that the reason is the lack of remedy over, it being impossible to sue God or strange enemies.[6] The Student denies

---

[1] 5 Co. Rep. 21b, Moo. K.B. 357, Cro. Eliz. 398. See also *Arundell* v. *Combe* (1566) Dyer 262a; *Tropp* v. *Bedingfield* (1591) Cro. Eliz. 532, and above, p. 107. For covenant see *Hyde* v. *The Dean and Canons of Windsor* (1597) Cro. Eliz. 552.

[2] The question whether medieval law adopted a principle of strict liability has been the subject of much controversy; see the literature discussed in Fifoot 187 et seq. To the cases generally cited may be added 18 Hen. VI, f. 21, pl. 6 and 5 Edw. IV, (Long Quinto) f. 26. Most writings on the subject are of extremely low quality.

[3] Aleyn 26, Style 47.   [4] Dial. II, c. 4.

[5] The same dogma is, of course, rampant in modern law.

[6] The leading medieval case on remedy over is the *Case of the Marshalsea*, 33 Hen. VI, H. f. 1, pl. 3, from which the examples are taken.

that this is the reason; it just happens to be the law. He takes this line in order to develop the view that a person may bind himself by private contract to being strictly liable in situations where the law would not impose such liability upon him:[1] *lex non* [*neminem*] *cogit ad impossibilia*, but the *individual* may so bind himself. The Doctor argues that the common law is unreasonable,

> 'For that law seemeth not reasonable that bindeth a man to an impossibility'.[2]

And the Student replies that a tenant can always refuse to accept a tenancy. The Doctor points out that this is not true of tenant to the curtesy, who becomes tenant at once on his wife's death; the Student parries by saying he need not have married a lady of property, and the Doctor scores a technical knock-out by suggesting that the marriage could have been contracted when the party was within age, or before the wife owned the lands. The discussion contains most of the arguments which were to recur in later cases. In discussion elsewhere of promissory liability the Doctor reports the canonist view, derived from Aquinas that promises should cease to be binding by 'casualty coming after', so here again common lawyers were made familiar with the canonist doctrine.

The next source is Dyer's Reports, which contain two relevant cases. The first is *Anon.* (1537),[3] involving a lease of lands adjoining the river Exe in Devon, and a covenant to sustain and repair the river banks. Action was taken on a bond to perform the covenant and the lessee pleaded that they had been broken down by a great, outrageous, and sudden flood. Fitzherbert and Shelley JJ. held that the defendant was not liable on the bond for the penalty, since he had the defence of act of God to breach of the covenant to sustain. However, he was liable to perform

---

[1] The classic statement is that of Illingworth in 8 Edw. IV, M. f. 9, pl. 9, 'A man by his own act can bind himself to do something which he would not be compelled by the law'.

[2] The reference is no doubt to the maxim *lex non coqit ad impossibilia*, or one of its variant forms. The maxim echoes the Digest 50.17.185 *impossibilium nulla obligatio est*. Littleton, *Tenures* 129, states the principle but not the maxim with the illustration of an obligation to provide a rose or a bushel of roses in midwinter. See also Co. Litt. 92a. 206a, and Noy, *Maxims*, No. 34. The maxim is related to *impotentia excusat legem*.

[3] Dyer 33a.

his covenant to repair in a reasonable time because he had bound himself to do this 'of his covenant'. The second case is *Richard le Taverner's Case* (1543),[1] which also deals with a lease, this time a lease of land and sheep; the sheep all died, and the question at issue was whether for this act of God the rent should be apportioned. Here the case was complicated by the general common law reluctance to apportion,[2] which tended against the tenant, and on the other hand by the notion that rent was conceptually reserved from the issues of the property leased, so that in such a case there was no source from which the rent (so far as the sheep were concerned) might come. The case was much argued, and no decision was reached though all thought that in equity and reason apportionment was right, but the majority view was that in law it was not possible,

'And some[3] were of opinion that it should not, although it is an Act of God, and no default in the lessee or lessor; as if the sea gain upon part of the land leased, or part is burnt by wildfire which is the Act of God, the rent is not apportionable but shall issue out of the remainder; otherwise is it if part be recovered or evicted by elder title then it is apportionable'.

No settled doctrine emerged from these cases, but it is at least clear that there was no general support for a move towards the extension of the defence of supervening impossibility, and a case in Dalison in 1553[4] dealing with the liability of a carrier who has voluntarily taken in hand goods to carry holds the carrier liable for robbery by a third party partly on the ground that he is not bound to carry, and partly on the ground that he has a remedy over. The earliest assumpsit case appears to be *Taylor's Case* in 1583[5] where the defendant promised to carry apples by boat from Greenwich to London, and the vessel sank through

---

[1] Dyer 56a.

[2] The general rule was that an entire contract could not be apportioned; the medieval cases are collected in Brooke, *Apportionment*, and the doctrine still affects the modern law. For its application in assumpsit see e.g. *Bret* v. *J.S.* (1600) Cro. Eliz. 756.

[3] Those against apportionment included Luke and Brooke JJ., those in favour Montague C.J., and Brown and Mervin JJ.

[4] Dalison 8, *per* Browne and Portman JJ.

[5] 4 Leon. 31 in the King's Bench.

a tempest. The report is inadequate but apparently the defendant pleaded act of God, and

> 'it was holden no plea in assumpsit, by which the [defendant] had subjected himself to all adventures'.

The decision may have been influenced by the notion that the term *assumpsit* connoted strict liability, but this is mere conjecture; it does involve a distinction between formal contracts, where supervening impossibility could be a defence, and assumpsit, where no such rule applied. *Saunders* v. *Esterbie* (1615)[1] possibly suggests that a promise was discharged by the death of the promisor, but is mainly concerned with the transmissibility of liability on a broken promise, at this time controversial, and since it was originally thought that such liability was intransmissible *a fortiori*, a promise was discharged by death.[2] Against this confused background we must consider the two leading cases on the subject—the well-known *Paradine* v. *Jane* (1648)[3] and the less well-known but equally important *Williams* v. *Hide* (1624).[4]

In *Williams* v. *Hide* an action of assumpsit was brought on a gratuitous bailment of a grey gelding which the defendant had promised to return on request. Before any request made the beast died without fault or negligence on the part of the bailee, and the action was fought on demurrer to a plea setting up this clear case of act of God as a defence. It was held by the court of King's Bench (Dodderidge *absente*) that the plea was good. The case was elaborately argued by Germain for the plaintiff, who argued that a promise to return a horse implied a promise to pay damages if the horse died; he further contended that the whole 'policy of assurances' would be overthrown if the defendant was not liable. Maynard on the other side contended that supervening impossibility through act of God without fault was a defence if there existed no remedy over; he relied on covenant cases and argued that an assumpsit is a covenant by words, and a covenant an assumpsit by deed so that it was irrational to apply a different law to formal and informal

---

[1] 1 Rolle Rep. 266.
[2] See below.
[3] Aleyn 26, Style 47.
[4] Palm. 548, W. Jones 179.

contracts. The court accepted Maynard's argument, and Hyde C.J. took the view expressly that there should be no difference between the two types of contract.

Twenty-four years later there was decided *Paradine* v. *Jane*, a case which has come in the course of time to be regarded as critical in that it laid down the rule as to absolute contracts. Debt was brought for rent due on a lease for years; the defendant pleaded specially that for some[1] of the period for which the rent was in arrear,

> 'Prince Rupert an alien, and an enemy of the King, invaded the land with an army . . . and kept him out that he could not enjoy the lands for such a time'.

The plaintiff demurred to the plea both as to substance and form. The plea was held bad, first because it did not aver that the army consisted of aliens unknown, so as to show that there existed no remedy over the lessee to recoup his losses. But the court went further than this and held that in substance the plea was in any event bad. In the report in Style it is simply said that he would have been liable in covenant on a covenant to pay rent if the land was surrounded with water, *a fortiori* on the facts of the case. The report in Aleyn is fuller, with this reasoning:

> 'And this difference was taken, that where the law creates a duty of charge, and the party is disabled to perform it without any default in him, and hath no remedy over, there the law will excuse him . . .[2] but when the party by his own contract creates a duty of charge upon himself he is bound to make it good, if he may, notwithstanding any accident by inevitable necessity, because he might have provided against it by his contract.'

It was then argued that he was plainly liable in covenant, and that reservation of rent on a lease 'being a covenant in law . . . it is all one as if there had been an actual covenant'. The two authorities relied upon for the second part of this doctrine were

---

[1] Another objection to the plea was that it confessed some rent due.

[2] Supported by authorities from the law of waste. The argument is plainly influenced by *Doctor and Student*.

a year-book case of covenant[1] and the case in Dyer in 1537, and these explain the words, 'he is bound to make it good, if he may'.[2] They are clearly suggested primarily by the case in Dyer —the covenantor in that case was not to forfeit the bond for failure to sustain the river banks, for this he could not possibly do. But he can make them good, and hence must pay damages if he fails to do so. Similarly there is nothing impossible in the lessee paying rent, or so goes the argument of the court. The argument on the other side for contending that the payment of rent is impossible is that rent issues out of the land, and when the lessee is not in occupation he cannot collect the profits from which the rent must come; this point was taken by Style *arguendo*, relying on a case in Coke,

> 'Next consider the nature of reservation, 10 Rep. 128.[3] A rent is not to be paid until it may be intended that the lessee might have received the profit of the thing for which the rent is to be paid'.

But the court rejected this.

Paradine v. *Jane* and *Williams and Hide* seem diametrically opposed decisions, and in basic approach they are; furthermore in the later case it is clear that the issues were directly before the court, for in argument it was said (and no doubt the report is truncated),

> 'Also by the law of reason it seems the defendant in our case ought not to be charged with the rent, because he could not enjoy what was let to him, and it was no fault of his own that he could not, and the civil law, the canon law and the moral authors do confirm this'.

Whilst in reply the court took the point that,

> 'as the lessee is to have the advantage of casual profits, so he must run the hazard of casual losses, and not lay the whole burden of them upon the lessor'.

---

[1] 40 Edw. III, H. f. 5, pl. 11, distinguishing trees from buildings blown down. Man cannot grow trees, but he can repair buildings, is the point being advanced, though the distinction between nature and art seems unconvincing today.

[2] Discussed without reference to their context by H. W. R. Wade in 56 L.Q.R. at 525.

[3] *William Clun's Case.*

But the two cases are not so far apart as appears at first sight. For *Paradine* v. *Jane* is not dealing with an act of God at all, nor does it seek to impose liability for failure to do what is wholly impossible.[1] Hence the decisions left open a limited scope for a defence of supervening total impossibility by act of God, a curious compromise.

3. The promise must be clear and certain

The rule that the promise must be clear and certain is intimately associated with the whole system of pleading to an issue, and, as Stephen explains, to 'the nature of the original constitution of the trial by jury', which led to the insistence upon certainty in the issue.[2] If in the action of assumpsit this certainty in the issue was to be achieved, the promise must itself be averred with certainty, and numerous cases illustrate this. The principle applied both to the promise sued upon and to a promise averred as a consideration, for the latter was not a good consideration unless itself actionable, and to be actionable it must be certain. Thus in *Tolhurst* v. *Brickenden* (1610)[3] an action was brought upon a promise to pay £100 within a short time in consideration for a promise to deliver two fat oxen within a short time.

> 'The Court all agreed that this declaration is not good, for the incertainty in it, for *per breve tempus* is as uncertain, what time this should be, as the case of forbearance *per paululum tempus* which was adjudged in the Exchequer to be no time, and so void for incertainty.'

The reference is to *Sackford* v. *Phillips*[4] and to an unidentified decision in 1610, dealing with a promise of forbearance 'for a little time' as consideration for a promise to pay a debt. The principle did not, however, exclude the averment of promises which though themselves uncertain could be reduced to a certainty, as in *Dockley* v. *Bury* (1612),[5] where action was brought on a reciprocal promise to bear half the loss in return

---

[1] Except on the basis that rent is a share of what issues from the land.
[2] Stephen, *Pleading*, pp. 132 et seq.
[3] Cro. Jac. 250, 1 Rolle Rep. 5, 1 Bulst. 91.
[4] Moore 689.
[5] 1 Bulst. 202.

for a promise of half the gain on a voyage to France. As Yelverton J. said,

> 'What more certainty can there be in an adventure? None at all; this possibility and uncertainty is now by this his return well reduced into a certainty; and so the same is good, being now all made certain by the account had and made of the gain and loss, being now by this all made certain'.

The requirement of certainty had also applied to the older contractual remedies, notably debt; it was not peculiar in an way to assumpsit.[1] In assumpsit actions, however, it was permissible, as we have seen, to sue on promises to pay *quantum meruit* or *quantum valebant*, and less particularity was required of a promise than was required of the grant of a debt, though eventually the law of debt was modified and brought into line with assumpsit.[2]

4. The promise must be co-hering, and agreeing in itself, and with the consideration

It is not easy to see what Sheppard has in mind in stating this principle, but I suspect that two distinct ideas are involved. The first is that a promise must not be absurd or internally self-contradictory; Sheppard in fact indexes a number of cases as illustrating the idea that promises must not be 'insensible' or 'repugnant'.[3] The second is perhaps a reference to the requirement that there must be a relationship between the consideration averred and the promise, so that it appears that the consideration can rank as a reason for the promise in question, an idea connected with the rule that consideration must 'move' from the promisee. Another illustration is a case such as *Traver* v. *Lord Bridgport* (1627),[4] where a declaration on a promise to pay money in consideration of the delivery of goods was held bad. For the goods might belong to the defendant,

---

[1] See *Johnson* v. *Morgan* (1599) Cro. Eliz. 758, above, p. 496, and on assumpsit, *Kete* v. *Michell* (1623) 2 Rolle Rep. 413. In forbearance cases actual forbearance as consideration must be distinguished from promises to forbear: in the former case problems of certainty did not arise. See *Cowlin* v. *Cook* (1625) Noy 83.

[2] See also *Sharp* v. *Rolt* (1625) Noy 83; *Whitlock's Case* (1619) Sheppard 92; *Burkin's Case* (1598) Sheppard 92; *Morris's Case* (1619) Sheppard 93.

[3] Sheppard 90, 91.

[4] Hetley 62, See above, p. 439.

in which case the delivery was no reason for the promise of payment. But there is no very clear evidence for this interpretation.

5. The promise must be serious and weighty

Here again it is by no means clear what Sheppard had in mind, and the principle seems to have had little importance. The examples given by Sheppard seem confused. One is concerned with uncertainty,[1] another involves a misunderstanding of a year-book case,[2] but the third, referring to a case in Hetley's Reports,[3] deals with a joke contract—a promise in consideration of 12d. to pay £5 to the defendant if the plaintiff does not have him whipped at the cross in Gloucester, and this was held not actionable. This case seems close to a wager, but wagers, perhaps the most obvious type of contract which the courts might have refused to recognize on the ground of frivolity, were regarded as actionable at common law. Indeed it is in connection with wagers that the common law first recognized the doctrine that a promise was good consideration for a promise,[4] so that wagering contracts so far from being anomalous have in fact been the source of an important contractual doctrine. The actionability of wagers originated with the rise of assumpsit, for debt never lay, and consequently *indebitatus assumpsit* could not be brought,[5] but only special assumpsit. It never seems to have been argued during our period that wagering contracts were bad at common law either on the ground of mere frivolity or on the ground that their enforcement was contrary to public policy, and statutory interference did not begin until 1664, the statute only operating against excessive gaming.[6] Nor did the court treat the contract in *James* v. *Morgan* (1663),[7] as void for frivolity: here a horse was sold for a

---

[1] Sheppard 92 (*Burkin's Case*).

[2] Sheppard 92 referring to 21 Hen. VII, H. f. 23, pl. 15.

[3] The reference to Hetley does not work.

[4] *West* v. *Stowel* (1577) 2 Leon. 54. See also *Andrews* v. *Herne* (1661) 1 Lev. 33, 1 Keb. 56, 65; *Hunby* v. *Johnson* (1663) 1 Chan. Rep. 243.

[5] See *Smith* v. *Airey* (1710) Holt K.B. 329; *Walker* v. *Walker* (1694) Holt K.B. 328; *contra Rowley* v. *Dad* (1679) Freeman K.B. 263, *Indebitatus assumpsit* was available against a stakeholder, however, see *Asser* v. *Wilks* (1707) Holt K.B. 36.

[6] 16 Car. II, c. 7, which limited the actionable loss on a single occasion to £100.

[7] 1 Lev. 111, 1 Keb. 569.

barley corn each nail, doubling for every nail. The quantity of barley involved was immense, since there were thirty-two nails in the shoes of the horse. The contract was held good, the jury, however, giving the value of the horse only in damages.[1]

Other possible grounds for invalidity

In modern common law the validity of an informal contract can be affected by a number of vitiating elements—mistake, fraud, innocent misrepresentation, duress, and undue influence. In our period there was little law on any of these topics and on some none at all. So far as the defence of error or mistake is concerned, there appear to be no cases at all in which the point was raised, and although the argument must of necessity be one from silence the explanation is fairly obvious. The requirement of consideration renders the recognition of an independent doctrine of mistake otiose. The requirement of consideration excludes the irrational promise, and granted that only promises given with a good reason are actionable there is no place for a doctrine of error. The link between *causa* and *error* is plainly made in St. Germain,[2] where it is the promise without a cause which is supposed to have been given in error, and it probably lies behind the link between the notion of consideration and deliberation in *Sharrington* v. *Strotton* (1566).[3] The idea that mistake could form an independent ground for invalidity belongs to the nineteenth century, when the theory of *consensus ad idem*, the meeting of minds, held sway.

Similarly it was not suggested during this period that fraud, much less innocent misrepresentation, should affect the validity of a promise. Again the explanation may lie in the acceptance of the doctrine of consideration; if the promise has been given for good consideration, why should it not be actionable, and what place is there for the *independent* contention that it was induced not by good consideration, but by fraud? For *ab hypothesi* it has been induced by good consideration. It followed that the defendant who wished to set up fraud as a defence should attack the consideration. However, the old action for deceit for breach of warranty had evolved in the late fourteenth

[1] See R. E. Megarry, *Miscellany at Law*, 229.
[2] See above, p. 389.
[3] Plowden 308b.

century in connection with the contract of sale long before the rise of the action of assumpsit and its associated doctrine of consideration, and it lived on somewhat anomalously to provide a remedy in damages for breach of a warranty inducing a contract (normally a sale). The transaction itself was not however, affected; indeed it was the fact that the plaintiff had been cheated into contracting which was the basis of liability, and if there was no contract there would be no deceit. With the possible exception of sales of victuals,[1] there had to be either an express warranty or an affirmation known to be false at the time of the sale. This appears to be the effect of the difficult case of *Chandelor* v. *Lopus* (1603),[2] where an action was brought against a jeweller who had sold a stone *affirming* it to be a bezoar stone, whereas it was not. A bezoar stone is an object somewhat similar to a gall stone, but formed in the intestines of goats, and was thought at the time to possess medicinal value. The action succeeded in the King's Bench, but judgment was reversed in the Exchequer Chamber, Anderson C.J. dissenting, upon the ground that no *warranty* had been averred; quite what would count as a warranty, as opposed to a mere affirmation, is left unclear, and was presumably a jury matter. A similar view is taken in the earlier case of *Harvey* v. *Yonge* (1602),[3] which did not appear in printed reports. However, it was also said that the seller would have been liable on a mere affirmation coupled with knowledge that the stone was not a bezoar stone at the time of the sale. This doctrine was applied in *Warner* v. *Tallerd* (1650)[4] and later in *Ekins* v. *Tresham* (1663);[5] later on, in the time of Holt C.J., decisions[6] were given assimilating affirmations to warranties and thus breaking down a distinction which must always have been somewhat artificial. But it was never suggested that either a fraudulent or an innocent misrepresentation would affect the *validity* of the sale, and until

---

[1] See F.N.B. 94C.

[2] Cro. Jac. 4, 2 Rolle Rep. 5, Dyer 75a *in margine*, 8 Harv. L.R. 282, Cro. Jac. 469, Kiralfy 220, *H.E.L.* VIII. 68. The dating of this case is obscure and so is the reasoning: I do not accept the view that here were two actions between the parties.

[3] Appendix, Case No. 16.

[4] 1 Rolle Ab. 91.

[5] 1 Lev. 102, 1 Sid. 146, and *Fowke* v. *Boyle* (1652) Style 343.

[6] *Crosse* v. *Gardner* (1689) Carth. 90; *Medina* v. *Stoughton* (1700) 1 Ld. Raym. 593.

Holt's time there was in general no liability in the absence of either a warranty or an affirmation known to be false.[1] Duress had been accepted in medieval law as invalidating acts in the law, and there was in principle no reason why cases of assumpsit involving duress or menace should not have arisen; there appear, however, to be no examples of the application of the medieval doctrines to informal transactions, and again the explanation may be that if the defendant wished to contend that he promised because of a threat or because of imprisonment his proper course would be to plead the general issue and give the circumstances in evidence as showing the promise was devoid of consideration. So far as the equitable doctrine of undue influence is concerned, it was yet to be invented

Jurisdictional limitations

We must notice finally that certain promises were not actionable upon jurisdictional grounds. Thus actions for breach of promise of marriage were spiritual in nature and consequently fell within the jurisdiction of the ecclesiastical courts. The earliest action at common law for straightforward breach of promise is *Stretch* v. *Parker* (1638),[2] where the action was allowed although the consideration was spiritual. In *Baker* v. *Smith* (1651)[3] it is noted that such actions had become common, and they were justified by Rolle C.J. on the ground that, although the thing to be done was spiritual, temporal loss might occur for which there ought to be a temporal action. After the Restoration, when the ecclesiastical courts were again sitting, the common law courts retained jurisdiction,[4] though in *Holder* v. *Dickeson* (1673)[5] Vaughan C.J. vigorously dissented from allowing such actions. So far as the substance of the matter is concerned, this development of a common law jurisdiction introduced a new liability for damages, which had never existed in the ecclesiastical courts, and this introduced an element of

[1] See *Harvey* v. *Young* (1602) Yelv. 20; *Roswel* v. *Vaughan* (1606) Cro. Jac. 196; *Bailie* v. *Merrill* (1615) 1 Rolle Rep. 275. The warranty had to induce the sale (see *Pope* v. *Lewyns* (1622) Cro. Jac. 630 and therefore had to be at the time of the sale. See also *Goldsmith* v. *Preston* (1605) 1 Rolle Ab. 96.
[2] 1 Rolle Abr. f. 22.
[3] Style 295, 303.
[4] *Rutter* v. *Hebden* (1664) 1 Lev. 147, 1 Sid. 180; *Cooper* v. *Witham* (1668) 3 Keb. 399.
[5] 1 Freeman K.B. 95, Cart. 233, 3 Keb. 148.

compulsion into the matter. In the canon law there was no question of enforcing a contract of marriage *de futuro*—that is an executory contract to marry—though there could be admonition and penance for breach of faith if there had been a pledge of faith. The other important jurisdictional rule concerned legacies, which were in principle ecclesiastical in nature and not recoverable by action at common law until the Commonwealth;[1] this gave rise to theoretical difficulties over actions on promises by executors to pay legacies.[2]

[1] *Butler* v. *Butler* (1657) 2 Sid. 21; *Nicholson* v. *Sherman* (1661) T. Raymond 23, 1 Sid. 46.
[2] See above, p. 440.

X

CONTRACTUAL CAPACITY AND AGENCY

FOR a variety of reasons the law may deny full or indeed any contractual capacity to certain classes of person, or treat them in some anomalous way. In the common law, infants, married women, and monks were the more important categories involved. Lunatics and drunkards form two other special categories, since it is in theory arguable that they lack the natural capacity to consent, but there was virtually no law developed in our period on their status.[1] Corporations, being non-natural persons, necessarily attract special rules as to how they can contract, and thus form another special category. The existence of persons with limited or non-existent contractual capacity is associated closely with the evolution of a law of agency—if, for example, a married woman cannot herself enter into contracts it may be that she can act as agent for her husband who can.

Monks

Monks professed were civilly dead,[2] as were friars, and as a general rule lacked all legal capacity. Thus, for example, a feoffment to a monk was void,[3] and a monk could not be party to any form of contract.[4] However, obviously monastic houses had to be able to purchase necessaries and make contracts, and this was achieved by allowing a monk to act as an agent who could, with his assent, bind his sovereign. In the fourteenth century a doctrine was developed whereby the Abbot would be charged on contracts made by his monks, but the basis of liability was the receipt of goods or money or whatever to the

---

[1] See *Beverley's Case* (1603) 4 Co.Rep. 123b. Other categories which I do not discuss are aliens, villeins, outlaws and persons attained: their history more naturally belongs to the history of status.

[2] The best account is Maitland's; see P. and M. I. 416.

[3] 12 Hen. VII, T. f. 27, pl. 7.

[4] 3 Edw. III, M. f. 46, pl. 32; 4 Edw. IV, M. f. 24, pl. 2; 16 Hen. VII, P. f. 17, pl. 10. There were respects in which a monk's 'civil death' was eroded by exceptions. So, for example, he could act as executor. On the method of trying whether a person was professed, see 9 Hen. VII, T. f. 2, pl. 3.

use of the house,[1] or, according to another view, the agreement to the receipt.[2] Originally it seems that this would only be so if the monk in question was an officer deputed to make purchases, such as a cellarer, but fifteenth-century case law apparently dropped this restriction.[3] The basis of liability in such cases is in reality more akin to restitution than contract proper; the house is held liable in order to prevent its being unjustly enriched at the expense of the other contracting party, and from time to time it was argued that a similar doctrine should be applied to acquisitions through servants and wives. The rules governing monks came, of course, to be obsolete under the Reformation, and have never been disinterred with the revival of monasticism in England in modern times.

Infants

After some vacillation it came to be settled in medieval law that, in general, contracts made by infants were voidable at the option of the infant[4] either at once or on attaining his majority. This doctrine was taken to the extreme point of saying that if, for example, an infant leased land he could either claim rent or sue for trespass; the lease was, however, clearly voidable rather than void.[5] He could on attaining his majority become estopped from disclaiming the contract, in a lease by accepting rent or in a contract of sale by suing upon it,[6] and according to Newton in a case in 1441,[7] an infant lessee who remained in possession was liable in debt for the rent—'the cause is that he has *quid pro quo*'—though presumably he could, by leaving the land before rent fell due, avoid the liability. The only major exception to the general principle was the infant's liability to pay for necessaries supplied to him, and this liability came to be accepted in the fifteenth century. It is not very clear

[1] 7 Edw. III, T. f. 35, pl. 35; 22 Edw. III, T. f. 8, pl. 9; 2 Hen. IV, T. f. 21, pl. 1.
[2] See 20 Hen. VI, H. f. 21, pl. 19.
[3] 11 Hen. VI, P. f. 30, pl. 16; 12 Hen. VI, M. f. 6, pl. 13; 21 Edw. IV, H. f. 19, pl. 21; M. f. 80, pl. 28.
[4] 21 Hen. VI, H. f. 31, pl. 18; 21 Edw. IV, P. f. 6, pl. 17; 1 Hen. VII, P. f. 14, pl. 2; 14 Hen. VIII, P. f. 25, pl. 7 at f. 29.
[5] 7 Edw. IV, P. f. 6, pl. 16; 18 Edw. IV, P. f. 1, pl. 7, and cf. 12 Hen. IV, H. f. 12, pl. 1.
[6] 14 Hen. VIII, P. f. 29, pl. 7, *per* Brudenell C.J.
[7] 21 Hen. VI, H. pl. 18 at f. 31.

how this happened. The first case dealing with the point is in 1431,[1] where Strange argues:

'When an infant within age has *quid pro quo* he will be bound by law. As in the case when an infant within age is at table with me to pay a certain sum each week, or when he buys clothes for his body, he will be charged by action of debt, because these things he must of necessity have.'

This confuses two quite distinct rationales of the doctrine, necessity and benefit, and it is not clear that the argument was accepted. Some years later Paston J. emphatically denied that an infant was liable for necessaries in reply to an argument that an infant could be bound by a contract which was beneficial to him. The context and terms of the discussion echo the earlier case, and make clear that the question had become a standard form doctrinal controversy. In 1478,[2] once again in repetitive terms, Vavasour, then a serjeant, states the modern doctrine:

'Vavasour said in secret to Littleton at the same time that if an infant be at table with me, I taking for his tabling twenty pence per week, or if he buys clothing of me or materials for his robes, I shall have an action of debt against him, and it will not be a plea for him to say "within age", because the law intends that he cannot live without food, drink and clothing, and consequently the law wills that he pay the money due to him in this case.'

The doctrine is restated in slightly different terms in Perkins's *Profitable Book* (1528),[3] in a passage primarily concerned with an infant's capacity to make a valid grant:

'And an infant will be bound by all acts done by him during his nonage which acts are to his advantage, except in special cases, and therefore if an infant of years of discretion makes an obligation for his necessary food and drink, or for his necessary clothing or covenants for his schooling, he will not avoid this, the reason being obvious, and so it will be in similar cases.'

---

[1] 10 Hen. VI, M. f. 14, pl. 46.
[2] 18 Edw. IV, P. f. 1, pl. 7 at f. 2.
[3] Perkins, *Grants*, 14.

Here again we find the conflation of two principles of liability—advantage and necessity. The common law doctrine is derivative of Roman Law, as developed in the medieval universities.[1]

There was some obscurity over the application of general principle to articles of apprenticeship. There was some suggestion that a covenant under seal for apprenticeship bound the infant at common law,[2] subject perhaps to a minimum age of 12.[3] But the view which prevailed was that an infant within age could not bind himself apprentice; however, the custom of London permitted this at the age of 14.[4] The use of simple covenants under seal, as opposed to penal bonds, in arranging apprenticeships may be connected with the fact that an infant could in no circumstances be liable on a penalty bond at common law and a custom permitting this would probably have been bad.

The post-medieval law followed the earlier precedents, and cases in the late sixteenth and early seventeenth centuries established that debt lay on a contract for necessaries (the court being the judge)[5] and that a simple bond or bill[6] for necessaries was binding, whereas a penal bond for necessaries was bad.[7] So far as the action of assumpsit is concerned, the propriety of using this form of action against an infant, thereby depriving him of the benefit of waging his law, seems to have caused some initial controversy, and according to Rolle,[8] there was a decision in 1614 to the effect that the action for this reason should not be allowed. However, there are precedents earlier than this permitting the action. In *Blackstone's Case* (1610)[9] a brewer

---

[1] I am indebted to Mr. J. L. Barton for some confirmation of my suspicion that the common law doctrine is derived from Roman Law. The starting point appears to be Digest 46.3.47.1: see also the gloss *contra senatusconsultum* to Codex 2.23.2. As elaborated the civilian doctrine was based upon a principle of enrichment coupled with a doctrine according to which necessaries were deemed to enrich.

[2] 21 Hen. VI, H. pl. 18, f. 31.

[3] 38 Hen. VI, H. pl. 4, f. 22.

[4] 21 Edw. IV, P. f. 6, pl. 17.

[5] Assumed in *Makarell* v. *Bachelor* (1597) Cro. Eliz. 583; *Rearsby* v. *Cuffer* (1613) Godbolt 219.

[6] *Aoliffe* v. *Archdale* (1602) Moo. K.B. 679; *Rearsby* v. *Cuffer* (1613) Godbolt 219; *Cupworth's Case* (1613) 1 Rolle Ab. 729; *Russell* v. *Lee* (1662) 1 Lev. 86, 1 Keb. 382, 416, 423.

[7] *Randal's Case* (1602) unrep. Godbolt 219; *Hutchin's Case* (1619) Dyer 104b *in marg*.

[8] 1 Rolle. Ab. 729.

[9] Dyer 104 *in marg*.

was allowed to sue on a promise to pay for drink supplied, and in *Dale* v. *Copping* (1610)[1] a promise by an infant to pay for a cure of the falling sickness was upheld as falling within the concept of necessaries. In *Tillet* v. *Buckstone* (1617)[2] it was held that assumpsit lay against an infant where debt lay, though it was doubted whether assumpsit lay against an infant upon a collateral promise. What counted as necessary was for the court to decide.[3] The normal heads were meat, drink, lodging, and apparel 'necessary and convenient to wear, according to his state and degree';[4] medical attention was also included, and after some argument schooling.[5] The important case of *Whittingham* v. *Hill* (1619)[6] settled that trading contracts of an infant were not binding upon him even though they concerned a trade by which the infant maintained his living.

There has been some discussion as to whether the infant's liability for necessaries is truly contractual or quasi-contractual. The early cases hardly concern themselves with this abstract question, and there are both cases where the action is brought on a promise to pay a definite sum[7] and cases including promises to pay a *quantum meruit*;[8] such a promise may or may not be fictional. In the absence of any express agreement the law would imply a promise to pay for lodging unless some third party had actually undertaken to pay on behalf of the infant.[9] Where an action was brought on an express promise to pay a definite sum for necessaries there was some suggestion in *Pickering* v. *Gunning* (1627)[10] by Hyde C.J. that the plaintiff must aver that the sum promised was deserved, though this was not in the event insisted upon. Eventually, of course, it came to be settled that the infant's liability was only to pay a *reasonable* price for necessaries, not the contract price as such.

The doctrine that an infant was bound not only by con-

[1] 1 Bulst. 39.
[2] 1 Rolle Ab. 729. See also *Delavel* v. *Clare* (1626) Noy 85.
[3] *Makarell* v. *Bachelor* (1597) Cro. Eliz. 583.
[4] *Ive* v. *Chester* (1620) Cro. Jac. 561.
[5] *Whittingham* v. *Hill* (1619) Cro. Jac. 494, 1 Rolle Ab. 729, *Pickering* v. *Gunning* (1627) Palm. 528.
[6] Cro. Jac. 494, 1 Rolle Ab. 729.
[7] e.g. *Blackstone's Case* (1610) Dyer 104b *in marg.*
[8] e.g. *Ive* v. *Chester* (1620) Cro. Jac. 561.
[9] *Duncomb* v. *Tickridge* (1649) Aleyn 94.
[10] Palm. 526.

tracts for necessaries but also by contracts to his advantage seems to have survived in seventeenth-century law as an explanation for the infant's liability to pay rent due on a lease.[1]

In the case of a contract by an infant which was not for necessaries the position was that the contract was enforceable by the infant at his election, whether or not he had performed his side of the agreement, so long as there was good consideration for the other party's promise. Thus in *Forrester's Case* (1661)[2] an infant sued by guardian; the jury having found in his favour, it was moved in arrest of judgment that since the consideration for the promise was the infant's promise to pay money, and this was unenforceable, there was no consideration. It was, however, said that even if the infant had not performed and could not be sued himself he could nevertheless sue; the consideration here was the promise, not its future performance.[3] Of course the decision would have been different if the promises had been mutually conditional. It is difficult to fit this opinion in *Forrester's Case* into any coherent theory, since the rationale of holding a promise a good consideration for a counter-promise was its reciprocal enforceability, nor is any satisfactory explanation found in the cases. Perhaps the idea was that infancy was a personal privilege upon which only the infant could rely. Later in the seventeenth century, in *Ball v. Hesketh* (1697),[4] it was held that a promise made after majority to pay a debt contracted in infancy was binding, but this decision, with its further theoretical obscurity, lies outside our period. The only earlier case which touches the point is *Stone v. Wythipol* (1588)[5] where it was argued that an infant's promise was not void, but voidable, and it would have followed from this that a promise to pay on attaining majority would be good. But this was rejected, though a promise on majority to pay money due by bond executed during nonage would be binding, an infant's bond being voidable and not void.

---

[1] *Ketsey's Case* (1613) Cro. Jac. 320; *Kettle v. Eliot* (1613) 1 Rolle Ab. 731 (infant remaining in occupation after 21 is liable for arrears accruing in infancy), *Rainsford v. Fenwick* (1670) Carter 215 *per* Sise Sjt.

[2] 1 Sid. 41.

[3] Followed in *Smith v. Bowen* (1669) 1 Vent. 51.

[4] Comb. 381.

[5] Cro. Eliz. 127, and see *Morning v. Knop* (1602), Cro. Eliz. 700.

Married Women

The classical common law denies to a married woman all contractual capacity during the subsistence of the marriage. How and why this came to be the law is somewhat obscure, and before the leading decision in *Manby* v. *Scott* (1663)[1] there is remarkably little case law dealing directly with the point: probably it was not one which often arose in litigation. This may be the reason why the rationale of the principle and its precise scope (which commonly depends in the common law system upon the assumed rationale) were not at all clearly settled in medieval law. Holdsworth, adopting a suggestion by Maitland,[2] thought that the reason for the married woman's lack of capacity was her lack of property:

'The married woman has no property, and therefore she can make no contracts.'

More precisely the married woman had no personal property, her chattels by marriage becoming her husband's—a married woman did have property in realty and chattels real, though her proprietary powers were suspended during the marriage. There is, however, very scanty direct authority to support this theory, except conceivably a case in Edward III's time,[3] where a husband and wife sued on a bond executed in their favour during the coverture; counsel objected that the husband should sue alone since

'no manner of chattel can be in the wife whilst her husband is living',

but this objection was not approved; the debt was a *chose in action* and not in possession. The case does little to support Holdsworth's view; at the most counsel suggests that the proprietary incapacity of the wife debars her from being the beneficiary of a contract, and even this is not accepted by the court. Another case which casts some doubt on Holdsworth's theory is found in 1375.[4] Here a husband and wife brought debt on a sale of land, and by counsel counted that they had been jointly

---

[1] See p. 549 below, n. 5.
[2] *H.E.L.*, III. 528; P. and M. II. 432.
[3] 43 Edw. III, H. f. 10, pl. 31.
[4] 48 Edw. III, T. f. 18, pl. 14.

seised of lands in Weston which they had sold to the defendant; the lands were the wife's. Persay offered a plea in abatement of the writ, objecting that the sale could not be the sale of the wife, but only of the husband alone; Hamun for the plaintiffs by way of demurrer said,

> 'And since we have counted of certain lands sold by us and our wife, which were in the right of our wife, and on account of this we have levied a fine in common, so that this duty belongs to the wife on account of the same lands, which were of her right, therefore we ask for judgement if our writ be not good enough . . .'

Wichingham J. thought the writ bad, though the demurrer was never entered and the defendant's counsel, in order to get his client out of prison where he was on a *capias*, tendered wager of law on the general issue. Here if the proprietary incompetence of the wife had been the rationale of her contractual incapacity the writ would have been good. Yet in spite of this case, there remains a certain plausibility in Holdsworth's view, for where a contract involved the transfer of chattels—for example, a sale of a horse—it could well have been thought that a wife, who could own no chattels, ought to be unable to contract. Furthermore the wife's lack of personal property, and her restricted rights over realty and chattels real, would necessarily have raised difficulty over the enforcement of contractual obligations, leaving little by way of remedy to the creditor except process of imprisonment against the body of the wife, a gross violation of the rights of her husband to consortium.

Slightly better support is found in the cases for the idea that the contractual incompetence of the married woman was thought to derive from the fact that marriage subjected a wife wholly to the dominance of her husband; what at least in law she lacked was not (so far as contract was concerned) property so much as a will and power. As it was put in *Bill* v. *Lake* (1652)[1]

> 'a *feme covert* is not capable of making any contract, because she is *sub potestate viri*',

or earlier by Luke J. in *Jordan's Case* (1536)[2]

---

[1] Hutton 106.
[2] 27 Hen. VIII, M. f. 24, pl. 3.

'for she has no will, for the will of the woman depends upon the will of the husband',

and in the same case Spilman J. agreed in terms with this. Similar statements are to be found in *Manby* v. *Scott*. The subjection of the wife's will in law to that of her husband relates back to the general evolution of the common law's view of the wife's status, which in all probability evolved out of a form of guardianship. This may explain the survival of the idea that although a wife without the consent of her husband could do nothing which operated to her prejudice or charge she could nevertheless be a party to legal acts which were to her benefit— for example, she could be a donee. This idea is well illustrated by a case[1] in which a husband and wife in debt for rent were sued jointly on a lease made to them during the marriage. Choke J. thought that this was correct, for in the eyes of the law a lease must be more beneficial than the rent due and issuing out of the land; *ergo* the lease was beneficial and the wife should be joined as a contracting party. Clearly this principle does not lead to complete contractual incompetence, as the case itself illustrates. The treatment of leases was, however, somewhat anomalous, and this makes it difficult to relate the cases to general principle. Thus both husband and wife could bring covenant against the lessor for ouster,[2] since the lease after the husband's death passed to the wife and not to the husband's executors—the rule here copied the rule governing actions for disseisin from freeholds.[3] But the wife was not liable for rent due from a leasehold during the marriage, though after her husband's death she might agree to the lease and thereby become liable retrospectively for arrears of rent accruing during the marriage.

Granted the contractual incompetence of married women (whether or not the general principle had exceptions) the question arose as to whether she could impose liability upon her husband. In medieval law there was some suggestion that a husband would be bound by contracts for the acquisition of

---

[1] 17 Edw. IV, H. f. 7, pl. 2. See also 3 Hen. VI, H. f. 23, pl. 2.
[2] 47 Edw. III, M. f. 12, pl. 11.
[3] So held in 3 Hen. IV, M. f. 1, pl. 4, *contra* 45 Edw. III, M. f. 11, pl. 7, though on the ground that the land, not the wife, was chargeable in debt, though not in covenant.

things which came to the use or profit of the husband;[1] the analogy being used here was the liability imposed upon a religious house by unauthorized purchases by members of the house. But this was denied by Newton C.J., who insisted that the purchase must be to the use of the husband—that is to say, expressly on his account, and later in the fifteenth century an even more restrictive view was insisted upon by Fineux C.J.:[2]

'For a woman during marriage can do nothing which turns her husband to prejudice or charge by her contract, but she is able to do a thing whereby her husband will have advantage. For if I give goods to a woman during marriage, this is good, and the husband can agree to this. But if a woman during marriage makes a contract or buys goods in the market, this is void, since it could be that this would be a charge to her husband. But my wife can buy a thing to my use, and I can agree to this, and thus if I command my wife to buy necessary things, if she buys them, I shall be bound by this general command. And if my wife buys things to keep my household, such as bread, and I have no knowledge of this, I shall not be charged although they are used in my household.'

This has all the air of a somewhat unworkable doctrine, and was advanced by Fineux to deny that a contract made without authority could be subsequently ratified by the husband. Not long afterwards in *Jordan's Case* (1535)[3] it was held in the King's Bench that subsequent ratification by the husband sufficed; the facts were that one Jordan had Tatam in execution in the Counter for debt; the defendant promised Jordan's wife that if Jordan would discharge Tatam, he would pay the debt. This agreement being reported to Jordan, he agreed to it and discharged Tatam. The court held the defendant liable, but there was some difficulty in explaining the theory of this—Luke J. thought that the defendant's promise was good until the husband disagreed, whereas Spilman J. employed a fiction: the agreement related back to the moment of the promise. What-

---

[1] See *per* Markham, Sjt. in 20 Hen. VI, H. f. 21, pl. 19.
[2] 21 Hen. VII, M. f. 40, pl. 64.
[3] 27 Hen. VIII, M. f. 24, pl. 3.

ever the theory, the law was that a husband could be bound by prior authorization or subsequent ratification.

There was also a tenuous line of authority suggesting that wives could in any event bind their husbands in contracts for necessaries.[1] In *Sir Nicholas Poine's Case* (1564)[2] the facts were that a wife, without her husband's consent, bought cloth from one Wheler and had it delivered to her tailor to make clothes on credit. The husband paid the tailor for his work, but not the mercer for his cloth, and Dyer C.J. was in much doubt as to the law, partly presumably because of the husband's partial ratification, and partly because the case could have raised the issue of the husband's liability for necessary apparel. In 1616 in *Thomas Gardener's Case*[3] it was held that a husband was liable for necessary apparel bought without his consent, but the case is only scantily reported in Rolle, and may turn upon desertion by the husband; there is also a similar decision in 1613 in *Sir Henry Compton's Case*,[4] but again the report is too brief to be illuminating.

The whole law on the position of wives was reviewed in the leading case of *Manby and Richards* v. *Scott* (1663).[5] The facts were that in 1646 Katherine Scott deserted her husband and lived away from him for many years. She then wished to return, but he refused to have her back. Her husband forbade the plaintiffs to trust his wife with any goods, and himself provided her with no maintenance. In 1658 the plaintiffs sold goods at a reasonable price to Katherine, the goods being necessary for her and suitable to the husband's degree (they were in fact clothes), and the question at issue was whether the husband was liable to pay for them. The case began life in 1659 before Mallett J. at the Guildhall, the jury finding a special verdict and leaving to the court the question whether on the facts found the husband was liable to pay. It was then argued in the King's Bench, where Mallett and Twysden JJ. thought the husband liable and Foster C.J. and Wyndham J. thought he was not, and discussed by the judges and serjeants in Serjeants Inn in Chancery Lane,

---

[1] 11 Hen. VI, P. f. 30, pl. 11 *per* Martin is the earliest suggestion of this.
[2] Dyer 234b.
[3] 1 Rolle Ab. 351, pl. 7.
[4] 1 Brownl. and Goulds. 47.
[5] 1 Lev. 6, 1 Mod. 124, O. Bridg. 229, 1 Sid. 109, 130, 1 Keb. 69, 80, 87, 206, 337, 361, 383, 429, 441, 482, Bacon *Abridgement*, Baron et Feme.

where the unanimous view favoured the defendant. It was then in 1661 adjourned into the Exchequer Chamber, where it was elaborately argued by counsel and by the judges on a considerable number of occasions between 25 January 1661 and 9 May 1663. Tyrrell J. of the Common Pleas joined Mallett and Twysden in favouring the plaintiffs, whilst the majority view was in favour of the husband; it is said in a note to Bridgman's report that Twysden J. eventually changed his view and joined the majority. The basic question at issue in *Manby* v. *Scott*, put in terms of contract law, was whether a wife possessed an inherent power as wife to bind her husband to the payment of the price of her necessaries (granted of course that she was not in desertion or had not, for example, committed adultery). Put more generally, the question was whether the common law recognized a legal liability in a husband to support his wife, or whether the only remedy was for her to go to the ecclesiastical courts. The decision was that there was no such power, and no such common law liability. The husband was only liable if he gave prior authorization or if he subsequently consented. The case left somewhat unsettled the circumstances in which a husband would be said to have consented by implication to his wife contracting so as to bind him, but where a wife was housekeeping such an implication would readily be inferred in the case of contracts for necessaries. It is clear that before *Manby* v. *Scott* there had been a practice, at least in the Guildhall, of holding the husband liable in similar circumstances.[1] In *Dyer* v. *East* (1669)[2] *Manby* v. *Scott* was called by Kelynge C.J. a hard decision, and it appears to have been restrictively interpreted as turning upon the fact that the wife eloped and the husband expressly forbade the tradesman to trust her; unless there was some positive ground in evidence for reaching the opposite conclusion, a jury was generally entitled to hold a husband liable for his wife's necessaries, and in practice no doubt much would turn on the form of the direction given.

Corporations

A corporation in medieval law possessed full contractual capacity, and would normally make important contracts under

[1] See the report on O. Bridgman at 25, *Stone* v. *Walter* (1661) O. Bridg. 618.
[2] 1 Mod. 9, 2 Keb. 554, 1 Vent. 42, 1 Sid. 425, though the reports differ.

its common seal, just as individuals made their contracts under seal. There was, however, a long dispute as to what, if anything, a corporation could do without a sealed instrument, granted that in general a sealed instrument was essential.[1] One suggestion was that for necessary things a sealed instrument was not required,[2] another was that for everyday things no sealed instrument was required.[3] In 1489[4] Townsend J. tried to state a reasonable compromise,

> 'Note that Townsend said that a body corporate can grant nothing without a deed, as it has been held in the new terms, but it seems that a body corporate cannot make feoffment lease or such like of their inheritance without a deed. But of an office, and those things which pertain to service, they can. For they can have a ploughman, and servants in husbandry without deed, and butlers and cooks and so on, and then depute their servants to do anything without a deed, this they can well do, for it is not in disinheritance, but solely concerning services.'

But Brian C.J. denied this. The position at the close of the year-book period was therefore somewhat uncertain, but there was some authority for saying that in matters of small importance (variously defined) a seal was not needed.[5] There was also authority for holding a corporation aggregate liable on a contract of sale made by its servant where the goods in question came to the use of the corporation.[6] This arose in a case in which the Provost and Scholars of King's College, Cambridge were sued for the price of two bells, which, it was averred, had been bought by a former Provost, Thomas [*sic*] Millington, through his servant Tho. F. In reality the Provost in question was *William* Myllington, appointed in 1443 the first Provost of King's College. He was deprived in 1447 for refusal to take an oath to honour new statutes of the college to which he objected, and he was succeeded by John Chedwall, defendant in the

---

[1] 22 Hen. VI, M. f. 4, pl. 6.
[2] 12 Edw. IV, f. 9, pl. 24; 18 Edw. IV, T. f. 8, pl. 11.
[3] 4 Hen. VII, P. f. 6, pl. 2 *per* Townsend J.
[4] 4 Hen. VII, M. f. 17, pl. 3. The reference is to 21 Edw. IV, H. f. 19, pl. 22, H. f. 75, pl. 9.
[5] 7 Hen. VII, H. f. 9, pl. 2, T. f. 16, pl. 3.
[6] 5 Edw. IV (Long Quinto), M. f. 70.

action (called in the year-book J.B.).[1] The case mainly turned upon the sufficiency of the plaintiff's count, it being objected *inter alia* that the removal of the Provost should be stated with more particularity. It was not, however, suggested that the college would not in principle be liable on such a sale so long as the bells came to the use of the college, and since King's employed the best possible legal representation this clearly shows that liability in such circumstances was accepted. The case is an interesting one in that records in the college's possession enable the whole story of the bells of King's to be traced in some detail,[2] and it is most unusual to be able to relate a year-book case to a litigant's own records.

There are hardly any cases in the immediate post-medieval period which deal with the requirement that a corporation must act by sealed instrument,[3] and so far as contractual liability is concerned little before the nineteenth century.[4] The right of a corporation to sue in assumpsit was established in the *Mayor of London* v. *Goree* (1676)[5] and *The Barber Surgeons of London* v. *Pelson* (1679);[6] both cases, however, involved actions of *indebitatus assumpsit* for money legally due independent of contract. There appears to be no case in which a corporation was sued in assumpsit, and only in such a case could its contractual liability in respect of contracts by parole be canvassed.

Agency

In the case of contracts under seal there was no difficulty in conducting contractual negotiations through an intermediary in such a way as to establish a contractual lien between the

---

[1] See the article in the *D.N.B.* and Emden, *Biographical Dictionary of the University of Cambridge to 1500*.

[2] See J. W. Clark, 'History of the Peal of Bells belonging to King's College Cambridge' (1881), *Camb. Antiq. Soc. Comm.* IV. 223. Clark was unfortunately not aware of the year-book case. The bells in question were probably supplied to the College through one John Langton, and it was Myllington's understanding (as he stated to the college in 1465) that they had been a gift from the Founder, Henry VI. Presumably the bell-founder had not been paid by the King and was now attempting to get the college to foot the bill.

[3] See *Dumper* v. *Symms* (1602) 1 Rolle Ab. 514; *Horn* v. *Ivy* (1669) 1 Vent. 47, 1 Mod 18, 2 Keb. 567, 604, 1 Sid. 441 and *R.* v. *Bigg* (1717) 3 P. Wms., the only cases of any importance.

[4] *Arnold* v. *Mayor of Poole* (1842) 4 M. & Gr. 860 deals with the older authorities.

[5] 2 Lev. 175, 3 Keb. 677, 1 Vent. 298.

[6] 2 Lev. 252. See also *Mayor of London* v. *Hunt* (1681) 3 Lev. 37.

third party and the principal. For example, if Robert wishes to lend money to Hugo, using Bagot as an intermediary, all that is needed is for Bagot to procure Hugo to execute a bond in favour of his principal Robert and hand over the money, and the job is done. Nothing of this will appear on the face of the instrument, and hence there will be apparently no law on the subject. To arrange for the collection of money through agents was also easy, and indeed the standard bond provided for the payment of the money to an attorney, whose appointment could be attested under seal. The flexibility of the sealed instrument largely explains the absence for any elaborate law of agency in medieval times, and not the fact that the use of agents was in any way uncommon, or legally impeded by the common law.

In the case of informal transactions, the law of agency developed around the relationship of master and servant, and depended upon two distinct principles. The first was that a servant's acts, if authorized by his master, ranked as the act of the master; quite literally *qui facit per alium facit per se*. The second was that a master might be charged on a contract made by his servant if property or money in consequence of the transaction came to his use with his assent.[1] These two bases of liability are, as we have seen, to be found at work in the law governing married women, monks, and corporations, and they survived into post-medieval law, which was firmly based upon year-book precedents.[2] So far as the former principle is concerned, the servant, unlike the married woman or monk professed, is not himself by status contractually incompetent, but where he did bind his master he himself was not liable[3] and was not conceived of as being a contracting party at all; as it was put in one case,

'nest forsque instrument et minister'.[4]

---

[1] 8 Edw. IV, M. f. 11, pl. 9, 27 Lib. Ass. M. f. 133, pl. 5, *Doctor and Student,* Dial. II, c. 42, 2 Edw. IV, P. f. 4, pl. 9, 14 Edw. IV, T. f. 8, pl. 15.

[2] See for the liability based upon receipt *Sir H. Dowckray's Case* (1614) Brownl. 64, and for the 'instrument' theory *Hewer v. Bartholomew* (1598) Cro. Eliz. 614, *Cally v. Kish* (1625) Noy 77, and cases cited below.

[3] See Brooke, *Contract,* 40, *Moore v. Moore* (1612) 1 Bulst. 169, *Woodhouse v. Bradford* (1619) 2 Rolle Rep. 77. But the servant must buy on behalf of the master— *Degeder v. Savory* (1671) 2 Keb. 812.

[4] 11 Edw. IV, T. f. 6, pl. 10 *per* Fairfax.

The servant did not make the contract on behalf of the master—it was the master who made the contract through the servant. The theory behind cases where the master was charged by receipt of property which came to his use, just as a religious house or college could be so charged, is not so clearly stated in the cases but must have been that the servant himself contracted. This is no doubt the explanation behind the case concerning the bells of King's College, where there is no suggestion that the contract for the bells needed to be under seal—the rationale must be that the contract was there supposed to have been made by the Provost's servant, the college becoming liable on the contract of another. The medieval law is well summed up in two much-quoted passages, one from a year-book and the other from St. Germain.[1]

> 'If I command my servant to buy certain goods, or I make a man my factor and my attorney to buy merchandise, in this case if he buys merchandise from a man, I shall be charged by this contract although the goods never come into my hands and although I have no notice of them, and the case is that I have given such a power to him, and it is my folly to do so.'

This is said by Pigot in 1469. St. Germain in 1530 states comprehensively,

> 'Also if a servant borrow money in his master's name, the master will not be charged with it unless it come to his use, and that by his assent. And the same law is, if a servant make a contract in his master's name, the contract shall not bind his master, unless it were by his master's commandment, or that it came to the master's use by his assent.'

In principle one might not expect the rise of assumpsit to make any very great difference to the law of master and servant. It had, however, to be settled that the same principles did apply in assumpsit as in the older actions, and once the principle was evolved that every contract executory imports in itself an assumpsit, it inevitably follows that assumpsit will lie in lieu of debt on the contract of the master made through his servant.

[1] 8 Edw. IV, M. f. 11, pl. 9; *Doctor and Student*, Dial. II, c. 42.

The first case imposing such liability appears to be *Petties* v. *Soam* in 1603,[1] a case turning on another point.

In actions of special assumpsit there could, however, be a theoretical difficulty; the point could be taken that although a contract made through a servant was the contract of the master, a promise made by a servant was personal to the servant. However, in the important case of *Senior* v. *Woolmer* (1623)[2] it was held that a master could sue on a promise made to his servant, who had been sent with express authority to contract, and said that a master would himself be liable on an assumpsit by the servant with authority—in short, that the old law applied to the new form of action. The matter seems never subsequently to have been doubted. Further to this it was said in an anonymous case in 1564[3] that where a servant contracted so as to bind his master and the servant promised to pay, the servant would be liable in assumpsit in addition to the liability of his master in debt on the contract. This idea, which remained undeveloped, involves a sort of suretyship which could not be imposed under the older action of debt, since one transaction was thought in medieval law to produce (cases of joint liability apart) only one debtor.[4]

Leaving apart liability based upon receipt, the liability of the master, and consequent immunity of the servant (subject to the exception just mentioned), turned upon the notion of authorization, which would normally have to precede the transaction. In *Senior* v. *Woolmer* (1623)[5] Dodderidge J., who was a particularly conservative lawyer, thought that subsequent ratification would charge the master, and this may long have been the law. The case law dealing with the scope of a servant's authority is not very consistent, some adopting a narrow view of the matter and others inclining to holding the master bound by all acts which came within the scope of the servant's ostensible authority. Thus a servant might have a general implied authority to sell goods,[6] and a bailiff was probably treated as having a general authority to carry out agricultural transactions

---

[1] Goldsb. 138, pl. 46.
[2] Godbolt 311.
[3] Dyer 230b.
[4] See above, p. 68.
[5] Godbolt 311.
[6] See cases cited above, p. 533, n. 1.

which would bind his master, if known as a bailiff.[1] Dodderidge J. in *Senior* v. *Woolmer* went so far as to say,

> 'For whatever comes within the compass of the servants' service, I shall be chargeable with, and likewise shall have advantage of the same'.[2]

A very wide view was also taken in *Petties* v. *Soam* (1603)[3] of the principal's liability for his factor:

> 'It appeared upon evidence . . . if one be factor to a merchant to buy one kind of stuff, as tin, or other such like, and the said factor hath not used to buy any other kind of wares but this kind only for his master, if now the said factor buys . . . other commodities for his master, and assume to pay money for that, now the master shall be charged in assumpsit for the money, and for that let the master take heed what factor he makes.'

Probably there lies behind such cases the idea, later developed, of a *general* authority, to be contrasted with a *special* authority for a particular transaction. A decision taking a restrictive view is the curious case of *Southern* v. *Howe*.[4] Here the defendant had some counterfeit but not valueless jewels which he gave to his servant, Saldock, to sell to the King of Barbary (*un barbarous roy*). Saldock procured the plaintiff, a merchant there, to conduct the sale, which he did in all innocence for a large sum. The King discovered this and put him in prison until the money was repaid, and he then sued the principal Howe, without success, since there had been no authorization by him of the act of Saldock in employing Southern. The case may turn upon the lack of any direct nexus between the parties, or on a general reluctance to impose liability on a master for a warranty by a servant.

The position over warranties was peculiar. Liability turned on deceit, and the deceit was the tricking of the plaintiff into the transaction. If the sale was the sale of the master (who had

---

[1] Brooke, *Contract*, pl. 40, *Trespass*, pl. 295.

[2] He appears to have taken a more restrictive view in *Delgeder* v. *Savory* 2 Keb. 812.

[3] Golds. 138, pl. 44.

[4] 2 Rolle Rep. 5, 26, Cro. Jac. 468, Popham 143, Bridgman 125. See also *Barton* v. *Sadock* (1610) 1 Bulst. 103, Yelv. 202.

not warranted) and not the sale of the servant (who had) there
was no liability, for the servant could not be said to have sold
with warranty and thereby deceived the purchaser.[1] To impose
liability there had to be an express authority not only for the
sale, but also for the warranty.[2] Difficulty also arose in cases
where the servant appeared to possess an authority which he
in reality lacked; for example, to buy goods on credit. If the
master forbad tradesmen to trust the servant, he was safe,[3] but
if he gave his servant money to pay cash, and the servant bought
on credit, this was apparently evidence that might exonerate
the master, at least in the absence of a previous practice of
purchasing through the servant on credit.[4] This whole branch
of the law was not reduced to any sort of order until Chief
Justice Holt's time.

[1] 11 Edw. IV, T. f. 6, pl. 11.
[2] Godbolt 311.
[3] *Sir H. Compton's Case* (*c*. 1612) referred to in Brownl. 64.
[4] *Rouse's Case* (1658) cited by Viner from *Trials per Pais*, 181; *Southby* v. *Wiseman*
(1676) 3 Keb. 625, 630.

XI

TRANSMISSION OF LIABILITY
ON DEATH

In medieval law, executors and administrators were not in general liable for simple contract debts, nor were they liable to be sued on account of wrongs committed by the deceased, for *actio personalis moritur cum persona*. One of the consequences of the rise of assumpsit was that very considerable inroads were made upon the immunity of executors, so that eventually the general rule came to be that liability for breach of informal contracts was passively transmissible to personal representatives.

Simple contract debts and executors

The action of debt, when brought on a contract not under seal, could not in general be brought against personal representatives. Nor could executors be sued on their own undertaking to pay the debt of the testator.[1] The theoretical justification for this rule was the inability of personal representatives to wage the deceased's law, and this inability was in its turn explained by saying that the representatives were not in a position to know whether a debt was owing or not, and therefore could not be admitted at their soul's peril to swear an oath on a subject about which they had no knowledge. With perfect consistency, the medieval courts allowed personal representatives to be sued where the deceased would not in his lifetime have been allowed to wage his law, as was the case in some exceptional circumstances, notably the case of servants' wages.[2] In such cases trial was by jury; the matter was within the knowledge of the country, and the knowledge was not lost when the debtor died. At the back of all this theory there also lay the idea that well-organized creditors took bonds for debts, and a creditor who could have insisted on a bond before extending credit but failed

---

[1] See above, p. 142, and for an attempt to bring debt on an undertaking (mainprise) by executors see 11 Hen. VI, T. f. 48, pl. 5. In *assumpsit* this device of course succeeded.

[2] See above, p. 140.

to do so was not entitled to much sympathy; a general relaxation of the law would only encourage fraudulent claims. The executor's immunity from suit in medieval law was not in any way connected with the doctrine summed up in the maxim *actio personalis moritur cum persona*—the doctrine that actions for personal wrongs died with the person. It was based simply upon the difficulty over wager. If you seriously believed that the swearing of a false oath might lead to hell-fire—real hell-fire, and not the refrigerated version which is popular today—it was not unreasonable to refuse to allow personal representatives to swear an oath that no debt was owed, when in the nature of things they could never be certain that their oath was a true oath. Scrupulous executors, out of fear of the spiritual consequences of perjury, might be led into paying under pressure when no debt was in fact due, preferring this alternative to defending actions of debt by wager. There was therefore something to be said in favour of the common law position.

On the other hand there was much that could be said against it. Creditors through the accident of death could be unjustly deprived of their rights, and, what was perhaps more important to the medieval mind, there was the soul of the deceased to worry about too. If his debts were not paid his soul might be in peril.[1] The position of the representatives in conscience was perfectly clear; they took the deceased's property to administer it to his use.[2] If the assets were sufficient they must make amends for the wrongs he has done, and they must pay his debts.[3] But they were legally compellable to do neither. The common law required them to pay debts which they were compellable to pay—debts of record, and debts due by specialty—so long as they did this, what they did about other debts and legacies was not the law's concern, unless they paid such debts before compellable debts and thereby ran out of assets.[4] If they did this they became personally liable to judgment *de bonis propriis*. The payment of legacies could be enforced in the spiritual

---

[1] For a discussion of the merits of the law see St. Germain, *Doctor and Student*, Dial. II, c. 10.

[2] See *per* Knightly in 27 Hen. VIII, T. f. 23, pl. 21, and for the view of Thomas Rotheram L.C. see 4 Hen. VII, H. f. 4, pl. 8.

[3] 11 Hen. VII, H. pl. 1, f. 12. On their liability if they made amends to a trespass see Statham, *Executions*, pl. 10.

[4] 9 Edw. IV, T. pl. 4, f. 13; 21 Edw. IV, P. f. 21 pl. 2; 11 Hen. VII, H. f. 12, pl. 1.

courts,[1] but not debts, for the spiritual courts could not meddle with the debts of the laity. However, it seems that simple contract debts were treated as having priority over legacies.[2]

Modifications of the strict legal position

It was natural enough that attempts should be made to alter the common law position, and to bring the law into conformity with current ideas as to the moral obligation of representatives. It could hardly be maintained that representatives *never* knew that a debt was due on a simple contract, only that they could never be certain that one was not owed. If they admitted knowledge, they could be held to have waived their immunity. Representatives were not often likely expressly to waive their immunity in the course of litigation, for if they wished to pay there was nothing to prevent their paying without litigation. They could, however, get into a position in which they could be said to have waived their immunity by impliedly admitting knowledge; the principle involved would today be called estoppel. Thus in a case in 1434 it was held that if executors, when sued on a simple contract, did not demur to the action, but pleaded in bar, they thereby admitted knowledge of the transaction, and could not at a later stage in the action reclaim their immunity by objecting in point of law to the action by motion in arrest of judgment or by bringing a writ of error.[3] But in the later fifteenth century this view was questioned, and it was suggested that where the executor did not demur to the action the court nevertheless had a power *ex officio* to stop the action, without waiting upon the motion of the party.

A more radical inroad into the immunity was made by the Exchequer, which, towards the end of the fifteenth century, began to allow personal representatives to be sued for simple

---

[1] It was settled in the thirteenth century that no action lay at common law to recover a legacy; see Bracton's *Note Book*, pl. 381. The legatee must await delivery at the hand of the executors or sue in the spiritual court. See 11 Hen. VI, T. f. 84, pl. 31; 2 Hen. VI, T. f. 15, pl. 17; 37 Hen. VI, f. 8, pl. 18, Brooke, *Devise*, pl. 27 (1532). In the case of a legacy of a certain or specific thing, the legatee could sue a third party in trespass if he took the thing. This was contrary to principle and Brooke thought it 'marvellous'. On the right of a legatee to take a specific thing see 27 Hen. VI, f. 8, pl. 6, 11 Hen. VI, T. f. 39, pl. 31. On the common law action in the seventeenth century see above, p. 440.

[2] See St. Germain, *Doctor and Student*, Dial. II, c. 10.

[3] Fitz., *Executors*, pl. 21.

contract debts by *quominus*.[1] The plaintiff alleged, fictionally, that he was unable to pay a debt due to the Crown because he had not been paid money which the deceased owed to him. The use of this fictional device was probably encouraged by the existence of the rule that wager of law was not allowed in the Exchequer on a *quominus*.[2] It is not, however, clear that this fictional device was still encouraged in the early sixteenth century, when the evidence becomes conflicting. Fitzherbert J. in 1535 somewhat vehemently denied that the remedy was available, but Fitzherbert when he said this was concerned to make a point, and perhaps may not be too reliable.[3] There war certainly pressure from petitioners for a remedy in Chancery, and by 1491,[4] if not earlier, the Chancery had succumbed to it. During Henry VIII's reign this continued to be the position; a note in 1524[5] states that on contracts made by the testator a subpoena is available against the executors, provided that assets descend to them, and the reason given is the absence of any remedy at common law.[6] Against this background it is clear that the evolution of a common law remedy by assumpsit in the sixteenth century did not represent a step forward; all that happened was that the common law courts took over a job previously done by the Chancellor.

The use of assumpsit

Since the use of debt against executors was blocked by the dead weight of medieval doctrine, the evolution of a common law remedy by means of assumpsit offered the best prospect of

---

[1] In 1494 (Y.B. 11 Hen. VII, T. f. 26, pl. 9) it was said, 'Note, that if a man is indebted to me by simple contract, and dies, I have no remedy by the common law against the executors, but I will have a Quominus in the Exchequer, supposing that I am in debt to the King. Which, note, is the practice according to Davers, and commonly in use.' 'Supposing' in fifteenth-century legal language means 'fictionally alleging'.

[2] Brooke, *Novel Cases*, 158 (1543)

[3] Y.B. 27 Hen. VIII, T. f. 23, pl. 21. Knightly in the same case asserted that the practice was in use.

[4] Y.B. 7 Hen. VII, f. 10, pl. 2. Barbour, pp. 102–4, reviews the evidence, and was unable to find a definite decision that a subpoena was available in the fifteenth century, though he thought that in all probability a remedy was given.

[5] Spilman's MS. Reports, B.M. MS. Hargrave, f. 202a.

[6] This continued to be the position in the sixteenth century; see *Peck v. Loveden* (1600) Cro. Eliz. 804. Holdsworth, (*H.E.L.* V. 318–21) took the view that Chancery jurisdiction over legacies was acquired reluctantly in the late sixteenth century, referring to Monro, *Acta Cancellaria*, pp. 10–11 (1591).

success. The use of assumpsit was not hindered by any difficulty over wager of law, since trial was by jury; furthermore the rule that debt did not lie could be turned to positive advantage. It could be argued that, because debt was not available and there was no other appropriate common law action, the action on the case ought to be allowed to fill the gap in the law, and this argument somewhat speciously got over the difficulty over alternative remedies. On the other hand the use of assumpsit could be regarded as objectionable on two grounds of principle. The first was that *actio personalis moritur cum persona*, and the action of assumpsit fell within the class of actions governed by this maxim; received maxims constituted the basic fabric of the common law, and to depart from them was to invite confusion. The second was that, as a matter of substantive law, simple contract debts died with the debtor. These two grounds of objection are quite distinct, and produce different results. If the first was accepted, the consequence would be that no action of assumpsit whatsoever could lie against executors, even if the action was not in lieu of debt (for example, an action for breach of a promise to perform a service). If the second only was accepted, only actions of assumpsit in lieu of debt were ruled out.

'Actio personalis moritur cum persona'

It was once thought that this maxim, which is not derived from the civil law, was invented by Coke in his report of *Pinchon's Case* (1612).[1] It turns out, however, that for once the old rogue is not to blame. Thus the maxim is quoted in a case in 1496,[2] in somewhat peculiar circumstances. A woman had been cited in an ecclesiastical court for defamation, and costs and damages had been awarded against her, so that by the judgment she owed a certain, quantified sum of money. The woman subsequently married, made her husband executor, and died without having made satisfaction. A citation was then

---

[1] See H. Goudy, 'Two Ancient Brocards', *Essays in Legal History*, (ed Vinogradoff) and *H.E.L.* III. 576 et seq.

[2] See Y.B. 12 Hen. VII, T. f. 22, pl. 2. The earliest use in the year-books is in 18 Edw. IV, M. f. 15, pl. 17, where the maxim is used as a basis for the argument that a personal action is not actively transmissible: the case is complicated by the fact that an Abbot was suing for a wrong done in the time of his predecessor, so a body politic was involved. This reference was found by Winfield; see 29 Col.L.R. 239.

moved against the husband as executor to recover the sum owed; the husband moved at common law for a prohibition to stop the proceedings, and the year-book reports the discussion (which was inconclusive) as to whether prohibition to the spiritual court should issue. Although admittedly defamation was properly within the jurisdiction of the ecclesiastical courts, it was arguable that once a certain and definite sum was adjudged due by judgment, this sum should be treated as a lay debt which was the concern of the common law courts. In the course of the argument Mordant introduced the maxim with this remark,

> 'For as for a trespass, or a personal thing done by the woman before or after the marriage, by her death all determines, *quia actio personalis moritur cum persona*'.

Mordant was here using the maxim to sum up the medieval rules under which, statutory provisions apart, liability for trespasses was neither actively nor passively transmissible. Although statute had made considerable inroads upon the common law rule which prevented executors from suing for trespasses done to the property of the testator,[1] their immunity from being sued remained unimpaired throughout the medieval period. Hankford, in a case in 1410,[2] had expressed the law by saying of a trespass action that 'the action dies with the person'. In 1440 Newton C.J. laid it down that,

> 'The Law is, if one does me a trespass, and dies, the action is dead also'.[3]

The case in 1479[4] is the first in which the doctrine is expressed in a Latin tag. Fineux C.J., who took part in this case, referred to the doctrine in 1521 with the tag *actio moritur cum persona*,[5] which is an inaccurate reference to the maxim. It was not, therefore, through the publication of Coke's *Reports*[6] that the

---

[1] 4 Edw. III, c. 7.
[2] Y.B. 11 Hen. IV, H. pl. 20, f. 46.
[3] 19 Hen. VI, P. f. 66, pl. 10. See also Statham, *Barre,* pl. 102 (30 Hen. VI).
[4] 18 Edw. IV, M. f. 15, pl. 17.
[5] *Oliver* v. *Cleymond* (1521) Y.B. 12 Hen. VIII, M. f. 11, pl. 3.
[6] *Pinchon's Case* (1612) 9 Co.Rep. 86b at 87a. A reference is found in 1590 in *Russel and Prat's Case* 4 Leon. 44. See also *Sir Brian Tuckes Case* (1589) 3 Leon. 241; *Maynard's Case* 3 Leon. 67; *Onlie's Case* (1576) Dyer 355b.

maxim became canonical, for it had been current long before, though Coke may well have popularized it further.

The expression *actio personalis* is peculiarly unfortunate, because it suggests a contrast between real and personal actions.[1] Now in medieval law the actions of covenant, debt on a specialty, and detinue were all transmissible in medieval law, and they were all personal actions as opposed to real actions; furthermore the action of debt *sur contract* was actively transmissible in all cases and passively transmissible in others where wager was not possible. Nowhere is it so much as hinted that the transmissibility of these actions constituted some sort of exception to the doctrine that personal actions died with the person, nor is there any reference to the doctrine in cases which dealt with difficulties over the transmissibility of debt, detinue, and covenant. It is clear that 'personal' here is not being contrasted with 'real', but is used in some special sense.[2] It means indeed nothing more than 'annexed to the person', and the maxim itself must, if its meaning is to be caught, be rendered into English like this:

'An action which is annexed to the person dies with the person'.

This is a trite and almost tautological remark, but then most of the maxims of the common law are not distinguished by their profundity.

Coke indeed makes this point perfectly clearly in *Pinchon's Case* (1612),[3]

'As to the objection that this personal action of trespass on the case *moritur cum persona*, although it is called trespass, in respect that the breach of promise is alleged to be mixed with fraud and deceit to the special prejudice of the plaintiff and for that reason is called trespass on the case; yet that doth not make the action so *annexed to the persons of the parties*, that

---

[1] Pollock (*Pollock on Torts*, 5th ed., p. 58 n. 6) suggested that we ought to read *poenalis*; his idea was that a rule about penal actions had been confused with a rule about personal actions. There is no evidence for this suggestion, which starts from the misapprehension that 'personal' in the maxim is being used in opposition to 'real'.

[2] The point that the maxim is only relevant to tort or trespass actions is expressly made in Y.B. 11 Hen. IV, H. f. 46, pl. 20.

[3] 9 Co.Rep. 86b *Pinchon's Case* is also reported in 2 Brownl. 137, Cro. Jac. 293, 294, Jenk. Cent. 290.

it shall die with the persons, for then if he to whom the promise is made dies, his executor should not have any action, which no man will affirm. And an action on assumpsit upon good consideration, without specialty to do a thing, is no more personal, *i.e., annexed to the person*, than a covenant by specialty to do the same thing'.

The idea that trespass actions were in general 'personal' in this sense of 'annexed to the person' probably arose for two reasons. One was the association between such actions and punishment; the criminal element in trespass was strong and persistent, and it is not surprising to find that liability to punishment should be personal and not transmissible passively to persons who had no part in the wrongdoing; the damages were conceived to be satisfaction for injury rather than compensation for loss. The law has never extended the representation of the deceased to the criminal visiting the sins of the deceased upon his heirs on representatives, except through the feudal doctrine of corruption of blood. The other is the idea that trespasses were injuries to the person of the victim, and to nobody else. This idea seems most rational in the case of an action for personal injuries; the representatives of the deceased may be thought to have no interest in injuries to a corpse which is now buried; it seems least rational when the trespass is to property, and here it was modified by statute, the executors being given a right to sue.[1]

'Actio personalis' and assumpsit

Since assumpsit was a trespass action, and furthermore, since in the action the plaintiff alleged that he had been deceived—which could be thought a wrong to his person—there was a case for saying that the action was neither actively nor passively transmissible. As far as active transmission is concerned, there are two cases bearing on the question in Henry VIII's time. The first was in 1523 in the Common Pleas.[2] A man had recovered in an action in the nature of an assize of *mort d' ancestor* in a manorial court, and had paid ten shillings to the steward of the court to enter the judgment on the roll of the

---

[1] 4 Edw. III, c. 7; 25 Edw. III, c. 5; 31 Edw. III, c. 11.
[2] Spilman's MS. Reports, B.M. MS. Hargrave 388, f. 42a.

court. The steward failed to do so, the man died, and his heir brought an action against the steward. The action failed, the reporter noting,

> 'And the Justices of the Common Bench were of one opinion, that the action could not be brought by the heir, seeing that the matter is only a personal tort to his father . . .'

A similar doctrine is put forward in 1527 in *John Style's Case* in the King's Bench,

> 'It is so in law and in experience, and agreed by the Justices of the Common Bank, that when a man recovers certain lands from anyone in a writ of mesne, and he who recovers gives certain money to the clerk to make an entry on the roll, if he does not do it, there it is agreed he will have an action on his case for the nonfeasance. But if he dies his heir will not have this action which his father could have brought, for it is a personal action and dies with the person'.[1]

Though these cases concern heirs and not executors or administrators, they would suggest that at this period the courts would not have allowed such personal representatives to sue. These cases, perhaps mercifully, never found their way into print; nor did an opinion of Dyer C.J. in a case in the Common Pleas in 1567, which is directly in point.[2] An executor brought an action of assumpsit against the executor of a deceased debtor, the action being based upon a special promise to pay the debt due by the testator on a simple contract, and the puisne Justices were in doubt as to the propriety of the action.

> 'But the Lord Dyer said that an executor cannot maintain an action on the case, for this does not lie at common law, and there is no statute made on this point such as the statute for goods taken away in the life of the testator . . .'

In later cases it seems to have been assumed without argument that personal representatives could bring the action.[3]

---

[1] Spilman's MS. Reports, f. 215b. Appendix, Case No. 8. The name of the case is, of course, only a substitute for *Anon.*

[2] Bodl. MS. Rawl. C. 112, f. 261.

[3] *Russel and Prat's Case* (1589) 4 Leon. 44; *Edwards* v. *Stapleton* (1596) Cro. Eliz. 551; *Browning* v. *Fuller* (1612) Cro. Jac. 299; *Lance* v. *Blackmore* (1655) Style 463; *Saunders* c. *Plummer* (1662) O. Bridg. 223.

The first case in which executors were held liable was *Cleymond* v. *Vincent* (1521),[1] a decision of the King's Bench, and this case provoked a controversy which lasted for nearly a century. The action was brought against the executors of a parole guarantor of a debt; though in the opinion of some lawyers debt *sur contract* would not have lain here in the lifetime of the testator, the question at the time of the decision was unsettled and controversial.[2] The action was allowed, and in justifying the decision Fineux C.J. commented on the *actio personalis* doctrine in this way,

> 'And Fineux Chief Justice said that this is outside the case where *actio moritur cum persona*; for this applies where the hurt or damage is corporal, as if one beats me and dies my action is gone, or if I die, my executors will not have an action. For the party cannot be punished when he is dead'.

It seems that Fineux's reasoning, which confined the doctrine by holding that it did not apply to actions for patrimonial loss, was generally accepted by lawyers in the sixteenth century, for although there was very considerable dispute over the correctness of the decision in *Cleymond* v. *Vincent*, there is no case reported between 1521 and *Pinchon's Case* in 1612, where the dispute turns upon the *actio personalis* doctrine. It is particularly striking that in *Norwood* v. *Read* (1558),[3] a very fully reported case, no reference whatsoever is made to this point. In *Pinchon's Case* the point was again taken, only to be rejected. Thus *Cleymond* v. *Vincent* removed one objection to the use of assumpsit against executors and administrators to recover debts, though the maxim may have been influential in the dispute over liability for other types of *assumpsit* where debts were not involved.

Simple contract debts die with the debtor

The objection which remained was that simple contract debts died with the debtor, and to allow assumpsit to be used when a debt was involved was simply to allow the evasion of a

---

[1] Y.B. 12 Hen. VIII, f. 11, pl. 13.

[2] See above, p. 265. The guarantee was gratuitous, and therefore the doctrine of *quid pro quo* did not happily apply.

[3] 1 Plowden 180.

substantive rule of law. This point was succinctly put by Anderson C.J. in *Stubbings v. Rotheram*.[1]

> '... for Anderson said, the reason why debt lies not against an executor upon the contract of the testator, is because the law does not intend that he is privy thereto, or can have notice thereof, and he cannot wage his law for such a debt as the testator might. And when debt will not lie, it is not fit that this action [i.e. assumpsit] upon a bare promise should tie him, *for it stands all upon one reason*, and if these actions should be allowable, it would be very mischievous'.

This could be answered on grounds of policy either by insisting on the peril to the testator's soul if his debts went unpaid, and the benefit which would accrue if they were, or by emphasizing the injustice to creditors, or by arguing that in the absence of legal liability the executors might enrich themselves unjustly. The force of these points would not be weakened by the realization that the Chancery would give a remedy anyway if the common law did not. More technically the objection could be answered by saying that the incompatibility was unreal, since actions of assumpsit were not actions to recover debts, or, more radically, by denying that simple contract debts did die with the debtor, and saying that the duty remained though it was not enforceable by writ of debt. Various permutations of these arguments feature in the cases.

Thus in 1535[2] Knightly asked the opinion of Fitzherbert J. on the question, arguing that executors who had assets sufficient should be charged in assumpsit,

> 'for seeing that the executors have assets in their hands of their testator's goods, this is a reason [or, it is in accordance with reason] that they should pay their testator's debts, for notwithstanding the testator is dead, yet the duty remains as a duty, just as before, and they have the goods to the testator's use'.

But Fitzherbert would have none of this,

---

[1] Cro. Eliz. 454, in the Exchequer Chambers. Anderson was Chief Justice of the Common Pleas.

[2] Y.B. 27 Hen. VIII, T. f. 23, pl. 21. This was not a case, but merely a discussion at the bar. The right of a serjeant to pose hypothetical questions to the judges was lost in 1641; see *Serjeant Pheasant's Case*, March N.R. 155.

'when the testator died, this debt which was due by reason of a simple contract is dead also'.

Knightly, not to be put off, returned to the attack, and drew attention to the practice of the Exchequer in allowing quominus against executors, and to the decision of the King's Bench in *Cleymond* v. *Vincent* in which Fitzherbert had been counsel for the plaintiff. But again Fitzherbert was not impressed. He denied that any such practice existed in the Exchequer, and vehemently denounced the case, advising the students to expunge it from their year-books:

'Mettez le cas hors de vostres livres, car nest ley, sans doubt.'

The dispute between the King's Bench and the Common Pleas

Notwithstanding such arguments, the King's Bench from Henry VIII's time onwards allowed the action;[1] the Common Pleas after some vacillation eventually did not.[2] The practice of the King's Bench was confirmed in that court after an elaborate debate in *Norwood* v. *Read* (1558).[3] An action was brought against the executors of the vendor upon the sale of fifty quarters of wheat. The wheat was deliverable in instalments, and payment was to be made on delivery of the purchase price. The purchaser had prepaid forty shillings for a promise and undertaking to deliver at the contract date. Delivery was never made, and the plaintiff had sold the wheat onwards, and could not perform this contract. He claimed 200 marks by way of damages, a sum considerably larger than the purchase price. The argument centred largely upon precisely what *Cleymond* v. *Vincent* had decided,[4] it being the only reported case in print

---

[1] See the precedents (i.e. records) cited in *Pinchon's Case* (1612) 9 Co.Rep. 86b.

[2] Brooke, *Accion sur le case* pl. 106 (1546). Dyer C.J. took this view in 1567; Bodl. MS. Rawl. C. 112 at f. 261. See the cases cited by J. H. Baker, 'New Light on Slade's Case' 1971 C.L.J. at p. 233. It appears that the Common Pleas rejected the action after c. 1588. There is a decision in that year, *Hughson* v. *Webb* Cro. Eliz. 121 and see Owen at p. 95.

[3] 1 Plowden 180.

[4] The case is extremely important on the history of precedent; it seems to be the earliest case in which the court is invited to attach critical importance to precisely what the *ratio decidendi* of an earlier case was. Plowden, who argued in the case seems to have been the first common lawyer to elevate the importance of those resolutions of judges upon which the outcome of a case depended, and to play down the importance of what judges said 'by the way'.

on the question. It was discovered from the record that in the earlier case the defendant had not demurred, but pleaded *non assumpsit* in bar to the action;[1] in consequence it was arguable that the point of law had never arisen for decision, since the executors, by pleading to the action instead of demurring had waived their immunity.[2] On the other side it was arguable that even in the absence of a demurrer the court had had the power to stop the action *ex officio*.[3] If this was correct, the opinions expressed by Fineux C.J. were relevant to the decision, and not mere dicta. After a rather inconclusive debate, the court allowed the action, presumably taking the view that *Cleymond* v. *Vincent* was an authority in favour of the decision. Plowden, perhaps the outstanding lawyer of the time, approved the decision in principle, but criticized it in one particular. The plaintiff had alleged that the executors had assets sufficient to pay all debts; Plowden considered this averment unnecessary, though he thought that if the executors did not have sufficient assets they could plead this in bar to the action.[4] This view ultimately prevailed.[5]

---

[1] *Protestando* that the action was demurrable; the point of thus pleading was to reserve the right to raise the question of law at a later stage in the action by way of a motion in arrest of judgment. Although there is no clear evidence on the question, a motion in arrest of judgment may have been made, and the year-book may be reporting the court's ruling on the motion. If this was the case, then the view of the court would be relevant to the decision of a question raised in the action.

[2] In conformity with the decision noted in Fitz., *Executors* pl. 21 (1434).

[3] The authority relied upon was Y.B. 15 Edw. IV, P. f. 25, pl. 7, which does not in fact decide the point. Brooke, *Executors*, 80, goes beyond the case; he may be relying on a different text. cf. Y.B. 22 Edw. IV, M. f. 23, pl. 2. The view that the court could stop the action *ex officio* was taken by the Common Pleas in *Hughson* v. *Webb* (1588) Cro. Eliz. 121. There debt *sur contract* was brought against administrators, who pleased *plene administravit* in bar; held the court could abate the action although the administrators had not demurred. In 1594 the King's Bench, characteristically, inclined to the opposite view in *Germyn* v. *Rolls*, Cro. Eliz. 425, 429.

[4] It was never suggested that personal representatives who behaved properly should be liable beyond the extent of the assets; all that was in question was a point of pleading. The averment of assets in actions against personal representatives in their representative capacity must be distinguished from the averments of assets as consideration for a personal promise to pay debts or pay legacies.

[5] But not without much controversy. In *Anon.* (1572) Dalison 89, pl. 4 and *Anon.* (1594) 4 Leon. 5 the averment of assets was treated as essential. A decision the other way was given in *Cottingham* v. *Hulett* (1588) Cro. Eliz. 59, and this decision was approved in *Pinchon's Case* (1612) 9 Co.Rep. at 90b, Cro. Jac. 293 under the name of *Codington* v. *Hulet* and in *William Bane's Case* (1611) 9 Co.Rep. 93b at 94a. See also *Fisher* v. *Richardson* (1603) Cro. Jac. 47; *Evans* v. *Warren* (1620)

From precedents cited in *Pinchon's Case* it appears that the Court of Common Pleas allowed the action in the 1580s, at least until c. 1588 following the lead given by the King's Bench; this position may have existed since 1545.[1] For a short time harmony prevailed, but in the 1590s the statutory court of Exchequer Chamber began to overrule decisions of the King's Bench upon the point, these reversals being cheerfully ignored by the King's Bench.[2] In *Pyne* v. *Hide* in 1601 Chief Justice Popham of the King's Bench suggested a solution:

'For the contrariety of opinion between the judges of the Common Pleas and us, we will make it an Exchequer Chamber Case, and try the law.'[3]

He was probably referring to the ancient informal court of Exchequer Chamber, but his suggestion does not seem to have been immediately accepted. But in *Slade's Case*, although the point did not arise, the assembled judges ruled upon it according to Yelverton's Report, resolving that, in future, actions of assumpsit were not to be allowed against executors. If the report is correct this represented a compromise, the King's Bench winning over assumpsit against living debtors, while the Common Pleas won over assumpsit against personal representatives; however a report recently published suggests that the matter was never resolved.[4] Ten years later in *Pinchon's Case* (1612) it was ruled by all the judges, that the practice of the King's Bench was correct. But, as in *Slade's Case*, the judges

---

[1] 9 Co.Rep. at 89b. The precedents cited in the King's Bench begin in 1522; the first in the Common Pleas is in 1572, but the case (*Beecher* v. *Mountjoy*) concerns a promise by an administrator, and not by the deceased; see also cases cited by Baker in 1971 C.L.J. at p. 233. The first instance of an action based upon the promise of the deceased is *Michel* v. *Vial* in 1581.

[2] *Mathew* v. *Mathew* (1595) Moore 702; *Hughes* v. *Rowbotham* (1593) Popham 30; *Griggs* v. *Helhouse* (1595) Cro. Eliz. 545, Moo. K.B. 691; *Pyne* v. *Hide* (1601) Goulds. 154; *Stubbings* v. *Rotherham* (1595) Cro. Eliz. 454, Moo. 691; *Serle* v. *Rosse* (1596) Cro. Eliz. 459; *Gowood* v. *Binkes* (1594) Owen 56. In the last case Popham C.J., who was party to the decision in the K.B. for the plaintiff, remarked that he expected the decision to be reversed. The matter was discussed in the Exchequer Chamber in *Kerchers Case* (1610) Godbolt 176, but inconclusively.

[3] Goulds. 154.

[4] See *Morgan* v. *Slade* Yelv. 20, and for the report in B.M. MS. Add. 25203 see 1971 C.L.J. at p. 67.

Cro. Jac. 604; *Davis* v. *Warner* (1620) Cro. Jac. 593; *Bothe* v. *Crampton* (1621) Cro. Jac. 613; *Papworth* v. *Johnson* (1613) 2 Bulst. 91.

also ruled that in actions brought against representatives the general *indebitatus assumpsit* form of declaration was not to be used.[1]

The limitations imposed by 'Pinchon's Case'

Over *Pinchon's Case*, as over *Slade's Case*, Coke's report is not as frank as it might be, and this has given the impression that after 1612 it was established that assumpsit lay generally against executors and administrators. This is not the case. Just as *Slade's Case* was concerned with actions of assumpsit in lieu of debt against living debtors, *Pinchon's Case* was concerned with assumpsit in similar circumstances involving debt contracts where the debtor had died, and where he could have been sued by writ of debt in his lifetime. Thus *Slade's Case* allowed assumpsit to supersede debt *sur contract*, making assumpsit into the basic contractual action (in the medieval sense of contract), whilst *Pinchon's Case* established that contractual liability was transmissible. This conformed to the line of authority in the King's Bench since *Cleymond* v. *Vincent* in 1523. *Pinchon's Case* did not decide that personal representatives could be sued for breach of *any* promise made by the testator. In Elizabeth I's reign the Court of King's Bench did allow such actions, where the deceased had owed no debt, but the practice was disapproved in the King's Bench in *Hughes* v. *Rowbotham* (1592)[2] by Popham C.J.,

'And he said, that the executor shall be charged with the contract of the testator by common course of the Court, which stands upon reason ... but if the testator upon good consideration assume to make assurance of land, or to do any such collateral thing which doth not sound in a duty of a thing payable, there the executor shall never be charged with such an assumption to render recompense for it. And such an assumption hath not been allowed in the King's Bench but of late time, and that but in one or two cases'.

In *Pinchon's Case* (1612) actions against executors on such 'collateral promises', as they were called, were expressly excluded from

---

[1] See the report (*sub. nom.*) *Puncheon* v. *Legate* in 2 Brownl. 137.
[2] Popham 30. In *Prichard's Case* (1581) Dyer 14a *in margine* it was said that the point had often been adjudged.

the scope of the decision.[1] Quite why it was thought that liability on such collateral promises should not be transmissible is nowhere clearly explained. It could be that the maxim *actio personalis moritur cum persona* was thought to apply, though this is nowhere said. More probably the objection was the idea of supervening impossibility. It may have been thought that a promisor took upon himself an obligation to perform his promise personally, himself; when he died it was no longer possible for the promise to be performed, and it was not fair to hold the estate liable for the breach of a promise which it was impossible to perform. Such reasoning would not apply to a duty to pay a debt, for the only ground upon which it could be said that such a duty had become impossible to perform would be if the executors lacked assets, and this they were entitled to plead as a special defence.

Not long after *Pinchon's Case* the question was raised again in *Sanders* v. *Easterby* (1616)[2] upon a writ of error in the Exchequer Chamber from the King's Bench, and after some doubt it was held that executors were liable on the collateral promises of their testator; Chief Baron Tanfield, who had been one of the judges in *Pinchon's Case*, dissented,

'for it had been oftentimes adjudged that upon such a meer collateral promise, the executor is not chargeable'.

The point was argued again a year later with the same result in *Beresford* v. *Woodruff* (1617),[3] and again in *Fawcett* v. *Charter* (1623).[4] The repeated raising of the issue indicates that there existed a serious doubt as to the propriety of extending the liability of executors so far, and Chief Baron Tanfield never abandoned his view that assumpsit ought not to be allowed in such cases. But by the end of James I's reign the principle was established, though the action for breach of promise of marriage remained an exception.

[1] See the report of the case in Cro. Jac. 293. The same decision had been given in the previous year by the Exchequer in *Herman* v. *Elliot* (1610), unreported; see Cro. Jac. 404, where the case is cited.

[2] Cro. Jac. 417. See also *Smale* v. *Boyer* (1616), 3 Bulst. 248.

[3] Cro. Jac. 404, 3 Bulst. 236, Rolle Rep. 433.

[4] Cro. Jac. 662, Palm. 329. See also *Bidwell* v. *Catton* (1617) Hob. 216, *Christopher* v. *How* (1649) Style 158.

XII

PLEADING AND PROCEDURE IN THE ACTION FOR BREACH OF PROMISE

T H E action on the case was essentially formless; in consequence the declaration and pleadings in an assumpsit action were not stereotyped, though the publication of Books of Entries such as Rastell (1566),[1] Coke (1514),[2] and Brownlow (1652),[3] containing forms drawn by acknowledged masters, inevitably discouraged individual experimentation. The basic structure of a declaration in assumpsit may be illustrated from William Brownlow's precedent for an action brought by one of his clerks against a client claiming payment of a *quantum meruit* for drawing a declaration.[4] This starts with the averment of consideration in that part of the declaration known as the inducement (i.e. 'the leading in').

> 'that whereas the aforesaid (such a day, year and place), in consideration that he, the said P, then and continually afterwards and hitherto one of the clerks of the aforesaid prothonotary [Brownlow], at the special instance and request of the aforesaid D, would draw for him the said D a certain declaration . . .'

The consideration here is executory or future. The next part contains the averment of the undertaking and promise:

> 'did assume upon himself, and to him the said P did then and there faithfully promise, that he, the aforesaid D, when after the drawing of the declaration aforesaid he should be thereunto required, would pay to him the said P such a sum of money as he the said P in that behalf should reasonably deserve to have . . .'

---

[1] Editions in 1566, 1574, 1596, and 1670, the collection of William Rastell.
[2] Editions in 1614 and 1671. There were numerous other such collections, and a leading treatise on pleading, Sampson Ever's *Doctrina Placitandi*, appeared in 1677.
[3] In English in editions of 1652, 1653, 1654, and 1659 and in Latin as *Latine Redivivus* in 1693, the collection of Richard Brownlow, Prothonotary of the Common Pleas.
[4] 2nd ed., p. 199, spelling modified and initials changed.

Having averred an executory consideration, the next step was to aver performance, for otherwise the declaration would fail to say that there yet was consideration for the promise:

'and although the said P upon the hope of the faithful performance of the aforesaid promise and assumption afterwards . . . did draw the declaration aforesaid . . .'

Having averred that he deserved 40s., the next step was to say that there had been breach,

'yet the aforesaid D, his promise and assumption aforesaid little regarding, but plotting and fraudulently intending him the said P of the aforesaid 40s. craftily to deceive and defraud . . . he hath not paid, or to him the said P in any manner contented . . .'

Further, since the promise was to pay on a request, there is included an averment of a *special* request (i.e. one with time, date, and place). Finally comes the averment of damage:

'whereupon he saith he is damnified, and hath damage to the value of ten pounds.'

This was the basic framework of a declaration, which could be varied according to need. Thus a precedent[1] for failure to pay a marriage dowry includes an averment of loss of profit of £100 through non-payment of the sum of 100 marks promised:

'by which he, the said P, divers commodities profits and advantages, which he with the aforesaid hundred marks by buying and selling, might have gained . . .'

Books of Entries provided the profession with a wide range of models—precedents for part-payment for wares sold,[2] breach of a promise not to overwork a mare loaned,[3] money won on a wager or at hazard, money promised as a reward to the public occasioned by a theft of goods;[4] all these could be adapted to

---

[1] Op. cit. p. 205.
[2] Op. cit. p. 202.
[3] Op. cit. p. 214.
[4] From W. Brown, *Methodus Novissima Intrandi Placita Generalia* (1699) at pp. 2, 29, 6.

the needs of particular litigants, and the drawing of declarations seems to have been a service commonly performed by court clerks as well as by counsel and attorneys.

The breach of promise

The gravamen of the plaintiff's claim is the breach of the promise, and a considerable body of law grew up as to what precisely had to be averred to show breach.

If the promise was subject to a condition precedent then the condition must, of course, be performed,[1] just as an executory consideration must be executed at the time of breach; in a conditional assumpsit the defendant could, if he wished, take issue specially upon the performance of the condition.[2] Although similar in effect, the rationale of the rule applicable to executory consideration and of that applicable to a condition precedent differed. In the former case there was no *consideration* until execution, and hence the declaration failed to aver consideration at all unless the pleader alleged execution. If a counter-promise, as opposed to its performance, was the consideration alleged, then the declaration was not objectionable as failing to show consideration simply because the promise was unperformed. In the second case of a conditional promise, there was no *breach of promise* if the condition was unperformed. Granted, however, a consideration for the promise, there was no general principle according to which the obligations arising out of a bilateral agreement were to be treated by implication as impliedly mutually conditional or dependent.[3] Either there was an express condition or there was not. The rationale of the mutual-promise cases was mutuality of remedy, as we have seen; each party had his action, and a bird in the bush was treated as a bird in the hand (*Qui actionem habet ad rem recuperandum, rem habere videtur*). This suggested an exception in cases where there was no mutuality of remedy, and there was some authority for implying mutual dependence in such cases, although the undertakings were not expressly mutually condi-

---

[1] *Raynay* v. *Alexander* (1605) Yelv. 76, *Paynter* v. *Paynter* (1630) Cro. Car. 194

[2] *Richards* v. *Carvamel* (1614) 1 Brownl. and Goulds. 10. At this date a plea of *non assumpsit* was thought to confess performance of the condition.

[3] The rule derives from covenant, see *Brocas' Case* (1588) 3 Leon. 219; *Everard* v *Hopkins* (1614) 1 Rolle Rep. 125; *Bettisworth* v *Campion* (1608) Yelv. 133; *Spanish Ambassador* v. *Gifford* (1616) 1 Rolle Rep. 3.

tional.[1] But an approach which turned upon the question 'did the parties make their promises mutually conditional as absolute?' was rather absurd when applied to informal promises, where the parties will rarely use language precise enough to indicate one way or the other whether their promises are mutually conditional (even assuming no difficulty over proof). One cannot apply to verbal promises doctrines derived from the earlier law of contracts under seal, for they depend upon the fact that written contracts under seal have a set text. Hence in time rules came to be evolved which fictionally attributed to the parties intentions to make certain types of promises mutually dependent, and these could be applied whatever the informality of the arrangement.[2]

Considerable controversy developed as to whether in cases where no date for performance was fixed it was necessary to aver a request for performance, and, if so, whether the request must be averred specially with a date and place, or whether a general averment (*licet saepius requisit*) was sufficient. The rule as eventually settled distinguished between promises to perform an existing *duty* (i.e. debt) and other promises; in the words of Houghton J. in *Hill* v. *Wade* (1618):[3]

> 'Houghton Justice took this difference: where a request is upon a duty, as if I can sell a house for five pounds to be paid on request, there a *licet saepius requisitus* is sufficient. And [on the other hand] where it is a collateral matter, for there he ought actually to allege a request, although issue be joined on the assumpsit.'

The distinction was particularly important over questions of limitations; in the former case the cause of action accrued at the time of the promise, in the latter at the time of the request. This illustrates the radical difference between *indebitatus assumpsit* and special assumpsit, the former involving a change of

---

[1] See *Cowper* v. *Andrews* (1612) Hob. 39 at 41.

[2] They are set out in the notes to *Pordage* v. *Cole* (1669) 1 Wms. Saund. 319 and originated outside our period.

[3] Cro. Jac. 523. See also *The Case of an Hostler* (1606) Yelv. 66; *Devenly* v. *Wellbore* (1587) Cro. Eliz. 85; *Morris* v. *Kirke* (1587) Cro. Eliz. 73; *Osbaston* v. *Garten* (1587) Cro. Eliz. 91; *De Bavoy* v. *Hassal* (1588) Cro. Eliz. 133; *Palmer* v. *Knight* (1634) Cro. Car. 385; *Freeborne* v. *Purchase* (1649) Style 107; *Williamson* v. *Mead* (1649) Style 207; *Birks* v. *Trippet* (1666) 1 Wms. Saund. 32 with note 2 at 32 and cases there cited.

procedure brought about by a promise to pay, the latter involving an independent promissory liability.

Pleading of defences

The general issue in assumpsit arose on the plea *non assumpsit*. After some doubt it came to be settled that the possible alternative, a plea of *not guilty* (*non culpabilis*), was demurrable, though if the defendant did not demur it was cured by verdict and could not therefore be objected to on a motion in arrest of judgment; not guilty in trespass actions was appropriate to cases of misfeasance, not to cases of nonfeasance.[1] The form and effect of the general issue in assumpsit is very peculiar. Where the action is brought to enforce a pre-existing duty, as in *indebitatus assumpsit*, it seems natural that the denial of the undertaking and promise should be the standard reply, since the cause of action in assumpsit can be regarded as arising when the promise is made. But in other situations (and arguably even in *indebitatus assumpsit*) the gravamen of the plaintiff's case seems to be the breach of promise and undertaking; consequently one might at first sight expect the standard defence to be a denial of the *breach* of the promise, rather than the promise itself. However, the difficulty inherent in such a plea may have been that a traverse of the averment of breach would of necessity take the form of a plea of performance of the promise averred, and such a plea would, in accordance with the ordinary principles of pleading, have confessed by implication the making of the promise. Hence, presumably, the preference for a denial of the promise by a plea of *non assumpsit*, which constituted in a sense a more radical attack upon the plaintiff's position, and one which conceded nothing. In terms, however, such a plea merely denies the promise and assumption, and it would be natural to expect the plea of *non assumpsit* to put in issue merely the fact that a promise had been made in the terms alleged by the plaintiff, or, in the case of a promise, implied by law, the facts giving rise to the implication; this indeed was the scope allowed to the plea under the Hilary Rules of 1834.[2]

---

[1] *Bradley* v. *Benney* (1606) Noy 114; *Glover* v. *Taylor* (1615) 1 Brownl. and Goulds. 8; *Elrington* v. *Doshant* (1640) 1 Lev. 142

[2] See Stephen, *Pleading*, App. n. 44.

There was, however, a movement in the seventeenth and eighteenth centuries to reduce the necessity and attraction of special pleading. This was furthered by widening the scope of the general issue and allowing defences which at certain periods would have had to be pleaded specially to be put in evidence before the jury on the general issue. The history of this movement has never been adequately investigated, but in all probability its source is to be found partly in a dislike of the over-elaboration of special pleading and partly in the growth of more adequate controls over the working of jury trial. At common law, as a result, the scope of the general issue in *assumpsit* as in other actions was much wider than its terms suggest The position came to be that the plea of *non assumpsit* put in issue first of all any defence which involved saying that the plaintiff never at any time had a cause of action.[1] Thus it was possible to give in evidence matter showing that the defendant never promised at all, did not promise in the terms averred, that there was no consideration, or that the consideration was unlawful, that he was an infant or within the coverture, that the promise was made under duress, that the promise itself was unlawful or had been discharged before breach. In seventeenth-century law (though the position later changed) in actions of special assumpsit a defence which involved conceding that there had once been liability, though liability which had later been discharged, had to be specially pleaded.[2] For example, a defence of accord and satisfaction, or payment, or performance, had to be pleaded specially, and could not be given in evidence on the general issue. In actions taken upon implied promises. however, this rule was not insisted upon, though a special plea which gave 'colour' (i.e. admitted an apparent right in the plaintiff) was good.[3] In later law even on an express assumpsit the plea of *non assumpsit* put in issue matters of discharge or excuse,[4] but never a defence based upon limitation, which always had to be specially pleaded.[5]

[1] See Chitty, *Pleading*, 3rd Ed. (1817), Vol. I.

[2] *Easte* v. *Farmer* (1641) March 100; *Abbott* v. *Chapman* (1672) 2 Lev. 81; *Fits* v. *Freestone* (1676) 1 Mod. 211; *Paramour* v. *Johnson* (1699) 12 Mod. 376, Ld. Raym. 366.

[3] *Milward* v. *Ingram* (1675) 1 Mod. 206.

[4] See Buller, *Nisi Prius*, 148.

[5] See for seventeenth-century law *Holford* v. *Gibbes*, Hetley 85. *Lee* v. *Rogers* (1663)

Damage and the action on the case

The trial of the issue in assumpsit was a jury matter, and if the jurymen found for the plaintiff they were responsible for assessing the damages and costs.

Though the action of assumpsit was an action for unliquidated damages, once the jury had given its verdict the sum due became certain, and so a debt became due by record; hence at common law promissory liability, like all other forms of civil liability in the personal actions, ended up as the liability of a debtor. This sharply differentiates common law civil liability from the liability of a defendant in a Chancery suit, where the unsuccessful defendant either submitted to the court or fell into contempt. The fact that assumpsit was an action for damages for a wrong—what is sometimes called its delictual character—has given rise to some misunderstanding, particularly in relation to the origins of the doctrine of consideration. For it has been suggested that the source of the notion that detriment suffered counted as consideration is to be found in the requirement, in actions upon the case, that damage must be proved; proof of damage was therefore of the essence of the action of assumpsit. Such a theory can be variously developed around the idea that a shift from a delictual to a contractual action alters the way in which the damage is viewed, so that it is transmuted into detriment consideration.[1]

There is no doubt that the fact of damage suffered was at all times an argument for allowing an action upon the case to be brought, though not a conclusive argument, for there might be *damnum sine iniuria*;[2] also the suffering of temporal damage was an important factor in justifying a temporal remedy.[3] But it is an anachronism to read back into the earlier common law the modern doctrine according to which a distinction is drawn

[1] See *H.E.L.* VIII. 10–11; Kiralfy 170–5; Milsom, 'Not Doing is No Trespass' [1954], C.L.T. 105; Fifoot 396.

[2] The classic case is 11 Hen. IV, H. f. 47, pl. 21, where the masters of the grammar school in Gloucester sued for loss suffered through competition from a rival school.

[3] See generally Kiralfy 12 et seq.

---

1 Lev. 110. Limitation defended upon the Statute of 21 Jac. I, c. 16 (1623) which imposed a six-year period. The doctrine that a subsequent promise to pay a debt barred by the statute is actionable is found in *Dickson* v. *Thompson* (1682) 2 Show. 126 and *Hyeling* v. *Hasting* (1699) 1 Ld. Raym. 389.

between actions (such as trespass *vi et armis* and libel) in which special damage need not be proved, the tort being actionable *per se*, and actions in which the plaintiff will fail if no such damage is proved. All this would be unintelligible to a fifteenth- or sixteenth-century lawyer, for it involves law developed around directions to juries, which were then either not given at all or not normally open to review. Nobody had to 'prove' anything in a medieval action of trespass or trespass on the case; hence legal rules about what had to be proved did not exist. However, it was indeed the invariable practice to aver damage in the declaration, and no pleader would deliberately fail to include such an averment: hence case law on the point is hard to find. However, there is no doubt that such an averment was in principle essential. *Musket* v. *Cole* (1587)[1] shows this. The plaintiff sued for breach of a promise to deliver to him bonds executed by his son; objection was taken in that he did not aver that there were any such bonds. The point of the objection was that if there were no such bonds 'then no damage'. But it was held that the pleading was sufficient, for

> 'the plaintiff had time enough for the shewing to the jury what bills or obligations [there were] for the instructing of the jury of the damages'.

The case assumes the principle. It is again assumed in the rule that the plaintiff could not by verdict recover greater damages than he had averred in his declaration,[2] though the jury could award less.[3]

Granted an averment of damages, it was in general at the discretion of the jury to award what damages the jurymen thought fit, subject only to minimal guidance by the court, and no doubt if they thought that no damage had been suffered they might award none. The conception of nominal damages as a right did not exist; legal presumptions of damage and rules as

---

[1] 1 Leon. 123.

[2] *Persival* v. *Spencer* (1604) Yelv. 46. On costs the matter was controversial, but there was authority allowing the jury to give costs and damages exceeding the damages claimed. See 1 Rolle Ab. 578 pl. 9, *Robert Pilfold's Case* (1613) 10 Co.Rep. 115a.

[3] *Farrer* v. *Snelling* (1605) 1 Rolle Rep. 335; the case also holds that an inconsistency in the declaration caused by false arithmetic was not disastrous, as it would have been in debt.

to the proof of damage had not yet been invented. There was indeed very little law about the principles governing the assessment of damages, and the considerable number of cases collected in the title 'Damages' in the early abridgements are hardly at all concerned with this matter. It is only against this background that damage may be said to have been an essential element in an action of assumpsit in the sixteenth and seventeenth centuries.

Damage, consideration, and the principle governing contractual damages

The possibility that the courts in some way confused detriment consideration with damage suffered is rendered very implausible by the fact that the averment of consideration comes physically at a quite different point in the declaration from that at which the averment of damage suffered comes, and this makes it almost inconceivable that contemporary lawyers could have been confused. The only case for identifying the damage for which the claim is made with the detriment suffered in reliance upon the promise is that there are situations in which both appear, on a simplistic view, to have the same economic value. For example, consider a gratuitous loan: the sum which the plaintiff parts with in reliance upon the borrower's promise looks the same as the loss he will suffer if the borrower fails to perform his side of the arrangement and give the money back. But, even in so simple a case as this, the identity can only be maintained by a refusal to *compensate* the lender for late repayment, a refusal which confines the action to a purely restitutionary function. The distinction is obvious in other cases; thus consider a payment of £100 in return for a promise of, a horse. The detriment suffered here is £100, whereas the value of performance is the value of the horse, which obviously can be quite different.

In an action for damages for a wrong the natural policy of the law is to put the injured person into the position he would have been in if the wrong had not been committed. The classic statement of the principle is that of Lord Blackburn in *Livingstone* v. *Rawyards Coal Co.*:[1]

---

[1] (1880) 5 App. Cas. 25 at 39, and see generally F. H. Lawson, *Remedies of English Law* (1973), Ch. IV.

'where any injury is to be compensated by damages, in settling the sum to be given for reparation of damage you should as nearly as possible get at that sum of money which will put the party who has been injured, or who has suffered, in the same position as he would have been if he had not sustained the wrong for which he is now getting compensation or reparation.'

Now in the action of assumpsit the wrong is breach of promise, at which date the cause of action accrued,[1] and it follows that primarily the compensation awarded ought to be the value of performance of the promise wrongfully not performed. The alternative would be to regard the making of a promise (subsequently not performed) as itself a wrong, that is as a deceitful trick whereby the promisee was cheated out of whatever it was he parted with on the strength of the promise. Although allegations of deceit and fraud were standard form in pleadings in assumpsit, it was the breach of promise, not the making of the promise, which was characterized as deceitful and fraudulent; a typical example is the pleading in *Slade's Case*,[2] where the defendant was said to have 'faithfully promised' and then,

'his assumption and promise aforesaid little regarding but endeavouring and intending the said John of the aforesaid £16 in that part subtilly and craftily to deceive and defraud the said £16 of the said John . . . hath not paid . . .'

A possible reason for the absence of actions in which the *making* of the promise is characterized as deceitful may be that a promise would probably have only been so regarded if it was not accompanied by an intention to perform, and intent was not in the fifteenth- and sixteenth-century law regarded as issuable. Whatever the explanation may be, the courts consistently treated the breach of promise as the deceitful wrong, with the result that the proper measure of damage was a substitute for performance.

The case law indicates that the principle of compensation as opposed to restitution or recuperation was always grasped. Thus

---

[1] *Shutford and Borough's Case* (1629) Godbolt 437.
[2] 4 Co.Rep. 91a.

PLEADING AND PROCEDURE IN

in *Orwell* v. *Mortoft* (1505)[1] one of Frowicke C.J.'s arguments
for allowing the action on the case to lie instead of the action
of debt involves the drawing of a clear distinction between the
recuperatory actions such as debt, and actions leading to compensation,

> 'but in my opinion the cause whereby this action is maintain-
> able is because the plaintiff is damaged by the non-delivery
> on the day according to the bargain, and although the plain-
> tiff can have an action of debt for the barley, nevertheless
> by that action he is not satisfied of the damages suffered'.

This distinction was used as one of the justifications for the
decision in *Slade's Case*, and was also relied upon in connection
with actions of assumpsit for money payable in instalments.
That the compensation should normally be a substitute for
performance is classically illustrated by *Colman's Case* (1595),[2]
where the defendant had promised to pay the plaintiff £10
(money due to him as damages in another action) in return for
a payment of 4d. Damages to be awarded were £10, not the 4d.
with which the plaintiff had parted. *Field's Case* (1619),[3]
which involved a wager, is another illustration of the award of
what are now called damages for loss of expectation. In consideration of 1s. given to the defendant, he promised to pay the
plaintiff Field £10 if he ran from Shoreditch Church to Ware in
four hours. Field achieved this feat and the jury awarded £10
as damages. The reporter Rolle notes that on any theory the
jury got it all wrong, for this was more than the plaintiff had
given the defendant, and less than the defendant promised,
presumably because the understanding in such a bet is that the
stake is returnable; hence the jury ought to have awarded
£10 1s. od. He concludes that the case illustrates the fact that
damages are within the discretion of the jury, but the compensatory principle upon which the jury acted is clear enough. A
contrary solution was, however, urged in *Anon.* (1588),[4]
though the report does not indicate whether it was accepted.
The case involved a promise to pay £100 if an act was not done

---

[1] Keilwey 69a. See above, p. 262.
[2] Moo. K.B. 419.
[3] 2 Rolle Rep. 113.
[4] Owen 34.

within a certain time in consideration of a payment of a French crown. The report suggests that in equity at this time only the stake was recoverable. But the chancery case was peculiar, and merited an exception,

> 'a Gentlewoman took the death of her husband so heavily that she said she would never marry again, and her son comforted her and said, "God will provide a new husband".'

The son then bet his mother £100 to £10 she would remarry, and, when she did, sued for his winnings.

> 'And the Master of the Rolls awarded ten pounds only, and said he would never give a penny more, because it was unreasonable to bar a gentlewoman from marriage.'

This plainly is an exception based upon public policy. Sometimes, however, the breach of promise can cause the plaintiff to be worse off in an absolute sense, so that merely to give him a substitute for performance is inadequate. *Nurse* v. *Barns* (1663)[1] is perhaps the first case which clearly recognizes the right of a jury to provide compensation in such a situation. The defendant had broken a promise to allow the plaintiff the use of iron mills for six months, the use being worth £10. The jury awarded £500 damages for loss of stock, and the court upheld this award.

Granted the general principle, the jury enjoyed a wide discretion in settling the sum, though in some exceptional circumstances the court would exercise control, as in the curious case of *Jones* v. *Morgan*,[2] the case where a horse was sold for a quantity of barley, one barley-corn for one of its nails, two for the next, and so forth, doubling up for each of its thirty-two nails. The judge, however, directed the jury to award the value of the horse, a mere £8, not the value of the barley. In general, the jury's award would only be questioned on the basis of what appeared in the pleadings,[3] and it was in general presumed that the jury had been properly directed on any question of law arising out of them. Thus it was clear that the jury could not award more in damages than the plaintiff claimed in his

---

[1] T. Raymond 77. From this case has been traced a right to recover damages based on a 'reliance' rather than an 'expectancy' interest. See L.L. Fuller and W. R. Perdue in 46 Y.L.J. 52.

[2] 1 Lev. 111, 6 Mod. 305, 1 Jones 131, and see Vent. 267.

[3] A good illustration is *Osborne's Case* (1613), 10 Co. Rep. 130.

declaration, for he of all people knew best how much he had
suffered. But it was open to argument whether the jury might
award in costs and damages more than the total sum claimed,
for the plaintiff at the time of settling the pleadings might
underestimate his costs; the eventual view was that the award
could not be interfered with if the costs inflated the sum
beyond that claimed.[1] Another area of controversy centred
upon agreements to pay money in instalments. For example,
in *Beckwith* v. *Nott* (1617)[2] the plaintiff declared that the
defendant was indebted to him £4, and promised to pay the
debt at 5*s.* each month; he paid nothing, and the plaintiff
sued after four months for damages of £6. The jury awarded
£4. The award was upheld, and to the objection that the plaintiff should only have claimed £1 (four instalments), or waited
until all the instalments were due, it was replied,

> 'here it [the action] is grounded upon the promise, which is
> broken by every non-payment according to the promise,
> and he doth not demand any sum certain, but only damages;
> and it is at the discretion of the jury, whether they will find
> the entire sum in damages, or only so much as is due. But
> when they give the entire damages, as here, Dodderidge
> said it is with an averment that it is given for the entire sum;
> and it shall be a good bar in a new action upon that promise'.

Although it was quite settled that in assumpsit, as contrasted
with debt, an action lay as soon as an instalment of an entire
sum was in arrear, it remained controversial whether or not the
jury could award damages for the whole sum, and, if they did,
whether the plaintiff was barred from suing again.[3] It is, however, important to note that law only evolved on the matter
because legal argument could be based upon what appeared
on the face of the record. There was a general reluctance to
interfere with awards which lay within the discretion of the
jury, which might of course award less than the sum claimed.

---

[1] See *Egles* v. *Vales* (1605) 1 Rolle Ab. 578 pl. 9, *Bigot's Case* (1496) Keilwey
21a, *Robert Pilfold's Case* (1612) 10 Co.Rep. 115.

[2] Cro. Jac. 505.

[3] See *Pecke* v. *Redman* (1552) Dyer 113a and cases *in margine*; *Joscelin* v *Shelton*
(1557) 3 Leon. 4; *Hunt* v. *Sone* (1588) Cro. Eliz. 118, 2 Leon. 107; *Foster* v. *Taylor*
(1600) Cro. Eliz. 776, 807; *Milles* v. *Milles* (1631) Cro. Car. 241; *Peck* v. *Ambler*
(1633) Cro. Car. 349.

For example, on a promise of £1,000 for a cure the jury could award less than the sum promised, if they thought fit,[1] in spite of the promise, and the same discretionary power is illustrated by the 'doubling-up' cases.

The effect of a judgment in assumpsit

Although the plaintiff in assumpsit quantified the damages claimed in his pleading, the action was conceived to be for an uncertain or unliquidated sum; the effect of a verdict in the plaintiff's favour and judgment was to convert this into a liquidated sum, that is to say a debt of record or judgment debt. Hence the defaulting party became the promisee's debtor, and although in general the history of methods of executing judgments lies outside the scope of this book, some brief account is necessary to appreciate the nature of promissory liability. The plaintiff possessed a choice of remedies, set out thus by Blackstone:

'Executions in actions where money only is to be recovered, as a debt or damages (and not any specific chattel) are of five sorts: either against the body of the defendant; or against his goods and chattels; or against his goods and the *profits* of his lands; or against his goods and the *possession* of his lands; or against all three, his body, lands and goods.'[2]

Taking the least severe measures first, execution against the goods and chattels was achieved by the issue of the writ of *fieri facias* which commanded the sheriff to take the goods and 'make of the goods' the debt, which he could do by sale. By writ of *levari facias* the debt could be levied from the chattels and profits of the debtor's lands. With the disappearance of debt slavery after the Conquest these were the only two common law procedures for enforcing the debtor's liability. Modification came through legislation. In 1285 by the Statute of Westminster II, c. 18, a procedure known as *elegit* was made available at the choice (hence the name) of the creditor. If the creditor wished, he could take possession of the debtor's chattels, excluding cattle and plough beasts, and the chattels were valued and went in satisfaction of the debt. If they were insufficient,

---

[1] *Anon.* (1670) 1 Vent. 65.
[2] 3 Blackstone 414. See generally Plucknett 389 et seq, *Legislation of Edward I*, 148 et seq.

then half the debtor's lands were delivered to the creditor by
way of security for the debt, he becoming 'tenant by *elegit*'; the
rents and profits went in discharge of the debt. The procedure
by *elegit* is, of course, related historically to the even more severe
system for enforcing recognizances established at about the same
time by the Statute of Acton Burnell (1283) and the Statute of
Merchants (1285) and later extended by the Statute of the
Staple (1353).[1] Here the method of enforcement was peculiarly
harsh, involving the immediate imprisonment of the defaulting
debtor and the eventual seizure of all the debtor's lands as
security for the debt. But the debtor had voluntarily to subject
himself to these proceedings by executing a recognizance in
advance, and the procedures were intended for the use of
merchants alone and not the public at large.

Execution against the person of a judgment debtor ought
historically to be the original method of execution, and it is
a curiosity of the history of the common law that as a general
remedy the imprisonment of the debtor at the suit of the creditor
is a relatively late development. It arose partly as a result of
statute and partly through the interrelation between statute and
common law principles. The writ for arresting and imprisoning
the judgment debtor was known as *capias ad satisfaciendum*, and
in the common law of the early fourteenth century this method
of execution was not as a general rule available in personal
actions, in particular in the action of debt. The Crown could,
however, as a privilege employ imprisonment against its debtors.
However, in trespass actions *vi et armis et contra pacem* arrest by
capias was available, for these were pleas of the Crown, and in
the early fourteenth century trespass actions in the royal courts
were all in this form. In 1352 the availability of *capias ad satisfaciendum* was extended in a curious way. By this date it appears
to have been established as a common law rule that if arrest was
available (by *capias ad respondendum*) to compel the appearance
of the party in court then *capias* was also available to execute
the judgment, *ad satisfaciendum*.[2] A statute in 1352 extended the
use of *capias ad respondendum* to actions of debt[3] and the conse-

---

[1] See above, p. 126.

[2] Y.B. 30 Edw. III, T. f. 8, pl. 15, 40 Edw. III, f. 25, pl. 28, 42 Lib. Ass. pl. 17
all assume the principle.

[3] 25 Edw. III, st. 5, c. 17. This also allowed *capias* in detinue of chattels and for
taking of beasts.

quence was that imprisonment for debt as a method of enforcing the judgment by *capias ad satisfaciendum* became generally available to creditors, whereas previously it had only been available exceptionally to the Crown and in the action of account. The converse principle, that *capias* could not be used to enforce the judgment unless *capias* was possible in mesne process, was also generally accepted legal doctrine.[1]

In the late fourteenth century the courts began to draw a distinction between actions of trespass *vi et armis et contra pacem* and actions for other kinds of trespass in which there was no breach of the peace and no overt crown interest; these became the purely private tort actions 'on the case', and they include the action of assumpsit. As we have seen, it is by no means clear why this distinction was insisted upon, but one possible reason is that the courts did not think it fair to subject defendants in such private tort actions to the stringent procedures appropriate to the violent and criminal wrongdoer, in particular process and execution by *capias*, and, even more grave, *exigent*, which led to outlawry.[2] Whereas, for example, the courts had at one time been ready to permit a careless smith to be sued by trespass *vi et armis* as if he had killed the plaintiff's horse like a criminal, they came, in about 1370,[3] to insist that such an action should be honestly pleaded as an action for careless conduct with no allegation of violent breach of the peace. The point of this may have been to provide a rationale on the pleadings for refusal of *capias*. A case in 1368[4] in which it is apparently held that *capias* is an inappropriate process against a negligent innkeeper lends some support for this view.

Trespass was brought against an innkeeper by the King and his escheator Thomas of Navenby, and the complaint was that the plaintiff, who was on the King's business, had lost goods when he was staying in the inn. The action alleged breach of

---

[1] 2 Hen. IV, f. 6, pl. 24, *Isabel's Case* (1605) Moo. K.B. 765, and for an exception see 2 Hen. VI, T. f. 12, pl. 4.

[2] To compel appearance outlawry went with *capias*, so that, if the sheriff on a writ of *capias* returned *non est inventus*, the next step was to proceed by *exigent* to outlawry. Outlawry by *exigent* after judgment and attempts to execute by *capias ad satisfaciendum* were not originally allowed. See 49 Edw. III, f. 2, pl. 5. But the rule changed in the fifteenth century. See 9 Henry VI, f. 13, pl. 20.

[3] See *Waldon* v. *Marshall* 43 Edw. III, f . 33, pl. 38, and Milsom 250.

[4] 42 Lib. Ass. pl. 17, which is the same case as 42 Edw. III, f. 11, pl. 13. For the record see Kiralfy 222.

the peace and contempt, and it was alleged that the loss had occurred through the innkeeper's default, third parties having broken into the inn *vi et armis* in the night. The plaintiffs won, and when the King's Serjeants asked for *capias ad satisfaciendum*, since the defendants had been brought by *capias ad respondendum*, this was refused, on the ground that *capias* should never have been used. There was, it was said, no fault in the defendant; he was not charged by fault, but by law.[1]

Whatever the explanation, it was settled by 1400 that *capias* was not available to enforce execution in an action on the case. But the position was changed by statute in 1503.[2] Thereafter a judgement in an action on the case could lead to execution by *capias ad satisfaciendum*, just as had been possible in an action of debt since 1352; furthermore outlawry was possible both in mesne and final process. This change in procedure, and particularly in the method of executing the judgment, may well have been of considerable importance in the rise of the action of assumpsit, encouraging attempts to supersede debt *sur contract*, for a less drastic method of execution would clearly have given assumpsit a built-in disadvantage as contrasted with the action of debt, and consequently hindered its development into a general contractual remedy.

Blackstone's fifth mode of execution is against 'his body, lands and goods', and this is intended as a reference to the procedure under statutes merchant and staple. There was in addition some complex law on the extent to which the various forms of execution were cumulative. Broadly the principle was that execution against the body of the debtor was regarded as more serious—'of a higher nature'—than execution against the land of the debtor, and thus more serious than execution against chattels. Once the debtor had been taken into custody on a *capias ad satisfaciendum* it was not permissible to have recourse to remedies of a lower nature, and this made *capias* a remedy of last resort.[3] If the creditor proceeded by *elegit* and the debtor had no lands and insufficient goods to satisfy the debt, then the creditor could use *capias*, but this was not allowed if there were

---

[1] See also explanations by Brooke, *Execution*, pl. 16 (*car nest tort en le def. mes laches*), pl. 87 (*car nest que fait del ley et nemy son culpe*), Exigent pl. 12 (*nest tort, mes negligence*).
[2] 19 Hen. VII, c. 9.
[3] 21 Jac. I, c. 24 allowed a new process to be sued on the death of the debtor.

lands of any value. If the creditor proceeded by *fieri facias* against the goods, then *capias* could be employed cumulatively in cases where the goods were insufficient. One could within limits move up the scale of severity, but not down.[1]

Imprisonment for debt

Once taken upon a *capias*, the debtor was to be kept in *arcta et salva custodia* and the classical statement of his unfortunate position is to be found in Plowden's Commentaries.[2]

'For if one be in execution he ought to live of his own and neither the plaintiff nor the sheriff is bound to give him meat and drink, no more than if one distrain cattle and puts them in a pound, for there the owner of the cattle ought to give them meat ... and if he has no goods he shall live of the charity of others, and if others will give him nothing, let him die in the name of God, if he will, and impute the cause of it to his own fault, for his presumption and ill behaviour brought him to that imprisonment.'

This was a statement made in a brutal age, and there is some authority for the view that in medieval law the gaoler was bound to provide food, though the duty was not directly enforceable.[3] In practice prisoners had to live of their own, or rely upon friends, or charity,[4] and providing for the welfare of prisoners was a common object of private charity. There was an attempt made to relieve imprisoned debtors by a county rate under statutes of Elizabeth I.[5] but this appears to have been ineffective. Under the Commonwealth attempts were made to reform the law, the most radical scheme involving the complete abolition of imprisonment for debt; this project failed, but the 'Five Pound Act, of 1649 enabled debtors worth less than £5 to take proceedings for their release from prison, though not from liability. Other legislation of the period considerably

---

[1] See Blackstone, III, Ch. 26.

[2] *Dive* v. *Manningham* (1551) Plowden 60 at 68.

[3] *Pinchon's Case* (1612) 9 Co.Rep. at 87b, relying on 28 Hen. VI, M. f. 4, pl. 21, on which see above, p. 141. *Contra per* Lord Holt in 12 Mod. at 683.

[4] See R. B. Pugh, *Imprisonment in Medieval England*, Ch. XV and *passim*.

[5] 14 Eliz. I, c. 5, cl. 38 (not mainly concerned with debtors), and 39 Eliz. I, c. 3, cl. 13, discussed *H.E.L.* VIII. 333.

enhanced the indigent debtor's chance of release.[1] After the Restoration this legislation lapsed, but the movement for reform lived on, culminating in an Act for the 'Releife and Release of Poore distressed Prisoners for Debt' in 1670–1.[2]

This Act established an elaborate scheme for alleviating the lot of poor but honest debtors, and the purpose of the legislation was set out in the preamble:

> 'Forasmuch as very many persons now detained in Prison are miserably impoverished either by reason of the late unhappy Times, the sadd and dreadful Fire, their owne Misfortunes, or otherwise, soe as they are totally disabled to give any Satisfaction to their Creditors, and soe become without advantage to any a Charge and Burthen to the Kingdome, and by Noysomnes (inseperably incident to extreme Poverty) may become the occasion of Pestilence and contagious Diseases . . .'

The debtor could swear an oath before a justice of the peace that he was not worth £10, could not pay the debt, and that he had not made any disposition to defraud his creditors. The oath being sworn, the justice was to give notice to the creditor to appear before the next Quarter Sessions, and if the oath was not then disproved the debtor was normally to be released. However, the creditor could turn up and insist upon continued imprisonment, in which case he was required to pay for the prisoner's reasonable maintenance as ordered by the justices at a maximum rate of eighteen pence per week; if the maintenance was not paid, the debtor was to be released. The debtor was to remain liable to execution against his lands or goods, but not his person; a new *capias* could only issue if the prisoner's oath is proved to be perjured. Various other provisions of the Act dealt with the multifarious abuses involved in imprisonment for debt, and the Act also set up an inquiry into the administration of charities in favour of prisoners. It also required debtors to be kept in prison separated from felons. The Act of 1670–1 is the first of a long line of statutes which at least attempted to grapple specifically with the problem of distressed debtors; the earlier

---

[1] D. Veall, *The Popular Movement for Law Reform 1640–1660* discusses the movement for reform and its effects at pp. 12–17 and 149–51.

[2] 22, 23 Car. II, c. 20.

Elizabethan legislation was concerned with poverty and vaga-
bondage generally, and was not specially concerned with
debtors. Eventually this legislation culminated in 1971[1] in the
abolition of the institution of imprisonment for civil debt,
though the major reform was by the Debtor's Act of 1869.[2]
The final outcome was a complete revolution in the nature
of contractual liability.

The legal consequences of imprisonment

The theoretical consequences of imprisonment for debt by
capias gave rise to some controversy. It was clear that, once the
debtor had been imprisoned, no other process of execution
could be employed against him, and there was no question of
capias issuing again. The imprisonment could be perpetual,
and there was no arrangement for fixing a term corresponding to
some scale of indebtedness. Once released at the instance of the
creditor, proceedings were at an end, no further execution being
possible against the debtor or his property.[3] At common law it
was a subject of controversy whether the death of the imprisoned
debtor left the creditor without any further remedy; it was held
in *Blumfield's Case* (1596)[4] that the creditor could thereafter
levy execution against the deceased debtor's land or goods,
and this view was confirmed by a statute in 1624,[5] though in
1609 in *Foster* v. *Jackson*[6] a long discussion of the theory of
imprisonment divided the court of Common Pleas. Given the
state of the law, various different theoretical views of the nature
of the remedy were possible. Thus one was to say that the
imprisonment itself was in theory a satisfaction for the debt; as
Blackstone put it:

'Confinement is the whole of the debtor's punishment, and
of the satisfaction made to the creditor.'

A more extreme version of this view was that the initial taking
of the debtor into custody is by itself a satisfaction which

---

[1] The Administration of Justice Act, 1970.
[2] 32 and 33 Vict., c. 46.
[3] See Blackstone, III, 415; 13 Hen. VII, M. f. 29, pl. 1, and 27 Hen. VIII, M.
f. 24, pl. 3.
[4] 5 Co.Rep. 86b.
[5] 21 Jac. I, c. 24.
[6] 2 Brownl. and Goulds. 311.

discharges the debt. This view was elaborately argued in a case in 1455,[1] where a bond was conditioned upon the party making satisfaction, and the question at issue was whether this condition had been performed by the taking of the party's body in execution. The decision was that it was not, and this could be made the basis of the theory advanced in *Blumfield's Case*—that the imprisonment of the debtor was merely a pledge for the debt rather than a satisfaction for it.

A more archaic view appears to have possessed enough vitality to cause difficulty in cases where the debtor escaped from custody. When this happened the creditor had an action against the gaoler as a sort of surety for the debt, though the basis of this action was controversial. According to one view, the proper form of action against the gaoler was case, and this existed at common law; another view was that debt was available[2] through the extension by equity of the Statute of Westminster II or a Statute of Richard II.[3] But granted that the gaoler was liable one way or the other, it was a question whether the debtor could ever be retaken into custody. If the taking into custody originally discharged the debtor from liability to his creditor, then it would seem that once he escaped from prison he ought to be free for ever from further proceedings at the creditor's suit, the creditor's rights being confined to an action against the gaoler. This view was taken by Fineux C.J. and the King's Bench in 1498.[4] But this left open the question whether the gaoler was entitled to recapture the prisoner, and if so whether this discharged his liability for the escape. In 1470[5] it was held that the gaoler remained liable, since the debtor was not in prison on the same execution, but a contrary decision was given in 1475 by the Exchequer Chamber;[6] this, however, only applied to negligent escapes, not voluntary wrongful release.[7] There was also some authority that the

---

[1] 33 Hen. VI, M. f. 47, pl. 32.

[2] On this controversy see 42 Edw. III, P. f. 13, pl. 20, 7 Hen. VI, M. f. 9, pl. 5; *Platt* v. *Sheriffs of London* (1550) Plowden 35; *Whiteacres* v. *Onsley* (1562), Plowden 36. *F.N.B.* 210C treats the actions as alternative.

[3] 1 Ric. II, c. 12, in terms gave debt only against the Warden of the Fleet prison. Westminster II, c. 12, only dealt with imprisonment of accountants.

[4] 14 Hen. VII, M. f. 1, pl. 1.

[5] 10 Edw. IV (S.S. 47, Neilson), 92-5.

[6] S.S. Vol. 64, (Hemmant) p. 34.

[7] 10 Edw. IV, T. f. 1, pl. 4.

gaoler could only retake if in hot pursuit,[1] though Fineux C.J. and his companions allowed recapture although the prisoner has escaped from view.[2] If the escape was voluntary then it was certainly the law that no recapture was possible, and the creditor himself did not acquire a right of recapture until it was given by statute in 1696.[3]

Common law and equity

Whereas common law provides damages as a remedy, equity in appropriate circumstances would order specific performance of agreements. The early history of this remedy is peculiarly obscure and lies outside the scope of this book, but it seems clear that specific performance was decreed in the case of contracts to convey lands in the mid-fifteenth century,[4] whether on account of sale or in consideration of marriage. Barbour indeed instances a petition requesting this remedy as early as Richard II's time, and an actual decree in 1456. The evolution of the doctrine that a bargain and sale of lands passes a use to the purchaser is in all probability a development brought about by the readiness of the Chancellor to order specific performance of such contracts, and it is possible that the doctrine in *Doige's Case* (1442) permitting an action for damages at common law where the vendor had conveyed the lands to a third party, arose in order to deal with the situation where the Chancellor had not yet evolved a remedy against the third party and could not compel the conveyance of lands which the vendor no longer possessed. So too the doctrine that a covenant in consideration of marriage or natural affection passes a use is in all probability a consequence of the specific enforcement of marriage dowry contracts in equity.[5] But it is not possible to demonstrate this form of connection directly, for the evolution of the principle that equity treats as done what ought to be done remains uninvestigated, and the absence of much direct evidence of the reasoning employed by the chancellors of the fifteenth century makes investigation difficult if not impossible.

[1] *F.N.B.* 130.
[2] 14 Hen. VII, M. f. 1, pl. 1.
[3] 8 and 9 Will. III, c. 27.
[4] Barbour 122, and cases there cited, Spence, *Equitable Jurisdiction of the Court of Chancery*, I, 643, *H.E.L.* V. 287. See above, p. 277.
[5] See above, pp. 259 and 348.

Chancery jurisdiction is normally referred to a number of distinct principles justifying intervention, and the specific performance of contracts by the Chancellor is categorized in the scheme as an example of jurisdiction in situations in which the common law, by awarding only damages, provides an inadequate remedy. But this can be rather misleading, for it suggests that specific relief was exceptional. This is not correct; all early Chancery jurisdiction involved the coercion of the person who declined to act in accordance with good conscience, and the function of the subpoena in all instances was to compel conscientious behaviour, whatever that might involve, for the avoidance of sin.[1] Hence if conscience required that the defendant pay money,[2] bring an action,[3] make a feoffment,[4] hand over a chattel,[5] or cancel a bond[6] the Chancellor would decree this. Hence the specific performance of contracts was only an illustration of the general mode of proceeding adopted in all instances by the Chancellor, an aspect of the principle that equity acts *in personam*. Furthermore, to award damages as a contractual remedy in Chancery would violate the general principle that the Chancellor only intervened when the common law provided no remedy, and the common law did award damages where an action lay at all. In those cases where the Chancellor did become involved with broken contracts for which the common law provided no remedy at all, there seems to have been no reluctance to make an order for the payment of money, if this was what good conscience required; with the rise of assumpsit, the need for a wider scheme of contractual liability in Chancery disappeared.

Where the petitioner wanted the contract performed, and this could be ordered, it would have been quite anomalous for the chancellor to acquiesce in a wrongful and unconscientious failure to perform a contract, and simply order the payment of damages (even assuming administrative machinery for their assessment). Particularly was this so since at the time the pay-

---

[1] See, for example, 8 Edw. IV, f. 4, pl. 11, 7 Hen. VII, P. f. 1, pl. 2, and St. Germain, *Doctor and Student*, Dial. I, c. 17, where this is assumed.

[2] Barbour 123, 127, 128 et seq.

[3] 2 Edw. IV, P. f. 6, pl. 12.

[4] 37 Hen. VI, T. f. 35, pl. 23.

[5] *H.E.L.* V. 287, and examples there cited.

[6] Barbour 88.

ment of damages was spoken of and viewed as a penal measure,[1] and to order what amounted to self-inflicted punishment would hardly count as ordering conscientious behaviour, which was the function of the decrees issued by the Chancellor.

Clearly the approach of the Chancery to contract differed radically from that of the common law; where the common law provided a remedy for breach of contract the Chancery took steps to see to it that contracts were actually performed, and if at the end of the day the defaulting party found himself in prison, a measure employed by both common law and chancellor as the ultimate weapon, the theory of why he was there differed. At common law all defaulters ended up as debtors and lost their liberty either as a satisfaction to the creditor or as a pledge for payment of what was due. But the defaulting party who ended up in prison on a subpoena was there because of his contempt, and could regain his liberty by purging his contempt. The differing approach of the two systems of jurisprudence meant that the common law in effect gave to the promisor an option to perform his contract or pay damages, which option equity denied. This distinction is well brought out in *Bromage* v. *Gennings* (1617)[2] where prohibition was sought to stop an action brought in the court of the Marches to compel execution of a lease. In the course of the case it was noted that a subpoena was usual in such a case in Chancery. Coke C.J., in criticizing this practice, said,

> 'that this would subvert the intention of the covenantor when he intended it to be at his option whether to lose the damages or perform the lease'.

Serjeant Harris went so far as to say that an award of specific performance was 'against conscience'. Looked at rationally, it seems reasonable to preserve an option not to perform in some cases—for example, in contracts of personal service—and not in others, and in the sixteenth and seventeenth centuries specific performance was largely limited to contracts to convey interests in land. Under the doctrine that a bargain and sale of lands passed a use, which the Statute of Uses executed, the scope for specific performance was necessarily limited in the main to

---

[1] For example, see *The Case of the Thorns*, 6 Edw. IV, M. f. 7, pl. 18.
[2] 1 Rolle 368.

contracts to settle land in consideration of love and affection or marriage, leases and agreements which for one reason or another were not within the concept of a bargain and sale. This may explain the fact that the remedy of specific performance was not much in evidence in our period.[1] Indeed the main contributions of equity to contract law in the sixteenth and seventeenth centuries was the establishment of the compensatory principle in actions on bonds, an ironical fact in view of the court of Chancery's own predilection for specific relief.

[1] See Yale in S.S. Vol. 73 at cii.

XIII

THE STATUTE OF FRAUDS

THE effect of the evolution of the action of assumpsit for breach of promise, and its victory over the action of debt *sur contract*, was to introduce into the common law courts an action for informal promises in which the issue was triable by jury, and not by compurgation which had once been the standard mode of trial both in the communal and in common law courts where a creditor lacked formal proof to support his demand. If the medieval common law, with its restrictive attitude to parole agreements, and its use of compurgation, had been excessively biased in favour of defendants, it was at least arguable that seventeenth-century law had come to be excessively biased in favour of plaintiffs. And in evaluating the law of the time it must always be borne in mind that contemporaries were, by modern standards, extremely litigious, so that opportunities to bring groundless suits were likely to be taken. The contemporary status of litigation is notably illustrated in Aubrey's notes of his life for the year 1656, 'This Yeare, and the last, was a strange year to me, and full of Contradictions: scilicet Love (M.W.)[1] and Lawe-suites'. Such a juxtaposition would hardly be possible today. Litigation indeed came close to a form of sanctioned aggression, and it was an aggressive age. The view that the law could go too far in encouraging litigation produced such bizarre legal doctrines as the *mitior sensus* rule,[2] which attempted to discourage actions on the case for defamation. In the field of contract law the same view prevailed in 1677 when the Statute of Frauds and Perjuries[3] was enacted. The broad policy adopted in this enactment was to require written evidence of important legal transactions as a prerequisite to their enforcement, to insist, that is, on a measure of formality in areas in which wholly informal transactions had come to be legally

---

[1] Mistress M. Wiseman had stolen Aubrey's heart.
[2] Discussed by Fifoot 129; the classic example is *Holt* v. *Astgrigg* (1607) Cro. Jac. 184.
[3] 29 Car. II, c. 3.

effective. Thereby the bringing of groundless suits would become more difficult, though inevitably at the cost of some injustice to plaintiffs unable to produce written evidence. As finally enacted, the statute covered six categories of contract. Five of these were embraced by section 4, which provided that

> 'noe Action shall be brought whereby to charge any Executor or Administrator upon any speciall promise to answere damages out of his owne Estate
> 'or whereby to charge the Defendant upon any speciall promise to answere for the debt default or miscarriages of another person or to charge any person upon any agreement made upon consideration of Marriage
> 'or upon any Contract or Sale of Lands Tenements or Hereditaments or any Interest in or concerning them
> 'or upon any Agreement that is not to be performed within the space of one yeare from the makeing thereof
> 'unlesse the Agreement upon which such Action shall be brought or some Memorandum or Note thereof shall be in Writeing and signed by the partie to be charged therewith or some other person thereunto by him lawfully authorized.'

The sixth was specified by section 16 as contracts for the sale of goods worth more than £10; such contracts were not 'to be allowed to be good',

> 'except the Buyer shall accept part of the Goods soe sold and actually receive the same or give some thing in earnest to bind the bargaine or in part payment, or that some Note or Memorandum in writeing of the said bargaine be made and signed by the partyes to be charged by such Contract or their Agents thereunto lawfully authorized'.

Other parts[1] of the Statute, which contains twenty-four sections, apply broadly the same remedy to conveyances, to leases for more than three years, to devises of land, to declarations and assignments of trusts, and to testaments, and in relation to all these matters the policy of the Statute is clearly stated in the preamble.

[1] Ss. 1, 2, 3, 5, 6, 7, 8, 9, 12, 18, 19, 21, 22.

'For prevention of many fraudulent Practices which are commonly endeavoured to be upheld by Perjury and Subornation of Perjury'.

Other provisions of the Statute do not fall under this policy; they deal with a variety of defects in the law which were reformed by the same enactment; for example, section 10 made lands of *cestui que trust* liable to execution in pursuance of a judgment. The Statute was in fact a general measure of law reform, and its somewhat untidy arrangement is largely explicable by the history of its draftsmanship; thus the last seven sections, all dealing with wills, were all additions by Sir Lionel Jenkins to an earlier draft.

The legislative history and authorship of the Statute

The immediate legislative history of the Statute has been very fully investigated by Hening[1] and Holdsworth.[2] The story begins in 1673 when the House of Lords gave a first reading to 'An Act for preventing many fraudulent practices which are commonly endeavoured to be upheld by perjury and subornation of perjury'.[3] This was probably drafted by Lord Keeper Finch, later Lord Nottingham. It provided that in all actions of assumpsit or debt on promises or agreements by parole there should be a limit to the amount of damages recoverable unless there was a memorandum or note or memorial in writing 'taken at the direction of the parties thereto'. This provision is qualified so as not to apply to actions taken on sales of goods, loans of money, *quantum meruit*, or promises arising by operation of law. The draft does not specify what the limit to damages should be, nor is there in it any requirement of a signature to the writing. The Bill was committed, but nothing further was done after the committee met and adjourned. The same Bill, as amended in Nottingham's handwriting, was reintroduced in April 1675, was read a first and second time and committed; North C.J. and Windham J. were ordered to attend the committee. It was the amendments introduced by this committee which

---

[1] C. D. Hening, 'The Original Drafts of the Statute of Frauds and their Authors', 62 Penn. L.R. 283.

[2] *H.E.L.* VI. 379 and App. I.

[3] Text in Hening and *H.E.L.* VI at 673. On Lord Nottingham's involvement see S.S. Vol. 79, p. 978.

substantially produced the final form of the Statute; however, the Bill lapsed through the prorogation of Parliament after it had been read a third time by the Lords and once by the Commons. Lord Nottingham's scheme for dealing with parole contracts was abandoned entirely by the committee, which substituted, at a meeting on 22 April, the solution finally adopted in Section 4 of the Statute—a list of five types of contract which were not to be sued upon in the absence of a signed memorandum. The immediate author of this new scheme seems to have been Sir Francis North, then Chief Justice of the Common Pleas, who may have been responsible also for the addition of section 16, though the internal evidence of the text suggests otherwise. However, the measure failed to become law, and it was again introduced in October 1675, committed and lapsed, no amendments being made in committee. The same Bill was reintroduced in February 1676 and after some amendment in detail became law as the Statute of Frauds 1677, after the failure of a proposal to make the Act temporary.[1]

So far as contract law is concerned, it is plain that Francis North was responsible for the solution adopted. In *Ashby* v. *Adby* (1678)[2] Lord Nottingham remarked that he had originated the legislation, but that 'it afterwards received some additions and improvements from the Judges and Civilians'. The reference here to the civilians is obviously a reference to the sections dealing with wills, which were the work of Sir Lionel Jenkins, and there is no reason to suppose that the civilians had anything to do with sections 4 and 16.

The Statute and jury trial

It is said by Roger North that Sir Mathew Hale,[3] who died a year before the final enactment,[4] was also in some degree responsible for the Statute. There is indeed some basis for this account, though it was doubted by Holdsworth. Under the Commonwealth Hale had presided over a Commission on Law Reform, the Hale Commission of 1652, which produced extensive schemes for law reform together with draft statutes to

---

[1] Fuller details of the passage of the Act are given by Holdsworth and Hening.
[2] 3 Swanst. 664.
[3] R. North, *Lives of the Norths* I. 141.
[4] Hale died on Christmas Day 1676, after retiring as Chief Justice of the King's Bench in February of that year on account of ill health.

carry these into effect.[1] These included a draft act to make debts assignable, which required the assignment to be 'made in writing under the hand of the party assigning', and it is just possible that this suggested the note or memorandum employed in the Act of 1677. More probably the reference is to cases in which Hale as Chief Justice of the Kings Bench had complained strenuously against the unsatisfactory state of the law. Thus in *Buckridge* v. *Shirley* (1671)[2] he said,

'It is come to that pass now, that every thing is made an action on the case, and actions on the case are become one of the great grievances of the nation; for two men cannot talk together but one fellow or other, who stands in a corner, swears a promise and cause of action. These catching promises must not be encouraged. It were well if a law were made whereby some ceremony, as striking hands etc., were required to every promise that should bind'.

Again in an anonymous case in 1672[3] he said,

'An executor was charged in his own right, upon a promise pretended to be made by him, without any cause or truth. He said he would always require marvellous strong evidence for such a promise and charge. For it had become a great grievance, two men can hardly talk together but a promise is sprung. He said it were well if a law were made that no promise should bind, unless there were some signal ceremony, or that wager of law did lie upon a promise. For the common law was a wise law, that men should wage their law in debts upon contract, and if they proved their reputation twelve handed should be discharged. That so things might be reduced to writing, and brought to certainty. And Slade's Case, which was hardly brought in (for it was by a capitulation and agreement among the judges) has done more hurt than ever it did or will do good'.

[1] See M. Cotterell, Interregnum Law Reform: the Hale Commission of 1652, 83 E.H.R. 689; Lord Somers, *Tracts*, I. 511; D. Veall, *The Popular Movement for Law Reform, 1640–1660, passim.*
[2] Treby's *Reports*, Middle Temple MSS. at 651. I am indebted to Mr. J. H. Baker for these references and transcripts of the texts. I have modernized spelling and punctuation.
[3] ibid. 747.

In another case in the same year he suggested 'the delivery of a piece of money or something like livery of seisin' as a possible solemnity.[1] Hale's view may well have been influential. Somewhat similar dissatisfaction with its formality had been expressed much earlier by Lord Ellesmere in 1603,[2] in relation to parole leases,

> 'that he nothing would help leases paroll in Chancery, and that it were good for the Commonwealth, if no lease paroll were allowed by law, nor promises to be proved by witnesses, considering the plenty of witnesses now a days, which [be] *testes diabolices qui magis fame quam fama moventur*'.

Opinions such as these reflect a general dissatisfaction with the operation of jury trial, and it was this dissatisfaction which gave rise to the desire to reform the law.

As Holdsworth[3] pointed out, the institution of jury trial was, in the seventeenth century, in a transitional state. Originally the jurors constituted a body of local witnesses, charged to speak truth upon an issue joined before them on the pleadings; the rules as to venue were intended to ensure that the jurymen would possess the local knowledge which was needed for them to discharge their function, and many rules of pleading were directed to placing before the jury some matter of fact of an appropriate character—something that is of which 'the country' could have knowledge. Only by slow degrees did the jury change into a collegiate judge of evidence presented to it, and as late as 1670 Vaughan C.J. in his famous opinion in *Bushell's Case*[4] relied heavily upon the contention that the jurors might decide a question of fact on the basis of their private information,

> 'Being returned of the vicinage, whence the cause of action ariseth, the law supposeth them thence to have sufficient knowledge to try the matter in issue (and so they must) though no evidence were given on either side in Court . . .'

---

[1] ibid. 775.
[2] Cary 27, and cf. Vaughan C.J. in *Edgecomb* v. *Dee* (1670) Vaughan 89 at 101.
[3] *H.E.L.* VI. 388 and IX. 177 et seq.
[4] Vaughan 135 at 147.

In seventeenth-century practice evidence was in fact presented to juries, and this could be done on oath,[1] but contemporary rules of law excluded much that would now be admitted, most notably the evidence of the parties themselves.[2] Whilst originally they could not give evidence on oath, they came to be unable to give evidence at all, and the law also excluded the evidence of persons interested in the cause and the spouses of the parties. Nor did the common law, once the practice of calling witnesses before the jury became normal, adopt the canonical rule requiring a minimum of two witnesses for proof of a fact; a single witness or in theory no witness at all would suffice, the plaintiff's declaration providing him with his sole opportunity to set out a set of averments which were not, of course, testable by cross examination or inquisition by the court. Against this background, and the inadequacy of methods of control over the jury, we must set the Statute of Frauds, and it is a mistake to judge the merits of the policy adopted by the Statute simply in the light of the difficulties of interpretation which the lawyers delighted to find in it.

Continental law and the Statute

It has, however, been argued by Rabel[3] with considerable plausibility that the ultimate source of the Statute should be sought abroad in continental legislation, and in particular in the Ordonnance sur la Réforme de la Justice of 1566,[4] commonly known as the Ordonnance de Moulins; in a less developed form the same contention is to be found in Mme J. Hayes's thesis, presented in 1924 to the University of Paris, 'Le Statute of Frauds en droit anglais', though with the qualification 'Bien que ces deux lois soient profondement divergentes . . .' There is no direct evidence of any connection between the Ordinance of 1566 and the other legislation which preceded or followed[5] it in France or elsewhere and the English legislation.

---

[1] See Thayer, *Evidence*, Chs. II and III *passim*, and *H.E.L.* IX.

[2] Settled by 1582; see *Dymoke's Case*, Savile, 34 pl. 81. For explanation see Wigmore, *Evidence*, §§ 575 et seq.

[3] E. Rabel, 'The Statute of Frauds & Comparative Legal History', 63 L.Q.R. 174.

[4] See Jourdan, Decrusy, Isambert, *Recueil général des anciennes lois françaises*, Tome XIV.

[5] Rabel refers to a considerable body of continental legislation some of which preceded and some of which followed the Ordinance of 1566. In particular he

His argument basically turns upon the comparison between the French and the English legislation, or alternatively upon a comparison with the *Édit perpetuel* (1611) of the Archdukes of Flanders which copied the Ordinance of Moulins.[1] The relevant parts of the Ordinance, in a somewhat modified form, were re-enacted in France in Louis XVI's reign in the Ordonnance civile touchant la reformation de la justice, made at Saint Germain-en-Laye in 1667,[2] and Rabel's argument allows for the possibility that this legislation, rather than that of 1566, may have influenced the English legislation. The validity of his argument, which seems to me to be slight, turns essentially upon the detailed consideration of the legislative texts involved.

The Ordonnance de Moulins was a comprehensive measure of reform, and only two of its many articles concern us. Article 54 recites its object in these terms:

'Pour obvier á multiplication de faits que l'on a vû ci-devant entre mis en avant en jugement, sujets à preuve de témoins et reproche d'iceux dont adviennent plusieurs inconveniens et involutions de procés[3]

and ordained

'que doresnavant de toutes choses excédans la somme ou valeur de cent livres pour une fois payer, serront passez contrats pardevant notaires et témoins, par lesquel contrats seulement, sera faite et reçue toute preuve esdites matières, sans recevoir aucune preuves par temoins, outre le contenu au contrat'.[4]

[1] Text in Boiceau, op. cit. xxv.

[2] *Recueil général*, Tome XVII, 103.

[3] Literally 'To avoid the multiplication of issues of fact such as one has seen hitherto brought forward in judgment [i.e. pleaded in legal proceedings], subject to proof by witnesses and challenge by the same from which arises much inconvenience and complication of procedure'.

[4] Literally 'that henceforth for all matters exceeding the sum or value of a hundred *livres* to be paid at one time, there shall be executed contracts before notaries and witnesses by which contracts alone shall be made and accepted all proof in the said matters, without receiving any proofs by witnesses [of matters] outside the contract'.

regards Statutes of Bologna (1453) and Milan in 1498 and 1552 as the immediate progenitors of the French legislation. See generally J. Boiceau (ed. Danty), *Traité de la preuve par témoins en matière civile*, ed. 1759, and J. Brissaud, *A History of French Private Law* (London, 1912), P. Viollet, *Histoire du droit civil français* (Paris, 1893).

This provision cannot be easily rendered into modern English, but its aim is to avoid a confusing situation in which too many issues of fact are brought before a court, these facts being subject to proof and challenge by witnesses. The solution adopted is twofold: first, to require the parties in more important matters to execute contractual documents before witnesses and a notary. Second, these 'contracts' are then to become the sole proof acceptable, and in litigation witnesses are not to be admitted to add or subtract from what is contained within the contractual document. There is little similarity between this and the provisions of the English Statute of Frauds, either in its original or eventual form, nor was the object of article 54 in terms the avoidance of perjury. It is true, however, that Jean Boiceau[1] in his commentary on article 54 of the Ordinance (1582) introduced the idea that the *ratio legis* was in part connected with perjury:

'The reason therefore of this Law is avoid many and diverse affirmations of facts, which could only be proved by witnesses, through which endless pleadings of suits and further pleadings daily arose, which were devised not so much with the intention of truly preserving the right [of the party] as with the tricks and devices of wranglers, which are commonly practised with suborning of false witnesses.'

But this gloss explains that confusion in legal proceedings is the evil against which the law is primarily directed. A century later under Louis XIV a modified version of the same scheme was enacted in L'Ordonnance civile touchant la réformation de la justice. Title XX deals with matters of proof:

'Des faits qui gisent en preuve vocale ou litterale',

and XX.2 provides

'Seront passes actes par devant notaires, ou sous signature privie toutes choses excédant la somme ou valeur de cent livres, même pour depôts volontaires, et ne sera reçu aucune preuve par témoins contre et outre le contenu aux actes, ni sur ce qui seroit allégué avoir été dit avant, lors ou depuis les actes'.[2]

---

[1] Cited by Rabel at p. 177; see Danty, *Traité de la preuve par témoins en matière civile*, p. 25, for the original latin text, which Rabel translated very defectively.

[2] *Recueil général*, Tome XVIII at p. 137. Literally 'let there be deeds executed

This modifies the system by allowing proof by a private signed document, and strengthens the requirement by including contracts of deposit, though there were exceptions to this.[1] The *Édit perpétuel* of the Archdukes of Flanders, enacted in 1611 in imitation of the Ordinance of Moulins, may to some extent have suggested changes incorporated in 1667. It provided for the use of signed documents as an alternative to documents executed before notaries and witnesses or before other public persons, and it expressly applied to testamentary dispositions, contracts of marriage, and all sorts of agreements and dispositions (*toutes espéces de conventions ou dispositions*).[2] The rule forbidding the variation by oral evidence of the terms of a written contract is also strengthened, but again there is only a very general similarity with the English legislation.[3]

The other relevant provision of the Ordinance of Moulins is article 58. This has indeed some connection with the avoidance of perjury, but there the similarity ends; it deals with arrangements for the registration of gifts:

> 'Et pour oster à l'avenir toutes occasions de frauds et de doutes qui pourroient estre mues entre nos sujets pour l'insinuation des donations qui seront ci-aprés faites, avons ordonné que d'oresnavant toutes donations faites entre-vifs, mutuelles reciproque, onéreuses, en faveur de mariage et autres, de quelque forme et qualité qu'elles soient faites entre-vifs, comme dit est seront insinuées és greffes de nos sieges ordinaires de l'assiette des choses données, et de la demeurance des parties dans quatre mois.'[4]

[1] Dealt with in Tit. XX. 3–5.

[2] Boiceau, op. cit. xxv; the limit was 300 *livres* Artois, and there is no reference to fraud or perjury as the *motif*.

[3] Earlier legislation is printed in Boiceau. A Statute of Bologna in 1453 (op. cit. xxxvi) forbids proof by witnesses for debts of over 100 *livres*, and this may well have influenced the French legislation.

[4] 'And to avoid for the future all occasions for frauds and doubts which might be raised between our subjects on account of the registration of gifts hereafter to be made, we have ordained that from henceforth all gifts made *inter-vivos*, mutual, reciprocal, onerous, in favour of marriage and others, of whatsoever form and

before notaries, or under private signature, for all things exceeding the sum or value of a hundred pounds, even for voluntary deposits, and let there not be received any proof by witnesses against or in addition to what is contained in the deed, whether that which is alleged to have been said is before, at the time of or since the deeds'.

There is no possible direct connection between this and the Statute of Frauds. All that can be said is that both French and other continental legislation was dealing with problems over the precise scope to be allowed to proof by witnesses on the one hand, and proof by writing or registered instrument on the other, and this not only in relation to contracts but also in relation to other matters, such as gifts and marriage articles, and even over the proof of monastic profession.[1] In a literate society where not everyone tells the truth there are inevitably problems of proof which will call for regulation; thus in the English world of property law the Statute of Enrolments of 1536 attempted to provide for registration of transfers of real property, and in the Interregnum in England the Hale Commission produced elaborate schemes for registration of gifts and transfers of property.[2] So far as contract law is concerned, the recognition of the actionability of informal agreements in a society where important contracts had normally been reduced to writing generated throughout Europe a reactionary movement, which insisted upon a requirement of formality once again. There is a sense then in which the English legislation forms part of a European phenomenon, but more direct influence is improbable. This improbability is increased by the fact that English legal arrangements differed considerably from continental ones, so that the legislation had a different context; for example, in England commoners could use seals, whereas in France they could not.[3]

The contracts listed in section 4 of the Statute of Frauds

Until the decision in *Leroux* v. *Brown* (1852)[4] it was settled that failure to comply with the provisions of section 4 rendered a contract void, not merely unenforceable, and the distinction was perceived by contemporaries and the point argued.[5] The

[1] See article 55 of the Ordinance of Moulins.
[2] See Somers *Tracts*, I. 515.
[3] The principle acted upon in the Ordinance of Moulins passed into the French Code Civil (arts. 1341 et seq.) and into the Prussian and Italian Codes.
[4] 12 C.B. 801.
[5] *Mowbray* v. *Bacon* (1680) S.S. Vol. 79, p. 852.

quality they be made *inter-vivos* as aforesaid, there shall be registered within four months in the record offices of our ordinary seats of justice the disposition [or, the location] of the things given, and the residence of the parties.'

selection of the five types of contract listed in section 4 for this drastic treatment seems at first sight somewhat curious, and it is arguable that no general principle lies behind the list; such explanations as have been offered seem unsatisfactory.[1] However, a certain unity becomes apparent if the Statute of Frauds is seen as a profoundly reactionary measure so far as contract law is concerned. We have seen how the rise of assumpsit involved in part the recognition of new contractual liabilities at common law, and in part the mere substitution of a new form of action for older mechanisms for the enforcement of common law obligations. The unifying feature of the types of contract listed in section 4 is that they became actionable at common law through the innovatory and not the substitutionary effect of the new action. Parole agreements to make marriage gifts to guarantee debts, to convey land, to perform contracts of service, to answer for the liabilities of the deceased—all such contracts were not recognized at common law at all through the medium of the older remedies unless formalized by sealed instrument. The Statute of Frauds put the clock back, substituting only the signature for the seal. An even more reactionary policy would have been to require written evidence in all cases; instead the legislature compromised by leaving matters as they were in relation to a category of less momentous contracts, defined by exclusion. Taking into account section 17, the major classes of contracts left out of the Statute are bailments, loans, the less important wholly executory contracts for the sale of goods, and all but very future-looking contracts of service; most service contracts would be of much shorter duration than one year. Although perhaps never very clearly thought out, there may be something approaching a principle involved here — one not very different from the doctrine of part-performance which evolved later.

Within section 4 the first two categories—special promises by personal representatives making them liable *de bonis propriis* and promises by way of guarantee—both involve the assumption by the promisor of a liability which is fundamentally that of another. Such liability was first recognized in Henry VIIIs reign, and could be wholly gratuitous.[2] It is possible that the

[1] See *H.E.L.* VI. 392, Rabel, op. cit. 185.
[2] See above, p. 265.

special promise by an executor or administrator was included in deference to the views of Sir Mathew Hale, for it was in just such a case that he was provoked to call for more formality in the passage already quoted from the case in 1672.[1] Actions of this kind had a somewhat controversial history, which continued until Lord Mansfield's time.[2] Normally, of course, the action against an executor or administrator would charge him in his representative capacity, *de bonis testatoribus* and judgment would be against the goods of the deceased, the residue of which the representative could keep if there was no residuary bequest. Actions charging the executor *de bonis propriis* could only be brought on the averment of a promise by the representative supported by good consideration[3]—normally consideration of forbearance to sue for a debt or legacy—and it was probably the law in the 1670s that in such actions no averment of assets was needed.[4] This state of the law, coupled with the fact that representatives must often have been harassed by creditors and legatees, and tempted to make some incautious promise to buy peace,[5] may provide an explanation for the feeling that some special protection was needed in this area, and insistence upon formality would serve to prevent actions being taken on promises never seriously intended. Another possible explanation is suggested by the curious wording of the Statute. The sort of promise so far discussed is more naturally described as a promise 'to pay a legacy' or 'to pay a debt'; the Statute, how-ever, talks of a promise 'to answere damages out of his own estate'. It is just possible that the reference is to a practice under which creditors agreed not to oppose a grant of letters of administration or probate, there being grounds for such opposition, in return for a promise by the executor or admini-strator to guarantee in effect the payment of debts; I have not, however, found evidence to support this conjecture.[6]

There is a further possibility—that one type of special prom-ise envisaged was a promise by an executor to guarantee the payment of legacies or debts in return for an undertaking by the

[1] See above, p. 603.   [2] See above, p. 440.

[3] *Forth* v. *Stanton* (1668) 1 Wms. Saund. 210, 2 Keb. 465, 1 Lev. 262. cf. *Russel* v. *Haddock* (1666) 1 Lev. 188, 1 Sid. 294.

[4] *Davis* v. *Reyner* (1671) 2 Lev. 3, 1 Vent. 120, and above, p. 441.

[5] As in *Frederick* v. *Wynne* (1715) 2 Eq. Cas. Abr. 456.

[6] See for a later period *Tomlinson* v. *Gill* (1756) Amb. 330.

testator in his lifetime not to alter his will, under which the executor was to benefit. Such a promise was regarded as binding in law and equity.[1]

The prevalence of contracts to make marriage gifts and their importance sufficiently explains their inclusion;[2] furthermore the very nature of the delicate negotiations preceding a marriage provide a clear rationale for the insistence upon written evidence; the inclusion of contracts for the sale of interests in realty explains itself, and falls into line with the policy of the earlier Statute of Enrolments of 1536, which required the registration of bargains and sales of land. More curious is the contract not to be performed within one year. It is just possible that this category is borrowed from Scotland, though there is no direct evidence of this. For in seventeenth-century Scots law contracts of service for more than one year required proof by writ.[3] But on the other hand, as pointed out by Lord Holt in *Smith* v. *Westhall* (1697):[4]

'the design of the statute was, not to trust to the memory of witnesses for a longer time than one year',

and this rationale does not conform to the rule of Scots law.

Sale of goods and the Statute of Frauds

The provision dealing with the sale of goods plainly represents a distinct provision which looks as if it has been added to a draft by a different author from the draftsman of section 4, and in particular the words dealing with the effect of non-compliance contrast sharply. Contracts which do not conform are not 'to be allowed to be good'. This difference was eventually to be made the basis for an argument that the effect of the two sections differed, section 4 making contracts unenforceable and section 16 making them void.[5] But this idea was only developed in the nineteenth century, for the original view was that both sections rendered offending contracts void. The source

---

[1] *Chamberlain* v. *Chamberlain* (1678) 2 Freeman 34, 2 Eq. Cas. Abr. 43.

[2] Originally this was thought to include promises to marry; see *Philpott* v. *Wallet* (1682) 3 Lev. 65, Freeman K.B. 541. But this view was abandoned: see *Harrison* v. *Cage* (1697) 1 Ld. Raym. 386, 1 Salk. 24, 12 Mod. 214.

[3] See Erskine, *Institutes*, III, Tit. II, *Introduction to Scottish Legal History* (Stair Society, 1958), p. 261, Stair, *Institutes*, Tit. X.

[4] 1 Ld. Raym. 316.

[5] *H.E.L.* VI. 386 n. 4 discusses the case law.

of section 16 cannot be established with any certainty. The class of contract affected, contracts for the sale of goods worth more than £10 does not seem to be derived from any foreign model, and the requirement of writing is no doubt transferred from section 4. The alternatives to writing—earnest, part payment, or acceptance and receipt of part of the goods—may be derived from William Sheppard's *Action on the Case for Deeds*, which was published in 1663 and again in 1675 and 1680.[1] In this somewhat disorderly work Sheppard, discussing consideration, wrote,

> 'If the contract be by word of mouth, or by writing not sealed and delivered, if there be no consideration, or no good consideration in it, it is no effect at all . . . But if one sell me a horse, or other thing for money, or other valuable consideration, and the thing is to be delivered to me at a certain day, and by our agreement a day is set for the payment of the money, or all or part of the money is paid in hand, or I give earnest money (albeit be but a penny) to the seller, or I take the thing bought by agreement into my possession, where no money is paid, earnest given, or day set for the payment; in all these cases there is a good bargain and sale of the thing, and the property is altered.'

This muddled passage conflates the rule requiring consideration with the late medieval rules[2] dealing with the perfection of a contract of sale and the passing of property—that is a right to possession—to the buyer. It could also be that there is some civilian influence, either through earlier common law cases or directly, but of this there is no real evidence.[3]

The interpretation of the Statute of Frauds: part performance

The interpretation gave rise to an immense body of case law, every word being subjected to minute and largely uninteresting

---

[1] On William Sheppard see the indifferent article in the *D.N.B.* and *H.E.L.* V. 391. Sheppard, a somewhat obscure figure, was admitted to the Middle Temple in 1620, and became a Sergeant in 1656. He died *c.* 1675, and was the author of a considerable number of law books, including possibly *The Touchstone of Common Assurances.*

[2] See above, p. 166.

[3] There is a certain similarity between the Statute and the law of Justinian.

discussion. Of little intellectual interest, this corpus of case law lies outside our period and its intricacy is of little relevance to an assessment of the merits of the Statute, for it is a characteristic of the common law system that the courts encrust any statute with an untidy jumble of legal decisions. Two issues of interest did, however, emerge which are related to the historical understanding of the Statute. The first is that the court of Chancery radically modified the operation of the Statute by evolving the doctrine of part-performance; the second is that it came to be suggested that the proper interpretation of the Statute was to remove the necessity of showing consideration where the agreement could be proved by written evidence.

The equitable doctrine of part-performance is something of a mystery. Although the first clear case applying the doctrine is *Butcher* v. *Stapley* (1686),[1] a decision of Jeffreys L.C., it is clear from *Hollis* v. *Edwards* (1683)[2] that the doctrine was by then in some form known.

> 'Bills were exhibited to have an execution of parole agreements touching leases of houses, and set forth that in confidence of these agreements the plaintiffs expended great sums of money in and about the premises, and laid the agreements to be, that it was agreed the agreements shall be reduced to writing'.

In discussion the Lord Keeper distinguished between necessary repairs and improvements, and money laid out merely at the fancy and humour of the plaintiff. No clear decision emerged, but plainly the basic ideas involved are appreciated. Numerous cases after *Butcher* v. *Stapley* illustrate the doctrine, and it was approved in the House of Lords in *Wankford* v. *Fotherby* (1694)[3] and again in *Lester* v. *Foxcroft* (1700).[4] In *Floyd* v. *Buckland* (1703)[5] and again in *Oldham* v. *Litchford* (1705)[6] it is said that Lord Nottingham made a decree giving effect to the doctrine.

> 'Where a deed was sealed for security for money borrowed, and the deed being absolute, the defendant promised to seal

---

[1] 1 Vern. 363, 1 Eq. Cas. Abr. 21.
[2] 1 Vern. 159.
[3] 2 Vern. 322, 2 Freeman 201.
[4] Colles P.C. 108.
[5] 2 Freeman 268.
[6] 2 Freeman 285.

such a defeasance, and afterwards refusing, a bill was preferred to compel him, and though he insisted upon the statute of frauds and perjuries, he was decreed to seal a defeasance though there was no agreement in writing for that purpose.'

In the second of these cases the transaction was said to have involved a mortgage; the act of part-performance may therefore have been either the loan of money or the conveyance of land. Lord Nottingham died in 1682 and sat little in the last year of his life; the decision was therefore very close to the Statute indeed.

It has been suggested[1] with some plausibility that the doctrine of part performance should not be viewed as an innovation whereby equity evaded the Statute; rather the Statute had never been intended to apply to contracts which had been in part executed and where equity had, before 1677, decreed specific performance. The draftsman had merely failed to make this clear. More simply the thesis is that the Statute was passed to reform common law procedure alone. So far as the precise text of section 4 is concerned, it speaks of 'actions' to 'charge' defendants, language plainly more appropriate to actions at common law; this might seem to provide some textual support for confining the operation of the Statute to the common law courts. But in no case is this point made. In *The Earl of Feversham* v. *Watson* (1677)[2] there is a curious statement by North C.J. to the effect that

'The Chancery will never force the execution of an estate, but either where the agreement is in writing, or else where a valuable consideration is paid or performed of one part, and it must not be a trifling consideration, as the payment of twenty shillings or the like: for this Court will not compel the execution or an estate thereupon where the agreement is not in writing'.

This statement by the man who may have drafted section 4 suggests that the idea that part-performance as an alternative

[1] E. B. Sugden, *A Practical Treatise of the Law of Vendors and Purchasers*, 8th ed. (1830), pp. 70 et seq., G. P. Costigan, 'The Date and Authorship of the Statute of Frauds', 26 H.L.R. 329 at 343, D.E.C. Yale in S.S. Vol. 73 at ciii.
[2] 2 Freeman 35.

to writing was then recognized in the Chancery as a pre-requisite to specific performance, and that the intention was that this should continue to be so; this would entirely explain the silence of the Statute on the matter, though at this time 'writings' might mean documents under seal. Unfortunately the other early cases do not provide any clear *rationale* for the doctrine.

It seems, however, to have been appreciated from the start that the Statute could work injustice and protect frauds, particularly when an agreement had been acted upon either by the expenditure of a large sum of money,[1] the delivery of possession,[2] or the celebration of a marriage.[3] This was most obvious when the action involved possessed an irrevocable character, which was classically the case where a marriage had taken place in reliance upon a parole contract of endowment. The notion that a change of circumstances should give rise to an equity has always been influential, and still is, and there may have been civilian influence upon the Chancery to accept the notion of an agreement becoming binding *interventu rei*.[4] There is also some indication in the early case law of two[5] other approaches to the problem of avoiding injustice in executed contracts. One was to allow the recovery of money paid, a solution only, of course, applicable where the act of part-performance was payment of money. The other was to treat an agreement to put a concluded parole contract into writing as itself enforceable as a pre-contract outside the Statute,[6] such a pre-contract being itself possibly actionable at common law. But this conceptual device came to be disapproved.[7] Behind these developments clearly lay a general policy of interpreting the Statute in such a way as to avoid and not assist the frauds against which the law was directed.[8]

---

[1] *Hollis* v. *Edwards* (1683) 1 Vern. 159, *Foxcroft* v. *Hunter* (1700) Colles P.C. 108.

[2] *Butcher* v. *Stapley* (1686) 1 Vern. 363, 1 Eq. Cas. Abr. 21.

[3] *Cookes* v. *Mascall* (1690) 2 Vern. 34, 200; *Wankford* v. *Fotherby* (1694) 2 Vern. 322, 2 Freeman 201; *Halfpenny* v. *Ballet* (1699) 2 Vern. 373

[4] See above, p. 383.

[5] *Hollis* v. *Edwards* (1683) 1 Vern. 159; *Leake* v. *Morrice* (1683) 2 Cha. Cas, 135.

[6] Sugden called this a 'floating opinion' of North.

[7] *Whitchurch* v. *Bevis* (1786) 2 Bro. C.C. 565.

[8] Illustrated also in *Thynne* v. *Thynne* (1684) 1 Vern. 296; *Alsopp* v. *Patten* (1687) 1 Vern. 472.

The interpretation of the Statute of Frauds: writing as an alternative to consideration

Lord Mansfield, in the well-known case of *Pillans* v. *Van Mierop*[1] (1765), suggested that at least in mercantile contracts writing and consideration were to be regarded as alternatives, and referred this notion to the Statute of Frauds,

'I take it that the ancient notion about the want of consideration was for the sake of evidence only; for when it is reduced into writing, as in covenants, specialties, bonds etc. there is no objection to the want of consideration. And the Statute of Frauds proceeded upon the same principle'.

This view was rejected in the opinion of Skynner C.B. and the Barons and Common Pleas judges advising the House of Lords in *Rann* v. *Hughes* (1778),[2] upon the ground that the Statute of Frauds merely operated negatively and did not give rise to liabilities which had not existed at common law before.[3] On the basis simply of the text of the Statute there is indeed no basis for Lord Mansfield's view, for the text does not mention consideration at all. Nevertheless there is a certain plausibility in the idea that the change in social practice brought about by the rise in the use of signed documents, as contrasted with sealed documents, coupled with the change in the law brought about by the Statute of Frauds, made it appropriate to review the place of the doctrine of consideration in the law of contract, especially if the rationale of that doctrine was to protect persons from being legally liable in consequence upon unconsidered words. This was the argument used by Wilmot J. in *Pillans* v. *Van Mierop*,

'There was no radical defect in the contract for want of consideration. But it was made requisite in order to put

[1] 3 Burrow 1663.

[2] 4 Brown. P.C. 27, 7 T.R. (Durnford and East) 350n. This case had been decided in the plaintiff's favour by Lord Mansfield, whose decision was upheld by the full court in banc on a motion for a new trial. The case came in error before the Exchequer Chamber where the Common Pleas judges and the Barons of the Exchequer reversed the King's Bench. Error was then brought to the House of Lords, where it was finally argued on 13 and 14 May 1778. The Lords took the opinion of the judges of the Exchequer Chamber, who advised unanimously in favour of upholding their own opinion, and the Lords therefore affirmed the decision of the Exchequer Chamber. See the Lords Journals for 1777 and 1778 at 259, 289, 337, 413, 455, 474, 483, and 485.

[3] Mr. Treitel's suggestion that the decision turned merely upon the Statute of Frauds (*Contract*, 62) seems incorrect in view of the opinion of Skynner C.B.

THE STATUTE OF FRAUDS

people upon attention and reflection and to prevent obscurity and uncertainty; and in that view, either writing or certain formalities were required . . . Therefore it was intended as a guard against rash inconsiderate declarations . . .'[1]

We have seen how the doctrine of consideration in its origin excluded from actionability promises which lacked a good reason, promises in a sense irrational, and how historically there is a basis for the interpretation placed upon the doctrine by Mansfield's court of King's Bench. But to allow the Statute to modify the law in so radical a manner involves an approach to the handling of legislation which is basically alien to the common law system, under which, at least in modern times, legislation is not assimilated into the system.

Lord Mansfield was no innovator in legal matters, though the contrary is often supposed, and his ideas commonly involved no more than a bold and striking affirmation of views expressed earlier by others. The view he and his brethren took of the function of consideration was current earlier. Thus in an elaborate unpublished work on contract law Chief Baron Gilbert, who died in 1726, explains the absence in the common law of solemn forms of verbal contract in this way:[2]

'but in our law we have no solemn forms in our verbal contracts as they had.[3] And the reason is manifest because our law respects the consideration only and the contract is invalid if founded upon no consideration. And therefore there was no need to establish solemn forms to shew whether the party intended to be obliged or not, for such serious intention was manifest from the consideration . . .'

The explanation of the irrelevance of consideration to contracts under seal was the corollary of this, and had long been common

---

[1] The context is a discussion of the doctrine that a nude pact does not oblige, and there are references to Vinnius, Grotius, and Pufendorf. Pufendorf's *Of the Law of Nature and Nations*, published in England in translation by the Oxford University Press in 1710, was much read and very influential. Pufendorf in Bk. III, Ch. V, ss. ix–xi. discusses the status of the promise made without a cause in terms which easily fitted the common law's conception of the promise lacking consideration; the reference to 'rash inconsiderate declarations' echoes a passage from Connanus quoted by Pufendorf.

[2] B.M. MS. Hargrave 265 at f. 65b. See also f. 396–40a. I have modernized the punctuation.

[3] i.e. the Romans. The reference is to the forms of the stipulation.

form. All that was needed was the modest step of assimilating the written contract to the sealed, and for this too there was some support, since it was not uncommon to refer to 'writings' without differentiating sealed and signed documents. And if we can rely upon North C.J.'s statement in *The Earl of Feversham* v. *Watson*,[1] there was at that date a practice in the Chancery of treating writing and consideration as alternatives, though this reference to 'writing' could be merely an example of a failure to distinguish clearly between signed and sealed documents. Viewed from a historical point of view, the Statute of Frauds gave the courts an opportunity which Lord Mansfield took rather too late; whether the provision of this opportunity was in any real sense the intention in 1677 is hardly a matter capable of strict proof.

The missed opportunity

The legislation of 1677 can thus be seen as critical in the evolution of English contract law, for it provided an opportunity for a general revision of the basic division of contracts: contracts by parole which required consideration, and contracts by specialty, which did not. A new look at this dichotomy could have led either to the emergence of a new body of law around the signed written contract or to the assimilation of such contracts to contracts under seal. The opportunity was not taken; by the time of *Case* v. *Barber* (1681)[2] the courts are moving towards the view that the Statute is not to be allowed a radical significance. It is in some ways remarkable and regrettable that this revision never took place. The year 1677 is also significant because the Statute of Frauds can be seen as a reactionary measure, in part aimed at restoring the substance of the old common law to what it had been in the medieval period before the rise of assumpsit; 1677 was the year in which a development which we today view as representing progress was in part reversed by contemporaries who took a less sanguine view. The passing of the Statute also coincided in time with the attack by Chancery upon the penal bond, and the recognition in consequence of the compensatory principle, already recognized in assumpsit throughout contract law. This too was a

[1] 2 Freeman 35.
[2] T. Raymond 450.

development which ought, in an ideal world, to have provoked something more radical in the way of doctrinal revision. But it is a characteristic of an intensely historically minded system of traditional law that such revisions are rare events, and so these things were not to be. It was many years before any basic modification of categories took place through the change in the nineteenth century to a conception of obligations arising out of a bilateral contract as contrasted with the essentially unilateral promise supported by consideration, and through the reception into the common law of a body of civilian doctrine.[1]

[1] See Simpson, 'Innovation in Nineteenth Century Contract Law' 91 L.Q.R. 247.

EPILOGUE

IN a system of law organized as the common law was, and indeed is, rapid change is more or less ruled out; law must evolve since evolution is the condition of its existence as law. So far as contract law is concerned, anything which might be called radical change is inhibited by the fact that the basic notions which underlie the social institution of contract in Western Europe were settled a very long time ago, and do not change over the centuries. If Bracton or Littleton could return and study Treitel or Cheshire and Fifoot on Contract they would, of course, find much to surprise and interest them, but they would start their reading with a firm grasp of what the subject was all about. During the period in which the action of assumpsit came to be the regular contractual remedy there were nevertheless important developments, more important in all probability than anything which has happened since then in the evolution of the common law of contract. We can appreciate these developments better if they are seen as falling into a number of distinct categories. *Firstly*, there was an important shift in jurisdiction, whereby the common law progressively extended its scope so as to include a wide category of informal agreements, agreements that is by parole; as the common law courts took on more contractual business, other jurisdictions inevitably contracted. *Secondly*, and in consequence, the common law courts evolved a mass of legal doctrine—in particular the doctrine of consideration—to provide the conceptual apparatus with which the new business was to be handled. We must look forward to the nineteenth century for any period as productive of contractual doctrine, and what was then introduced had, because of the nature of the system, to be conflated with the accumulated doctrine of the past. *Thirdly*, there was a procedural change of great importance in the establishment of jury trial as the normal mode of settling contract disputes, a procedural development which lasted until the late nineteenth and early twentieth centuries and the virtual disappearance of jury trial in civil actions. *Fourthly*, there was change in the mode of execution, the first steps being taken towards an eventual abolition of the institution of imprisonment as the ultimate sanction against the contract breaker. *Fifthly*, the evolution of assumpsit and the intervention of the Chancery began to shift the centre of gravity of contract law away from the conditioned bond, and at the same time led to the general acceptance of the compensatory principle in contract law. *Finally*, and at the end of our period, the Statute of Frauds tried to put back into the law of the new action some of the insistence on formality which had characterized the earlier common law's approach to contract. These were all very significant changes, and all but the fourth can be viewed as developments internal to the common law, though the mechanism of the last was legislation.

APPENDIX OF CASES

CASE No. 1   *The Case of the Humber Ferryman* (1348)[1]

Bylle de transgressio   John de S queritur per billam qe G de S certein iour et an a B sur Humbre il avoit empris de carier son Jument pris etc. en son batew outre lewe de Humbre sain et sauf per lou le dit G, surchargeant la dite bateu dautres chivalx per quel surcharge le dit Jument perist, a tort et as damages etc. Richmond iugement de bille que suppose en nous null tort einz prove qil avera accion per brief de Covenaunt plus que per voie de trespas per que etc. Bankwell, il semble que vous lui fistez trespas quant vous surchargiez le batew per qi son Jument perist etc. per qi respondez Richmond de rien coupable prest etc. et alii econtra etc.

Bille de transgressio   John de Burton se plaint per bille que G de F, certein iour et an, a B sur humbre, avoit enpris a carier son Jument etc. en son batel outre lewe del humbre sane et sure, per lou le dit B surcharge son batell dez auters chivalx per quel surcharge son jument perist, a tort et as damages Richmond iugement de bille que suppose en nous null tort mez prove qil avera accion per voie de Covenaunt et nemye per voie de Transgressio per que etc. Bankwell il semble que vous luy fistez transgressio quaunt vous surchargiez vostre batell per qi son jument perist per que respondez Richmond de rien coupable prist.[2]

John of Burton made his plaint by bill that G of F, on a certain day and year, at B on the Humber, had undertaken to carry his mare in his boat over the water of the Humber safe and sound, whereas the said B overloaded his boat with other horses through which overloading the mare perished to his wrong and damages. RICHMOND: Judgment of the bill which supposes no wrong [*tort*] in us but proves

---

[1] First text from Bodleian Library M.S. Bodl. 364, f. 90b. Second text from MS. Exeter College, Oxford. 134, f. 1v. Both transcribed by Mr. G. D. G. Hall, second text translated.

[2] The incident probably occurred between North and South Ferriby where the ancient route crosses the Humber.

that he will have an action by way of covenant and not by way of trespass. BANKWELL J.: It seems that you did him a trespass when you overloaded your boat whereby his mare perished; therefore answer. RICHMOND: Not guilty, ready.

CASE No. 2   *The Parker's Case* (1465)[1]

A writ of annuity was brought by a man, and he claimed an annuity in respect of [*per cause del*] the office of park keeper granted to him for term of life to have such annuity, and this for keeping the office of parker. And it was pleaded by the defendant how this office was granted to the plaintiff etc., and to have so much etc., and that there had existed such an office there from a time whereof memory does not run, and that all men who had held the office of parker had also had the guardianship of the woods and the savage beasts as well as the park itself. And that on such a day, to wit the second day of July in the second year of the present King up to the fourteenth day of July next following, twenty-two savage beasts were killed through the negligence of the plaintiff by strangers unknown to the defendant, and that throughout this time the aforesaid keeper of the park was negligent in this matter. And he demanded judgment whether the action lay. And this plea was challenged upon the ground that there was nothing shown whereby the plaintiff ought to lose his annuity, for it is shown that the wild beasts [*savages*] were not killed by the advice or consent of the plaintiff, but by strangers, against whom the plaintiff will have no action, but the defendant can have his remedy. . . . YONGE: for the defendant. It appears that by our plea that there is default in keeping and negligence in the plaintiff in his office, for it is shown how, through his negligence in the performance of his office, and through his default from a certain day to another, so many wild beasts were taken and killed by strangers, in which case this negligent keeping of his in his office will make him lose his fee. . . . CHOKE J.: The defendant's pleading seems good enough, for by the plea of the defendant there appears default in the plaintiff in the performance of his office, for if through the plaintiff's negligence in park keeping the wild beasts in the park or alternatively the woods are wasted, it is not reason to give him his fee, for the parker is bound to keep reasonably. But to say that he should be there every day, this he is not bound to do as it seems to me, but it suffices for him to occupy the office three or four days a week, and not to be there each day. For if he is guarding the park and performing his office three times in four days or three days a week, this is sufficient keeping for him. DANBY C.J.: It is hard to take issue on the matter alleged by the defendant unless he says more.

[1] Text from Y.B. 5 Edw. IV, Long Quinto f. 26.

CHOKE J.: Yes sir, issue can be taken on this and it can be traversed perfectly well, for if it be as the defendant has said—that through the negligence of the plaintiff etc., and through his negligent keeping the defendant's park is wasted—it is reason that the parker be punished for his default, and this can only be done through the extinction of his office and of his annuity, for through nonfeasance of an office the officer will lose his annuity, and so will it be if he misuses it. ... [CHOKE goes on to reject the argument based on the defendant's having an alternative remedy against the poachers.] NEDHAM J.: A parker is not bound to be in the park every day, but to guard it reasonably suffices for him, for on feast days or at the week-end he ought to be at divine service. And also at night he is not bound to guard, but to take his rest, and also each day to take his meals. And at such times, and other reasonable times he is not to answer nor to be punished, nor kept from his annuity for non-feasance or failure to keep at such times, for he is not bound each day to guard it, but on reasonable days and at reasonable times. And also if a number of people come against him with force, six or eight or twenty against him in the park to take wild beasts or to destroy the park, where this is against his will and where he cannot deal with this or repel them [he is not liable], for neither law nor reason compels him to fight, and drive them out with force, for he is not capable of doing so. But if he does his part reasonably in accordance with his ability, this is sufficient. And he is not bound each day, or any day, to find six or seven men, or more or less, to guard the park, but he is bound solely in his own person that he should do what is reasonable in his own person, and certain days and reasonable times suffice for him. For no law compels him to do more. But if at reasonable times or days the park is wasted through his default or negligence, then it is in accord with reason that he should answer for this, and for such cause and such default he can lose his office. For in *Brandon's Case* recently concerning the Marshalsey he guarded his office day and night, but he misused his office, for he let several condemned prisoners go at large, and this by his own act and negligence. And for this he lost his office for term of life, which he held through previous grant, for the grantor entered into the office and granted it to another. [He goes on to discuss the position of a gaoler.] So it is in the aforesaid case of a parker, he will answer for his negligence and default, for he will be punished if the park be wasted through his default at a reasonable time, or through his negligence. Thus this is a proper issue, namely to show that they were killed by strangers unknown to him at an unreasonable time— for example at night—or at some other time in the day by a multi-tude and by force, *sans ceo que* they were killed by his negligence or his default, and this will be a good issue, for he will answer for his negligence and default. . . . DANBY C.J.: How can the pleading be in these words—that through the negligence of the plaintiff the wild beasts were taken and killed by persons unknown? YONGE: The pleading is, that the party the plaintiff from such a day to such a day, namely within twelve days, one after the other, *custodire parcem praedictum neglexit*, during which time twelve wild beasts were taken and killed by strangers. DANBY C.J.: It is hard to uphold this pleading, for this is not certain matter, and what do you mean by this word *neglexit*? YONGE: That he was negligent in the guarding of this park.

TOTA CURIA: That is not an issue, for *neglexit* means that he did not guard [*denia a garder*] the park from such a day to such a day. DANBY C.J.: It is well that you pay some more attention to this pleading, for to say this is uncertain—that is that he did not guard the park from such a day to such a day. YONGE: Then we will say that from such a day to such a day *parcem praedictum non custodivit*, and in the mean time the wrong was done etc. DANBY C.J.: This is the better pleading, and much more certain etc. [Here the case ends, so presumably the amended plea was accepted by the court.]

CASE No. 3   *Anon.* (1441)[1]

In a writ of trespass on his case the plaintiff counted how he made a bargain with the defendant to the effect that the defendant should enfeoff the plaintiff of certain lands of which the defendant was then seised before a certain day, and how the day is passed, and that he has not enfeoffed him, a tort, and to his damage, etc. MARKHAM: This bargain sounds in covenant more than in trespass. Therefore show what you have of the covenant. Fortescue showed nothing. ASCOGH: It seems that this bargain is entirely a covenant, for if I make a bargain with a carpenter to build me a house before a certain day, which he does not do, on such a nonfeasance I shall not have a writ of trespass but an action of covenant if I have a specialty. And otherwise I am without a remedy. But if a carpenter makes my house and makes it badly on such a misfeasance I shall have a writ of trespass on my case. But in this case there is nothing done, and therefore, etc. BROWN (the second clerk): If a man prepays any sum of money that a house be built for him etcetera and he does not do it, now he will have an action of trespass on his case because the defendant has *quid pro quo* and so the plaintiff is damaged. And this was privately denied to him, etc.

[1] Text from Harvard MS. 156, unfoliated, Michaelmas Term of 19 Hen. VI. In the King's Bench.

CASE No. 4 *Anon.* (1443), probably *Tailbois* v. *Sherman*[1]
In a writ of trespass the plaintiff counted that a bargain was made between the plaintiff and the defendant for the delivery of five casks of wine, and that he [i.e. the defendant] ought to transport the five casks to the plaintiff at a certain place before a certain day, and that he did not transport them there to his damage. CHINGHAM: Judgment of the writ, for it well appears from his action that he ought to have a writ of covenant and not a writ of trespass, for a man will never have a writ of trespass without supposing a tort committed by the defendant, and he has not supposed any tort committed by him. Thus it seems to me that the writ should abate. ASCUE: If my arm is broken and I make a covenant with another to apply ointments to this and he does not do so and so as a result my arm is lost I shall have an action of trespass on the case, etc. DAVERS[2]: If he makes a covenant with me to make a house before a certain day, and if he makes no part of the house by the said day I shall never have an action of trespass but a writ of covenant. But if he cuts my timber and does not make the house, or if he makes part of the house but not all, or if he makes it badly, I shall have an action of trespass on my case, etc. And the opinion was that this plea went to the action and not to the writ, and so the defendant took leave to imparl.

CASE No. 5 *The Surgeon's Case* (1375)[3]
A woman brought a writ of trespass against one H a surgeon of London, and the writ said that her right hand was wounded by one F and the defendant undertook [*emprist*] to cure her, whereas by the defendant's negligence her hand is perished, whereby she is maimed, to her wrong and damage, etc. And note that no place was put in the writ, where he undertook, etc., but in her count she declared it, to wit at the Strand Cross. HASTY: He did not undertake to save her, ready to wage his law. PERSAY: This is an action of trespass which lies in the knowledge [notice] of the country, therefore wager of law is not available. FYNCH: But it is not law, etc. to answer [that when the writ is] not *contra pacem*, so that it seems that wager of law is available. But it seems that the action does not lie for she was not maimed by the defendant but by the person who did it to her, and if she recovers damages now against us she will recover on another occasion against the person who maimed her, and thus twice, etc. Nevertheless ready, etc. [i.e. ready

[1] Text from Harvard MS. 169, unfoliated, Paschal 21 Hen. VI. See Y.B. 21 Hen. VI, f. 55, pl. 58, for *Tailbois* v. *Sherman*.
[2] Presumably Danvers J.
[3] Text from Statham, *Abridgement, Accions sur le Case*, pl. 9.

to wage law]. And the other side to the contrary. HASTY: Now judgment of the writ because no place is put in certainty. PERSAY: You affirm the writ to be good by the tender of issue. Yet the writ was abated.

CASE No. 6   *Pickering v. Thoroughgood* (1532)[1]

Richard Pickering, a brewer of London, brought an action on his case against John Thoroughgood, and counted that the defendant on the thirtieth day of October in the twenty-third year of Henry VIII in London in the parish of St. Giles outside Cripplegate, in the ward of Cripplegate, for £5 13s. 4d. previously paid to him and for £5 13s. 4d. to be paid at the feast of the Purification next following, bargained and sold to the plaintiff forty quarters of malt, to be delivered in London in the said parish before the said feast, and assumed and promised to deliver it accordingly. And he counted that he, the plaintiff, being in hopes of this, made less provision for malt to maintain his art of brewing, and that the defendant did not deliver the malt before the aforesaid feast, whereby the plaintiff was without malt, and was compelled to buy malt at a very much greater price to continue and maintain his art of brewing, to his damage £20. And the defendant traversed the promise and the assumption, and this was found against him. And the plaintiff prayed judgment. And the other party by his counsel—Cholmeley and Hinde, Serjeants, alleged in arrest of judgment that this action did not lie because an action of debt lay, and where a general action lies there, in the same case, a special action on the case does not lie.

SPILMAN J.: It seems that an action on the case lies, for when a man has a tort done to him, and has sustained damage, he can have an action, but for this reason: when the defendant broke his promise and assumption, he did a tort to the plaintiff, and the plaintiff has sustained damage by the failure to deliver the malt. Therefore the law will give him an action, and no action lies on this except an action on the case. And therefore the action lies. And in some books a difference has been taken between nonfeasance and malfeasance, so that on the one an action of covenant lies, and on the other an action on the case. This is no distinction in reason, for if a carpenter for £100 covenants with me to make a house, and does not make it before the day assigned so that I am deprived of lodging, I shall have an action on my case for this nonfeasance just as well as if he made it badly. And as for the fact that he could have an action of debt, this makes no difference, for that action is based on the debt and detinet. But this action is based upon the other person's tort, that is, on the

---

[1] Text from B.M. MS. Hargrave 388. See SS 93 4, 94 at p. 247.

breach of promise. And if a man sells me his land for £100 and promises to make me an estate before a certain day, and if he enfeoffs another, I shall have an action on my case for this deceit, and yet covenant lies because he has performed no part of his promise. But such an action is based on the covenant broken, and the action on the case is based upon the deceit with which he has enfeoffed another. And in the same case if he had retaken an estate, and before the day he had enfeoffed me, the action on the case lies if he had warranted to him and his heirs and assigns, for by the taking of the estate he is in of another estate, and so the warranty is void as regards me. And if a man bails goods to be looked after, and he converts them to his own use, in this case he can also have an action of detinue, but this is based on the bailment and on the detention. This was the case between Bowser and Chapman (1530) where Bowser delivered a chest of plate with a bag of money to one who was his executor, and then the chest and bag came into the hands of one Chapman, and he broke the chest and the bag and converted the plate and the money to his own use. And in an action on the case brought by Bowser the issue was taken on the conversion to his use. It was found for the plaintiff, and the plaintiff had judgment to recover; and yet he could have had an action of detinue, but this made no difference. And the reason is clear, and therefore, etc.

MASTER PORTMAN J.: To the contrary, that this promise is part of his covenant, and all one, and no act done by the defendant but solely the non-delivery for which detinue lies.

CONINGSBY J. and FITZJAMES C.J.: It seems that the action lies, and it is at the election of the plaintiff to choose one action or the other, for they are based upon different points as SPILMAN has said. And if a man bails money to one to bail to one B, and he does not bail it, it is at the pleasure of the bailor to bring debt, account, or an action on his case, for the actions are based on different points. If a man bails his robe to me to look after, and by my carelessness the robe is eaten by moths, on this negligence and ill-keeping he will have an action on his case and also a writ of detinue at his pleasure. And although in the action of detinue I can wage my law, but cannot in the action on the case, yet this makes no difference, for in the case of Chesman [i.e. Chapman] above, which is good law, he was ousted of his law which he could have had well enough in an action of detinue. And there are many precedents where a man has bailed goods to be looked after, and where the bailee has converted them to his own use or has looked after them badly, and the bailor has had an action on the case, yet he could have had an action of detinue in which the bailee could have waged his law. And so why should he not have this action, granted that he could have had an action of debt in which the defendant could have waged his law.

And therefore judgment was given for the plaintiff that he should recover damages.

CASE NO. 7 *Anon.* (1542)[1]

Action on the case was brought, and the plaintiff declared how he delivered to the defendant twenty quarters of barley, and how the defendant assumed upon himself to deliver to the plaintiff in place of the twenty quarters of barley twenty quarters of malt before a certain day, and how the day is now passed and he has not done so, and so he has brought his action. The defendant came and said that the plaintiff at a certain place in another county sold the said twenty quarters of malt to a stranger, and he delivered them to him, and asks judgment whether the action, etc. [Objection was taken to the plea by Townsend on technical grounds.]

SHELLEY J.: It seems to me that there is another matter in the case, for I believe that the action does not lie here, for action on the case lies in no case except where the plaintiff is without another action, but here he can have an action of detinue. But I perceive your purpose in bringing this action—because he cannot wage his law in this action as he can in an action of detinue, etc. But supposing that the action does lie I am of the same opinion as you are, that the plea is not good. Which WILLOUGHBY J. conceded.

CASE NO. 8 *John Style's Case* (1527?)[2]

The case was that a man delivered an obligation to one John Style to safely guard it, who assumed upon himself to do so, and promised. The seal came off it when it was in the custody of J.S. and on this the obligee brought an action on his case against J.S. The question was if he should have an action on the case or a writ of detinue, and it was held by all except Inglefield that he should have an action on the case if he wished. And as to the objection that was taken that where he could have had an original writ at the common law there he would not have an action on the case, this was held not to be so, for he could have the one or the other. But never for the point raised here could he have an action at the common law. For example in detinue if he brought an action on the case and declared on the detention of the bond this would be no good, for he has an action of detinue on this point. But the taking off of the seal and misordering

---

[1] Text from Library of Congress MS. Gell at f. 15. This collection of year-books once belonged to Anthony Gell, and is mentioned in the Ninth Report of the Historical Manuscripts Commission.

[2] Text from B.M. MS. Hargrave 388, f. 215b.

of the bond is a different thing suffered by him, for which different thing he will have an action on the case. And it was said that the defendant had only committed a nonfeasance for which he would not have an action on the case. To this they said that if this nonfeasance amounted only to a *nudum pactum* then this was a good objection —for example if I promise you to build you a house by a certain day, which is not done, this is only a *nudum pactum* for which I will not have an action on the case and have suffered no tort by this nonfeasance. And if he has suffered a tort by this then it is otherwise, as if I am bound in an obligation in £40 to pay £20 by a certain day and I deliver the £20 to a stranger and he promises to deliver before the day, and he does not pay this before the day, so that I have forfeited my obligation, there for the nonfeasance I shall have an action on the case, for he has done wrong [*tort*] to me. The law is the same if I give certain money to one to make me a house by a day, and he does not do this by the day—there this is a consideration [*sic*] whereby there for the nonfeasance I shall have an action on my case. The law is the same in experience, and agreed by the justices in the common bench, that where a man recovers in ancient demesne certain lands, and he who recovers gives certain money to the clerk to make entry of the matter so recovered, which he does not do, there it was agreed that he should have an action on his case for the nonfeasance. But if he dies his heir will not have this action which his father could have, for it is a personal action and dies with the person [*cum persona*].

CASE No. 9 *Sukley* v. *Wyte* (1543)[1]

In an action on the case brought by Sukley of London against Wyte, etc. the plaintiff declared that the said defendant came to him with a *capias* on the first day of May in the thirty-second year of the reign of our lord the King who now is, the said plaintiff then being one of the sheriffs of London, and begged that the writ be served on one J.S. To which the plaintiff said that the said J.S. was a burgess of Parliament, and so he was not able to serve it. And the defendant said to him that he was willing to guarantee him without damage if he was willing to arrest him, by force of which the said plaintiff, then a sheriff, arrested the said J.S., then a burgess of Parliament. And because of this arrest he was in the Tower and lost his office and so was put to great damage by this arrest, on which matter he had commenced his action.

BROMELEY: It seems to me that the action does not lie, and the cause is because his action is grounded on a nude promise, and there is no specialty nor any money given in the covenant, but it is

[1] Text from Library of Congress MS. Gell at f. 13.

nothing more than a promise, on which promise he cannot have his action.

HALES: To the contrary, and as it seems to me the action lies. And as to what has been said, that a man cannot have an action on a promise, this is not so. For if I promise my brother Sanders that I shall make him a house, if I make part of it and not all he can have an action on his case against me. Or if the house is not as long as I promised he can have an action. Or if a smith promises me to shoe my horse and not for money paid before, if he injured my horse I shall have an action on my case. Or if a surgeon takes on himself to make me well of my disease, if he does not make me well but I fall into other diseases I shall have an action on my case against him. And also if I sell my horse to one J.N. for a certain sum of money and a stranger is with him, and I say to J.N. that I am not willing to trust him for the sum of money, and the stranger takes upon himself that if J.N. does not pay that he is willing to pay, and the purchaser dies before he has paid the sum, and the stranger makes his executors and dies, and the seller brings an action on the case, and the action was well maintainable, and so here etc.

SHELLEY J.: This last case is a doubtful case, and as it seems to me the action on the case does not lie against the executors on a promise made by their testator, which all the court as it were affirmed, but *quaere*.

WILLOUGHBY J.: It seems to me that the action at the bar is well maintainable, for I am willing to show a case which is very like it and is in a book. If the sheriff takes the beasts of one J.S. in Withernam, and the said J.S. says to the sheriff that if he is willing to deliver the beasts to him tomorrow that he is willing to guard him without damage, and he delivers them, and after the sheriff is amerced, in this case he can have an action against him, and so here.

SHELLEY J.: This is a good case, and great erudition can be developed by this case, for strong arguments can be made in favour of both parties. For on the one side a man could say that this action is not maintainable because the defendant took upon himself to guard the plaintiff free of damage for nothing except a thing that he was entitled to do by law, that is for the arrest. For the arrest was good, and a man can arrest a burgess of Parliament, and this arrest is good, but it can be avoided by *supersedeas* or by plea (and thus bar him so that he does not have to answer), and in consequence if the defendant took upon himself to guard him free from damage for a thing which was legal, he has no cause of action against him etc. But notwithstanding these reasons I am not prepared to say definitely that the action does not lie, but I wish to be advised on this for it is a doubtful case. So *quaere*. And then it was adjourned.

CASE No. 10 *Lord Grey's Case* (1567)[1]

An action on the case against Arthur Lord Grey whose father was indebted to the plaintiff. The defendant in consideration of this and of two shillings paid to him by the plaintiff assumed upon himself to pay him the same debt. And GAWDY demanded of the court whether the consideration of two shillings was traversable, or, if we were to traverse here by plea of *non assumpsit modo et forma*, whether the plaintiff ought to prove the consideration.

DYER C. J.: No, for this is only alleged as a matter of course, and it is alleged now so faintly in the King's Bench that it is too late to stop this there.

GAWDY: Then we are put to a mischief, for he has no other consideration to charge us, for the son is not chargeable with the debt of his father. But I understand that whenever the assumption is the cause of the debt, there the action lies well, as where negotiations for a bargain are held between two people, and they are agreed on the sum and the day of payment and everything, but one mistrusts the credit of the other—there if I am willing to say 'Do not doubt, if he does not pay on the day I shall', this is a good assumption and will charge me. For the other would not have been willing to give credit had it not been for my promise. But when the debt was due before it seems to be that it is not reason to charge a man by such naked words without any consideration.

DYER C. J.: The case which you have put is much clearer. And so it is that if a man is in execution at your suit, and I say 'Discharge him, and if he does not pay I am willing to do so', this is a good consideration if you discharge him to charge me in an action on the case, for there because of my promise you discharged the execution as in *Tatam's Case* in twenty-seven Henry VIII. And it seems to me that it will also be the same when there was a debt in existence before, for the discharge and ease of my friend is a good consideration to charge me without more. And therefore if my brother, cousin, or friend is indebted to you, and I say to you 'If he does not pay you I shall', here if you forbear because of this to sue and charge my friend, this is a good consideration to charge me, for what you did in ease of and for the benefit of my friend is to my ease and benefit also. Therefore etc. To which Weston J. agreed.

CASE No. 11 *Marsh v. Rainsford* (1587)[2]

An action on the case on assumpsit was brought by Marsh, a leather seller, of London against one Rainsford of the County of Essex, and he declared that there was a communication between himself and

---

[1] Text from Bodl. MS. Rawl. C. 112 at f. 292.
[2] Text from Harvard MS. 16 at f. 393b.

Rainsford concerning the marriage of Marsh with Rainsford's daughter and it was [proposed] by Rainsford to the plaintiff that he should have £200 with her, but they could not agree upon the day of payment. And then Marsh stole away Rainsford's daughter, and married her without the knowledge or consent of Rainsford, yet after this he consented to it, and said that in consideration that he had married his daughter he promised to give him £200. And on this promise Marsh brought the action, and showed how there had been talk about the marriage beforehand, and how he had proffered £200 with his daughter, but he founded his action on the promise after the marriage. SOLICITOR EGERTON: The action does not lie, for the consideration upon which the action should be founded ought to be to be executed in the future, and not precedent, and here he supposes the promise to be made after the marriage had and executed. Also he showed that there was a communication of marriage before, but he has not shown that he acted in pursuance of this, but independently he stole Rainsford's daughter. If I promise my daughter £100 at her marriage nevertheless he cannot have an action for this £100. 10 Eliz. 272 [*Hunt* v. *Bate*] my servant is arrested in London, and another because of his goodwill towards me bails him, and then I hear of this; I say to him that for the friendly consideration I promise and assume to save him harmless against the party of all damage and costs if any be adjudged. Then he is sued to condemnation, and the surety pays, and on this he brings action on the case. And it is held that the action does not lie— see the reason. But there in another action on the case on a promise made for £20 by the defendant to the plaintiff in consideration that the plaintiff had at the special instance of the defendant taken the cousin of the defendant to wife, there it was a good consideration, although the marriage was past and executed before the assumption and promise, because the marriage followed upon the defendant's request. And also land can be given in frankmarriage as well after the marriage as before, for the marriage can be understood to be the cause. And so there is a distinction between these two cases, which he compared to our case here. And according to him if I covenant to be seized of certain land to the use of my daughter the use by this is raised, at once, but if I say that I will give £100 to my daughter at her marriage I will not be charged by an action on this, for such a promise on such a consideration is not sufficient to ground an action although it is sufficient to raise a use. FULLER: Although there was a communication and talk of marriage, and nothing was certainly determined, yet this is a good consideration in conscience, and therefore it is good to have an action on his case. For just recently this case was ruled: if an infant requests another to be bound for him, and promises him to save him harmless, and he is bound, this consideration which is here precedent is only good in conscience [text has 'in consideration'] and not in law. And when he comes to full age he says to him 'In consideration that you are bound for me, I will save you harmless' on this assumpsit he will have an action on the case. SOLICITOR: I concede this case; but if I say to my servant 'In consideration that you have given me good and faithful service I shall give you £20' this was adjudged not such a consideration on which an action can be founded. WRAY C.J. took a distinction, viz. where the defendant requests the plaintiff to do something and then he does it, and then when it is done he says 'In consideration that you have done the thing for me I promise, etc.', there he will have an action on the case on this promise made on consideration precedent. But there the request ought to be alleged in fact. But if no request be made on the defendant's part, but the plaintiff does the thing off his own head, although he promises afterwards that in consideration that he has done such a thing, etc., yet no action can be based on this promise. And as to the principal case here he believed the action not to be maintainable, for there it is solely alleged that there was a previous communication, and not a request at the instance of the defendant whereby, etc.

On another day this term the case was moved again by POPHAM, Attorney, and he was representing the plaintiff, and he said that the natural affection of the parents to their children that the marriage be consummated is a good consideration to have an action. SOLICITOR: I concede that it is a consideration, but not such that an action can be grounded upon it—that is a personal action by the child against the parent. POPHAM: He can have a subpoena on a covenant to be seised to the use of his daughter in respect of natural affection and therefore by the same reasoning he can have an action on the case on such a promise on such consideration. If I be of counsel with one, and he, before I give him counsel, promise nothing, but after says 'Seeing that you have given me your counsel, I promise you £10', I shall have an action for this as the case was ruled in the Exchequer. COOKE: To the same effect. There are numerous actions in this court which are founded on similar promises, as 'whereas the plaintiff had delivered to the defendant so many goods, he promised to pay him so much money' and on this infinite actions have been maintainable here. SOLICITOR: I concede the case put by Popham of a promise in consideration of counsel, for there is always understood a precedent retainer, and after when he promises this it is in pursuance of his previous retainer. As for the case put by Cooke it is not the same as our case. If I exhort or request one to marry my daughter and promise nothing, and he marries, and then I say to him 'In consideration that you have married my daughter I shall give you £100', he shall have an action for this. COOKE: If one who is a physician and my good friend, knowing that my son is ill, comes to him and cures him, and then when I hear of this, I say to him 'Seeing that you have cured my son I shall give you £20', he shall have an action for this. As for the case of a delivery, previously vouched by me, it was between Stile and Smith in this court. DANIEL: To the same effect. 29 Edw. III, a bailiff of a manor made a good account to his master, upon which the master said to him 'Seeing that you have been ... and have yielded a good account to me I shall give you £10'. He had debt; therefore it is the same if I say to you 'Seeing that you have built me a house, I shall give you ten pounds'. So here.

At another day it was moved again, and for the plaintiff it was shown that at the instance of Rainsford there had been a communication held of marriage, and that then he married the daughter of Rainsford, and in consideration of the premisses he promised Marsh, etc. SOLICITOR: He has not alleged that he married at the instance of Rainsford, and there ought to be other consideration concurrent with the promise or future consideration. POPHAM, Attorney: Natural affection remains [i.e. continues] and this is sufficient consideration to make frankmarriage after the marriage and to raise uses, and so in our case here, and for this reason the conclusion of the case in 10 Eliz. [*Hunt* v. *Bate*] is against us if it be well. ... WRAY C.J.: When I promise him so much money in consideration that he has married my daughter this also is understood to be included in my promise, that he ought to use my daughter well, and this is future and executory, and thus it seems to me that the consideration is sufficient. GAWDY J.: The marriage cannot be understood to be against his will, for the communication before marriage was at his instance, and since he married her then did he promise, which proves his consent. Therefore it appears to us that the marriage was in pursuance of the communication. [REPORT-ER:] And as I gather the better opinion of the justices was that if one marries my daughter without my request, or without any communication had with me, or against my will, nevertheless if after the marriage I say that in consideration of his having married my daughter, I shall give him so much money, that on this he will have an action, for the natural affection is sufficient. Yet query, for Wray C.J. said when Egerton first moved this case in the court, that there had been a common distinction drawn to this effect: that if a man marries the daughter of J.S. with his consent and privity, and after the marriage had J.S. promises him in consideration of this to give him £100, now assumpsit will lie, whereas if the marriage is had

without consent and afterwards the father promises him in consideration of this to give him £100, now assumpsit will not lie. . . . Afterwards Wray with the assent of his brothers said 'Enter judgment
for Marsh £100.'

CASE NO. 12 *Fuller's Case* (1588)[1]

A promises to an elder son that if he should be willing to give his
consent that his father should convey his land [i.e. the father's land]
to someone, that he would be willing to give him forty shillings; now
if he gives consent, although no estate is conveyed, nevertheless he
can have assumpsit. And it was the case of Fuller. But on another
day Periam said that in this case the son ought to promise to give
his consent in consideration of the other promise, or otherwise A
has no remedy if the son is unwilling to give his consent, and if it is
thus the case that each one has a remedy against the other it is a
good assumption. And in the following Hilary term Serjeant Fermor
spoke in arrest of judgment on this special verdict. And he said that
since the undertaking was only on one side, and the other was free if
he wished to give his consent or not, although he consents he will
not recover. Also the promise was that he should be willing to
consent that his father should make assurance to him, and here it is
made to A to the use of the defendant and his wife in tail, so that he
varied from the first consideration. . . . Serjeant Shuttleworth to the
contrary, and he said that seeing that he had performed this by
giving his consent, then, he having performed, it is irrelevant he was
not under an obligation to do so by reciprocal undertakings to do so.
But if he will not give consent, he will get nothing. And at last
judgment was entered for the plaintiff. And Periam, in speaking
on this case, doubted whether if a man agrees to convey an estate to
A, and the conveyance is to the use of A, if this would be good or not.

CASE NO. 13 *Anon.* (1588)[2]

I having a term sell this to J.N., and then I continue my possession
as before. And then a third party promises me to give me £20 in
consideration that I should be willing to assign to him all the interest
that I have in the land. I assign this and then bring an action on the
case on an assumpsit. And it was held by the justices that it did not
lie because it is a nude pact. For I have nothing, and it is only in a
manner of speaking that I made this assignment of the land of J.N.
. . . And here they held that the defendant could plead *non assumpsit*,
and give in evidence that there was no *quid pro quo*, and he shall not
be compelled to plead the special matter.

---

[1] Harvard MS. 16 at f. 229a.
[2] Harvard MS. 16 at f. 423a. In the King's Bench.

Case No. 14　*Megod's Case* (1586)[1]

Megod brought an action on the case against two, and the case was as follows. One Mounson enfeoffed two persons of land to the intent that they should convey this land to whoever he should sell it to subsequently. And then he sold it to the plaintiff, and they did not convey it to him accordingly, and on this he brought this action. And it was argued for the defendants that the action did not lie, seeing that there was no consideration as between the plaintiff and the defendants, but this was solely between the said Mounson and the defendants. GAWDY J.: No one is damnified except the plaintiff. SHUTE J.: There is no consideration as far as he is concerned, for when they were enfeoffed there was no knowledge as to to whom it should be sold and it would be hard by matter *ex post facto* to raise a consideration between him and the defendants, they being uncertain to whom it should be sold. On another day Rokeby for the plaintiff said that the benefit is not reserved to the feoffor himself, but to the person to whom it should be sold. Also they have good consideration, for they are to take the profits in the mean time before he bargains and sells, which is a good consideration. GODFREY: The consideration does not arise between the plaintiff and the defendants, therefore the action does not lie. I concede that the bargain and sale made by the feoffor to the plaintiff is a good consideration between them, but not between the plaintiff and the defendants. SHUTE J.: There is no consideration between the plaintiff and defendants to raise the action, and therefore it does not lie. GAWDY and CLENCH JJ.: The action lies well, for they said that this is a good consideration, seeing that there is a trust placed in them that they should make an assurance to the other. And where there is a good consideration in the Chancery, on this an action on the case can lie here. And judgment was entered that there was good consideration and that the action lies well. In Cowdray's Reports, the defendants never made a promise to the plaintiff to make assurance of this land. Query, for it would seem that the contrary was the case according to their argument and the reasons given here.

Case No. 15　*Harwold's Case* (1586)[2]

An action on the case by Harwold against another on an account between the plaintiff and the defendant. The defendant was indebted to the plaintiff in £10 and promised him that if he would postpone the day of payment of the said £10 for a little time, that he would be willing to pay him when required by him. And the case depended in law upon a special verdict on the question whether this was a suffi-

---

[1] Harvard MS. 16 at f. 338a.
[2] Harvard MS. 16 at f. 254a.

be bound to take back that horse from the said R de H, provided
that it was in good condition, when asked to do so by the said R de H,
and to do so for the same sum of money paid to the said R de C less
six shillings and eightpence, yet the same R de C has utterly refused
to take back the said horse, which is in good condition, on the terms
stated above, though he has often requested to do so, to the damage
of the said R de H forty shillings, as he says.

cient consideration for him to have an action of assumpsit, a
adjudged that it was. And yet it was urged that a little ti
be a quarter of an hour, which is no consideration. But
and Periam said that the consideration of 'a little time' i
much material, but the debt is the chief matter and the
the action. And according to Periam if a man is indebte
the sum of £10, and he says that he is willing to pay n
and such a day, and does not say 'inconsideration that he
to me in a sum of £10 he is willing to pay' nevertheles
lies well.

Case No. 16 *Harvey v. Yonge* (1602)[1]

S having a term sold this to B for £150. S affirmed this
value. B placing his faith in this gave the money to
wards offered to sell this term to another, but was only a
£100 for it. B therefore brought an action on the case
of deceit, and on a plea of not guilty a verdict was
plaintiff. And it was held that an action does not lie
this B on the naked assertion of S, and it was his foll
willing to give this to him. But it would be otherwise
ranted the term to be of such value, for the warranty
inducing confidence.

Case No. 17 *A Writ of Trespass on the Case for Nonfe*

... ostenturus quare cum idem R de H quendam equ
R de C in parochia sancti Dunstani in Fletestrete I
certo viagio per ipsum R de H tunc faciendo pro
summa dicto R de C soluta emisset ita quod ex
praedictus R de C equum illum dummodo in bon
praefato R de H per eadem summa exceptis se
denariis praefato R de C resoluenda cum per ipsu
hoc foret requisitus recipere teneret idem R de C e
in bono statu existentem in forma praedicta r
sepius requisitus fuerit penitus recusavit ad dam
H lx s. ut dicit.

... to show why, whereas R de H [the plaintiff] {
money bought a certain horse of the said R de
in the parish of St. Dunstan in Fleetstreet, Lo
journey which was then about to be made by th
the terms that when that journey was over the

---

[1] Harvard MS. 105.
[2] From Harvard MS. 26, f. 90a, a Register probably be
in the fifth year of either Henry V or Henry VI.

INDEX

Printed in the United Kingdom
by Lightning Source UK Ltd.
119726UK00001B/1